PRAISE FOR

The Candy Bombers

"Absorbing and lucid." —*Publishers Weekly*

"A successful work of popular history . . . an enjoyable, timely narrative."
—*Dallas Morning News*

"Writing with the flair of a novelist, Cherny tells the story of the Berlin
Airlift . . . Cherny dramatically weaves together the conjoined fates of
numerous characters. . . . The author skillfully delineates the airlift's role
in dramatically improving Germans' and Americans' attitudes toward
each other, with significant consequences for the Cold War."
—*Kirkus Reviews*

"A fine eye for character and detail." —*Bloomberg News*

"*Candy Bombers: The Untold Story of the Berlin Airlift and America's
Finest Hour* is the definitive telling of the amazing story of the airlift. . . .
Andrei Cherny tells this story vividly, placing it on the broader canvas of
the incipient Cold War." —Michael Barone, *U.S. News & World Report*

"Everything one could want from a work of history—engrossing, inform-
ative, and stirring. . . . Cherny takes readers inside the eerie last days of
Franklin D. Roosevelt's presidency, the jubilant first meetings of Allied
soldiers astride a defeated Germany, the quick pivot to the Cold War
footing, the four-way 1948 presidential race and, chiefly, the intricacies of
surmounting the Soviet blockade of American-occupied Berlin to bring
food to the starving city, and the manner in which unplanned acts of
kindness won over the people of Germany and the world. The author
does a beautiful job with both the arc of history and the minutiae of the
lives of those making it." —*The Washington Post (Express)*

D0380563

"A gripping, suspenseful narrative history about the U.S. Cold War–era pilots determined to help the freedom-strangled citizens of West Berlin survive Soviet tyranny. Cherny succeeds in making those harrowing days of Berlin circa 1948–1949 come alive. As a historian, he reminds me of Stephen Ambrose at his best."

—Douglas Brinkley, Fellow, Baker Institute, Professor of History, Rice University, and author of *The Great Deluge* and *Tour of Duty*

"The early Cold War era was as tense as the days after 9/11. Andrei Cherny captures, in vivid detail, the excitement and drama of the U.S. response to the Soviet blockade of Berlin. You will have a hard time not cheering—or feeling moved—when America rescues its former enemy in the name of freedom." —Evan Thomas, author of *Sea of Thunder*

"Superb scholarship, thrilling storytelling."

—Jonathan Alter, author of *The Defining Moment*

"One of the finest narrative histories that I have read in years."

—Lawrence Kaplan, editor of *World Affairs*

ALSO BY ANDREI CHERNY

The Next Deal

THE

CANDY

BOMBERS

The Untold Story of the Berlin Airlift
and America's Finest Hour

ANDREI CHERNY

Berkley Caliber • New York

THE BERKLEY PUBLISHING GROUP
Published by the Penguin Group
Penguin Group (USA) Inc.
375 Hudson Street, New York, New York 10014, USA
Penguin Group (Canada), 90 Eglinton Avenue East, Suite 700, Toronto, Ontario M4P 2Y3, Canada
(a division of Pearson Penguin Canada Inc.)
Penguin Books Ltd., 80 Strand, London WC2R 0RL, England
Penguin Group Ireland, 25 St. Stephen's Green, Dublin 2, Ireland (a division of Penguin Books Ltd.)
Penguin Group (Australia), 250 Camberwell Road, Camberwell, Victoria 3124, Australia
(a division of Pearson Australia Group Pty. Ltd.)
Penguin Books India Pvt. Ltd., 11 Community Centre, Panchsheel Park, New Delhi—110 017, India
Penguin Group (NZ), 67 Apollo Drive, Rosedale, North Shore 0632, New Zealand
(a division of Pearson New Zealand Ltd.)
Penguin Books (South Africa) (Pty.) Ltd., 24 Sturdee Avenue, Rosebank, Johannesburg 2196,
South Africa

Penguin Books Ltd., Registered Offices: 80 Strand, London WC2R 0RL, England

The publisher does not have any control over and does not assume any responsibility for author or third-party websites or
their content.

"Ol' Man River" by Jerome Kern, Oscar Hammerstein II © 1927 Universal—PolyGram Int. Publ., Inc. Copyright
renewed. All rights administered by Universal—PolyGram Int. Publ., Inc. / ASCAP. Used by permission. All rights
reserved.

PRINTING HISTORY
G. P. Putnam's Sons hardcover edition / April 2008
Berkley Caliber trade paperback edition / June 2009

Berkley Caliber trade paperback ISBN: 978-0-425-22771-8

The Library of Congress has catalogued the G. P. Putnam's Sons hardcover edition as follows:

Cherny, Andrei.
    The candy bombers : the untold story of the Berlin Airlift and America's finest hour / Andrei Cherny.
        p.   cm.
    Includes bibliographical references and index.
    ISBN 978-0-399-15496-6
    1. Berlin (Germany)—History—Blockade, 1948–1949. 2. United States—Foreign relations—1945–1953.
3. United States—Foreign relations—Germany. 4. Germany—Foreign relations—United States. I. Title.
    DD881.C495   2008   2008000856
    943'.1550874—dc22

PRINTED IN THE UNITED STATES OF AMERICA

10 9 8 7 6 5 4 3 2 1

TO STEPHANIE,
WHO MAKES MY LIFE SWEET

Two middle-aged ladies were sitting at the table behind me that day, the only other customers of the meal. They had come, they said, because when the Americans liberated Paris, a young American lieutenant had slept in their house. He had brought coffee, soap, food, butter when all Paris hungered at the mention of them. When he moved off with his company they asked him what they could do to repay him. He said there was nothing they could do for him, but if, someday, they ever got the chance to visit Omaha beach and the cemetery that was going to be built there, would they put some flowers on the graves of a few friends he had left behind. They said they would, and so, seven years later, they took a bus from Paris to put flowers on American graves, not because they remembered history and the Liberation, but because they remembered coffee, food and human kindness.

THEODORE H. WHITE

Things all go past and they fade away
After each December there comes another May.
POPULAR GERMAN SONG, 1942

CONTENTS

PART III: THE BRIDGE
1948–1949

Prologue

SEPTEMBER 2001

On the lower tip of the island of Manhattan, fires trapped deep beneath the twisted metal girders were still burning. In great cities around the globe, people gathered to express their outrage and their sympathy. Hundreds of Londoners stood in silence when Big Ben rang at noon. When the guard changed at Buckingham Palace, the band played a song about the American flag still waving after a failed British assault on Fort McHenry. In Beijing and Amman, bouquets and wreaths piled high at the gates of the American embassies. In Dublin, the stores closed in commemoration. Children in the West Bank held candlelight vigils. In Paris, the newspaper headline was "We Are All Americans."

But nowhere was there a greater outpouring of humanity and emotion than in the German capital of Berlin. There, 200,000 people gathered along the broad avenue leading through the Tiergarten to the Brandenburg Gate. No one was quite sure why so many turned out.

The crowd felt young. Men and women in their twenties wore backpacks and shorts under the late summer sun; parents pushed strollers and held children by the hand in the enormous throng.

One woman stood still, alone in the crowd, lost in her thoughts as families and couples marched past her. She was old and stooped. Her hair was wild and she wore a dark, heavy coat even on the warm day. She was quietly sobbing.

Two young men approached her and asked why she was crying. She seemed startled, as if roused from a slumber. "I love Americans," she said quickly, in a way that was so imploring they understand that it grabbed them and shook them by their lapels. She started to go on, to say more, to explain, but before the words came out, her gaze widened and warmed, the tears replaced by an ineffable joy. Her shoulders straightened just a bit. The wrinkles seemed to flee her face.

A distant, happy memory danced across her eyes as she looked upward, toward the sky. She began softly, in a whisper. "You see, I was a girl during the Airlift. . . ."

JUNE 24, 1948

Years later, long after the bunting and banners had been torn down, delegates to the 1948 Republican convention would fondly remember the busty blonde in the rowboat. It was Wednesday night, June 23, 1948, and the floor in Philadelphia was open for nominations. For the first time in twenty years, a convention was meeting with neither economic depression nor global war as a backdrop. Instead, Americans—in those bursting, jubilant years after the end of World War II—were living in a period of plenty and progress that would have been unimaginable only a few years before.

Outside the convention hall, Philadelphia was hot and humid. After only a few moments of walking about, the delegates felt as if a heavy velvet had been draped over their skin. But they rushed between the various candidates' headquarters in a mood of delirious excitement. Harold Stassen, the young former governor of Minnesota who was the favorite of Republican voters across the country, handed out red-white-and-blue buttons and 1,200 pounds of cheese. Robert A. Taft, the grandson of an attorney general and son of a president and chief justice of the Supreme Court, passed out buttons in the shape of a four-leaf clover. With a pained expression, the favorite of conservatives acceded to his advisers' request and shook hands for the cameras with a baby elephant named Little Eva. The pachyderm was draped with a blanket on which was written "Renounce Obstinate Bureaucracy, End Roguish Tactics, And Tally Americanism, Freedom, Truth," a catchy slogan whose acronym just happened to be "Robert A. Taft." Over at the Bellevue-Stratford Hotel, New York governor Thomas E. Dewey put them all to shame. His campaign gave away cigarette holders, ashtrays, and matchbooks; lipstick, luggage, and lingerie; unlimited bottles of pop provided by the president of Pepsi-Cola; chewing gum, boxes of chocolate, and 5,000 rolls of Life Savers. Thus, of course, Dewey was the convention's frontrunner.

The air of abundance was evident on the convention floor, where two marching bands, Scottish bagpipers, and men with megaphones all competed for attention. The statuesque sailor in the eye-popping outfit, there on behalf of Stassen, moved through the sea of delegates atop a float, greeted with chants of "Man the Oars and Ride the Crest, Harold Stassen—He's the Best." "To Steer Our Craft, Let's Take Taft," came the shouted answer. To make the speakers' voices heard above the commotion, the arena installed what H. L. Mencken called "a loud-speaker system that is to any loud-speaker system of the past as the range of Himalayas is to a crabcake." For weeks leading up to the convention, newspapers and magazines had carried ads for television sets that read "Meet Your Next President on RCA Victor." The new phenomenon of television carried the proceedings from gavel to gavel since it was an inexpensive way to fill airtime. Ten million people, including President Harry S Truman sitting in front of a television in the White House, watched the convention—more than had witnessed every previous political convention in America combined. It was then the largest television audience in history.

The Republican convention had a plethora of seemingly everything, but what it had most—and this fairly oozed from the delegates—was confidence. The Democratic Party had been split by the issue of relations with the Soviet Union, resulting in what the *New York Times*' chief political correspondent described as the country's "general conviction that the nominee of the convention will become the next president of the U.S."

But in the pivotal year of 1948, it was not the campaign of Thomas Dewey to capture the White House that would dominate the newspaper headlines. Another event would seize the public's attention and ultimately deny Dewey his victory. It was the battle for Berlin.

IT WAS 4 A.M. in Philadelphia, almost dawn, when the convention adjourned and the delegates stumbled bleary-eyed into bed, not realizing that while they had been in the hall a global crisis had arisen that threatened to spark World War III. Berlin, a city divided up between the victors of the last world war, lay deep within the Soviet-occupied parts of Germany. At 6 A.M. there on June 24, 1948, as the cheers for Taft were dying down in Philadelphia, the Russians, in order to capture control of the entire city, halted the trains, trucks, and barges that brought food, coal, and every other supply into the western portions of the capital on a daily basis. Two and a quarter million people in Berlin—the biggest city in the world—were cut off from everything they needed to survive.

To Colonel Frank Howley, the bombastic head of America's occupation government in Berlin, it was "a wicked decision, the most barbarous in history since Genghis Khan reduced conquered cities to pyramids of skulls." That morning, a gentle drizzle was falling on the capital, but Howley rode to work in an open car so that the knots of worried Berliners he passed could see he was unafraid. There was another reason he rode with the top down in the rain. He thought there was a chance that assassins might be lurking in the shadows waiting to kill him in advance of a Soviet attack on western Berlin. He liked to dare them to take their best shot.

Howley drove through a city that had once been among the most elegant and sophisticated in Europe. American and British bombs from high above and a brutal Russian invasion had all but flattened Berlin. By 1948, the distrust and enmity between the conquerors and the conquered had barely begun to thaw, and Berlin had barely begun to rebuild. It was a city, wrote a reporter at the time, "which lacks everything but ruins." In the three years since the end of the war, Berliners had lived with the pains of hunger and cold every day—and this made the prospect of no more food and warmth all the more terrifying.

When the blockade was announced, a frisson of panic leapt through the city. Since dawn, Soviet radio had been announcing that the water supply would be cut off next. In the city's sixteen water plants, the gauge levels were plummeting as Berlin's mothers filled up every available container with all the water they could hoard—bathtubs, buckets, even their own chamber pots. Around Berlin, taps began to dry out. Howley phoned the broadcast chief of the American-run radio station and gave him very precise instructions. Minutes later, Berliners heard the announcer make an unusual request. "Give your baby a bath. All of you take baths. Use as much water as you want. There's plenty of it." And around Berlin, households turned off their water and emptied their bathtubs. Almost instantaneously, the city's water supplies returned to normal.

But the fear that truly seized Berliners that morning was not a lack of water, it was war. Many believed the blockade was a precursor to a Russian invasion of the western sectors of Berlin. Howley himself went on the radio that afternoon to reassure the city. With all the considerable bravado he could muster, he addressed the Red Army commanders directly, spitting out his words as if they were gristles of rancid meat in his mouth: "If you do try to come into our sector, you had better be well prepared. We are ready for you." The bluster was meant for Berliners' comfort rather than as a threat to the Russians. It was a bluff and not at all a convincing one: The military forces of the Western democracies were outnumbered 62 to 1 in Berlin and its surrounding areas. The Soviets had more troops within a few hours of the city than America had in the world. "Militarily, we didn't stand a chance," Howley would admit. The Russians could have "liquidated us before you could say 'Politburo!'"

FOR THREE YEARS, America had watched as the Communists took control of the nations of Eastern Europe, one after another, but so far, the Soviets had only captured governments in the areas already under their thumb. Much of western Berlin was American territory—in the struggle there the U.S. and the U.S.S.R. would face off directly for the first and only time. It would be the testing place that would determine whether the Soviets could conquer the rest of Europe or whether democracy could hold its ground; whether there would be a hot war or a cold peace.

The Americans and their British and French allies quickly concluded that they had three options on that morning of June 24, 1948. They could retreat from Berlin and leave the entire city and its people to the Russians. However, "withdrawal would snuff the last candle of light east of the Iron Curtain," wrote the *Christian Science Monitor* that week. "And it would set ablaze new fires of Communism to the west." It would be a death sentence for the democratic leaders in Berlin, and it was widely assumed by the top officials in America that a retreat would mean that Communists would capture control of Italy, France, and the rest of Germany next. As the *New York Times* put it, an evacuation "would inevitably entail the surrender of all Germany and of Europe." They might well have been right—certainly NATO would never have been born and the Marshall Plan would have died in its early infancy.

They could try to hold their ground in the city, watching helplessly as Berliners steadily starved in the streets in front of the eyes of the world, knowing that it would be only a matter of time before they would rise up against the Allies and force them out simply to survive.

Finally, they could try to bring food into the city by force, likely bringing about a new world war against an enemy of vastly superior strength. "All the Russians need" to overrun American forces in Germany, said Bob Lovett, America's acting secretary of state at the time, "is shoes." If this had occurred, the Red Army would have raced across Western Europe—it was estimated that the Russians could reach the English Channel in forty-eight hours—and America would have had no choice but to raze Moscow, Leningrad, and other Russian cities with atomic bombs.

"Never before had a city been summoned to surrender before the threat of starvation, civil war within, or a bigger war without," wrote an American newsmagazine that week. The general in charge of American forces in Europe and of the occupation of Germany, Lucius Clay, took a look at the alternatives that morning and confided to a journalist, with a snap of his fingers, "I wouldn't give you that for our chances."

THESE WERE THE choices on June 24, 1948. What happened next is as much an American fable as that winter in Valley Forge, the last desperate stand of the Alamo, or the bus boycott in Montgomery. It was a turning point in the nation's history, the moment America came to fully accept the mantle of leader of the free world. But more than that, it was the moment when America became beloved by the very people it had defeated in battle and whose cities it had leveled—and was revered by people around the world who looked to the United States as a source of decency and good.

This book does not aim to be a comprehensive history of the Berlin blockade and the American response. Able scholars have trod that ground before. Rather, using recently declassified documents, new interviews with those who were there, unpublished letters, and unexplored details, it is the story of when Americans learned—for the first time—how to act at the summit of world power. Some aspects of this story, if not the particulars, may be familiar: the president written off for reelection, an allied response to the siege of Berlin, a secretary of defense battling America's demons and his own. Even the account of a kind American pilot who dropped candy to the children of Berlin has been referred to often in passing as a warmhearted human interest story. But these are not separate threads. Instead, in the course of a year, these stories were woven together into a single fabric—each strand tied into the others—that is the forgotten foundation tale of America in the modern world.

It is a story of America at her best, but it is by no means a simple story or a straight line. Those who are accustomed to the jerky, flickering, black-and-white newsreel images of Harry Truman and his advisers might be surprised by the people they will meet ahead. Freed from their imprisonment in bronze statues and marble busts, they turn out to be at times shortsighted, petty, crassly political, calculating, often miscalculating. They were, it turns out, human—and it is their very humanity that makes what they accomplished so extraordinary. For despite their foibles and failings, they were able to heal the wounds of a terrible war, save the world from the advances of a new threat without firing a shot, and bring freedom and democracy to a place that had never known them and was thought to be unsuited to them.

Three years after the end of the most terrible war the world had ever seen, the appetite for great men had disappeared along with the confetti and the kissing in Times Square. The men who broke the siege of Berlin were the misfits, the leftovers, history's second-stringers. Hal Halvorsen, a lovesick pilot who had served far from the conflict, not in dogfights over Normandy or on bombing runs over Dresden but in the backwaters of a global war—flying transport missions on the outskirts of the headlines. Lucius Clay, a general who had spent World War II on the home front in charge of defense procurement; frustrated, overlooked, haggling over spare parts instead of commanding troops in battle. Bill Tunner, a superb military organizer who had achieved great glory in commanding the most successful air transport mission in history but, with the war's end, with his family falling apart, had been sidelined to a desk job in a forlorn corner of the Pentagon. James Forrestal, a secretary of defense ignored and flailing. Harry Truman, an accidental president, derided by his own party, headed toward defeat, who had proved to be little match for the eloquence and elegance of his predecessor.

Yet in the year after that June day in 1948—long after the postwar parades had passed, after the ticker tape had been swept away, after all the heroes had supposedly been minted—it was these unlikely men who improvised and stumbled their way into inventing a uniquely American approach to the world that married the nation's military and moral might. Clay's stubbornness in standing against the American foreign policy establishment would save a city; Tunner's zeal would achieve what no one else thought was possible; Forrestal's vision would define the nation's outlook even as it consumed him; Truman would find victory at home and abroad because of his decisions in Berlin; and Halvorsen, the ordinary young pilot, would almost single-handedly transform how the citizens of defeated Germany's capital saw the United States.

Their story has powerful resonance for our own time. In confronting the Berlin blockade, America went to battle against a destructive ideology that threatened free people around the world. In a country we invaded and occupied that had never had a stable democracy, we brought freedom and turned their people's hatred of America into love for this country, its people, and its ideals. Never before—or since—would America be so admired around the world and stand so solidly on the side of light.

Those were the years when people thought that atomic bomb shelters and air-raid drills would be parts of daily life forever. But because of the legacy of the Candy Bombers, this turned out not to be true. Today, in a time of metal detectors and air marshals, their legend and its lessons can help guide our way forward.

THE STORY BEGINS in the spring of 1945. In Germany, Hitler's Thousand Year Reich is falling, order itself is crumbling, and, on the broad plains of Central Europe, the two greatest armies in history are converging on open fields where, after a long winter, the green grass of spring brings a new hope.

Part I

THE BANKS

Spring 1945

What does he care if de world's got troubles?
What does he care if de land ain't free?

"OL' MAN RIVER" BY OSCAR HAMMERSTEIN II

1

THE END

Lieutenant Buck Kotzebue's boot splashed into the Elbe, sending ripples down the river as the water washed away the dirt and grime of war. He had come from halfway around the world. Crossing a rough ocean and a jagged channel, he and his men had been deposited onto the beaches of France. They had huddled against one another in the back of railroad boxcars and in open trucks that sped through nights of driving, icy rain. They had marched through the snows of the Low Countries and across the River Rhine. In small hamlets and in yawning green valleys, they had fought their way from the west, crushing remnants of the once fearsome Wehrmacht and Waffen SS. Now, behind him, as Kotzebue began to cross the river, was all of America's army in Europe, 3 million strong. In front of him, on the other side of the swollen Elbe, flowing cold and quick as the winter snows on the Giant Mountains melted in April's spring, was a small group of Russian soldiers, their tan tunics speckled with medals that shone in the midday sun. The Russians had fought their way from the east through the bloodiest battles in history. To get to this grassy riverbank, they had tramped over hundreds of miles, sometimes pulling themselves by their elbows through mud so deep a man could drown. On both sides of the waters lay years of tragedy and destruction. But now soldiers of the world's two great armies had found each other, for the first time, on the outskirts of a tiny village in the heart of a Nazi Germany on the brink of defeat. And only a powerful river separated them.

Kotzebue had come to this moment of history by accident and insubordination. He had been instructed to lead a patrol from the town of Trebsen, twenty miles west of the Elbe. His orders were clear and strict: He was to go no more than five miles and then return. Rumors had spread that the Russians were somewhere nearby. It was said that General Dwight Eisenhower was busy planning for a momentous ceremony that would mark the first meeting of East and West, a juncture tantamount to final victory over Germany. Yet this, as with so much else, was uncertain. Hitler had promised his Reich would last a thousand years, but, in the spring of 1945, it was confusion that reigned in Germany.

The morning had been cool and gray. Low clouds hung over the land. The dirt roads of the German countryside were so choked with surrendering German soldiers that Kotzebue's patrol, a gaggle of jeeps crowded with GIs, could only creep forward. The German troops, dazed and staggered, all but begged the Americans to capture them, preferring shame and imprisonment to the more awful fate they faced if forced to fight in the climactic battle then being waged for Germany's capital, 125 miles to the north. Yet when Kotzebue and his men pushed into the little farm towns, they found them deeded to the ghosts. White flags bowed from windows, unfurling in April's breeze, but no people could be seen. The inhabitants cowered behind closed doors, fearing the awful wrath they had been told to expect from Germany's invaders.

Kotzebue reached the five-mile point, but down the road the unknown that lay past the next bend beckoned. So he decided to push on. And then came a hill, and another ridge, and each time, Kotzebue, instead of turning back as he had been ordered, pressed on just a little farther. The road passed a sturdy farmhouse, and Kotzebue told his men to hang back while he went to inquire inside. He was lanky, even gangly, like a young Jimmy Stewart, but he squared his thin shoulders, breathed in deeply, and looked suddenly older as he slowly stepped toward the front entrance. The heavy, dark wood door sat ajar and Kotzebue sensed a trap. Standing back from the portal, he pushed the door open with the barrel of his rifle and cringed as it creaked on its old hinges. He stepped into the house. There, sitting around the family dinner table, were the farmer, his wife, and their three beautiful children. It could have been the very picture of bucolic, placid pastoral life. The only sign that indicated it was a time of war was that they were all dead of poison. They had decided to kill themselves rather than suffer the terror of life under the oncoming foreign hordes.

With a few glum words, Kotzebue got back into the jeep and the patrol moved farther down the road. Soon they ran across another tuft of Nazis, who offered to show them the way to the Elbe. Kotzebue had them sit on the hoods of the jeeps and told them to hold on as they rumbled onward. Up ahead, a lone horseman in a fur hat disappeared into a deserted courtyard. Kotzebue gave chase and they cornered the man on horseback in a pack of refugees. The man would say little, but he waved his arm toward the next town, indicated the Russians were there, and quickly rode off. A Polish prisoner of war, recently freed from the camps, eagerly offered to show the way. Kotzebue told him to climb aboard the lead jeep's hood as well.

The convoy picked up speed, kicking up a train of dirt behind it as it raced along the unpaved paths. The morning fog had lifted and, for the first time that spring, the day was sunny and warm. As the river grew closer, lilacs burst across the fields like firecrackers. The Nazi troops and the freed Polish prisoner sat side by side, gripping the hood of the American soldiers' scudding jeep; the conquerors and the conquered, the oppressors and the oppressed, all moving together toward the rendezvous up ahead. In Kotzebue's jeep the atmosphere was light, almost giddy. They joked that they were drawing near the River Jordan; up ahead was Canaan. They were about to cross into the Promised Land.

JUST PAST THE town of Strehla, the Elbe loomed in sight. They had barely rolled to a stop by the banks when Kotzebue bounded out and ran toward the river. He put his field glasses to his eyes and there, on the other side, he saw men in brown shirts. Someone had told him that Russians wore their medals into battle, and these men's chests glittered. He ordered a private to fire two green flares into the sky. The Russians loped toward the riverbank and gazed across intently. The Pole began to jump up and down, gesticulating madly, yelling, *"Amerikanski! Amerikanski!"* The Russians motioned for the Americans to cross the river to their side.

The rude pontoon bridge that had once spanned the waters had been destroyed. Half of it still jutted uselessly out into the flood. But Kotzebue saw that four boats were chained to the riverbank, and he made his way toward them. Pressing his foot against the damp soil, he pulled at the chain to free the boats, but it would not budge. Telling his men to stand back, he took out a grenade, carefully balanced it on the knot of chains, pulled the pin, and ran for cover.

The blast freed the boats. Kotzebue and six others spattered the water as they climbed into one and began to make their way across the river. Using loose boards and the butts of their rifles as makeshift paddles, they fought against the rushing current to make it to the other side.

Reaching the Elbe's eastern bank, they leapt out of the boat to discover that the land they had reached was not one of milk and honey, but of still more sadness and death. The river they had crossed was not the Jordan, but the Styx.

In their thrill at seeing the Russians on the ridge overlooking the river, they had not noticed the scene on the bank itself. There, surrounding them for hundreds of yards, were dozens of dead German civilians. Their wagons and carts were blown to pieces nearby; their suitcases and their clothes were spread about. "Here we are, tremendously exhilarated, and there's a sea of dead," recalled one of Kotzebue's soldiers, Private Joe Polowsky. The ground was "literally covered with bodies—of women, old men, children. I still remember seeing a little girl clutching a doll in one hand—it was right there. She couldn't have been more than five or six years old. And her mother's hand in the other. They were all piled up like cordwood."

Three Russian soldiers were easing their way toward them down the steep bank. To meet up with them, the Americans had to step carefully through a knee-deep heap of dead bodies. The two groups approached. The massacred innocents lying crumpled at their feet served only to underscore what was about to occur. But no one who was there—no one even in either of their countries—needed a reminder. For half a decade, the war unleashed by German terror had opened a bloody, deep gash across the earth. In the winter of 1941, the Nazis had been camped on the outskirts of Moscow; on a clear December day, they could see the Kremlin's cupolas shimmering in the distance. Sitting up late into the night, as was his habit, Joseph Stalin could hear the rumble of German guns from his home. That same December, Germany's Pacific ally, Japan, unleashed its surprise attack on Pearl Harbor, shattering America's sense of isolation from a messy world.

In the three and a half years since that bleak December, so many perished that, more than sixty years later, experts' estimates on casualty figures diverge by the tens of millions. But the Russians and the Americans had pushed back against the tide from each direction and, in the war's waning hours, were about to join up on a luminous spring day. They had begun the war as second-rate powers among the nations of the world. They had been big, boastful adolescents, hungry and undisciplined. Once the sophisticated states of Europe had carved up colonies and decided the fates of faraway countries in plush, hushed drawing rooms. Now the grand and the refined were shattered. London, unbowed through it all, had survived the Blitz and seen its finest hour, but would never regain its dominance. Paris had fallen to the Nazis with barely a fight, only to be liberated by American farm boys. Berlin was about to taste the full bitterness of its own fate. The world's future lay with the two nations whose young men were now walking toward each other with the dead children of their defeated enemy at their feet.

Kotzebue and his men moved up the riverbank and the three Russians came down the incline. They met. It was shortly after high noon on April 25, 1945. They exchanged handshakes and salutes. And then they did not know what to do next. Kotzebue "couldn't talk Russian. The Russians couldn't talk English," remembered Private Polowsky. "We couldn't understand each other," agreed Lieutenant Grigori Goloborodko. Having come from opposite ends of the earth, across hell and rivers, they found themselves united in victory and separated by half a world of differences amid the death and confusion of civilization coming apart. So they simply stood in silence and stared.

Three hours later, at Torgau, sixteen miles to the north of Strehla, Lieutenant Bill Robertson climbed to the top of a tall watchtower in an old town castle sitting on the banks of the Elbe. Robertson scaled an ancient wooden ladder up through a trapdoor out onto the roof of the tower and stuck his head out to look around. On the other side of the river, Russians, thinking he was a German, began to fire in his direction, missing him by only a few feet. He pulled out a bedsheet on which he had used colored powders stolen from a pharmacy to paint five red stripes and a field of blue in the upper corner. He waved it over his head, yelling: "*Tovarich! Amerikanski!* Moscow! America! Don't shoot!"

The day was blustery and the river between them was raging, loudly dashing against the ruins of Torgau's bridge. Robertson was only about 500 yards away from the Soviet troops on the other side of the river, but amid the wind and noise the American and the Russians could not hear each other. "They shouted. I could not understand. I shouted. They could not understand." But he saw a small group of Russian soldiers making their way toward the fallen bridge and he ran down to meet them.

Crawling out onto the girders from either side, the waters swirling violently below them, Robertson and the Russians met in the middle of the bridge. Unlike Kotzebue's stilted encounter downriver, at Torgau the meeting was immediately celebratory. Robertson and two other Americans greeted the Russians on the riverbank. "We just said 'Hiyah! Here's to you!'" he recalled, and they stood about "laughing, shouting, pounding each other on the back, shaking hands with everyone." The Russians produced biscuits and sardines, schnapps they had taken from

Germans, pieces of chocolate they had saved. They toasted one another, their ally's courage, their nations' leaders, the defeat of their enemies. They drank to words they did not know, "but the commonality of feeling was unmistakable," Robertson would remember. "We were all soldiers, comrades-in-arms. We had vanquished a common enemy. The war was over, peace was near." A German civilian came upon the Russians and Americans celebrating together, looked at the scene in despair, put a gun to his head, and shot himself dead.

IN THE FINAL hours of April 25 and into the next day, Americans and Russians would meet all along the Elbe, and for the soldiers of both armies the tension of a thousand nights of trouble melted away. "Men on both sides of the river tossed their caps and helmets into the air and cheered loudly," a then-twenty-three-year-old veteran of Stalingrad recollected. "We smiled happily, eyes shining. . . . Far away from our own homelands, on the bank of a German river, we sang songs, cracked jokes, laughed and reminisced together." Even near Strehla, the initial awkwardness that surrounded Kotzebue's meeting dissipated into a joyous celebration that Joe Polowsky would long remember. "We drank and there were accordions and balalaikas and music and dancing." The Russians broke into a harmonica factory in Torgau, and they all seemed to know how to play. Ann Stringer, a journalist, was swept up in the Russian-organized merriment. "We drank toasts in cognac. Then wine. Then schnapps. Then vodka. Then another liquor which I couldn't quite identify, although it tasted like grain alcohol." It was "the best time I ever had in my life," crowed Private Leo Kasinsky to a reporter. "We had about sixty toasts. Boy, they don't even drink like that in Brooklyn."

The language differences proved more difficult to surmount than the Elbe. The Russians could do a little better than the Americans—one kept approaching GIs and exhausting his repertoire of "How do you do? How old are you? What time is it?"—but "they seemed instinctively to like each other," reported an Associated Press correspondent. "We were on the same side. Everyone was a friend," said one GI, but there was more to it than that. The two sides looked at each other, and in light of the very human emotions of the moment, saw something familiar. The Steppes seemed much the same as the Plains; Ukrainians not all that different from Iowans. Young *Stars and Stripes* reporter Andy Rooney wrote on April 26, 1945, from Torgau as if the Russians were silly Kansas farm boys: "It is impossible to imagine a regimented, goose-stepping Russian." The "Russian soldiers are the most carefree bunch of screwballs that ever came together in an army. They could best be described as exactly like Americans only twice as much." The theme repeated itself over and again. "We waited for them to come ashore," Luibov Kozinchenko would remember. "We could see their faces. They looked like ordinary people. We had imagined something different." Al Aronson would concur: "I guess we didn't know what to expect from the Russians, but when you looked at them and examined them, you couldn't tell whether . . . you know? If you put an American uniform on them, they could have been American!"

The optimism and hope flowed as freely as the vodka and the schnapps. "You get the feeling of exuberance, a great new world opening up," Andy Rooney reported. It was a "mad scene of jubilant celebration." They had come so far, survived so much, seen such horrors, and felt such fear, that all they wanted to do was exhale. The sweet scent of waxing apple blossoms flushed the patios where they sang and drank and ate chocolate. American women war correspondents danced with Russian soldiers; Red Army nurses danced with American GIs. For some reason, soldiers would find themselves laughing—constantly, seemingly uncontrollably, even hysterically—at jokes and quips and slapstick pantomimes they barely understood. Freed from a German POW camp where he had been held since 1944, Private Frank Bartz watched the goings-on and shook with so much laughter that he cried as he asked, "Say, is this war over or has everybody just gone crazy?"

Americans taught the Russians "Swanee River"; the Russians, in turn, played one of their favorite ballads: "If There Should Be War Tomorrow." No one there could imagine that such a thing was possible. At one Elbe celebration, a Russian major who spoke little English rose to make a toast: "Today we have the most happy day in our lives. At

Moscow and Stalingrad in 1941 and 1942, we have the most difficult days of our lives. Our great friends, the Americans! We have met one another. It end up the enemy." Which was not what he meant to say at all.

We've been waiting a long time," General Omar Bradley said into the telephone upon receiving word of the meeting on the Elbe. He hung up the receiver, popped open a bottle of Coca-Cola, and drew a tight circle around Torgau on the map hanging on his wall.

Around the world, the news of the linkup on the Elbe was met with a joy that matched that of the soldiers. "East and West have met," intoned the announcer for the BBC. "This is the news for which the whole Allied world has been waiting . . . the forces of liberation have joined hands." In Moscow, the maximum salute of twenty-four shots was fired from 324 guns to celebrate the "victory of the freedom-loving nations over Germany." In New York, there was singing and dancing in Times Square.

But in the White House, the president was solemn. Over the radio, he told Americans there were yet more hard tidings ahead. "This is not the hour of final victory in Europe, but the hour draws near, the hour for which all the American people, all the British peoples and all the Soviet people have toiled and prayed so long."

He was right. There were long hours still to come. The war was not yet over. The bliss on the Elbe was premature. One more titanic battle remained. Twenty-year-old Alexander Olshansky had been the first Russian to greet Kotzebue on the river's bank. His skin was caked with mud and his uniform was thin and threadbare at the knees and elbows. He had been through much in his short life, but while he rejoiced at the linkup, he met the Americans with solemnity and did not give in to the abandon. He understood that the brutal war's final act had not been played out: "From the Don to the Elbe, I covered many thousands of meters under enemy fire, often crawling or sprinting. I was wounded three times and shell-shocked twice, but I knew that the way home lay through Berlin."

2

TOMBSTONES

John McCloy jiggled anxiously as he waited to enter the Oval Office. As assistant secretary of war, McCloy had been in many meetings with the president to plan military operations and discuss questions of diplomacy, but through all the years of World War II, they had never met one-on-one. McCloy, the portly, balding son of a single-mother hairdresser, had distinguished himself, first on Wall Street, and then as an aide to Secretary of War Henry Stimson, through a relentless work ethic and a quiet efficiency. He had made his mark as an able assistant to the powerful, always a step behind those at the forefront of action. So when he received an urgent call to visit the White House on the morning of March 22, 1945, he was nervous, uncertain what to expect. Outside the paneled door, he shuffled his feet and paced about the West Wing. The door swung open in a hush and McCloy was ushered in. Sitting behind the desk was President Franklin Delano Roosevelt with his arm held stiffly in front of him in a Nazi salute, yelling, *"Heil hoch Kommissar für Deutschland!"*

McCloy was startled at the sight. Roosevelt delighted at the face frozen in shock. With a broad smile, he said, "I've made up my mind, McCloy, that you're going to be the first high commissioner for Germany.

We have got to have somebody there who can have an impact on the direction of the country. And I have a mind you're the fellow to do it." McCloy was staggered, but even in his astonishment he had the presence of mind to know that this was a job that he was determined to decline.

As German resistance was disintegrating, McCloy had played a central role in hard-fought debates within the Roosevelt administration over Germany's future, debates as fundamental as they were inconclusive. At least a dozen prominent men had found their names put forward for the slot of American administrator in postwar Germany. Each had found some way to dodge the honor of taking this impossible, thankless position. One, former senator and former Supreme Court justice James Byrnes, then the so-called assistant president, with broad powers over America's wartime economy, begged off with the less-than-convincing excuse that he could not possibly do the job, since he did not speak German. McCloy now had to find his own way out.

He began to slowly step away from the curved wall and toward the center of the room. Like any good lawyer, McCloy marshaled his arguments—and then let them all loose, hurling them out without pause until he found one that worked. "Mr. President, we haven't won the war. I'm up to my ears in that. We haven't won the war with Japan yet." He gasped for air. "Furthermore, I think you would probably be making a mistake to put a civilian in there right away after the victory. The great heroes, the military heroes, will be marching and countermarching around. It will be primarily a military problem at first."

McCloy could tell by Roosevelt's expression that his excuses were making little headway, but he continued to spill out every point he could think of. "Moreover, it will be a problem of keeping body and soul together. There won't be too many political decisions of any consequence first off. And the person who goes in there is going to find himself in a situation like a Mississippi River disaster. Where are the rations going to come from? How are people going to be fed? Basic logistics." For the first time, Roosevelt seemed to be engaged, so McCloy continued in this vein of argument: What was needed was someone with administrative, rather than diplomatic experience. "And with all the armies there, with the military conquest so recent, I think a civilian there might be submerged," he recapped. "He is going to have to call on the Army to do it. So why not let the Army do it?"

He stopped, and in the moment of still that followed, studied Roosevelt. The brio and zest the president had displayed when McCloy first walked in had drained away and—as if a shadow had passed over him— he was now a shriveled figure, halfway hidden behind the knickknacks and bric-a-brac that blanketed his desk. McCloy noticed that Roosevelt's shirt collar hung loose around his neck, as if the shrinking person before him was wearing a larger man's clothes. Outside the Oval Office window, a cold breeze shook the young buds of the magnolias. After a week of warm, even hot, days, the thermometer had dropped a dozen degrees overnight and the temperature hovered in the midforties, a final blast of winter before spring took hold. Roosevelt looked up at him with haggard eyes. "McCloy, I'm too tired to argue with you. I think you're wrong," he sighed, defeated, "but you tell me: Amongst the soldiers, who could do this job?"

For just an instant, McCloy paused.

AT THAT MOMENT, in late March of 1945, a month before they would meet the Russians, American troops were only days away from crossing the Rhine, but little progress had been made on planning for Germany's future after the end of the war—except, perhaps, in the private thoughts of Franklin D. Roosevelt.

Roosevelt, alone, considered himself an expert on Germany. As a young boy, he had visited the country with his parents eight times— once bicycling through Bavaria—and then had spent his honeymoon with Eleanor touring in high style. The problem of Germany, he was convinced, was less one of national policy than of national psychology. A strain of militarism had infected the peaceful, poetic Teutonic people he had known as a child in the privileged spas where his parents cavorted. The world would not know peace until the German mind-set was radically reformed.

The failure to do this, Roosevelt believed, was the tragedy of

Versailles. In the first years of the twenty-first century, the conventional assessment of the accord ending the First World War was that by imposing harsh reparations and economic burdens on Germany, the Versailles Treaty created the bitter resentments that boiled into the rage of the Third Reich. Roosevelt's verdict on Versailles, instead, was that the Allies' failure had been one of treating the defeated Germans too lightly. Where, at the end of the Great War, President Woodrow Wilson had been determined to avoid occupying Germany and had stated he had "no desire to march triumphantly into Berlin," Roosevelt, then his young assistant secretary of the Navy, was convinced that "the one lesson the Germans will learn is the lesson of defeat." In the decade that followed, as he lay in bed for long hours, defeated in politics and wracked by paralysis, Roosevelt studied newspaper accounts of the struggling Weimar Republic and grew ever more convinced that America should have occupied Germany and taught its people the ways of democracy at the point of a gun.

As president, he was resolved that he would not allow America to make the same mistake again. Among the three wartime allies, something of a bidding war broke out over who could vow the harshest treatment toward Germans after the war. At their Tehran conference in 1943, Roosevelt had told Stalin that it was "very important not to leave in the German mind the concept of 'the Reich.'" Indeed, "the very word Reich should be stricken from the language." Stalin replied it was "not enough to eliminate the word. The very Reich itself must be rendered impotent, so as never again to plunge the world into war." When Winston Churchill declaimed that postwar Germany should be stripped of all its aviation and armament factories, Stalin said this too was not enough: "Furniture factories could be transformed into airplane factories. Watch factories could make fuses for shells."

Returning from Tehran, Roosevelt reported on what had happened in a wartime fireside chat on Christmas Eve. The Allies had "no intention to enslave the German people. We wish them to have a normal chance to develop, in peace, as useful and respectable members of the European family. But we most certainly emphasize that word 'respectable' for we intend to rid them once and for all of Nazism and Prussian militarism and the fantastic and disastrous notion that they constitute the 'master race.'" Americans had learned the errors of the past. "After the Armistice in 1918, we thought and hoped that the militaristic philosophy of Germany had been crushed; and being full of the milk of human kindness we . . . lived on pious hopes that aggressor and warlike nations would learn and understand and carry out the doctrine of purely voluntary peace. The well-intentioned but ill-fated experiments of former years did not work. It is my hope that we will not try them again. No—that is putting it too weakly—it is my intention to do all that I humanly can as president and commander in chief to see to it that these tragic mistakes shall not be made again." But Roosevelt believed that while Americans wanted to see the war won, they would not stand for a long-term commitment of troops in foreign lands. Such an involvement would run counter to the entire history of the nation. En route to Tehran, Army Chief of Staff General George Marshall had asked Roosevelt how long American soldiers would stay in Europe after the war. "For at least a year," Roosevelt announced and then hedged, "maybe two."

While Roosevelt had struck a note of mercilessness, his cabinet members fought with one another over the tenor of America's policies of occupation. The discussion quickly settled into two camps. Secretary of War Stimson led one. He was committed to the rebuilding of Germany in the spirit of "Christianity and kindness" in order to stave off further chaos. On the other side of the debate was Secretary of the Treasury Henry Morgenthau, who, confronted by evidence of the Holocaust while the war still raged, had waged an ultimately unsuccessful campaign to convince war planners to attempt to stop the genocide. As it became clear that the Allies would prevail in the conflict, Morgenthau became fixated on the idea that Germany must never again be able to rise up and wreak havoc on the world. Working feverishly, he and his staff produced a plan to strip Germany of its industrial strength and leave it a "land of small farms" where men would lift rakes but never again rifles. "To return Germany as a respectable member of the family of nations is to put Germany in a position where she will again endeavor to become master of the world," he argued in the summer of 1944. "Twice in our generation she has tried, and the third time, she may well be successful." For many, the acrid, severe Morgenthau Plan was hard to swallow. Roosevelt appeared to lap it up. "If I had my way," he said publicly in August 1944, "I would keep Germany in a breadline for the next 25 years." Election-year statements by a consummate campaigner can be discounted, but even privately he told his cabinet members that same month that Germans could "live happily and peacefully on soup from soup kitchens."

The argument over postwar Germany continued for months and, as he so often would, Roosevelt chose to allow the debates to fester and the decisions to be delayed. There were many reasons for his avoidance. Consumed by the work of leading a nation and an alliance in fighting a total global war, he had little time to plan for the peace. By nature superstitious, he shrank from making firm plans for a nation he had yet to conquer. A master politician, he stalled at committing himself to decisions too early, preferring an *ad hoc* governing style that kept decision-making firmly in his own hip pocket.

But there was another, more human reason why planning on Germany's post-Nazi future had slowed. By the winter of 1944, the architects of American policy were decaying and exhausted. Stimson was nearing the age of eighty and flagging in his energies. Secretary of State Cordell Hull was secretly living in the Bethesda Naval Hospital—a tall tower on the outskirts of Washington—because he had advanced tuberculosis and diabetes. Roosevelt himself was a broken shell of a man, unable to conduct the business of government for more than two to four hours a day. He often arose after 11 A.M. and was back in bed by 6 P.M. He had created an administration where he alone made all major choices and where no one else had the full information or the president's complete trust. Without his active engagement, decision-making could not go forward and vigorous debates could not be resolved.

With the stalemate dragging on, the factions agreed to draft a document for Roosevelt's signature that took a tough tone on Germany's future but allowed a future American postwar administrator large discretion to make the real decisions. In effect, they punted the final judgment into the hands of an individual who had not been selected.

For months, the job of presiding over postwar Germany went unfilled. As those mentioned for the position balked, a dangerous vacuum developed. Supreme Commander Dwight Eisenhower's ambitious and ruthlessly efficient chief of staff, General Walter Bedell Smith, worked fervidly to secure the post. The gleam in his eyes was a glitter. His plan was to divide up captured Nazi gold among his fellow American generals as war loot. "Can't some of us quietly arrange some of our own bonuses?" he wondered.

In that March of 1945, with Germany collapsing, Roosevelt's generals and advisers pleaded with him to make a decision on who would be appointed. He changed the subject by telling tales and offering up reminiscences. Perhaps he himself would "like to try" his hand at serving as overlord in conquered Germany, he would muse before repeating his oft-heard stories about bicycling through Bavaria long ago. Leaving the Yalta conference the month before, he had jauntily told Stalin, "We will meet again soon . . . in Berlin!" But as the American army drove toward its meeting with the Soviets in the heart of the Nazi Reich, the question of who would put in place Roosevelt's stern policy toward the Germans was still undecided.

"WHO?" Roosevelt pressed McCloy again.

With barely a breath, McCloy blurted out, "Lucius Clay." The reply came from someplace deeper than thought. He had not given the answer a moment's consideration. He hardly knew the man. While throughout the war he had heard reports of the general's great effectiveness in securing supplies and weapons for the troops in the field, "these reports," he would remember, "were sometimes accompanied by vivid accounts of his somewhat arbitrary or brusque methods of operating." And so, for the rest of his life, John McCloy would often wonder why it was that he suddenly and fatefully uttered the name of Lucius D. Clay.

Roosevelt stared at McCloy blankly. McCloy, having not been immediately rebuffed, launched into his sales job. "You must have heard of him. He's Jimmy Byrnes's right-hand man. He's been doing all the procurement for the Army. And to me he's the real factor in that area. Furthermore, he's an Army engineer. He has dealt with disasters of this kind. He knows how to distribute food, and keep body and soul together." Roosevelt had not said anything, and McCloy, resolved not to let the president get a word in edgewise to turn down Clay, continued his filibuster. "Furthermore, he is a very interesting man. He is the son of old Senator Clay, and he was a page boy in the House of Representatives."

For the first time in the conversation, Roosevelt—an unashamed celebrator of idyllic American boyhood—perked up. "Oh, is that so?" For a brief moment, this biographical nugget seemed to change Roosevelt's entire countenance, but the shadow passed over again. "Well, as I said before, I'm too tired to argue with you, McCloy. I haven't changed my mind, but I'll think it over."

McCloy left the Oval Office and walked to James Byrnes's small East Wing office. He thought Byrnes might refuse to part with Clay. Instead, when McCloy recounted the conversation, Byrnes said, "You're absolutely right. I think Clay would be the man." Though McCloy did not know it, Byrnes—still stung by Roosevelt's machinations at the previous year's Democratic convention, which had denied Byrnes the vice presidential nomination and instead swung it to a little-known senator from Missouri—was planning on leaving his position within days. "Talk to Marshall and Stimson about it," he told McCloy. "I'll take care of the boss."

A couple of days later, Byrnes went into the Oval Office to tell the president he was resigning. They fell into a long conversation about peace and war. Roosevelt ambled aimlessly through his stories, getting lost in familiar terrain. He wandered from tangent to tangent and blinked helplessly when the thread of his thinking would slip out of his hands. When the discussion came to postwar Germany, Roosevelt said he planned to send McCloy to run the occupation. Byrnes replied as if the commander in chief were a dense child. No, he said slowly, the War Department had decided that Clay should be sent. Roosevelt, tired and wan, sighed and acquiesced. He asked only to have Clay come by so that he could meet him. Byrnes, who had kept the intrigue from Clay to this point, left to go break the news. He knew he would have to be gentle.

On March 28, 1945, Lucius Clay sat at his desk shuffling papers, waiting for the phone to ring. His office, across from the White House, on the top floor of the Hoover-era Reconstruction Finance Corporation building on Lafayette Park, fluttered with activity. Purposely small and informal, with only seven or eight staff members at any one time, the Office of War Mobilization had been given full reign over America's wartime industries and daily life on the "home front," thereby freeing Roosevelt to concentrate his limited energies on military and diplomatic efforts.

Managing its operations was Clay, the General Patton of white paper, a bureaucratic warrior who barreled over anything or anyone deigning to stand in his way. He had been appointed to the deputy position in December 1944, shortly before both Roosevelt and Byrnes departed for Yalta, and in their absence, Clay—a general whom few had heard of—was perhaps the most powerful government official in America. He made full use of that power, putting in place a series of measures that made his name—often preceded by a curse—a common expression in homes across the country.

With victory in sight, and after years of rationing and sacrifice, Americans were eager to begin returning to normal ways of life, to leisure and laughter and the occasional splurge. Clay, to whom Byrnes delegated much responsibility even after his return from Yalta, would have none of it. Instead of easing up, he turned on the screws. War involved all, not just the troops in the field, he believed, and all Americans would do their part—whether they wanted to or not. Clay and Byrnes asked for legislation that would have given the government the ability to draft young men into important industries at home just as surely as it put them into uniform and gave them a gun. Despite active campaigning for the measure by Roosevelt—the debt of those that did not serve in this moment, he said, would be repaid "with the life's blood of our sons"—the bill passed the House of Representatives only to be defeated in the Senate by an odd coalition of labor unions and the far right.

When he was free to exercise his powers by edict, Clay was more successful—and more comfortable. He enforced brownouts and night-time curfews in major cities to conserve energy. He shut down horse racing, arguing that Americans should not be wasting gasoline and tires to drive to the track. When New York City mayor Fiorello LaGuardia balked at an order to close nightclubs and bars at midnight, Clay sent military police in every night at the appointed hour to tell men in uniform to go home. The other patrons, shamed, would invariably follow. *Time* magazine proclaimed Clay "the military's conscience pricker on the Home Front."

These were the matters—draft boards and draft beers—that concerned Clay that late March day in 1945. But as his young assistants ran about the office suite bringing him papers to sign, Clay would, every so often, look intently at the heavy black phone that rested on his desk, ready to leap on it like a grenade the moment it rang. He had waited thirty years for this call, growing gray and impatient. Now he was sure it was coming. If it did not come now, it never would.

His thoughts were interrupted by his secretary's announcement that a Mr. Robert Murphy was there to see him. They had never met, but in an era when diplomats were famous, Robert Murphy was, in some quarters, infamous. The so-called "Lawrence of North Africa," Murphy had—dressed in a knit turtleneck, sneakers, and a baseball cap—welcomed a covert American military mission onto the beaches of Algeria in advance of the Allied invasion. He had been a spymaster and President Roosevelt's personal representative, and the wartime revelation of his secret negotiations to win over the loyalty of the Nazi-collaborators of Vichy France had earned him recognition along with opprobrium.

Clay instructed the secretary to show Murphy in and wondered why the diplomat could possibly have come. As Murphy walked in, Clay rose to meet his guest. Murphy, towering over the diminutive Clay, was the kind of tall man who carried himself with a stoop so as to try to make himself inconspicuous. His shoulders hunched and chin seemingly fused to his chest, Murphy crossed the room toward Clay in great strides and flashed a friendly grin. Clay was curious, but cordial, greeting him, in Murphy's words, with "a somewhat puzzled air." They shook hands. Murphy looked about the room. Where most offices of the powerful in Washington were well decorated with a beautiful Oriental rug spread across the floor, nothing covered the cold, humdrum tile of Clay's office. The walls were bare. It was the mark of someone who was more interested in exercising power than in creating the appearance of it. Or perhaps someone who was not planning on staying around for long.

Murphy began to speak pleasantly. Within moments, Lucius Clay's most fervent dreams had been destroyed.

LUCIUS DUBIGNON CLAY was born in the final years of the nineteenth century—a Southerner who grew up among the memories of a vanished world. When he was a young boy, the conversations he overheard in the front parlor of the large rambling house with a white veranda were so often about lives that once had been and then were destroyed amid the terrors of military occupation and the terrible burdens of defeat. He later would joke that he "had to go to school in the North to learn that the North had won the war." But that could not have been less true. His hometown of Marietta had been burned to the ground by Union soldiers who set off from there on their March to the Sea across the state of Georgia. Only two buildings had survived, and when Clay was born in April 1898 it was into a town that had been rebuilt from the ashes. The war had ended more than thirty years earlier, but it suffused the atmosphere as surely as the scent of the willows.

Clay was, by far, the youngest of six children born to Alexander Stephens Clay and his wife, Frances. In 1896, two years before Clay's birth, his father had been elected to the United States Senate. Clay grew up surrounded by politics and learned its ways as naturally as he learned the alphabet. An endless round of local dignitaries served as regular guests for suppers where "politics," according to Clay, "was always the conversation of the day." To outsiders, life behind the great white veranda seemed idyllic. But it was a house divided.

Steve Clay was a progressive voice in a state struggling to escape its history. To the dirt farmers of northern Georgia who were his devoted supporters, he represented a new type of leader who rejected much of the sordid past. His maiden speech in the Senate had been a denunciation of American imperialism in the Philippines. He was an advocate of the progressive income tax, the first chairman of the Senate's Select Committee on Women's Suffrage, and a proponent of the free delivery of mail to rural communities as a way of binding the nation together. "We should be broad and liberal in our policy, tolerant in our spirit," he would say, and he won his elections without appealing to racism and without waving the tired, tattered, bloody flag of Dixie.

Yet if Lucius Clay's father sought to represent Georgia's future, his mother was never willing to shake her allegiance to the past. "She was very bitter about the North, and didn't like Yankees," remembered her grandson. She founded the Marietta chapter of the United Daughters of the Confederacy. And when, every April 26—to commemorate the day of the Southern surrender to Sherman, which ended the war in Georgia—Clay and the other children of the town would march together through the streets carrying a "flower of love" to deposit on the grave of a war dead, it was Clay's mother who ensured that the Confederate flag flew overhead at the cemetery. "The Civil War was always with us when I was growing up," said Clay. Indeed, it played out in his very home.

It was not just the continuing battles of the War Between the States that raged in the Clay household but skirmishes of a more prosaic nature as well. Clay watched helplessly as his family spiraled out of control. "His brothers all had the world at their feet," Clay's nephew would say, "and they went haywire. He saw that, plus unbelievable fits of emotion." A flowerpot was set up on the front porch just so that his older siblings could kick it over when they were upset. Four of his older siblings would eventually see their lives ruined by alcoholism; the fifth died before he reached that point.

In later years, however, the childhood Clay spoke of—and quite possibly the childhood he remembered—was the one he constructed for himself. It was a lavender life of surrey rides to church on Sunday, ten-cent shows at the movie house, ice-cream sodas with a date at the drugstore, and summer concerts in the town square where a third of Marietta would gather to hear music played under the bandstand. He treasured the constant stream of august dinner guests and the serious conversations they had with his father, but all his happiest memories came when he escaped the high ceilings and high tension of that white-steepled house.

He would run down the painted steps of the wraparound veranda and out past the two magnolias that stood guard over the house. The Clays owned thirty-five acres of land, and ten of those had peach trees, and he would sample the crop. At Brown's Creek, he would build a dam—his friends were amazed at how easily he did it—and wait for the water to back up and then swim and splash. But of all the happy memories of childhood he carried with him like keepsakes, the times he probably cherished most were those spent catfishing in the Chattahoochee. On the banks of the river, sheltered by the whispering hemlock, he would watch the blue heron play and wait for the catfish to bite. He would while away hours—alone, happy, and far from home.

If fishing and scampering through the foliage was one escape for young Lucius Clay, traveling with his father to Washington was another. Their small suite in the Normandy Hotel was no match for peach trees and catfish, the hours of stentorian debate in the shadowy Senate chamber did little to capture his interest, even the visits to the columned mansion down the street where his father's friend Theodore Roosevelt lived and once gallantly pulled a rose from his lapel to present to Clay's sister were not what the boy loved most about life in the nation's capital. Rather, he would remember, "the thing that impressed me more than anything was the Library of Congress, where, as a member of a senator's family, I could get all of the books I wanted to read."

At least once a week he would crawl into the library's stacks, devouring six or eight books at a time. Straining to read by the flicker of gas lamps, he developed a twitch in his right eye but was hardly slowed. He would read stories of chivalry, of knights clad in armor going off to do battle. But much of the time, he read about the Civil War. He studied the battles intently, learning the positions of the lines and the strategies of the generals. With stacks of books under his arms, Clay could dream of picking up the fallen standard at Gettysburg, charging up Cemetery Ridge, pushing past the copse of trees, and leaving the High Water Mark behind as he headed north in glory; of reversing the history of failure he had been bequeathed, the whispered shame and anger that filled his Marietta home.

When Clay was twelve, his father died, and he was left in that veranda-moated house with his domineering mother and older siblings rapidly descending into potomania and pathology. The trips to Washington ended; the esteemed worthies no longer came by for supper. Clay lashed out in rebellion and anger. He ran around town with a gang called the "Filthy Five"; at fourteen he became upset with his chemistry teacher and pushed him out of the schoolhouse's first-floor window. "He was strong-willed and he was very strongly opinionated and if you got into a discussion with him, his view was the correct one," said one of his closest friends as a young man. "He would persist and it was pretty hard to try to change his mind." If Clay were to escape his brothers' fate, he needed to replace the chaos of their home with a sense of order, to find an outlet for his belligerence more satisfying than endless arguments and more useful than manhandling chemistry teachers, to fling open the doors of his imagination that had once been unbolted by those dusty volumes in the marble library in Washington. In the summer of 1914, a month before the archduke of Austria's driver made a wrong turn in Sarajevo and happened by the café where a Black Hand terrorist named Gavrilo Princip was eating a sandwich, Lucius Clay was appointed to West Point.

CLAY ARRIVED AT a military academy that was holding tight to bygone ways. West Point's curriculum had not changed fundamentally in over a century. While hundreds of thousands of young men were dying in brutal trench warfare in the fields of Flanders, America's future generals were being drilled in the same cavalry tactics that had been created for Spotsylvania, not the Somme. The West Point program emphasized rigid, ridiculous discipline and rote memorization of the useless and trivial. For an intellect as powerful as Clay's, the work was laughably easy. He made some basic effort at studying in his first year; after that he never cracked open a textbook. Ignoring his prescribed studies, he spent hours reading Balzac, Zola, Dickens, and Dumas. He ended up ranked 27th in his class, a more than respectable showing among the 137 graduates. But the number hid the true story: He was ranked first in English, first in history—and 128th in conduct.

Had he simply withdrawn into his own interests, he could have easily floated through his time in the school without causing a fuss. Such was not his way. He chafed against the medieval caste system on campus and refused to show the deference to his elders that custom required. Demerits were handed out liberally for the smallest infractions and paved the way to expulsion. Clay collected them as others did postage stamps. The boy who had run with the "Filthy Five" in Marietta now grew into the ringleader of a group called the "Dirty Dozen." In a derelict part of the cadet canteen, they set up a clubhouse where, after football games, with a windup phonograph playing in the background, they danced with girls, drank beer, and smoked cigarettes. Clay's smoking habit was "a source of infinite demerits." When one of his instructors invited a pretty date to a weekend dance, Clay stole her away, accumulating another sixty demerits. Seven weeks from the end of his third year at West Point, he was four demerits away from being expelled.

Had he returned for a fourth year, he would almost certainly not have managed to graduate. Fortunately for him, senior year for Clay's class was canceled on account of the Great War. For Clay this was thrilling news. As much as he had chafed at West Point's authority system, his greatest discomfit came from his yearning for battle. When Clay's class was graduated a year early, in June 1918, America had already been in the war for more than a year, and there was clamor all along Germany's western front. That spring, the kaiser's armies had advanced to within 75 miles of Paris. It was America's greatest conflict since Appomattox, and Clay was driven to distraction by the idea that, having decided to devote his life to the military, he would then miss "the war to end all wars." "I thought we ought to be let out and go into the war," he said, "and staying at West Point seemed a rather useless waste of time really." Clay had decided to enter the artillery and left school wearing their crossed cannons. "The greatest thrill I could imagine was taking a horse-drawn battery and putting it into action." He went home to await his orders.

AFTER ONLY ONE week in Marietta, the orders came. But something was horribly amiss. Instead of being assigned to a battle unit headed for the front, the cable he received was addressed to "Lieutenant Lucius D. Clay, Corps of Engineers" and directed him to report immediately to Camp Humphreys in Virginia. He contacted the War Department under the assumption someone had made a terrible error in the paperwork. "I wired the adjutant general and told him he'd made a mistake. I was in the field artillery. He wired me back that he knew what he was doing and I'd better follow orders." He reported in at the end of June. The Armistice came a continent away that November.

If there was any gilded lining to missing the Great War, it was that during that summer of 1918, Clay had been able to continue a courtship that had begun at West Point. When his best friend was sick in the infirmary, Clay—always helpful—volunteered to go to the bus station to retrieve the young lady who was coming up from the city to be his date for that weekend's prom. As Marjorie McKeown, a Barnard coed and daughter of a New Jersey button magnate, descended from the bus, Clay saw immediately that she was a stunning beauty with blond hair and blue eyes the size of dinner plates. She must have been similarly impressed—or perhaps the step was just slick—for she slipped coming down and fell directly into Clay's arms. They were engaged that Labor Day and married two weeks later.

Bored at backwater installations in the slighted military of an era that saw diplomats signing treaties to outlaw war itself, Clay's obstinance became a defining characteristic of his years as a junior officer. While efficiency reports routinely lauded his abilities, there was a persistent, nagging question in his evaluations: "mercurial temperament," "sensitivity to criticism," "tenacity in pursuit of his own ideas." Clay saw little future in the military, but was unsure of what other direction to take. He responded to want ads in the *New York Times* and considered applying to law school, but mostly by force of inertia he remained in the Army. In 1929, he was stationed in Panama. After two years, he was sent to Pittsburgh and returned to a country in the throes of the Great Depression. He walked amid the shantytowns that had sprung up in that once-bustling industrial hub and rejoiced in the election of Franklin Roosevelt in 1932. Three months after Roosevelt's inauguration, he was called to Washington to become the number-two man in the Rivers and Harbors Division of the Corps of Engineers. With it came a promotion—the first he had received in fifteen years.

The new job placed Clay in a military division that had once been disregarded but now was becoming a central part of the New Deal's Works Progress Administration. As a young boy in Washington, lost amid the stacks of Jefferson's library in the nation's athenaeum, he had thought more of Cemetery Ridge than Capitol Hill. At West Point, he had been trained for battles very different from those in a bureaucracy. But the senator's son quickly saw the possibilities of his new job and knew instinctively how to make the most of it. In a hungry nation, Clay was dispensing huge sides of pork. From his office in the dark Old Munitions Building, he greeted a parade of congressmen who, with the Depression ravishing their communities, inquired about—in fact, pleaded for—construction of public works projects in their districts. He made himself indispensable to them. He was always ready to provide snippets of information on plans being made and enough scraps of advice on how to get the project moving through the bureaucracy to send them scampering off toward the Hill sated and obliged. He made the acquaintance of a junior senator named Harry Truman whose home state happened to have a number of rivers—among them the Missouri and the Mississippi. When floods tore through Paducah, Kentucky, in 1936, Clay sent a Corps of Engineers boat to save Senator Alben

Barkley's mother. Most important, that same year he worked with Congressman Sam Rayburn on a massive flood-control bill, and because of this, he would recall, "I don't think anyone in Washington was as close to Mr. Rayburn as I was at the time." When Rayburn would repair to his "Board of Education" with other members of Congress to drink bourbon and branch water, Clay was one of the few outsiders invited along.

In 1937, Clay spent a year in the Philippines analyzing hydroelectric power for Douglas MacArthur and his deputy, Dwight Eisenhower, before being summoned to construct the immense Denison Dam on the Red River in the district of now–Majority Leader Rayburn. By September 1940, Europe was at war and Clay was called back to Washington to head a titanic effort to build airports across the country. When he began the job, there were only 36 airports of any real significance in America. A year later, 457 were being built, including Washington's National Airport, Newark Airport, Chicago's O'Hare, and Los Angeles Airport. The airports were purportedly built for civilian use—Congress refused to anger an isolationist public by spending any large sums for defense preparedness—and so Clay worked out of the Civil Aviation Division of the Department of Commerce. By this time, Clay was only nominally a military officer. He did not even wear a uniform through most of the 1930s, but rather could be seen about town in three-piece wool suits and slicked-back hair and, were it not for his intense, piercing eyes, could have been mistaken for an easygoing young executive.

ON SUNDAY, DECEMBER 7, 1941, Clay was sitting in the commerce secretary's box at Griffith Stadium watching the Washington Redskins tromp the Philadelphia Eagles. One by one, admirals sitting in the stands were called by name over the public address system and asked to report. A quiver of curiosity shot through the crowd. Sportswriter Shirley Povich came up to the box to report the rumor that Pearl Harbor had been bombed. Impossible, declared Clay. "Pearl Harbor is impregnable."

That night Clay pulled his uniform out of storage and, though it was outdated, wore it the next day. With America at war, he was sent immediately to Brazil to build an important airport at Natal on the Atlantic.

He soon returned, ready to finally go off and fight. Instead, he was assigned to the War Plans Division. "I don't think that's my talent," he told his friend Dwight Eisenhower. "Well, in any event, you take a desk here for the time being," Eisenhower responded. Finally, George Marshall announced that Clay would be chief of matériel in the new Services of Supply. Clay, put into an office job when he finally had the chance to go to war, ran immediately to see his new boss and told him of his unhappiness. General Brehon Somervell's reply was succinct: "That's too goddamned bad." Defeated, Clay then asked for directions on what do in his new position. "Your job is to find out what the Army needs and get it," Somervell answered. "As a matter of fact," Clay would note later, "those are the only instructions I ever had from him."

For the next three years, Clay was responsible for every element of supplying an army of 8 million men—from negotiating contracts to supervising research and development to demanding that schedules be met. He oversaw everything from building 88,000 tanks to sewing 229 million pairs of pants. The work, and the sense of responsibility, consumed him. He was at his desk at the Pentagon at 7:30 in the morning and would stay at work until 10 or 11 at night. Often he would work seventy-two hours straight through, leaving only for quick trips home to shower and shave.

He expected the same level of commitment and devotion to duty from all other Americans. A lipstick manufacturer fought plans to convert his factory to making machine-gun cartridges with the argument, "We must keep up the morale of American women." Clay's face darkened: "Yesterday, the sons of several hundred American women died in battle. Perhaps some of them would have lived if they'd had all the cartridges they needed. I'm interested in the morale of several million other American mothers. I demand that this plant get into the war." Looking back a few years later, another businessman would observe, "After I had been battling with Clay for several months, I concluded that it must have been someone just like him who originally inspired the association of the adjective 'grudging' with the noun 'admiration.'"

The admiration came not only from his commitment to the cause, but also from the skill with which he worked. He had become a first-rate Washington hand. Byrnes recounted that in wartime Washington he had "found no man more capable than Clay and no Army officer who had as clear an understanding of the point of view of the civilian," meaning, from his perspective, the point of view of civilians like him: accomplished political power players. John Kenneth Galbraith, who had been deputy head of the Office of Price Administration, remembered him as "one of the most skillful politicians ever to wear the uniform of the United States Army."

Kept away from the front, Clay turned the conference room into a battlefield. When backed into a corner in an argument, he would come out fighting with a ferociousness far out of proportion with the stakes. "He had a mind that was splendid in his capacity for logical and clear thought," recalled a young lawyer on his staff. "But when he got into an argument he was really quite outrageous. You would make a statement, perhaps a peripheral overstatement that was not quite accurate, he would not hit you on the subject that was central, but would grab hold of the misstatement, error, or weak statement and essentially seek to best you in that like a debater rather than coping with the subject." In a dispute, he would never concede a point, even if afterward he would adopt the other's position as though it had been his own all along. "He liked to fight to a Mickey Finn" was how McCloy would later put it. "Clay has incurred the wrath of junior and senior officers, prominent and powerful civilian industrialists and politicians," wrote the *New York Times*. "He has in most of his arguments been proved right in time. This, one feels, is all General Clay cares about. He gives the impression of not giving a hoot about public or private opinion of Lucius Clay."

Clay was crucial to the American war effort, but he was miserable at being kept away from the battlefields for which he had waited his entire career. His friends were leading assaults at places like El Alamein and Anzio. He read about it in the papers. His own grown sons were in the thick of combat; one fought in North Africa and up through Italy, the other flew seventy bombing missions against the Nazis. Clay worked in the quiet of the Pentagon. "Day after day," Marjorie Clay would remember, "he came home complaining about the misfortune of being denied a combat command." In the spring of 1943, he attempted to transfer to the Persian Gulf command. He was denied. That December, five days before Christmas, he wrote a long, overwrought letter to Somervell asking to be sent into the field. Military procurement had been successfully ramped up and now someone fresh could better do the job, he argued. Having been promoted quickly during the war, he even offered to take a large demotion in rank—from major general back down to colonel—in order to be sent to the front. Somervell responded the next day in two terse sentences, which concluded that "the needs here in Washington are too pressing to permit favorable consideration of your request." When Dwight Eisenhower was put in charge of the invasion of Europe, he offered his friend Clay the job of chief engineer on the cross-Channel crossing. Once more, Clay's transfer was blocked. In August 1944, two months after D-Day, Clay sent another telegram to Somervell: "PRODUCTION DIFFICULTIES LESSENING. CLAY SAYS NOW MAY HE PLEASE GO TO WAR." Again the answer was no. Clay was despondent. "I am afraid that my almost thirty years of military service is going to wind up with me still behind a desk filled with papers, while you and others are doing the things that are really worthwhile," he wrote a friend serving with MacArthur. "I really feel quite hopeless and blue about it."

Then, just as the winter of 1944 was setting in, Clay's situation finally brightened. Eisenhower's supply lines had broken down and his troops were running low on everything from ammunition to gasoline. The drive that had begun on the cliffs of Normandy had been stymied by a lack of American bullets more than by the force of German arms. The French port of Cherbourg, the only real avenue for bringing in matériel, had become a bottleneck. Eisenhower asked for Clay to come to Europe—and this time the move was approved. When Clay arrived, Eisenhower promised him a combat division if he would clean up the breakdown at Cherbourg, then being called "the most important port in the world." He was given three weeks. About a week later, General James Stratton—who had been a fellow young officer in the 1920s—came to visit Clay. He found him sitting alone in a quiet room reading a book. "For Christ's sake, Lucius, don't you have anything to do?" Clay took him on a tour of a port that was now bustling with activity.

Two weeks after Clay had arrived, Eisenhower called him back to Paris. The supreme Allied commander was apologetic. While Clay would still get the division he had been promised, Eisenhower needed him first to make a quick trip back to Washington to check on a slow-down in delivery of artillery ammunition. Clay spoke slowly, heavily: "They will not let me come back." Not to worry, said Eisenhower. He wrote out a personal letter to General Marshall stating that Clay needed to be sent back to Europe as quickly as possible.

Clay arrived back in Washington on a Thursday; by Friday afternoon the problem was on the way to being solved and he prepared to return to Europe on Sunday. That Saturday, Clay was sitting at a desk at the Pentagon before he planned to head off to Baltimore for the Army-Navy football game. The phone rang and Clay lifted the receiver to find James Byrnes, who had just been put in charge of the home front, on the line with the news that Clay had been assigned to be his deputy. "I'm sure you're mistaken," Clay said almost desperately. "I have a letter here from General Eisenhower asking that I be returned immediately."

Byrnes was tender, almost remorseful. "I think you're coming with me."

Clay appealed immediately to Marshall, to no avail. "I am afraid that I failed to appreciate fully" the Army football victory that afternoon, he would later write. In fact, he was devastated. "I never saw a sicker man," said a colleague of Clay. "It was a wound that never healed, it bit into his soul," said another. More than thirty-five years later, Marjorie would look back across the years and remember with a wife's tenderness, "It ruined his life." All that kept him going was the promise that the job would only last four months. This meant that while he would miss the war in Europe, he would receive combat command for the long slog that would be the deadly, difficult invasion of Japan. By the end of March, on that day Robert Murphy walked into his office, it had been three months and twenty-six days since Byrnes's call. And Clay was expecting the phone to ring with his new assignment at any moment.

———

MURPHY SMILED BROADLY and casually said he had just wanted to stop in to congratulate Clay on his new job. Clay looked at him blankly, tiny furrows of terror beginning to gather on his brow. Murphy, undaunted, kept talking. He was looking forward, he said, to working with Clay when the general took up his position in charge of the military government of postwar Germany. Clay's face sank. Murphy, realizing, blanched. No, Clay gasped in a cry of anguish that sounded as if he had been run through with a spear. There must be some mistake, he snapped, as, in Murphy's words, "his politeness vanished." But he knew it was true. Silence hung over the office. "After an awkward moment," Murphy managed to excuse himself and showed himself out the door, leaving Clay standing there, alone, stunned.

Clay dropped into his chair. A few minutes went by before the phone rang. It was Byrnes asking Clay to come to his office in the White House. The walk across Lafayette Park and bustling Pennsylvania Avenue was short, but Clay took his time, feeling the weight of each step. Byrnes told him the news. It is unrecorded whether Clay pretended to act surprised.

What is clear is that he moved quickly to try to reverse the decision. He drove immediately to the Pentagon to see Somervell as well as McCloy. He practically begged them to find someone else. "I had been a soldier in two wars, and like any other professional soldier, I believed that my career would be a failure without combat experience," he later wrote. "My plea was ineffective."

The following day, March 29, Byrnes brought Clay to see Roosevelt, honoring the president's modest request. On their way to the West Wing, Byrnes prepared Clay, listing some trick questions Roosevelt might pose. It was an important meeting. Roosevelt had frozen real work on the planning for postwar Germany while the armies were still fighting and because of this, as well as the administration's internecine conflicts, any major decisions on the occupation were locked away in the president's head. Vast powers over the direction of Germany had been invested in the position of America's administrator, but the person chosen for the job—by the Pentagon and not by the president—had no relationship with Roosevelt. Clay's chief qualification appeared to be that he was unobjectionable.

Instead of a presidential audition or a serious conversation, Clay and Byrnes walked into the Oval Office to find Roosevelt in a discursive mood. He retold favorite stories about childhood trips to nineteenth-century imperial Germany with his parents. He linked the end of his presidency to its beginnings by launching in on a long discussion of his idea of constructing a vast Teutonic version of the Tennessee Valley Authority that would power all of Europe. Through it all, Clay stood silently at attention.

When they walked out, Byrnes, in his Carolina lilt, ribbed Clay, "General, you talk too much." Clay did not respond. Byrnes smiled, and tried again, "You didn't say very much."

"The president didn't ask me any questions. But I'm glad he didn't, because I was so shocked watching him that I don't think I could have made a sensible reply." He turned to look Byrnes squarely in the eye. "We've been talking to a dying man."

That evening, Roosevelt left Washington by train for Warm Springs. All he wanted to do, he wrote a friend, was "sleep and sleep and sleep."

A month later, on the banks of the Elbe, a Red Army lieutenant rose to toast his new American friends: "My dear, quiet please. You must pardon I don't speak the right English, but we are very happy so we drink a toast. Long live Roosevelt!" A fellow Russian soldier rushed up to whisper something to him about "Harry Truman." The speaker looked at him for a long instant, as if he were an idiot or a lunatic speaking gibberish. He shook his head and repeated, "Long live Roosevelt! Long live Stalin! Long live our two great armies!"

3

VISIONS

At 1:15 P.M. on April 12, 1945, when Franklin Roosevelt complained of "a terrific headache" and slumped his head to his chest, he was a military leader preparing to cross over into a world of peace. On his desk in Warm Springs, Georgia, that morning's *Atlanta Constitution* announced that America's Ninth Army was approaching the Elbe and was only "57 Miles from Berlin." At the hour of Roosevelt's death, the *New York Times* would declare the next morning, "the armies and fleets under his direction as Commander in Chief were at the gates of Berlin and the shores of Japan's home islands." Though American forces were conquering Germany without a plan for the occupation, they knew how Roosevelt thought a world at peace should look. He had told Churchill and Stalin of America's determination to realize this vision; he had worked to advance it all during the war; he had described it to Americans many times before. On April 12, he was planning to speak of it again the following day in a broadcasted Jefferson Day address. "The mere conquest of our enemies is not enough," his prepared remarks read. "We must go on to do all in our power to conquer the doubts and the fears, the ignorance and the greed, which made this horror possible." America sought "more than an end to war, we want an end to the beginnings of all wars—yes, an end to this brutal, inhuman and thoroughly impractical method of settling the differences between governments." For six years, an average of 20,000 soldiers and civilians had died every day in the war. Roosevelt's promise was that out of this cataclysm a more just and peaceful world would be created—one where people and peoples chose their own rulers, where open markets spread prosperity and the reach of ideas, where nations abided by the rule of law, and where international institutions resolved conflicts at the bargaining table instead of the battlefield. Americans thrilled to the idea. But they had heard it before.

The men who guided America through the war with Nazi Germany were serious and tough-minded, but when they were young they shared a beautiful dream. They had been called to service on behalf of deep ideals by a president, and that call would resonate the rest of their lives. Three decades earlier, New Jersey governor Woodrow Wilson had defeated a president and a former president in a campaign where he promised to slough off America's self-satisfied contentment and send the country racing into the still-new century. The contest had engaged the passions and interest of the nation. On the night of Wilson's election, hundreds of Princeton students poured out of the dormitories in what one observer called "as wildly enthusiastic a collection of young men as this village ever saw, even after a big football victory." They paraded down streets lit by fires and jammed onto Wilson's front lawn. The entire Princeton marching band showed up and brayed loudly. The crowd yelled for him. As midnight approached, Wilson came out to speak to them. Standing on a chair on his front porch, he said, "I am quite sincerely glad to see you. I have a feeling that something has just happened in which you men will play a great part in carrying forward." With "a feeling of solemn responsibility," he intoned, "I look almost with pleading to you, the young men of America, to stand behind me and the Administration. The purest impulses are needed." Indeed, he told the throng, the task would not be accomplished through "a single man, nor a single session of the House of Congress, but by long processes running through the next generation."

When the Great War came, Wilson broke with both the balance of power politics of the colonialist crowned heads of Europe and Teddy Roosevelt's foreign policy based on "blood and iron," and instead sent America into the conflict to "bring peace and safety to all nations and make the world itself at last free." He vowed that the United States would walk forever in the sunlight of moral virtue and take up the special task that God had laid before the nation—to spread justice and democracy to the entire globe. Young Americans of the day responded with frenzied excitement. Captain Harry S Truman, a middle-aged Missouri farmer with thick glasses, stood on his toes, straining his short frame, to catch a glimpse over the heads of cheering Parisian crowds of Wilson coming out of the Hôtel de Crillon. In his last, sad days in the White House, Wilson—by then a broken man who had led the country into what would become an unpopular war and then lost the peace—could count on junior congressman Jimmy Byrnes of South Carolina as one of the few officials in Washington who still stood by him. In March 1921, while thousands were watching Warren Harding's inaugural parade, a young lawyer named Dean Acheson joined a small clump of admirers who gathered to watch a slumped Wilson make his way into his new home on S Street in Washington. During much of his bedridden 1920s, Wilson's assistant secretary of the Navy, Franklin Roosevelt, would devote himself to organizing the Woodrow Wilson Foundation, keeping alive the flicker of the fires his generation's president had once lit.

On that election night in 1912, when Wilson had called a new generation to act on their ideals, a young man named James Forrestal had been there to catch the initial spark. He stood just a few yards away from Wilson on the Princteon lawn, in the middle of the crowd of his fellow students but somehow not entirely of it. Even in torchlight parades, he marched a little bit off from all the rest. It was not so much that he walked to his own beat. It was that something—some nagging voice deep inside him—kept him from stepping in time with everyone else.

FORRESTAL WAS PECULIAR. Born in the working-class township of Fishkill on the banks of the Hudson in Dutchess County, New York, just down the river from the rolling green hills of Franklin Roosevelt's Hyde Park home, Forrestal cut a broad swath at Princeton—popular, grades far above the Gentleman's C, a member of the right eating club, editor of the *Daily Princetonian*. The world was open to him, but he seemed reticent, as if he had squirreled something away and was nervous someone would catch on, as if he had rooms in the house of his soul that were closed off and tightly locked. Even the inebriated, frivolous sons of privilege he befriended took notice. His classmates voted him "Most Likely to Succeed"—as well as "Biggest Bluffer" and "The Man Nobody Knows." Nevertheless, he had worked his way into the good graces of the graceful and powerful and been tapped by them for easy success. Then, in the spring of 1915, something went horribly wrong. Just weeks before graduation, Forrestal dropped out of Princeton. The reason would never be known.

Forrestal found work moving boxes in a warehouse of the New Jersey Zinc Company and then found another job selling cigars on Manhattan's Upper East Side. Many of his customers were fellow Princetonians, and in hearing of their work in the world of finance, he found his ambition rekindled. He became a successful bond salesman, and when the Great War came, Forrestal, like so many of his generation, was swept up in the patriotic fervor of Wilson's call for service. He joined a group of Princeton friends and earned his wings as a naval aviator.

After the war, he returned to Wall Street and scurried up the ladder of financial glory at the famous firm of Dillon, Read. The conflict had knocked out the last of the props that had held up the old America with its strictures and boundaries. In the swirl of the 1920s, the lives of young, rich Americans like Forrestal became fully untethered from the moorings of the past. They could build lives not from experience and heritage but the wisps of imagination and desire. Forrestal's boss, Clarence Dillon, the sophisticated, pipe-puffing "Baron" of Wall Street, had been born in San Antonio to a Jewish clothes peddler named Samuel Lapowski. Forrestal took things one step further. Not content to be self-made, he became self-remade; self-invented from whole cloth. All that had been handed to him, he rejected, obliterating his past. His mother desperately wanted him to be a priest; Forrestal abandoned the Catholic Church entirely. As a boy, he was forbidden even from watching the boxing matches that were Fishkill's most popular source of entertainment; not only did he become a boxing enthusiast, as a young tycoon he would spend up to two hours a day sparring at a gym at Forty-second Street and Broadway, fighting with such ferocity that his opponents twice broke his nose. By the 1920s, he never spoke of his family and never made the short trip from New York to see them. His children would not meet their relatives until they were grown—and after their father had died.

Forrestal's high-toned friends searched for a way to describe this man apart who attended the same operas and played tennis at the same clubs but never seemed wholly part of their world. They frequently settled on the word "different." They sensed his face was a façade. Yet they did not seem to mind. To have paid it much heed would have been to allow a cloud to pass over the bright, sun-splattered days spent summering in Long Island's Locust Valley; happy days consumed with swimming and polo and golf, soft nights of elegant parties and hard cocktails. Forrestal rented a summer house with Bob Lovett, another young Wall Street comer and World War I veteran. There, as in the New York of the rest of the year, Croesus and Eros met and Forrestal bedded a succession of young women, quickly discarding them like spent shirts before they grew too close.

One of them stuck. At a cocktail party on the Left Bank of Paris, Forrestal saw Josephine Ogden, a vivacious beauty with dark eyes. She was a young divorcée, a former chorus girl in the Ziegfeld Follies, and then a fashion columnist covering the flapper era for *Vogue* magazine. At the time of the party in Paris, she was twenty-five and had been dating one of Forrestal's closest friends for five years. They stole away together that night and began a clandestine affair that lasted for a year. The secrecy of their liaison fueled their passion. They were married in New York's Municipal Building with no family or friends present, which was appropriate for the life they had chosen to lead. James Forrestal would spend his days poring over ledger sheets in the company of serious men of finance and law. In 1928, at the age of thirty-six, he helped engineer the merger of Dodge and Chrysler and he was called Wall Street's "boy wonder." When darkness fell, however, he lived another life. He would accompany Jo into the New York night, becoming a familiar figure in the speakeasies and dancing clubs of Manhattan. At the Stork Club or at "21," he would drink and laugh with the writer John O'Hara or Eddie Cantor, the vaudeville star. They would think he seemed happy and light, never realizing that though the house of his soul was now a mansion, some doors were still barred. "Jo is the secret side of Jim's life," said Diana Vreeland, her friend who would eventually become editor of *Vogue*. Vreeland summed it up: "He is crazy about her."

BY 1940, FORRESTAL had conquered the world of high finance. As for many young men of his generation and others before and since, youthful idealism had been, if not tempered, temporarily laid aside. But now, Hitler was marching across the continent, and when Roosevelt searched for businessmen to help prepare America for a time of war, Forrestal volunteered. He first went to the White House as one of the small number of staff members the president was then allowed by Congress. He cultivated the affections of his new boss by reminding Roosevelt of their shared roots in Dutchess County and the help his father had given the president in his first campaign for the State Senate in 1910. A man with some modicum of self-awareness might have found a degree of irony in the idea that it was the very roots he had so long disdained and tried to obliterate that were now his greatest calling card. It is unlikely the thought ever crossed Forrestal's mind.

In the summer of 1940, with Britain endangered, Roosevelt appointed Republican Frank Knox—one of Teddy Roosevelt's Rough Riders, the editor of the *Manchester Union-Leader* and *Chicago Daily News,* and the GOP's vice presidential nominee in the previous election—as secretary of the Navy. After less than two months of work in the Executive Office Building next to the White House, Forrestal asked for and was given the newly created post of undersecretary.

It quickly became apparent that while the aging Knox added a glow

of bipartisanship to the war preparations, the actual work of building a
Navy ready for war would fall to Forrestal. He reveled in it. He and Jo
rented a large Washington home where a bevy of the powerful would
gather around Forrestal each night for dinner and cigars. The conversation was lively and important, their host genial with frequent flashes of
mordant wit. When the *New York Times* profiled Forrestal they described
a "very pleasant, easy, pipe-smoking man who makes a great point of
never being hurried or fussed no matter how pressing the day's duties."
On the Sunday morning it ran, Forrestal proudly read and reread the
article. It was December 7, 1941. Forrestal's duties were about to
become far more pressing. And the pleasant pipe-smoker's easy personality would not survive the war.

THROUGH MOST OF the war, Forrestal worked on questions of production and procurement, managing defense contracts and battling
admirals to streamline the Navy's operations. When Knox died in April
1944, Forrestal was the clear choice to replace him. Roosevelt
announced his decision, and *Time* magazine wrote that not since before
the war "was there such unanimous approval of a Presidential appointment." It was not an overstatement of the esteem in which Forrestal was
held. "He has a great aversion for conversation and making himself
popular," wrote Joseph Goebbels's newspaper, *Das Reich,* of Forrestal
five days after D-Day. "He is proud of the fact that even in the midst of
the most harassing business he does not lose his calm." As with so much
else, the Nazis were wrong. Forrestal was not unflappable. The stress of
war was beginning to grate on him, as was the strain on his own personal
home front.

Jo's move to Washington had been an unhappy one. She had left
New York society, with its fabulous people tossing off glittering *bons
mots,* to come to a still-sleepy town of rumpled men discussing bombing
missions. There were no restaurants, no real theaters; 21 was not a club,
but the number of guns in a presidential salute. She began to drink, and
she did not stop. She would pass out with her head on the table at formal embassy dinners; her friends took to pouring her drinks into flower-

pots at parties. She always got a refill. The depression, the loneliness, the boredom, the alcohol, the hothouse of a capital at war jostled something loose in her, something terrifying and grave. She lost control, castigating friends in the most vulgar terms. "Wives would literally flee when they heard she was in town," said one of Forrestal's friends.

Jo was diagnosed with schizophrenia and subjected to electric shock. The treatment did not take. She became pallid; her large brown eyes turned desperate. A White House aide thought that, with her ebony hair, she was the spitting image of Morticia from the Addams Family cartoons in *The New Yorker.* But the condition was serious. She would scream and curse at any moment. In the middle of his workday, Forrestal was called with news Jo had been walking down Connecticut Avenue and kicked a child. Her symptoms included hallucinations, vivid visions of danger to herself and to her husband and their school-age children. When no one believed her, she grew ever more distraught. She repeated her cry over and over, growing louder and more brittle: The "Reds" were coming to get them.

Forrestal's friends all remarked on how much compassion and understanding he showed for her.

WITH HIS LIFE at home erratic and with his new broader responsibilities as Navy secretary, Forrestal began to travel widely across the fronts of war. He was offshore during battles in the Marshall Islands in the Pacific, met with Eisenhower at a secret location near the troops a month after the invasion of Normandy, visited the Fifth Army along the Arno in Italy, and landed on the French Riviera on the day of the American invasion of southern France. Forrestal "exposed himself to the dangers of warfare as no other United States official of his rank did in World War II," observed one war correspondent. He was drawn to the places where the war was fiercest, to those spots where shrieks pierced the silence and death was in the air. And so he went to Iwo Jima.

Forrestal sailed with the armada from Saipan. On February 19, 1945, American troops began streaming onto the island's soft volcanic sands. The first waves of Marines came on shore without opposition and more rolled in behind. It was a trap. The Japanese waited until the beaches were filled. And then they unleashed hell. From pillboxes, blockhouses, and bunkers, from the top of Mount Suribachi overlooking the beach, came machine-gun bullets falling like raindrops; mortar, shrapnel, and shells tearing the soldiers apart. Forrestal, with his binoculars pressed tightly up to his eyes, watched it all unfolding. For three days, he saw wave after wave of landing craft come onto Iwo Jima's beaches and saw thousands of young men die in the most horrible, tragic, painful ways possible. On the fourth day, he said he wanted to join them on the island. Admiral Kelly Turner tried to talk Forrestal out of it. "I don't think it's wise," Turner said. The beaches were "hot," they had been shelled just that morning, it was not a safe place to be. Forrestal looked out with his binoculars again. "Aren't those men I see on the beach?" he asked grimly.

The landing craft carried Forrestal and a few others onto the beach at 10:30 in the morning. He wore a safety vest and helmet, his binoculars hung around his neck; his face was screwed into a scowl. As they scurried into the nearest trench for cover, he saw body parts of dead Americans all around him—remains of young boys with their limbs torn off like a petulant child's doll, of teens whose torsos were severed and thrown fifty feet away from their legs. A stack of a hundred bodies was piled up nearby. Just as they reached the trench, over his left shoulder, Forrestal saw Marines raising the flag over Iwo Jima on Mount Suribachi. "There goes the flag," men yelled. There were cheers and men waved their helmets in the air. Ships blew their whistles in approval. After about half an hour, Forrestal was convinced to leave the island.

Many men had seen and experienced worse in World War II. But other men were not as driven and divided, as acquainted with the darkness, as Forrestal already was. The war, the mounting troubles and tensions in his home, had caused him strain, but Forrestal had, it was generally agreed, taken to the challenges of politics and bureaucracy with incredible skill and even glimmers of joy. He was a popular figure; bluff, tough, visionary, hopeful. That Jim Forrestal never made it off Iwo Jima.

No one knew it at the time. He seemed to return as he had left—serious and determined and strong. But Iwo Jima was the chink in the dam holding back the tormented waters Forrestal had contained only through sheer force of will. It was not a gash, it was only a crack, but it was the kind that grows. At first only drops appeared; eventually there would be a river. In the weeks and months after his return from the Pacific, though the war was ending in victory, the creases in Forrestal's brow grew deeper. The tense expression he wore on the landing craft seemed to have stuck in place. He laughed less, if at all. No photograph appears of him with a genuine smile after Iwo Jima. "We cannot go from Iwo to Iwo," he told Rear Admiral Ellis Zacharias shortly after the battle. "We must find a formula to sustain peace without this endless, frightful bloodshed." Finding this "formula" became his central purpose and eventually his obsession. But as his hero Woodrow Wilson had learned, there was no exact formula for peace. Try as he would, there was no equation that Forrestal could divine that would yield the result of no more Iwo Jimas. There were no tables of figures in oversized ledger books like those he had studied on Wall Street that would show him the way and convince others to follow his lead. His frustration would lead to catastrophe.

IN THE EARLY months of 1945, around the time he went to Iwo Jima, Forrestal had come to be thought of as one of the two great future leaders in Roosevelt's cabinet. His name was being discussed as a possible governor or senator on the way to an eventual run for the White House. Shortly after he returned from Iwo Jima, he listed in his diary what he thought were the chief requirements of a successful candidate for president. The other man to watch was Secretary of Commerce Henry Wallace, who had been—until that January—vice president. Though extremely popular among the rank and file of the Democratic Party for his messianic liberalism, Wallace seemed to exist on a different moral and practical plane from the bosses and industrialists who brought the party votes and money. While he personally admired Wallace, Roosevelt did not have the time and energy in the summer of 1944 to fight to keep him on the ticket. Instead he settled for the safer choice of Senator Harry Truman from Missouri, a straightforward man from the heartland who seemed to inspire as little love as he did loathing. Forrestal had been one of those cheering Wallace's demotion. Indeed, on the Fourth of July in 1944, just days before the convention opened, Forrestal had lunched with Senator Truman and told him it was his duty to take the vice presidential nod to prevent Wallace from being renominated.

The differences between Forrestal and Wallace were readily apparent. Forrestal's father had been an immigrant carpenter; Wallace was the son of a former agriculture secretary. Forrestal was a wealthy and successful banker, and was seen as a conservative within the Democratic Party; Wallace, though rich in his own right from his prosperous agribusiness company, was the self-styled advance agent for a new "Century of the Common Man." Forrestal felt most at home, if anywhere, with the bluebloods of Wall Street and Princeton; it was no surprise to anyone who took an instant to size up Wallace's rumpled appearance and quiet demeanor to learn he came from the plains of Iowa. His childhood memories—like the long walks he took as a five-year-old in the woods around Ames with Iowa State college student George Washington Carver—were illuminated by the last languid lights of the dying agrarian empire of the nineteenth century. Wallace retained his country ways even in Washington. Among the comfortable set that came to Forrestal's elegant dinner parties, there were peals of laughter whenever someone mentioned Wallace's habit of lecturing people at great length on the virtues of eating raw garlic or the hour a day he spent—while vice president or as a cabinet member—tending to his strawberry plants.

More than anyone realized, however, Forrestal and Wallace had their similarities as well. They were both, on a basic level, ill at ease among others. Forrestal was charming on occasion, but he was tightly coiled and seemed physically incapable of friendly banter. Wallace could be winning, but he was deeply uncomfortable in social situations. He once told a friend that when he met with people in small groups he felt as if a cold snake were curled up inside him. Sometimes he dealt with this by falling asleep in the middle of important meetings. When, as vice president, the presiding officer of the Senate, he would pass a senator in the hallway of the Capitol, he would look down at the marble floor or up at the murals on the ceiling in order to pretend he did not see him and thus avoid having to stop and exchange pleasantries.

Wallace was also profoundly strange. In his *Wallace's Farmer*, which he edited in Iowa before coming to Washington, he had run articles on mystical religion side by side with practical agriculture advice. He believed that the future could be foretold by markings on the Great Pyramid of Egypt and convinced President Roosevelt to put the pyramid of the Great Seal, with the all-seeing eye floating above, on the dollar bill. While in the cabinet, he fell in with a sect of theosophists, led by Russian émigré Nikolai Konstantinovich Roerich. Wallace placed Roerich on the payroll and put him in charge of a secretive mission to Inner Mongolia. When Wallace's letters to Roerich, addressed "Dear Guru," became public, they bolstered the notion among the urban bosses and Senate bulls who ran the Democratic Party that he was simply not one of them. More than half a decade after they had been leaked, Forrestal would still get great enjoyment from reading the goofy letters aloud to friends.

"When Henry looks at me with that global stare, I really get frightened," Forrestal said of Wallace. Wallace, the Midwesterner, was more polite. Forrestal was "a very fair and decent kind of fellow," he would say but then add, in a telling afterthought, "unless deeply touched emotionally." But along with their social discomfort, Wallace and Forrestal shared their idealism. They were both true believers, each seeing himself as a keeper of Wilson's dream in a government of those who, by turning their back on it, would bring about another, even more terrible war. However, like bickering Freudians, they had very different interpretations of the meaning of that dream.

As long as Roosevelt was alive, their argument would take place on the sidelines. But at ten to six on the evening of April 12, Forrestal— then meeting with the secretary of state and the attorney general— received an urgent call that they were all needed at the White House. A shaken Harry Truman greeted them, along with Wallace and the other members of the administration in the Cabinet Room. "I can only say that I will try to carry on as he would have wanted me and all of us to do," he said of Roosevelt. Shortly after seven, beneath a large portrait of Woodrow Wilson gazing thoughtfully on the scene, with Forrestal and Wallace standing shoulder-to-shoulder behind him, Truman took the oath of office. As he finished, Justice Harlan Stone reached out to shake hands with him. Truman, instead, bowed deeply to kiss the Gideon Bible before taking Stone's hand.

Neither Forrestal nor Wallace thought much of the new president. As the cabinet members filed out of the room, leaving a dazed Truman behind, Forrestal muttered to Secretary of the Interior Harold Ickes, with something between condescension and compassion, "Poor little fellow. Poor little fellow." Two days later, Truman asked Wallace—the man who but for an accident of timing would have been president after Roosevelt's death—to stand beside him on the platform at Union Station in greeting the fallen leader's body. Wallace appreciated the sentiment, but aboard the funeral train heading for Hyde Park, he happened upon Truman huddling with oil lobbyist and Democratic Party fund-raiser Edwin Pauley—the man who had been the ringleader of the dump-Wallace movement the previous summer. He was shocked and wondered what such big-money conservatives "would do to the putty which is Truman."

Truman was not as helpless as Forrestal and Wallace might have thought—or hoped. But as he tried to, in his words, "carry on" Franklin Roosevelt's policies and further Woodrow Wilson's dream, he would find that Forrestal and Wallace were each pulling him in a different direction. Forrestal harbored dreams of being elected to the Oval Office in his own right. Wallace had been robbed of a presidency he felt should have been his. These two men, and their viewpoints, would end up at war at a decisive moment—and in the crucible of that conflict the course of history would be set.

4

FLIGHT

On that tragic Sunday in December 1941, the day that found Lucius Clay at the Redskins game and James Forrestal reading about himself in the *New York Times,* twenty-one-year-old Hal Halvorsen returned home from church and hung up his good suit neatly, as poor boys know to do. It was a warm day for December, and Halvorsen gloried in it. There had been a record early dusting of snow in October, but it melted quickly and autumn weather had lingered on in Utah's high desert. The day was clear and comfortable enough that Halvorsen could go outside under the midday sun to wash his car. He filled the bucket and poured in the soap. He took a rag and dunked it deep and rejoiced in the way the suds oozed through his fingers as he worked his way across the hood of the red Ford V8. He turned the car radio up loud and hummed along to the music. The worlds and worries of men like Forrestal and Clay were far from those of a farm boy untouched by distant rumblings, and he could not imagine that his life would intersect with theirs. But shortly after noon, the Sunday program playing on the crackling car radio, with its static hovering above the line of notes like a piccolo in a marching band, was interrupted by a special news bulletin. For Hal Halvorsen, that tune—and so much else for him and his generation—would never be resumed.

GAIL S. "HAL" Halvorsen was born in 1920, the year after the signing of the Treaty of Versailles. His mother's parents had pushed handcarts across the plains to come West; his father had left school at fourteen to work full-time as a mucker in an Idaho gold mine and then drove a horse-drawn Wells Fargo wagon. The family moved every few years in Halvorsen's boyhood, either to escape economic disaster or to chase a better opportunity—the piece of land a couple miles down the road or across the Idaho state line that promised easier farming and less struggle. Their Mormon faith snugly bound them into the rural communities they entered as newcomers. At harvesttime, men from surrounding farms would take turns threshing the wheat on one another's land while their wives baked mincemeat pies. When suppertime came, the men would file up to the house and they would all eat together, the steaming pies washed down with cool glasses of milk.

The Halvorsens grew wheat, potatoes, alfalfa, grain, and green peas on their land, but the crop that dominated their lives was the sugar beet. From the time he was young, Halvorsen had worked at reaping the yield. This required him to hunch over or crawl through the dirt on his knees, with the dust flying up into his face, lifting the beet up with his left hand and chopping it with a long-handled beet hook with his right. The work of farm life felt seemingly endless to Hal: crops to harvest, kindling to chop, chicken coops to clean. He would fish and hunt to help provide for the family, knock down apples from the tree to feed the hogs, and pick huckleberries for his mother's pies. By the time he was six years old, Halvorsen was so good at milking cows that he could shoot a stream of milk from the cow's teat into a cat's mouth clear across the stable.

But amid the work, there were moments of idyll. Halvorsen was the undisputed champion in local onion-eating contests. In summer, he would watch the lightning shows as thunderstorms rolled through the Snake River valley and splurge a nickel on firecrackers for the Fourth of

July. In fall, when the maple trees surrendered to an assault of crimson, Halvorsen would spend hours wandering through the hills with Old Shep, his black cattle dog, walking by his side. In winter, the snow would fall heavy, covering the tops of the fences. The wood-spoked wheels of their Model T were no match for the deep drifts, and so his family went to town in bobsleds pulled by horses. "I remember those rides well," he recalled, "and especially if we had to leave town after dark and as we left the streetlights with the soft snowflakes falling and the sleigh bells jingling and, going into the dark outside of town, the horses would always find their way." A Boy Scout, he spent winter nights teaching local children how to ice-skate and play hockey. At Christmas, he would receive oranges as gifts—a delicacy at that time and in that place. One year he got a book about King Arthur and immediately sat down and read it through, ignoring his friends' pleas to go out and play. Once, he was given a windup train. Another Christmas, his relatives in California sent him a board game based on the book *Pollyanna*.

Sunny and kind, he made friends easily. Every year, his father pulled him out of school for two weeks to work on the farm at harvesttime, and so, on his tenth birthday, he was topping the sugar beets, upset that his absence meant his classmates would ignore the milestone, when he heard the approach of young voices singing "Happy Birthday" and a group of his friends came up the hill with gifts of work gloves, candy, and gum.

Halvorsen lived at the very end of the American frontier, just a couple dozen miles from Promontory Summit, where the Golden Spike uniting the transcontinental railroad had been driven into the ground. As the striving modernity of the West Coast and the mature sophistication of the East moved slowly inward along the tracks, northern Utah was one of the places they came to last. Even when he was a teen, Halvorsen's family lived in a home without indoor bathrooms or running water or electricity. He brought hot bricks to bed with him for warmth. Though there could be hardship and sickness and tragedy on the farm, though sometimes the snows would fall deeper and the river waters would flood, there was, like the turning of the seasons, a certainty that pervaded his young life. On the farm, "everything was in its place," he would recall. "Neat bales of stacked hay, corn growing clean and tall." It was a world Halvorsen knew and loved. And he was desperate to escape it.

AS HIS HIGH school graduation neared, Halvorsen dreamed of going to college, but was needed on his father's farm. Instead, he took correspondence courses in refrigeration and air-conditioning and worked ten-hour days, six days a week, farming sugar beets. In his spare time, he devoured geography books to fuel daydreams of distant lands. One summer day in 1939, Halvorsen was at work in the fields when he heard the crescendo of an approaching whir, first high like the flit of a bumblebee, then deeper, until he looked up to see a biplane coming toward him, not high above but just over the level of the low trees nearby. He stood transfixed, staring at the plane and its spinning propellers as if they held a hypnotic power until, right as it seemed to be about to crash, it pulled up and away into a vertical climb, straight into the sky.

Halvorsen had never been that close to a plane, and immediately flight and all the faraway places it could take him consumed his imagination. The following weekend, a high school classmate of his, Art Hansen, cocky and from a wealthier family, came by to pay a visit. "How'd you like that, Seymour?" he said, needling Halvorsen with his middle name. He admitted it was he who had buzzed the Halvorsen farm. "Sure beats playing nursemaid to a sugar beet!" taunted Hansen, the kind of amateur pilot who wore a white scarf thrown around his neck. Halvorsen earnestly asked if there was a way he could learn to fly. Sure, "all you have to do is go to college, qualify as a sophomore, pass a test, and they will enroll you in the beginners' part of the flight program," replied Hansen, knowing full well that this was out of reach for Halvorsen. "If you pass that phase, you will get a shot at that little Waco biplane jewel I dusted you off with last week."

But already the force of a coming war was being felt in this isolated corner of northern Utah. At the time, the Army Air Corps was training only about 500 pilots a year. In Washington, in 1940, the decision was made that America needed more airplane pilots, with or without college degrees. Thousands of young men, including ten from northern Utah, would be chosen for scholarships to flight schools. Halvorsen immediately entered the competition and, after a series of tests, was chosen from a field of 120 for the sixth slot of the ten.

After training at the local airport, he was ready for his first solo flight. Halvorsen bounced down the runway in a plane made of fabric and cables with less than half the horsepower of a twenty-first-century compact car. Lifting off, he made a straight line for the family farm. His parents and Old Shep were outside. Halvorsen, proud of himself, was not sure whether they would know it was him up above, so he climbed to 9,000 feet and then plunged the plane in a spin toward the ground. He pulled up in plenty of time and headed toward the airport. As he looked back, Shep was running in circles. His parents were standing motionless. He returned home that evening to find his father angry: "You are through flying. You almost did your mom in," he yelled. "She's still not herself." Halvorsen begged for forgiveness. He was only trying to make sure they understood it was him. He promised he would never do it again. Instead, they would have a signal. Halvorsen would gently roll the plane's wings back and forth, lifting the left side, then the right, so that the plane would wiggle in the air.

When the war came, Halvorsen knew little about America's enemies. His high school agriculture teacher, however, had told him that it was Germans who developed the sugar beet. This alone would have been enough to send Halvorsen into battle.

Soon after Pearl Harbor, Halvorsen enrolled as an aviation cadet in the Army Air Forces. He was sent into the reserve as a pilot while waiting for an active-duty flight training slot. In the meantime, he had earned enough money working on a construction job to enroll at Utah State University in the fall of 1942. It was there, a couple of months into the semester, that a friend introduced him to a sophomore named Alta

Jolley. Halvorsen was, from the very first, smitten by the girl he called "the neatest, best-looking, most popular, smartest, least stuck-up coed" on campus. Alta was, by any measure, a beauty, with brown curls falling past shapely shoulders and big, alluring chocolate eyes. And though Alta was, in Halvorsen's estimation, "one of the queens of the campus," she immediately took a liking to the balding, poor farm boy who had just arrived at college three years after graduating from high school.

It was, significantly, Alta who made the first romantic overture. She asked him to be her date for a sleigh ride, but, when the appointed day came, there was no snow. Instead, they tooled around town in the red Ford. When he got up the nerve to ask her out again, Halvorsen thought she said yes because she liked the car. For the next few months, they saw each other regularly. Their affection was mutual and undeniable and it grew in strength in the pressure-cooker atmosphere of war as young couples they knew debated whether to get married before the boys shipped out. But they felt their relationship was too new and tenuous to consider the prospect. "The chemistry seemed to be right, but he was on his way to fight a war and I still had one more year of college" was how Alta would sum up the situation.

In March 1943, Halvorsen finally received the long, thin envelope with orders calling him up for duty, but by then the occasion was papered over with sadness. Nevertheless, on March 23, Halvorsen said goodbye to Alta on her front stoop in Logan. She cried softly into his shoulder, they promised to write, and he left for the train station. A cold wind flogged the platform. Around him there was wailing. Young husbands clutched tightly to their new brides in the last moments before they went to battle on distant shores. Halvorsen, standing alone in the midst of the tumult, saw "devastation on the faces of the young married couples, some with babes in arms." The heightened ardor of the moment made his feelings for Alta seem smaller, less solid. They had known each other for only a few months and, in saying goodbye, he had stumbled over his words, unable to find the right phrases, unequal in his fresh love to the full measure of devotion and fidelity he now saw in the tears of those around him as men hung out from the train's open windows, locked in embraces with loves who ran alongside the cars as they moved slowly down the track.

Halvorsen was quickly thrown onto the assembly line from which American pilots were made. There was no position open to an American of that era that was more glamorous than that of a flying ace. Seven out of ten Americans in 1941 had never flown in an airplane. In the first half of the twentieth century, pilots were treated with a reverence and awe that would be reserved for astronauts a few years later and that would be without analogy as a self-consciously jaded twenty-first century began. Pilots like Charles Lindbergh and Jimmy Doolittle were the preeminent national idols of the years between the wars. Even movie stars—Clark Gable, Jimmy Stewart, Tyrone Power—found greater glory in the air than they had ever enjoyed on the screen.

Halvorsen was transferred from base to base in Texas and Oklahoma as he continued his training, impatient as he waited to go to war. The young man who dreamed of shaking off the dust of the farm towns he knew so well had been thrown into a great adventure, swept up alongside young men from places so different from anywhere he had seen. They traveled together across the broad expanse of the country, singing patriotic songs on the train rides. "This is it!" he wrote to Alta on the morning of Friday, August 13, 1943, as he waited to be shipped out from the muddy field that was the base in Stillwater, Oklahoma. "The hum and bustle of excitement is high. . . . It's not hard to be cheerful around here. I pity those Axis bums when we get our 'wings.' I hope/I can't wait to get off to Solomons, China, India etc. besides Tokyo. It's a long way from over. Keep writing." But the bums would be safe from Hal Halvorsen.

At the beginning of World War II, the United States had only two basic types of military airplanes: bombers and fighters. And though other categories were added, throughout the war the fighter pilots and the bombardiers were the heroes of the air. Halvorsen was neither. Dutiful, careful, a self-described "stickler for rules," Halvorsen was assigned to be a transport pilot: ferrying people, planes, and supplies to forgotten spots far from the battlefields. Transport pilots were anonymous, second-tier; fame, glory, attention, the chance for advancement flowed to the combat pilots, who, in turn, mocked the Air Transport Command, joking that its initials stood for "Allergic To Combat" or "Army of Terrified Civilians." Halvorsen had set out to be an ace; he ended up flying lumbering old planes. Pilots found that folks back home would perk up at word that their local boy had gone off to be a military pilot. When they heard it was merely flying transports, they were crestfallen. One pilot remembered, "'Oh,' was their answer with obvious disappointment." The fighter and bomber pilots were the war's dashing idols. Halvorsen spent the war as a truck driver of the sky.

Combat pilots were valued and honored to the extent that they were willing to take risks that endangered them and their planes. The bigger the risk, the greater the danger, the more they were called heroes. Yet what made someone a good transport pilot was an aversion to risk. All that mattered was getting the cargo to the destination safely. Halvorsen's ability to methodically obey directions made him exceptionally good in this type of flying. Even while still in training, he was chosen as senior cadet of his class, drilling and parading the men under his command. When, after they had spent a couple of years flying C-47s, every man in his squadron asked for the chance to fly the newer, larger C-54, it was Halvorsen who was selected. "I should explain to you that I don't consider you to be the best pilot," his squadron commander told him as he announced his selection, but "the most important thing for me, given you have enough skill, is to trust that you will heed my counsel on how I want that aircraft flown." With Halvorsen, there was little worry he would step out of line.

Halvorsen was initially assigned to go to India, to take part in the effort to fly supplies to American troops over the Himalayas, but as he was on his way, stopping over in Natal, Brazil, the plans were changed and he was told to wait at the transport base there. He would be stuck there for two years—the rest of the war. From Brazil, he would fly routes up to Miami and across the Atlantic. Three times a week, he would deliver a C-54 troop carrier or a bomber plane used to attack Germany to Ascension Island in the Atlantic. He would take off from Brazil at ten at night and use the stars to guide him to that small, isolated, five-mile-by-seven-mile speck of land in the sea by sunup. The places Halvorsen had dreamed of, curled up with geography books under the hiss of gaslights on cold Utah nights, came alive. In northern Africa, he landed in Marrakech and was haunted by German POWs singing a mournful version of "Lili Marlene" that sent chills down his back. In England, he delivered cargo in advance of the invasion of Normandy. At stops in Haiti, street urchins surrounded him, begging for candy and pocket change. And most everywhere he went—from football games in Brazil to the cockpit of flights over verdant islands—he carried a small movie camera with him to record what he had seen.

All through those years of war, Halvorsen, like so many others, dreamed of the life he would build when the war came to a close. He desperately wanted that life to be with Alta, but—shy and uncertain—he was unable to tell her. The letters kept coming, and once he managed to place an international phone call to her from Natal. But since those few months together before he left, they had not seen each other except for a ski trip with friends when he returned to Utah on leave in February 1944. "I wish you were going to be home for Christmas, but even though you can't, my prayers are all for you and the hope that it won't be long before we can spend every day together," she wrote him in the last December of the war. "Did I ever tell you how very proud I am of you and how very, very glad I am that you are the person you are? Remind me to tell you often but you don't have to remind me to appreciate it because I never forget—not for a second. I've been disillusioned in so many people, people I believed in and people I thought had what it takes that life seems pretty cruel. Then you come shining through with all your wisdom, ideals, and will power, and then life takes on a new meaning and I start out again with renewed hope and vigor for I know there's someone I can sincerely admire."

Alta would hint broadly that he needed to tell her his intentions for the future. In one letter, she made an offhand mention of a school paper she had to complete on how to create a "permanent peace" and then wrote, "Speaking of peace and post war plans, we really should come down to earth and talk about something we can do something about. Instead of wishing you were here maybe it would help if we knew what we'd do if you were here. What do you want to do when you come home?" Halvorsen, oblivious or conflicted, let the bait float by.

They had not seen each other since the ski trip when, in February 1945, on a flight to Miami, Halvorsen's plane had mechanical problems and he was told it would be a few days before he could fly back to Brazil. Alta had joined in the wartime migration to New York City, living with a friend and working as a waitress in a Schrafft's ice-cream parlor. Within an hour, Halvorsen had hitched a ride in the plastic nose cone of a B-17 heading north. He landed at LaGuardia Airport and caught a cab to the YWCA dorm where Alta was staying. The girl at the front desk gave him Alta's number and he called her on the lobby phone. "Just thought I would give you a call and see how you are doing."

She shrieked with glee, "How are things in Natal?"

"Pretty good but rather warm. Why don't you come downstairs and let me tell you about it?"

There was a pause.

"Downstairs, where?"

"Right here in the YWCA."

"You are not here!" she said as the phone slammed down. Moments later, she burst into the lobby and flung herself into his arms. For the next few days, they traveled through the city together, visiting the Statue of Liberty and going to the top of the Empire State Building. He bought a big, brown military coat to keep warm. She wore a bright red coat that, along with her skirt, drifted just below her knees, and a hat pushed back on top of her curly locks. They walked down the broad avenues arm in arm, she holding him tight as the wind whipped through the canyons, he beaming in proud delight. But the time passed quickly, and soon he was gone.

A FEW MONTHS later, the war was coming to an end. On the morning that the Russian and American armies met on the Elbe, 3 million American troops awoke in Europe. Within weeks, they were tripping over themselves to return to America and to leave military service. On some days, 35,000 soldiers, sailors, and Marines were discharged; in some months, 800,000 men were demobilized—nearly twice the total number of soldiers on active duty in the beginning of the twenty-first century. Here was where Hal Halvorsen—who had been in so many ways typical of a generation of young men plucked from quiet lives and thrust into the tumult of far-off battles—suddenly diverged from his peers.

On the farm in Utah, Halvorsen had dreamed of escaping the tight confines of the world he had known. Now men were streaming home from war, eager to restart the lives they had put on hold. Halvorsen wanted something more, a bigger life than farming sugar beets, but he was not sure what that would be. He wanted to complete his college education, but thought he was too old to afford to take time away from drawing a salary to do so.

Though Halvorsen appeared confused—about Alta, about his future—there was at least one point on which he expressed a fair amount of certainty. With the war ending, he told friends that he was eager to return to civilian life. Those who wanted to stay in the Army Air Forces had to receive a regular, peacetime Army commission, which was awarded to pilots who scored highest on a battery of tests. Halvorsen claimed to have no interest in such an assignment. But when the team of Army examiners arrived on their base in Brazil, he let his friend, Bob Heath, convince him to spend a few of his days off taking the tests, as he put it, "for the heck of it." Heath could not have been too surprised by the outcome; neither could Halvorsen. Only one pilot at Natal was offered a regular Army commission, and Halvorsen was chosen for the honor. He immediately turned it down.

A few days passed before the Army major in charge of personnel appeared at Halvorsen's barracks. "I am surprised to see you turned down the regular commission," he said. "Are you aware of some of the benefits?"

"No," replied Halvorsen resolutely. "I have other plans."

"I see from your records that you don't have a college degree," the major noted. "Did you know that if you are a regular officer and don't have a degree, the Army will send you to a college of your choice, pay your full salary, let you continue to fly, pay your tuition, and even buy your books?"

Halvorsen was incredulous. "That can't be so."

If the major had been Beelzebub there to bargain for Halvorsen's soul, he could not have dangled a shinier promise. "Immediately, visions began flashing before me of the ability to support a wife, the opportunity to continue flying military aircraft, going to a university to complete my meager education, and getting to see different parts of the world."

The major waited for a response. Halvorsen asked for a couple of hours to think it over. Alone, on a foreign continent far from home, he returned to his barracks to ponder his decision without anyone to talk to about it. He wished his parents or Alta were there to counsel him. Instead, he knelt on the hard barracks floor and prayed for guidance as the minutes passed, knowing that the decision would be irrevocable. "After a time," he would recall, "I'm not sure how long, I felt a warmth in my bosom and a peaceful, calm reassurance that to me was the answer." He got up and went to go sign on the line.

But Halvorsen had not read the fine print. Priority for college went to those officers who could finish school in two years or less. Halvorsen had only two semesters under his belt. So as unquestioningly as he had followed orders in the air, he dutifully waited his turn.

Alta was waiting too. Earlier in 1945, in Rio, Halvorsen had bought a diamond for an engagement ring. He carried it with him in his wallet, wrapped in wax paper, intending to give it to her, but was never able to bring himself to make the commitment. When she left New York in that summer, Alta traveled to West Palm Beach to see Halvorsen as he stopped there briefly before returning to Brazil. She told him that Florida was on her way back home to Utah from New York. He seemed to believe her. Their time together was brief. They talked of their future and she gave him every opportunity to make his intentions clear. Neither of them was willing to lay bare their soul. He was hesitant, she was anxious, and the meeting ended on an unsatisfying note. Their time was up. He had to leave. They said their goodbyes yet again. He climbed into his plane. She stood off to the side of the tarmac before beginning her lonely journey home. As Halvorsen took off from the runway, watching Alta's shrinking figure wave goodbye, he felt his chest tighten and throat constrict. He pointed the plane toward South America. The flight was routine but, somehow, Hal Halvorsen—uncertain about his love, aimless in his life—felt lost.

5

THE DESCENT

Lucius Clay was not one to feel lost, but he was confused by the mysterious phone call he received on May 6, 1945, as the slowly setting sun streamed through the large windows of his office in Versailles. It was a sumptuous, though inauspicious, place to be planning the postwar future of Germany, but in the month he had been there, Clay had found little time to enjoy his surroundings. Before his appointment, several hundred experts had divided themselves into study groups and spent many months drawing up procedures to take over the government of Germany. Clay arrived in France and, in short order, tossed their blueprints to the side. The scholars had "lived too cloistered and academic a life to face the realities of the problem," he wrote a friend. Reports from soldiers on the front lines in Germany were spotty, but they told of "very much more destruction than most people at home realize." If so, there would be no government left in Germany to capture. Of course, he pointed out judiciously, the accounts could simply be the yarns of overwrought soldiers. "Careful investigation may indicate the apparent destruction to be much less than it now appears." In fact, the intelligence Clay was receiving drastically understated the extent of the devastation. As Allied troops made their way to Berlin, the country was not just being conquered, it was collapsing. The fall of the Nazi Reich was bringing down with it any sense of order. To govern Germany—a huge, modern nation in the heart of Europe—the Allies would have to do what no invading army had ever had to attempt in such circumstances: create a government of occupation from scratch.

Walter Bedell Smith's afternoon phone call to Clay was cryptic. He asked Clay to come immediately to Eisenhower's headquarters, in the northeast French city of Rheims. It was 6 P.M. by the time Clay's car, kicking back pebbles in its wake, pulled up to the three-story red brick schoolhouse that served as the command center for the American and British forces in Europe. Clay strode through the arched entry, past the guard, and toward the office he kept in the building. He opened the door and there, sitting at his desk, in a uniform heavy with decorations, was a Nazi general.

Clay stood frozen in shock. Not believing his eyes, he squinted, blinked, and backed out of the door.

He went to find out what was going on and was told that, because he had been in Versailles, his empty office was being used to hold General Alfred Jodl, there to negotiate the final surrender of Germany.

The negotiations stretched into the night. Jodl asked for a cup of coffee and a map of Europe. Clay stayed up playing poker with his friend General "Tooey" Spaatz, who had directed the strategic bombing of Germany. Refusing to deal directly with the Germans, Eisenhower paced in his office down the hall. As the clock neared 3 A.M. on May 7, in a cramped pale-blue room that had once been the students' play area, the Germans signed the documents ending the war. After signing the papers, Jodl shot up from the flimsy wooden chair as if he were about to leave. But then he stood at the table looking at General Smith, who had accepted Germany's surrender on behalf of the Allies. In English, he said, "I want to say a word." There was no response, but he continued. "General," his voice caught as he seemed to be holding back sobs, "with this signature the German people and the German armed forces are, for better or worse, delivered into the victor's hands. In this war, which has lasted more than five years, both have achieved and suffered more than perhaps any other people in the world. In this hour, I can only express the hope that the victor will treat them with generosity." The room fell into an uncomfortable silence. After a moment, Smith gave a slight, tentative nod, and it was then that Jodl dropped his head in defeat. Without another word, he turned and left the room. He had delivered his plea to the wrong person. The man who would be responsible for America's treatment of the defeated Germans was the one in whose office he had sat hours earlier.

A FEW MINUTES after the surrender, Eisenhower called General Omar Bradley to tell him the news. "Brad, it's all over." Bradley walked to the window of his bedroom in the German spa town of Bad Wildungen and threw open the heavy blackout curtains, illuminating the dark street below. The lights began to come back on all over the world. Big Ben in London and the Capitol dome in Washington were bathed with floodlights once again; the torch of the Statue of Liberty was lit for the first time in over three years. In great cities and tiny hamlets, the victory over Germany was greeted with jubilation. Never before in human history had so many in so many places marked a single event.

After years of tension, people felt a release. Red Square, Trafalgar Square, and Times Square were jammed with celebrants. Cannon boomed and confetti flittered in Paris. In the Vatican, church bells rang. Muscovites yelled "Long live America!" as loudspeakers blared the "Star-Spangled Banner." In Boston, women took off their blouses on the street while roisterers sat on the ledges of high-rise apartments, fourteen floors up, waving buoyantly down to the crowd. "World gone nuts!" said an observer. In New York, a woman ran down Twenty-third Street shouting "It's over! The war's over!" When they did not have ticker tape, revelers threw playing cards and pages from telephone books out of skyscraper windows. They fluttered to the ground past flags still at half-mast in honor of Roosevelt. Garment workers shredded bales of fabric and added them to the downpour. The strands of silk and wool "turned and squirmed in the thin morning sunlight," wrote the *New York Times.* "Within the hour, Sixth, Seventh and Eighth Avenues, and Broadway, were eight to ten inches deep in multi-colored fabrics." Under the deluge of paper and floral prints, a crowd of over a million danced without music.

But after so much suffering and death, relief was not the only emotion. There was anger as well. A girl walking her two dachshunds on Park Avenue near Fifty-fifth Street was assaulted by a gang of schoolboys throwing sticks and yelling, "Get those German mutts off the street!" The girl pleaded with them, "They're not German. They were born here."

And there was solemnity and sadness. In the French Quarter of New Orleans, bars emptied and there was quiet as men and women filed into churches to drop to their knees and pray for the dead and for peace. In homes with Gold Star banners paling in windows, women softly sobbed. Instead of a chest-thumping editorial of braggadocio and triumph, the tabloid New York *Daily News* printed the text of "*Te Deum Laudamus,*" the Latin hymn of praise.

Most of all, even amid the excitement, people looked forward. There was a sense of having attained a hard-fought, well-earned measure of hope. In the White House, it was the new president's birthday. "The flags of freedom fly over all Europe," Truman announced in what was then the most widely heard radio broadcast ever. And Americans expected those flags to fly in peace. A Gallup poll soon after the war's end revealed that a substantial majority of Americans did not think there was the possibility of another war for at least twenty-five years. They believed that if they held tight to Wilson's dream of spreading democracy, if they followed Roosevelt's policy of cooperation and friendship with the Soviets, there would be little danger of a return to the horrors of battle. "We must work to bind up the wounds of a suffering world—to build an abiding peace, a peace rooted in justice and in law," Truman said in his speech. "We can build such a peace only by hard, toilsome, painstaking work—by understanding and working with our allies in peace as we have in war."

THE MORNING AFTER the Germans surrendered, Eisenhower held a lunch for his top officers in honor of the victory. Clay looked around the room at the couple dozen men, American and British, who toasted each other, laughing with cheer. He smiled with them, but no doubt felt small. These were the generals who had guided the Allied liberation of a captured continent and defeated Hitler's forces. Clay, instead, had three stars on his shoulder and not a single combat decoration on his chest. He had served his country in the Army through two world wars and never seen a battle. The men around the table had sent young men into enemy fire and put countless Germans in their graves. The only blood-shed Clay had experienced was the result of paper cuts.

Before long, the merriment of the victory lunch began to fade. What had begun as a celebration soon became a farewell for a group of brothers-in-arms who had worked and lived closely together, amid the most trying conditions, for months and, in some cases, years. "All of a sudden this group of generals recognized they no longer had a job," Clay recalled. The men began to say goodbye to one another. Eisen-hower spoke to each of them, tears in his eyes. Clay, who had just arrived, must have felt like receding into the background with embar-rassment. Eisenhower's men had been single-minded in their pursuit of a grand objective whose achievement now left them adrift. Clay thought it anticlimactic; he called it "a terrible letdown." But that was only his arm's-length diagnosis. For him, the work was only beginning.

The news of Clay's appointment as military governor for Germany had been well received by a war-weary American public—primarily for the relief it would offer them to have him out of the country. "Life will be hard for the German citizen," proclaimed the *New York Herald Tri-bune,* "but things may be a little easier for the Americans." *Time* maga-zine concurred: "His grim insistence on war priority, his sometimes arbitrary ways of getting it, gave some civilian officials and even some of his army colleagues a feeling that he had forgotten that the United States, even in war, was a democracy." "General Clay's exceedingly high abilities are better suited to the German situation than to our own," opined the *Washington Post.* "That task calls for authoritarianism." The *Baltimore Sun* wrote that it "served the Germans right for losing the war." A prominent businessman who had dealt with Clay groused gracelessly to *Look* magazine, "They've found the right place for him. Ruling over enemies."

In the days before he left Washington, friends warned Clay that the task of occupying, rebuilding, and, in fact, remaking Germany was an impossible one, that "the job would ruin the best man's reputation." As he would later recount, "There was not anyone of requisite size who would volunteer to take the job or would take it except an army officer who you could tell to take it." His availability was one of the few features recommending him for the position. By most measures, Clay seemed the wrong man for an important job. He had been chosen, in large part, because he had played no role in—and expressed no opinions on—the roiling administration debate over the future of Germany. In fact, he left Washington not having read the Morgenthau Plan or the final compromise document outlining Germany's future. An authoritarian personality who appeared to relish rule by fiat, he would have to root out the vestiges of pervasive Nazism from Germany and do what many thought was impossible: plant the seeds of democracy on the fallow fields of despotism, in a country whose only experiment with popular rule had led to disaster. He had no experience in foreign battle or with the affairs of nations, but few expected these to be much of a concern. He was being sent to oversee a rebuilding operation—what McCloy had told Roosevelt would be something much like the aftermath of a Mississippi River flood. No one conceived that Clay would ever face a military crisis or have to undertake high-stakes diplomacy. After all, the occupation of Germany would be shared with the Soviets, the British, and the French—America's allies. In the few days before he left Washington, Clay went to see McCloy, Secretary of War Stimson, Army Chief of Staff Marshall, and John Hilldring, the Pentagon general in charge of civil affairs. He telephoned Treasury secretary Morgenthau to enlist his help in providing economic advisers. But he did not speak to anyone in the State Department—and no one thought to suggest that he should.

A WEEK AFTER the German surrender, Clay held his first press conference as military governor. Sitting at a long table at the Hotel Scribe in

Paris, with Murphy at his side, Clay showed how deeply the Roosevelt-ian vision of harsh treatment toward the defeated Germans and expansive friendship with America's Russian allies had seeped into the consciousness of the country's wartime leaders. "I would like to make it perfectly clear that the government we propose to set up in Germany is going to be a military government, and that the Germans are going to know that it is a military government," Clay said. Those responsible for the German atrocities "will pay for their crimes with their lives and their liberties and their sweat and their blood." Germany would be divided up into zones of occupation between the four victorious powers of World War II, but these would be merely administrative divisions. The country would be ruled by an Allied Control Council where each nation would get one vote—and each of the four nations had a veto.

While they sat in Paris, the first session of the United Nations was being held in San Francisco. It had begun, to much fanfare and ruminations on the meaning of the coincidence, on the same day that the Americans and Russians had met on the Elbe. Roosevelt had told the American people repeatedly that they were fighting and sacrificing—that they were sending their children to their deaths by the hundreds of thousands—not only to avenge Pearl Harbor or to defeat the threat of rising fascism, but to promote a vision of the possibilities of a postwar world made new, for a United Nations that, in Roosevelt's conception, was no mere global gathering but an international force that would finally bring harmony to nations. At the press conference, the reporters pressed Clay on whether four-power cooperation would be successful. "It's got to work," Clay said, slamming his fist into his open palm. "If the four of us cannot get together now in running Germany, how are we going to get together in an international organization to secure the peace of the world?"

In the final weeks of the war, as Russian and American forces had each closed in on Berlin, one from the east, the other from the west, Eisenhower had been under enormous pressure, especially from Churchill, to capture the German capital before the Soviets arrived. It was a strategic and political decision that should have been made by Roosevelt, but the president was in his tired last days. So it fell to the Allied commander, who decided that the city was not worth the blood of the tens—if not hundreds—of thousands of GIs who would be expected to die in the final battle of the war. No one was quite sure of the situation in Berlin, but after 363 American and British bombing raids, it could only be assumed that the capital had received a severe blow. When General George Patton tried to convince Eisenhower to make a push to conquer the city first, Eisenhower blithely asked, "Well, who would want it?" Patton, who would die before the year was out, placed his hands on Eisenhower's shoulders, looked steadily into his eyes, and said calmly, "I think history will answer that question for you."

Berlin was the epicenter of an earthquake that had shaken the world. It was there that the work of remaking the German psyche and rebuild-ing the economy would be most difficult. Berlin—which the Allies had decided they would govern jointly until a German peace treaty was signed and a new government was chosen—would be the place where the four powers would rub up against one another on a daily basis. To lead their part of the military government of the city of Berlin, the Americans chose Colonel Frank L. Howley. They did not know what they were getting.

At a time when Americans were meeting Russians in Germany with hugs along the Elbe, Howley greeted the first Russian soldier he saw with a left hook.

Making its way to Berlin in the first detachment of Americans to enter the city, Howley's open car was crossing a pontoon bridge over a small stream when, out of the corner of his eye, he saw a soldier in a for-eign uniform leaping onto the car's running board. He threw a punch to the man's jaw, knocking him to the ground. The soldier turned out to be a Russian POW who had escaped the Germans and was trying to make his way back to his unit. Howley's reaction said much about the measure of the man. He struck the soldier not because he was scared. It was sim-ply his natural first response.

Howley was a sophisticate who carried himself as a street tough. A member of Philadelphia's high society who went on to be a "five-letter man" at New York University, in the late 1920s and early 1930s he lived the life of a Parisian expatriate—studying history at the Sorbonne and art at Parson's, carrying on in the cafés with fellow students from around the world, bicycling for hours through the French countryside. Returning to Philadelphia, he became an advertising executive, first with a major firm, then successfully putting out his own shingle. However, for all his veneer of schooling and comfort, Howley never quite fit in among the cosmopolitan set. His whole personality drove him to warfare. He joined the Army Reserve in 1932, soon after returning to the United States from France. When his unit was called up in 1940, he had a career, a business, a wife and small children, but he went off happily, even joyfully. Yet speeding down a dirt path in the back country of Georgia, on maneuvers before heading oversees, his motorcycle flipped out from under him. He broke his back and pelvis. After five months in the hospital, about to be released from the Army, Howley was given two options: take the discharge as unfit for duty in combat, or accept a transfer to a desk job in a unit charged with organizing the military government of conquered territory. He landed on Omaha Beach four days after D-Day.

Howley was directing the Army's civil affairs section in Paris, in the fall of 1944, when he was told he was getting the post of running the military government in Berlin. He accepted it eagerly, and with near-total ignorance about what it would entail. "We knew little of Berlin," he later wrote. The city had been shrouded in the fog of war, concealed under the dust of bombing, hidden behind the curtain of the total control of the Nazi Reich. But this much was clear: "I knew pretty well that Berlin was getting the real treatment and was going to be a mess."

Howley began to build a team of highly trained men to run Berlin. It would eventually grow to 350 officers and enlisted men. Unlike the youth of most Army units, his men were, on average, forty-two, Howley's age as well. Many of them were at the peak of their careers—a California state judge, a former mayor of Gary, Indiana; there were engineers, policemen, and accountants. Howley brought them all to Barbizon, a secluded village by the forests of Fontainebleau. It was a spot where, he told his diary, his initially small group of twenty-five officers "could live like Gentlemen, study like scholars, and train like soldiers." At Barbizon, they scrutinized aerial photographs of Berlin to determine the location of sewers and water lines, investigated information on the city's schools and hospitals, and examined bomb damage assessments to try to determine how much of the city was left. They developed what Howley termed "a one, two, three, four, five series of steps of what would be done by each officer upon his arrival in Berlin." Believing they would be surrounded by defeated Nazis determined to kill their American invaders, they had a handful of judo experts teach them about hand-to-hand combat and they practiced their marksmanship with pistols and rifles.

Howley, usually keyed up and driven, had a sense of what lay ahead. He told his men to use this time as "a rest period." He thought it was important to "give each officer and man a chance to communicate with his own soul." Howley worked hard at his preparations in those months in Barbizon, but though American soldiers were fighting and dying just hours away in the Bastogne and the Bulge and elsewhere, he also saw them as a time to relax and steel his psyche for what he would confront in Berlin. He caught up on neglected correspondence, played poker, drank cognac, and went to "walk out through the most beautiful forest in the world." He built up reservoirs of calm. They would be quickly drained.

SOON AFTER DAWN, on the morning of June 17, 1945, the first contingent of American troops heading for Berlin began to make its way toward the capital, with Howley at the lead. "We moved along in a gala spirit," he remembered. Howley rode in front of a long column of trucks and troops in an open Horch roadster, a gleaming German driving machine that had once belonged to a high-ranking Nazi functionary and been found hidden in a haystack on a burning farm. The front of the long black convertible, with its high-mounted headlights, stuck out far ahead of the windshield like the nose of a racehorse reaching for the finish line. Two baby boars—whose mother had been killed by the Americans on a hunt—had been adopted as mascots and were along for the ride. It was a sunny summer day. His convoy had 114 vehicles— jeeps, ten-ton trucks, half-tracks with machine guns mounted on top, all freshly painted. They carried radio equipment, food, tents, cameras, mimeograph machines, and hand grenades. Howley had arranged for a small American flag to be placed on the right side of the fender or wind- shield of each. "It was my intention to make this advance party a spectac- ular thing. It would be the first ground party of Americans to go through the Russians into Berlin, and I wanted it to look as such." Howley's jet- black hair was bristly like a wire brush and the wind whipped up the bouffant in which he combed it even higher. His big ears stuck out from the side of his head like sails. The morning was warm. He smiled— content, with purpose and anticipation. The pigs squealed with delight.

The war had been over for more than a month, but the Americans' entry into Hitler's capital had been postponed as negotiations continued over how to administer the city and how it would be divided. Germany itself had been carved by the Allies into four zones. The British zone was in northern Germany—the home to much of the nation's industrial might. America had a southern zone of Germany, which included Bavaria. The French—not really among the victorious powers of the war but important to the occupation for political reasons—were given a dumbbell-shaped appendage on their border with Germany, to the west of the American zone. To the east was the Soviet zone, and deep within it—much closer to Poland than to the Western zones—lay Berlin. Like a Russian nesting doll, Berlin would be a miniature version of the Ger- many in which it lay, also divided up by the World War II Allies into four sectors. The negotiations, which might have gone smoothly—after all, the Americans were only planning to stay for the few months, until a postwar peace treaty had been concluded—had instead dragged on for weeks, bogged down over tiny details that the Russians claimed were crucial. If the Americans had not known better, if so many had not been convinced that the Russians were their allies and the brothers-in-arms they had embraced along the Elbe, they might have thought that something terrible was happening in Berlin, something horrible beyond words, that the Soviets did not want the Westerners to see.

Such suspicion did not seem to occur to Howley. As his column moved toward the Soviet zone, he thought of the Russians only "as big, jolly, balalaika-playing fellows, who drank prodigious quantities of vodka and liked to wrestle in the drawing room." At Dessau, a hundred miles from Berlin, they reached the Elbe, and Howley slid forward on the Horch's leather seat as the bridge over the river, and into the Soviet zone, came into view. On the Russian side of the river, a great arch had been erected, with large portraits of Lenin and Stalin and a banner with the inscription "Welcome to the Fatherland" draped below. It was "as though this were no longer Germany but already had been annexed by the USSR," Howley thought. As they crossed the river, just miles from where the Russians and Americans had first met nearly two months earlier, Howley discovered that the few, sparse regiments on the Elbe had been replaced by a substantial amount of activity. Signs of Soviet occupation had sprouted up all over, with roadblocks, traffic officers waving multicolored flags, and armed Russian guards stationed every twenty yards alongside the highway. "There was a hellava lot of excitement and confusion," he observed.

A Russian officer approached the convoy and addressed Howley: "You must stop here. You are expected at headquarters." Howley was only too happy to oblige and offer his respects to the local Soviet commander. So began what he described to his diary as "the most extraordinary trip of my life."

The entire convoy followed the Russian's car until it reached a small house by a dirt road. The car came to such a sudden stop that it got rear-ended by Howley's Horch. Howley, a fellow officer, and a translator followed the Russian past a guard, into the house, and up a creaky set of wooden stairs to the second floor. There, a Soviet colonel greeted them with elaborate and eloquent pleasantries. Wouldn't they join him in a champagne toast to the great friendship of their nations? The Americans smiled, sat, drained their glasses, and prepared to take their leave. "Ah, you cannot go just yet," the colonel said nervously. "There is a formality."

Howley sat back down to wait. A Russian sergeant entered the room and, without so much as a nod in the direction of the Americans, sat down at a piano in the corner and began to beat away at it with bawdy beer hall tunes. After a while, Howley got ready to try to leave again when the colonel, looking out the window, asked him, "How many vehicles, officers, and men do you have?"

"Roughly, five hundred officers and men and a hundred twenty vehicles," Howley answered.

"The agreement," the colonel announced, "says thirty-seven officers, fifty vehicles, and one hundred seventy-five men."

"What agreement?"

"The Berlin Agreement," the colonel replied as if that settled the matter.

Howley said he had never heard of any such agreement, that he had his orders, and in any case, this was simply the first wave of thousands of American soldiers that would soon be on their way to occupy Berlin. "Oh?" said the colonel. "Then I must check headquarters."

Howley told him to go ahead, not realizing that the nearest telephone line was twenty miles away. It was two hours before the colonel returned with a response: the decision stood, the "Berlin Agreement" must be enforced. By that point the champagne had run out and had been replaced with warm beer, the piano player had worked through his entire repertoire and was repeating himself, and Howley's patience—something never in surplus—had been exhausted. "Look," he said to the colonel, "my orders say go to Berlin. They don't say with your permission. Let's be frank. You are keeping us from going to Berlin and I want to know who is responsible."

"My superior ordered this."

"Then let us speak to your superior," said an exasperated Howley. The Russian smiled, happy to oblige, and set off down the road to make the request while Howley waited. By the time a one-star general showed up at the shabby little country house, forty-five minutes later, Howley's men were lying down in the dirt outside out the building and even the piano player had grown tired and quit.

He got no further with the general: "The agreement is for thirty-seven officers, fifty vehicles, and one hundred seventy-five men."

Howley tried to threaten him with "serious repercussions" and the specter of an international incident. The general seemed somehow less than cowed. Howley asked for the general's superior and—after another interminable wait—a two-star general arrived singing from the same hymnal: "thirty-seven officers, fifty vehicles, and one hundred seventy-five men." Howley, with nothing to lose and evidently curious on how long he could keep this up before Joseph Stalin himself marched up the creaky stairs, asked to see the two-star general's superior, and—the wait by this point was superfluous—a three-star general eventually arrived.

"My colleagues have explained to you that you are to take into Berlin only thirty-seven officers, fifty vehicles, and one hundred seventy-five men. You have more than that. What is your decision?" This time, Howley folded and contacted his own superiors for instructions. After another few hours, he got word back telling him to comply. It was almost nightfall when Howley walked back down the stairs and left for Berlin with a convoy of thirty-seven officers, fifty vehicles, and one hundred seventy-five men.

"THE ROAD TO Berlin was the high road to Bedlam," remembered Howley of the journey toward the city. As his convoy moved along in a stately procession, they passed streams of refugees. Railroad tracks had been bombed, locomotives destroyed, fuel was all but nonexistent, so millions of the wretched and dazed set off on foot, pulling wagons or simply trudging along dirt roads with the miserable remains of their worldly possessions on their backs, walking across a continent in a search for family members, villages—a world—that had disappeared. "Strange sights were all over," he wrote in his diary. "A ragged man with holes in his pants leading three beautiful horses. Groups of people along the roads cooking." On the American side of the Elbe, Howley had seen 200,000 German prisoners of war being held on a hillside without GI guards but only by the promise of food. As they neared Berlin, it was easy to forget how close they were to the hub of Germany's war-making machine. Green hills rolled by, fecund pastures stretched before them, cows masticated contently, white clouds hung quietly over village churches. But as if the reverberations of what had happened in the capital had driven them away, Howley looked about to find the fields deserted of people: "Eerie silence drenched the countryside. The land was empty and desolate, the crops unattended."

Howley did not mourn their absence. He thought of the Germans he would rule over in Berlin with a cold loathing instead of sympathy. "As I rode on the Autobahn to Berlin in 1945, hate had hardened my conscience." His brother had been crippled fighting the Germans during World War I; many of his friends had perished during the present conflict. Feelings of revulsion came easily to Howley. He was someone who would be described frequently as possessing what was called, tactfully, a "dramatic" personality. Yet his outlook merely represented a common emotion among Germany's conquerors. "Two years of war have built up an intense hatred among front-line troops for the Germans," wrote a *New York Times* correspondent embedded with the First Army in October 1944. The antipathy spread beyond the soldiers. Though Americans' attitudes toward Germans stopped a step short of the racist tinge with which wartime propaganda treated the Japanese, many of those on the home front were convinced there was something vile innate in the German national character. "The Germans have an inborn love for regimentation and harsh discipline," declared Frank Capra's popular series of documentaries *Why We Fight*. The image of bloodthirsty, war-loving Prussians was used so often it became a cliché.

Animosity was not directed solely at the Nazi Party as if it were an alien force that had lorded over subservient citizens and flung them unwillingly into war. Responsibility, many Americans believed, lay at the feet of individual Germans—and to some degree, with an earlier generation of Americans who had treated a defeated Germany with kindness and compassion instead of the harsh severity they had earned. *A Pocket Guide to Germany*, prepared for distribution to soldiers entering the country, reminded them not to "forget that you are ordered into Germany now partly because your fathers forgot so soon what the war was about last time. They took it for granted that the friendly reception the Germans gave them after the Armistice in 1918 proved that Germany meant well after all. Our whole country let down its guard too easily last time." Americans arrived convinced that this time things would be different, that it was their duty to treat Germans with such sternness as to ensure that they had been thoroughly degraded. "Whether you fight your way in, or march in to occupy Germany under armistice terms, you will be doing a soldier's job on the soil of the enemy," read page 1 of the *Pocket Guide.* "The occupation of Germany will give you your chance to build up a personal guarantee that as soon as you turn your back to go home, the German will not pick up his shooting iron and start throwing lead and lies at an unsuspecting world once more."

Thus GIs received strict orders not to converse with or even smile at Germans, and grave punishments were meted out to those who violated this command. Treating Germans with humanity was seen as the surest way to bring about another chapter in the saga of Teutonic destruction. "If in a German town you bow to a pretty girl or pat a blonde child," warned Armed Forces Radio in an announcement run frequently in the summer of 1945, "you bow to Hitler and his reign of blood . . . you caress the ideology that means death and persecution."

The Germans, continued the *Pocket Guide,* "have sinned against the laws of humanity and cannot come back into the civilized fold by merely sticking out their hands and saying—'I'm sorry.'" As Americans drove further into the defeated country, as they discovered that those violations of humanity's laws were even more egregious than most of them had understood, their anger at the Germans grew instead of abating. On April 12, just hours before Roosevelt died, Eisenhower toured a death camp, Ohrdruf Nord, for the first time. "I never dreamed that such cruelty, bestiality, and savagery could really exist in this world," he wrote to his wife, Mamie. America's occupation of Germany was designed to ensure that the malignancy in the German national character that made this possible was torn out for good. Two weeks later, the day after the linkup at the Elbe, Eisenhower issued a directive to American troops: "Germany will not be occupied for the purpose of liberation but as a defeated enemy. The principal objective is to prevent Germany from ever again becoming a threat to the peace of the world." It was an audacious goal—and the plan was to accomplish it through unremitting strictness.

As he left Ohrdruf Nord, Eisenhower turned to a U.S. Army sentry and snarled, "Still having trouble hating them?" Few of the Americans—back in the United States or in the occupation force in Germany—had any such difficulty. For years, their disgust and revulsion had festered. And though America's loathing was directed at the Nazi nation in general, it had a focal point: Germany's capital city—the home to Hitler and his government, the command center for all that had come to represent evil in the world. During the war, posters calling on Americans to achieve "MORE PRODUCTION" showed soldiers loading bombs into an airplane with the simple and self-explanatory words "Bundles for Berlin." Howley looked toward the capital he was about to enter and rule, "full of hate for what we considered the black heart of Prussia."

Not since the pinnacle of Rome had one city ruled over so much of Europe. Never—not even when Rome was pillaged by barbarians—had a city fallen from such heights so quickly. And when Berlin's invaders came, it was not a civilization that was destroyed, but civilization itself—or at least its crude veneer—that vanished.

Once—before—when the bonfires and the bombings and the rubble and the rapes were still unimaginable, Berlin had been a city of statues and eagles, of streets choked with trolleys and big black cars, of women with nice hats rushing to gossip in the café. When Hitler was still delivering his deluded rantings in the sticks, Berlin was the largest city in the world in terms of size and third-largest by population. More than only its expanse, Berlin represented, to people everywhere, what was most modern and advanced about the Industrial Age, the very possibilities of

progress and improvement that thrilled so many in those first decades of
the last century. "It is a new city; the newest I have ever seen," wrote a
visiting Mark Twain. At the Romanische Café, across the street from the
Kaiser Wilhelm Memorial Church, writers, actors, and rabbis stayed up
into the dawn hours discussing the hopes of the world. Berliners walked
hand in hand through the Tiergarten—the city's large park—enjoying
its statues of generals and its marble paths. The city had the world's
fastest subways and more taxicabs during the 1930s than Boston and
Philadelphia combined had at the start of the twenty-first century.
There, in 1931, Konrad Zuse built the first computer to make calculations with binary codes of ones and zeroes. By 1933, the city had
500,000 telephone lines, the highest ratio of lines to residents anywhere.
With 149 daily periodicals, Berlin, during the 1920s, was nicknamed
"Newspaper City." Berliners raced about and jabbered and discussed—
and it struck some that there was something unsettled about it all.
"There is no city in the world so restless as Berlin," wrote British diplomat Harold Nicolson in 1932.

London and New York still had more people, but no city had the
kind of people who came to Berlin. Berlin was the home to Dadaism,
Expressionism, and particle physics. It was in Berlin that Vladimir
Nabokov spent his days giving tennis lessons to girls and nights translating *Alice in Wonderland* into German. Berlin was where Marlene Die-
trich sang "Falling in love again, never wanted to. What am I to do? I
can't help it." It was Berlin that a young W. H. Auden, full of clever
hopes, moved to directly after graduating from Oxford, arriving in time
to see Mack the Knife swaying on the opening night of *The Threepenny
Opera*. There, in Berlin, Walter Gropius threw up walls of glass in the
Bauhaus style, and Ludwig Mies van der Rohe built homes of steel, saying "less is more" and "God is in the details." There, a fifty-year-old
Albert Einstein sat in the audience of the Philharmonic Orchestra listening to a twelve-year-old Yehudi Menuhin playing selections from
Bach, Beethoven, and Brahms, and was so taken that, as the crowd
screamed in adoration, he rushed backstage and—with his hair wild and
eyes bulging—grabbed the boy and shook him, exclaiming, "Now I

know there is a God in heaven!" Where some found the divine in Berlin, others found the satanic; where Werner Heisenberg explored uncertainty, others found they had all the answers. "This city is a melting pot of everything that is evil—prostitution, drinking houses, cinemas, Marxism, Jews, strippers, Negroes, dancing and all the vile offshoots of modern art," said young Joseph Goebbels on arriving there in 1926, and the Nazi's revulsion would surely have made Christopher Isherwood smile, at first.

But all the modernity, all the refinement and freedom of which Berlin's residents were so proud, was hollow, rotten at its core. If, in later years, Berliners would point out that they had given Hitler and the Nazis a few percentage points less of a plurality than in other parts of Germany, that they thought of themselves as a city occupied by a political force springing from the hinterlands, that they had been too sophisticated to be taken in by the enthusiasms of the less cynical, it was a tinny defense drowned out by the shouted *"Heils"* with which they greeted one another on the street; the crackle of the flames of books by Jack London, H. G. Wells, and Helen Keller burning in giant bonfires; the *"Ja!"* which they yelled as one when Goebbels asked a packed Sportpalast, "Do you want Total War?"; the castanet click of goosesteps on cobblestone as Berlin's young men proudly went off to die in the name of a monstrous cause. It was Berliners who, on their way to the market, blithely brushed by the doctors forced to walk the streets carrying a placard reading "I AM A FILTHY JEW"; who quickened their step to hurry past the SS and SA buildings where the music was turned up loud in a vain attempt to muffle the wails of the tortured; who gleefully reported on and rounded up their neighbors and dispatched them on the first available cattle car to hell.

As grand as their city was, Berliners saw a future where their capital—like that of the pharaohs—would reach glories yet untold on the backs of the enslaved. At night, after the work of conquering continents and annihilating millions was done for the day, Hitler would call for his architect, Albert Speer, and together they would pore over plans for turning Berlin into Germania, a new capital of the world, crisscrossed with massive highways and grotesque, gargantuan monuments. "These buildings of ours," announced Hitler in 1937, "should not be conceived for the year 1940; no, not for the year 2000, but like cathedrals of our past they should stretch into the millennia of the future." His own offices were to be fitting to his new power. "All who enter the Reich Chancellery must have the feeling that they are visiting the masters of the world." When he said this in October 1941, such visitors might have been excused for thinking this could soon be true. The new Chancellery had a main hall twice as long as the Hall of Mirrors in Versailles—a final kick of dirt on Woodrow Wilson's grave.

Under Speer, Potsdamer Platz—already among the busiest intersections in Europe and home to the continent's first traffic light—was to be turned into an enormous city square to dwarf Paris's Place de la Concorde. Flanked by big neoclassical buildings, its center would be a sunken pool with four pillars of water shooting up high into the sky. Surrounding the fountain would be ornate statues built at four times human scale. A thousand cars could find a space to park around the square. Speer designed a palace for Hitler that was to be 150 times the size of Bismarck's residence, with a dining room that could fit thousands. Hitler and Speer envisioned a statue of a German woman taller than the Statue of Liberty. In Speer's plans, Germania would be dominated by a three-mile-long central axis. At the north end would be a mammoth pantheon seventeen times larger than the dome of St. Peter's and able to contain numerous U.S. Capitols within it. At the south end, the plan was for a triumphal arch into which the Arc de Triomphe would fit forty-nine times.

In 1934, the Nazis built a new airport terminal at Tempelhof so that it would be aligned with the proposed arch. It was designed to welcome the visitors from around the world whom Hitler expected would come to marvel at his capital. Tempelhof, close to the center of the city, had been an airport since the early 1920s, and its place in the history of flight stretched back even farther. When, in 1909, Orville Wright showed off his flying machine to Crown Prince Friedrich Wilhelm and the German people at Tempelhof in a nineteen-minute flight, Tempelhof had already been used as field for launching dirigibles and hot-air balloons for a century. Stretching out in a mile-long arc, the new air terminal was constructed to resemble, from the skies above, a German eagle in flight; its administrative buildings represented the bird's body and its semicircular hangars formed its spread wings. In case the point was missed, a huge black eagle with a swastika emblazoned on its chest was carved into the building's façade. But the terminal's dominant feature was not its design but its size. It had 5,000 offices and a multifunctional roof designed to provide a bird's-eye view for up to 80,000 people at party rallies where Goebbels organized immense celebrations, complete with parades and painstakingly planned "spontaneous demonstrations of joy" on the field below. As befitted its place in Germania, Tempelhof was, upon its construction, the largest building in the world—so large that, more than forty years after it was built, only the Pentagon and the World Trade Center were larger. By 1938, it was Lufthansa's main airport, with 250,000 passengers passing through each year and flights departing to twenty-seven German and forty-three international destinations. Tempelhof was designed to be the gateway to the new capital—Berlin's link to the rest of the world. There the dirty and degraded representatives of lesser peoples would arrive to visit Hitler's palace and his stately, treasured dome and bow in homage and awe before the new order. They would come to a Berlin that by most every measure had been one of the world's great cities for many years and whose glory seemed to be only at its dawn.

AND THEN THE war came. From Berlin—and from Berliners—came a flood of death and disaster unlike anything the world had ever known. The wave came from the splendid villa on the Wannsee where the Nazis built a bureaucracy for extermination; from the red-marbled Chancellery where Hitler plotted the conquest of Europe; from Opernplatz on Unter den Linden, the city's most refined boulevard, where Berlin's youth hauled volumes from every major library, dancing maniacally around a bonfire that threw monstrous shadows of undulating celebration onto the gray walls of the city's university. The surge crashed against

London and Leningrad; it flooded Paris and Prague, Antwerp and Amsterdam, Budapest and Bucharest and a thousand other storied cities. Angry rivulets of dark water flowed past the tiny spots as well, the points not even on a map, places few had heard of but whose names would soon be full of meaning; past Babi Yar, past a fishing village named Dunkirk, past the small Polish town of Oświęcim whose pronunciation was the least of what the Nazis would butcher there when they called it Auschwitz. And when the waters had spread so far and risen so high that it seemed for a moment as if all the world would be covered by the deluge, the tide began to turn and the waters began to recede, fleeing from the very forces they had let loose. And the awful hand of vengeance came down on Berlin.

They came first with the bombs. From the air, British and American planes dropped a rain of fire onto Berlin. Beginning in 1940, but then in earnest in 1943, they let loose 156 million pounds of explosive terror. On the nights of November 11 and 12, 1943, bombing raids killed or injured 9,000 Berliners and left nearly 300,000 homeless. Firestorms swept through the city. The Kaiser Wilhelm Memorial Church was destroyed, the hands of its clock charred into place forever. On February 3, 1945, the homes of 125,000 Berliners were destroyed along with much of the city center, including the Reich Chancellery, the Gestapo headquarters, the People's Court in Kleist Park, and the great buildings along Unter den Linden.

Through days and nights of bombs from above, Berliners huddled in air-raid shelters and cellars, shivering in fear. When the fires subsided and they could emerge from hiding, they picked through the remains of their once-magnificent city in disbelief. To deal with the carnage and devastation, with the bombing raids occurring every few days, Berliners deployed their unique wry, ironic sense of humor. When explosions illuminated the night sky, they would nudge the person next to them and crack that the Allies were lighting up the Christmas tree again.

As the war progressed, air attacks on Berlin became commonplace. Allied planes had destroyed the Luftwaffe and now owned the skies. They were able to fly over Nazi Germany with impunity, approach the capital with ease, and drop explosives with more destructive power than that of centuries of human combat combined. American and British planes killed or grievously injured 150,000 Berliners, and destroyed one-third of the city's buildings. The pilots who let loose this barrage of death onto Berlin began to treat their work as routine. By war's end, they referred to bombing raids as "milk runs."

AS HIS CAPITAL was coming down around him, Hitler was obsessed with the well-being of Germany's children. More so than even Speer's monuments, they were his legacy—a master race he hoped would advance the ambitions of his Thousand Year Reich. "Each mother who has given birth to a child has struck a blow for the future of our people," Hitler told the Germans. But it was not enough to bear young Aryans, they had to be molded as well, inculcated at the youngest age with values and views that would define the rest of their lives. "This youth of ours," Hitler said in 1938, "is going to learn nothing but how to think German, how to act German." To accomplish this, Hitler left little to chance. Nazi indoctrination began in kindergarten. Every subject in school was twisted. "An aircraft drops a bomb from a height of 2,000 meters at a speed of 108 km per hour. After what lapse of time and at what location does the projectile hit the ground?" read one math question. Another word problem stated that if "an airplane flies at the rate of 240 km per hour to a place a distance of 210 km in order to drop bombs . . . when may it be expected to return if the dropping of the bombs takes seven and one-half minutes?"

Yet to truly train Germany's children in his ways, Hitler needed to gain total control over them. For this, his deliverance came from the same place as his destruction. Beginning in September 1940, just days after the first bombing raid over Berlin, the Nazis began evacuating the children from the city—supposedly for their safety. Over the next years, 5 million German children—one-half of the nation's youth—were sent to 12,000 camps throughout rural Germany and occupied countries. As bombers continued to attack the country's cities, the move did indeed save many of their lives, but there were added benefits for the Nazis as well. Run by Hitler Youth brigades, the camps were devoted to brainwashing children with the purest, most wicked form of the Nazi ideology. Lessons revolved around the benevolence and wisdom of Adolf Hitler and the depravity of Germany's enemies. Children were forced to write letters home filled with lavish praise of *der Führer* and boundless devotion to the Nazi cause. Life in the camps was regularly rocked by word of the deaths of parents and siblings in bombing raids or on the battlefield, and the emotional wreckage of the children—alone, disoriented, abandoned—was put to use. The children were taught to think of Americans as evil incarnate and blame the GIs for their suffering and loss. It was, one young girl would recall, "a steady rape of children's souls."

Hitler and his regime drilled Nazism into Germany's children until the very end. In Berlin, on April 20, 1945, Hitler's birthday, all ten-year-olds were required, as they were every year on that date, to swear an oath of undying allegiance to the Nazi leader: "I promise in the Hitler Youth to do my duty at all times, in love and loyalty to our Führer and our flag." But by that time a roar was growing steadily in the east, and on the horizon the sky was the color of fire.

ONE OUT OF every ten bombs dropped on Germany landed in Berlin. Under the torrent of American and British bombing, Berlin was staggering, its feet wobbly. Then the Russians came and knocked it down.

By early April, two and a half million Russian troops were massed and ready for the Battle of Berlin. The Germans were outnumbered five to one and outgunned fifteen to one. It was only delusional fanatics who thought a last stand was sensible, yet—despite the privations of war—Germany did not suffer shortages in that department. Other Berliners scoffed as hasty trenches and makeshift roadblocks were erected on the outskirts of the city. "It will take the Russians two hours and five minutes to get past a roadblock in Berlin," went the joke. "Two hours laughing at it and five minutes pushing it aside." After the long years of war, most simply wanted it to be over, no matter how painful the final few days would be. Better an end of terror, they said, than terror without end. They had no idea what terror truly meant.

On April 21, central Berlin came under Russian artillery attack for the first time. Shells hurled into a crowd of people outside of the Karstadt department store on Hermannplatz. Soviet tanks poured into the city's suburbs. The nightingales left the Tiergarten. An ice-cold wind came down on Berlin as the Russians approached.

For many, the years of tension and bombing from above, the rain of shells and the torture of fear over what still was to come, finally took their toll and they cracked under the strain. The thought of Russians smashing into Berlin, of the fall of the Reich, gave the city an atmosphere of apocalypse. It seemed as if they were living in the end times. When a shell exploded in the middle of a line of women waiting to collect their rations, those behind stepped forward over the bodies of the dead without breaking their order. At the city clerk's office, a woman showed up with the body of her dead fiancé and demanded they be married. Something in her eyes, in her tone, or perhaps just the sense of resignation in the air, led the clerk to acquiesce. Exactly sixteen years to the day that Einstein had felt the presence of God as Menuhin played the violin, the Berlin Philharmonic performed a final concert. The only lights came from the lamps on the music stands. It was cold in the hall and the audience—including many of the highest-ranking Nazis—wore their overcoats. The orchestra played Beethoven's Violin Concerto, Bruckner's Eighth Symphony, and the finale from Wagner's *Götterdämmerung*— "The Twilight of the Gods." As the concertgoers left the hall, the music of the end of the world still ringing in their ears, they filed out past children dressed in their Hitler Youth uniforms who had been assigned to helpfully hold out baskets filled with cyanide capsules for the crowd.

On April 25, the same day the Americans and Russians met on the Elbe, the Russians encircled Berlin and were ready to begin their full attack on the city. In Berlin, would-be Davids readied their slingshots for the tanks. Berlin's men were gone—dead, captured, mortally wounded. Authorities estimated that of the 2.7 million people still in Berlin, 2 million of them were women. Of the males that were left, there were very few between the ages of eighteen and sixty, and of those most were invalids or otherwise useless in battle. So the Nazis conscripted those who were left—the very old and the very young—into the Volkssturm, the home guard. The elderly were of some help—there was even a battalion for old men who were hard of hearing—but they had grown weak and tired in the war. So in the final battle of World War II, the weight of defending Berlin was placed on the slender shoulders of twelve-year-old boys. Once, the Nazis' empire stretched far beyond that of Napoleon or Caesar; it had seen victories in the Ukraine and its U-boats off Coney Island, and the mere sight of its fearsome troops inspired terror in great armies. But by the end of April 1945, it was reduced to a few square miles, and its last stand would be little children on the barricades of Berlin.

With the Red Army just outside the city, young boys and even some girls were sent out toward the front with antitank grenades strapped to their bicycles. They improvised roadside bombs to stop the rolling armor. When the Russians approached closer, the children—some who would be captured were as young as eight years old—were handed rifles to hold off Soviet tanks. Boys were ordered to "man" the antiaircraft guns ready to take down any American bombers flying overhead.

In other circumstances, someone who happened on the Volkssturm might have thought they were simply children playing war. They wore oversized uniforms and leftover metal helmets far too big for their heads. Some of the boys were walked to the barracks by their mothers. Others would go home at night and arrive at the fortifications the next morning with lunches that had been packed for them. But it was real. One out of every nine Soviet citizens had died in the war the Nazis had unleashed, and the Russians were mad for revenge. They were told that Berlin was "the City of the Devil," and they attacked with the fury of Lucifer invading Hades itself. With the Germans completely outnumbered, with all of Germany doomed, there was no way Berlin could stand, but the city's defenders fought back with a ferocity untethered by any rationality. The boys flung themselves in fearsome rage at the Red Army, convinced, in the hubris of youth, that they could turn back the invaders and avenge the deaths of their fallen fathers and brothers. Five thousand boys and girls under the age of sixteen were estimated to have fought in the defense of Berlin. Five hundred survived.

———

A GREAT ARMY of soldiers—the kind that once would have moved gracefully across vast plains and gone into battle on stately fields—now slammed into one of the largest cities on earth, a twentieth-century metropolis of highways, subways, and streetcars. The Russians used 22,000 big guns in the attack; shells came down in the center of Berlin every five seconds. The troops and tanks rolled into the city and the fighting was furious. A German Panzer officer kept a scribbled diary during the fighting, its staccato entries hinting at the cataclysm of urban warfare: *"April 25th, 5:30 A.M.:* New, massive tank attack. We are forced to retreat. Heavy street fighting—many civilian casualties. Dying animals, women fleeing from cellar to cellar. We retreat again, under heavy Russian air attacks. Deserters hanged or shot. What we see on this march is unforgettable. Heavy fighting in the business district, inside the Stock Exchange. The first skirmishes in the subway tunnels through which the Russians are trying to get behind our lines. The tunnels are packed with civilians."

Berliners cowered as the debris fell around them. The steady shocks were too much for some. Babies would die of hunger and be left lying on the floor by parents too dazed to know what to do with the corpse. At Tempelhof, the airport's commander received orders to blow up the terminal so that it did not fall into Russian hands. He killed himself instead. One shell hit the riding stables of the Tiergarten, sending a herd of shrieking horses stampeding down the city's streets with their manes and tails on fire. A lion escaped from the zoo and trod past the Gestapo headquarters. A zebra was seen grazing in a Berlin graveyard, but by then the entire city had become a cemetery of bodies buried in rubble. The Russians would lose 305,000 troops in the last 42 miles approaching Berlin—about the number of American army soldiers who died in all of World War II. Of the 125,000 of Berlin's civilians who died in the Russian attack, 6,400 were suicides; they simply could not bear to live through it any longer.

Many of the front-line troops of the Red Army seemed to have an otherworldly quality about them to European eyes. "These men have come from the back of beyond, from the far Ukraine, the farther Urals, from Siberia and Mongolia, and the impressive, ghostly feeling they exude is one of being nowhere yet everywhere at home," observed one British occupation officer who arrived a few weeks after the battle. The Siberians washed their faces in the toilet, believing that this was what they were for. Unaccustomed to electricity, they would marvel at light-bulbs. They demanded that the glowing orbs be handed over, held them delicately, packed them away carefully, and planned to unveil them back home, in front of their awed family and friends, to be used to light their squalid huts on the steppes.

The Russian soldiers would nap in straw-filled wagons with lambs, goats, and pigs; they had pulled their food supplies into Berlin with them. Many should have felt at home among the animals. They stole everything they could get their hands on; wristwatches and bicycles were their favorites. Their government began immediately to rip away Berlin's industrial might and cart it off to the Soviet Union. And with the ransacking came the ravishment. As they entered Berlin, while still killing off the last of its German defenders, the Russians indulged in an orgy of rape and rage beyond the bounds of human imagination. Over the course of ten days, about 130,000 women were raped—and most were violated repeatedly by various soldiers. "The Russian soldiers were raping every German female from eight to eighty," reported a Soviet correspondent who entered the city with the Red Army. "It was an army of rapists."

The assailants were brutal. *"Frau, komm!"* ("Woman, come here!") they would call, and under threat of death, they would rape girls in front of their fathers; wives in front of their husbands, all the while smiling through yellowed stubs of teeth and smelling of dung and loam. *"Frau, komm!"* they yelled and then shot anyone who interfered, even when it was a little boy defending his mother. A soldier who was bothered by a baby crying while he raped its mother swung it by its legs and crushed its head against a pole. *"Frau, komm!"* they would snarl and sever the tendons of women so they would not try to run away. Women would cut their hair to disguise themselves as boys or smear muck on their faces to try to make themselves less attractive, but the Russians, having come so far for vengeance and booty, did not mind a little dirt.

Berlin's women dealt with the aftermath in different ways. Many girls, having been taught that when honor was lost, all was lost, did to themselves what American bombs and Russian shells had not; they chose the fate they had avoided by tearfully submitting to the angry, vodka-drenched soldiers who reeked from crossing two continents without taking a bath. On their own, or sometimes under instructions of their shamed fathers, they hanged themselves from the rafters and drowned themselves in the river. "Poison or bullet, rope or knife. They are killing themselves by the hundreds," wrote a Berliner in her diary on May 6. In fact, it was by the thousands.

Others were almost matter-of-fact about the assaults. For some, the rapes became so routine that the women would find themselves worrying during the attack about their only undergarments being torn to shreds. In the weeks after the fall of Berlin, women would see old friends on the street and casually begin conversations with "How many times?" No further explanation was needed. Yet, as horrific as the rapes were, as shattering as the fear could be, many were able to rationalize the violations in light of all Berlin had experienced. They chose the hiss of *"Frau, komm!"* over the roar of American planes and their bombs from above. "Better a Russian on the belly," went the saying, "than an American on the head."

ALL WARFARE BECOMES primitive—the gloss of technology does little to camouflage the blood and brutality of human death—but there was something especially jarring about this elegant, modern city first serving as the capital for the most vile, evil regime in history and then getting sacked by hordes from the east thirsty for carnage, lucre, and revenge. It was as if the most dateless fears of Europeans had come to life, sweeping savages into Berlin in a rhyme of ancient memories. The scene in Berlin was so chthonian that, if asked to describe it, even Dante would have drawn a blank. "Ruins, craters, burned-out tanks, smashed guns, tramcars riddled with holes, half-demolished trenches, heaps of spent cartridge shells, fresh graves, corpses still awaiting burial, masses of white flags, crowds of glum and hungry inhabitants lie before our eyes," catalogued a Soviet correspondent arriving with the Russian troops. "The Tiergarten is burning; trees crack and writhe in flames."

Ernest Leiser of *Stars and Stripes* reached Berlin on May 5, one of the first Western journalists into the city. "Berlin, the capital of defeat, today is a charred, stinking, broken skeleton of a city," he reported. "It is impossible to imagine what it looked like before. It is impossible to believe that the miles of disemboweled buildings, of cratered streets, of shattered masonry once could have been the capital of Greater Germany and the home of four million people. Only a handful of the four million still remain as the last clatter of machine-gun fire echoes through the hollowed city." He was wrong. They were there, millions of them, living in the skeletons, hiding amid the rubble of their homes, waiting to come out from below to consider what was left of their great city after they had reaped the whirlwind.

World War II ended in a battle for a single building, Germany's Reichstag, the parliament building whose destruction by arson in 1933 had provided the pretext for Hitler's suspension of freedoms and civil liberties. At 8:30 A.M. on April 30, the Russians began an artillery barrage on its burned-out shell. An hour and half later, the first infantry wave began its assault on the 7,000 German troops defending the building. It was shortly after 1 P.M. that Russians made it up the steps and broke through the front doors. Then began hours of bloody hand-to-hand combat as the final battle for Germany was waged corridor by corridor, room by room. By 2:30, the Red Army made it to the second floor. Nearly 5,000 men died in the battle for the building. It was not until 11 P.M. that Sergeants Mikhail Yegorov and Meliton Kantariya raised the red flag over Berlin. In the dark night of a city without power, it might have flapped unseen, but it was illuminated by a capital enflamed by the orange glow of conflagration. The sky of Berlin around the Reichstag had been brightened by fires that had burned throughout that day and night—including the flames from the shallow ditch in the nearby Chancellery garden, where forty gallons of gasoline had incinerated the bodies of Adolf Hitler and his new wife, Eva.

In those final, manic days in the bunker, it was not the wedding of

Adolf and Eva—with the bride in black and a reception of cake and liverwurst—that was Hitler's happiest moment. Rather the moment of exhilaration had come the day after Franklin Roosevelt's death. Hitler learned the news on Friday, April 13, and saw it as an omen of good luck. Goebbels was ecstatic: "My Führer, I congratulate you! Roosevelt is dead. It is written in the stars." It was the turning point they had been waiting for. On January 30, 1933, the day Hitler took power, an astrologer had predicted that war would break out in 1939 and that, after initial success, there would be great hardship lasting until the middle of April 1945. At that point, Germany's course would change. For the next three years there would be a very difficult time, but beginning in 1948, the German people would rise again. With Roosevelt's demise, Hitler was now buoyed by the prediction. But the Germans did not send the Red Army fleeing from the Motherland, the roar of cannon only grew louder with each passing day, and Hitler died thinking the astrologer had been wrong.

Howley's shrunken convoy reached the outskirts of Berlin after the hundred-mile journey from the Elbe to find that, with negotiations between the Allies over the occupation still continuing, Russian guards had orders to keep them out of the city. The Soviets told the Americans that they had to wait to enter until the Red Army "restored order" and "cleared mines." For two weeks, Howley waited just outside the city, growing angrier and more impatient. Finally, on July 1, 1945, America's troops were allowed to enter Berlin.

They rode in wearing their most resplendent dress uniforms but, without having an advance party able to scout out barracks and offices, had nowhere to go. Instead of entering the city that day, they set up camp in the Grünewald, a vast forested park in the southwest part of Berlin. "The ground was high and dry with plenty of fine trees and shade about," Howley noted. But then it began to rain and the ground turned wet. They parked their trucks and jeeps in a protective circle as if they were in a wagon train heading across the Great Plains. Men stood under trees to shield themselves from the driving downpour. That night they would use their helmets as pillows and sleep in the mud in their finest uniforms. Howley lay there fuming. "I had managed to avoid pup tents throughout World War II and here I was, with the war over and making a triumphal entry into Berlin, established in that dreaded form of shelter under most dreary and uncomfortable conditions," thought one of Howley's aides. "This was undoubtedly history's most unimpressive entry into the capital of a defeated nation by a conquering power."

The next day, July 2, Howley and General Floyd Parks, who was in charge of American troops in Berlin and was nominally Howley's boss, went to meet with Parks's Russian counterpart, General Alexander Gorbatov. Howley, still steamed at the Soviets for the delays and insults along the way to Berlin, took an immediate dislike to the "beefy, red-faced" Red Army commander. Gorbatov produced a map of Berlin divided up by the victorious powers' sectors and asked the Americans when they would be ready to take over their area. The long days of planning at Barbizon were now worth it. Howley said he needed only one day for his men to do reconnaissance and be prepared to assume responsibility. So July 4 was chosen as the day that America would take control of its sector of Berlin. With the work done, Gorbatov invited Howley to join the others at tea. Howley was about to decline—it was 3 P.M., there was much work to be done, and he had no desire to sit with the Russians—when the more diplomatic Parks jumped in. They would both be honored to accept the invitation, he said, shooting Howley a stern look. Gorbatov smiled amiably and opened a door to a room where a table groaned under the weight of a vast spread of food and drink. "I couldn't swear that there was no tea, but I sure as hell didn't see any," Howley wrote in his diary. Wanting nothing to do with the Russians, he gathered a plate of food, found a corner, and went off to sit. Eventually, a Soviet general sat down in the empty seat next to Howley. Rank-conscious, the Russian visibly shuddered when he realized he was sitting next to someone of much lower position. "I see you're a colonel," he said through an interpreter. Howley looked up from his plate and grumbled, "I see you're a general. Here, have some salami."

OVER THE NEXT days, Howley and the other Americans got their first look at Berlin. They entered the city under huge banners that hung overhead proclaiming, "The Red Army Has Saved Berlin." It seemed to Howley a curious use of the term.

"It didn't look like a city anyone would deliberately come into," Howley wrote in his diary of his first view of Berlin. "The whole center of the city was completely gutted." The apartment buildings, offices, shops that had filled chic Berlin had been replaced by empty, jagged ruins that appeared as if they had been fashioned of rotten Swiss cheese. It was a dark city—only 4,000 of 125,000 streetlamps were left. Berlin's Philharmonic Hall—where a wild-maned Einstein had heard God's revelation, where children in tan uniforms had held out baskets of cyanide—was gone. In its place was a dead, bloated white mare atop a heap of boulders. The debris was piled in mountains two and three stories high, and everywhere Howley went "uncertain, ragged, many-times-violated women were clearing the rubble, passing one brick at a time," their fine hats supplanted by mangy scarfs as they dug through the wreckage of the big city. As Howley rode into the city center on Berliner Strasse, he passed an area where only 604 of the 11,075 residential buildings remained standing. Farther down what was once one of the city's most gracious boulevards, he saw "a dead horse being torn apart by hungry women." They would rip the meat off the decaying animals and bring the flesh home to their families with pride. "Berlin is a shambles," Howley told his officers after his first view of the city. "It's not worth an acre of good land with cattle on it."

A great twentieth-century electric city—beating, racing, vain—had come undone, and millions were at loose ends. Telephone poles and wooden doors were papered over with nailed-up handwritten notices inquiring after relatives who were nowhere to be found, dead or separated by thousands of miles with no way to reach home. Without walls in their apartments, Berliners had nowhere to leave their belongings, so anywhere they went they carried with them whatever meager possessions they had left. "Wretched, walking skeletons of what remained of the Wehrmacht, in a Russian chain gang, limped by" Howley's Horch, "carrying rails." Amputees, men with turbans worth of bandages on their heads shuffled down the street, newspapers stuffed in their shoes, their hands out begging when no one had anything to give. "Were these the crack soldiers who goose-stepped so arrogantly through Poland, France, Russia?" wondered an American correspondent in his diary.

As July of 1945 tramped in with the American troops, an oppressive heat hung over Berlin, as stifling as a woolen blanket. For days on end, not even the lightest breeze would tiptoe through the city. A scent of decay grew in strength; sweet, sickly, intensifying with each passing day. Anyone who was in Berlin in the spring and summer of 1945 would remember many things, but none would ever be able to forget the smell. Those who still possessed such quaint artifacts of bygone ways would hold their handkerchiefs to their noses as they made their way home. One witness wrote, "All Berlin stinks to high heaven. Wherever one looks there are heaps of rubbish covered with flies—flies and more flies, black, blue and fat." Howley, driving by in his open car, felt woozy from the stench. He knew its source. The stink of rotting corpses, of body parts blown apart by bombs and shells, came from below the colossal piles of rubble. Bodies floated in the canals. With hundreds of thousands dead and no coffins in Berlin, the corpses were pulled through the streets on great carts. They would be wrapped in rags or paper and buried in shallow graves in the faint hope they would rest in peace more soundly than they had in war.

There was no water for bathing or cleaning—the water mains had been broken in 3,000 places. Raw sewage flowed through streets filled with gigantic rats. The rivers of foul-smelling excrement, like the regiments of foul-smelling Russians, brought with them the scourge of pestilence. Dysentery, diphtheria, and typhoid fever were marching their way through the capital. Only 9,300 of Berlin's 38,000 hospital beds remained, at the moment they were needed most. In the months after Berlin's fall, the death rate climbed to levels unseen since the Thirty Years' War three hundred years earlier. Of babies born alive and in hospitals during that month of July 1945, 92 percent would die within ten days.

In war it is always the youngest who pay the most terrible price. Many had not survived the conflict; only one in ten Berliners was under the age of thirty. Those that did live to see the end of the war had lost much along the way. Fifty-three thousand orphans roamed the streets, lost and scared. Eight-year-old veterans of the Volkssturm wandered around with one eye or one leg—and there were no doctors and no anesthetics for the amputations.

Howley passed under the Brandenburg Gate and came upon the Tiergarten. There two million had gathered to celebrate Hitler's fiftieth birthday. Now it was barren. All but a few of its trees were gone. Children in the park were gathering grass and pine nettles to bring home for their mothers to boil or use for a salad. The more energetic and able tried to trap squirrels or ravens. Hungry, malnourished, underweight, they were covered with sores—the slightest bruise would fester and refuse to heal. "The hollow-eyed children," remembered Howley, "looked at us quietly." The children, having known no life but that of Hitler's Reich, the Allies' bombing, the Russians' savagery, were broken, as razed and ravaged as their city. Doctors in 1945 would report that one of Berlin's children's favorite games was "rape." When they saw a man in uniform—even a Salvation Army uniform—they would start screaming hysterically. The sight—or merely the low rumble of the sound—of an American plane flying overhead could send them into a panic. *"Terror-Fliegen!"* they would screech. "Terror flyers!"

"Enjoy the war," read the graffiti left on Berlin's walls. "The peace will be terrible."

ON THE FOURTH of July, with a band playing, a row of Sherman tanks standing at attention, and a few words from General Omar Bradley, American troops moved into the Adolf Hitler Barracks and, under a setting sun, formally began their occupation of Berlin. That evening, the Russians sent a message telling the Americans that the assumption of control in their sector would have to be delayed again, since the governing council for Berlin had not been put in place. Howley argued to Parks that they should ignore the note and proceed according to their arrangements. "Go ahead as planned," Parks replied, "but don't get into too much trouble." It would be a prescient, fruitless order.

Lucius Clay arrived in Berlin a couple of days later and began to set up offices for the occupation of Germany. "Wherever we looked we saw desolation," he noted of his first visit to Berlin. "The streets were piled high with debris which left in many places only a narrow one-way passage between high mounds of rubble, and frequent detours had to be made when bridges and viaducts were destroyed." When his car passed, "Germans jumped out of the rubble like frightened rabbits. When we looked at them they jumped back in again." Robert Murphy, who was with him, observed that "two months after capitulation, Berliners still seemed stupefied."

The military capital that America's high officials in Washington had debated over had not simply been vanquished, it had vanished. To Clay, "it was like a city of the dead." There was no more question over reindustrializing or pastoralizing Germany—over whether Stimson or Morgenthau was right. The question was simply one of survival: Would they let Germany starve? "Something that is worse than anything probably that has ever happened in the world" had occurred in Germany, McCloy told Truman after an inspection trip. There was no sense in discussing whether to send Germany back to the nineteenth century. A quick look around Berlin showed that American bombing and Russian invasion had already sent it reeling back much further than that.

By July 7, American military government was, according to Murphy, "officially opened for business in Berlin." That day, Clay prepared to meet with Marshal Georgy Zhukov, the Russian general who had stopped Hitler's advance at the gates of Moscow, helped defeat the Germans at Stalingrad, battled retreating Nazis across Russian territory scorched under Hitler's army, and taken Berlin. Clay and Zhukov, who was now in charge of the Russian forces in Germany, were to hash out the structure of the new occupying government of Berlin. An "Inter-Allied Governing Authority," or Kommandatura, was to be the ruling body over the German capital—much like the Allied Control Council was to administer the country as a whole. In advance of Clay's meeting, Parks had asked Howley to prepare a plan outlining the organization and powers of the Kommandatura. What Howley offered up was a proposal that would allow the four-power body to act as an umbrella council but left much discretion to each individual nation's sector commander. Just as each military governor of Germany had supreme authority in his own zone, Howley sought similar powers for each sector commander in Berlin.

Before the meeting with the Russians got under way, Clay, Murphy, and various other American and British generals met to go over their unified strategy. A lowly colonel, Howley was told to wait outside. He was "wandering aimlessly around headquarters" when he was asked to join the group. "When I arrived in the room the tail end of the discussion was going on and General Clay was about to wash his hands of our agreement." Clay was in the middle of a tirade, lecturing Parks at length about the deficiencies of Howley's plan. Clay would not accept a proposal that anticipated anything less than unanimity among the World War II allies—and he would not allow an American officer to act like a pasha in Berlin.

It did not require sophisticated antennae to immediately pick up the mood in the room. Howley failed to do so—or did not care. He tried to interject: "If I may say something—" But the conversation continued over him. Howley thought they had not heard him. It was more likely that they were simply ignoring him. He was undeterred. The lowest-ranking officer in a room with men whose uniforms had enough stars to form a constellation, he interjected again, and this time the room froze. Howley spoke directly to Clay, one of the top generals in the Army and someone he hardly knew. He had no interest in setting up a little kingdom in Berlin, he retorted, but there had to be a way to have some flexibility to act in areas where total agreement with the Communist Soviets was not possible, such as religion or education.

There was silence when he finished. Clay glared at him, his small black eyes narrowing as if he were a jungle cat about to pounce. "You are entirely wrong," Clay said icily. "I have just come from Washington, and it certainly is the intention of our government to administer Berlin on a unanimous basis." He launched into a long lecture aimed directly at Howley. "General Clay jumped all over me," Howley recorded in his diary. The free world depended on nations working together, Clay believed, on a model "of world leadership which is not based on demand, but is based on consultation, cooperation, and the coordination of efforts." This had been Roosevelt's faith and Wilson's dream, and Clay was determined to put it into effect in Germany.

When the meeting with Zhukov began, the Americans and British were without a plan for the Kommandatura. The Russians were not at a similar loss. Zhukov produced a one-page document that set up a single administrative unit for Berlin and gave the occupation sectors the task of carrying out the policies arrived at in the Kommandatura on a unanimous basis—in other words, with each government having a veto. Howley was asked to step outside of the meeting with a translator and make sure the Russian-language document held up. He returned to the room and handed the sheet to Clay, who half-turned to Howley and asked, "Is it okay?"

"Well, as a legal document, it stinks," Howley answered, "but as a rough note on what you've been talking about, it's all right." Clay smiled at Zhukov, took out his pen, and signed across the bottom of the page. Howley was disgusted. "Even Henry Wallace couldn't have asked for more appeasement," he later complained.

AS ROOSEVELT HAD said in his farewell to Stalin at Yalta, the plan had been to hold the first meeting of the Big Three allies after the fall of the Nazis in Berlin, but there was no Berlin left in which to hold a meeting. So Truman, Stalin, and Churchill met in Potsdam, just outside the city, instead.

Flying into Berlin from Paris, Secretary of the Navy Forrestal's eyes grew large as he saw the capital from above. Anything resembling a city—buildings, streets, signs of life—was gone. The next day, Forrestal toured Berlin. Along with him on the trip was John F. Kennedy, a well-connected young journalist whom Forrestal had just recently discharged from the Navy. "Went into Berlin," Forrestal wrote in clipped, unemotional prose in his diary. "Stories of destruction not overdone. City a skeleton of prewar Berlin. Very little of it untouched by bombing."

After the tour, the party went to have lunch with Clay. The conversation focused on the level of devastation in Berlin. Some wondered whether there was any hope or reason to try to start again. "One of the debatable questions now in Berlin is whether Berlin will ever be built up again into a large city," Kennedy noted in his diary. American bombs had made a desert and now they wanted to walk away and call it the cost of war.

Soon after he arrived in Germany, Truman went into Berlin as well. He drove under the charred, bullet-ridden Brandenburg Gate. He rode down Unter den Linden where Napoleon had marched in triumph. The smell of the putrid corpses tweaked his nose. "A more depressing sight than that of ruined buildings was the long, never-ending procession of old men, women, and children wandering aimlessly," he remarked. He looked at them, but instead of showing some reaction to the sight of their conqueror driving by, they simply stared blankly as if they were looking past him or through him. "This is a hell of a place," he wrote to his wife, Bess, "ruined, dirty, smelly forlorn people, bedraggled, hangdog look about them. You never saw as completely ruined a city. But they did it."

Americans believed that once before they had let German militarism wreak havoc on the world without exacting a harsh enough penalty, but now they had learned the lesson of history and would not make the same mistake again. "The Russians have recognized good and bad Germans," Howley would write in his diary. "We have recognized bad and less bad Germans." Americans saw the suffering but had little inclination to do very much about it. "The coming months are going to be a hard test for you. You will have to be tough—there is no alternative. Every sign indicates a severe shortage of food, fuel, housing, and transport," Eisenhower said in a message to the German people. "These are all your problems. Their solution depends entirely on your own endeavors." The conquerors and the conquered looked at each other with eyes of loathing. The defeated Germans were "full of resentments," *Time* magazine reported in June. "Most of all they resented the bombing of their homes and cities. The Americans, they felt, had gone much too far beyond the evident necessities of war. Deep in many a German heart, the conviction grew that Americans were unfit for human society." Considering the source, Americans were far from troubled by the sentiment.

ON JULY 20, Truman went to the American sector to officially raise the American flag in conquest over the German capital. Clay had established an American headquarters in the leafy, residential neighborhood of Zehlendorf, in a large gray building dwarfed by a tall flagpole and set back from the street by a long driveway. When the Americans had arrived, there were dead horses out on the street and much scrubbing to do to clean up after the Russians, who had camped there, defecated in closets, and cooked their meals in fires on the wooden parquet floors.

The ceremony was brief. Truman wore a dark double-breasted suit and a white Stetson. Next to him stood the heroes of America's greatest war: Eisenhower wearing the jacket that bore his name; Patton in riding boots and a metal helmet, his gloves clutched lightly in his left hand; Bradley, the "GI General," in simple Army green. Behind the heroes, in the second row, stood Clay. Under a big sun, they watched as a flag that had flown over the U.S. Capitol on that December day in 1941 when America went to war was slowly raised over the capital of the enemy. There was a jerry-rigged sound system with a small speaker wired to a microphone, and Truman stepped forward to say a few words. Speaking without notes, he reminded all there about why they had waged the war. They were there "to raise the flag of victory over the capital of our greatest adversary," but "we are not fighting for conquest. There is not one piece of territory, or one thing of a monetary nature that we want out of this war. We want peace and prosperity for the world as a whole. We want to see the time come when we can do the things in peace that we have been able to do in war." They were fighting for "a world in which all the people will have the opportunity to enjoy the good things in life and not just a few at the top." If they won this victory, "we can look forward to the greatest age in the history of mankind."

It was, wrote the *New York Times,* a "simple, homely declaration of the faith that had sent millions of American boys into battle far from home." It was this faith that Roosevelt had bequeathed to his nation and his successor, a progressive vision of what it meant to go to war, one that sought to transform the world by bringing freedom and prosperity to those who had never felt its warmth. For a generation, Wilson's dream had been deferred; now it would be tested. No one listened more carefully to Truman's brief statement than Lucius Clay, the man who was charged with transporting Germany from Nazism to democracy. That day he was awed by the declaration that America would, in his words, "work only to secure a world of peace and mutual understanding." Years later he wrote, "While the soldier is schooled against emotion, I have never forgotten that short ceremony as our flag rose to the staff."

AMID THE RUIN, there was hope. Truman saw a golden age ahead. In Berlin, as spring gave way to summer, among the shallow graves, lilacs began to grow, their subtle scent mixing with the stench of the fetid corpses and felled buildings. When Thornton Wilder's *The Skin of Our Teeth* became one of the first American plays to open in Germany after the war, it was a sensation; half a million Germans went to see it. Its title had been translated as *We Managed to Pull Through Again.*

Above all else, hope sprang from the conviction that, at long last, the great powers of the world would be working together for the betterment of mankind, that laws and treaties would replace bullets and bombs. The two strong nations left in the world had publicly committed themselves not simply to working together but to forging a real friendship. Kennedy wrote in his diary of meeting with a Colonel Frank "Howlie" and even the bouffant-topped officer told the young man that while some had been suspicious of the Russians early on, the chill had lessened, and there was cause for optimism about the future. "We are on very good terms with the Russians," Howley told the *Manchester*

Guardian that month. In a public opinion poll that year, Americans predicted that postwar problems—such as there would exist—would be more serious with Great Britain than with the Soviet Union. No dissent to the certainty of amity with the Russians was brooked. On June 8, on his way back home from Moscow, Charles Bohlen, a high-ranking American diplomat, stopped off in Frankfurt to meet with Eisenhower and his generals. At the meeting, Clay spoke with great conviction about the need to work with the Russians. The key to getting along with the Soviets, he said, was that you had to give trust to get trust. Bohlen had heard the same refrain from others. As he left, he told Clay privately what he did not want to say in front of the others. Within a few months, or certainly within a year, Bohlen predicted to Clay, he would become one of the officials in the American government most opposed to the Soviets. Clay looked at him quizzically, as if the diplomat had begun speaking in tongues in the middle of the conversation.

TWO DAYS LATER, on June 10, the Americans welcomed Marshal Zhukov to their zone of Germany for a gala party in his honor. Without any Soviet emblems on hand, they had a team of seamstresses work twenty-four hours straight so that there would be red flags at the airport and lining the streets of Frankfurt. The day was warm and pleasant and the lunch was held outdoors. A swing ensemble played in the background. Soviet and American officers stood about in the grass, socializing and reminiscing. Above, 1,700 American fighter and bomber planes flew in a demonstration of respect. Zhukov presented Eisenhower with the Soviet Order of Victory, the first time a foreigner had received the honor. It was a five-pointed star encrusted with rubies and diamonds—an appraiser back in the United States would estimate its value at $100,000.

Though the Americans did not know it, the good cheer was only a mirage. While Zhukov was in Frankfurt, an order—Soviet Military Order No. 2—was being issued in his name that authorized "anti-Fascist democratic" political parties, otherwise known as Communist parties, to form and begin to operate. Primed for the step, the German Communist Party would begin operations the next day.

But the Americans in Frankfurt were unaware of this, and would have overlooked it to maintain their alliance even if they had known. Instead, they laughed and embraced once again as they had on the Elbe. Zhukov in his toast praised Allied unity and spoke of his "hope that in the future work of the four Allied Commanders in the Control Council we will be just as unified." Eisenhower responded with evident feeling: "This war was a holy war, more than any other in history." It had been fought so that around the world, "the people might live a little better next year and the next." Now "we are going to have peace, even if we have to fight for it."

The lunch came to an end, and a gospel choir, visiting from America, began to sing. Eisenhower had landed at Normandy and fought his way from the west. Zhukov had beat back the Germans from the outskirts of Moscow and, in howling terror, fought his way from the east. Their armies had met in a defeated Germany, surrounded by the deaths of millions. Now the soldiers stood arm in arm, singing or humming, along to the choir. Clay, who knew the song well, sang louder than most:

I gets weary, an' sick of tryin',
I'm tired of livin', an' scared of dyin',
But Ol' Man River, he just keeps rollin' along.

Part II

THE BEND

Spring 1948

You an' me, we sweat an' strain,
Body all achin' an' racked wid pain.

"OL' MAN RIVER" BY OSCAR HAMMERSTEIN II

6

CHASM

Waves crashed against the hull of the troop ship crossing the Atlantic toward Europe. Belowdecks, a young GI had gathered the attention of a rapt group of his fellow soldiers. "With just a few packs of cigarettes, you can pick up any *fräulein* in Germany," he promised. Most were duly impressed and visions of willowy sure things danced in their heads. One soldier, near the back of the pack, would have none of it: "Okay, okay, but how do you like us sending all that dough to a lot of krauts? The same krauts that were shooting at us a couple of years ago."

In the dark of thousands of movie theaters in 1947, Americans heard the stern voice of Westbrook Van Voorhis, the newsreel's narrator, over images of rag-wearing, haggard men and women picking through rubble: "Today, Hitler's erstwhile master race is living abjectly—without initiative, without dignity. Its grandiose aspirations reduced to an endless struggle for mere existence, for enough fuel to keep from freezing, for enough food to keep from starving."

There was little reason to feel sympathy for this evil nation. "Americans are discovering that the Germans are still far from ready to settle down as a peaceful and law-abiding people," Van Voorhis said. The Germans, the Americans who watched this *March of Time* newsreel were told, were simply paying "lip service" to and "mechanically going through the motions of democracy." Over footage of men desultorily drinking beer from large white steins while listening to a fat, sweaty man drone on at a podium, Van Voorhis described the Germans as "attending election rallies as an appeasement gesture," but finding "them strangely unexciting—sadly lacking in the fire and fury of Nazi rabble-rousing."

Two years after the end of the war, the broadly held conviction that the United States' occupation of defeated Germany would be quick had been discarded. "America has resolved to continue the occupation until the Germans give conclusive proof of regeneration—if necessary, for forty years. For of adult Germans, deeply affected by Nazism, little can be expected." But then Germany's children, the ones who had been molded by Hitler's regime, were shown eating a hearty dinner at a table laden with food. The music crescendoed. The newsreel's final words were spoken over the image of a young girl excitedly clapping her hands as she was handed a steaming mug of hot chocolate. "Any hope that Germany will ever become a responsible peace-loving nation centers on the very young who have not been corrupted by Hitler's doctrines of treachery and aggression, who may still be taught that Germany can find greatness only through freedom and democracy in peaceful cooperation with the rest of mankind." Van Voorhis's voice thundered the famous closing: "Time Marches On!"

The lights came up in the theater and the moviegoers shuffled out, blinking at the sunshine of a new world.

When World War II ended, the boys came home to an America that was relieved but anxious. After both the Civil War and World War I, a wartime economic boom had been followed by a peacetime bust. With memories of the Great Depression still vivid, Americans expected that the country's greatest war would be followed by a long and deep slide back into joblessness and stagnation. For a time it appeared as if these fears would be realized. Soon after the war, nearly 2 million workers were on strike; meat and housing shortages were rampant. But the great bust never came. Instead, a decade and a half of pent-up demand was met with a treasure chest of supplies. As 1948 began, Americans were living in the midst of unparalleled plenty. "The year's harvest was the biggest in history. With few exceptions, everyone who wanted a job had one," *Time* magazine declared in looking back at the year's end. Americans had trudged through the tunnel of more than a decade of economic catastrophe and global war and come out into a world that promised gleaming new automobiles in their driveways and televisions in the living room. According to popular magazines, personal helicopters and weekend trips to the moon were only a few years away.

The late 1940s were the time between the swing of the big bands and the twist of rock and roll; bebop was king, Dizzy Gillespie was its troubadour, and Americans were content to listen to its mismatched chords and sit the dance out. They simply wanted to unwind. "At last they could fill their gasoline tanks, use a second chunk of butter, watch the long lazy curl of a fishing line flicker in the sunlight, or get royally tight without feeling that they were cheating some GI in the flak over Berlin or on the bloody ash of Iwo Jima," historian Eric Goldman would remember. Americans had known hardship and sacrifice for so long that their search for comfort and ease was almost frenzied. The first couple of years after the end of the war saw the introduction of resealable Tupperware and prefabricated Levittown; of Minute Maid frozen orange juice, Maxwell House instant coffee, Ragú jarred spaghetti sauce, Tide laundry detergent, and Nestlé's Quik. At the end of World War II, there had been 100 drive-in movie theaters. By 1950, there were 2,100.

As 1947 turned to 1948, America was in a flighty, silly mood. Bob Hope and Bing Crosby's musical romp *Road to Rio* was champ at the box office, packing tired holiday shoppers into the movie theaters. The Oscar for Best Supporting Actor of 1947 would go to Edmund Gwenn for his portrayal of Kris Kringle in *Miracle on 34th Street*. The editors of the United Press voted and chose "the high cost of living" as the top

story of 1947, what with the average family spending $20 a week on
food and the cost of a New York subway fare about to double from a
nickel to a dime. When the Associated Press asked society editors in
February 1948 to pick America's most eligible bachelors, Jimmy Stewart
came in first, tycoon and aviator Howard Hughes followed at second,
and there was a tie for third between freshman congressman John F.
Kennedy and FBI director J. Edgar Hoover. It was a frothy moment in
American life. "Zip-A-Dee-Doo-Dah" was one of the biggest hits of
1947; the manic cackle of "The Woody Woodpecker Song" raced up
the charts in the first half of 1948. It would be the year of the bikini and
big tail fins on Cadillacs; of factories for Slinkys and a blizzard of new
Dairy Queens.

That spring, a fifty-three-year-old man named Alfred Pittlik walked
into a New York bar wearing a Luftwaffe commander's jacket. The veterans inside put down their drinks and beat him bloody. It was only later
that the police determined he was simply a confused Polish immigrant
who had bought the jacket at a pawnshop. But most of the time, as 1948
got under way, the old passions of war and politics were all but forgotten, put away in the back of the closet with carefully folded uniforms
and ribboned bundles of love letters. The major controversy in Washington seemed to be whether Truman had the right to build a second-
floor balcony on the White House.

Roosevelt had told Americans they were fighting the war so that they
could open an era of lasting peace, and initially many thought they had
succeeded. Harold Russell, the double-amputee amateur actor who
clutched an Academy Award with his hooked hands in 1946 for his portrayal of a GI struggling with homecoming in *The Best Years of Our
Lives,* would recall those years with fondness. "I can look back at that
period now and say they truly *were* 'the best years,'" Russell would say
three decades later. "The guys who came out of World War II were ideal-
istic. They sincerely believed that this time they were coming home to
build a new world. Many, many times you'd hear guys say, 'The one thing
I want to do when I get out is to make sure that thing will never happen
again.' We felt the day had come when the wars were all over."

But some began to harrumph at the misguided idealism of the hand-shakes and hugs on the Elbe. "It's all very well to win a war with Social-ist New Dealers and Bolsheviks having a love fest, but what follows then?" grumbled conservative Nebraska senator Kenneth Wherry. In 1946, the Republican Party had won a huge election victory and retaken control of Congress for the first time since before the New Deal on a platform of big tax cuts and a retrenchment from vast expenditures on foreign entanglements. Their slogan in that election—"Had Enough?"—meant many things, that was its beauty, but surely one of its meanings was an end to the burdens of caring about, as well as caring for, people in faraway places. "Get Germany off the American taxpayer's back" was the call of conservatives in Congress.

Americans could be forgiven if they wanted to shrug off global respon-sibilities, if they wanted to, in diplomat Averell Harriman's description, simply "go to the movies and drink Coke." Men came home from World War II driven to live the lives they had dreamed of while hunched in a muddy foxhole half a world away from anywhere they had ever known. Cold and scared, with a frigid rain battering their helmets, drenching their clothes, chilling the hands with which they gripped their guns, they shiv-ered as shells burst and friends died at their feet. And through it all they dreamed not of great mansions or exploding flashbulbs trailing them on red carpets. Rather, theirs had been simple dreams that were audacious under the circumstances. Survivors of America's Great Depression and the world's greatest war, they dreamed in those foxholes of pleasant homes and sturdy jobs, of warm, soft wives and happy children playing catch on a green front lawn. And, having come home to achieve those dreams in numbers unimaginable in any previous generation, they were determined to hold on to them tightly and not let go.

Dawn came late on winter mornings in Berlin. Lucius Clay rose before the sun did. By this, the first week of January 1948, he had been in Berlin for exactly two and a half years and his routine was set.

He would be out of bed by 6:30 A.M. and eating breakfast by seven. While he fed crackers to his Scottie, George, under the table, Clay perused the day's *Stars and Stripes* newspaper with his morning meal. He "contrived generally to give the impression that he ate fire for breakfast and enjoyed the taste" wrote a British reporter in Berlin. And as he smoked the first cigarette of the three or four packs he would go through that day—and washed it down with this first of his twenty daily cups of coffee—the impression was not far from the truth.

Clay's home in Berlin was comfortable but by no means grand. During the war, it had been the home of a leading German businessman, and when Clay arrived in 1945, it was littered with a collection of Nazi propaganda and decorated with photographs from the parties that had once been held there, with smiling men in Nazi uniforms mugging for the camera. A three-story house with ivy-covered walls leading to a long sloping roof, it was surrounded by a garden of green grass and forget-me-nots and yellow tulips, of poplar and beech trees that begged for the home's master to sit under their shade and while an afternoon away. They were sorely disappointed.

Seven days a week, a Fleetwood Cadillac the color of the morning sky was waiting for him in front of the house before eight. It took only a few minutes to pull up to the long driveway of the headquarters of United States Military Government in Germany, a two-story building of gray stone and concrete with tall windows on the second floor. Outside, where Harry Truman had outlined American hopes for a world after the war, the American flag flapped from the tall pole. Inside, the refuse of bombing and the Russians' occupation had been replaced by a tidy organization that, even in the early hours of the day, buzzed with activity.

Upon his arrival each morning, Clay was handed, along with a hot cup of coffee, forty feet of overnight news ticker tape, folded into long strips. He sat down at his desk, put on his thick, dark reading glasses, curved behind the ears, and began reading, throwing the parts he had finished over the front of the desk and onto the floor so that an aide could scurry to pick them up.

This mammoth walnut desk dominated the office. It was big and brown; its dark wood was polished to a blinding gleam. On top of it, he had placed an oversized nameplate facing toward his visitors that read "Gen. Lucius D. Clay" as if someone might wander into the office of the absolute ruler of American-occupied Germany by accident and not know whom he had happened upon or if some poor Godforsaken staff member might, in mid-sentence, lose his train of thought and momentarily forget who the glowering man behind the desk was.

A slight, slender, physically unimposing man, Clay might have been dwarfed by the large tanklike piece of timber, but he dominated every conversation. Reporters would note his "sad brown eyes." Those who worked for him saw something very different. "He looked up at you with his big eyebrows and his big black eyes and you just trembled," remembered one of his assistants. When he became enraged, according to a frequent visitor, his "eyes contracted until they were opaque black pools of anger."

It was not an uncommon sight. The *eminence grise* of one of Chicago's top law firms, a distinguished man in his mid-sixties of "fine reputation and a high standing," came to Berlin to discuss an important matter with Clay. He emerged shaken. "I can still remember, and this is what he said himself," one of Clay's aides, Robert Bowie, would recall, "that he would go into a discussion with Clay and he was almost frightened by him; and here was a man who dealt with all sorts of large legal matters. But the focus of Clay's personality and his intensity when he contested or argued something—it was almost like a physical blow." When staff members walked into his office, "he would pick their brains and tear their papers apart," remembered another aide, Edloe Donnan. "He would work them over, up and down, down and up." He deployed what Bowie would delicately term "a very succinct command of the language" and expected those who worked for him to accept the verbal blows. "You couldn't help but saying 'yes, sir,'" recalled Donnan, "but there were times when you'd like to hit him right in his nose. You know, standing up in front of his desk."

———————

THOUGH CLAY'S MANNER was imperious, it was not imperial—and the distinction was important. Through the Allied Control Council, the four military commanders who ruled over Germany coordinated broad policy, but in the thousand daily decisions that constituted government in their own zones each held absolute power. "It was the nearest thing to a Roman proconsulship that the modern world afforded," said John McCloy of Clay's position. "You could almost turn to your secretary and say, 'Take a law.'"

Like Douglas MacArthur in postwar Japan, Clay held dictatorial power in a nation that respected its exercise. But the differences between the two men were telling. In Tokyo, MacArthur lived in a great white house stuffed with silk sashes, bejeweled cigarette boxes, and dark lacquered fans. He relied on Japanese mysticism and the nation's historic authoritarianism to enhance his power by setting himself off from the people as a khaki-clad emperor. When he made his way to his headquarters every morning, traffic lights were turned green, cars were stopped, and Japanese policemen stood at salute as his Cadillac and its motorcycle escorts moved through the streets. He arrived to a well-choreographed display of military splendor from his guards. MacArthur left Tokyo only twice in the five years between the end of World War II and the beginning of the Korean War, and he never spent a night away from the Japanese capital.

Clay, in contrast, sought to undermine traditional Teutonic authoritarianism and create a foundation for democracy. He proudly took credit for having introduced the concept of a press conference into German political life, and when German journalists asked him the kind of fawning softballs that had once kept them out of Dachau, he continually prodded them to ask tougher questions. In meetings with the elected officials of the Länder—the German regional states—Clay would tell them they had to make their own decisions when they looked to him for guidance. Clay's home was simple; on its front door, Marjorie Clay—who joined him in Berlin in 1946—had stuck three stickers of Army mules to represent Clay and his two sons, all West Point graduates. At night, during his frequent inspection trips around the American zone, he and Murphy would stroll into pubs in small German villages, dressed in civilian clothes, to glean clues as to the public mind. Murphy, who spoke fluent German, would order them beers and they would sit unobtrusively off to the side—a languid tall man and an intense-looking short one—drinking their brew while, under his breath, Murphy translated the conversation for Clay.

CLAY WOULD DRINK another pot of coffee by ten and still another by noon. All through the morning, staff members would come in to his office looking for a decision and he never appeared to hesitate. When he first began to work with Clay, Murphy said, "I was dismayed to learn that he knew virtually nothing about Germany," though he came to believe that such "information about Germany's history, its former financial and industrial ramifications, its prewar personalities, and so forth might have cluttered" Clay's mind. Unburdened by such seemingly relevant facts, Clay acted with a decisiveness and self-assurance that caused some men to recoil. "He makes up his mind by himself with the almost mystical belief in his rightness," remarked one aide. A friend would recall having a discussion with Clay about a complicated matter and being exasperated by how definite Clay's quick opinions could be. Every answer was "Good or bad. Yes or no. Finally, I said, 'Jesus Christ, Lucius, there's a word "maybe" in the English language. Don't you ever use it?'"

The truth was Clay had to be decisive. His job was more difficult than MacArthur's. In Japan, the occupiers inherited an imperial government that had capitulated in fear of firebombs and mushroom clouds. Germany's government had been eviscerated—nothing of Hitler's regime remained, and the Americans had made an early decision that those who had been Nazis had no place in the governing of postwar Germany.

Clay and America's occupying forces had been sent to Germany to remove what Roosevelt had called "a cancer" from its national character—something deeper than even Nazism, a disease that broke down a country's immunity to the blandishments of a Hitler. In its place, the Americans were to install a thriving democracy. And then they were to wrap up and go home. If such a task ever did sound simple, it did not take anyone involved much time to realize it was not.

"There is no parallel in history for what we are trying to do," Clay wrote to his friend Bill Draper, the Army undersecretary charged with serving as a liaison to the occupation, in the last weeks of 1947. Never before had one nation been ruled over by another not as a colony but in order to create a democracy so that the conquered could, in short order, be given the task of governing themselves.

Two million former Nazis were put on trial and nearly one million punished. Debates swirled in the American press about whether the denazification efforts were too harsh or too soft, but the entire apparatus of prosecuting the petty party members for their crimes was a sideshow. Getting rid of Nazis was easy compared with getting rid of Nazism—and inculcating the habits of democracy was an entirely different matter itself.

Clay was unembarrassed about his belief that the purpose of the occupation was "to establish and maintain democracy—American style," and he threw himself into this effort. By the beginning of 1948, American-occupied Germany had dozens of newspapers up and running and an American-sponsored radio station, Radio in the American Sector (called "RIAS" by its initials), that was listened to by 80 percent of Berliners. Under Clay's watch, 126 "Amerika Haus" libraries were set up around Germany to provide reading materials and cultural events, and nearly three million Germans visited them each month. Clay encouraged the work of the American Civil Liberties Union in Germany and spurred the creation of trade unions to serve as building blocks of democracy, even having an official of the American Federation of Labor serve on his staff to speed the process. To demonstrate to the Germans the importance of the rule of law, he discontinued the use of wartime tribunals for Nazi officers and instituted standard legal proceedings with protections for the accused. Clay oversaw the replacement of Hitler's textbooks in German schools, and children learned of math problems that did not involve bombs, and history that did not revolve around hatred. He ordered the renaming of all streets, parks, and buildings that had been christened in honor of the martial leaders of Germany's past, and street signs with Bismarck or Kaiser Wilhelm came down all over the nation. And Clay successfully demanded that free elections be held just months after the end of the war. "Early elections are an American CREED," he wrote to Frank Howley in advance of Berlin's first postwar municipal elections in 1946, underlining the capitalized word with a deep pencil mark that burrowed into the paper.

The Americans tried everything they could think of to build a democracy, often eschewing subtlety; one American air base in southern Germany sponsored a children's essay contest on the subject of "What Can I Do to Help My Country Improve Its Present Situation and Assist in Creating a Democratic and Peaceful Germany for All Time?" First prize was clothes.

But despite all their efforts, by the beginning of 1948 Clay and the Americans in Germany had been stymied in fashioning that "democratic and peaceful Germany." The master engineer, the autocratic organizer, had difficulty when it came to the work of soulcraft; the work of building not dams and airports but bonds of trust and confidence among Germans in the ideas of freedom and self-government. "Anyone who seriously believes in democracy knows that it is not a commodity that can be neatly packaged, distributed with food rations, and digested with magical effects," he would say in justifying his frustration.

It was only later that he would learn of the magical properties of tiny packages.

INDEED, PROFESSIONAL PUBLIC opinion surveys conducted by social scientists in the employ of the military government showed that as the months of the American occupation continued, the regard in which Germans held democracy plummeted. Six months after the war had ended, a bare majority of Germans had agreed with the statement that Nazism was "a good idea badly carried out." By the summer of 1947, the number who believed this had risen and the number who disagreed had dropped. Around the country, American GIs were finding walls graffitied with the number "88." Initially, they were confused. Eventually they realized the numbers stood for the eighth letter of the alphabet: "88" was "HH"—"Heil Hitler."

By those first days of 1948, it was no mystery to Clay why the drive for democracy was failing, and why Nazism or Communism looked to be attractive alternatives. Germans were very clear about the matter. In survey after survey, the hungry, cold Germans were asked whether they preferred a government that provided "economic security" or one that guaranteed "free elections, freedom of speech, press and religion." Their answers were remarkably consistent: they chose the guarantee of a full stomach over freedom and democracy by two or more to one every time. In Berlin, the margin was 70 percent to 22 percent.

Of this Clay was certain: "You cannot build real democracy in an atmosphere of distress and hunger."

CLAY USUALLY ATE a small sandwich for lunch at his desk. What for him was a few nibbles would be a family's feast just blocks away.

By the beginning of 1948, Berliners had been hungry for three years, if not longer—and it was a pang to which people did not grow accustomed. In fact, the food situation, despite Clay's efforts, had become worse, not better, as time progressed. The economy in Germany had faltered, crops had failed, and Americans had not provided the massive shipments of foodstuffs needed to feed their former enemies.

During the Great Depression—the so-called "Hungry Years"— Americans had consumed an average of 3,260 calories a day. After the war, the United Nations relief agency had reported that the minimum a working male needed to consume was 2,650 calories a day. No German had received this much in rations since before the fall of Berlin.

It had been decided early on that each power would be responsible for feeding those in its zone of occupation and in its sector of Berlin. Since Berlin was completely encircled by the Soviet zone of Germany, the three Western powers had to transport all the food and supplies for their sectors of the city. In the first few months after the war, the Americans pledged an official ration of 1,550 calories, which would include a piece of meat or fish "one half the size of an egg." Every day, long trains, rumbling trucks, and heavy river barges moved toward Berlin carrying all the provisions they could bring—tens of millions of pounds of potatoes and bread, shoes and socks and overcoats, newsprint and matches. It was not nearly enough. A year after the end of the war, the Americans' daily distribution of food was 1,180 calories, and still another year later it had dropped to 1,040 calories a day.

Ration amounts were tiered based on age for children and the amount of physical labor performed by an adult. People doing heavy work got relatively higher rations to keep them going. For the unemployed, the old, the sick, or those doing less physically demanding labor, there would sometimes be only dry bread and cereals for weeks at a time. They would not even receive a pat of butter. Those who performed the hardest work, and received the most food, such as miners, would often furtively hide away a potato or a hard roll to give to their families. The economy slowed under the lethargy and illness of too little nourishment. Housewives received the lowest ration levels for adults; they were given what was called a "death card." In the first six months of 1946, the death rate in Berlin was six times that of the birth rate—stunning considering the period marked nine months since the Russians' assault on Berlin's women. Even by 1947, Berliners were dying at almost three times the rate they were being born. The average adult German over the age of forty was 30 pounds underweight, and the average man in the American zone weighed 112 pounds.

Hunger became an all-consuming concern for Germans, the lens through which they saw everything they did. When Berliners happened upon a friend on the sidewalk, the conversation immediately turned to the subject of food and where to acquire it. The military government's public opinion researchers asked Germans, "What are your chief cares and worries at the present time?" Answers revolving around hunger and food had placed at the top since the end of the war, but as the occupation dragged on they became an obsession. Six months after the surrender, Germans volunteered food-related answers 20 percent of the time. By early 1947, it was 40 percent of the time, and as 1948 began, food-related answers accounted for half of all answers, with shortages of fuel, clothes, and shoes following behind. Berlin was, of course, worse off than the rest of Germany. The percentage of its residents who cited food as their chief concern had already been at half in February 1946. By July of 1947, Berliners gave their hunger as their main worry 74 percent of the time. Hunger crowded out every other concern. In the spring of 1948, 80 percent of Berliners said they were not getting enough nutrition to be able to perform their jobs well. When they were asked about the biggest problem in educating their children, 42 percent mentioned a lack of food. Shortages of teachers and textbooks and bombed-out classrooms trailed far behind.

Germans began to fixate on food, compulsively tracking what they ate like a flying ace notching his kills. When, in early 1948, Marjorie Clay served some chocolates to a few pale and pasty German children at a small party she held, one thirteen-year-old girl wrote to thank her ecstatically for "the second sweeties that I have got after the war." For her tenth birthday, another girl in Berlin received ten slices of bread, which her mother and sister had slowly saved for her. The hunger shaped everything people did. Years later, in an interview, a German woman who had been happily married for decades to an American she met when he was a GI recounted going "to the NCO club at the base for a 4th of July celebration. We roasted marshmallows and put them on Hershey chocolate between Graham crackers. I thought I had died and gone to heaven, not ever had I eaten anything like it. Another time we were invited to the house of his Warrant Officer and the lady served cherry pie which I had never eaten before." The question she was responding to was "When did you realize you were falling in love?"

The Germans found ways to augment their rations. Many—an estimated 80 percent of all train travelers—were so-called calorie seekers, spending their days scouring the country looking for food on the black market. Clutching their children and carrying their suitcases, they would wait for hours on crowded station platforms for a dark, cold train to take them hundreds of miles in pursuit of an often chimerical rumor of a village overflowing with potatoes. A visitor from Switzerland in 1947 watched a gray mass of pallid Berliners stuffing themselves into crammed trains: "The people are squashed into the carriages like sardines in a tin. Such is life in Germany today. The German goes hungry. He sees his children die. He becomes like a helpless, hunted animal."

Berliners created a primitive barter economy—trading wood or bars of soap for a haircut, rags for a book. In Potsdamer Platz, split down the middle between the American and Russian sectors, or at the edge of the Tiergarten, in the shadow of the Reichstag and the Brandenburg Gate, flourishing black markets sprang up, with thousands gathering each day. Cigarettes and chocolate bars became currency. A few once-discarded, half-used-up cigarette butts could buy bacon for a family. In the summer of 1947, a Hershey bar that cost 5 cents in America was worth about 20 percent of a German's monthly wages. It was much too expensive for almost anyone to afford to actually eat it.

Pleasures of the loins as well as those of the stomach were available for purchase with chocolate and cigarettes. By early 1948, the standard price for a rushed grope with a street prostitute in the ruins of Berlin was a pack of cigarettes or a bar of chocolate. Women in their twenties and thirties had been the only group in American-occupied Germany to register a weight gain during 1947. A GI would cruise down Kurfürstendamm Strasse and take his pick. The young lady would bring him home and introduce him to her parents and younger siblings, and they would repair to the only bedroom. A short time later, he would emerge and take a moment to say his goodbyes—having left a few cigarettes and a piece of chocolate behind. By the beginning of 1947, it was reasonably estimated that one in four of Berlin's women was professionally or occasionally trading in sex. "I know very fine people who would have done anything," remembered one woman, Ursula Gay, admonishing those who would judge them in later years. "How could you blame a starving girl?"

YET IT WAS not simply that Berliners were hungry or suffering. In the years after the war, they had lost their bearings. What Clay saw around him in the capital was different from the conditions in the rest of Germany. "They really looked beaten, frightened, whipped. I guess they'd had a pretty tough deal with the troops coming in there. The rubble . . ." His thought trailed off. "The town was of course badly damaged, but so were a lot of other towns." The difference was not in the buildings, but in something less tangible. "The people of Berlin were really beaten down."

Berlin was a city of wreckage pockmarked by the buildings that still stood and stood out, lonely and forlorn, in a sea of rubble. Two and a half years after the fall of the Third Reich, little rebuilding had taken place. Many streets were still not passable; mountains of debris piled up where taxicabs used to jam. An estimated 2 billion bricks were being carried away by hand—by long chains of Berliners standing shoulder to shoulder, cleaning the city brick by brick. With the small number of able-bodied men needed for other jobs, 70 percent of the "rubble workers" were women—many were former Nazi Party members barred from other work, some were mothers in search of a better ration card. Some worked in peasant skirts, others in high heels and tattered silk dresses, frayed reminders of lives they had lost. The women threw themselves into the task with a devotion that was in part traditional German tidiness, but with a tinge of something deeper as well; it was an impulse that Lady Macbeth, furiously scrubbing the blood from her hands, would have found familiar. All through the day, month after month, the women hauled off the chunks of debris in ceaseless effort. In March 1948, Germans calculated that there was 1.765 billion cubic feet of destruction left to clear. After three years of difficult work, they had rid themselves of 71 million cubic feet.

Hurled down from the summit of civilization, Berliners called themselves "ruin dwellers." They lived primitively, figures in apartments that looked like a child's dollhouse, with one of the four walls of a room simply not there. Three-fourths of Berlin's housing had been destroyed, so three families often huddled into a single apartment with five or six people sleeping in a room. A visiting correspondent described a Berliner's home: "The ceiling seemed on the point of falling; only half the doors were left; in the middle of the room stood a bathtub which gathered rain water that fell through the holes in the roof; next to the tub, a billiard table on which two people slept. A huge chandelier might be standing meaninglessly on the floor; it could not be used because it would have consumed too much current, but the people did not want to part with it because it was, after all, an object of value." Blown-out windows were covered up with cardboard. At the going rate of glass deliveries, the last window was scheduled to be replaced in 1988.

"It seemed as if the fates had conspired against defeated Germany," observed Emil Schäfer, a historian, in those years. They were already living exposed to the elements when next came the cold. The winter of 1947 was the coldest in a century. Temperatures plunged to more than 20 degrees below zero Fahrenheit. The Elbe was covered in ice for a hundred days instead of the usual twenty-two. The water-supply pipes in Berlin froze shut. Twelve thousand Berliners died in the cold. Suicides spiked. Hunger in the forests drove packs of wolves into the capital; they roamed the streets at night with the hookers and the housewives picking through garbage cans. On the famous balcony of the Reich's Chancellery, from which Hitler exhorted mobs of Berliners warmed by torch fires, someone chalked, "Blessed are the dead, for their hands do not freeze."

Amid rubble, hunger, and cold, order all but broke down. Once Berlin had been called "Newspaper City"; it had been where artists came for inspiration and scientific advancements thrilled the world. By 1946, Berlin had acquired a new nickname: "Crime Capital of the World." Even with a puny, thin police force, there were 2,000 arrests a month in Berlin in 1946, compared with 3,000 in all of 1935. Every day there were six assaults, five murders, and 240 robberies. There was, of course, nothing to steal. The saddest part of the crime wave was that all the thieves would make off with was a few extra potatoes that had been saved for a special occasion or a badly bent brooch whose only remaining value was sentimental.

Berlin had become unglued. At the end of 1947, Curtis LeMay—an architect of the American bombing missions of World War II—came to Germany to become head of the U.S. Air Force in Europe. The situation was growing worse instead of better. The Germans "looked like zombies, like the walking dead. They went unheeding and aloof across the streets. An automobile would be coming . . . they didn't care, didn't look, didn't even turn their heads when the screech of brakes exploded behind them. There was an eternal nothingness about the place; nothing happening, no work going on; nothing much to eat at home. People sat and stared. A little girl would be crouched on the steps of a half-ruined house, or maybe two or three little girls; and one of them might be holding a toy, but she wouldn't be paying any attention to it; neither would the others. When you passed, their eyes followed you, but blankly, blankly. There was no response, no enlivening humanity in any countenance. The place was bewitched."

As Lucius Clay sat in his office in those first days of 1948, Berlin was in ruins—three days before Christmas a strong rain had knocked over a home, killing six people inside. The Berliners were degraded—another thirteen had committed suicide over that Christmas. Rival gangs fought bloody battles among the wreckage. Food had grown scarce and people had become desperate. One ice-cold night, a young woman was stopped by a blind man in the deep dark of a Berlin street. He asked her for directions to an address scrawled on a letter he clutched in his gnarled hand. She looked at this pitiful man wearing an old battered German army tunic, tapping his way through the rubble with a white cane, and offered to deliver the letter for him. It was not far at all. She was headed in that direction anyway. He seemed to hesitate for a moment, uncertain whether he could impose on her, but then he accepted and thanked her for her kindness. She said it was no trouble and went on her way, but after walking a few yards, she hesitated; something made her look back, and she saw the blind man scurrying away quickly with the white stick tucked under his arm. Suspicious, she stopped off in a nearby police station, and the officers inside decided they would deliver the letter themselves. They found the address to be simply a shoe store run by a respectable-looking married couple. Downstairs, however, they found a cellar filled with fresh meat, on large grimy hooks, clearly meant for sale on the black market. The officers were slack-jawed. Such a large supply of meat was unheard of in Berlin, where a pound was worth a small fortune. They handled the cuts and on close inspection they discovered the color and texture of the meat was unfamiliar. It was neither beef nor lamb nor venison. One of the officers realized that, in all the commotion, they had forgotten about the envelope the blind man had given the young woman. They ripped it open to find a single piece of paper on which was written a single short sentence: "This is the last one I will be sending you today."

The story was repeated endlessly. Most thought it was apocryphal. What made it—and Berlin—so scary was that no one could be sure.

The plagues on Berlin had come first with bombs from above. Then a rain of shells and an invasion of soldiers and the death of children on barricades and then rape. There had been an assault of rodents and a march of pestilence that felled Berliners by the thousands. They had turned on one another in desperate acts of crime and, when they could least withstand it, they had been struck with the most frigid cold. Berliners, Melvin Lasky wrote from the city in 1948, were "a ruined, poverty-striken, brutalized people, with little to eat, everything to fear, nothing to hope for." As the year began, their only cause for optimism was that, having lived through nine terrible plagues since the end of the war, they could only assume that their misfortunes had run their course.

FROM HIS FIRST days in Germany, Clay had vowed to operate under what he called a "goldfish bowl policy"—the door to his office would be open to aides and news correspondents who had permission to stop in whenever they had need to see him. By the early afternoon of a typical workday, the path to his door would have been well traveled. Delegations of American politicians and pastors and businessmen would show up at Clay's office to preen before him on fact-finding missions in search of evidence to buttress their preconceptions and prejudices. But weeks, months could go by without a Berliner making it anywhere near the big desk in Clay's office.

Clay himself was his mother's son and, even in the early days of the occupation, treated the crushed Germans with a basic decency that came naturally to one who had been reared among the shadows of the vanquished. "We are not here as carpetbaggers," he announced when he first arrived in Germany, as if he were depositing yet another flower on the graves in Marietta. But Clay was profoundly uncomfortable around them. Neither he nor any of his top military officers spoke German, yet his German-language interpreter only performed that duty part-time. "He didn't meet with many Germans," remembered Robert Lochner, and "he had no social contacts whatsoever." When the occasion did require Clay to confer with high-ranking Germans, the interactions were stilted and awkward. Soon after arriving in Germany, someone had told Clay that professional men were customarily addressed as "Doctor." He proceeded to greet just about every German he met—no matter who they were—as "Doctor" for the rest of his time in the country.

Two and a half years after the end of the war, GIs and Germans still glared at each other over a gaping chasm of distrust and even hatred. "In heart, body and spirit, every German is Hitler," American troops had been instructed as they entered Germany. "Don't make friends with Hitler." As months went by and the invasion turned into occupation, the same spirit remained. Beginning a year after the war's end, the reinforcements that came to Germany after the first waves of warriors had gone home were required to attend a special six-hour information program. The instruction series was designed to make sure the American troops understood what was at stake in the occupation. "Germany cannot be trusted," they were told. American soldiers were told not to walk through the streets alone at night for fear of getting their throat slit and ending up in the river. And the smallest Germans were thought to be the most dangerous. After all, Nazi children "had been reared in Nazi schools" and had taken up arms against the Allies in the final days of the war. "Most young people," the postwar GIs were taught, "are Germans trained to think only as the Nazis wanted them to think."

Many of the soldiers arriving in Germany, however, needed little encouragement in their loathing. They had arrived "angry as hell toward the Germans," in the words of one postwar GI. Major Everett S. Cofran, a military government official outside of Munich, hung a sign reading I HATE ALL GERMANS on his wall and kept a large card with the number of America's war dead on his desk. A small group of soldiers decided, that first December after the war, to erect a Christmas tree in Berlin, topped with a tiny Statue of Liberty, as a goodwill gesture to Germany's children. They began to save up their candy rations to distribute to the kids. Yet when the high command of the occupation received word, the reaction was swift. The American GIs were warned, it was reported, that "it would be illegal to give the Germans a speck of army food or a stick of chewing gum from the post exchange." On mess walls in the early days of the occupation, warnings read, "Notice to U.S. troops: American taxes pay for your food—it is forbidden to give, sell, or trade it to the natives." When bread grew stale, the Americans would douse it with gasoline and burn it to keep the Germans from scrounging for it. Outside the mess, children would line up and, gulping hard, watch wide-eyed as hot cocoa was poured down the drain in front of them. Most had never tasted the drink.

"In the midst of ruins and near starvation, we lived well," recalled Arthur Kahn, an intelligence officer then in his mid-twenties. "We wined and dined as we had never done at home. Like conquerors, we affected fancy uniforms and fancy leather boots. The most beautiful women in Germany we had at our price. There were servants to minister to our every need. For a few packs of cigarettes, we even had music with our meals. And on the streets, before the opera, groups of Germans gathered to fight for our cigarette butts." Even at the time, some Americans were disgusted by the display. George Kennan, a Foreign Service officer stationed in Moscow, passed through Germany and experienced "a sense of sheer horror at the spectacle of this horde of my compatriots and their dependents camping in luxury amid the ruins of a shattered national community," creating a "disparity in privilege and comfort between themselves and their German neighbors, no smaller than those that had once divided lord and peasant in that feudal Germany which it had been our declared purpose in two world wars to destroy." Certainly, the opulence was somewhat sybaritic, but in its iciness there was a touch of revenge—in some cases, more than others. One twenty-two-year-old staff sergeant ruled over the city of Bensheim, south of Frankfurt, in the months after the surrender. He lived in a castlelike villa whose owners he had evicted, and he was driven through town in a white 1938 Mercedes-Benz he had confiscated. He had a maid, a housekeeper, and a German cook who prepared him his favorite meals. But what was most delicious for young Henry Kissinger was that Bensheim stood about 150 miles away from Fürth, the town from which he and his family had fled persecution only seven years earlier.

As time went on, however, the hearts of some Americans could not but help soften at the sight of the Germans scurrying after the GIs' cigarette butts or hoping for a dropped crumb. On Severino DiCocco's first morning in Germany, he was standing in formation when he "saw a Catholic nun behind the mess hall holding her habit up on her right arm and she had her whole right arm in the garbage cans 'fishing' for any chunks of food she could find." As regulations about fraternization loosened, the Americans began to do more to help the foraging Germans—at least in a limited fashion. Instead of destroying the leftovers, the Americans labeled the metal trash cans outside the mess halls "Edible Garbage" and "Non-Edible Garbage." Some made a special effort. Jim Spatafora, a young airman, would plop extra helpings onto the stainless-steel trays in the dining hall and "duplicate the food like a double-helix. Corn over here, corn over there. Roll over here, roll over there. And then I would it put in the trash. Nuns would appear and they would be feeding three orphanages."

Millions of defeated Germans were being fed by their American conquerors—through the individual efforts of troops throwing away extra trash and, on a much larger scale, by an American military government distributing rations. But Clay's military government was doing just enough to keep the Germans alive. In the months ahead, Clay wrote to McCloy early in the occupation, Germans would experience "much cold and hunger. Some cold and hunger will be necessary to make the German people realize the consequences of a war which they caused. However, between the cold and hunger which is necessary for this purpose and the cold and hunger which brings about human distress is a wide range. We may not be able to avoid the latter, but certainly it is our duty to attempt to do so."

Soldiers may have tossed away an extra biscuit for a nun, but for Germans such an act from the Americans was the exception; it did not capture the spirit of the occupation. Six months after the war, 70 percent of Germans thought the Americans were helping in the reconstruction of Germany. By August of 1947, only 44 percent agreed with this sentiment. The American military government was making enormous exertions to bring Germans whatever food it could, and those who received it were rightly grateful, but tasted something was lacking. The Germans fully realized they were being fed not because Americans felt they shared some basic humanity with them, but because, as Clay put it, "there is no choice between becoming a Communist on 1,500 calories and a believer in democracy on 1,000 calories." Clay would try to provide food for the Germans; he would do what he could to make sure their children did not freeze to death in the winter. But he would do so, he explained, because it was in the best interest of the United States, not because he cared a whit for the people he ruled. He would proclaim he was "not at all sympathetic to the Germans" and that he "had no desire to do things because it was for their good." And, in Berlin, they knew it.

MOST AFTERNOONS, MURPHY would come by Clay's office and sink into a plush leather chair in front of the outsized desk, and the two men would discuss the day's events over a few hands of gin rummy. In their years together in Berlin, the two men had become close friends, and Clay had come to rely heavily on the insight of his diplomatic adviser. He had little choice. International relations had turned out to be a much

larger part of Clay's job than anyone could have imagined when he left
Washington in the last spring of the war.

While MacArthur had near-total power over occupied Japan, in Germany America was one of four countries sharing equal control. Three
times a month, the four military governors met at the Allied Control
Council. The sessions were held in an upstairs hall in the building that
once had housed the Nazi's "People's Court." It had been the site of a
direct hit by an American bomb, but was rebuilt soon after the war.
Perched at the edge of a large grassy lawn in Kleist Park, the Control
Council building was a maze of corridors leading to 546 rooms. Even in
the brightest daylight, shadows would creep across the passageways; on
the hottest day, the marble balustrade on the stone staircase leading
upstairs would be cool to the touch. Inside the meeting room, eight
columns capped by elaborate golden cornices emerged from the walls.
The floor was inlaid mahogany. On the ceiling a fresco of plump
cherubs looked down on the scene below.

When the Control Council met, four long tables would be arranged
to make a square. In the center sat stenographers. Around the outside
were more than thirty generals and diplomats. The matters discussed in
the Control Council were complicated and controversial, but an air of
camaraderie took hold early among the four military governors. On the
occasion of the one-year anniversary of the formation of the council,
Clay drew a sword and, with a flourish of ceremony, cut a birthday cake
in four—just like Germany. At Christmastime, the Americans decorated
the meeting room with garlands and candles; they set up an electric
model railroad and the generals took turns making the train go around
the track to much mirth and laughter. After each meeting, whichever
nation held the rotating chairmanship of the Control Council that
month provided for an elaborate buffet.

With the departure of Zhukov soon after the war's end, Marshal
Vasily Sokolovsky became the Soviet commander. Six foot four inches
tall, with forty medals arrayed across his chest, Sokolovsky had the puffy
good looks of an aging movie star. He was the son of poor Russian peasants, and had been a schoolteacher when the Revolution had broken

out. He loved to read Jane Austen and could quote the Bible, to Clay's astonishment, "more accurately than anybody I'd known." In their first years in Berlin, they built a close relationship, greased by Sokolovsky's bluff charm and Clay's devotion to friendship between their nations. When one of Clay's sons was married in Berlin, Sokolovsky accepted the invitation to attend the wedding. Long after the other guests had departed, Clay found Sokolovsky was still there, singing soldier songs in a clump of young American officers. The two men and their wives would have dinner together and watch movies in each other's homes. "And after dinner," remembered Clay, "we'd have a nightcap together and chat and talk. Sometimes until very late."

When meeting in one of their offices, Clay and Sokolovsky did not bring their own interpreters and instead confidently relied on the other's. Even as it became apparent that their countries were approaching a break over Germany, Clay and Sokolovsky were able, for a long while, to remain more than civil. They would insult each other with abandon during sessions of the Control Council, and when the meeting was over, according to one observer, "out they would go to the bar, arm in arm, and have a drink." But by 1948, it was just for show, two men lying to the world.

BY 1948, ROOSEVELT'S dream of a postwar friendship between the Russians and the Americans lay dead in the graveyard that was Berlin. The German capital was to have been the place that showed all nations that the great powers could work in concert and harmony. Instead, Berlin became the place where Russia and the West found themselves locked in the same cage, slamming against each other and, in the process, setting off a global ideological struggle that would bring them to the brink of a new world war.

The Soviets had, in the final days of the war, begun a program of expansion that was moving steadily outward from Russia's borders. Iran and Greece and Turkey were threatened by the force of Communist arms, and in the nations of Eastern Europe democratically elected governments were replaced one by one with Soviet-backed coups.

The Russians seemed methodical. As one Communist leader, Hungary's Mátyás Rákosi, explained it, eliminating democratic opposition was "like cutting up a salami, thin slice after thin slice"—soon it would all be gone. All through 1947, the West watched with growing horror and fear as the carving took place. In January 1947, in Poland, elections distinguished by massive voter fraud gave the Communists 93 percent of seats in the parliament and sent the democratic Peasant Party leader Stanisław Mikołajczyk—who had promised to bring Franklin Roosevelt's "Four Freedoms" to the country—fleeing into exile. In June of that year, Hungarian prime minister Ferenc Nagy, whose Smallholders Party had won 57 percent of vote compared with the 17 percent received by Communists in 1945 elections, was also driven from office and out of the country after the Communists kidnapped his four-year-old son. In July, Romania's aging, pro-Western opposition leader Iuliu Maniu was arrested for treason and sent to a dingy prison, where he would die. In September, Bulgarian democrat Nikola Petkov was convicted in a quick show trial and, within days, was swaying from a rope. Among the nations of Eastern Europe, as 1948 got under way, only Czechoslovakia remained free. For those who had lived through Hitler's early victories—and tallied up their later cost—the steady advance of this new menace was fearsome in its implications.

Though Soviet expansionism in Eastern Europe and elsewhere supplied the heavy drumbeat of Western fears, it was the argument over Germany's course that provided the lyrics. Clay had arrived in Germany believing that the great powers would quickly negotiate a treaty that would reestablish an independent Germany and allow American forces to return home having won a peace. But in meetings of the Council of Foreign Ministers, where American secretaries of state conferred with Russian, British, and French foreign ministers, no agreement on Germany's future was reached.

Clay had held to the vision of amity he had brought with him to Europe long after most had given up on it. He opposed an effort by the U.S.-backed, Russian-language Radio Liberty to beam anti-Russian propaganda into the Soviet zone. When antipathy toward the Russians began to increase back in America, he bemoaned the rise of "the old Red scare." Berlin was a city crawling with spies from many nations, including the United States. Clay could not have been less interested in what they were learning. Between the end of the war and the end of 1947, he met with the chief American intelligence officers in Berlin three times—and each was on the occasion of their escorting a high-ranking American visitor.

Clay's faith that an accommodation could be found with the Russians grated on Frank Howley, his military government commander in Berlin. Of the top officers who had come to Berlin in 1945, Clay and Howley were the only ones who remained in early 1948. They were, in some fashion, too similar to avoid butting heads. "He could indeed be very unpleasant," said one of Howley's staff members. "He was a real Irishman with a temper." When the two men interacted, the results could be combustible.

Howley—the scion of Philadelphia high society, the military reservist who had been kept out of combat, the former Parisian art student—made a fetish of demonstrating his toughness. The men under his command took to calling him "Howlin' Mad" Howley. His harsh treatment of Berliners earned him the sobriquet "The Beast of Berlin" even in American newspapers not disposed to treat the Germans lightly. "If we bring food into Berlin," he proclaimed early in the occupation, "the only reason is that we don't want their rotten corpses to infect our troops."

A few months after the war, the mayor of a suburb just outside the American sector of Berlin came to tell him that there were a thousand women and children living in his village and that the food was running out. "Why do you come to us?" demanded Howley. "Your town is in the Russian zone." The mayor replied that the Russians had refused to help the villagers. Howley turned the man away.

"And what happened to the people in that town?" a reporter later asked.

"I don't know," Howley shot back. "I believe in being tough with the Germans, and I don't blame the Russians for being tough. When that mayor returned to my office and begged me to go with him to look at his starving children, I told him to get out and never come back again." But for all the virtue Howley would make of his hardness, it was only a protective shell over what lay within. "I have children of my own," he told the reporter, "and I do my job here best by keeping completely away from children."

Howley's harsh treatment of the Germans was matched only by his disdain for the Russians. Clay had saddled Howley with Kommandatura rules that required agreement by all parties before any action could be taken. Berlin would be governed as a whole. To make the city function, the Kommandatura had set up a complex system of joint subcommittees covering all aspects of life in Berlin stretching from those on cultural affairs and monuments and fine arts to those dealing with concerns such as coal and food. "I was in closer contact with the Russians than any other American in Europe," he averred. "I met thousands, from Marshal Zhukov down to field privates."

Howley did not think much of the Russians while being kept in the ramshackle house on that first day of his journey to Berlin. In the three years since, he had sat through two thousand hours of Kommandatura sessions, and the longer he spent with the Russians, the more his esteem for them plummeted. "We came here with a job to do—to get this city operating," he complained to the foreign editor of *Newsweek,* visiting in October 1946. "It wasn't any concern of ours whether the Germans wanted to be Communists or Hottentots or what have you. We just wanted to get the job done. But we've found that our program for getting the job done runs into obstacles at every turn and the obstacles always come from the Russians." That same month, Howley was even more forceful in his diary. The Russians "have, in less than two years, converted the American admiration and love which was built up during the war by their magnificent resistance, to a hatred of their stubborn, uncompromising greed."

Like Clay, Howley had attempted—at least halfheartedly—to create a personal relationship with his opposite numbers, but it never took. "I have wined and dined them, wined and dined with them, swapped bourbon for vodka and chicken *à la Maryland* for chicken *à la Kiev,* but the politeness of the gala night always disappeared in the bitterness around the Kommandatura table the next morning."

If the Soviets had wanted to find a counterpart for Howley sure to send him into paroxysms of annoyance—and perhaps they did—they could not have chosen better than General Alexander Kotikov. He was, in Howley's incensed description, "the epitome and the quintessence of the evil doctrines Moscow preaches. A big, bulky man, with flowing white hair, icy blue eyes, and a mouth like a petulant rosebud, his mind turned on and off automatically with switches operated in the Kremlin." Kotikov would arrive at Kommandatura meetings armed with an hour-long speech outlining American misdeeds. Howley would listen with rising fury, and grow sputtering angry in his reply as he eagerly enumer-ated the Russian's falsehoods. Kotikov would watch the spectacle in quiet triumph, only to return with another speech, on another topic, the following week.

Their battle was not confined to the Kommandatura sessions. How-ley was an adman who knew good copy, and his preening air of self-satisfaction and quotes as carefully primped as his pompadour made him a perfect subject for newspaper profiles. The press loved him—and he shared their affection. In the privacy of his diary, he would write, "I have had to openly speak frankly and forcefully to the American press," and that it was all part of his job "to inform the American people as to the nature of the Soviets and Communists." For too long, Americans had not understood—as he had—the grave threat posed by the Soviets. "Therefore, my 'blasts' during the past three-and-one-half years have gone directly to the American people, and to the President of the United States by way of his morning newspaper." It is likely that Howley, who would often refer to himself in the third person, enjoyed reading his pithy quotes in the morning paper more than Harry Truman did.

"The Russians are the world's most colossal liars, swindlers, and cut-throats," Howley would charge. Soviet-controlled radio took to refer-ring to "Jesse James Howley" in their broadcasts. The battle between Howley and Kotikov raged from the newsstands to the conference table. "It would take a wheelbarrow to bring here all the insults published about the Americans in the Soviet sector," Howley charged in one Kommandatura session.

"A ten-ton truck wouldn't be enough to haul all the insanities and calumnies the press carries in your sectors," Kotikov replied childishly.

The arguments in the Kommandatura ranged from the consequential to the trivial. At one point, work ground to a halt as they fought over what image would appear on Berlin's postage stamps. But while the subjects may have been unimportant, the mood was never light. An air of danger pervaded Berlin, and it seeped into the Kommandatura. In one session, Kotikov and Howley were trying to settle the question of what color Berlin's automobile tags would be. Kotikov dove into a stem-winding sermon on Marxist dialecticism and "the world class struggle." Howley cut him off: "Look, let's get down to business. You and I won't live to see the end of the class struggle, but we can settle this automobile tag business today."

Kotikov grinned grimly through a mouth full of gold-capped teeth. "Maybe *you* won't live to see the end of the class struggle, but I will."

In postwar Berlin, such a shot carried with it a sense of menace. In the last weeks of 1947 and first weeks of 1948, 1,600 Berliners—a large number of them anti-Communist activists—had simply disappeared, vanished without a trace. Sometimes their "crime" would be as simple as reading an American newspaper. The Soviets paid little attention to the sector boundaries. Cars would come screeching down the street of the American sector and plainclothes men would snatch their victim off the sidewalk, stuff him into the sedan, and hurry back over the border into Soviet-controlled areas. Sometimes, an agent would slip something into a victim's cocktail in a bar, hustle him out with the explanation that "he had had too much to drink," and put him into a waiting car to take him to Soviet Berlin. On some occasions, a Berliner would receive a phone call luring him to the Russian sector to see a friend or family member who had suffered a sudden accident. Other times, there would just be a knock at the door, late at night. Whatever the means, the end result was they would often never be heard from again. Occasionally, there would be a perfunctory show trial, but the Soviets rarely went through the motions. Howley issued public instructions to Berliners on responding to kidnapping. The city's newspapers regularly ran the growing list of Berliners who had disappeared and provided their readers with checklists of what to do if Soviet secret police came to kidnap them: "Remember their badge numbers," "Attract as much attention as possible so your next-door neighbors, family members and people in the neighborhood notice," "Fight back." Just a few dozen miles from Eastern European nations falling into Communist control, the pattern in Berlin seemed familiar. The "reign of terror," Howley warned Berliners, was coming there next. Life in the city, wrote a Berliner, had become "a dance on the edge of a volcano."

AS IN THE nations of Eastern Europe, the Soviets' goal was to capture control of the government. By the beginning of 1948, they had found themselves frustrated in that ambition. A few days after they had taken the city, the Russians appointed sixty-seven-year-old Arthur Werner, an innocuous former municipal employee and schoolteacher, as Berlin's mayor. Berliners joked it was because he was the only person left who still owned a frock coat. The Soviets were more interested in the real levers of power. They placed loyal functionaries in control of the key departments, including the police, where Paul Markgraf, a decorated Nazi soldier turned rabid Communist, was made chief. The Americans and British demanded that free elections for a new city government of Berlin be held. Kotikov vetoed every attempt to set a date. But when the matter was taken up by the higher-level Allied Control Council, Sokolovsky overruled his subordinate, believing the Communists would sweep in through the ballot booth. In raped, looted Berlin, it was the height of overweening delusion.

As the October 1946 elections approached, the Soviet-controlled Communists blanketed Berlin with propaganda in newspapers and over the radio, but, taking sprightly to electoral politics, also gave Berliners what they really wanted. Voters were invited to parties at election headquarters where brimming platters of food and flowing bottles of booze were the main attraction. The Communists passed out lumps of coal—a treasured gift under such circumstances—with their party's name branded into them.

The election could not be bought. In their first free election in more than a decade, 92 percent of Berliners showed up at the polls. And they gave the Communists only 20 percent of the vote. The Soviets were stunned. Two Western-leaning parties, the Social Democrats and the Christian Democrats, together took 71 percent of the ballots. The new City Assembly, the governing council of the city, appointed Otto Ostrowski as the first postwar mayor chosen by Berliners. His primary goal was to avoid offending any of the occupying powers. "My name is Ostrowski," he told Howley, "but the Russians say it ought to be Westrowski. As far as I'm concerned, I'd like to change it to Centrowski." But as the two sides began to play tug-of-war over Berlin, neutrality proved impossible. Facing impeachment by Berlin's democrats for giving in to Soviet demands, Ostrowski resigned.

In his place, the Social Democrats—the most strongly pro-Western party in Berlin, who had nearly captured an outright majority of the splintered vote—nominated Ernst Reuter as the new mayor. It was a decisive step. Reuter was a legendary figure in Berlin. By 1947, he had spent forty years crusading against injustice. With colossal ears, big lips, and huge black eyebrows, Reuter had an improbable face that looked as though it had been assembled by a committee whose members were not speaking to one another. He was rotund as he neared his sixties, and his jowls sagged; whenever people saw him they thought instantly of a basset hound. Topped off with his trademark beret, he was a comical sight, but in 1947 it is entirely possible that there was no European leader the Kremlin feared more.

Born in a tiny town on the Baltic coast to a professor of navigation, Reuter had set a course as a persistent critic of the powerful from a young age, working as a human rights and peace activist in Berlin before the First World War, writing vituperative, anonymous attacks on the kaiser's policies. When he was identified, he was quickly sent into the brutal trench warfare of the eastern front as an infantry private. There he was wounded and captured by the Russians. On the train to the POW camp, he began teaching himself the Cyrillic alphabet by studying the signs in the train stations he passed. When his wounds had healed, Reuter was sent with his fellow POWs to work in coal mines, where, as the only one of more than 400 prisoners who could read Russian, he would read to the camp every night from the newspaper. Word quickly reached Moscow of a brilliant young German with great leadership potential, and Vladimir Lenin personally sent for him. Reuter was trained and indoctrinated and then dispatched to take charge of a settlement of Germans who had lived on the Volga near Saratov since the reign of Catherine the Great. He was given the title of first commissar of the Independent Soviet Republic of the Volga and reported directly to the minister of nationalities, a rising functionary named Joseph Stalin.

When World War I ended, the Soviets sent Reuter back to Berlin. "The young Reuter is brilliant, but strong-willed, a little too independent," wrote Lenin to German Communist leader Clara Zetkin. He proved this in 1921, when as general secretary of the German Communist Party, he quit the party after watching with disgust as the idealism of the Russian Revolution was replaced by the thirst for the consolidation of personal power. Instead, he focused on a career he thought would be less wrought by politics: municipal government. By 1926, he had become head of Berlin's transportation and public utilities department. It was under his leadership that great leaps were made in completing Berlin's growth into a twentieth-century metropolis.

In 1930, Reuter was elected to the Reichstag, where he eventually became a prominent anti-Nazi and, for his dissident activities, was thrown into one of the first concentration camps. Sentenced to a year but released early under pressure from the Catholic Church, he survived, he would remember, "by looking stupid, saying nothing and obeying every order." An intensely proud man, he forced himself to obey the orders with perfection: "I cleaned the latrines so beautifully!" In 1935, he was arrested again, tossed into solitary confinement, and freed only when the London City Council made a special plea for the release of this renowned innovator of urban government. He knew he would never live to tell of a third apprehension.

With a small suitcase and ten reichsmarks, Reuter escaped across the Dutch frontier and made it to London. He could not find a job in England, so when he received an offer to work for the Turkish government's transportation ministry in a low-level bureaucratic position in Ankara, he and his wife departed for the hills of Anatolia. Reuter was no longer the young teen who had taught himself Russian from signs in train stations. It took him three years to learn the language. He had been scarred by experience, tossed about by the tides of history, and, amid the swaying fig trees and sweltering summers, was profoundly depressed. All his attention remained on the home he had escaped, perhaps forever, and he closely followed the minute details of political developments, looking for the stray strands of possibility that might lead to his return. Reuter hoped for a military coup that might overthrow the Führer, he thought a crisis might lead the German people to rise up against the Nazis, and, most faithfully, he believed the countries of the world would, at long last, unite to defeat Hitler's regime. But all through the 1930s, as Germany rearmed, recaptured the Rhineland, annexed Austria, and prepared for war, he suffered in shaking disappointment. In the hot September of 1938, Reuter sat with the shades pulled down in their small hotel room in Ankara, listening hopefully to BBC reports from Munich. When news of the capitulation came, his disappointment boiled over into fury. He snatched an andiron from the fireplace and began to bash the venetian blinds, slamming them again and again with his face contorted in anger. His wife shrieked, begging him to stop. "Never have I seen 'the fat one' in such a rage," she would recall.

Seven years later, the war ended. Reuter had to wait another year and a half before he received a visa to return home. He arrived in Berlin a famous name from the city's once-glorious past, an unsullied reminder of what once had been. The man who had criticized the kaiser and the Communists and the Nazis alike was trusted by Berliners above all others for his independence and honesty. Ostrowski resigned only a few months after Reuter had returned from Turkey, but the Social Democrats immediately put his name forward for mayor. The Soviets panicked at the thought of their wayward disciple taking power in Berlin. "Do you want a Turk for Mayor?" read posters that went up on walls all around the city. Nevertheless, all the parties in the City Assembly, save the Communists he had once led, united behind Reuter and elected him mayor with 82 percent of the vote.

Three days later, Kotikov vetoed the City Assembly's decision in the Kommandatura. Howley was furious, decrying this subversion of democracy. The veto was appealed up to the Allied Control Council— and there, Clay, still trying to keep the peace, sided with the Russians. He told Howley that someone who was so bitterly opposed by one of the four powers would not be able to function as mayor.

Berliners and the Russians had reached an impasse. Letters to "Mayor Reuter" sent to City Hall through the Soviet-controlled postal system were returned with a notation that no such person existed. The Berliners, however, stood their ground. Louise Schroeder, the first woman elected to the Reichstag, now, at age sixty, sickly and gray, was Reuter's deputy and next in line to be mayor. But she refused to occupy the office and instead maintained she would be acting mayor only until Reuter could take the position to which he had been elected. Reuter himself was also, characteristically, uncowed. A convert's zeal being nothing compared to a defector's, Reuter, instead of trying to placate the Russians by making himself more amenable to them, redoubled the daily invective he hurled in their direction. When he was advised that his only hope was "to be on a good footing with all four powers," he replied sharply, "It is not my business to act like a terrified rabbit staring at a snake." He ordered up a new set of business cards: "Ernest Reuter, the Elected but Unconfirmed Mayor of Berlin."

FOR HOWLEY, CLAY'S decision to allow the Russians to reject Reuter's election was another blow to his faith in the military governor. It "was a new low for American prestige," he believed. He was disgusted, unable to understand why Clay should care about upsetting the Soviets. Their conversations grew heated. Howley forgot his place. "I am not afraid of you, so why in hell should I be afraid of a Russian general," he, a colonel, shouted at Clay, a four-star general.

Clay let the incident pass, yet Howley's antics—with Clay or the Russians—were not helping his career. Since 1945, Howley had served, officially, as the director of military government in Berlin, but as only the deputy American commandant in the city. During that period, eight men had served briefly as commandant, usually acting only as figureheads and allowing Howley to make the most important decisions. While common practice was for a deputy to move up into an open position, Howley was rejected for promotion every time. The only reason he was given was that the job required someone more "diplomatic."

By the fall of 1947, Howley had come to feel that his "thinking was in complete disagreement with American policy in Berlin and, logically, I could expect no personal advancement." He began planning to return home—if only so that he could quit before he was fired. His relationship with Clay had continued to fray. In September, Howley had jailed a handful of Communists for planning a meeting in the American sector by using an obscure, unenforced regulation issued by Eisenhower at the end of the war that prohibited gatherings of three or more Germans without prior approval. Clay summoned Howley to castigate him for the action, accusing him of imposing Gestapo-like measures. Howley denied it and walked out on him.

Still steaming when he returned to his office, Howley could not leave the matter alone. He wrote Clay a long letter justifying the arrest and telling him why he was wrong. This, he admitted in his diary, "was probably a bad idea because it resulted in my being called on the mat the second time and invited to go home if I couldn't follow" Clay's orders. The meeting was "a bit stormy." Howley again defended his actions and his overall record in Berlin in rough language. Outside Clay's office, assistants listened in to hear the low-ranking officer yell at the commander of American Armed Forces in Europe. Howley rose to leave again. Clay tried to smooth things over. "I want you to know, Frank," he sighed, "that I wouldn't call you up here if I didn't think the world of you."

Only a couple of weeks passed, however, before Clay and Howley were battling again. The subject was a familiar one; the same ongoing disagreement they had been having since their first meeting in 1945. Howley had drawn up a report criticizing Clay for operating under a "false premise." Russia, he wrote, "was neither a friend nor an ally." Clay lectured him again on the Roosevelt vision. Howley had heard enough. "I was fed up." He offered his resignation.

Howley planned to return to Philadelphia where political leaders were trying to draft him to run for mayor on a "Crusader Reform" ticket. Two days before he was scheduled to leave, Clay called him into headquarters once again. They made small talk for a few minutes. Howley began to head toward the door when Clay stopped him. "Frank, how would you like to come back on active duty as commandant?" he asked.

"Clay can be irresistible," Howley would remark. The new position brought little change in duties and no promotion in rank, but it matched Howley's sense of self. It was not that Clay was so irresistible. He simply knew his man.

THE SUN HAD long set over Berlin by the time Clay returned home for dinner. Among the reasons he had chosen to live in such a modest house instead of the ample villas that were available to him was that it made it difficult to accept overnight guests. A stream of American dignitaries flowed through the capital—government officials, movie stars, and other famous personages—all there to view the ruins, assess the occupation, and have their picture taken alongside rubble and grinning GIs. There were regular visits from congressional delegations so that the politicians could return home to declaim to their constituents about the "problem of Germany" from a position of expertise. But what they saw robbed them of the ability to spout easy answers. Thirty-five years later, Richard Nixon would remember his 1947 visit as a freshman congressman as "among the most sobering experiences of my life. . . . We found thousands of families huddled in the debris of buildings and in bunkers. There was a critical shortage of food, and thin-faced, half-dressed children approached us not to beg but to sell their fathers' war medals or to trade them for something to eat." Another freshman congressman, John F. Kennedy, made a return trip to Berlin, but his visit paled in Clay's memory to that of the congressman's two sisters, whose freedom had to be secured by the military government when they were picked up by the Russians and held for hours after having wandered deep into the Soviet zone by driving to the wrong city of Frankfurt.

Occasionally, Clay would have to entertain at dinner, but because he despised talk of work when he was trying to rest, often only Marjorie would join him. At dinner, as during the rest of the day, Clay was the undisputed master of his life. A buzzer was installed under the dining room table and German servants would come running when he pressed the button. Otherwise they were to leave him alone.

Clay's respite at home was brief. By eleven o'clock, he would return to headquarters and, late into the night, would confer by teleconference with the policymakers in Washington over the future of Germany. As his time in Germany stretched on, Clay found himself increasingly out of step with the official policy of the United States.

In 1947, Truman made General George C. Marshall his secretary of state. Soon after Marshall took office, he went to Berlin en route to a Moscow meeting of the Council of Foreign Ministers. He brought with him a large entourage in which the strongest voice was that of John Foster Dulles, the Republican Party's chief foreign policy expert. Marshall had been appointed secretary of state the same month that the new Republican Congress, elected in a political tidal wave the previous November, took office. Dedicated to pursuing a bipartisan foreign policy, Marshall made sure that Dulles was given a say in all major decisions.

At a guesthouse by the Wannsee lake, Marshall convened a meeting on the future of Germany. He asked Clay to report on the state of affairs. Clay reviewed the situation and expressed his faith that democracy could be brought to a united Germany. Dulles was ready with a prepared statement of his own, drafted in advance. Clay had been set up. Dulles explained that the world had entered a mortal struggle between the forces of Christian civilization and godless Communism. As Germany had shown that it could not be considered an ally of Christian civilization, it needed to continue to be divided and subjugated. Clay shot back that to combat Communism, Germans needed to have an economic recovery and a sense of hope for better days ahead. Without that, they would turn to the Soviets.

Far from the pleasant evasions of diplomacy, this was a raw, emotional argument. Whether the other members of the delegation agreed with Clay or Dulles was unclear. With the Republicans on the ascendancy, they sat in silence, none of them willing to cross the likely next secretary of state. As for Marshall, he let the argument rage, and then when he finally spoke, he was openly dismissive of Clay's views, condescendingly accusing him of suffering from "localitis" and not being able to see the global big picture.

One aspect of Dulles's idea went unsaid in the argument, though the implication was clear to all in the room. If Germany was to be divided, then the western half of Berlin—deep within the Soviet zone and reliant almost completely on the democratic nations of America, Britain, and France for its food and supplies—would have to be given over to the Russians. It was, Dulles believed, not only a worthless pile of debris but a strategically indefensible outpost.

When Clay arrived in Moscow a few days later, Walter Bedell Smith was at the airport to greet him. Now ambassador to Moscow, he still nursed his ambition to hold Clay's job—and he just happened to be closer to the reserved, austere Marshall than anyone save the new secretary of state's own family. Alighting from the plane, Clay suppressed a smile at the sight of his rival. Smith's white hair had turned pink because a Moscow hairdresser had confused his request for hair tonic with hair dye. But any silent joy Clay might have felt was overwhelmed by his anger at discovering that Dulles's plan was now undisputed American policy. Clay found on the ride from the airport that "Bedell Smith was for it, because he thought it was probably a good idea to be for whatever Mr. Dulles was for." Frustrated, Clay lashed out. He forced the delegation to spend a full day debating the definition of democracy. When Marshall appointed Clay the American representative to a four-power subcommittee in Moscow to deal with German issues, Dulles instructed him not to make any commitments without receiving the blessing of the entire delegation. Clay's eyes congealed into black dots. He was, he told Dulles icily, the military governor of Germany and had been dealing with such issues for two years while Dulles had, in fact, no real say. Dulles responded that if his wishes were not obeyed, he would speak out against the Moscow conference's decisions to the Republican-controlled Congress now setting the course in Washington. Clay threatened to resign. "Blood was all over the floor," said one observer.

"GENERAL CLAY, THERE has been a lot of talk in Moscow about the possibility of Germany being split down the middle. Are we making any concrete plans for facing this alternative?" asked the *New York Herald Tribune*'s Marguerite Higgins at a press conference when Clay returned to Berlin from Moscow.

Clay, dejected but publicly playing the good soldier, tried to avoid a direct answer about whether the United States would abandon Berlin. "I just went out to plant some garden seeds in Berlin yesterday."

"Were they perennials or annuals?" cracked *Newsweek*'s James O'Donnell.

It became a running joke. "Sir," Clay was asked at a press conference six months later, "could you tell us whether you are making plans for your Berlin garden next spring?"

"As a matter of fact," he replied, "I am glad you brought that up because I want to put down a note to bring fertilizer back from Washington." But by then Clay knew that regardless of whether the United States stayed in Berlin for the long term, he would not.

Clay had returned from Moscow in April convinced that Marshall was about to replace him with Smith. "The sooner the better," he told Marjorie. If he was not pushed, Clay resolved to soon leave the post on his own.

Clay offered his resignation, by a conservative count, eleven times while in Germany—and this list does not include the mere threats to resign that piled up like the bricks in Berlin's rubble. Usually those threats came not over great questions of national policy but over the slightest of slights: He bristled when overruled on some matter of food distribution. He would refuse to attend international conferences when he felt his views were not requested ahead of time and then summarily depart when he felt they were being ignored as the negotiations proceeded. He wanted to quit when the State Department ordered up its own independent study of the German situation, as well as when Secretary Marshall overruled him on an industrial production question of concern to the French. Often the threats of resignation would be accompanied by an offhand statement that "a tour of catfishing looks awfully good," as if he could still run out past the great white veranda in Marietta when tension inside the house rose too high and drop his line into the Chattahoochee.

Though the resignation was rejected every time, some of the highest officials in American government had, since the end of World War II, been forced to spend a great deal of their time convincing Clay not to quit his job in a huff. After one such episode, Byrnes, Truman's first secretary of state, had invited Clay and Marjorie to come dine with him in Paris so that he could massage the general's ego. "How you could take time to raise my spirits in the midst of your worries is almost unbelievable," Clay wrote in a handwritten note to Byrnes the following day. "I want you to know that until you say the word I shall continue to do my best to carry out my part of the task in Germany. I would be ashamed otherwise."

Facing a new irritation, he resubmitted a request for early retirement two days later.

After another threat of resignation, Eisenhower was enlisted to beg Clay to stay in his position. "I thoroughly understand your sense of frustration," Eisenhower cabled, reminding Clay of their "long and close personal friendship." However, "you and I have served too long in this Army to contemplate seriously the laying down of a task simply because things sometimes go at sixes and sevens through no fault of our own. Times are too critical for anyone to move out of a post in which he can serve our country's interest. As a final word please remember that now abide Faith, Hope, and Charity, these three, and greater than any is a sense of humor."

"I am not temperamental," Clay wrote in reply, which must have sent Eisenhower chortling. Plaintively, he continued that Eisenhower himself would not have remained in his job as supreme commander of the Allied Expeditionary Force if his prerogatives had been as trampled as Clay's. "I have never run out on an unfinished job," he wrote, ignoring all the positions in wartime Washington he had tried to jettison in order to see combat, but "leaving a job under such circumstances might well be in the best interests of the job and not 'running out.' . . . Nevertheless, I value your friendship and good will too much not to accept your advice. If you think that my departure would be running out of the job and failing in my obligation to an Army which has been more than good to me, that is enough to keep me here."

It would be eleven days until he attempted to resign again.

By the fall of 1947, all involved in the discussions over Clay's future had decided the time was approaching for him to go home. The official reason was that it was now possible for Franklin Roosevelt's initial vision of civilian control of the occupation to be put in place. The truth was that Marshall and others in the administration in Washington had tired of Clay's impetuousness and petulance. They wanted someone they could direct, rather than have to plead with. Marshall told Walter Bedell Smith to prepare to take up a new post in Berlin.

Clay announced at a press conference at the end of October 1947 that he would be leaving his post toward the end of 1948. It would be a "full and complete retirement—I am going to go catfishing." That fall, in London, Clay bought his first set of civilian suits since before Pearl Harbor.

THAT WEEK IN early January, Clay returned home from his teleconferences with Washington hours after midnight. He was tired. For years, he had worked seven days a week. Even on weekends he worked twelve hours a day. "Clay is a fine fellow when he relaxes—the only problem is he never relaxes," one of his assistants would quip.

Once, on a Saturday evening, he had been having dinner at Murphy's home when one of the diplomat's daughters said, "Oh gee, it would be wonderful if we could go down to Bavaria skiing. It must be wonderful down there."

Clay, who had not taken a vacation since returning from the Philippines in 1938, said, "Well, God damn it, let's go tomorrow morning." They left by train for Bavaria at 5:30 A.M. Clay had never skied before in his life. He did not have ski clothes or equipment and none were available. He went out onto the slopes in his uniform and combat boots and simply stood there on the snowy mountainside. He returned to Berlin. And he never took another day off in Germany.

Subsisting on cigarettes and coffee, he had lost thirty pounds off his already slim frame since arriving after the war. He began to look like the gaunt Germans over whom he ruled. What could not be seen, and what Clay kept a secret, was that he was suffering from painful ulcers, developed under the strain.

Marjorie, long asleep by the time Clay returned home from headquarters, was intensely worried about his health. She was not alone. On his way back home from a trip around the world, James Forrestal had spent an hour with Clay in Berlin. Upon his return to Washington, he had written a memorandum to Secretary of War Bob Patterson stating, "I think you should order General Clay to take a ten-day or two-week holiday—nothing else will make him do it—and if he doesn't get some break, he runs the risk of blowing up entirely."

Had Patterson known he was being advised by an expert, he might have taken the recommendation.

On January 8, 1948, Clay's routine was upset when his assistant handed him a wire service ticker bearing the public announcement from George Marshall that the State Department would take control of the German occupation that spring. Neither Clay nor the Pentagon had been notified in advance. Clay had recently assured British military governor Brian Robertson and German leaders that he would stay in office until the later part of the year. "Secretary Marshall's announcement certainly came as surprise," Clay said to Bill Draper at the Pentagon in a teleconference the following day. "I would like to have beat the gun on it." Clay had long wanted to leave Berlin, but now he was aghast at being fired in disgrace.

Within days of the announcement, Clay received a letter from Smith vowing a smooth transition of responsibility. Clay could only purse his lips and reply that he and the others in Berlin would "do whatever you want us to do."

A schedule for the transfer of authority was drawn up and a State Department team was sent to lay the groundwork. Marjorie began sending their furniture and belongings home. The Army officially agreed to a date for Clay's retirement. It would be April 1, 1948.

7

MARCH

The lights in the garret of the Czernin Palace, perched high on a hill above the west banks of Prague's Charles River, burned into the night. There, on March 9, 1948, in the long room that doubled as his bedroom and study, Jan Masaryk, the foreign minister of Czechoslovakia, worked into the night on a speech on Polish-Czech cooperation he was to deliver the next day. A cool breeze lifted up the curtains by the large window that opened onto the narrow, winding, medieval paths leading to the ancient Prague Castle. The streets were still. The tumult and din of the previous weeks had ended.

Jan Masaryk's father, Tomáš Masaryk, had been Czechoslovakia's first president, its founding father, and he had left his son the legacy of serving as a living reminder of the country's promise. Czechoslovakia, cobbled together in the drawing rooms of Versailles after World War I, was by 1948 one of the few lasting successes of Woodrow Wilson's dream—a nation pried from the rule of the Habsburg Dynasty, living proof of the power of self-determination; a vibrant, open democracy sprung to life amid thousand-year-old spires. Wedged into a tiny spot between the great nations of Central and Eastern Europe, the Czechs thought of their country as a bridge between East and West.

Jan Masaryk thought of himself in the same way. His mother had been an American and, years before Czechoslovakia had been born—when his father was still a dissident philosophy professor living in a dreary, cramped apartment—Jan had set out for his mother's land with less than a hundred dollars in his pocket. He spent ten years living among other Eastern European immigrants in New York, Bridgeport, and Chicago, working in dimly lit factories by day and playing the piano to accompany silent movies at night. He returned to Prague before the outbreak of World War I and by the mid-1920s was appointed as the new Czech nation's ambassador to London, representing his father's government there for thirteen years. With perfect English and a garrulous manner, he was the shining face of a hopeful nation, a well-known and well-liked figure in the halls of Westminster, though, he explained, "I spend most of my official time in there explaining to the gentlemen inside that Czechoslovakia is a country and not a contagious disease."

By the late 1930s, it was Nazism that was spreading across Europe and, in London, men in dark suits used noble words to justify infecting others to inoculate themselves. "How horrible, fantastic, incredible it is that we should be digging trenches and trying on gas masks here because of a quarrel in a faraway country between people of whom we know nothing," said Neville Chamberlain before he and Hitler carved up Czechoslovakia in Munich. Masaryk sat dejected in the gallery of the House of Commons as Parliament cheered Chamberlain for buying peace at whatever the price. He went to confront the prime minister and foreign minister in person: "If you have sacrificed my nation to preserve the peace of the world, I will be the first to applaud you. But if not, gentlemen, God help your souls."

AFTER WORLD WAR II ended, Edvard Beneš, who had succeeded the elder Masaryk in 1935, was restored as president and Jan Masaryk became his foreign minister. Once again, Jan Masaryk tried to make Czechoslovakia into a free nation that was neither East nor West, a democracy that respected "the right of Jew and Gentile to read *Das Kapital* and *Mein Kampf* in Prague streetcars." In 1947, as the other nations of

Eastern Europe were falling under Soviet control, he convinced the cabinet—split between democrats and Communists—to send Czech representatives to the organizing conference for the Marshall Plan. In the streets of Prague, Czechs cheered and embraced total strangers at the news. The Russians were enraged. Stalin called Masaryk to Moscow and forced him to stop cooperating with the Americans. "The fate of a bridge is to be walked over," Masaryk said.

"I left as a minister of a sovereign state but have come back as Stalin's stooge," Masaryk lamented. He plunged into terrible bouts of depression, which would send him into the sterile confines of mental institutions for long periods. "He was extremely unstable," his girlfriend, Marcia Davenport, an American, later wrote. "I felt his judgment weaken and sway and wheel from desperate hope to more desperate hopelessness." She asked him, "How does Stalin treat you?"

He answered casually. "Oh, he's very gracious. Of course, he'd kill me if he could. But very gracious."

General elections were scheduled for May 1948; the Communists were expected to lose seats; and Masaryk hoped their power would wither. But on February 13, 1948, the Communist interior minister fired the last non-Communist divisional police commanders in the country. The majority in the cabinet protested this power grab and ordered that it be reversed. The Communists refused to obey. On February 20, the democratic ministers in the cabinet, with the exception of the nonpartisan Masaryk, made a grave mistake. They submitted their resignations to force a showdown. Czech Communist leader Klement Gottwald demanded that Beneš accept their resignations and replace them with Soviet loyalists.

At first, Beneš refused. As the Communist-controlled police looked on, mobs of thugs stormed into the president's office. He told them he would not "let the streets decide." The police themselves raided the headquarters of non-Communist parties and stood guard on street corners with machine guns in hand. A Soviet fixer, Deputy Foreign Minister Valerian Zorin, arrived in Prague from Moscow to oversee the Communist campaign. Busloads of protesters were brought into

Prague's squares, where they chanted slogans and sang the Communist anthem, the "Internationale." The Communists gained control of the radio and newspapers. They barred the democratic ministers from entering their offices. When students marched to the castle to demonstrate their loyalty to Czech independence, Communist squads fired into the crowd. On the Czech border, 18,000 Red Army troops massed. On February 25, Beneš capitulated and the Communists captured Czechoslovakia.

That night, 8,000 armed men marched in victory through St. Wenceslas Square. For days, Beneš was silent. He made no statement to his country. All his scheduled public appearances were canceled. When his new Communist minders allowed photographers to come take a picture of him working late at night, he had a single book on his desk. In large block letters, the English title on the spine, placed just so to face the cameras, was "DICTATORSHIP."

The next day, Beneš was sent off to his summer home. "The president is very tired and it is not known when he can come back to Prague," announced Gottwald's press secretary. Across the country, factories were nationalized, political parties disbanded, and professors dismissed from universities. Organizations, including the Boy Scouts and the football league, were purged.

Masaryk told Marcia Davenport he was going to go into exile. She should go ahead to Claridge's Hotel in London. He would meet her there in about ten days. She left Prague on Sunday, March 7. It was Tomáš Masaryk's birthday and Jan went to visit his father's grave in the small town of Lany. He knelt by the stone and cried for forty-five minutes. Then he lifted himself off the dirt and said goodbye.

The next day he began to burn the papers in his office and on March 9 he drove out to visit Beneš. Masaryk told the president he would be trying to escape the country.

That night, when he finished his work on the Polish-Czech cooperation speech, Masaryk went over his schedule for the next day with his secretary and said that after he delivered the speech, he planned to leave Prague for a two-week visit to a spa.

He ate dinner and climbed into bed. As he did every night, he took two of the sleeping pills from the bottle by his bed.

JAN MASARYK'S DEAD body, clad in blue silk pajamas, was found the next morning at 6:45 on the cold flagstones of the snowy palace courtyard, a few dozen feet below the tiny window of his apartment's bathroom. Inside his apartment, the sheets had been torn off his mattress, chairs were overturned, shards of glass from broken bottles were on the floor. The ashtrays were full of cigarettes. His father's Bible was opened to the fifth chapter of the Epistle to the Galatians. The chapter began:

Stand fast therefore in the liberty wherewith
Christ hath made us free, and be not entangled
Again with the yoke of bondage.

In the cramped bathroom, the contents of the medicine cabinet had crashed onto the floor, the bathmat and towels were piled into a corner, one pillow from his bed was in the bathtub and another was under the sink. Safety-razor blades were tossed about the tiled floor. A long rope fashioned by knotting together the drawstrings of several pairs of pajama pants hung from a hook on the door.

In his bedroom, the large window was still open and the bottle of sleeping pills was still almost full. Under the carefully manicured fingernails of Jan Masaryk's corpse, there was plaster, as if he had struggled frantically to hold on to the ledge of the window in the garret high above.

"All winter, confidence in peace has been oozing away," wrote a Chicago journalist in March 1948. "With the Czech coup, it practically vanished." Less than a decade had passed since the democracies of the West had allowed Hitler to capture Czechoslovakia. In the late 1930s, the fall of the Czech regime to totalitarianism had been the last resting point on the road to war. After Masaryk's death, many Americans believed it would serve the same function again.

That conviction was also shared by many of the top officials in American government. Among them, no one was more troubled by the creeping advance of Communism across the map of Europe than James Forrestal.

In less than three years, the spirit of the Elbe had dissolved into the specter of war. Americans had come to see terror when they looked toward the Soviet regime. Forrestal had seen it first. He viewed himself as a modern-day Paul Revere warning that the Reds were coming. Yet, so often, his cries went unheeded. Even those wise mandarins of American foreign policy who agreed that a stronger stance against the Soviets was needed believed that Communism was a mere "fig leaf" disguising a Russian expansionist tendency that was fueled by that country's fundamental insecurity, a result of its being invaded over and again. Forrestal, the secretary of the Navy, held a different view of the nature of the threat from the Communists. America was facing not simply a new great power on the globe, a nation-state seeking security and territory, but a dogmatic religion untethered from the bind of borders, a dangerous ideology whose adherents could be hiding in the corners of capitals around the world. "Nothing about Russia can be understood without understanding the implacable and unchanging direction of Lenin's religion-philosophy," he wrote to his former Wall Street boss, Clarence Dillon.

On a winter weekend in 1946, George Kennan, then a little-known diplomat in the Moscow embassy, received a routine query from the Treasury Department on the subject of Soviet attitudes toward the International Monetary Fund. Kennan was sick in bed, woozy from powerful antibacterial medications whose most common side effects were nausea and mental confusion. Like Forrestal, he was frustrated that his warnings about the Russians were being ignored. He began to dictate a reply to his secretary and eight thousand words streamed out of him. The Soviets, he informed Washington, were "a political force committed fanatically to the belief that with the US there can be no permanent modus vivendi, that it is desirable and necessary that the internal harmony of our society be disrupted, our traditional way of life be destroyed, the international authority of our state be broken, if Soviet power is to be secure."

This "Long Telegram" received praise from the State Department, but when Kennan's boss, then-ambassador to Moscow Averell Harriman, showed it to Forrestal, power and principle met. Were it not for Forrestal, Kennan's telegram would have been—much like his previous attempts—largely forgotten, and its author could well have served out his days as a brilliant but anonymous Foreign Service officer. Instead, with Forrestal's efforts, it signaled a turning point in America's approach to the Soviets.

Ignoring the aspects of its analysis with which he disagreed, Forrestal saw, in the intellectual rigor of Kennan's dispatch, a distillation of all he had been attempting in vain to convey to the country. Forrestal distributed thousands of copies of the telegram, sending them to Truman and the cabinet, members of Congress, journalists and columnists, and senior military officers around the world, including Clay in Berlin. Forrestal was so taken with Kennan's thinking that he arranged for the diplomat to be transferred to a teaching position at the National War College, a new institution created by Forrestal to foster strategic thinking on national security issues. With the backing of his new patron, Kennan exchanged the dark snows of a Moscow winter for palatial quarters that opened up onto a broad, green lawn overlooking the Potomac. "I greatly appreciated his interest in my work, and his confidence," Kennan admitted.

Forrestal began to use Kennan, still basically unknown beyond the rarefied circles of the foreign policy elite, to provide answers to troubling questions—and no matter was more troubling to Forrestal than the threat posed by the expansion of Soviet Communism around the world. He prodded Kennan to write him a paper on the ideological dimensions of the Soviet threat. Kennan balked. Pushed to do so again, Kennan produced a draft. Forrestal rejected it as not sufficiently in line with his own views. His staff had Kennan "take another crack at it." The next draft was much more to Forrestal's liking. Kennan—never much hobbled by consistency—flitted about in his analysis of the Soviets, sometimes raising alarm bells, other times decrying considerable overreaction, but this paper clearly reflected the intellectual mark of his new boss, emphasizing the Soviet Union as an ideological, quasi-religious adversary to America's Wilsonian democratic vision. As he later acknowledged, it was written in response to "what I felt to be Mr. Forrestal's needs at the time."

In July 1947, a few months after Kennan delivered the analysis to Forrestal, it was published in the journal *Foreign Affairs* as an article entitled "The Sources of Soviet Conduct." Since Kennan had been hired by George Marshall—with much encouragement from Forrestal—to work in the State Department, the article had to appear anonymously under the byline of "Mr. X." The piece was a sensation. Excerpted in *Life* magazine and *Reader's Digest,* it was seen as the clear encapsulation of the nature of a new Soviet threat to America and the world. "The main element of any United States policy toward the Soviet Union must be that of long-term, patient but firm and vigilant containment of Russian expansive tendencies," Kennan wrote. This idea of "containment" of Soviet expansion—a modern-day version of the biblical injunction, "Thus far you shall come, but no farther"—became the touchstone for a new American foreign policy.

At every turn, Forrestal, by force of his energy and intellect, was at the center of the work of shaping this new policy. On the day Marshall returned, by way of Berlin, from the Moscow conference where Clay and Dulles had fought so bitterly, Forrestal buttonholed him at a cabinet lunch. Europe was sinking into despair, Marshall believed. Hungry, cold, and divided, the continent was becoming a petri dish for Communism. Forrestal—as he always seemed to—had a ready solution that he had just happened to have been working on for weeks. "Economic leadership" was required from America. In the name of national security, "an all-out effort" was needed to restore areas destroyed by war and make them viable and vibrant again. He pressed Marshall on the point. The Russians could offer nothing but anger and misery; America could give destroyed nations a chance to rebuild. Marshall seemed interested. This was just the type of project that Kennan could be helpful with, Forrestal added. The following morning, Marshall summoned Kennan to his office and told him to come up with a way to save Europe. A little over a month later, in a speech at Harvard's commencement, Marshall announced the plan for economic recovery that would come to bear his name.

That same year, Forrestal also came up with the idea of a committee in the executive branch that would coordinate foreign and military policy. He pushed for the committee's inclusion in legislation then being considered in Congress. The idea was put into law, but with a modification. It was decided that the new National Security Council should report to President Truman and not to Jim Forrestal.

The 1947 National Security Act, however, would be remembered not for what Forrestal had proposed but for the idea he opposed: the unification of the various branches of the military under a single civilian official—a secretary of defense. Since the country's founding, the Army and Navy had been not just separate branches of the military but separate departments of the government. The secretary of war and the secretary of the Navy both sat as equals at the table of the president's cabinet. But the World War II experience of combined operations such as the amphibious landing at Normandy, and the need for a unified bureaucracy to run an organization as large as the modern military, convinced Army leaders that the direction of the armed forces should be united under a single individual and department. Naval leaders vehemently disagreed, fearing that they would not only play a secondary role to the Army but would also lose funding to the popular and exciting Air Force, which would be made its own independent military branch.

As secretary of the Navy, Forrestal backed the myopic, self-serving position of his senior officers and played a virtuoso game of congressional politics to block Truman's unification plan. He authored a compromise proposal, one that—in traditional Washington fashion—was worse than no action at all. Under Forrestal's idea, which became law in 1947, there would be a new position of secretary of defense. However, instead of running a single Department of Defense, the secretary would be head of a nebulous coordinating agency for the armed forces called the "National Military Establishment." The secretary of defense would oversee the Army, Navy, and Air Force; the Chiefs of Staff of the various branches; the Munitions Board; the Research and Development Board; and most other aspects of the military, but his actual powers over them would be minimal. He would have almost no staff to speak of, other than those detailed from the various branches to which they maintained their loyalty. There were no deputy or assistant secretaries of defense. It was a position that had been emasculated by Forrestal, designed to make it impossible for anyone who held it to succeed.

If Harry Truman had been a person of lesser character, he would have appointed Forrestal to the position of America's first secretary of defense solely out of a delicious sense for revenge. As it was, he insisted that Forrestal take the job for other reasons—his singular abilities and widespread popularity, among them—but it is hard to imagine that the irony of the offer did not cross his mind.

Forrestal's appointment in the summer of 1947 was another great achievement in a fast-rising public career. For the first time in American history, the duty to direct and organize the nation's entire armed forces was placed in the hands of one member of the president's cabinet. But it was responsibility without authority, a terrible combination. Forrestal seemed to sense this. "This office will probably be the greatest cemetery for dead cats in history," he wrote to Robert Sherwood, Roosevelt's former speechwriter, upon taking over. That same month he joked to his wife Jo's former psychiatrist that he would need the attention of "the entire psychiatric profession by the end of another year." He was a few months off.

WITH THE END of World War II, almost all of Franklin Roosevelt's top lieutenants returned to the law firms and banks from which they had decamped in the hours of their country's need. Of the officials running the major wartime cabinet departments, only Forrestal had remained in office. Forrestal was a singular figure in postwar Washington. With his fedora cocked slightly to the left, his double-breasted suits, and the flat-tened nose from his boxing days, he strode about town as if a creature out of a Damon Runyon story. The top of his brightly colored tie tugged out from his pinstriped vest as if it were a sail pulling him through the hushed halls.

In July 1946, Forrestal had arranged for the Navy to test an atomic bomb on an atoll in the Pacific called Bikini. Of course, he had to be there in person. It was already hot when the bomber pilot began his approach at 8:50 in the morning, and the sun beat down on Forrestal as he stood looking into the distance from the ship's deck eleven miles away. At exactly nine A.M., the ship's loudspeakers boomed, "Bomb away! Bomb away! Bomb away!" It was so loud that Forrestal shook. For a full minute, nothing happened—silence save for the sound of the waves lapping against the hull of a warship out at sea. Then the sky of the bright sunny day lit up a million times over. Forrestal removed his protective glasses after the initial explosion had passed to see a pillar of fire, streaked with purple and scarlet, racing toward the heavens. Forty seconds after the explosion, the blast's force reached the ship and For-restal felt its rancid warmth crawling over his skin.

Forrestal was the highest-ranking government official ever to witness an atomic explosion, and by the time Masaryk's tangled body was found on the cobblestones of Prague, he was consumed by the horror that mil-lions of Americans might soon be annihilated because of his own inabil-ity to convince others of the full danger of the Soviet threat. Everywhere Forrestal looked he saw the steady approach of the Communist menace. The same week as the coup in Czechoslovakia, Stalin invited the Finns to negotiate a pact of friendship—twisting notions of an "invitation" and a "friendship" beyond recognition. Finland's old, frail president agreed to allow Russians to base their troops on Finnish soil. Early that March, Norway's foreign minister disclosed to Washington that he had received intelligence from Moscow indicating his country was next. In Italy, the Communists were showing signs of great strength going into the April elections. In France, Communists had organized campaigns of looting and vandalism in major cities and a mammoth strike, at the end of 1947, involving 3 million workers that brought the country's economy to a virtual stop. Thirteen thousand troops had been needed in Marseilles to restore order after its mayor was pulled from his office by a Communist mob that threw him to the ground and set upon him, viciously beating and kicking him, all the while screaming "*à mort, à mort, à mort!*" In his diary, French president Vincent Auriol fretted, "We are on the edge of the abyss."

The pressure on Forrestal grew. He became obsessed with the circumstances of Masaryk's death. In the weeks and months after the coup, Forrestal would repeatedly recount to friends the manner in which the Czech's body had been discovered smashed into the stone below the open window. He was fascinated by the most minute details of the fateful plunge, repetitively returning to the conversation as if it were some puzzle he could not solve. For long periods, he would be silent and then he would bring it up again, working it over in his mind as a child runs his tongue over a loose tooth. He continued to read widely on the Communist threat. When Forrestal discovered the novel *Darkness at Noon*—Hungarian exile Arthur Koestler's story of a man imprisoned in a tiny cell by Communists as he awaits his execution—he sent copies to Supreme Court justice William O. Douglas and FBI director J. Edgar Hoover, among others. In early 1948, shortly after Omar Bradley succeeded Eisenhower as Army chief of staff, Forrestal invited him to play a round of golf at the Chevy Chase Club. "He arrived in his usual state, wound tightly as a clock spring," recalled Bradley. Forrestal rushed through nine holes in an hour and ten minutes, hardly saying a word. He lost his appetite, having his meals brought to his desk but only picking absently at the food on his plate. Jo was often away on long trips, and at night he sat alone and awake, unable to sleep; he would see the mutilated Marines on Iwo Jima, feel the heat of the atomic bomb on his face, hear the thunderous "Bomb away! Bomb away! Bomb away!"—and he would shake once again.

FORRESTAL HAD EMERGED from World War II with the conviction that there was only one way to prevent another war: military strength. "I pray to God that we have learned the lesson that peace without power is an empty dream, that it is an invitation for evil men to shake the very foundations of society," he said on CBS radio the day Japan surrendered. "Now more than ever before we must make it our business to see that the means to wage war be kept in the hands of those who hate war." Others in Washington kept their desks crammed with the memorabilia and mementos of power and happiness: doodads and curios that carried special meaning and sentimental value, dull aphorisms ("The Buck Stops Here!") picked to present just the right impression to an impressed visitor, the talismans of connection and contact with history and the renowned. Forrestal had none of this, not even a framed photo of a stiff handshake with the president or of his arm thrown awkwardly around his wife and kids. His office was an expanse of blankness save for a framed quote resting above his desk: "We will never have universal peace until the strongest army and the strongest navy are in the hands of the most powerful nation."

But under Forrestal's watch as secretary of the Navy and then secretary of defense, the world's most powerful nation had let peace become endangered by shuttering its once powerful military force. Within two years of victory in World War II, defense spending was less than a sixth of what it had been during the war. The share of the American economy devoted to the military plummeted by more than 90 percent. Army personnel went from 8.27 million to just 530,000 by 1948. Like a beachside ice-cream shop being boarded up when the summer season ends, the American military closed for business.

The American army of occupation in Germany was just a sliver of the great military force that had invaded the Third Reich. Curtis LeMay arrived there in 1947 to take charge of the United States Air Force in Europe having achieved great fame as a bomber in World War II. Because of his pioneering efforts in the air attack on Germany, he had shot up through the ranks, moving from a one-star to the Army's youngest two-star general in just four months in 1944. At a wartime news conference at the Pentagon, LeMay was introduced to reporters as the "Number One Menace" of America's enemies. But even in a country geared for all-out war, his firebombing campaigns on Axis cities were so ferocious that they proved controversial. On the day the war ended, the *New York Times* would refer to his "wholesale slaughter of civilians." LeMay was unapologetic. "There are no innocent civilians," he barked. "So it doesn't bother me so much to be killing innocent bystanders."

When victory in World War II was declared, LeMay was so famous that the governor of Ohio offered to appoint him to a vacant seat in the United States Senate. LeMay turned him down. There was more important work to do. The "next war," he said, "will be launched in and from the air" and it will make Pearl Harbor look "like a quiet day in the country." Unless Americans were prepared, the result would be "our cities leveled, our homes destroyed, our people killed in massive attacks from the air."

Instead of preparing to fight, however, LeMay found himself with little to do in Germany, the nation whose cities he had bombarded. He worked only a few hours a day and would spend long stretches hunting boar in the German wilderness. He lived in a 102-room mansion that had once belonged to a German industrialist whose daughter had married Hitler's foreign minister. With the house, he inherited thirty-eight servants. Economizing, he decided he could get by with only eighteen. When he did work, it was largely on the dispiriting task of disposing of what was left of a once mighty Air Force. "No one was getting anything much done, except some administrative work of getting the Air Force disbanded, closing up bases, discharging people, trying to take care of the vast amount of property that was scattered around all over the world, getting it properly disposed of, and things of that sort," he summed up later. At the end of the war, the Air Force had 64,000 aircraft. In the months that followed, thirty to forty planes a day would be parked on a field, filled with explosives, and blown up. It was less expensive to demolish the planes than to pack them up for return to an American airplane graveyard or to guard them while they sat unused. To mark the day Eisenhower, Zhukov, and Clay had celebrated their friendship arm in arm, 1,700 airplanes had flown over Frankfurt. When LeMay arrived in Germany, the Air Force had fewer planes than this in its entire worldwide fleet. By early 1948, the American Air Force in Europe amounted to 275 airplanes. "At a cursory glance," he observed, it looked like they "would be stupid to get mixed up in anything bigger than a catfight at a pet show."

The same month that the Communists captured power in Prague, the Munitions Board reported that the Army was so lacking in rudimentary parts and equipment that it could provide for only half its divisions over any time in the next eighteen months. It was not just a shortage of manpower and matériel, it was that the military—which had bought into what LeMay called "the God-bless-our-buddy-buddy-Russians-we-sure-can-trust-them-forever-and-ever philosophy which flowered back in the Roosevelt Administration"—had not given any real thought to how to fight a new war.

At the end of 1947, a five-member commission of prominent businessmen established by Truman to investigate America's preparedness in the area of airpower tried to arrange a meeting with the Chiefs of Staff to review the nation's war plans. They were repeatedly rebuffed and put off. Finally, they were able to schedule a briefing with the great military leaders of World War II: Admiral Chester Nimitz, Admiral William Leahy, General Hoyt Vandenberg, and General Eisenhower. When the commission members arrived, they were handed a thick strategy document composed of reams of unintelligible jargon. The military men began to explain its content. The presentation was contradictory and meandering, and the longer it went on, the more the commission members were confused. They began to ask questions, trying to understand the basics of the plan, and the chiefs stumbled about in their answers. "I'm sorry, I guess my mind is worse than I thought it was," said Eisenhower, leafing through the pages of the document. The commission members were too awestruck by the imposing military leaders to address them in tones that were anything less than respectful, even fawning, but they grew perplexed the more their queries were met with evasions. They wondered whether they were simply out of their depth in the presence of such wartime giants. Their uncertainty was plain on their faces. Finally, Eisenhower dropped the ruse. Turning to his colleagues, he said, his voice now strong instead of befuddled, "Gentlemen, these five civilian gentlemen who are here are just patriotic American citizens trying to do something they've been asked to do by the president. I think we owe it to them to tell them that there is no war plan."

When Bradley took over as Army chief a few months later, he had the same realization. "Ike had left me an administrative rather than a military force," he wrote. "Actually, the Army of 1948 could not fight its way out of a paper bag."

One year after the death of Franklin Roosevelt, only two of his cabinet members remained in office: James Forrestal and Henry Wallace. They were political rivals—the two most obvious options for the Democratic Party's future once Harry Truman, the accidental president, was out of the way. As early as October 1945, the *New York Times* wrote that since, at the next Democratic convention, labor unions and liberals were expected to attempt to put Wallace back on the ticket, those more conservative elements that opposed him had begun "to look for an alternative. More and more often the name of Mr. Forrestal is heard."

Forrestal and Wallace had come to be seen as the paired poles for progressives. In a moment when old truths were being jumbled, in a capital jammed with pragmatists shifting in the wind and responding to events as they came, both men had a deeply held ideological vision of how to prevent World War III. Forrestal was convinced that the Soviets were on the march, knocking down governments in Eastern Europe and heading steadily west toward Germany and Italy and France until all of Europe would be subjugated as a base for their conquest of the world. America needed to show strength—military and otherwise—to convince the Russians to halt their advance before it was too late. Wallace, in contrast, was just as sure that Franklin Roosevelt had been right, that the Soviets could be America's allies. To preserve the peace, the United States should drop the notion of "establishing democracy in Eastern

Europe, where democracy by and large has never existed," wrote Wallace in a July 1946 letter to Truman, ridiculing the idea that American-style democracy could exist in a place where Western values were so foreign. Filled with fervor and certitude when everyone else was confused, Forrestal's and Wallace's diametrically opposed views would face off in a battle whose outcome would define America's role in the world for years to come.

From the very first, Wallace's presence as secretary of commerce in Truman's cabinet had been awkward. Truman had campaigned to replace Wallace on the Democratic ticket—first supporting Byrnes, and then allowing his own name to be placed in nomination. Wallace had fought back hard at the convention, coming within 100 votes of retaining his place alongside Roosevelt. Those 100 votes would have made him, instead of Harry Truman, president in 1945.

But though Truman may have usurped the Oval Office, many of the most liberal Democrats believed that Wallace was Franklin Roosevelt's true heir. "How I wish you were at the helm," wrote Minneapolis mayoral candidate Hubert Humphrey to Wallace after Roosevelt's death. Despite a flurry of good feelings toward Truman when he took over the presidency and soon thereafter presided over victory, by the summer of 1946 many Americans had decided that he simply could not fill the job. Presidents were supposed to be big men who inspired reverence and brought about great achievements. This had been true of Roosevelt. He would cast a shadow across the rest of the century—and he positively eclipsed his successor. Roosevelt had spoken to a trembling nation in sonorous tones; Truman's high-pitched staccato was more strained than stentorian. It was, in the phrase of one British politician, "like a village fiddler after Paganini." Truman had managed to alienate labor unions by his methods of combating the wave of postwar strikes. He had angered Southern Democrats with his forward-leaning stance on civil rights. He had disappointed urban liberals by lacking Roosevelt's urbane style. By August 1946, a Gallup poll showed Democrats preferred former vice president Henry Wallace to sitting president Harry Truman as their party's 1948 nominee.

As Truman's administration was coming closer to embracing Forrestal's view of the Soviets, Wallace was feeling increasingly out of place. On September 10, 1946, Wallace visited Truman to let him know about a speech he was planning to give two days later at a Madison Square Garden rally to kick off the fall campaign to defeat New York governor Thomas Dewey. Wallace went through the speech page by page, and Truman nodded along—though probably he was not listening. When the press got advance copies of the speech, they asked Truman at a press conference whether he endorsed the remarks and whether they were a break with the administration's policies toward the Soviet Union. The questions should have been clues for Truman that something was amiss, but, jovial and confident, he did not pick them up. "I approved the whole speech," he assured the reporters.

In fact, the speech was an attack on Truman's opposition to the Soviet Union's expansionist moves. America had "no more business in the political affairs of Eastern Europe than Russia has in the political affairs of Latin America, Western Europe, and the United States," Wallace said in his speech. "Whether we like it or not," he continued, "the Russians will try to socialize their sphere of influence just as we try to democratize our sphere of influence." The firestorm was immediate, within the administration and without. At first, Truman tried to wriggle out of trouble with the clumsy lie that he had only intended to approve of Wallace's right to give the speech, not the words themselves. No one was satisfied. Then he hoped Wallace would decide on his own to resign, but in a long conversation in the Oval Office, Wallace seemed unfazed. "Henry is the most peculiar fellow I ever came in contact with," Truman wrote to his mother on September 19. "He is a pacifist one hundred percent," he wrote in his diary that same day. "The Reds, phonies, and the 'parlor pinks' seem to be banded together and are becoming a national danger. I am afraid they are a sabotage front for Uncle Joe Stalin. They can see no wrong in Russia's four and one half million armed forces, in Russia's loot of Poland, Austria, Hungary, Rumania, Manchuria. They can see no wrong in Russia's living off the occupied countries to support the military occupation" of Germany. Finally, eight days after the speech, as public and private pressure mounted, Truman fired Wallace. There were low whistles and audible gasps from reporters when he announced his decision. After the correspondents had left the room, Truman sank into his chair and turned to his press secretary: "Well, the die is cast."

The next day, Truman wrote again to his mother, reveling in opposition from liberals: "Now he's out and the crackpots are having conniption fits. I'm glad they are. It convinces me I'm right." Truman was becoming lonely in that conviction. The chaos surrounding the Wallace firing constituted "the most astounding and disturbing series of errors to come out of the White House in a generation," wrote the *New York Times*' James Reston. When Truman took office in the spring of 1945, 87 percent of Americans approved of his job in a Gallup poll, and only 3 percent disapproved. A year later, in the spring of 1946, the number had declined to a still respectable 50 percent approval. In the wake of the Wallace debacle, public perceptions of Truman's presidency plummeted. By the first week of October 1946, a month before the midterm elections, Truman had a 32 percent approval rating in the Gallup poll. Republicans pounced on the Democrats' disarray. National chairman B. Carroll Reece framed the campaign as a "fight basically between Communism and Republicanism"; the Democratic Party's heart had been captured by "a radical group devoted to Sovietizing the United States." Republican campaign pamphlets showed the Democratic donkey wearing a turban decorated with a hammer and sickle. The Republicans' leader in the Senate, Robert Taft, said that in the wake of the Wallace and Truman fight, the Democratic Party was "divided between Communism and Americanism." That November, Democrats lost 55 seats in the House and 12 in the Senate, giving Republicans control of Congress for the first time in fourteen years.

ALL THROUGH 1947, the gulf between Truman's and Wallace's positions grew. In March of that year, Truman told Congress in a special address that "at the present moment in world history nearly every nation must choose between alternative ways of life"—that of democracy and freedom and that of "terror and oppression." He asked for military and economic aid for Greece and Turkey to prevent their falling to the Communists. Henceforth, it would be the "policy of the United States to support free peoples who are resisting attempted subjugation by armed minorities or by outside pressures."

Wallace responded in a nationally broadcast radio address the following day, attacking this new Truman Doctrine for dividing the globe in half and interfering in the domestic affairs of sovereign countries. "America will become the most hated nation in the world," he declared. That same day, Truman wrote to his daughter that Wallace, along with "the actors and artists in immoral Greenwich Village," were members of the "American Crackpot Association."

Yet the ranks of those attracted to Wallace grew in the wake of Truman's address. In forging a bipartisan foreign policy with the Republican Congress, Wallace charged, Truman had abandoned the Democratic Party's deepest principles and failed to give Americans a clear choice. Democrats disgusted with what they saw as a militaristic attitude toward America's Soviet allies were drawn to Wallace's banner. In his new role as editor of the *New Republic,* a political magazine with a storied past and ambiguous political leanings, Wallace set out on a cross-country speaking tour to address his followers. He spoke in large auditoriums and sports stadiums. The rallies required an admission fee that averaged $1.50 (equivalent to nearly $15 a ticket sixty years later), but in May of 1947 alone, 100,000 Americans paid that rather steep price to see Wallace in person. In the Windy City, 22,000 packed into Chicago Stadium—the site of the 1944 convention where Wallace had been ejected from the vice presidency. In Berkeley, 10,000 showed up to scream their approval for him. In Los Angeles, Katharine Hepburn warmed up a crowd of 30,000 and, as Wallace declared that "an ugly fear is spread across America—the fear of Communism," Charlie Chaplin dropped a hefty donation into the passed collection plate.

No one had ever seen anything like the rush of Americans to Henry

Wallace's rallies in the spring of 1947. The challenge was taken with the utmost seriousness by the White House. In early April, a cabinet meeting discussed at length the question of how to deal with Wallace, especially his upcoming trip to England, where he planned to continue his assault on the Truman administration's attitude toward the Russians. As usual, Forrestal was in the forefront of the attack on Wallace and his views. The administration should deny Wallace a passport so that he was prevented from leaving the country, he argued. Truman thought this was going too far; refusing to allow a former vice president and cabinet member his right to travel abroad would subject them to severe criticism. Forrestal was unbowed. He would rather take the public censure, he replied, than allow Wallace's attacks on American policy to go on unabated.

By the end of 1947, no one was surprised when Wallace announced his candidacy for president in the following year's election as a third-party candidate with what would come to be called the Progressive Party. Nor was anyone surprised by the driving issue of his campaign. That fall, newspaper columnist Walter Lippmann had published a book whose title was now on everyone's lips, *The Cold War.*

His candidacy, Wallace said, would give liberals a real choice, so that they would no longer have to "vote for the lesser of two evils." He knew he could not win, but all the polls showed that by running he would split the Democratic Party vote and deny a victory to Truman. There was an element of revenge in his campaign, but he claimed that what drove him was a desire to send the Democrats a message. "The bigger the peace vote in 1948," he said in his announcement address, "the more definitely the world will know that the United States is not behind the bipartisan reactionary war policy which is dividing the world into two armed camps and making inevitable the day when American soldiers will be lying in their Arctic suits in the Russian snow."

Democrats had abandoned the Roosevelt policy for Forrestal's anti-Communist fervor, and from his campaign's beginning, Wallace called on Truman to fire "his Wall Street–military appointees," directing his attack on Forrestal with greater vehemence than at Truman, as if the defense secretary were a sinister shadow pulling the strings of the unsophisticated rube in the White House. Though it would be Truman's name on the ballot, Wallace was largely running against Forrestal's policies.

ON FEBRUARY 24, the day before democracy fell in Czechoslovakia, Democratic senator Glen Taylor of Idaho announced he would become Wallace's vice presidential running mate. Taylor had been a traveling minstrel in vaudeville acts who, happening upon a political speech in Idaho, had decided he could do a better job entertaining the masses, and thereby winning votes, than the hapless politician on stage. Known as "The Crooning Cowboy," Taylor had won election to the Senate on his fourth try by hooking his banjo to a sound truck and strumming serenades such as "Oh, give me a home by the Capitol dome" for farmhands on the fringes of Idaho's potato fields. He had come to Washington as a ready-made character for the press with a gap-toothed smile and a toupee he had fashioned himself with felt and part of an aluminum pie tin.

Taylor quickly became a spokesman for the most liberal ideas. Upon arriving in the Senate in 1945, he introduced a resolution calling for the establishment of a "World Republic." It did not pass. In 1947, he had set off across the country by horse to "dramatize the issue of peace." He got as far as Texas when he was called back for a special session of Congress, but he still rode up the steps of the Capitol on his horse, wearing a checkered shirt and waving his Stetson. In his announcement speech as Wallace's running mate, he excoriated Truman for allowing his party to fall into the hands of militarists like Forrestal. "I didn't leave the Democratic Party," he proclaimed, "the Democratic Party left me."

At the time Wallace announced his candidacy, Truman had climbed back from the trough of low poll numbers in the fall of 1946 to achieve a degree of popularity. Throughout 1947, his approval ratings in the Gallup poll had hovered near 60 percent. Yet with Wallace in the race, Democrats were divided. When asked in a Gallup poll to name who they wanted as president, 17 percent said Harry Truman. Wallace was not far behind at 10 percent. The same week that Wallace announced his candidacy, *Look* magazine asked fifty-seven top Washington political journalists who they thought would win the White House. Most named Dewey; Truman was the fourth pick behind Eisenhower and Taft. That Truman was given so little chance of victory in the coming election was only partly due to the assumption that Americans were tired of sixteen years of Democratic rule or the embarrassments and errors that continued to spring from Truman's administration or because the Republicans had won such a titanic victory in 1946. Even with all this, Truman might have had an outside possibility at winning another term. It was because Democrats were split, because two of Franklin Roosevelt's vice presidents were competing for the mantle of his legacy, and because Wallace was attracting so many liberals to his cause (he was winning double-digit support in crucial states such as California) that the prognosticators were convinced that Harry Truman did not stand a chance in 1948.

But it was not only the Democrats who began 1948 cleaved by the issue of how to handle the new Soviet threat. That same February, on the day before the Czech coup began in earnest, Dewey had delivered his first campaign address of the year. The young, vigorous, moderate governor of New York had gained enough national attention as the crusading prosecutor who had sent mobster Lucky Luciano and the corrupt former head of the New York Stock Exchange to jail to have been a serious candidate for the presidency in 1940 at age thirty-eight. His career had continued to ascend. He was elected governor of New York at age forty, shocked the world as the Republican nominee for president at age forty-two by holding Roosevelt to 53 percent of the vote in the midst of World War II, and then was reelected as governor in 1946 by the largest margin in Empire State history. In office, he had banned racial discrimination in hiring and doubled state education funding while cutting taxes. As the Republicans' front-runner for president, he promised a more fiscally responsible version of the New Deal. He began his campaign, however, with a frontal assault on Truman policies that had advanced the "Soviet ambition to rule the world" and "resulted in surrendering two hundred million people in Middle Europe into the clutches of Soviet Russia."

Most Republicans knew their best bet of a presidential victory for the first time in twenty years lay with the moderate Dewey. But the heart of their most passionate adherents was with Robert Taft—so beloved by his party's faithful followers that his nickname was "Mr. Republican"— and that February he too was launching his campaign with a national speaking tour. Taft promised Americans that their days of being enmeshed with the problems of Europe could come to an end. "We should not be actuated by purely altruistic desire to improve the condition of a lot of other people who have failed for centuries to do the job for themselves," he told the Inland Press Association in Chicago on February 10.

Both Taft and Wallace, in different ways, promised an America at peace that would not challenge the Soviet tide. With the news from Europe so frightening, it was an appealing notion. Dewey concentrated his attacks on the Democrats' lack of competence. Only Truman had remained quiet about how his answer to the Russian threat would figure into the upcoming campaign. But he could not do so for long. "Before an election," Taft declared to the Detroit Economic Club that February, "it is the duty of both parties to present their foreign policies to the people and say what they will do if they are entrusted with the conduct of the government." The time to do so had now come, he said. "The campaign, gentlemen, is on."

Harry Truman was on vacation in the Florida Keys when the Communists seized control in Prague. For days, as Americans were transfixed by the news, he had made no comment on the coup. Finally, on March 1, 1948, before a morning of sunning himself on the beach and an afternoon of deep-sea fishing, Truman held a quick news confer-

ence. He was jaunty, bantering with the reporters as if the cares of the
world had been blown away by the soft ocean breeze. "Mr. President,
Czechoslovakia and perhaps Finland seem to be going down the drain
in the classic style," yelled one correspondent. Truman begged off every
chance to comment on the Czech crisis, but hinted he might have something to say soon. Instead, he defended himself from criticism of his
untimely vacation. "I have been in touch with the State Department
every day since we have been away," he protested. "We have direct wires
that go there, and I get a pouch nearly every day, and sign just as many
documents and make just as many decisions as if I were sitting at the
desk in the Executive Office."

Inevitably, in light of the broadsides from Wallace, Dewey, and Taft,
he was asked about his own candidacy in 1948. "I am so darned busy
with foreign affairs and domestic affairs and other situations that have
developed that I haven't had any time to think about any presidential
campaign," he replied and then joined in with the newsmen in the ensu-
ing laughter.

THE TRUTH WAS that Truman's breezy demeanor masked a raging
squall. Two days after his press conference, he sat down to write a long
letter to his daughter, Margaret, that was very much unlike the quick
missives he usually dashed off. In page after page, he poured out his
anger about Russian actions in Germany and Eastern Europe and his
feeling of dismay about attacks from the Republicans and from Wallace.
He traced his stewardship of relations with the Soviets up to that
moment. "Now we are faced with exactly the same situation with which
Britain and France were faced in 1938–9 with Hitler. A totalitarian state
is no different whether you call it Nazi, Fascist, Communist or Franco
Spain. Things look black," he wrote.

> *A decision will have to be made. I am going to make it. I am sorry to*
> *have bored you with this. But you've studied foreign affairs to some*
> *extent and I just wanted you to know your Dad as President asked*
> *for no territory, no reparations, no slave laborers—only peace in the*

world. We may have to fight for it. The oligarchy in Russia is no different from the Czars, Louis XIV, Napoleon, Charles I and Cromwell. It is a Frankenstein dictatorship worse than any of the others. Hitler included.

I hope it will end in peace. Be a nice girl and don't worry about your dad's worries—but you'll hear all sorts of lies about the things I have told you—these are the facts.

I went to Potsdam with the kindliest feelings toward Russia—in a year and a half they cured me of it.

Lots of love,
Dad

With the fall of Czechoslovakia, the enormous expanse of land from the Elbe River east across Europe and Northern Asia to the shores of Alaska was now controlled by the Communists, ruled ultimately from the Kremlin. In all that vast area there was only one tiny speck of land that remained free of Communist domination: the divvied city of Berlin.

France and Italy were thought to be endangered, but it was Berlin where the Soviets were assumed to be turning next, and it was there that the war that so many anticipated was expected to come. The manner of the Russians' move was a mystery—perhaps the Red Army would move into the western sectors, overwhelming America's and Britain's tiny garrisons; perhaps the Communists would foment a coup that would topple the democratically elected city government—but whatever the method, Berlin was in danger. And unlike in the countries of Eastern Europe, a Soviet move there would mean direct conflict with the United States. How to respond was the decision weighing on Truman's mind. As he pointed out to his daughter, it was he who would have to make it.

IN BERLIN, FROM Lucius Clay's perspective in early March as he shipped home his and Marjorie's clothes and crated their furniture, the decision was fairly straightforward. Like Truman, he had come to see the situation facing America as similar to that confronting Britain and

France in the 1930s—and he had decided that the United States was in danger of repeating the mistake of appeasement. In his iron-cased engineer's mind, the situation came down to cold numbers. American forces had not simply been demobilized, they had been demolished. At the beginning of 1948, the United States, Britain, and France had a combined total of 6,500 soldiers in Berlin. The Russians had a force of 400,000 in and around the city. America had 60,000 soldiers in Europe as a whole, and as commander of those troops, Clay knew that all but 10,000 of them were administrative, support, or military government personnel in no way ready to do battle. The Soviets had 2.5 million soldiers in Germany and in the nearby states of Eastern Europe.

The numbers were so overwhelming to Clay in those first months of the year that they made military considerations irrelevant. A few days after being fired, he sent a cable to the Pentagon that made his position clear: "If USSR has decided it will fight to drive us from Berlin, then we will be driven from Berlin. If we have decided that we will not be driven from Berlin except by force, then we will remain in Berlin regardless of appeasement on the one hand or annoyances on the other. The reality of our position in Berlin depends upon our determination to stay in Berlin unless we are driven out by acts of war."

Once, the notion of war with the Soviets would have been inconceivable to Clay. By early 1948, this was no longer so. In Berlin, the kidnappings continued. Americans who crossed over legally into the Soviet zone were being arrested on various pretexts, forced to scrub the floors and walls of Soviet jails, and then released hours later. Non-Communist newspapers and magazines were banned in the Soviet sector of Berlin and burned in the Soviet zone of Germany. Beginning in January, the Soviets had begun to take picayune steps to harass and interfere with the daily traffic of food and supplies into Berlin. The Soviets would occasionally and unpredictably make elaborate inspections of cargo. Roads would suddenly be closed for repair and vehicles would be sent on long detours through the German countryside. Sometimes a set of official documents would be judged insufficient to pass through the Soviet zone and a truck would be sent back into the western part of Germany. The next day, the same documents would be acceptable.

With tension rising in Berlin and the nearby government in Prague tumbling in a coup, Clay was apprehensive. But then Sokolovsky—who had usually followed up his anti-Western tirades in Allied Control Council meetings with signs of friendship—began to merely give a curt nod in the direction of the other military governors. At this point, Clay became terrified. "Somehow I felt instinctively that a definite change in the attitude of the Russians in Berlin had occurred and that something was about to happen."

For months, Clay had maintained a secret, coded correspondence with George Marshall about the situation in Europe under the guise of writing about the condition of "Lieutenant Peters' health." In late February, Clay decided a clearer statement on what was happening in Germany was needed. In the first couple days of March, he told Lieutenant Steven Chamberlain, the director of Army Intelligence, in Berlin on an inspection mission, that he had a sense that war was becoming more likely. Chamberlain said if this was the case he should notify Washington. Clay demurred. He had no real evidence to pass along that would justify a formal report, merely a gut feeling, so he asked that Chamberlain simply convey Clay's concerns. Chamberlain pressed him again for a written cable that he could share with others in the Pentagon, but Clay was reluctant.

By the morning of Friday, March 5, Chamberlain had returned home. Sitting in his Berlin office, Clay recounted the conversation to his own chief intelligence officer, Major General Robert Walsh. Walsh, who, like Frank Howley, had been in agony during the long months that Clay continually acquiesced to Soviet demands, leapt at his commander's change of heart. "Lucius, if you feel there's a good chance of war, we had better get the word to Washington," he said as he began to rummage about Clay's spartan office looking for some paper. Clay was hesitant, unsure whether his suspicions justified a statement. Walsh insisted that Clay could not keep such a worry to himself. So Clay began to dictate, with Walsh scribbling along on a long yellow pad of paper. When he was done with the draft, Clay edited it, reordering some sentences. He checked with Howley to confirm a similar shift in attitudes in the Kommandatura. At 3:15 in the afternoon, the cable was sent by double-encrypted code to the Pentagon.

It was morning in Washington as the cable clacked through:

FROM CLAY EYES ONLY TO CHAMBERLAIN

FOR MANY MONTHS, BASED ON LOGICAL ANALYSIS, I HAVE FELT AND HELD THAT WAR WAS UNLIKELY FOR AT LEAST TEN YEARS. WITHIN THE LAST FEW WEEKS, I HAVE FELT A SUBTLE CHANGE IN SOVIET ATTITUDE WHICH I CANNOT DEFINE BUT WHICH NOW GIVES ME A FEELING THAT IT MAY COME WITH DRAMATIC SUDDENNESS. I CANNOT SUPPORT THIS CHANGE IN MY OWN THINKING WITH ANY DATA OR OUTWARD EVIDENCE IN RELATIONSHIPS OTHER THAN TO DESCRIBE IT AS A FEELING OF A NEW TENSENESS IN EVERY SOVIET INDIVIDUAL WITH WHOM WE HAVE OFFICIAL RELATIONS. I AM UNABLE TO SUBMIT ANY OFFICIAL REPORT IN THE ABSENCE OF SUPPORTING DATA BUT MY FEELING IS REAL. YOU MAY ADVISE THE CHIEF OF STAFF OF THIS FOR WHATEVER IT MAY BE WORTH IF YOU FEEL IT ADVISABLE.

Chamberlain was handed the cable and immediately recognized its importance. He practically ran from his office down the halls of the Pentagon and broke into a meeting that Omar Bradley was holding to show the chief of staff the warning. Bradley read over the cable and his eyes widened. Clay's alarm "lifted me right out of my chair," he would recall. Bradley told Chamberlain to show the cable to Forrestal and Army secretary Kenneth Royall—and no one else. A few hours later, Bradley and Forrestal met to discuss Clay's warning. That evening, Royall hosted a buffet dinner for Forrestal, the other service secretaries, and the members of the Atomic Energy Commission. Those who were not privy to the cable were somewhat taken aback when Royall opened the evening's conversation by wondering aloud how long it would take to move atomic bombs into place for use in Europe.

ON SATURDAY, MARCH 6, the day following Clay's cable, Marshall informed Truman that the situation in Europe was now a "world keg of dynamite." Truman scribbled his thoughts in the margin of Marshall's memo: "Will Russia move first? Who pulls the trigger? Then where do we go?" He was not wondering whether there would be war, but how it would come—and what it would mean.

Truman was in a dark mood that weekend. America was on the brink of war while, on Capitol Hill, the Marshall Plan—his last, great hope for preventing a conflict—was being held up and pared back. The first years after the end of World War II had seen the triumph of an explicitly nonpartisan foreign policy forged by members of Congress like Republican senator Arthur Vandenberg and the Truman administration. But as the presidential election approached, the spirit of cooperation broke down. And as Americans grew scared, the country grew divided.

George Marshall had entered into the job of secretary of state as the most respected living American. Dubbed "organizer of victory" by Winston Churchill for guiding the American army during the war, Marshall was to have led the invasion force across the English Channel before Roosevelt decided he was too valuable to be given a command. "I feel I could not sleep at night with you out of the country," he told the magisterial general. Marshall was silver-haired, with a low rumble of a voice. His only known vice was a weakness for maple sugar candy. When they met for the first time, Roosevelt had called him "George" and slapped him on the back. The response was withering and he was never again referred to as anything but "General Marshall" in the Oval Office. When Truman nominated him as secretary of state in 1947, Congress did not even bother to hold hearings on his nomination. It took less than an hour for his appointment to pass through the Senate Foreign Relations Committee and onto the Senate floor, where it was approved unanimously.

But a year later, the plan that bore his name was sinking. Seven months passed before hearings were even scheduled, and both the plan and its author were under fire from the most fervid and vocal on both the left and the right of American politics. That March, Wallace called on Truman to fire Marshall—as did Harold Knutson, the Republican chairman of the House Ways and Means Committee. Testifying before the House Foreign Affairs Committee on the same day Taylor became his running mate, Wallace declared that what he referred to as the "Martial Plan" was "a blueprint for war." Wallace was no isolationist; he thought it vital that Europe get aid to rebuild. But he believed that rather than exercising power unilaterally, America should work in concert with other countries and through the United Nations. Taft opposed the Marshall Plan from the right for his own reasons. To him and many other Republicans, it was a "European TVA"—a global version of the New Deal—welfare payments to foreign nations. His ally, John Taber, the Republican chairman of the House Appropriations Committee, charged that the plan to rebuild Europe was nothing more than "a world-wide relief program" created in "a series of after-dinner conversations in which Administration economists let their imaginations run wild." The very day that Clay sounded his alarm, Taft was one of a half-dozen prominent Republicans who threw up legislative roadblocks to the Marshall Plan's passage and tried to dramatically scale back its scope in order to fund new tax cuts.

The usually taciturn, understated Marshall struck back. The vote of Congress on the European Recovery Program would be "the greatest decision in our history." If America was "unable or unwilling effectively to assist in the reconstruction of Western Europe, we must accept the consequences of its collapse into the dictatorship of police states," he declared. "There is no doubt in my mind that the whole world hangs in the balance." But even this stern warning from Marshall could not move the politicians. Something more would be required, and with Clay's cable, Forrestal now believed he held the answer in his hands.

THE SAME WEEKEND Truman was jotting his worries onto Marshall's solemn memo, Forrestal was engaging in a classic game of Washington subterfuge. Truman had proposed rebuilding military manpower, but the Senate Armed Services Committee had refused to authorize the plans. Quietly, Forrestal shared the contents of Clay's cable with the committee members. On Monday, March 8, Forrestal testified before the senators and found their attitude had changed significantly. They voted unanimously to begin hearings on the Truman proposals.

Forrestal was not done yet. Mysteriously, magically, the warning fell into the hands of prominent members of the press. By Wednesday, March 10, reporters were asking Forrestal about rumors of "a certain Clay letter to you." Forrestal would not confirm such a letter's existence. But by then, Clay's words seemed almost moderate. That morning, Jan Masaryk's body had been found crumpled on the cobblestones of Prague. At a press conference a few hours after the news hit Washington, Forrestal made an announcement: He was summoning the Joint Chiefs of Staff to an emergency meeting in Key West the next day to hammer out a common plan for military action.

For the next five days, America's highest-ranking military officials met in secret to try to forge a unified response to the Soviet aggression they thought might be soon approaching. "Recent developments in world situation," Bradley cabled to Clay and MacArthur from Key West on March 12, "make it advisable . . . to survey your current emergency plans and insure that such implementing instructions as might be required to expedite placing these plans into effect are prepared." They should be ready for the outbreak of war at any moment.

They were not the only ones who were girding for attack. In his diary entry that same day, Forrestal made an offhand notation: "Bevin suggests a meeting in Washington between British and American representatives next week." There was little to indicate that from this meeting would come the greatest shift in American foreign policy in the nation's history.

IF ONE PICTURES the caricature of a haughty, dapper British diplomat, Foreign Secretary Ernest Bevin was its precise opposite. He had dropped out of school at age eleven and found jobs washing dishes, conducting a streetcar, and driving a horse-drawn delivery wagon. By the time he reached his thirties he was an active union organizer, and he eventually became one of the founders of the Transport and General Workers' Union—Britain's largest labor organization. In 1940, Churchill appointed Bevin minister of labor and national service in his war cabinet. When the Labour Party defeated Churchill's Conservatives in the last days of the war, he had become Britain's chief diplomat.

Weighing in at 250 pounds, Bevin smoked, drank, and ate prodigiously. He suffered from all manner of ailments. A doctor performing an examination on him in 1943 announced that he had, after a thorough search, been unable to find a solitary sound organ in the man's body. Moreover, he was singularly unrefined. Instead of the elegant tones of Eton, Oxford, and Cambridge, which the world had come to expect from a British foreign secretary, Bevin "never bothered about the difference between the singular and the plural," said Prime Minister Clement Attlee. "Aitches were of no consequence."

"He murdered the King's English," Clay would recall. He did about the same for His Majesty's decorum. While the foreign ministers were meeting in London in 1947 to consider their next steps in Germany, a formal reception was held in their honor at Buckingham Palace. Clay and General Robertson were there, talking to each other off to the side, when Bevin spotted them, grabbed each by the arm, and pulled them over toward King George VI. Lifting his head in His Highness's direction as if he were hailing a taxi in front of Paddington Station, Bevin said, "King, 'ere are a couple o' my boys I want you to meet." The sovereign was delighted.

Yet, though coarse and without formal education, Bevin would become the most successful British foreign secretary of the twentieth century. He was an instinctive Wilsonian in his foreign policy, summing up his vision for the world as being "able to take a ticket at Victoria Station and go anywhere I damn please." Bevin became an implacable opponent of Communists while battling their infiltration of British labor unions. He took special joy in fencing with Vyacheslav Molotov, the sniffy, stuffy Soviet foreign minister who had presided over Stalin's murderous purges in the 1930s and then signed the nonaggression pact with Hitler that unleashed World War II. Bevin would routinely address the Russian as "Mowlotov," and each time Molotov would stiffen and flush, and, in a proper tone, correct Bevin's pronunciation. "'At's right: Mowlotov," Bevin would repeat cheerfully.

It was Bevin who had, before anyone else in Europe, seen the importance of the Marshall Plan and organized a unified continental response to it. Now, with Soviet Communism toppling governments one by one, Bevin was plotting yet again. By the end of 1947, he had become convinced that without a military alliance with the United States that committed the Americans to defend the democratic nations of Europe, the Soviets would soon overrun the continent.

In late January 1948, Bevin had approached the State Department, asking that the United States "consider with Great Britain a general commitment to go to war with an aggressor." Bob Lovett, Forrestal's roommate in those golden summers on Long Island long ago and now George Marshall's deputy, said such a move was politically impossible. A peacetime alliance with Europe would undermine the most sacred and basic tenets of America's historic foreign policy. The Truman administration was proving unable to get even the economic assistance of the Marshall Plan through an isolationist Congress. "If it became known in Congress that, in addition to the economic commitments involved in the European Recovery Program, the United States is being asked to assume new and extensive military and political commitments, it might well adversely affect the prospects for approval" of the Marshall Plan, Lovett replied to Bevin. Instead, Lovett suggested, if there was "an arrangement under which various European countries are prepared to act in concert to defend themselves," the United States would "carefully consider the part it might appropriately play in support of such a Western Union." Lovett was playing for time. The Europeans would have to move first.

In late February, talks began in Brussels between Britain, France, Belgium, the Netherlands, and Luxembourg regarding the creation of a military alliance. The French—facing surging Communist agitation at home and fearful of standing against the Soviets—were hesitant, dragging their feet with procedural delays. When the Czech coup struck, their doubts were quickly cleared up. Masaryk died on the morning of March 10. On March 13, the Treaty of Brussels was completed after only two weeks of negotiations. These five nations of Western Europe would stand as one against a Soviet invasion.

The idea was laughable. The treaty's only contribution to military defense would have been if it were rolled up and used to bop an advancing Red Army soldier upside the head. The Western Europeans were, in fact, militarily helpless. The only nation that could help them was unready and unwilling to do so.

IN KEY WEST, the military chiefs were haggling over unification issues. Yet what became apparent, once again, to Forrestal was just how weak America's armed forces were in the face of the rising danger. He returned to Washington on the afternoon of Monday, March 15, and reported in to Truman that evening. A buildup of military manpower and matériel was crucial, he said. The previous day, the Army's intelligence division had reported of the Soviet armed forces that "with 4,100,000 men, they are twice as large as in the late 1930s, when Soviet security was under immediate threat from Germany and Japan." In contrast, America did not have the strength to deploy more than a division of about 15,000 troops if trouble arose. As preparedness stood, Royall told Truman that evening, "If we got into trouble, we would lose all our troops in Europe and Japan."

Truman cut his military advisers off. He had already been told of the conclusions the generals had reached in Key West and he had come to a decision. The situation was so dire, he said, he was going to call for the reestablishment of the military draft, which had been discontinued after World War II.

Since the early days of the Czech coup, Forrestal had been urging Truman to speak to the nation about the crisis and about the importance of a robust response. It was the only way to convince Congress to pass the Marshall Plan and new military spending. Truman's political advisers were asking him to do the same, for their own reasons. "Pres. *must* for his prestige, come up with a strong foreign speech—to demonstrate his leadership—which country needs and wants," White House staffer George Elsey wrote in a memo to his boss, Truman political adviser Clark Clifford, the same day that Clay had sent his warning from Berlin. Now Truman told Forrestal he was going to make such a speech. He had intended to do so at a St. Patrick's Day dinner in New York, but in a noon meeting earlier that March 15, Marshall had argued that such a raucous event was not suitable for such a solemn announcement. Truman had decided that while he would still go to New York for the dinner on March 17, he would make an extraordinary address to a joint session of Congress earlier that same day. They now had one day to write the speech.

FORRESTAL AWOKE THE next morning to find he was caught in a waking nightmare. The terrors he had worked so hard to prevent since Iwo Jima and Bikini were coming to pass. "Papers this morning full of rumors and portents of war," he wrote in his diary. "Wallace in New York interview yesterday charged that United States was fomenting war and the Czech *coup* was an act of desperation by the Communists to which they were driven by threat of a Rightist *coup*. Nothing could be sillier, but such statements, even from Wallace, will have their effect. The fact is this country and its government are desperately anxious to avoid war. It is simply a question of how best to do it. If all Europe lies flat while the Russian mob tramps over it, we will be faced with a war under difficult circumstances, and with a very good chance of losing it."

It was madness, he continued, even for "the gang who run Russia" to start a war, "but one always has to remember that there seemed to be no reason in 1939 for Hitler to start war, and yet he did." Now the only remaining hope was "to try to make the Russians see the folly of continuing an aggression which will lead to war, or, if it is impossible to restore them to sanity, that we at least have a start which will enable us to prevent our being caught flat-footed as we were in 1941." As the tension grew, Forrestal seemed to be an unlikely source for sermons on sanity. In meetings that went on for hours at the White House and in the Pentagon, he appeared to be trying to contain some hidden tempest. As he squirmed about in his seat, the other men watched him pour himself glass after glass of water, and gulp them down. He would press his lips together as if he were trying to keep something inside that was fighting to escape.

THAT SAME MORNING, Tuesday, March 16, Truman's aides and advisers gathered in the White House to draft the two speeches he would deliver the following day. The country was facing a grave crisis. "All last week in the halls of Congress, on the street corners, U.S. citizens had begun to talk of the possibility of war between the U.S. and U.S.S.R.," observed *Time*.

But in the two days before Truman's addresses, Taft and Wallace attacked his policies in strikingly similar terms. In overthrowing the Czech government, the Soviet Union was simply "consolidating its sphere of influence," said Taft. Since he had "no knowledge of any Russian intention for military aggression," there was no need to spend vast amounts on military preparedness or to rebuild Europe under the Marshall Plan. For his part, Wallace wrote, in a message to members of Congress, "There is no evidence that any nation has threatened acts of aggression against us or threatens our national security." He charged that "military and cartelist members of the Administration," such as Forrestal, had fanned "a war hysteria" which was engulfing the country.

Truman believed that if he did not convince Congress to act, "the country is sunk." If he did not convince Democrats that Wallace was an unacceptable alternative, the same would be true for his own candidacy.

Yet Truman had, thus far, never called out the Soviet Union or Henry Wallace by name. On March 16, as the speechwriters were drafting, he decided that the next day he would attack both head on.

Marshall was apoplectic. Such rhetoric against the Russians might prove to be the very action that would set off war. Charles Bohlen was sent by Marshall to tell Clark Clifford that the speechwriters should "drop intemperate language"; the address should be "simple, businesslike, no 'ringing phrases'—nothing warlike, or belligerent." Marshall said that if a tough speech was delivered, it might "pull the trigger." Truman overruled his secretary of state, saying it was "better to do that than to be caught, as we were in the last war, without having warned the Congress and the people." It was not only the lessons of Munich, but those of Pearl Harbor that had been seared into him and his entire generation. He was determined not to allow either mistake to be made again.

As if to buttress Truman's decision, a memo was brought to the president, hand-carried from the offices of the infant Central Intelligence Agency, in existence for less than six months. Since they had received word of Clay's cable, the analysts at the agency had been drawing up their own assessment of the Soviet threat. On March 16, they reported to Truman that "the weight of logic, as well as evidence" pointed to no military action by the Soviet Union—in the next sixty days. Beyond that, they could make no predictions and, they admitted, even during the next two months there was "the ever present possibility that some miscalculation or incident may result in war."

Forrestal arrived at the White House in the morning on March 17 and, with other members of the cabinet, met with Truman in the Oval Office. They accompanied him on the ride up Pennsylvania Avenue. Taking his place in the front row of the House chamber, the defense secretary must have had some satisfaction in the knowledge that the address the president was about to deliver had been fundamentally shaped by the truths he had been preaching for years.

No sooner had Truman announced he would be delivering his address to a special joint session of Congress than a frigid wind had blown into the nation's capital, sending temperatures plunging overnight. The climate inside the chamber matched that outside. When Truman's arrival was announced shortly after noon, the members of the Republican-controlled Congress rose as one, but the applause was perfunctory. Truman appeared not to notice. He marched to the rostrum, opened a brown notebook, and without the barest of opening pleasantries for those before him or listening on the radio, began delivering his speech.

He started at the Elbe. "Almost three years have elapsed since the end of the greatest of all wars," Truman observed, "but peace and stability have not returned to the world." It had been thought that "the Allies of World War II were united in their desire to establish a just and honorable peace," but, unfortunately, "one nation" had "actively sought to prevent" such a peace; "one nation" had "persistently ignored and violated" postwar agreements; "one nation" had "obstructed the work of the United Nations."

But then he dropped the euphemism. For the first time in his presidency, he referred to America's new antagonist by name: "We have reached a point at which the position of the United States should be made unmistakably clear." Since the end of the war, he charged, "the Soviet Union and its agents have destroyed the independence and democratic character of a whole series of nations in Eastern and Central Europe. It is this ruthless course of action, and the clear design to extend it to the remaining free nations of Europe, that have brought about the critical situation in Europe today. The tragic death of the Republic of Czechoslovakia has sent a shock throughout the civilized world."

In response, he asked for prompt passage of the Marshall Plan. But this was no longer enough. "The free nations of Europe realize that economic recovery, if it is to succeed, must be afforded some measure of protection against internal and external aggression." As the United States faced a new enemy of vast reach and ambition, and the threat of war, Truman said the burden of response should be shouldered squarely and evenly by all American families. He called on Congress to pass legislation that would enact universal military training, where every eighteen-year-old male would spend a few months becoming prepared to enter the armed forces if war came, followed by service in reserve duty. And he said the crisis was so serious that it was necessary to reinstitute a peacetime draft. "There are times in world history when it is far wiser to act than to hesitate. There is some risk involved in action—there always is. But there is far more risk in failure to act."

Truman finished his speech, closed the brown notebook, and walked out, leaving the shocked congressmen behind. He had "entered the chamber in a postwar atmosphere," the New Republic wrote. "He left in a prewar atmosphere."

IN BRUSSELS, THAT same day, the foreign ministers of the five Western European nations had put aside ancient rivalries and mistrust to sign their military alliance. The men were sullen and tense. They had entered into the mutual defense pact not with confidence but with the resignation of men holding hands as their ship sagged into dark depths. One of the foreign ministers predicted that the Russians would be in Paris by August. With a sigh of resignation, Georges Marie Joseph Revers, the chief of the staff of the French army, said he agreed. With little ceremony, they inked the document and then, together, repaired to a side room. They gathered around a shortwave radio and leaned in to listen, over the static, to the broadcast of Truman's address. The mood lifted.

TRUMAN WENT STRAIGHT from the Capitol to Washington's National Airport. His plane took off shortly before 1:30, and an hour later he had landed at LaGuardia in New York. "Are you happy over your speech?" a reporter shouted on the tarmac. "I'm not happy about it, but it was necessary and it had to be said," Truman snapped. When he reached the St. Patrick's Day Parade reviewing stand at Fifth Avenue and Sixty-fourth Street, the band from St. Michael's struck up "Now Is the Hour." A stiff wind blew from the south and it seemed to those present that every window had an American flag flicking in the breeze. There was not a cloud in the sky. "Brass instruments glittered and winked and soaring batons caught the sun's fire," wrote a newspaperman.

Truman was the first president to attend the St. Patrick's Day Parade—but, after all, it was an election year. Already waving from the platform when Truman got there was Governor Dewey, the Republican front-runner. The men moved toward each other for a handshake. Each was wearing a shimmering green necktie. Dewey had a sprig of shamrock in his lapel, Truman a green carnation. "You've had a trying day, Mr. President," Dewey said in greeting. Truman's response went unrecorded in the clamor of the crowd.

WHILE TRUMAN WAS on the reviewing stand in New York, Lucius Clay was in the midst of his nightly teleconference with officials at the Pentagon. It was, at least, some relief to him that he was almost done with his service in Germany. His belongings were being boxed up. He had begun to consider job offers in business. Earlier that week, the *New York Times* had carried the breaking news that Walter Bedell Smith was "the definite choice" to replace Clay. "At first, General Smith was reluctant but President Truman and Secretary Marshall have refused up to now to accept a negative answer," it wrote.

Smith's arm had not been twisted so badly that he could not write frequently to Clay outlining what he required when he took over. Clay, an immensely proud man publicly fired from his high position, summoned all the graciousness he could muster. He offered to fix up his residence so that it would be ready once he and Marjorie left. Smith told him not to bother. He planned instead to take one of the splendid mansions on the Wannsee lake for his use.

Clay continued to work his same long hours—and he continued his long-distance wrestle with Washington. That afternoon he too had listened to Truman's speech on the radio. That evening, as usual, Clay returned to the office late at night and descended into the subterranean chamber where the secure teleconference equipment was kept. The Army's top generals were in a similar room in the Pentagon.

Bradley's deputy opened the conversation, his words flashing onto a screen in Berlin and coming through on a teleprinter. With "the tensing international situation," they were wondering if it might not be time to evacuate dependents—the family members of American troops—from Germany, to get them out of the way in case war came or the United States had to quickly retreat from Berlin.

Clay wrote out his answer in longhand, scratching it out with a No. 2 pencil and handing it to a code clerk, who then entered the text into a teletype. He was, at first, patient, even sympathetic to their distress. "From a strictly military viewpoint," pulling Americans out of Berlin and the rest of Germany "is logical and cannot be argued against." But there were other concerns to consider. Such a move "would be politically disastrous and perhaps harmful to military situation by creating new problems. For instance, withdrawal of dependents from Berlin would create hysteria accompanied by rush of Germans to Communism for safety." If they withdrew family members from the American zone of Germany first, it "would create panic in dependents in Berlin. This condition would spread in Europe and would increase Communist political strength everywhere."

Clay denounced an evacuation from Berlin in the most absolute terms. The generals on the other end of the line did not even bother to address his points. They simply moved on to logistics. Should the evacuation from Berlin "be done abruptly or gradually? What would be the Soviet reaction? What would be the reaction to morale to troops? What would be the effect on German people? What would be the reaction in neighboring countries? What cover for such action would you suggest?"

They were talking past one another, willfully. "Again from strictly military viewpoint alone, evacuation is logical but here withdrawal would be ruinous politically," Clay answered. "We are here now and must take consequences with our neighbors. If done, it should be abruptly as there can be no concealment. Soviet reaction, again, would be to use as propaganda and have that we are deserting Europe's non-combatants while we plan for war."

With Clay leaving Germany, the generals in Washington were not much interested in his advice on policy. Just moments after he had finished scratching out this impassioned tirade, their response flashed up onto the screen: "Should this evacuation include civilian employees male or female?" Clay, fed up, replied that he had already answered the question.

The teleconference wrapped up. In Washington, they told Clay that they were "simply reviewing their plans" and "just wanted to let you know we were thinking of you."

Clay was less than moved by the sentiment. It was nice to know, but there was something he wanted more than their good wishes. In closing the conference, he had one more thing to say, and it made clear that as tensions rose he was thinking of something very different from retreat: "Bazookas are badly needed to knock out Soviet tanks. We have nothing for the infantry soldier which would dent them."

IN THE GRAND Ballroom of the Hotel Astor, 2,800 "Friendly Sons of St. Patrick" made their way through courses of fish followed by pork loin followed by chicken. They lingered over "Grapefruit Erin," "Salad Shamrock," and "Sherbet Emerald Isle." With a not insignificant number of the speakers blessed with a touch of blarney, it was 10:30 by the time Truman arose to give the dinner's final address, broadcast on both radio and television.

Truman began by rehearsing the arguments he had made to Congress earlier in the day. The Soviet Union, he said, "has steadily expanded its control over its neighbors. It is a tragic record." Drawing out each foreign name, he called the roll of terror: "Latvia, Lithuania, Estonia. Poland, Rumania, Bulgaria. Yugoslavia, Albania, Hungary. And now Czechoslovakia. One after another they have been brought under the domination of one nation. Nor is this the whole story. For that nation is now pressing its demands upon Finland. Its foreign agents are fighting in Greece and working hard to undermine the freedom of Italy. Free men in every land are asking: 'Where is this leading? . . . When will it end?' I can bring you tonight no simple or easy answer."

But this much he did know: "We must beware of those who are devoting themselves to sowing the seeds of disunity among our people." In the year and half since Wallace had been fired and had set out on a nationwide tour attacking the administration, Truman had not ventured a criticism. In the three months since Wallace announced his campaign for president, Truman had not mentioned his candidacy. Now he did— and it was an attack of force and vehemence. "We must not fall victim to the insidious propaganda that peace can be obtained solely by wanting peace," he said. With his voice rising, Truman continued, "I do not want and I will not accept the political support of Henry Wallace and his Communists." The crowd, which had been tepidly applauding at that late hour, erupted into thirty seconds of sustained cheers. Truman held up his hands to quiet them. "If joining them or permitting them to join me is the price of victory, I recommend defeat." There was more clapping, but Truman raised his hands again. He wanted to get to the punch line. "These are days of high prices for everything, but any price for Wallace and his Communists is too much for me to pay," he said, thwacking the podium. "I'm nqt buying." The Friendly Sons of St. Patrick, fervent anti-Communists all, erupted into an ovation at finally hearing Truman denounce Wallace and the Russians by name. Had they not all been wearing green, they would have pinched themselves to make sure they were not dreaming.

Despite the joyous occasion, Truman ended the speech on a note that was sober, even somber. "We will have to take risks during the coming year—risks perhaps greater than any this country has ever been called upon to assume." That evening he could not have known how true those words would be, but as his train home pulled out of Penn Station at one minute to midnight, he must have realized that this had been the day in which the crisis of 1948—and the campaign of 1948—had begun in earnest.

On Friday, March 19, two days after Truman's twin addresses on St. Patrick's Day, the House Appropriations Committee—where the Marshall Plan had long been trapped—finally approved the measure. On the House floor, in light of Truman's appeal, there was hardly a vote against the aid package. Truman's speeches had succeeded, but the stress and worry over war was taking its toll. "He looked tired, as I have hardly ever seen him, and under strain," noted one administration official who saw Truman that day. "He has been through a *week*."

Though the Czech coup and Truman's response had forced Congress to adopt the Marshall Plan, his calls for a new draft and universal military training were deeply unpopular in Congress. "There was scarcely anything Harry Truman could have recommended that could have aroused more controversy," wrote the *New York Times*. For Truman, conscription was a civic duty, a "time tax" that young Americans should pay in exchange for the blessings of American life. Once again, the right and left united against him. The former thought the military spending required would prevent further tax cuts, the latter wanted the money for spending on social programs such as housing and health care. Both thought the draft was a threat to constitutional protections. A coalition of organizations such as the conservative Young Men's Christian Association and the progressive American Civil Liberties Union came together to oppose the Truman call for national service. Bob Taft had declared that universal military training "is contrary to the whole concept of American liberty." Liberals—the very voters who were drawn to Wallace's campaign, the ones Truman desperately needed to court and coax back into his camp— were especially irate. "For the United States to accept conscription in time of peace is a momentous political act, a violation of very deep traditions and habits of mind," declared the editor of *The Nation*.

The usual response of Americans to an international crisis is to rally around their president. Against the backdrop of emergency, the commander in chief always seems to gain in stature. But in March of 1948, the very opposite happened. With war apparently in the offing, Truman was judged the wrong person to lead the nation. "The simple fact is that Truman isn't the type of strong man to whom folks turn in time of national danger," wrote prominent columnist Richard Strout after the St. Patrick's Day speeches. The House majority leader, Charlie Halleck, declared that Truman was the worst president in history. Some questioned his intelligence. The left-leaning *New Republic,* no longer affiliated with Wallace, offered Truman its sympathies, since he was clearly someone who had a "known difficulty in understanding the printed word." The right-wing *Chicago Tribune* offered him its congratulations: "Mr. Truman has won his place in history. His title is beyond challenge. He is by long odds the most inept and incompetent President this country has known. If there was any doubt about it before his address to Congress, there isn't any now. By the same token, George Marshall is the worst blunderer ever to occupy the office of Secretary of State."

Scared by the Soviet advances, Americans seemed to concur with the editorialists. A couple of weeks after Truman's speeches, a Gallup poll reported that Truman's public approval ratings had dropped below 50 percent for the first time in more than a year. In fact, they had plunged down to the point where only about a third of the country approved of the job their president was doing.

A s the Communists moved across Europe, western sector Berliners watched the steady advance with the trepidation of a child building a sand castle as the tide inches nearer. The fall of Prague "has led to many heart-searchings among Berliners concerning the extent to which their situation may be similar to that of the Czechoslovaks," reported the *Christian Science Monitor.* They were "confused, apprehensive, and uncertain regarding their future," and most felt that "due either to the apparently untenable strategic position of their city, surrounded as it is on all sides by the Soviet Zone, or the weakness of the three Western democracies here—that the Russians still may succeed in enforcing their totalitarianism here whenever they choose."

Were it not for the joint occupation of Berlin, the city would already have been controlled by the Communists. And following the collapse of the Czechs' democracy, the Soviets used their power to spread a message to Berliners: the days of that joint occupation were coming to an end. On March 14, the Soviet-controlled *Berliner Zeitung* alerted residents to the "unpreventable withdrawal of the Western Powers which may some day soon occur very suddenly." On the radio, on loudspeakers placed on busy street corners, the Soviets announced that soon the United States would be leaving Berlin. Well-acquainted with the methods of repression, the Berliners knew the implication: they had better demonstrate their fealty to the Communists before it was too late.

When, the same week that the Beneš regime was being deposed in Prague, American, British, and French officials met in London to make plans to create a new west German nation from their three occupation zones, it was felt by many—on both sides of Elbe—that Western claims on Berlin were soon to be traded away. In these discussions, Germans were merely pawns, their fate controlled by distant governments. "The ugly sound of saber rattling arises over Germany. And because Berlin is the focal point, it is loudest here," wrote journalist Ruth Andreas-Friedrich in her diary. "We feel powerless in the face of approaching disaster, and even more powerless to try and prevent it."

THREE TIMES A month, the Allied Control Council met in a pantomime of government, occasionally making decisions for Germany but usually only providing a stage for mutual denunciations. But while its function had all but ceased, its forms continued, sad reminders of hopes for friendship that had been stomped out in the years since the last war. The chairmanship of the council still rotated among the four powers and, on March 20, three days after Truman's address to Congress, when Marshal Sokolovsky entered the Allied Control Council meeting room, he sat himself in the chairman's seat of honor in front of the hulking fireplace. In the next room, since it was their turn, the Soviets had blanketed a buffet table with refreshments for after the meeting; the lobsters were bright red, the caviar was black, the champagne was pink.

But from the moment Sokolovsky entered the chamber, it was clear to Clay that something was amiss. Sokolovsky's fog-colored eyes darted nervously about the room. Chain-smoking long-stemmed black cigarettes, one after another, he shifted uncomfortably in his chair as he launched into a round of rote accusations. Before him on the table, where everyone could see it, he had placed a typed sheet of paper, leaving it there like a warning.

Sokolovsky called on the council to take up a resolution attacking Western policies in Germany. Joseph-Pierre Koenig, the French military governor, dismissed it as outside the purview of the body. Sokolovsky went on the attack: "This only proves once more that the United States, British, and French representatives here no longer consider the Control Council as quadripartite authority in Germany. They regard it as a suitable screen behind which to hide unilateral actions in the Western zones, actions directed against the peace-loving people of Germany."

British general Brian Robertson bristled at the rudeness. "I wish to protest against the strong language the chairman has used in describing the attitude of his colleagues."

Clay jumped in. "I will not even attempt to reply to these charges. A mere casual examination of the record will show when, where, and by whom the Control Council's efforts to govern Germany have been blocked."

Sokolovsky next asked for a report on the decisions the three other countries had made at their meeting in London. Clay replied that while the request was reasonable, he needed permission from his government before making any announcement. Sokolovsky looked over at him and then, with a slight sigh, reached for the document sitting in front of him. "In view of the fact that the members refuse to give information on the conference in London, I am compelled to make the following statement."

He began to read from the sheet a denunciation of Western actions in Germany. He raced through the recitation as if trying to make it through a distasteful duty. The stenographers in the center of the square formed by the four tables clack-clacked to keep up with him. He spoke so fast the interpreters fell behind. Clay petted George, his Scottie, as he listened to the diatribe.

"The Control Council no longer exists as an organ of government," Sokolovsky said in a monotone voice without inflection, the kind a hostage uses to signal he is being forced to deliver a statement. "Since the British and the United States members refuse to report before the Control Council on matters discussed at the London Conference, I see no sense in continuing this meeting and declare it adjourned." He gathered his papers and pushed his chair back from the table. In the still room, it scraped against the parquet floor. He rose and marched out with his staff trailing behind him. The other delegations sat in silence, listening to the echo of the Russians' hard shoes as they marched down the stone steps of the sweeping staircase, across the tiled entryway, and out of the building.

For minutes no one said a word. The waitresses in dark uniforms and thin white gloves stood by the untouched buffet shuffling their feet. Even the chubby cherubs on the frescoed ceiling seemed to have had the wind knocked from their cheeks. Finally, Clay spoke up. "Well," he said casually, "I don't know what this means."

THE TRUTH WAS Clay and everyone else in Berlin knew immediately what Sokolovsky's move meant. The veneer of four-power occupation of Germany had been destroyed. Germany was split in two, with the Americans, British, and French occupying the western part and the Soviets the eastern. The Elbe now marked the border of their division.

Only in Berlin, nestled in the Soviet zone, were the four powers still tied together like gladiators in the arena, bound at the wrist with knives drawn. The situation was heading toward a climax. The Berliners knew it. "Nearly every hour brings more alarming news," worried Ruth Andreas-Friedrich in her diary the day after the Control Council breakup. Clay, his Army uniforms packed away, his new civilian suits tailored and pressed, knew it too. "I don't know how many times it is necessary to repeat it," he fumed in frustration to the press. "I have said it before and I say it again. We have no intention of leaving Berlin." And in Washington, Truman and his military officials knew it as well. Two days after Sokolovsky walked out of the Control Council, Truman met with Marshall and Pentagon officials to discuss Clay's impending retirement. With the situation in Berlin reaching a crisis, taking the general out of his post as military governor seemed an increasingly risky proposition. With Berlin in danger, Marshall had little choice but to back down.

The next afternoon, Clay was summoned to an urgent teleconference. "It is very important that we keep this matter secret until it is released by the president," Army secretary Royall said in opening. "It was decided yesterday afternoon that State Department will not take over" the occupation of Germany. He sent Clay a press release that was about to be distributed in Washington, which stated, "Following a review of the present situation, it has been decided that it would be inadvisable to make any changes in our present arrangements for Germany."

There was a long pause in Washington as they waited for Clay's response. Eventually it flashed up on the screen in the Pentagon: "In view of recent development, decision is wise." Royall said he hoped Clay would stay in place through the end of the year. "I am an Army officer as long as the Department feels I am needed," Clay responded.

Clay went home to tell Marjorie the news they would be staying. "You can't," she said. "You haven't any pants."

IN THE DAYS following the collapse of the Control Council, the Russians did everything they could to stoke Berliners' alarm about a coming attack. On March 24, the day after it was announced Clay was staying on, Soviet troops began field exercises just outside of Berlin. Thirty thousand new troops had arrived over the previous days. Soviets began an ostentatious survey of schools and hotels and other large halls within five miles of the border of the western zones, as if they were scouting for staging areas. Every day, they scurried into the American zone and kidnapped Germans, taking them back over the border and conducting detailed interrogations on Western troop strengths before releasing the scared civilians so they would return home and tell their tale. Border personnel were given battlefield equipment and several days of rations. Private homes near the border were requisitioned for use by senior Red Army generals, who were said to be on their way. Within sight of American observation posts in Berlin, troops were marched in formation multiple times, circling back out of sight in an attempt to trick the watching GIs. Marshal Zhukov, the conqueror of Germany, showed up for inspections in the border towns that American and British trains passed through to reach Berlin. In the capital, Valerian Zorin, hot off his victory in Prague, arrived to supervise preparations.

On March 25, Clay held a formal press conference. "General, the people here live in fear," said a German journalist. "The people are afraid that the Russians will overwhelm them. The people are afraid the Americans do not have enough troops." Clay tried to be reassuring. Panic was exactly what the Russians were trying to create. He was "not in the least bit apprehensive or nervous." He was asked about "the possibility of the autobahn being closed down to Berlin." He said, "I have no fear of any such event happening." But then he was asked whether war was now likely. He paused. "I am not expecting any conflagration to break out tomorrow or the next day, by any means" was the best he could do.

It sounded like the rapid fire of distant guns. Ken Royall awoke in his bed, unsteady, blinking in the darkness. The phone rang again. He got up and walked across the suite in the Mayflower Hotel that was his home. He lifted the receiver and croaked a greeting. The intelligence duty officer on the other end immediately apologized for waking the secretary, but they had just received reports in from Germany that the Red Army was about to invade.

It was around 4 A.M. on Wednesday, March 31. General Bradley had already been notified. Royall, still in his pajamas, stood by the window

looking out onto Connecticut Avenue, the glowing streetlamps illuminating the deserted street below. He called the president's aides to notify
them, dressed quickly, and went to the Pentagon. Shortly after dawn, he
went to the White House to brief Truman.

It proved to be a false alarm. The Russian troop movements had produced their intended result. In Germany, the night before, Clay had
received a letter from the Soviet occupation command, and its content
was the subject of swirling rumors. At 7 A.M., the Pentagon received a
heavily encrypted cable from Clay. Two hours later, when Bradley began
a teleconference with Clay and others, it had still not been decoded.

They began the conversation discussing other matters: new regulations
for disposing of scrap and salvage material, the return of art treasures to
Germany, appropriations bills working their way through Congress. It
was 9:13 in Washington when the cable was delivered to Bradley. "Recent
message from you just brought in," he told Clay. "Please wait."

Bradley began to read Clay's cable. The Soviets had announced that
new restrictions on trains running through the Soviet zone to Berlin
would begin at midnight on April 1. The thirty-two daily trains bringing
food and supplies into the city for Berliners could go ahead as they had
been, but all Western military personnel traveling to Berlin had to submit themselves for inspection, and permits would be required for
freight trains bringing supplies to occupation forces in the capital. Clay
proposed that the Americans agree to hand over passenger lists and
freight manifests, but not give up on their right to freely bring supplies
into their sector of Berlin. "It is my intent to instruct our guards to open
fire if Soviet soldiers attempt to enter our trains," Clay's cable read.
"Obviously the full consequences of this action must be understood.
Unless we take a strong stand now, our life in Berlin will become impossible. A retreat from Berlin at this moment would, in my opinion, have
serious if not disastrous political consequences in Europe. I do not believe
that the Soviets mean war now. However, if they do, it seems to me that we
might as well find out now as later. We cannot afford to be bluffed."

Bradley was furious. Shooting at the Russians would almost certainly
result in war. "Had I enough hair on my head to react, this cable would

probably have stood it on end," he recalled later. Holding his temper, he
told Clay that he would have to discuss his proposal with others in the
Pentagon and asked to have another teleconference in a few hours.
"Delay train until you hear from me," he ordered.

By 11:40 that morning, Forrestal had gathered the highest-ranking
officials in Truman's government in his Pentagon office for an emergency meeting over lunch. Royall and Bradley were there as were the
rest of the Joint Chiefs of Staff. Clark Clifford had come from the White
House. Eisenhower had come to lend his counsel. With George Marshall having fallen ill after the pressure of the previous month, Bob
Lovett was there as acting secretary of state. Someone proposed that
Truman send Stalin a letter asking him to rescind the new regulations
before they led to war. As the civilians discussed what the letter should
say, Air Force Chief of Staff General Tooey Spaatz scribbled his proposed language on a piece of paper and passed it to Lovett: "Stalin, you
crazy S.O.B., what do you think you're doing?" Lovett, deadpan, turned
to him and said, "General, you should know better than to call a head of
a sovereign state crazy." But then, more seriously, Lovett told the group
he opposed the idea of a note to the Soviets. It would give them exactly
what they were looking for. A White House meeting with the Republican and Democratic leaders of Congress was suggested, but this was
rejected because it would add to "the creation of a war hysteria."

The meeting turned to whether and when Clay should be allowed to
give his men permission to open fire. They failed to come to a conclusion.
Some thought the Americans should be allowed to fire if Russian troops
boarded their trains, others said they should be instructed to fire only if
fired upon first. It was quickly agreed that the Soviets had decided to try
to push the Western powers out of Berlin, but the men gathered in Forrestal's office were divided as to whether war was imminent or simply
possible. If war did come, American forces in Germany—undermanned,
unprepared, and all but unarmed—would be quickly overrun.

They summoned Major General Kenneth Nichols, who had recently
succeeded Leslie Groves, the architect of the Manhattan Project, as the
commander of the military's nuclear program. In the event of war, were

they in a position to be able to attack Russia with atomic weapons? They were not, Nichols answered. The only assembly teams were in the Marshall Islands preparing for a test on the atoll of Eniwetok. Eisenhower, whose placid public persona masked storms of anger behind closed doors, reacted with fury. As Nichols would recount it, Eisenhower told him "in very definite terms" to "improve the situation at once."

In the three years after Hiroshima and Nagasaki, America had produced 50 atomic bombs. Within a few months of this meeting, the number would grow to 133. The United States had only 30 of the B-29 bombers that could deliver the bombs. That day, Forrestal asked the Air Force to begin bringing the bombers out of storage. The nuclear arms race—though still one-sided—began in earnest at that lunch on March 31, 1948, because of the situation in Berlin.

All during lunch, Forrestal was firm and forceful. It was a bravura performance. But the others at the table could not help but notice that while he was participating in the conversation, Forrestal was compulsively dipping his fingers into his water glass and wetting his lips over and over again. He did not seem to realize it, nor did he pick up on their shocked stares. It was almost as if he were not in control.

AT 1 P.M., BRADLEY was back in a teleconference with Clay, this time with Royall and others in tow. Clay was annoyed at being second-guessed. He had passed on his intentions simply "for your information." He was not asking for their approval. "Urge I be permitted to proceed on my judgment."

There was not a chance. Instead, Royall told him that the options being considered were a letter to Stalin from Truman or letting the trains go forward, but "in no event shall there be shooting. What do you think of this?"

"Any weakness on our part will lose us prestige important now," Clay responded. "If Soviets mean war, we will only defer the next provocation for a few days. For that reason, I do not think either realistic."

"If you had to choose between courses," Royall attempted again a few minutes later, "which would you prefer?"

Clay replied snidely, "I would prefer to evacuate Berlin and I had rather go to Siberia than do that."

Royall said they should speak again at 4 P.M. Washington time (10 P.M. in Berlin), when they would know more. Clay said that the French and British military governors were waiting at his house for dinner but that he would come back. "I am sure that a strong stand here now is essential and will win issue. Please believe this my sincere conviction," Clay implored in closing.

"Continue to hold train," Royall replied. "Nothing further here."

WHEN THEY RECONVENED, Forrestal, Lovett, Clifford, and Royall had met with Truman and come to a decision: The Russians should not be allowed on board the trains, but should not be resisted by force. "If our action now should provoke war, we must be sure that fault is not ours," Bradley told Clay. "It is important that our guards not fire unless fired upon."

"I do not agree that this is a fair instruction to a man whose life may be in danger," Clay answered. "Our reply will not be misunderstood by forty-two million Germans and perhaps two hundred million Western Europeans." In this situation, "there is no middle ground which is not appeasement," but he would "of course, accept and carry out instructions to the letter."

Three Western trains entered the Soviet zone at midnight on April 1. On one, the train's commandant became scared and allowed the Russians to come aboard. They let him through to Berlin. The other two were stopped at the zone's border. Onboard the "Berliner," three hundred American soldiers were crowded together. Under the station lights, those aboard could see Soviet troops massed around the train armed with pistols, rifles, and short metal ladders. A Russian lieutenant announced the train would not be allowed to pass until every travel document had been inspected. The American commandant shouted back that if the Russians attempted to board, his military police would shoot them. Neither side made a move.

All day long the train stayed in place. The men got off and brewed coffee on fires they set on the tracks. They visited with British troops on a nearby train also trapped there. Together they cooked canned steak and kidney puddings in their tins and ate them with toothbrushes and nail files. At 8:20 that evening, the train began to move. But instead of heading toward Berlin, it chugged backward, returning to the American zone under the direct orders of Clay. He had found no choice but to order a retreat.

That day, Clay asked the commander of Tempelhof how many cargo planes were available in Europe. There were thirty-six of them stationed at Rhein-Main Air Base just outside Frankfurt; however, with maintenance problems, only about twenty-five were operable. That was sufficient for what Clay needed. He ordered that the one daily flight between Rhein-Main and Tempelhof be increased to thirty so that enough food could be flown to feed the 10,000 American troops, employees, and family members stuck in Berlin.

April 1 had been the day Clay was supposed to have returned home. It would be understandable if, when it finally came, he wished that he had.

On the same St. Patrick's Day that Truman delivered his attacks on the Soviets and Wallace, the Hells Angels bicycle gang was organized in California. There was a parlous, unsettled sense in America in those first months of 1948. In the middle of April, a Gallup poll asked Americans to volunteer what they thought was the most important issue facing the country, and 65 percent mentioned something involving matters of war and peace. At the end of the month, *Business Week* would devote a special section to the topic of the "Economic Consequences of a Third World War."

The fear of war hung over the country like a funereal crape. It was so real that the most powerful men in America could feel it drawing down around them. The speaker of the House of Representatives, Republican Joseph Martin, next in line to the presidency, announced that there were thousands of terrorists hidden in the country waiting to "execute a sudden coup and take over the Government." They would "sabotage our American freedom and bring our people and our Government under the sway of an alien ideology and a foreign clique of rulers."

Henry Wallace saw a different threat coming. He had responded forcefully to Truman's broadside, seeing it as an attack on his patriotism and an attempt to stifle dissent. "The men who speak of reigns of terror in Europe are fast introducing a reign of terror here at home," he said in an address nine days after Truman's speech in New York. "They are trying to silence all opposition to their program of regimentation and preparation for war by intimidation, threats, and by using every available means to frighten the people into silence. I tell you that the greatest threat to American freedom today comes from within our own country."

Wallace's popularity had not abated after Truman's attack. Twenty thousand of his zealous supporters filled Chicago Stadium on April 10 for a rally called "The Background of American Freedom." It was broadcast nationally on CBS radio with Studs Terkel as the host. Six days later, in St. Cloud, Minnesota, his running mate, Glen Taylor, predicted that "if war comes, because America does things bigger and better than anyone, we shall have bigger concentration camps and better roasting ovens." He could feel the onset of war like the approach of a winter storm. His wife had begged him not to bolt the Democrats in order to run with Wallace. He was a United States senator, by far the best-paying job he had ever had. He was finally able to provide for his family, perhaps be able to send the children to college. Taylor became enraged. He and Wallace were the last hopes to preserve peace. "If there is an atom bomb attack," he yelled, "it doesn't make much difference if they are educated or not."

Forrestal too felt threatening forces closing in on him. He had been worried about war and Communism longer than anyone else in government, and now he asked the National Security Council staff to make an urgent report "on the problems of our internal security, including the probable scope of the dangers, the strategy and the strength of the subversive elements in the event of an emergency, and the proposed countermeasures." With the Italian Communists gaining momentum in advance of the April 18 elections, Forrestal threw himself, in the words of a fellow cabinet member, into "masterminding the American effort to keep Italy on our side." He worked closely with the Catholic Church, which feared the Vatican falling behind the Iron Curtain. Prominent Italian archbishops proclaimed that anyone who voted for the Communists would not be allowed to receive holy absolution. Forrestal raised money from the Italian-American community and had Nazi loot laundered through the IRS to help fund democratic parties in Italy. In the days before the voting, he ordered Navy planes to fly over major cities in a show of force. When the election came, the Communists were defeated.

For Forrestal, it was only a reprieve. On April 2, the CIA had issued its "Top Secret" definitive statement on the "Possibility of Direct Soviet Military Action During 1948." As to the major question of whether the Soviets would start a war, the document punted. "The logic of the situation" indicated they would not, but the "possibility must be recognized" that they would. If they did launch an attack, their military forces were "estimated to be combat ready and generally so disposed that they could launch an immediate offensive" that had the "capability of overrunning all of Western Europe and the Near East to Cairo within a short period of time." When the United States tried to strike back, it would not be island-hopping or invading Western Europe, as they had in the last conflict. In World War III, "the US would be faced with the manpower and space of the Eurasian land mass." Forrestal knew there was only one way the United States could win such a war.

"APRIL! SEEMS INCREDIBLE, can't seem to fathom the speed of time. Many things keep me busy but there seems to be a great void following me about even in the midst of work," wrote Hal Halvorsen to Alta at the beginning of the month. He too felt uneasy in those weeks. Only two days before his letter to Alta, military commands had been informed to be on alert. All during that March of crisis, he and his fellow officers had been given extensive briefings about the worsening situation. With the fall of the Czech government to the Communists, they were told that "West Berlin was next and then the rest of Germany." But Halvorsen assumed that even if war came, he would be kept on its outskirts, just as he had the last time.

He was a Flying Dutchman, doomed to travel between ports in the Caribbean, racked with what he described to Alta as "loneliness," with plenty of time to do "a lot of thinking of the past and a little wishing on the side." At Easter, on a mission to Puerto Rico, he had attended sunrise services, standing by himself, surrounded by families and couples. In the middle of the month, he returned to New York to pick up a new, shiny red Chevrolet. On this visit, he walked the streets alone, carefully retracing the steps he had taken with Alta that weekend together so long ago. "Stayed near where they are going to put up the U.N. Building on the River," he wrote her. It was not far from the YWCA dorm where she had lived. He went to stand in front of the dorm. "Closed my eyes and it seemed like it was back when we were there together. RCA Bldg., outside skating rink, and all. Strong feeling."

In the end of February, he had opened his heart to her. "Alta, as I look back and think of good times and good hopes, they all seem to interweave with you. Sure is my conviction that you'd be astonished at the number of times per day pleasant thoughts of you course my mind and how many things that daily happen reflect my thoughts to you and the wonderful person you are." But months passed and they still did not get the chance to see each other. They had dated for a few months five years earlier. Since then they had only had brief visits on three occasions. Their letters came to have a routine, formulaic quality: a discussion of how fast time was passing, an apology for not writing more often, a wish that they would see each other soon, a detailed, running discussion of the weather as the seasons went by, a wistful reference to some now hazy memory of the few days they had spent together since the middle of the war. They were running on the fumes of a passion they had shared for a short time, more than half a decade earlier, and Halvorsen seemed to sense the relationship was running out of gas.

Now stationed at Brookley Air Force Base in Mobile, Alabama, Halvorsen was popular among his fellow officers. He had childlike, open features and a wide grin, but was prematurely bald—twenty-seven years old and with a bare dome—and the combination was like an old man joyfully licking an ice-cream cone. It was hard not to like him for his friendly manner. But he did not quite fit in. When the other pilots chased skirts, he stayed in the barracks to write moony notes to a girl for whom he had been carrying an engagement ring in his wallet for three years. When they called for a round of beer, he—the good Mormon—ordered up a glass of milk.

The American military, like Halvorsen himself, had been ignored and without direction in the years after World War II, lost in an uncertain world. But as the threat of war became palpable in March 1948, Americans' attention turned to the state of their arms. And yet, for Halvorsen, Germany felt as far away in 1948 as it had in 1944. The weather grew warmer, and he would swim out into the Gulf alone, spending hours floating like a cork in the sea under an awesome sky. But his happiest moments in those first months of 1948 came when his friend Pete Sowa, another pilot, invited Halvorsen to join him and his wife for home-cooked Sunday dinners. She had just delivered twins and their home was tiny, a brick structure with a metal awning in a wooded area at the edge of the base. The clouds would roll in off the water and seem to swallow the little house whole. Yet Halvorsen, without a family or a real home of his own in Mobile, loved those Sundays spent eating with the Sowas. Sitting around the small table, with two screaming newborns close at hand, Halvorsen found peace.

FIVE DAYS AFTER the Brussels Treaty had been signed on the day of Truman's dual addresses, British, Canadian, and American officials began meeting in the underground levels of the Pentagon to discuss whether the United States would enter into a military alliance with the nations of Western Europe. The conversations concluded on April 1. Lovett brought Truman their recommendation that the United States guarantee the security of western Germany, France, England, and the other smaller countries from the threat of Soviet invasion. Truman said he could not do it. He had had a difficult enough time passing the economic assistance of the Marshall Plan, and that took the crisis set off by the Czech coup before it was finally approved on April 2. To convince Congress to enter into a military alliance would be all but impossible without an imminent threat of war. Besides, Truman pointed out to Lovett, it was an election year.

In London and Paris and the other capitals, faith in America was ebbing. The Europeans wondered whether they would be able to rely on the Americans. The Marshall Plan had been passed but the millions promised had not been appropriated by Congress. The Americans were encouraging about the Brussels Treaty, but there were great doubts as to whether they would commit their troops to fight for European nations once again. In western Germany, political leaders were reluctant to move forward with establishing their own nation, because they worried whether the Americans would stay or be able to defend them when the inevitable Soviet response came.

The Russians, however, knew the Americans were serious. Great efforts had been taken to ensure the secrecy of the treaty meetings in the basement of the Pentagon. The diplomats entered through a hidden parking garage, they ate their lunch at the conference table, and no one was allowed to take notes. The Americans did not invite the French because they did not trust them to keep the talks a secret. But they did not account for the fact that sitting in the British delegation was Donald Maclean, a Soviet spy reporting all the proceedings to Moscow.

Since the end of the war, while the Russians had successfully placed vast tracts of Europe and Asia under Communist control, Americans had looked inward, tearing apart their military and caring more about amassing consumer goods. But now they had been awakened. In the space of a single month, America had announced a proposal to create a democratic west Germany, had passed a plan to rebuild the economies of free nations in Europe, had begun to reconstitute its military might, and was considering guaranteeing the security of Western Europe from Soviet invasion. The Russians' moment to spread their control across Europe was passing. If they wanted to move, they had to do so quickly.

THERE WAS WORRY in Moscow and in Washington—for different reasons—but fear was greatest in Berlin. After a British and a Russian plane collided in the skies over the city on April 5, the Russians had quickly lifted their rail restrictions, but there was the pervasive sense that it had all only been a dress rehearsal. As the United States, Britain, and France were putting together plans for a west German state, the Soviets were preparing for an east German state. Berlin would be the battle-ground where the West and East would meet—with the Berliners caught in between. "A struggle for Berlin is going on," wrote Ernst Reuter in April. "It may be that the Berliners will not be able to determine the final decision in this struggle." In a city where many had not been able to rebuild their homes, Berliners began to build bomb shelters.

That spring, high-ranking Soviet officers could often be seen being slowly driven by the houses in the western sectors in which allied leaders lived, as if they were making a show of picking out the best spot for their future residences. Howley would receive crank calls in the middle of the night. The doorbell would ring and when he or his wife or children opened the door, no one was there. He was implored to get armed guards, but refused. Instead, he slept with a pistol under his pillow.

From Washington, Bradley continued to press Clay to send American civilians and dependents home from Berlin. It was simply a reflection of the political pressure that the Pentagon was under, he claimed. "We are receiving many inquiries from Members of Congress as to why we do not evacuate dependents from Berlin," he said in a teleconference on April 2.

"Evacuation would play into Soviet hands and frighten the rest of Europe," Clay repeated. They went in circles on the subject. Clay calcu-lated it would take only thirty-six hours to evacuate all personnel by air if the decision were made. The only worry, he indicated, was if the Sovi-ets made a surprise military strike on the city. With Clay refusing to budge, Bradley transferred his own son-in-law, his daughter, and his grandchildren out of Berlin and back to the United States. "If the Russians overran the city and captured them," he explained, "the personal blow to me might be incapacitating."

IF WAR TRULY was to break out over Berlin, then, according to the CIA's estimates and the most obvious comparisons of military strength, it was a war that the United States would, if not lose, win only by unleashing an atomic attack that would destroy huge swaths of land and leave Europe in years of darkness. Therefore, if Berlin was the bone stuck in the Soviet craw, it made some sense to let them have that city in the center of their own German zone.

On April 10, Bradley had a private teleconference with Clay classified "Eyes Only." He laid out his case, gingerly. They were in a weak position in Berlin. "Will not Russian restrictions be added one by one which would eventually make our position untenable unless we ourselves are prepared to threaten or actually start a war to remove these restrictions?" After the events of the past ten days, there had been a running conversation among the highest officials of the country about whether America was ready for war. "Here we doubt whether our people are prepared to start a war in order to maintain our position in Berlin," he said, putting the onus for trading away the city on the public at large. "If you agree," he told Clay, "should we not now be planning to avoid this development" and determining under what conditions—he gave the example of setting up a west Germany with its own capital in Frankfurt—they could "announce withdrawal and minimize loss of prestige rather being forced out by threat." In effect, Bradley was proposing that the United States pull its troops out of Berlin under the guise of declaring victory in the occupation. Bradley recognized that there would be some cost to America's standing in the world, but the price that the conquered Berliners themselves would pay did not seem to factor into his thinking.

Clay, as a matter of fact, did not agree. He exploded into a torrent of words and pent-up anger. "Why are we in Europe? We have lost Czechoslovakia. We have lost Finland. Norway is threatened. We retreat from Berlin." His eyes narrowed and his pencil dug into the paper as he wrote out his response, handing sheet after sheet to the teleconference operator. "After Berlin, will come western Germany and our strength there relatively no greater and our position no more tenable than Berlin."

"If we mean that we are to hold Europe against Communism, we must not budge. We can take humiliation and pressure short of war in Berlin without losing face. If we move, our position in Europe is threatened. If America does not know this, does not believe the issue is cast now, then it never will and Communism will run rampant. I believe the future of democracy requires us to stay here until forced out. God knows this is not a heroic pose because there will be nothing heroic in having to take humiliation without retaliation."

No, said Clay, "I do not believe that we should plan on leaving Berlin short of a Soviet ultimatum to drive us out by force if we do not leave." Even under those circumstances, the Americans would have to "resolve the question as to our reply," to consider whether they would withdraw or try to stay and fight despite being so colossally outnumbered. In fact, as his pencil scratched out his outraged, forceful, determined reply to Bradley, Clay could only envision one scenario that, in his mind, should cause the United States to retreat from Berlin. "The only exception which could force us out would be the Soviet stoppage of all food supplies to German population in western sectors." But that, of course, would never happen.

Part III

THE BRIDGE

1948–1949

Show me dat stream called de River Jordan,
Dat's de ol' stream dat I long to cross.

"OL' MAN RIVER" BY OSCAR HAMMERSTEIN II

THE BRIDGE

1964-1965

8

JUNE

One by one, they filed into the office of Admiral William Leahy, Truman's top military adviser. When America's foremost military men and diplomats had settled into the straight-back chairs and plush leather couches, an FBI agent brought in the man they had all come to listen to—a shifty nomad from the mists of Central Asia named Boudikine. He had spent the past thirty years showering his loyalty on a succession of great powers: serving in the Russian army, the Italian navy, and then advising the British in World War II. "He is an intelligent man, a Moslem, and he appears to be telling the truth," observed Leahy.

Boudikine was directed to a chair, sat down, and looked around the room. He twisted his hands in his lap. He let a silence float over the scene for just a moment. And then he began his tale. He had been walking in a London park one night, long after dark, when he heard a Russian general and a Russian admiral, both of them drunk, boisterous in the confidence that no one could understand them, spell out the details of the most massive military operation the world had ever known. Fortified by their vodka, they had discussed the minute specifics of an invasion of America. It would begin with Soviet bombers, attacking from hidden airfields in Canada, obliterating major military installations in the United States. Soviet speedboats and submarines would sink the entire U.S. Navy. At the same time, 50,000 Russian sleeper agents—carefully biding their time in the shadows of American life—would, together with "disaffected Negroes," bring a tidal wave of terrorist attacks all across the country. President Truman, George Marshall, and Douglas MacArthur would be assassinated immediately. Dwight Eisenhower would be kept alive, the inebriated Russians revealed, because he "could be controlled." In Leahy's office, Eisenhower's embarrassed colleagues tried to avoid meeting his eyes.

The significance of the yarn of this fabulist from the Caucasus lay not in whether it was true or not, or even whether it was believed, but in that—to the most powerful men in America—it was believable enough to be heard. This was the atmosphere of a Washington that in the first half of 1948 had decided it was on the verge of war.

A s spring gave way to summer in June 1948, the sense of crisis that accompanied the Czech coup and the breakup of the Allied Control Council had dissipated into a slow-burning, pervasive fear. In March, it had felt as though war was about to break out. Men had readied themselves for battle. But when it did not happen, no one relaxed. It was, wrote the *Christian Science Monitor,* probably "just a lull between storms." In Berlin as well as in America, people felt they had received not a pardon but a stay—and having steeled themselves once, they now waited, opening the paper every morning wondering if this would be day the hangman rapped on the cell door.

On May Day, Communists held demonstrations around the world—from Paris to Seoul. In New York, the parade lasted six hours with marchers walking seven across carrying placards with letters that together spelled W-A-L-L-A-C-E. In Moscow, the May Day parade lasted six hours as well. Stalin stood atop Lenin's Tomb watching twice as many troops and tanks pass by as in previous years and five times as many long-range bombers fly overhead. In Berlin, the Communists gave full meals with schnapps both before and after the demonstration. Each marcher also received a half-liter bottle of schnapps to take home and extra ration cards for food or shoes. A quarter of a million Berliners marched through a Brandenburg Gate that had been decorated with large portraits of Marx and Engels, though at least one group of marchers was seen marching past the reviewing stand twice. Berlin's democrats held a counterdemonstration just past the gate, by the remains of the Reichstag. Only 75,000 came. Their slogan for the year was "*Freiheit und Brot*"—"Freedom and Bread." They did not realize they would soon have to choose between the two.

For more than three years, Berliners had lived in the jagged place between subsistence and starvation. By the middle of 1948, the daily ration for adults was two cups of milk, two tablespoons of vegetables, two tablespoons of meat, three small potatoes, three slices of bread, a small slice of cheese, and a lump of sugar. German students protested with placards that read, "Even a dog needs 1,700 calories."

Health officials in Berlin estimated that the health of 70 percent of the city's residents had been impaired by hunger. Since the beginning of 1946, a full third of all deaths in the western zones of Germany had come from malnutrition. The illnesses that preyed on starving bodies grew in strength. In the first half of 1948, the tuberculosis rate in the capital was more than twice what it had been in 1945 and 1946. Nine times as many Berliners were being diagnosed with jaundice than in the previous three years after the war's end.

Berlin's children were the most vulnerable. Six days a week, the American and British military governments served them a thick porridge that provided 300 calories. Occasionally, they were able to include a roll. The average child between ten and fifteen years of age had been permanently stunted from lack of food.

While Berliners worried about hunger, their occupiers squabbled behind closed doors. When Sokolovsky had stalked out of the Control Council, the only four-party body that had been left in operation in

Germany was Berlin's Kommandatura, which meant that the last vestiges of Allied cooperation in conquered Germany were in the hands of
"Howlin' Mad" Howley. If the Kommandatura—whose meetings now
regularly lasted up to eleven hours—disbanded, the Soviets would claim
the sole right to control Berlin. "For six weeks," Howley wrote in his
diary in May, "the Russians have ceased cooperating, have concentrated
their efforts to reading into the minutes attacks upon the Western Powers and the inability of the Kommandatura to function. When the time
is right, as they have planned it, they can walk out of the Kommandatura
and announce its termination and blame its failure on the Western Powers." If the four-power body did indeed dissolve, the Soviets would
argue that the Americans, French, and British had no more rights in
Berlin. Western soldiers and civilians in the city could become
hostages—or worse. "They can load us on cattle cars bound for Siberia
any night they want," an American officer told a visiting journalist.

In May, the French began to quietly but rapidly evacuate the family
members of their troops and officials from Berlin. It was an open question whether they would quit the city altogether. Their ambassador in
London had, on behalf of his government, pleaded with British officials
to support a complete Western withdrawal from Berlin, deploying an
argument identical to the one Bradley had made to Clay. "It would be
far more ignominious," he said, "to be driven out by Russian pressure
than for us to withdraw in good order and of our free will."

In early 1948, the Americans and British forged ahead with plans to
craft a West Germany and to create a new currency in the western zones
as a first step to halting the barter economy and black markets that had
stymied any hopes of recovery. The French balked. As they gathered
power in Eastern Europe, the Communists were gaining strength on the
rest of the continent. "Don't make it too hard for me," French foreign
minister Georges Bidault begged the American ambassador to Paris.
"Tell your government I am on your side and in the long run I am sure
we will work something satisfactory out, but at the same time I must
think about public opinion here."

But as the events of 1948 unfolded, the French faced a threat even greater than that of domestic politics. As one of their top diplomats told Clay in the weeks after the Control Council collapsed, "War with the Soviet Union within the next two or three years is inevitable—and that may mean this year." As the negotiations between the three Western allies continued in London, it became apparent that the French were not dragging their feet primarily because they worried about a resurgent Germany or about Communist pressures at home or about associating too closely with the Americans. The French were avoiding taking a strong stand on Germany because they did not want to provoke the wrath of the Soviets at a time when America was so weak. If war did come, the paltry number of American troops in Germany would be quickly overrun as the Red Army rolled west toward the Rhine. "The United States does not plan to defend Western Europe," Bidault groused to an American general, "but will abandon this area to the Soviets and base its defense lines possibly on the Pyrenees but chiefly North Africa." Of course, the Americans would eventually win World War III, he said; their monopoly on the atom bomb ensured that. But until then, "the Russian hordes will occupy the area, raping women and deporting the male population for slave labor in the Soviet Union." The price of standing up against the Soviets, the French foreign minister concluded, would be his country being first "occupied and devastated" by the Russians and then "atomized by the United States." The French pursued their policy of appeasement not only because they wanted peace but also because they feared America was not ready to fight an all-out war. "If we were sure you would drop atomic bombs fast enough and often enough, we would not be so worried but we doubt you will," Bidault confided to the American ambassador in Paris on June 2. "It would be easy for the Russian armies to overrun France and we shudder to think of what would happen to our beautiful country. We are defenseless, you know."

AMERICAN ACTIONS IN May and early June did little to reassure the Europeans. The legislation for the military draft was still winding its way through Congress, and Republicans in the House of Representatives were voting to slash the appropriation of funds to the Marshall Plan.

"The Nations of Europe Are Learning They Cannot Trust America," read one German headline in response. Then, worried that events were hurtling toward war, Marshall, with Truman's approval, sent Walter Bedell Smith to privately approach the Soviets with the message that the Americans were willing to talk. Smith met with Molotov on May 4 and presented him with a statement saying that "as far as the U.S.A. is concerned, the door is wide open for full discussion and the composing of our differences." Everything was negotiable, including, presumably, Berlin's future.

On May 9, the Russians released the contents of the note to the world and said they would accept America's invitation to begin bargaining. There was immediate shock and worry in London, Paris, and Berlin that the United States was about to sue for peace and walk away from Germany and Europe. Marshall backtracked, telling the press that there would be no negotiations, that he and Smith were military men and clumsy with the language of diplomacy.

But Henry Wallace took the opening. On May 11, speaking again at Madison Square Garden, he announced that he had sent an open letter to Stalin presenting his own plan for peace, which included student exchanges and an "outlawing of all methods of mass destruction." To a cheering, stamping crowd, he declared, "There is no American principle or public interest, and there is no Russian principle or public interest, which would have to be sacrificed to end the Cold War."

Within a week, Joseph Stalin replied to Wallace, planting both feet squarely in the 1948 presidential campaign. "No statesman caring for peace and cooperation among the peoples" can ignore Wallace's proposal, "since it reflects the hopes and strivings of the people toward consolidation of peace, and it doubtless will have the support of many millions of ordinary people," Stalin declared. The Soviet Union was bypassing the United States government and corresponding instead with the president's election opponent. Wallace was ecstatic. "The policies of Truman, Vandenberg, Marshall, and Forrestal have stained the world with blood," he charged at a California rally, but because of his efforts there was now a chance for peace.

Yet events were overtaking words. In early June, the London conference ended with the announcement that plans to create a western German state would be put in place and a constitutional convention would
be convened on September 1. Working in secret, Clay prepared to introduce a new currency in the three western zones—the Deutschmark. In
April, Congress had passed—over Truman's veto—a massive tax cut.
Soon after, Truman met with Forrestal to tell him he was, nevertheless,
still committed to balanced budgets. Despite the rising tensions, he told
Forrestal, money for the armed forces would have to be limited. Forrestal
would be allowed to spend no more than $15 billion for the next fiscal
year. It would be up to Forrestal to make Truman's military budget work.

It was ten in the morning on Wednesday, June 16, and Frank Howley
was already sour. The four Berlin commandants made their way into
the Kommandatura's oak-paneled meeting room and sat down in the
softly upholstered sling-back chairs that surrounded the long table of
inlaid wood. There was British general Edwin Herbert, with his slicked
hair and large moustache, and French general Jean Ganeval, his face
all angles. But Kotikov was not there. His deputy, Alexei Yelizarov,
announced that the Russian commandant was ill and he would sit in his
place. By his side, silent but watchful, was a shadowy Soviet political
adviser, a man Howley knew only as Maximov.

The agenda items were mundane: prison personnel, court reorgani-
zation, the parcel post. Translation involved a multilingual version of
the child's game of telephone. Behind each commandant stood an interpreter. When Howley spoke, his remarks were translated into French by
that country's interpreter, and then from French into Russian by the
interpreter standing behind the Soviets. The Russian interpreter pretended not to speak English.

The meeting dragged on past noon with only a half-hour break for
lunch. The commandants cycled through the same repetitive arguments. A standing fan buzzed in the corner of the room, swirling the

cloud of cigarette smoke hanging above the table. The room was stuffy. Howley's disdain was palpable. There was, at least, a handsome-looking official portrait of him hanging on the wall, which pleased him.

By the late afternoon, Howley had stopped paying attention. He gazed longingly outside the window at a lark flitting about in the azure sky.

At 7 P.M., a Russian commissar walked into the room. He wore an elaborately embroidered Ukrainian blouse under his dark, boxy coat. Howley had never seen the man before and never would again. Yelizarov and Maximov grew immediately tense.

The commissar sat next to the Russian delegation and whispered something to them. Usually unexpressive, they bolted straight up in their chairs. Yelizarov allowed the trace of a smile to hook up from his lips like a coiled curlicue of smoke from a cigarette shoved into an ashtray. Maximov's eyes scanned the room as if he was afraid someone had overheard them. Howley stared right at him.

Yelizarov immediately asked for a brief recess, which was granted. The other officials, with the exception of the Soviets, went upstairs to a dining room, where sandwiches and coffee were served. They mingled and stretched their legs. Howley casually moved toward the window. He watched Maximov, three stories below, stand outside in the courtyard smoking a black cigarette in a long holder, pacing nervously back and forth. The commissar approached him, and Maximov came to a stop. For a minute, they exchanged words, and then the commissar climbed into a dark, elegant roadster and drove away.

When they reconvened, Yelizarov immediately unleashed a torrent of calumny. The mood, reported one of the Americans there, "grew steadily heavier." By 10:45, Howley had reached his limit. The meeting was approaching the thirteen-hour mark, he noted, and he was tired. He proposed they adjourn at 11. The Russians could not have been happier if he had donned a fur hat and called for a proletariat revolution. But they hid it well. Yelizarov refused to adjourn. He had some important new business for the Kommandatura to consider that evening: a discussion of General Kotikov's eight-month-old "Fourteen Points for the Amelioration of Working Conditions of the Workers of Berlin." The

British and French generals took him seriously and began to rehearse their arguments against the Communist plan. Howley sat and steamed. Yelizarov watched him intently, waiting.

Finally, Howley asked to be recognized by Ganeval, who was presiding as chair. "It is now quarter past eleven," he said. "Half an hour ago, I suggested we end our meeting. I am tired. I'm going home and I'm going to bed. With your permission, General, I will leave my deputy, Colonel Babcock, to represent me." Ganeval gave his assent. Howley turned to Yelizarov and said, "You have reduced the dignity of the Kommandatura to a point below which the Kommandatura shouldn't be lowered." He stalked out, slamming the door behind him. In the quiet of the breezeless, still night, the others heard his car peel away.

At that point, Maximov turned to Yelizarov with insistent instructions. Yelizarov stood up and threw his papers onto the table. "I consider it impossible to continue this meeting after an action that I can only claim as a hooligan action on the part of Colonel Howley," he yelled. Ganeval began to reply that Howley had been properly excused, but Maximov had grabbed Yelizarov by the hips and was pushing him toward the door. "We haven't set a date for the next meeting," Herbert called after him. Yelizarov had a helpless look on his face. He raised his left hand as if he wanted to speak and then shouted something back to the group, but no one could make out what he said.

Howley was not so exhausted that he was unable to pay a visit to the American Press Club to hunt for his favored reporters and a strong martini. The bar was closing and only a few correspondents remained for a last round. German waiters in jackets of yellowing alabaster emptied ashtrays and washed out glasses. Howley ordered a martini on the rocks and began to recount the meeting's boring details. A steward approached with a message. Babcock had called for him on the phone in the lobby. Howley went out of the bar and received the news that the last ties between the four occupation powers in Germany had been severed and that he was being blamed. It was the occurrence the Americans had assumed would presage a Russian attempt to capture the entire city.

Howley's response was to go back into the bar and tell the press. "If any joker thinks the British, Americans, and French are going to be dealt out of Berlin, they have another thing coming," he said.

It was only when he had finished dispensing his pithy quotes that Howley decided to call Lucius Clay. It was now long past midnight, but Clay was still awake. At eleven that night, he had begun sensitive negotiations at his house with the French, who were once again flinching at the plans for a new currency. When Howley called him from the lobby phone in the Press Club to tell him what happened, Clay flew into a rage. "Get over here fast," he commanded. "I want to see you right away."

Howley arrived at Clay's house and was greeted with the words "You have done a terrible thing." Howley said nothing. Clay continued to berate the colonel for allowing the Soviets to bait him into leaving the meeting and giving them a pretext for dissolving the Kommandatura. Howley stood at attention, betraying no emotion, staring straight ahead. "And the worst part of it is, you're not even sorry about it."

"You're damn right I'm not," Howley exploded. Clay told him to get out and come back the next day at 8 A.M.

The following morning, June 17, the Soviet-controlled newspapers were full of stories castigating Howley. "The American commandant's contribution to the workers' question" had been to declare he was going to bed "in a condescending and flippant tone." Howley had slammed the door "as if in a horse-stall." Howley sat in the deep leather chair in Clay's office as the general paced in front of him, again cataloging the ways in which the Kommandatura's collapse would harm American interests. Howley's explanation was not complicated: "I have taken all I can stand from the Russians."

"Your job is to sit there and take it," Clay growled.

"I thought my job was to keep them from stealing the city of Berlin."

A silence fell over the room. Clay's ebony pupils shriveled. Howley expected to be fired on the spot. Long moments passed. Clay seemed as if he were not even breathing. Finally, he nodded slowly. "All right, Frank. I guess you've had your quota of conferences for one day. Go home and get some rest."

The next week felt crowded, like the last moments spent scurrying about the house before embarking on a journey. On June 18, after furious arm-twisting and in the face of a new wave of Communist riots and strikes, the French National Assembly approved the plans to begin creating a West Germany by a close vote of 300 to 286. That night, a Friday, on a special 8 P.M. German radio broadcast, Clay announced through an interpreter that he was instituting a new currency for Germany at 7 A.M., Monday morning. The Deutschmark would be effective in all three western zones. Since Berlin was governed jointly by all four powers, it was not included in the reform, the broadcast emphasized.

Just moments after the radio broadcast ended, in the afternoon in Washington, senator and vice presidential candidate Glen Taylor stepped behind a desk on the floor of the Senate to begin a filibuster against Truman's proposed military draft. For the next eight and half hours, he inveighed against this threat to the Constitution and peace. "We are in the process of losing all our ancient liberties," he declaimed, pleading with his colleagues not to be fooled by the chimera that "it is possible to have peace by getting ready for war."

Truman administration officials had conducted a furious lobbying effort to pass the conscription measures. With the president limiting military expenditures on new ships, weapons, and planes, they believed increased troop levels were vital to sending a message of strength to the Russians. Omar Bradley said the stakes were high. Passing the draft was "an eleventh-hour chance to erase tension." Marshall announced that a rejection of the draft "might lead to that which we are trying so hard to avoid—that is, war." For Forrestal, the tension was rising with each passing minute. He invited Taft, one of the two likely Republican nominees, to dinner at his home to personally press his case that "without Selective Service our defense establishment might really become a hollow shell as a result of the competitive wages offered by industry, the 'peace' campaign of Wallace, and many other considerations." As the night went on, he had another message for Taft, none too subtle. He said that he "hoped whoever became the nominee of the Republican Party" at the upcoming convention "would immediately assign several members of his staff to make a study of the National Defense Establishment." It was the kind of study that would be undertaken when a new party prepared to take over the White House. Like the rest of Washington, Forrestal understood that with the Democratic Party split by Wallace's "peace campaign," Truman had little chance at reelection. The Republicans, Forrestal indicated to Taft, should begin planning for the transition, and the secretary of defense was looking to be helpful to the new regime.

It was past 1 A.M. on Saturday, June 19 when Taylor handed the filibuster over to another draft opponent, Republican senator William Langer of North Dakota. Langer carried on through the rest of the night before giving Taylor back the floor shortly before dawn. At 8:29, reading from a telegram from a supporter, Taylor inadvertently violated a Senate rule that barred the impugning of other members' motives. The presiding officer ruled him out of order and the filibuster was broken. Taylor sank into his seat and, for long minutes, hung his head down with his eyes closed and pained. The Senate quickly passed the draft by a voice vote. That evening the House of Representatives passed it as well, with the most conservative and liberal members voting against the measure. Later that night, after midnight, Congress finally approved an appropriation to provide funds for the Marshall Plan to begin operations. The stalemate had been broken only because the Republican members of Congress needed to leave Washington. Their national convention was to begin the next day in Philadelphia.

ON SATURDAY, JUNE 19, the day after the announcement of the Western currency, the Soviets retaliated by placing new restrictions on western travel into Berlin. Passenger service on the rail lines was curtailed; only one train was allowed through at a time. Freight was carefully inspected. The bridge over the Elbe—a link between Berlin and the West—was suddenly closed for repairs.

Clay wanted to send a protest note to the Soviets stating that the restrictions were unacceptable. The State Department rebuffed him. It was not an "opportune" time. The British and especially the French were reluctant to cause a stir. "Unilateral action," Marshall felt, "would reveal a lack of unity." The United States had to work with its allies, the Americans were convinced. They could not strike out alone.

In Berlin, that weekend, GIs danced with *fräuleins*. They drank Cokes and smoked cigarettes. Curtis LeMay flew to Madrid to watch the bullfights. The others in his party were bored or horrified. He was entranced. "Three different bull fighters killed two bulls each during the evening," he marveled in his diary.

By now, the Americans in Germany had learned to live with crises. Yet there were signs this one was different. In his statement denouncing the new Western money, Sokolovsky had made clear it would have no value "in the Soviet occupation zone of Germany," as well as "in Berlin, which is part of the Soviet occupation zone."

"CAMPAIGN TO BE Fought over Domestic Issues," read the headline in that Sunday's *New York Times,* but the following day, the Republican convention opened with a harsh attack on the foreign policy failures of the Truman administration. On Monday, June 21, Representative Clare Boothe Luce, picking up on Truman's weary remark in Oregon ten days earlier that he personally had liked "old Joe" Stalin at Potsdam, reminded the television audience of the administration's failure to stem the tide of Communist expansion. "Good old Joe! Of course they like him. Didn't they give him all Eastern Europe, Manchuria, the Kuriles, North China, 'coalitions' in Poland, Yugoslavia, and Czechoslovakia?" That night, in the convention's keynote address, Illinois governor Dwight Green sounded the same theme. Roosevelt and Truman's "futile policy of appeasement of Communist Russia set back the clock of Polish freedom two centuries and paved the way for the destruction of the republic of Czechoslovakia." It all traced back to that warm embrace on the Elbe, the Republicans charged. The Cold War, Green said, was "the lusty child of the New Deal's rendezvous with Communism." Now

America was to pay the price. The Democratic Party, a "motley collection of embittered failures, back-alley revolutionaries and parlor anarchists," had "promised peace again and again and again when it knew war to be inevitable. Apparently the only promises that were really kept were those it gave to Joe Stalin."

There was a joyous buoyancy on the streets of Philadelphia. A huge inflatable elephant sat above the entry to the Bellevue-Stratford Hotel. Girls in summer dresses stood at intersections to give directions to visiting delegates. The little tinkle of bells filled the air as men in white pushed carts of Eskimo Pies down the street. In the hall, a sixty-two-piece band played "Anchors Aweigh," "California, Here I Come," "Can't Help Loving That Man of Mine," and "Ol' Man River." The Republicans had every reason for cheerfulness. The split in the Democratic Party was continuing. In January, a Gallup poll had given Wallace 7 percent of the vote. That June, it had given him 6 percent. He was holding steady. "The fact" was, Governor Green reminded the delegates, that the Democratic Party needed those Wallace voters. "It cannot win without them."

THAT SAME DAY, Monday, June 21, the Soviets matched the Western allies by announcing they would introduce their own currency in their zone. The question of what would happen in the four sectors of Berlin remained unresolved when representatives of each of the occupying powers met there on June 22 to discuss the currency stalemate. Negotiations continued through the day. By afternoon, the allies blinked. Under French pressure, the Americans and British made a remarkable concession. They offered to allow the Soviets to make their money the accepted legal tender for all of Berlin. With that right would come a powerful lever of control over the city's daily life and its ultimate fate. The Soviets turned them down cold. They would not agree to any decision that was announced jointly by the four military governments; only "Russian legislation must apply to all sectors of Berlin." The Soviets were not looking to resolve the currency issue. They were looking for a pretext to force the Western powers from the capital.

It was the week of the summer solstice, and in Berlin, high up near the Baltic Sea, the days stretched on without flagging. It was still light at nine that night when Acting Mayor Louise Schroeder was called to City Hall by the Soviets and notified that the following day the new Soviet money would become the official currency for all of Berlin. The Americans, British, and French, in turn, announced that now they would introduce their own currency into the western sectors. The City Assembly, meeting the next day, would have to decide how to reconcile the two conflicting orders.

"Something dangerous is brewing. Strangers talk to each other on the street, worriedly discussing the precarious situation. At four o'clock the city council is supposed to hold a special meeting," wrote Ruth Andreas-Friedrich in her diary on June 23. Berlin's City Hall had long been called the "Red City Hall" for the color of its bricks, but the building's location in the Soviet sector gave the term new meaning. As the city council members made their way to the session, they found the streets around City Hall choked with thousands of protesters. Red flags were waving above the crowd. Loudspeakers perched on vans blasted the speeches of Communist functionaries. The "Internationale" was being sung, seemingly in rounds. Just four months after the Czech coup, it all felt very familiar. Andreas-Friedrich, caught up in the mob, recorded what happened next:

> People are yelling. Their faces twisted as if they're suffering convulsions. The crowd surges forward. Trampling, pressing and pushing ahead like a stream of lava. There! Shoving, pushing, a flood of people surges forward. "They're storming City Hall," screams a woman.
>
> The stream carries us away. "They broke in the door," I hear someone shout. "They're taking over the assembly hall."
>
> Bastille! I think, alarmed. It's do-or-die now. We have entered City Hall. The surge sweeps us over stairs and hallways. In vain [Otto] Suhr, the Social Democratic chairman of the city council, tries to make himself heard. "We shall not begin the session before the spectator stands have been cleared," he shouts into the crowd.

For two hours, the democratic leaders of Berlin's City Assembly tried to quiet the crowd so that they could conduct their business. The horde in the galleries ignored them, chanting Communist slogans. One of the council members called for police protection. Communist police commissioner Paul Markgraf's officers ignored the summons. Finally, a Communist Assembly member told the mob to wait outside. They obediently filed out of the chamber.

Once the session began, the tide was overwhelming. By lopsided margins, the City Assembly voted to allow the Soviet currency only in the eastern sector and the Western currency in the other three sectors. Berlin's division had begun.

By 7 P.M., when the City Assembly was adjourned and its members began to go home, the throng outside had withered to around three hundred Berliners standing about halfheartedly waiting for something to happen. Many were hired thugs trucked in by the Soviets. The sight of the democratic politicians stirred them again. When one council member headed toward his car in the parking lot, a pack of hoodlums followed him, shoving him and taunting him as he tried to escape. Another council member ran from them and dove into the backseat of his friend's waiting car. One of the toughs slammed the car door on the council member's leg. The police pointed out the most prominent City Assembly members to the mob so that it could go after them. In the excitement of the moment, some of the hired goons began to forget that they were just there to get paid. When a boy picked up a rock to hurl at a fleeing council member, an older man next to him shook his head and told him, "Don't do it, kid, don't take this all too seriously." The young man dropped the rock to the ground. But not all of the hooligans received such good counsel. When Jeanette Wolff, a well-known Jewish council member whose fiery speeches against the Communists had earned her the nickname "The Trumpet," appeared, the mob met her with catcalls of "traitor" and "old Jewish pig." She was set upon and beaten roundly, her bones snapped by the blows.

Scattered reports of the riot were making their way to Clay's headquarters. Murphy sat in his office composing an urgent message to

Marshall and Lovett at the State Department. "Communist demonstrations of some proportion now occurring outside City Hall," he wrote in the cable. "General opinion is city government in present form cannot long survive." For three years, the tension between countries that had once been allies and then had become bitter enemies had been building. A new global conflict between two very different ideologies had arisen, and now was focused on Germany's capital, a once-great city, toppled by its own evil and hubris, where the Soviets and the Americans had trapped themselves together like scorpions in a bottle. Now the decisive hour had finally come. "Political developments in Berlin," Murphy wrote, "appear rapidly moving toward climax."

It was shortly before midnight on Wednesday, June 23, that the teletype machines in Berlin's newspapers began to whir. Urgent news bulletins began to stack up. "Transport Division of the Soviet Military Authority is compelled to halt all passenger and freight traffic to and from Berlin tomorrow at 0600 hours because of technical difficulties. . . . Coal shipments to Berlin from the Soviet zone are halted. . . . Water traffic will be suspended. . . . Soviet authorities have also ordered the central switching stations to stop the supply of electrical power from the Soviet zone and Soviet sector to the western sectors due to technical difficulties at the Czernowitz Power Station. . . ." The reporters still in the newsroom late at night began to gather around the large bulky machines, reading out the bulletins as they came through. "Here it is," said one. "This time it's final. A blockade has begun." Every day, by river, rail, and road, the allies had been bringing 31 million pounds of supplies to the 2.25 million Berliners who lived in the western sectors of the city. Now those supplies—food, clothes, medicine, coal for energy and heat—were cut off.

As soon as the electricity was shut down, the nighttime lights went out all over Berlin and raw sewage was discharged into the city's Spree River. By morning, backup power from coal-burning plants in the western sectors kicked in and, over the radio, Berliners learned of their fate. In a city already suffering from years of hunger and privation, people gasped at the news. In those early hours, the Russians stoked fear and confusion. Word spread through the city that Russian soldiers were about to invade again; the Red Army conducted exercises right outside the city limits. On Soviet-controlled radio stations, the announcer breathlessly informed listeners that "Babies are dying from lack of milk. . . . The Americans will be the first to leave. . . . Mrs. Howley is packing her silver. . . . Food riots are sweeping through west Berlin. . . . Stores are being looted and houses are in flames. . . . Western forces are firing on German crowds with hundreds of Berliners lying dead in the street." American troops made a show of force to tamp down any uprising among the Germans, as well as to try to reassure them. Wearing steel helmets, they rode through the city in armored vehicles with machine guns mounted on top. Military police officers toting rifles patrolled the streets. It was the most martial atmosphere in Berlin since 1945—a reminder of disaster that only added to the terror.

The gravest questions in western Berlin on that very first day of the Soviet blockade were whether there would be food and whether the Western allies would retreat from the city. From Washington and London, from Clay's headquarters in Berlin, there was silence. General Herbert went on the radio to try to calm Berliners. "There is enough food to avoid immediate anxiety," he announced. It was an occasion when British understatement was less than reassuring.

Howley waited all morning for some official word on America's answer to the blockade. Nothing came. Worried about the tension in the city, at 2 P.M. he drove to the studio of RIAS, the American station, to address Berlin on his own. There Colonel Frank Howley, speaking through an interpreter, took it upon himself to announce America's policy in the most dangerous crisis since World War II. "We are going to stay," he said. "I don't know the answer to the present problem—not yet—but this much I do know: The American people will not stand by and allow the German people to starve."

It was bravado without foundation, but for some it worked. " 'We

American lieutenant Bill Robertson embraces Russian lieutenant Alexander Sylvashko near Torgau on the Elbe in April 1945. (*National Archives*)

Truman raises the flag of liberation over Berlin in 1945. Dwight Eisenhower and George Patton stand to his right. Omar Bradley stands to his left, toward the front of the group. Lucius Clay is in the second row, over Truman's left shoulder. (*National Archives*)

Berlin after the war was a destroyed, dangerous, barely stirring city. (*National Archives*)

Berliners attempt to garden in the Tiergarten, their destroyed central park. The hulking mass of the burnt-out, shelled Reichstag looms in the distance. (*National Archives*)

After each session of the Allied Control Council, American, Russian, British, and French officers gathered for elaborate buffets. (*National Archives*)

American relief efforts attempted to feed Germans in the years after the end of the war, but it was not enough. (*National Archives*)

Wherever and whenever American occupiers threw away their trash, Germans would appear to pick through the refuse. (*National Archives*)

General Lucius Clay, the American military governor of Germany. (*National Archives*)

James Forrestal, who as America's first secretary of defense had greater total responsibility for national security than any previous cabinet member in American history. (*National Archives*)

Colonel Frank "Howlin' Mad" Howley at a meeting of the four-power Kommandatura that ruled occupied Berlin. (*Getty Images*)

Howley's nemesis, Russian general Alexander Kotikov. (*Getty Images*)

Ernst Reuter, the most popular politician in postwar Berlin. When the Russians vetoed his election as mayor, he passed out business cards reading "Ernst Reuter, the Elected but Unconfirmed Mayor of Berlin." (*Getty Images*)

German workers unloading C-54 Skymasters at Tempelhof. (*Halvorsen private collection*)

The insidious approach into Tempelhof brought the Airlift over a cemetery and above a tall apartment building perched at the edge of the airport's short runway. (*National Archives*)

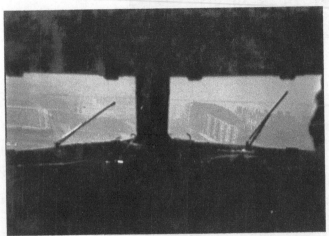

The view from the cockpit of an Airlift plane attempting to land at Tempelhof. (*National Archives*)

Even before arriving to save the Airlift, General William Tunner had acquired the nickname "Willie the Whip." (*National Archives*)

A plane overshoots the rainy runway and explodes into flames on Black Friday, August 13, 1948. (*National Archives*)

From left to right, Hal Halvorsen, Herschel Elkins, and John Pickering. (*Halvorsen private collection*)

The children Hal Halvorsen met at the Tempelhof fence. He gave them two sticks of Wrigley gum and promised he would return the next day to drop candy from his plane. (*Halvorsen private collection*)

Halvorsen at Rhein-Main preparing to make his first candy drop over Berlin. He is holding one of the first parachutes he fashioned out of handkerchiefs. (*Halvorsen private collection*)

Eventually, Airlift planes would come to drop hundreds of candy parachutes at a time to Berlin's children. (*Halvorsen private collection*)

On September 9, 1948, more than 300,000 Berliners gather in the shadow of the Reichstag to protest the blockade. It was the largest gathering since the end of war. (*Getty Images*)

Thousands of Berliners would gather to watch the Airlift planes land. Only a few years earlier, American military aircraft had brought Berlin death and destruction. Now, they represented the city's deliverance. (*Getty Images*)

Clay meeting with John Foster Dulles and an aide in his Berlin office in October 1948. Dulles, the presumed next secretary of state, came to Germany on a preelection publicity visit. "Ice existed between Dulles and Clay," Howley observed. (*National Archives*)

Twelve days before the election, Clay shows up presidential frontrunner Thomas Dewey at the annual Al Smith Memorial Dinner. (*Getty Images*)

On October 3, 1948, "Lt. Gail Halvorsen Day" at Tempelhof, Halvorsen throws candy to children from aboard his plane, the *Island of Christmas*. (*Halvorsen private collection*)

Halvorsen swarmed by young Berliners, who had lived through the war and its aftermath. These were the children Hitler had thought would be his legacy. "Take care of yourself," wrote 10-year-old Helma Lurch to Halvorsen, "and remember us children and we will remember you our whole life." (*National Archives*)

In a publicity shot taken during his trip to New York, Halvorsen points to a map showing the air corridors into Berlin. (*Halvorsen private collection*)

Halvorsen, surrounded by boxes of donated candy bars, reads through a batch of letters. (*Halvorsen private collection*)

With bags of coal beside him, Halvorsen shows how the candy parachutes are tossed from a Skymaster's cargo hold. (*Halvorsen private collection*)

To prevent pilots from leaving their planes at Tempelhof during unloading, Tunner brought a mobile snack truck to them and stocked it with hamburgers, coffee, and the prettiest young women in Berlin. (*National Archives*)

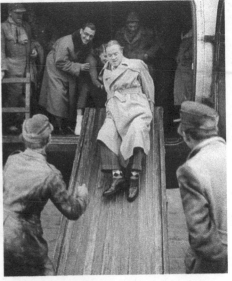

Bob Hope clowns around by sliding down an Airlift coal chute. Irving Berlin, in glasses, crouches over his right shoulder. (*Getty Images*)

Crew at Rhein-Main waiting for the fog to break for takeoff. Just when clear skies mattered more than at any moment in Berlin's history, the worst fog ever recorded engulfed Europe. (*National Archives*)

The blockade is lifted. (*National Archives*)

Young fliers at Rhein-Main— from Houston, Salt Lake City, and Yonkers—celebrate the victory of the Airlift. (*Halvorsen private collection*)

"Hurray, we're still alive." (*Halvorsen private collection*)

Truman honors Lucius Clay in the Rose Garden upon his return after the victory of the Airlift. Marjorie Clay watches from behind. (*National Archives*)

Halvorsen shows off one of his parachutes to Alta in a press shot after their engagement. They would be married for nearly fifty years. (*Halvorsen private collection*)

shall not let the people of Berlin starve,' he affirms loudly and clearly," wrote Ruth Andreas-Friedrich in her diary. "We are relieved. . . . We hope again! Because so far Colonel Howley has always kept his promises."

Others were less convinced. That evening, Berlin's democratic parties held a rally at a sports stadium in the French sector to show solidarity after the events of the previous two days. A large banner proclaimed, "Berliners: Fight for Your Freedom." When Jeanette Wolff appeared, hobbling on a cane and battered from her beating, there was thunderous applause. "None of us can be kicked down for long," she shouted. "This is not Prague, this is Berlin! We shall not bend till freedom is secure." Speaker after speaker delivered the same message. But there was one statement none of them could make. Not one said they thought that the Americans and other allies would stay.

AT 3:30 THAT afternoon in Philadelphia, House speaker Joe Martin's big gavel came down on the podium to begin the second ballot for the Republican presidential nomination. After the first round, the results had been Dewey with 434 votes, Taft with 224, Stassen with 157, and many other long shots and favorite sons trailing far behind. "The secretary will call the roll," he boomed. "Alabama, fourteen votes." Alabama cast nine votes for Dewey and five for Taft.

The roll call went on. In the White House, Truman watched flickering black-and-white images of the men with funny buttons announce their delegations' decisions. Taft was the clear emotional favorite of the delegates, and when his name was put forward there were genuine and sustained cries of joy from the galleries. Party leaders climbed atop chairs and rang cowbells. Men yelled until their voices grew hoarse. His supporters emphasized his experience with placards that read "To Do the Job, Let's Back Bob" and "Guard America with Taft." Stassen boasted of his ability to inspire a rising generation with slogans such as "The Man the People Want" and "Six Million New Voters Want Stassen." Dewey, a man who demanded that he get four fresh pencils sharpened to exactly the same length each morning, was not promising to inspire anyone. Nominated for his competence as "America's greatest administrator," he put forward no great vision and was carefully unobjectionable. But because of this he seemed to be offering what the delegates—starved for the White House after sixteen years of exile— really wanted. His signs read "Win with Dewey." When the voting was over, Dewey was within 33 votes of the nomination.

Truman knew Dewey would clinch it on the next ballot. He turned off the television and, at 5:40—his lips cracked and forehead sunburned from a cross-country speaking trip—sat down to sign the draft into law. The previous day, the legislation had been hand-carried to Philadelphia and back by a special courier so that Speaker Martin and Vandenberg, the Senate president pro tempore, could provide their official signatures. The new law called for 225,000 men between nineteen and twenty-five to be conscripted in its first year. The president was also given broad powers to seize factories that refused to or failed to follow the government's orders to produce weapons in case of emergency. As word from Berlin began to reach Truman in the White House, it appeared that the emergency was upon him.

IN THE CONVENTION hall in Philadelphia, few knew of the blockade of Berlin. After a break, the voting resumed with a stampede of support for Dewey. As delegation bosses announced their support for the New York governor, the galleries, packed with Taft's diehards, groaned.

Outside, the warm weather became muggy. The sky turned dark. The clouds broke and the applause of the delegates was punctuated by claps of thunder. A summer storm blew through with such force that it broke windows. The giant elephant balloon on top of the Bellevue-Stratford popped and deflated. By the time the squall passed, Thomas Dewey had been selected as the Republican nominee and—by the estimation of just about everyone who mattered in America—the 34th president of the United States.

While Dewey made his way downstairs from his hotel room to his waiting limousine, the skies cleared. As the car drove the short distance to the arena where he would to accept his nomination, the arc of a large rainbow hung in the west.

Four years earlier, Dewey had run in a period of total war and broad national purpose. This time, he had expected to be campaigning at a time of atomic peace and bitter partisan divisions. He and his advisers had settled on a theme of salving divisions and a strategy of, at all costs, remaining above the fray. His brief acceptance speech, which had been mimeographed for the press long in advance, mentioned the need for "unity" nine times. "The unity we seek is more than material," Dewey declared. "It is more than a matter of things and measures. It is most of all spiritual. Our problem is not outside ourselves. Our problem is within ourselves. We have found the means to blow our world, physically, apart. Spiritually, we have yet to find the means to put together the world's broken pieces, to bind up its wounds, to make a good society, a community of good will that fits our dreams." They were fine words, well practiced and polished to a shine, carefully modulated and conceived to win an election, but suddenly they were inadequate to a world on the brink.

THAT EVENING OF June 24, Clay arrived back at Tempelhof Airport after a full day of troop inspections in the American Zone. Berlin was on edge, uncertain; frozen in "a state of suspended animation," explained one Berliner. Save for Howley's boasts, there had been no reaction to the blockade from any American official. In the streets of the western sectors, Berliners debated the relative merits of starvation, war, and life under Russian control. As Clay descended from the airplane, the four stars on the shoulder of his dark-green uniform gleaming under the foundering sun, newspaper correspondents clambered about him to get a quote. He tried to calm the situation and said he did not believe that the Soviets would go through with their threat to truly blockade the city. "Do *you* think the Russians want to starve two million Germans?" he asked a reporter with withering disdain. The Soviets, Clay believed, simply wanted to scare the Berliners and Western powers into a capitulation. Marguerite Higgins, the twenty-seven-year-old correspondent of

the *New York Herald Tribune,* asked whether the Russians would succeed, whether America would bow to the demands. Clay seemed to hesitate for a moment. Then he said no, "the Russians are trying to put on
the final pressure but they cannot drive us out of Berlin"—and then,
realizing he had gone too far—"by any action short of war." Was there
some other way to bring food into Berlin? Clay practically guffawed. "It
is absolutely impossible to supply the city by airpower alone."

Clay arrived back at his Berlin headquarters to find his staff bitterly
divided between those who thought there was little choice but to make a
quick evacuation and those who thought America should use military
force to break the Soviet blockade. "If your hand is in the fire, why not
pull it out?" argued one aide. Murphy disagreed. The American military
was strong enough to force its way through to Berlin with supplies. The
Russians were bluffing and would not shoot. "Physically all that has
happened," he pointed out, "is a pole across the road guarded by two
Mongolian soldiers. *This* is the blockade, no more."

Clay kept his thoughts to himself in the meeting, but he had already
made up his mind. Everything in his character and makeup drove him
to take a stand against the Russians. After the meeting ended, Britain's
General Robertson arrived to discuss the blockade and coordinate their
nations' responses. Clay told him of his plan. He would send an armed
convoy of 6,000 men with tanks and with artillery guns down the autobahn by breaking through the Soviet barricades. The Russians would
not dare shoot. Robertson turned ashen. "If you do that, it'll be war—
it's as simple as that." Clay did not say a word. The British general
pulled himself up to the fullness of his formality: "In such an event, I am
afraid my government could offer you no support."

Robertson went home. It was late and Clay was left alone, dejected.
He must have realized at that instant that the officials of the Truman
administration, who so highly prized the principle of working in concert
with Britain and France and other allies, would be unlikely to approve
his convoy plan if it meant America would be isolated while bringing
about a new world war. The only other alternative he saw was an evacuation, which, it was widely assumed, would quickly result in all of Europe

falling to the Communists. This too would lead to the outbreak of war with the Russians. There was not much time. He believed that Berliners, already living the most difficult of lives, would "begin to suffer in a few days." A few hours earlier, Acting Mayor Schroeder, still shaken by the preceding day's events at City Hall, had told one of Clay's officers that if the Americans did not break through the blockade quickly, the Soviets would find "no need to stage riots as it will be a case of real riots" in which hungry Berliners would rise up to throw the Americans out.

Clay dangled a cigarette between his fingers and winced at the pain in his stomach. For one of the few times in his life, his confidence abandoned him. A retreat from Berlin seemed as if it might be inevitable. He called Marguerite Higgins and pleaded with her not to publish his pledge that America would stay in Berlin unless forced out by war. He told her it had been off the record—which was beside the point. He claimed she had misunderstood the context—which was not true. She agreed to allow him to clarify the quote for her readers. "If the Americans *only* were concerned, the Soviets could not drive us out of Berlin short of war but there is, of course, the fate of the Germans to consider," he claimed to have meant to say. In the dark of night on the most dangerous day the world had seen since the end of the war, Lucius Clay had lost his nerve.

A Manhattanite who dropped three pennies on the newsstand to pick up a copy of the *New York Times* on the morning on Friday, June 25, would have found the front page divided among stories about the new draft, Dewey's nomination, and the blockade. From that day on, the possibility of war, the election of 1948, and the siege of Berlin would be inextricably linked. "While the eyes of the American people are turned to the presidential campaign, a new drama is beginning to unfold itself in Germany which holds ominous potentialities for the United States and the world," began the editorial in that day's edition.

By the time Clay arrived in his office that morning, the shadow of doubt he had wrestled with the night before had passed—at least temporarily. The same flushed fury Clay had exhibited with his staff members and wartime industrialists took over, and the general who had missed action in two wars now wanted to send the pitifully weak American army into a face-off with the most powerful military in the world.

The Truman administration was, on that first day of the blockade, puzzled over what to do in Berlin, but their first concern seemed to have been making sure that the general in charge of U.S. forces in Europe did not start World War III. Clay was sitting at his desk composing a long message to Secretary of the Army Royall making the case for a convoy when he received word that the secretary wanted to speak to him immediately on a teleconference. Clay made his way downstairs into the windowless room filled with telecommunications equipment. "I am having conference with State Department and with Forrestal this morning. Until you are advised further, I would not want any action taken in Berlin which might lead to possible armed conflict," Royall began.

"I do not expect armed conflict," Clay replied. "Obviously, conditions are tense. However, our troops and the British are in hand and can be trusted." At that moment, it was not the troops that those in Washington were worried about.

The Pentagon and State Department officials had developed a set of offers, such as slowing the introduction of the Deutschmark, that they hoped might convince the Soviets to back down from the blockade. Clay rejected them immediately. "We have to sweat it out, come what may. If Soviets go to war, it will not be because of Berlin currency issue but because they believe this is the right time. Certainly we are not trying to provoke war." But he could not help himself to remind Royall of the stakes of withdrawal: "I can only say that our remaining in Berlin means much to our prestige in Germany, in Europe, and in keeping high the courage of western Europe. To retreat now is to imply we are prepared to retreat further."

As Clay walked back up the stairs to his office, the weight of the danger sat on his shoulders. For the second time in as many days, the general who had threatened to resign every time someone doubted his decisions now second-guessed himself. He sent a message, marked "Urgent" and "Top Secret," to Royall. They had little time. Berliners' "suffering will become serious in two or three weeks." So while he was "still convinced that a determined movement of convoys with troop protection would reach Berlin and that such a showing might well prevent rather than build up Soviet pressures which could lead to war," he was also willing to try to compromise with Sokolovsky over the currency. But even as he wrote out the message, he knew he did not fully believe what he was writing. His language was riddled with evasions and qualifications: they could "*probably* afford to compromise to prevent the severe punishment of Berlin without *serious* loss of prestige." Clay had not come to see appeasement in a different light; he had simply blinked.

ROYALL GRABBED THE transcript of his teleconference with Clay and brought it to the White House. Truman had awoken that morning to newspapers declaring the 1948 election over. Dewey's victory in November was "certain" according to "political observers," announced the *New York Times*. The energetic New York governor was "about to cap a distinguished public career with the Presidency of the United States," opined the *Los Angeles Times* without even considering the prediction dicey enough to need a justification or qualification.

After a ten o'clock cabinet meeting, Royall, Forrestal, and Lovett—who was again serving as acting secretary of state on behalf of the ailing Marshall—stayed behind to meet with Truman on how to handle Berlin. It was a brief conversation wedged in before Truman's meetings with various members of Congress. The press was told it was a meeting with Forrestal on implementing the draft. They began by complaining about Clay having publicly raised the specter of war to Marguerite Higgins the night before, but then quickly turned to weighing their options. It did not take them long to realize they were facing a series of terrible choices. It was decided the advisers would hold a meeting with Bradley that weekend to discuss the military possibilities in Berlin, and then report back to Truman on Monday. Other than that, Clay was informed, "no decision was reached except to maintain the status quo pending further developments and further discussions of the problem."

It seemed, that first day after the imposition of the blockade, that everyone with any responsibility to reply to the crisis blanched at developing a response. Clay had in Berlin. Truman, Forrestal, and the rest had in Washington. In London, Bevin, cutting short a vacation on the Isle of Wight, made a speech on the situation that was so cautious and ambiguous that afterward he was asked by a member of Parliament whether Britain planned to stay in Berlin. His answer was, "I prefer not to add to my statement with the delicate situation which exists now." Only the French were certain over what should be done. That day, French officials told the American ambassador that while they would follow America's lead, they felt the difficulty of "maintaining the economic life of the western sections would be almost insuperable." They would be better off, the French were convinced, in surrendering the Berliners to the Soviets.

AS DREW MIDDLETON of the *New York Times* made his way around Berlin on June 25, he found the initial shock of the announcement of the blockade had given way to the constant prattle of a city on the verge of a breakdown. Daytime electricity was being shut off in the city, its paltry economic life was coming to a halt, the everlasting search for food now seemed to be pointless. "About 2,250,000 Germans in the western sectors of Berlin came face to face with the grim specter of starvation today," he observed. So many small groups of people gathered on the streets, the city's *Telegraf* daily reported, that all of Berlin looked like London's Hyde Park. Discussions of newspaper articles on street corners turned into violent arguments. Having suffered so much over the past three years, Berliners, it seemed, would be unable to bear up against this most serious blow. "The Berliners of 1948 are not equipped physically or emotionally to withstand the sort of siege the Soviet measures foreshadow without some indication of outside assistance," Middleton wrote that day for the *Times'* front page.

Clay—again trying to convince Washington to allow him to send his armed convoy through the Russian lines—wanted to make sure that the Berliners would be able to hold up if such assistance came. He sent for Berlin's most popular politician, Ernst Reuter—the man whose election as mayor he had once allowed the Russians to veto. The two men hardly knew each other. Clay had delegated the responsibility of speaking to Berlin's leaders to Howley, and he must have wondered at the sight of the fat man on a thin cane who walked into his office accompanied by his young aide, Willy Brandt. Reuter sank into the leather chair in front of Clay's big desk. He held his brown beret in his hands. Deep-furrowed wrinkles were scribbled across his forehead. Clay told Reuter that he was committed to staying in Berlin and would do whatever needed to be done to bring food into the city. But even if the convoy worked, Berliners "are going to be very cold and feel very miserable. Unless they are willing to take this and stay with us, we can't win this," he said. "I don't want to go into it unless you understand that fully, unless you are convinced that the Berliners will take it."

Reuter leaned forward on his cane and, in his perfect English, responded, "General, I can assure you, and I do assure you, that the Berliners will take it." Then, with all the sensitivity and diplomacy he could muster, he told Clay he thought it was doubtful that the Americans and their allies would be able to supply the city under the blockade, but no matter what, the Berliners would fight on again to the bitterest of ends. "We shall, in any case, continue on our way. Do what you are able to do—we shall do what we feel to be our duty. Berlin will make all necessary sacrifices and offer resistance—come what may."

When Reuter left, Clay made a phone call, almost as an afterthought. Robertson and Albert Wedemeyer, an American general visiting from the Pentagon, had urged Clay to load up transport planes with supplies and send them into Berlin in order to somewhat supplement the slowly dwindling stockpiles in the city. From the first news of the siege, the idea of supplying Berlin from the air had been widely considered and quickly dismissed. "The blockade left the air the only way to get food in to the 2,000,000" western Berliners, read an Associated Press bulletin that day. "Allied experts said that would prove unworkable in the long run."

The *New York Times* that day had stated that while "it may be possible to supply the allied personnel in Berlin by air," as had been done for a few days in April, "that method becomes wholly inadequate when it comes to supplying the whole population of the western zones."

Nevertheless, Clay thought that flying some supplies into the city might buy him time to press for the convoy and lessen the sense in Washington that they needed to quickly write Berlin off. Lifting the scrambler phone on his desk, Clay barked, "Get me General LeMay in Frankfurt." At the time, the legendary bomber chief was planning for a surprise first-strike attack on Russian air bases in Germany. As the conversation was recounted in the years to come, Clay said, "Curt, have you any planes there that can carry coal?"

"Carry what?" LeMay asked.

"Coal."

LeMay was a man of war, not a freight train operator; he saw his job as dropping bombs, not delivering packages. "General, we must have a bad phone connection. It sounds like you are asking whether we have planes for carrying coal."

"Yes," replied Clay, annoyed. "That's what I said. Coal."

There was a long pause on the phone before LeMay responded, "The Air Force can deliver anything."

So the legend has been retold. In fact, the next day, LeMay sent a message to the Air Force command in Washington: "General Clay queried me yesterday as to my capabilities" to supply Berlin by air. "My estimate to him was that my maximum sustained capability during good weather months is approximately 225 tons daily." Before the blockade, Berlin had been bringing in 31 million pounds of supplies a day—1.8 million pounds of potatoes, 1.3 million pounds of flour, 12 million pounds of coal to fire its factories and heat its homes. The most that LeMay believed could be brought in by air was less than half a million pounds a day—just over one percent of Berlin's meager preblockade supplies. The puny Air Force of 1948 could not "deliver anything." In terms of what Berlin needed, it could deliver almost nothing.

On Saturday, June 26, Clay met with Howley to discuss plans for dealing with the blockade. "Frank, I'm ordering some planes in," Clay said as casually as if he were ordering a ham sandwich. "There won't be many, but they will be planes. How fast can you get ready to accept them, and what do you want brought in first?"

"We'll accept cargoes as fast as they come in," Howley answered. "And we'll have flour first, please."

In western Germany, LeMay was trying to pull together a cargo transport operation with little in the way of resources and even less in terms of experience. His primary transport plane was the C-47, a military version of the celebrated Douglas DC-3. Before World War II had begun, the DC-3 had been the luxury liner of the sky. It carried twenty-one passengers and, by making possible travel between New York and Los Angeles in less than twenty-four hours, had popularized the idea of air travel in the United States. Once the war began, production lines had been converted to building the planes as C-47s that could each carry about 6,000 pounds of cargo. More than 10,000 had been built. In June 1948, there were 102 left in Europe, and 70 of them were in working condition. What LeMay really needed were the bigger C-54s. Each of those could haul 20,000 pounds of cargo. Of those, he had two.

They used whatever planes they could in those first days. Jack Bennett, a senior pilot with American Overseas Airlines, a division of American Airlines, received a phone call from LeMay's office asking if their plane could be chartered. "You're going to be shocked at the cargo. It's coal for Berlin."

Bennett balked. Coal dust would destroy the elegant interior of the passenger plane. LeMay's staff officer continued to prod him. "Is it that serious?" Bennett asked.

"It's that serious," he was told, and the plane was off to Berlin.

———

"WE ENDED THE week with a note of vaudeville," Murphy wrote to the State Department on June 27. That Saturday, a big, black Russian car blew past a speed trap in the American sector going 65 miles per hour in a 20 mile-per-hour zone. The driver refused to stop for an American jeep patrol. They pursued the limousine for two miles as it raced "to beat hell," in the words of an American military police officer. The troops radioed ahead for an armored car to intercept the speeder. Finally, three jeeps, two of them with machine guns mounted on top, pulled the car over and surrounded it. The Russian driver got out and, waving his arms, yelled "Marshal! Marshal!" The passenger, a tall man in a Russian uniform with a chest full of medals, stepped out as well. Another Russian car arrived on the scene and from it emerged a gaggle of Red Army troops with tommy guns. They headed toward the Americans. A young GI jammed his gun into the pit of Marshal Sokolovsky's stomach and told the Russians to back off. Sokolovsky nodded slowly and the Russians dropped their guns.

Sokolovsky was placed under arrest and taken to a military police station. There a sergeant phoned a lieutenant, who called a colonel, who finally identified the commander of Russian forces in Germany. The colonel called Clay and told him what had happened. "Using appropriate language," as Murphy put it, Clay ordered them to release Sokolovsky immediately. He was taken back to his car and drove off at 20 miles per hour.

The young American soldiers would claim that the Russian car did not have markings and that they did not know the identity of the general they had in custody. This could well have been true. But the row upon row of medals on the Russian's uniform might have given them a clue. It was a hint they chose to ignore or, more likely, one that emboldened them. The American troops in Berlin, reported *Time*'s bureau chief that week, "are spoiling for a fight. They are tired of being pushed around."

THIS WAS THE worry in Washington that Saturday—that war would begin not by orders from the White House or the Kremlin that sent armies moving across a frontier, but in a chain reaction from the mistake of a green GI with a nervous trigger finger or from an uncontrollable general determined not to lose face. That morning Forrestal called Lovett at the State Department to ask, "Any news?"

The latest news from Berlin showed the situation to be "hotter than a firecracker," Lovett told him. Events were spiraling out of control "and nobody exercises any influence over Clay."

Forrestal wondered, Was it time to fire Clay?

Not yet, said Lovett. To do so then would be seen as a "sign of weakness." But that afternoon Clay was sent detailed "Eyes Only" orders to make sure he understood the official stance of the American government and would not deviate from it. His job, Clay was told, was to "maintain US establishment in Berlin, to concert a united force with the British and French, and to resist force with force, but not to initiate a use of force." He was reminded that the "possibility of a communist revolutionary people's movement to seize power from the Berlin city government cannot be excluded" and that he should prepare himself for the fact that a continuing blockade would make the "western position on Berlin eventually untenable." After all, "the Western Nations can supply their Berlin garrisons by air but cannot supply the German civilian population with adequate coal and food."

THAT FIRST DAY of the airlift, thirty-two flights landed at Tempelhof, bringing 160,000 pounds of fresh milk in glass bottles, bags of flour, and serums and vaccines. The British Royal Air Force brought in another 26,000 pounds. Howley went down to Tempelhof to watch the planes arrive. What he saw were "old, tired, and patched" planes—not much longer than a school bus, many of them still painted in a dusty hue from service in battles in North Africa or with the three stripes that marked them as veterans of Normandy. To Howley, they were winged augurs of deliverance.

"They wobbled into Tempelhof, coming down clumsily through the bomb-shattered buildings around the field," Howley recalled, "but they were the most beautiful things I had ever seen. As the planes touched down, and bags of flour began to spill out of their bellies, I realized that this was the beginning of something wonderful—a way to crack the blockade. I went back to my office almost breathless with elation, like a man who has made a great discovery and cannot hide his joy."

The next day, on Sunday afternoon, four days after the blockade had begun, the top officials of American government finally met in Army secretary Royall's office to discuss how to respond to the crisis. Around the table sat Forrestal and Lovett—the secretary of defense and the acting secretary of state—as well as the highest ranks of the civilian and military leadership of the Pentagon.

They reviewed the situation. "Today, the two great power groups of the West and East are moving toward a showdown across the shattered capital of the enemy they joined to defeat," that morning's *New York Times* had announced. In Berlin, that weekend, the Soviets were employing the same tactics of disturbance they had used to such powerful effect in Prague. "Shock-troop speakers" would stand on busy corners and begin yelling about the treachery of the Western nations, gathering a crowd around them like traveling medicine men. "Agitation autos" filled with young Communists were distributing propaganda leaflets. The leader of Berlin's Communists proclaimed that the standoff "will not end until the western allies leave." But to win the affections of troubled Berliners, he announced the Communists would make a special distribution of prunes.

Advice was flooding in from around the world. The *New York Times* opined that the "surrender of Berlin would be such a blow to the democratic forces" that it "would inevitably lead to the loss of Germany," which "would in the end mean the loss of Western Europe." The paper endorsed an armed convoy to avoid "at least as grave a menace as was ever posed by Hitler." In turn, the *Washington Post* advocated a retreat, saying that there was no logic in keeping an outpost in Berlin. The previous day, in England, speaking before 100,000 at a Conservative rally at Luton Hoo, Winston Churchill, who knew something of the subject, said "we should all have learned by now that there is no safety in yielding to dictators, whether Nazis or Communists." The issues were, he said, as "grave as we now know were at stake at Munich ten years ago." If the Russians forced the Western powers out, the Germans under their control would live under a "reign of totalitarian terrorism." Privately, Churchill had sent word that he believed America should use its nuclear monopoly to tell the Soviets that it was they who had to leave Germany or face having their cities razed by a preemptive atomic strike. In contrast, the French were so worried about offending the Russians they were shrinking from even sending a strongly worded diplomatic note. "Let us continue our conciliatory action without excluding anyone," said French prime minister Robert Schuman.

To Omar Bradley, the choices that Sunday were fairly straightforward: "get out, fight, or try to stand on quicksand." None of the options were good ones.

The "fight" option was Clay's idea of an armed convoy that would call the Russians on their presumed feint and force them to fire upon the Americans or let them through. The group quickly dismissed this proposal. Even if the tank column did make it through, what happened then? A single wagon train down the autobahn could deliver a million pounds of food and fuel—a fraction of what Berlin needed every day. Would the Soviets allow caravan after caravan to break past their border guards? Would American forces have to capture and hold the Soviet highway?

Clay was putting his confidence in military intelligence reports that said that there were no signs that the Soviet military was making the preparations that would naturally accompany a decision to wage an all-out war. But what if the intelligence reports were wrong? Or what if war happened without either side planning on it? An errant shot by a raw Red Army soldier tautly clutching his rifle would unleash an immediate response. American soldiers were unquestionably allowed to return fire if fired upon. And once a battle had begun, once blood had been spilled, was it reasonable to believe that the lit fuse leading to the powder keg could be snuffed out in time? The Russians had twenty divisions nearby. The Americans, together with the British and French, could muster only three. To men like Bradley, who had led America through the complicated calculations of a global war, this was basic arithmetic.

Even if the convoy did not lead to war, some in the meeting argued, it might simply lead to embarrassment. All the Russians had to do was blow up a bridge on either side of the convoy and the entire line of trucks would be trapped in place. "The Soviets would just sit up on a hillside and laugh," said Lovett.

The "get out" option appeared inevitable. The night before, Murphy had sent a personal cable to Marshall pleading with him to stand firm. If they would "docilely withdraw now, Germans and other Europeans would conclude that our retreat from Western Germany is just a question of time. US position in Europe would be gravely weakened, and like a cat on a sloping tin roof." The officials in Royall's office agreed with the sentiment, but they felt they had no choice but to begin laying the groundwork for a retreat. Whether or not this crisis passed, Bradley believed, Berlin was militarily indefensible in the long run and it was better to leave sooner rather than later, to march out rather than be pulled under by the quicksand. They delved deeply into the relative merits of the cover stories they could use to reduce the humiliation of a withdrawal. They would try to delay the reckoning as long as possible, but by summer's end, they knew it would come. That morning, Bradley had received a "Top Secret" memo from Berlin stating that "food stores for 30 days are on hand." By the time it had been handed to him, the 30 was crossed out by hand and replaced with a 21. It was estimated that the airlift could extend those supplies already stockpiled by a few days. If the city was switched to consuming only dry food, they might be able to stretch out their time to 60 days. This meant that the Western allies had until September 1 to retreat. Nevertheless, they decided that Forrestal, Lovett, and Royall would lay the three options before Truman the next day. The meeting had begun a few minutes after four. By 7 o'clock, the men were done and on their way home for dinner.

On Monday, June 28, at half past noon, Forrestal, Lovett, and Royall went in to see Truman. The president was quiet, almost subdued. His cabinet members began to all talk at once about the blockade. It was a scene of general confusion, with the three of them arguing among themselves and interrupting one another. Truman let them continue on for a long while and they laid out the three alternatives they had discussed the previous afternoon. Finally, as Lovett began to describe the steps to take for a withdrawal, Truman cut him off. "We are going to stay. Period." The three men looked at him and a silence hung over the room.

Royall, his brow creased, began to explain the nuances of the situation and the consequences of what that would mean. He said he had "some concern" as to whether Truman had fully thought through what he was saying. If America committed itself to Berlin, they might have "to fight our way" into the city.

"We will have to deal with the situation as it develops. We are in Berlin by the terms of an agreement, and the Russians have no right to get us out by either direct or indirect pressure," Truman said.

Truman made two other decisions. He wanted to reinforce the airlift "even if it takes every Piper Cub in the United States." He also approved a plan to station B-29 bombers in Germany and England. These planes—commonly referred to as "atomic bombers"—were the kind that had flown over Hiroshima and Nagasaki. The decision marked the first time that an implicit threat of nuclear attack was to be made. In the three years since the end of the war, the atomic bomb had been in America's holster. Now the gun was put on the table—where it would remain for forty years. The entire meeting lasted only fifteen minutes.

THAT MORNING IN Berlin, Clay visited Sokolovsky to personally apologize for the speeding arrest that had occurred on Saturday. It was the first time they had seen each other since Sokolovsky walked out of the Allied Control Council three months earlier. The friendly bonhomie and banter was long gone. Sokolovsky received Clay coolly and correctly. He claimed that the arrest had been deliberate. "For the first time in the history of our meetings, no refreshments were offered," Clay reported to Royall.

But as the conversation continued, Sokolovsky seemed to be looking at Clay with pleading eyes, hoping that the American had come to offer a way out. "I was under the impression that he is set on his present course but is by no manner of means happy or confident. I was also of the definite impression that he had hoped I was bringing some proposal with me and that he kept waiting for me to offer such proposal."

Clay had no compromise to present. He was determined that the Americans would stay in Berlin; Sokolovsky was equally determined that they would leave. They each thought they were headed toward a confrontation where one of them would have to back down or there would be war. But that day, though neither man paid enough attention to it at the time, the airlift was on its way to exceeding what LeMay had thought was its maximum. It was still only bringing in a pittance, far less than what Berlin was consuming even on its severely scaled-back rations, but that night the airlift went on a twenty-four-hour schedule. For the first time since the bombing raids of the war, the quiet of the night in Germany's capital was interrupted by the hum of American planes flying overhead.

"UNITED STATES AIRCRAFT, which four years ago brought death to the city, will bring life in the form of food and medicines to the people of the Western sectors, whose food supplies have been cut off by the Russians," reported an American correspondent in Berlin. "It will be possible to keep Berlin fed but not for long and it is felt here that nothing is to be gained by hanging on as at present until the food stocks have become exhausted." That moment was fast approaching, and Harry Truman knew that with it would come the need to make grim decisions. His two top military advisers—Bradley and Leahy—told him that Monday that the situation in Berlin was "hopeless" and that the United States would probably "have to withdraw." The director of the Central Intelligence Agency informed him that "Soviet inspired terrorism is expected" in the German capital. The west Berliners had no love for the Russians, but "if their determination were weakened by hunger and continued unemployment," he told Truman, "the people probably could not be counted upon to offer serious resistance to Communist action."

In Berlin, food stockpiles were plummeting—there were twenty-five days of flour left, eighteen days of potatoes, nineteen days of milk.

Neither Truman nor his advisers had said a public word about Berlin. There was little reassurance they could offer, and panic would only make matters worse—both at home and in Berlin. Though the newspaper headlines pointed to an approaching emergency, Americans enjoyed halcyon days of summer. On Saturday, Hal Halvorsen had returned to Mobile from a mission to Panama. He wrote Alta that he had "kinda expected a temporary call to Germany on that Berlin food crisis," but it had not come. Instead he went swimming in the pool on base that had just opened for the season. He "stayed in an hour too long" and got sunburned on his back. He had no sense that he was about to be swept up in a whirlwind. "Not much going on around here," he wrote. "Been swimming at the Gulf a couple of times—Pretty nice out there. Watermelon time here—sure are good."

That Monday evening, Truman and Bess ate their dinner out on the South Porch of the White House. It had been a hot day, with temperatures rising to near a hundred degrees. Usually talkative, Truman sat quietly looking out on the new Jefferson Memorial through a gap in a line of trees off in the distance. The sun hung in the sky over his right shoulder, trying to decide whether to fall beneath the horizon. In the center of the great South Lawn a fountain, rimmed by petunias, burbled. A robin flitted between the trees. He could hear the cheers of young people playing their summer baseball games out on the Ellipse. Out across the Potomac, he saw the planes take off and land from National Airport. Truman thought of his predecessors, of how John Quincy Adams could while away hours swimming in the river. "It is a lovely evening," he noted in his diary. But his reverie was interrupted as he recalled the burdens he was facing. Over the past week, Thomas Dewey had been all but anointed as his successor in the coming election, he had been forced to bring back the military draft, and the Soviets had laid siege to Berlin, giving him the option of abandoning democracy in Europe or beginning World War III. "I wake up, go upstairs and go to work and contemplate the prison life of a President. What the hell!"

9

JULY

On the morning of June 29, General Curtis LeMay—bombing hero of World War II, commander of the United States Air Force in Europe—sat at the controls of a fully loaded C-47 waiting for a junior enlisted man in the control tower to give him the green light to take off toward Berlin. He was ready to go at 10:45, and he sat steaming until he was given his clearance at noon.

That afternoon, in Berlin, he met with Clay to discuss how they could bring more food into the city. LeMay reminded Clay that he thought this effort was wrongheaded—it was not what an air force was for, and he did not want to be wearing out his bomber fleet on such a sideshow to the coming real war. But he would follow orders.

The cargo being flown into Berlin was only a fraction of what Berlin needed to survive. Clay's office calculated that doling out to Berliners the bare minimum of rations they needed for survival would require 8 million pounds a day. Throwing all they had into the effort, that day the Americans and the British would fly in about 750,000 pounds.

The problem was, LeMay told Clay, that the C-47 was too small to carry much bulky cargo like coal. Even their two C-54s, the so-called Skymasters, though three times bigger, would not carry enough. What they needed, LeMay said, almost giddily, was the B-29—the bomber LeMay had sent into combat in World War II. There was only one problem with his plan, he admitted. Berlin's Tempelhof Airport, located smack in the middle of the city, had runways far too short to land a big B-29. This was, however, easily solved, LeMay said. He knew exactly what to do. They would open up the bay doors and drop the bags of coal down on Berlin.

LeMay began to put in place plans for the drops. He needed a wide-open area where the coal could fall. The British proposed that the stadium that had been the home to the 1936 Olympic games could act as a gigantic "catcher's mitt" for the coal and other supplies. A group of high-level officers gathered for a test run. The coal was dropped from an RAF bomber, and pulverized on impact. The wind carried the dust toward the officers, covering their light summer uniforms in a fine black soot.

THE BERLIN AIRLIFT never truly began. It was simply a temporary measure to furnish some extra food and supplies for the city's rapidly depleting stockpiles that dragged on and grew in importance. No one involved in even the most remote way in the decisions being made over Berlin thought it was possible to feed the city by air. The operation was being used largely as a way to stall those decisions. The more cargo that American and British planes were able to bring into Berlin, the more time Clay would have to lobby for his armed convoy plan and the more time those in the Pentagon and State Department would have to convince Truman that there was no real choice but to abandon the city.

If dropping supplies into the city would not work, the Americans and British would have to fly in what they could as freight. LeMay appointed one of his deputies, General Joseph Smith, to organize the operation. LeMay told Smith the duty would not last more than a couple of weeks. Among Smith's first decisions was to provide the military code name for the operation. His officers proposed "Operation Lifeline" or "Operation Airlane." He thought these were too pompous for a modest effort to provide a relatively small amount of extra provisions to Berlin until, one way or another, the crisis passed. "Hell's fire," he supposedly said, "we're hauling grub I understood. Call it 'Vittles' if you have to have a name."

LeMay's men scurried to fly as many supplies as they could into Berlin. Often LeMay himself would be found at the controls of the planes. His officers were combat veterans whose bombs had destroyed large areas of the Nazi Reich and brought the Empire of Japan to its knees, but they had never bothered to learn about the dreary details of air transport. The major that Smith made air cargo officer of Operation Vittles spent part of his first days on the job trying to find out the basic fact of how big a load a C-47 could carry.

But it took them no time at all to realize they did not have nearly enough planes or pilots to make a real difference in Berlin. With the planes that LeMay had at hand, he now estimated that the maximum he could haul was 1.4 million pounds a day. It was time, he told Clay, to "send up a smoke signal back home." The alert flashed to Air Force bases around the world: "Prepare to release all available C-54 Skymasters to the United States Air Force's command in Europe."

———

The same day that LeMay flew to Berlin to discuss the airlift with Clay, the City Assembly met to review the situation. The body was riven as it had never been before in the aftermath of the attack on the deputies a week earlier. Jeanette Wolff rose in favor of a measure to create a secure area around the City Hall so that the council members could come and go in safety. She was heckled by the very men who had directed the thugs that beat her. She answered their catcalls directly: "I was not afraid of the Gestapo which destroyed my family. I kept on working, and gentlemen, I am not afraid of the 'consequences' with which you threaten. For I have only one life to lose, and this life belongs to freedom. And if it should cost my life on your account, gentlemen, and Berlin could remain free, I declare myself ready for death."

The exchange was dramatic, but the real work of the session was to determine how to respond to the blockade. With the previous night having been the first in which allied airplanes flew round the clock, the Communists raised a terrifying specter to Berliners who well remembered the work of American and British bombers just three years earlier. An armada of 3,000 planes was on its way, their chief spokesman claimed, "of which possibly each one is to bring an atom bomb to Berlin."

The democrats in the body thought better of the Westerners' intentions, but less of their capabilities. Deputy Mayor Ferdinand Friedensburg told the City Assembly that they could not rely on the allies and that an airlift could not save Berlin. "We hear with joy and satisfaction that a certain substitute traffic by air has been introduced, and we shall hope that this emergency traffic will be greatly expanded in the future. But, ladies and gentlemen, in that way—and I want to speak very openly in order to leave no doubt about the seriousness of the situation—in that way at best only a portion of the food supplies can be assured. It is impossible, as far as I am able to judge, to deliver all the necessary food supplies, and it is completely impossible to assure the coal supply by air." Berliners had been cheered by the arrival of planes full of food but, he said, this should not distract them from facing forthrightly the deadliness of the circumstances they were confronting. "It may be that our population has not yet appreciated the entire seriousness of the situation. Ladies and gentlemen, I would understand it if even in our own circle we would hesitate to look the Medusa head of this emergency straight in the eye. It is something so unheard of, something so unthinkable, something so unprecedented, that in peacetime a city, or a large portion of a city of 2.1 million inhabitants should no longer receive the necessities of life." It was natural, he continued, that they "think instinctively that things cannot be so serious, that the threat must somehow be averted, that such a possibility will simply not be tolerated by the world." But it was real and it was upon them. That day—against the wishes of Clay's military government—they passed a direct appeal for action by the United Nations.

The Berliners were right to wonder about how much they could rely on the allies. Nearly a week had passed since the blockade began and it had been met with official silence from Washington. The only public response from top officials there had been a "No comment." But working behind the scenes from London, Foreign Secretary Bevin had been trying to stiffen the Americans' wobbly first response. On June 30, in a hushed House of Commons, he declared that Britain would not retreat from Berlin. "We recognize that as a result of these decisions a grave situation might arise. Should such a situation arise, we shall have to ask the House to face it. His Majesty's Government and our Western allies can see no alternative between that and surrender—and none of us can accept surrender." He was clearly speaking of war, but the word—in a Britain still mourning its dead from the last conflict—was too horrible for him to let pass his chunky lips. Winston Churchill sat nodding sternly. In the gallery, men clutched the former prime minister's new book, the first volume of his World War II memoirs, titled *The Gathering Storm.*

Bevin had pleaded with the Americans to make clear that they would not abandon Berlin. It would be helpful if Marshall "could say something appreciative" about the stout Berliners "and their steadfastness." Later that same day, June 30, Marshall made the American government's first statement to the press regarding the week-old Berlin blockade: "We are in Berlin as a result of agreements between the Governments on the occupation in Germany and we intend to stay." It was hardly definitive—and it did not say a word about the Berliners. America would try, at least temporarily, to bring supplies to the city because it was in the nation's own interest, not for the sake of the conquered Germans.

The American military, all but ignored in the years since the end of the Second World War, was awakened from its slumber. In downtown Honolulu, Navy airman William Glatiotis was having a beer when a sergeant walked by and shouted out, "Hey, Greek, you're shipping out in two hours' time." It was midnight on Guam when a colonel stopped the music at a Saturday night dance and read from a message he had just received: "Your group will proceed immediately from Guam to Hawaii, California, Massachusetts and Wiesbaden, Germany to form part of an airlift to Berlin." When no one stirred, he added, "Gentlemen, we leave in two hours' time." On Johnston Island, Captain Ted Harris was coming back from the operations center at midnight when a jeep's headlights approached. His navigator slammed the breaks and called out, "Ted, you've got to get yourself together in thirty minutes! We're going to Berlin." At Elmendorf Air Force Base in Alaska, the commanding officer walked into the base's movie theater and shouted, "This is what we've been waiting for!" Someone cracked, a bit too loudly, "Maybe *you* have . . ."

On Saturday, July 10, Hal Halvorsen had a head cold—the kind of summer cold that lingers for weeks. He was supposed to have been on a mission to Puerto Rico, but it had been postponed for airplane maintenance, so he had the day off. He and his friends went to swim in the pool at the Officers' Club. They frolicked with the flight nurses. Halvorsen did diving stunts off the board as everyone laughed. Big Larry Caskey did a cannonball and everyone got wet.

That afternoon came word of an emergency meeting for all C-54 pilots. Halvorsen had been selected to pilot the plane during the war based on his ability to follow the rules, but had since moved on to the larger C-74. With the pool clearing out, however, he followed the others to listen in on the briefing. Four C-54s from the base, it was announced, would be leaving immediately to Rhein-Main Air Base in Germany to take part in the airlift to Berlin. The crews would be gone for about three weeks, until the operation was over. The colonel began to read off the names of the thirty-six pilots and navigators who would be going.

Pete Sowa's name was one of those called, but he did not answer. At that moment, he was on a flight returning home from Panama. He would need to take off for Germany soon after he landed. Halvorsen called Sowa's wife and told her the news. She crumpled in despair. He could hear the twins in the background crying in the tiny house. She asked why he was not going, and he explained to her that he was in a different squadron and he flew a different kind of plane, but it felt empty as soon as he said it.

The Sowas had been so kind to him—those Sunday dinners had been such a source of comfort—and all that Halvorsen had holding him to Mobile was his new Chevrolet. Besides, the Berlin mission sounded like an adventure—a chance to finally be where the action was. Halvorsen went to his commander and asked to be transferred to the C-54 squadron to go to Germany in Sowa's place. He agreed and Sowa's commander, Lieutenant Colonel James Haun, did as well. Halvorsen was given temporary duty orders "not to exceed seventy days."

He packed quickly, carefully wrapping his spring-wound eight-millimeter Revere movie camera and throwing all the handkerchiefs he could get his hands on into a big duffel bag to care for his running nose. He parked the Chevrolet under a copse of pine trees and hid the keys.

Pete Sowa arrived as Halvorsen and the others were loading their gear into their plane. "What in the world is going on here?" he asked, and when Halvorsen told him, Sowa could not stop thanking his friend. Just a couple of hours after Halvorsen had received permission to take Sowa's place, he was heading down the runway on board the Skymaster. As the plane took off and left Alabama behind, he caught a glimpse of the sun reflecting off his red roadster, veiled beneath the sheltering pines.

On July 3, Clay and his British and French counterparts traveled to Sokolovsky's headquarters in the Berlin suburbs near Potsdam for the first meeting of the four military governors since the breakup of the Allied Control Council. In the days after the blockade began, Sokolovsky had maintained the ruse that "technical defects" were the reason trains could not make it to Berlin from the west. "All measures in their power are being taken by the Soviet transport organizations in order to eliminate these difficulties," he had written to Robertson. He had gone so far as to smarmily tender his appreciation for "the measures which, judging by the press, are so energetically now being taken" to supply Berlin by air while the repairs were being made. Now Clay and the others would have the chance to confront him directly.

They each drove out separately. As soon as their cars passed the city limits, Soviet escort vehicles pulled up alongside them. They were brought to Sokolovsky's anteroom and waited there until they were summoned. Finally, Sokolovsky greeted them properly. In his office were three men Clay had never seen before but who he assumed were Soviet minders. Robertson expressed "concern over the deterioration of our relationship." There had to be some way to fix things, he pleaded. Sokolovsky interrupted him and said evenly that "the technical difficulties would continue" until the allies abandoned their plans for a west German government. Even when the current technical problems on the railway were fixed, others might develop. No mention was made of the new Western currency as a reason for the blockade. It was clear that, as Clay had argued to those in Washington, it had simply been a pretext. The Soviets were looking to upturn the entire situation in Europe—by forcing the West to retreat from Berlin or give the Russians a say over the rest of Germany. "It was evident that he was confident we would be forced to leave Berlin and that he was enjoying the situation," wrote Clay. "We were not." Clay thanked Sokolovsky for his time, and they left the room. "Our farewell was as cold as our reception," he reported to Washington.

Three days later, the Soviet ambassador to Washington was summoned to meet with Marshall at the State Department. Thirteen days after the siege of Berlin began, the United States—along with France and Britain—lodged a formal protest. Reporters were informed that Marshall had handed the ambassador not just a note but a "very serious note." It reasserted the allied powers' right to be in Berlin, demanded that the Soviets allow supplies to flow into the western sectors once again, and offered to open up the subject of the future of Germany to negotiations once the blockade was lifted.

At that very moment, in an adjoining office, Bob Lovett, Marshall's deputy, was sitting down with representatives of the Brussels Pact governments to begin the first real negotiations over a military alliance with

Europe. He began with a lecture. The discussions they were about to begin had to be kept secret. "A leak, particularly during the political campaign in the United States, might throw the whole enterprise into jeopardy—political heat in this country will increase up to election day and scars will be left over afterwards and any leak might cast a cloud over the whole plan." The *New York Times* speculated the European ambassadors might be there to discuss an arms transfer, "a military assistance program, perhaps resembling Lend-Lease."

The truth was there was nothing to leak. What had been true in March was even more true in July. No progress would be made on a treaty committing United States forces to fight European wars until after the election. Already in political danger because of the Marshall Plan, Truman could ill afford to take this even larger step. Moreover, the evacuation of Berlin, which Lovett thought likely, would color any discussion over such a defense pact. That week in July, and for the next four months, Lovett employed every trick—from misdirection to classic diplomatic circumlocution—to slow the negotiations over America's defense commitments to Western Europe. It was, he believed, something the Dewey administration would have to deal with itself after November.

After stops at Westover Air Force Base in Massachusetts and in Newfoundland, Halvorsen's C-54 headed over the Atlantic. They flew through the night toward the Azores, and at daybreak "a puff of cloud could be seen dead ahead, perched like a floppy hat on the crown of the tallest visible peak." As they came over the island, the dark blue of the waters gave way to green fields surrounded by high stone walls that led to the runway. After landing, they climbed up a tiny hill to the Officers' Club past women in bandannas, blue-and-white stucco churches, and windmills spinning in the ocean breeze. Halvorsen was new to the squadron, but he snapped photos of the other men and they warmed to him. With his bald head and big grin he looked like a junior version of

General Eisenhower. When they got to Germany, they would be divided into crews of three. Halvorsen would be the pilot of his crew. His co-pilot would be Captain John Pickering, a big man with a gregarious nature. Their navigator would be young Sergeant Herschel Elkins, nervous and green. Halvorsen made a point to talk with them on the flight and on the island. Soon after eating lunch they were on their way toward Europe.

As their plane approached Germany, Halvorsen listened in to the control tower chatter on a set of large headphones. Tuning in to the Rhein-Main channels, he heard shouting and mayhem, a cacophony of confusion as the traffic controllers attempted to order the chaos in the skies over the base. They circled for forty minutes before they were cleared to land.

At the southern foothills of the Taunus Mountains near Frankfurt, the Rhein-Main Air Base was a single runway on open land cleaved out of the forests. The area had once been the home of giant dirigibles that blotted out the sun in cities around the world. From there the *Graf Zeppelin* had taken off to circle the world. It was the last home for the ill-fated *Hindenburg* before it departed for Lakehurst, New Jersey. During World War II, Allied bombs had landed on the base, and it had then been destroyed by the Germans themselves in advance of the arrival of American troops.

Halvorsen's Skymaster landed and pulled off the runway. They opened the door of the aircraft to a scene of mass commotion. Trucks and jeeps and airplanes all rolled past one another on the apron, men in uniform dodging their way between them, screaming orders. It was not clear whether anyone was listening. It was raining, hard and steady. As soon as they parked the plane, a junior officer ran up to them with a clipboard full of papers curling in the rain. His first words to them were "Welcome to Rhein-Main. Who will be the first crew to Berlin?" Without waiting for an answer, he said, "Let's go," and began to lead them to the operations center. Planes—some C-47s, some C-54s—were lined up in long rows, the nose of one only inches from the tail of the next. Halvorsen craned his neck as they walked past displaced people, refugees in rags, gathered in groups of ten in the back of flatbed trucks backed up to the planes, yelling to one another in strange tongues, as they threw large bags of flour into the cargo hold. The filthy smell of rain on asphalt mixed with the exhaust of engines. The rush of the men and the roar of the planes carried with them a sense of purpose that Halvorsen found electrifying.

Another crew from Halvorsen's group was selected to fly their first mission to Berlin. They took off in a loaded C-54 an hour and half after they had landed in Germany. In the meantime, Pickering had gone off to find out some information about where they would be housed. He returned with another officer who had bad news. Within the past couple of weeks, hundreds of new people had moved onto the base—not just pilots but everyone else needed to support them and the massive operation. It had been an established truth since the war that it took ten men on the ground to keep one man in the sky. Now, overflowing its capacity, Rhein-Main had the worst living conditions of any American air base in the world. Halvorsen and the others were given a choice between tents and tarpaper shacks. They chose the shacks.

It was forty-five minutes before a weapons carrier arrived to take them to their new home. While they waited, Pickering dozed off amid the hubbub. By the time they climbed into the back of the truck, a few more new crews had landed on base. They headed off toward the shacks. En route, they drove past the base's low, wood-frame buildings, now mired in muck. "I thought for a while this was the Klondike," said one of the first airmen to arrive. "Rain, mist, and cold." The three combined for the worst July weather since 1910. It had been raining for days—not the light drizzle of summer but a nasty cold downpour that chilled the men and turned the unpaved roads into rivers of sludge. The first aircrews to arrive had taken one look around at the disgusting slush and dubbed the base "Rhein-Mud."

The tarpaper shacks were on the far side of the autobahn from Rhein-Main, at the edge of the deep forest in a clearing enclosed by barbed wire. As they pulled up, they watched as war refugees, the current occupants of the shacks, were herded out to make room for the American fly-boys. The displaced persons shuffled out meekly into waiting trucks, carrying their few belongings with them. They had clearly been moved often and did so again more in resignation than in gloom. "By their haggard looks and disheveled mixed dress," observed Halvorsen, it was clear they "had seen happier times." He assumed they were survivors of the Nazi slave labor sites and concentration camps of which he had heard so much.

Halvorsen and Pickering stepped down from the carrier and walked toward one of the shacks. Their feet sank into the mud past their ankles. At the center of the structure was a potbelly stove, and it was surrounded by rows of metal cots whose thin mattresses reeked from dirt and death and the sweat of terrible nightmares. The floor was littered with debris. The raindrops played the roof like a snare drum.

Other newly arrived crews had converged on the same spot and were rushing to place their gear on the cots of their choice. As Halvorsen went to retrieve his duffel bag from the truck, he spotted something in the distance. "What is that big building at the other end?" he asked a captain. "It looks like a barn."

"That's exactly what it is."

"Well, is there any place in there I could put a cot?"

"I don't think so. It's full of old machinery and junk."

Undeterred, Halvorsen and Pickering went to check out the large gray brick structure with a tall sloping brown roof. The first door was closed. They walked around to the side. The rain came off the eave, dripping down cold onto their heads. The side door was open. It was dark inside. Pickering struck a match. The downstairs was a shambles of discarded junk but they saw a wooden ladder leading upstairs to a loft. They climbed up and found it to be decked in cobwebs but otherwise dry. Joined by a few others, they made it into their home.

Halvorsen lay down in a makeshift bunk that night. The barn was at the edge of the runway, and all night long he could hear the planes land and take off. Less than a day had passed since he had left Alabama and now he found himself under a foreign sky. He thought of Alta and his family. It occurred to him that he was suddenly on the other side of the world, disoriented and lonely, and no one who loved him even knew he was gone.

THE NEXT MORNING, at eleven, they were driven back to the base, where, in the small red brick operations center, they were given their instructions and a map of how to get to Berlin. At the end of the war, air corridors for planes to travel from the western zones over the Soviet zone to Berlin had been negotiated by the Allies. There were three—one from the north, one from the center of Germany, and one from the south near Frankfurt—that converged onto the capital. Each was only 20 miles wide.

They reached their assigned plane and found it had already been loaded with 138 bags of flour. "If we go down we are going to have plenty of pancakes," cracked Elkins. They were among the fortunate to be carrying something useful. In the early days of the airlift, planes were filled with any supplies at hand, a scattershot approach to throw whatever was available at a needy Berlin. Early cargo loads included 5,000 pounds of mimeograph sheets. Another plane was full to the brim with shrubs to help Berlin's reforestation campaign. One pilot flew a load of watermelons and French wine. This merlot mission caused such an uproar among the pilots that a delegation of insulted Frenchmen—whose country was not contributing to the airlift effort—arrived at headquarters with a presentation explaining why wine was as important to their troops in Berlin "as potatoes to a German, black bread to a Russian, or ketchup to a Texan."

Halvorsen climbed into the cockpit. He began to flip switches above his head, turning on the plane's four engines, one at a time. From his left to his right, the propellers, two on each wing, began to spin, billowing out smoke as they got started. The plane headed down the runway, slowly at first, gathering speed, vibrating violently as it rumbled toward takeoff. Under the weight of the flour, the heavy plane strained at the end of the runway, finally heaving itself into the sky with the groan of a fat man leaping. "Gear up!" Halvorsen told Pickering, who raised the wheels, filling the cockpit with the smell of burning rubber as the spinning tires rubbed against the stopper in the wheel wells.

A series of Morse code beacons directed them into the corridor. Below Halvorsen stretched a paisley patchwork of green and brown-hued fields and forests, sprinkled with the red roofs of German villages, rolling out clear to the ebbing horizon. Planes were supposed to be following one another at a regular pace, like soldiers marching past a reviewing stand, but as the airlift began, crews were often waiting twenty-five minutes for air traffic clearance. Once in flight, Halvorsen learned, pilots were racing one another to win bets on who could reach Berlin first.

After half an hour, they were over Soviet territory. With no radio contact available, they used highways, railroads, and mountain ranges below to guide them. The cabin was not pressurized, so it was not only cold inside, but loud. The grumble of the engines alone would have been noisy, but they flew with the windows open in the cargo compartment behind them in order to suck out the flour dust that gathered in the plane.

After forty minutes over the Soviet zone, they began to descend into Berlin. The voice of Tempelhof's tower came over the radio to guide them. Up ahead loomed the city. As they approached, the view, Halvorsen remembered, "just about took our breath away. Nothing I had read, heard, or seen prepared me for the desolate, ravaged sight below." It was, William Shirer wrote after seeing Berlin from up in a plane, "a great wilderness of debris, dotted with roofless, burned-out buildings that look like mousetraps with the low sun shining through the spaces where windows had been."

"Where in the world do the two million people live?" Elkins asked. Halvorsen and Pickering simply shook their heads. A few days later, Halvorsen would write home—after having by then seen the honey-combed city a dozen times—and he still could not come to grips with what he saw below. "Berlin is a shell of a city," he wrote. "I think how easily it would be for Detroit, New York or any U.S. city to look the same way, and I hope and pray we may be wise enough to prevent it, with the help of the Lord. I shudder every time I think of it and I think of it every time I see their black walls pointing skyward."

The flight path into the city had been laid out precisely, and any deviation from its particulars was strictly prohibited. They passed over Zehlendorf, where Clay had his headquarters; over the once fashionable boulevards of the city; over Spandau Prison, where Hitler's aides, including the architect of Germania, Albert Speer, were jailed; and over the Kaiser Wilhelm Memorial Church. As they neared the center of the city, they closed in on Tempelhof.

"As we came in looking for this place all we could see were bombed-out buildings all around," Halvorsen recalled. "Then we spied this grass field—it seemed more like a pasture than an airfield." He could see Tempelhof's orange-and-white control tower in the distance at the end of the runway. What lay in between was perhaps the most devilish landing approach that dumb luck and poor planning would ever devise. The flight path to Tempelhof's runway was obscured by two huge structures that pilots had to avoid in order to land—dual monuments: one to a German's intransigence, the other to Nazi incompetence.

On the left side of the approach was the tall 400-foot smokestack of a local brewery. As soon as the airlift began, the American authorities had pleaded with the brewer to let them tear it down since it was obstructing the flights. He refused. Berliners, he would say, needed his beer to survive. So the Americans slunk away defeated without ever pointing out to him that there was no malt for beer in blockaded Berlin anyway.

The obstacle on the right was even more insidious and dangerous: a seven-story apartment building sitting nearly on top of the runway. To land at Tempelhof, the pilots had to come down right over the building at a sharp angle. They were able to easily look into the apartments of the people who lived there as they were landing, coming so close that when they peered into the windows they could see not only that it was dinnertime, but learn what was on that night's meager menu. Some of the building's residents would later claim there were skid marks from airplane tires on the roof.

Of all the troubles the airlift pilots would face—and they would be formidable and manifold—none vexed them like this apartment building. They considered it as Ahab did the whale. The pilots would curse the Nazis again for having had the stupidity of leaving such a structure flush with an airport. They would wonder how it had been that American planes had flattened so much of the city but left this building standing. "If I'd known what I was going through on the airlift, I would have managed to drop some eggs on that building, believe me," said one pilot who was a veteran of bombing runs on Berlin. "If I had me a BB gun, damned if I wouldn't shoot out a window, at least," said another.

To the ironic pilots, it made perfect sense that the only spot of open space between the brewery smokestacks and the apartment building was a cemetery. It was not just that the apartment house was so tall, it was that the runway was so short. Loaded to capacity with coal or flour, the planes needed its entire length to slow down and come to a stop. That meant that the Skymaster had to dive down from the top of the apartment building to the start of the runway on a glide path more than twice as steep as Army regulations allowed.

Halvorsen came over the top of the building, chopped off the plane's power, pushed the yoke forward, and pulled it back. In the slice of a second between the time they peaked over the top of the apartments and when they slammed onto the Tempelhof runway, Halvorsen saw—gathered in the few feet between the building and the airport's barbed wire—something that barely even registered at the time: about twenty-five children gathered on a grass strip.

LANDING AT TEMPELHOF reminded Halvorsen of "the feeling that a crop duster would have" back home "landing on a high road or in the pasture he's dusting." They slammed onto the runway in a belly flop and the plane's brakes shrieked as if in pain. Hitler had built Tempelhof's terminal building to be the largest structure in the world. He was less concerned with the usefulness of the airport's runways. One was simply sod—this one was used by the planes for takeoffs. The other—the one used for landings—was made of mats of pierced steel laid on top of a bed of crushed rubble.

The steel planks, with holes the size of hockey pucks, had held up fine when Tempelhof had a few flights a day. But after weeks of steady beating from hundreds of landings of heavy planes, they were beginning to come apart. Women from Berlin were hired to stand by the runway and pour a mixture of tar, sand, and rubble into the gaps. LeMay ordered his staff to keep the runway open even if it meant placing "German workers one yard apart on either side of it." He was not far off. Crews of 225 women stood just off the runway as the planes came in. After each one landed, they ran onto the steel mats with shovels and wheelbarrows and patched up the breaks. They then ran back off the runway and knitted while waiting for the next plane to land.

As Halvorsen's plane reached the end of the runway, a yellow jeep with a sign reading "Follow Me" on its rear pulled in front of them and led them to an unloading area near the shade of the terminal's overhang, the large structure dwarfing the big planes. There was a banging on the cargo door, and Elkins ran back to open it. There, standing in the bed of a truck, were twelve men ready to unload the flour. By their tattered coats and strange combination of unfamiliar uniforms, Halvorsen saw immediately they were Germans—probably veterans of Hitler's army.

The call for German workers to come work on the airlift had been one of necessity in early July. Hundreds lined up at Tempelhof's gates for every dozen openings. Those selected were guaranteed not only pay but a hot meal, which most took, at least in part, home to their families. Fights broke out over places in line. The crowd turned into a mob pushing into the recruiting office, smashing a window and a door as they surged forward. Weak and thin from hunger, they had to show they could lift and carry a 220-pound bag of sugar up on their shoulders. Dieter Hahn, age sixteen, almost collapsed under the bag, his legs buckling from the weight. It would have cost him the job for which many others behind him were waiting. He managed to haul the bag to a waiting truck, he would remember, "but the path I took—that was determined by the sack."

Halvorsen acted skittish around the Germans, sizing them up suspiciously as they threw the bags of flour down a wooden chute into the truck bed. He looked for evidence of everything he had been taught and thought about the Germans during the war, for signs of "the monster, the hardened stare, the 'superior' eye, or the defiant look." Instead, he saw them looking at the bags of flour as if they had been brought by "angels from heaven delivering the news of the resurrection." They must have sensed his standoffishness, for one of them put out his hand and smiled. Halvorsen hesitated for the merest second before he took it.

For the pilots who arrived on the airlift, it was a common conflict. They had come to hate the Germans during the war and now were being asked to save them. "I flew milk runs to Berlin during the air war in Europe," one pointed out. "Now I'm flying milk there." Another told CBS News, "Four years ago, I was trying to kill all these Berliners. Now I'm flying myself to death trying to keep them alive." In fact, a number of the men flying the airlift had failed in the mission they had been assigned only a few years later: to bomb Tempelhof Airport out of existence.

Some dealt with the paradox better than others. One of the pilots who slept in the loft with Halvorsen had seen two of his crew members killed in a firefight over Germany. Halvorsen asked him how he could reconcile this with their new mission. "When defenseless women and children are involved, it cancels out a lot of the past," he told Halvorsen. "I didn't feel good about dropping the bombs. Now maybe I can do something about the food."

Yet the noble sentiment was by no means universal. The reaction the Germans anticipated, the one they felt they detected in those first weeks of the airlift, was that held by so many of the other pilots. "First you bomb them, then you feed them," said one veteran. "I wonder what my navigator's widow out in Kansas thinks of it." Asked by a reporter for his opinion of the Germans, another GI griped, "I've never found a Nazi or anyone who ever knew a Nazi, and neither have any of the other boys. For a guy who was all by himself, Hitler fought a helluva of a war." Still another pilot had a plan. "What I try to do now is fly one flight a day instead of two. That way I beat those bastards in Berlin out of 10,000 tons of coal." The attitude was not surprising to the Berliners.

After all, they had lost the war. The huge effort to feed the city was appreciated, but a survey conducted that week in mid-July showed that more of the city's residents thought the Americans were interested in strengthening their power than thought they cared about the welfare of Berliners.

THERE WAS A wait before they were ready to return to Rhein-Main. In the meantime, Halvorsen and his crew walked around Tempelhof. Out on the ramp, the scene was similar to that on the other end of the lift, a bustling garboil of hustling soldiers and flagging planes. The apron was made of marble, and as the planes were unloaded in the wet, the crews slipped about on the smooth surface, only adding to the sense of bedlam.

They headed inside the operations center to fill out the forms required for takeoff, check on the weather, and buy a hamburger at the snack counter. They saw that many of the windows on the terminal had been blown out in the war and had still not been replaced. On the outside of the terminal, facing the street, the big eagle that adorned the side of the building was still there. Its swastika had been painted over with a shield of red and white stripes. Its head had been painted white and its beak had been colored gold.

It would be an hour and a half after Halvorsen, Pickering, and Elkins arrived at Tempelhof before they were able to head back to Rhein-Main. They returned at 6:30. An hour later, after a quick dinner, they took off for Berlin for the round trip once again, flying into the night.

The airlift had been functioning on excitement and caffeine, but by the middle of July the effects of both had begun to wear off. A pilot named Hugo Krenek remembered the early days of the operation: "Things were pretty confused. After a while they seemed less confused and just plain rugged. Then a little while later, things weren't rugged anymore; we all just seemed to be exhausted." Flying time is draining. As if in some Einsteinian parable of relativity, time stretches out in the cockpit. Four hours flying was—in an article of faith—held to be as taxing as eight hours of work on the ground.

Pilots were sleeping for seven out of every thirty-six hours, returning home, as one of them recalled, to quarters that "were so crowded that it was common for two or three pilots to share the same bed, sleeping in shifts. With schedules erratic, it was impossible to separate crews flying at night from those flying days. People were constantly coming or going inside barracks. Aircraft engines were roaring around the clock outside, making uninterrupted sleep virtually impossible." A British reporter found that the "barracks were a seething, dead-weary dormitory in which there was no night and no day, only constant getting up and feeding and going to bed of men who ticked off hours flown on their schedule sheets like boys marking off the days to the end of the term."

The problem with the jumble and mess of the airlift was not simply its inefficiency—flying watermelons and wine to a city on the brink of starvation—but the havoc it wrought on the pilots. They would be awoken with a shake in the middle of the night to be told that their flight schedule had been changed and they were about to leave. They would sit disoriented on the edge of their bed unable to remember whether they had just got up or were about to go to sleep. And then they would sit on the tarmac for hours waiting for a delayed takeoff, growing hungry and becoming sick with fatigue.

Flight surgeons found that pilots were "jagging badly on too much coffee." But this was not the most dangerous part of the exhaustion. In the third week of the airlift, entire crews started falling asleep, awakening only when the planes' falling altitude jarred them from their slumber. That first day flying on the airlift, Hal Halvorsen collapsed back onto his cot in the loft of the barn at three in the morning.

In the White House, President Truman slept fitfully as well. "Never been as tired and groggy in my life," he wrote to Bess on the morning of Friday, July 9. The Democratic convention was three days away, and as it approached, party elders were working feverishly to drop him as the nominee and replace him with someone, really anyone, else. A disparate group that included Senate candidate Hubert Humphrey, Senator

Strom Thurmond, New York mayor William O'Dwyer, the leaders of the American Federation of Labor and the United Auto Workers, and Franklin Roosevelt, Jr., were trying to replace Truman with Eisenhower. None of them knew anything about the general's views on most of the major issues of the day, but they were willing to climb on board an empty vessel if it meant that Democrats could retain power. That Friday before the convention, Eisenhower again declared he would not run, saying his decision was "final and complete." In Jersey City, boss Frank Hague crumpled his cigar and said, "Truman, Harry Truman. Oh my God!"

As Truman met with his advisers to plan for the convention, however, he was also monitoring the deteriorating situation in Berlin. That July 9, there would be 1.6 million pounds flown into the city—far below even the 8 million pounds a day the allies had calculated was the bare minimum Berliners required. The stockpiles were dwindling. Murphy sent a note to the State Department that day stating that "within a week or so we may find ourselves faced with a desperate population demanding our withdrawal to relieve the distress."

The airlift had bought them a couple of weeks of time, but it was merely delaying the inevitable choice between retreat and an armed response. Truman's hopes lay with the Soviets' willingness to step back from the chasm. He awaited their response to the allied note. "We are in the midst of grave and trying times," he wrote Churchill on Saturday in a letter thanking him for a copy of *The Gathering Storm.* The Berlin decision would come at the same time that he was "going through a terrible political 'trial by fire,'" he groused to the former prime minister. "Too bad it must happen at this time."

CLAY HAD BEEN "as happy as a kid," according to Marjorie, at the news that the first wave of C-54s was coming to Germany in late June and early July. But these planes and the exhaustive efforts of Hal Halvorsen and all the others still had not been enough to provide for Berlin's basic needs. That Saturday, July 10, Clay cabled Bradley to say that the Americans were flying in about 2 million pounds of food and supplies a day. He believed that with another fifty C-54s, they could double that, and he requested that the Skymasters be sent immediately.

Clay went back upstairs and ran through another pot of coffee and another pack of cigarettes. His ulcer burned away steadily in his stomach. Unsettled, he paced like a caged jungle cat. He went back downstairs and cabled Bradley again. Clay realized that even if the American airlift doubled and the British were able to fly in 2 million pounds a day themselves—neither of these being a guarantee—the effort would still fall short of the bare minimum. Moreover, even if somehow this bare minimum could be attained, it would impose such severe hardships on a city already suffering grievously that it was doubtful that Berliners could hold out for long before they gave in to the Soviets and demanded the allies leave. They needed to convince the Russians to lift the blockade, and the way to do this, he said again, was an armed convoy "to make our right of way into Berlin usable." While he realized the fear that this would lead to war, he argued that if the Russians wanted war they would easily be able to start one and if they did not they would not allow the situation to blunder into a conflict. "If the Soviet Union does intend war," he told Bradley, "it is because of a fixed plan."

Clay had received intelligence reports that the Soviets were bluffing, that they would back down rather than risk war against an America with atom bombs. "I am still convinced that the Soviets do not want war. However, they know that the allies also do not want war," Clay wrote to Bradley that day. This was the nub of the problem. Each side was convinced the other would be forced to give in. The question was who would be first to swerve to avoid the collision. The allies were slowly realizing the greatest virtue of an airlift: On the ground they had the burden of making an initial hostile move. In the sky, it was the Russians who had to shoot first.

Two days after sending Bradley his request for fifty more Skymasters, Clay had still not heard a reply. He tried again. "While I know you are doing everything possible, would appreciate answer soonest to request for additional C-54s," he cabled. There was a steady "deterioration in overall stock position. Each day of delay will make our position more difficult." He was met with silence.

THAT SAME SATURDAY, July 10, Forrestal sent Truman a memo containing an idea. Instead of trying to fit the nation's military strategy into a budget figure, why not do the reverse? "Since the entire reason for the maintenance of military forces in this country is the safeguarding of our national security, their size, character, and composition should turn upon a careful analysis of existing and potential dangers to our security," he wrote. The National Security Council should develop a document stating "national policy . . . particularly as it relates to the Russians." From that basis, they could come up with a budget number. Truman replied the following Tuesday, and he could hardly have been colder in his response. It was an interesting intellectual exercise, but he had been clear with Forrestal about what he wanted: a military budget of no more than $15 billion. So "the proper thing for you to do is to get the Army, Navy, and Air people together, and establish a program within the budget limits which have been allowed. It seems to me that is your responsibility."

On Wednesday, July 14, the Democratic convention prepared to nominate Harry Truman for president. The expense of wiring a hall for television equipment was so great that in 1948 both parties, and Wallace's Progressives, had to hold their conventions in the same place. As the Democrats began to gather in Philadelphia, there was a natural contrast to the preternatural cocksureness the Republicans had exhibited three weeks earlier. "There is no enthusiasm, no jubilation, no confidence; rather a 'what else can we do?' air of resignation," wrote the *Philadelphia Inquirer.* In place of the inflatable elephant, a giant papier-mâché mechanical donkey was now perched above the door to the Bellevue-Stratford, with a nodding head, ears that moved back and forth, and eyes that lit up in a fiery glow. After the first couple of days of festivities, it shorted out in a flash thunderstorm, and it sat there soaked and limp for the rest of the convention. At the city's hotels, vacancies mounted as Democrats decided to steer clear of the dour week ahead. "We got the wrong rigs for this convention," said a cabdriver. "They shoulda given us hearses."

Unable to afford their own, the Democrats had asked the Republicans to leave up the flags and bunting from their convention. The Republicans had graciously agreed. But by mid-July, they were faded and worn. On the convention floor, while the speakers droned on, the delegates milled about in a desultory fashion. "We Are Mild About Harry," read one sign. "He is Human, our Harry Truman," read another. Millions watched the scene at home. It was the year that caught the conventions between the politics of cigars and cameras. The Democratic National Committee handed out instructions to delegates telling them how to behave on television. It asked them not to doze off in their chairs and to refrain from drinking from bottles of alcohol while they were being filmed. Big, fleshy party leaders were convinced to wear pancake makeup when they stepped to the podium to deliver their quadrennial harangues against the Republicans and big business. To light the room for broadcast, ten 10,000-watt lamps were placed up in the galleries and another ten 5,000-watt lamps were hung above the speakers' platform. Some delegates wore sunglasses indoors. The gladiolus festooning the dais withered under the lamps' heat. The power of the lights was "very little less than that of an atomic bomb," reported H. L. Mencken. "The initial sensation was rather pleasant than otherwise, for it was a good deal like that of lolling on a Florida beach in midsummer. But in a few minutes I began to wilt and go blind, so the rest of my observations had to be made from a distance and through a brown beer bottle."

THE SOVIETS CHOSE that day of Truman's nomination to reply to the allied note that had been delivered eight days earlier. If there had been any hopes that the blockade might be short-lived, they were now put to rest. "Berlin lies in the center of the Soviet zone and is a part of that zone," the Russians wrote. The allies, by their actions in Germany, had undermined "the legal basis which assured their right to participation in the administration of Berlin." The Soviets were willing to negotiate—as long as the future of all of Germany was on the table—but they made no offer to lift the siege. They had little reason to budge. "Time is still working entirely in favor of the Soviets if they desire to make the position of the Western powers untenable," wrote Walter Bedell Smith from Moscow.

That afternoon, Truman was preparing to make the trip up to Philadelphia to accept the Democratic nomination. In the White House, he watched on his black-and-white television as a group of liberal Northern Democrats, led by Hubert Humphrey, waged a fight on the convention floor that replaced the tepid language on civil rights of the 1944 party platform with a more courageous plank praising Truman's own agenda for integration. Truman was livid, referring to Humphrey and the other liberals as "crackpots." Southern Democrats, including Birmingham police commissioner Eugene "Bull" Connor, were reacting by organizing an effort to bolt the Democratic Party. With the Wallace split already having, in the minds of most observers, extinguished Truman's chance at reelection, a further division in the party would most likely be devastating.

As Truman was following news of the civil rights fight and working on his speech for that night, Bohlen arrived to discuss the Soviet note. Truman had already read it and gave the obvious assessment: it was a complete rejection of every Western demand. Bohlen said that he and Marshall agreed. Truman told Bohlen that he wanted the National Security Council to fully discuss the American response at a meeting the next day.

IN BERLIN, CLAY'S response to the Soviet rejection was unsurprising. "The intransigent position as indicated in the note should be tested and I see no way in which it can be tested except by proceeding promptly with the movement of the armed convoy as I have recommended previously," he cabled Washington.

News of the Russians' firm stance spread quickly through Berlin. At a rally held that day, visiting British politician Anthony Eden—who had famously resigned as Neville Chamberlain's foreign secretary to protest the policy of appeasement—appeared alongside Franz Neumann, the most passionate orator of Berlin's democrats. Neumann, whose speech was being translated into English one sentence at a time, observed that it was Bastille Day. "And on this great French holiday in Berlin we honor the ideals of Fraternity, Equality, and . . . ," the British translator said and then, with a befuddled look, asked Neumann to repeat that last word again. The Berliners bellowed in laughter. Neumann thundered in German, "We here in Berlin know what it is! Liberty!"

AT 7 P.M., TRUMAN and his family and aides left by train for Philadelphia from Union Station. He felt beleaguered. The final chance that the crisis in Berlin might come to a quick end had been extinguished. That day Dewey, in one of his first substantive statements since winning the nomination, had charged that the Democrats' "extremely partisan and provocative assertions concerning foreign policy" may cause the "tense Berlin situation" to become worse. And, Truman learned on the radio as the train stopped along the way to Philadelphia, the Alabama and Mississippi delegations to the convention had walked out in protest of the party's new civil rights plank.

Truman arrived in Philadelphia at 9:15 P.M. but—after the civil rights fight—the convention was running late. He waited in a back room. Hours of seconding speeches dragged on. Without air-conditioning, temperatures soared into the nineties. Truman went to sit on a wooden chair on a ramp outside the arena overlooking the railroad yards. The ground below him was littered with trash and debris. Freight trains rumbled by. He thought of Berlin.

It was 1:30 in the morning by the time Truman was finally brought to the stage. The television viewing audience had long since gone to sleep. As Truman and his new running mate, Kentucky senator Alben Barkley, appeared, the crowd burst into sustained cheers. Confetti and streamers were thrown into the air. A Democratic National Committeewoman from Pennsylvania presented Truman with a life-size Liberty Bell made of flowers in the hope that he would bring "peace in our time, and peace for all time." Inside, there was a surprise. At her signal, the bell was opened and forty-eight of what she called "doves of peace" were released. Things did not go as planned. They were not doves at all but ordinary pigeons. Two of them had died in the heat. The rest were so bewildered by the bright lights that they crashed into bunting and rafters and swooped down on the platform. Former speaker Sam Rayburn had to fight off one that tried to alight on his head. "Get those goddamned pigeons out of here," he could be heard shouting on television. The birds expressed their own feelings toward the convention delegates below in the most unsubtle manner.

When the fuss died down, Barkley introduced Truman. The president came forward. He carried a small black binder filled with notes. His white suit blazed under the blinding lights. Almost all the men in the hall had doffed their jackets long before. A lifelong early riser, he was tired and strained by the hour and the events of the day. As he stepped to the podium, he appeared nervous, out of sorts. He fidgeted with the black notebook. The crowd was waiting for him to begin. The big television microphones perched on top of the lectern blocked his view of his text. He pushed them up. Someone in the crowd yelled that now they could not see him. He should put them back down. The delegates laughed at the hapless Truman. "I can't. I have to have them up where I can see," Truman said plaintively, his first words to the audience. He continued his apology, tripping hesitantly over his phrases. "I'm sorry that the microphones are in your way, but they have to be where they are because I've got to be able to see what I'm doing." He paused, a thought clearly raced across his face, and with a sly smile and deepened voice he added, "As I always am able to see what I'm doing." The crowd exploded, and he was off.

"Senator Barkley and I will win this election and make these Republicans like it—don't you forget that!" Truman vowed. He said he was calling Congress back into a special session on July 26—"Turnip Day"—to deal with unmet domestic needs. But he did not mention Berlin and devoted only a few sentences to any of the questions of war and peace that were so dominating the news and Americans' concerns. He told the delegates it was a purposeful decision. "As I have said time and time again, foreign policy should be the policy of the whole nation and not the policy of one party or the other. Partisanship should stop at the water's edge, and I shall continue to preach that through this whole campaign." So he would, but it was a feint. Preaching was one thing; practicing, it would turn out, was something different entirely.

IT WAS 5:30 A.M. by the time Truman returned to the White House from Philadelphia, usually the time that he woke up. He stayed awake until after six, listening to news coverage of his speech on the radio, and then went to sleep. He was dressed and in the office before ten.

The National Security Council meeting began at eleven. Now that the Russians had rejected a compromise, the Americans had to finally choose their course. The final decision over whether to send the B-29s to Europe had been put off while they waited for the Soviet reply. Marshall argued they should go forward with the deployment, as it would not only send a signal to the Russians, but reassure the British and help offset the French tendency "toward weakness or appeasement." They could pass it off as a "routine training mission." Royall argued that such a flimsy excuse "would convict us of insincerity," but the rest told him not to worry about that.

The larger question was what to do with Berlin. Both of Clay's requests—more planes and the permission to send an armed convoy through the Russian lines—were on the table. Marshall began the discussion by arguing that Americans would not accept a military action when the Russians had taken no such provocative moves. He repeated a remark Rayburn had recently made: that the American people were "sold on the need for strength," but had a "strong fear of war." Therefore they should not "adopt too militant a course."

Forrestal disagreed sharply, but tried to soften his words. He said he "would analyze the reaction of the American people a little differently." His worry was that Americans would feel the administration was "not treating this matter as seriously as it warrants." He now thought—and others agreed—that if the airlift was augmented with more planes, they could postpone the final day of reckoning until the middle of October. At that point, winter weather would set in, choking off the flow of planes into Berlin just when the temperatures would begin to dip and the city would need more coal for heat. They had until then to prepare the American people for the use of armed convoys and the real possibility of war.

Representing the Air Force at the meeting was Assistant Secretary "Sonny" Whitney—Cornelius Vanderbilt Whitney: a financier of *Gone With the Wind* and Pan Am Airlines, three-time polo champion, and owner of Phalanx, the horse that had won the previous year's Belmont Stakes. He had come armed with numbers. The Air Force had studied the data and decided an airlift was impossible. At that moment, the Americans and British combined were flying 3.5 million pounds to Berlin a day. If, he said, they decided to send every single transport plane they had to Germany, the maximum they could move was 8 million pounds a day. To do this they would have to build a whole new airport in Berlin. Already, "Tempelhof is breaking up under its present load" and the planes themselves were "deteriorating rapidly since we have no facilities there to support proper maintenance." With "everything over there," he lectured the group, "it would be a serious question as to how many would be caught on the ground and destroyed if hostilities broke out." Most crucially, he added, even if they did all this and were able to transport 8 million pounds a day, it would still be less than the city's minimum requirement of 10.6 million pounds.

Royall jumped in first. Actually, Clay had said they only needed 6 million pounds a day. Lovett argued that maybe the 10.6 million pounds included building up Berlin's stockpiles. Whitney thought they were missing the point. He put it to them simply. The Air Force "was firmly convinced the air operation is doomed to failure."

Lovett agreed that the airlift was "an unsatisfactory expedient." Furthermore, it was "obvious the Soviets know that flying weather will be too bad for this operation to continue beyond October."

Royall concurred that "the airlift could not carry through the winter," but was very concerned by the confusion about the numbers. They needed to find out what the real figures were so they could make a firm decision, but it was his belief they should give Clay more planes in order to put off a verdict about the armed convoy until October. Sonny Whitney was infuriated. Increasing the number of planes devoted to this effort would "be dipping into planes which are required in emergency war plans" and it "subjects our planes to the danger of destruction." The airlift, he believed, was a political sideshow. The military was there for fighting wars, not to be used in this type of charitable effort.

The conversation was going nowhere. They resolved to put off any decision for a few days. They would meet again on Monday.

When the meeting had begun, Forrestal had been energetic and engaged. As the discussion over war had gone on, as it had become clear to all—though none would come out and say it—that they had no real options, he became withdrawn. He hardly said a word for the rest of the meeting. He stared off into the distance. As he well knew, that summer the Joint Chiefs of Staff were planning for the day the Soviets acquired an atomic bomb and unleashed an attack on America. They were working on a paper—"Strategic Vulnerability of Washington D.C."—which imagined a scenario where the Russians detonated one atomic bomb on the Federal Triangle just north of the Mall and another right above the Pentagon. They estimated that 66,000 government employees would die immediately and another 34,000 would be injured. Fires would race across the capital, broken only by the rail yards leading into Union Station, Rock Creek Park near Forrestal's home, and the lawn of the Mall itself.

The question of the atomic bomb hovered over the room. No one mentioned it—even implicitly—in this or almost any other meeting during the crisis, but it cast a spectral shadow over every decision. It was the reason they had some confidence the Soviets were not intending to go to war or that Clay's convoy plan was at all possible. "Nothing but the 'equalizing' power of the atom bomb stands between America's European occupation forces and annihilation if current tension over the Berlin blockade results in an armed crash with Russia," wrote the *Washington Post* that month.

Forrestal had the growing worry that, however events played out, it was a weapon they would soon have to use. He and Marshall stayed to speak to Truman after the meeting. Despite sleeping less than three hours, "the President was chipper and in very good form and obviously pleased with the results of his speech at the Convention last night," Forrestal noted. Truman's good mood would not last long. Forrestal said the time had come to meet about the question of custody of atomic weapons. After the war, Truman had transferred control of nuclear power from the military to a civilian Atomic Energy Commission. Forrestal thought the time had come to discuss getting it back.

Truman was annoyed. He wanted to make sure that only he would decide when the bomb was to be used. He did not want "to have some dashing lieutenant colonel decide when would be the proper time to drop one." Forrestal assured him that no one "thought of denying him freedom of action on this subject" but a decision on who controlled the bomb needed to be made. They agreed to meet on the subject the following week.

Royall had been stunned that the officials of the National Security Council were trying to make decisions without even a basic grasp of the facts in Berlin. On Friday, July 16, the day after the meeting, he cabled Clay. "I feel it essential that you should return within the next few days to discuss with General Bradley, the State Department and myself, the entire Berlin situation."

It appeared that America's journalists had been robbed of their thesaurus. Or perhaps it was that only a single word summed up the feeling of the moment. "Hold on to your seat, folks," wrote *The New*

Republic's Richard Strout. "This is the showdown." The *New York Times'* Raymond Daniell wrote for that Sunday's paper that "this is an uneasy week-end in Europe. Deep in the consciousness of everyone there lies the conviction that the time is fast approaching for a show-down between Western Europe and Soviet Russia." That same day the *New York Herald Tribune* noted, "On all sides it seems generally agreed that the Western powers stand today in Berlin at essentially the same crossroads that intersected in Munich just ten years ago. One road means retreat and appeasement; the other leads to showdown." Even the newsreels had the same idea. "The showdown is at hand. The airlift however successful and spectacular is no real answer to this Berlin business. The situation is pure dynamite," Jay Sims of *News of the Day* boomed in the singsong of a track announcer when the horses come down the stretch.

On Monday morning, July 19, at 9 A.M., John Foster Dulles showed up at the State Department. He had been conferring with Dewey on Berlin once or twice a day in the month since the Republican convention and the beginning of the blockade. Since he was likely to be the next secretary of state, Marshall and Lovett thought it was important to get his views on what should be done. While sitting in Marshall's office, they told Dulles that Truman had decided they would not retreat, but that this was the day they would have to choose what steps they would take to keep the city alive. They asked Dulles to sit down with the experts of the State Department's Berlin working group and then give his position on what course the government should take. He asked how much time he had to get back to them. Marshall and Lovett said they needed an answer by noon.

Lovett deposited Dulles into a room where Bohlen, Kennan, and others were hashing out the options. They told Dulles the situation was grim. The military would not agree to devote more of its planes to the airlift. In any case, the effort had only until October, when bad weather and the need to haul more coal for heat would make it impossible to continue. The group talked through all the facets of the situation. When his time was up, Dulles told Lovett they should begin to negotiate over Berlin and Germany with the Russians—and send a convoy through in the meantime. That same day, the other Republican foreign policy leader, Senator Arthur Vandenberg, also told Lovett the United States should begin to negotiate its way out of the mess and give up Berlin. "Let's keep in mind that our 'basic position' is that we cannot be FORCED out of Berlin by duress," Vandenberg wrote. "It's not that we will not GET out of Berlin voluntarily under satisfactory circumstances."

At 11:45, Marshall and Forrestal met again with Truman about Berlin. Marshall exhibited what passed for optimism in the circumstances. If war came, there "was some chance of containing the Russians in Western Europe." Forrestal, naturally, was far less hopeful. A military buildup could not happen until the next spring or summer.

Both men repeated the now common points about the dire characteristics of the situation. Truman was exasperated by them. "I'd made the decision ten days ago to *stay in Berlin*," he wrote in his diary. "We'll stay in Berlin—come what may."

The president was especially frustrated with Forrestal. "Jim wants to hedge—he always does." The two men were misunderstanding each other. It was not that Forrestal was equivocating. It was that late at night, when Washington was quiet and the rest of the government was asleep, he sat alone in a large mansion, drinking his booze and seeing what none of the others could: the horror of an atomic war.

That day, on the force of ill tidings from Berlin, the stock market in New York had its largest plunge in nearly two years.

———

The situation in Berlin was darkening, like a candle about to expire. By the middle of July, the stockpiles were falling so fast that new cutbacks were announced almost daily. In the city's hospitals, they were sterilizing and reusing bandages. Berliners were now limited to twenty-five minutes a day of gas from a single burner. On its best day thus far, the airlift had brought in just over a quarter of the coal Berlin usually imported every July day of previous years. Street lighting at night was cut by 75 percent. The subway stopped running between six in the evening and six in the morning. Each household received electricity for four hours a day—two during the daytime and two at night. The power came on in a rotating schedule by neighborhood. Some weeks it was ten to midnight, others it was two A.M. to four A.M. "Many industries face complete shutdown, and even the essential industries allowed to operate part-time will be forced to discharge majority of workers," Murphy cabled to the State Department.

It was not just food and coal that Berlin was missing, however. After the defeat of the war, after the terrible years of eking out a miserly existence, the blockade rattled any confidence left in the city that somehow their future might be better. The west Berliners were reliant for their very survival on occupiers they did not trust and who they felt loathed them. "There is a slow but steady deterioration," wrote the *New York Times* that week, of both the "living conditions and morale" of Berliners. If the allies deserted the city, said the head of the largest hospital in the American sector, "we will have a wave of suicides worse than in 1945." One German woman was known to be wearing a vial of poison around her neck wherever she went. A social worker summed up Berlin: "The energies of the people are spent in pursuit of a loaf of bread and a pair of shoes. Hope is alien."

For Hal Halvorsen, the first days of life on the airlift had been a blur. With the constant flights—two, sometimes three round trips to Berlin a day—and lack of sleep, he quickly came to see the mission as a slog; the exhausting, aerial equivalent of a march through hundreds of miles of barren, miry terrain. But there were moments, even from the very beginning, that shook him so that he was reminded something larger was at stake than the mechanized rush of hundreds of airplanes and millions of pounds of food. One morning, as they made their way to the shower in the small shed on the other side of the compound—Halvorsen with his towel around his neck, Pickering wearing his leather bomber jacket over his bare back—they saw some of the officers who lived in the tarpaper shacks being passed packages by German women through the barbed-wire fence. They asked what was going on and learned that the women did the Americans' weekly wash for the price of one candy bar and one package of gum. That same night, they returned from their second flight of the day to learn their third flight had been canceled. Relieved, they ate dinner in the mess hall just before midnight. When he was full, Halvorsen scraped his leftovers into one of the trash barrels outside the building. As soon as he turned, three German men, shrouded in rags, descended on the bin and fished out the scraps. The sight of "a fellow human being stripped of his dignity, relegated to animal instincts to survive, and totally oblivious to whoever might see, almost left me sick," Halvorsen would later recount.

One reason many pilots became disconnected from the larger stakes of the airlift was that almost none of them saw anything of Berlin other than from the sky. "Berlin wasn't there," one pilot would say later of what they all saw from above. "Occasionally you could see part of a wall or someone walking." They did not have time to leave Tempelhof to explore before they had to take off again. But Halvorsen, who had as a boy taken to geography books like a steaming stack of flapjacks, wanted to see more. The rumor was he might not have much of a chance to do so. In the mess hall, in bull sessions in the barn loft, along the flight line, the word was that the mission would soon be ending; high-level negotiations were happening somewhere; it was all being worked out; they would be sent home as fast they had been sent there. For more than a decade, Halvorsen had read about and seen images of the sites of Berlin. They had been part of the vocabulary of his time and "the thought of missing out on a close-up look at Hitler's bunker, the Reichstag, and the Brandenburg Gate after so many trips to Berlin didn't sound so good." With the eight-millimeter movie camera he had brought from Mobile, he wanted to make a record of the city that he would be able to show to the kids he hoped to have with Alta one day. He resolved to find a way to get into Berlin while he still had the opportunity.

On July 19, Halvorsen got his chance. He and his crew had been flying since the middle of the night and were done with their flights for the day by early afternoon. They had about ten hours off to eat and sleep before beginning their next day with a flight at two A.M. As he was standing around the tarmac, Halvorsen saw that Lieutenant Bill Christian, one of the men who shared the barn loft with him, was getting ready to take off. Halvorsen asked if he might come along for the ride. "We could use some company," Christian answered.

As Halvorsen timed it out, by skipping sleep he could go to Berlin and make it back to begin another sixteen-hour shift. He retrieved the movie camera and told Pickering what he was planning to do. "I'll be back for our next flight. Get some sleep for the both of us." Pickering nodded, dumbfounded. Stowing away on airlift flights was against the operation's rules. A small infraction, to be sure, but for a straight arrow like Halvorsen it was unexpected. And it was the kind of petty offense that often leads to more serious violations.

WHEN THEY LANDED at Tempelhof, Halvorsen used the phone in the base operations office to call a sergeant that fellow pilot Larry Caskey had told him could take him around Berlin in a jeep. The sergeant said it would be an hour before he could leave. To make use of the time, Halvorsen decided to get some shots of the planes zooming down onto the runway from above the apartment building. He headed toward the area along the airport's fence, where he could stand right under the planes' bellies as they appeared overhead in a sharp dive.

It was a two-mile walk to the other end of the airport and Halvorsen hurried, stopping along the way to film the women filling gaps in the pierced-steel runway. It took twenty minutes for him to reach the apartment building, and he looked for the best spot to catch the planes popping out overhead. He had filmed a couple of them when he noticed a group of about thirty children standing in the small grassy area between the apartment house and the fence. They had come to watch the planes land. Now, silently, they watched the strange American soldier with a film camera instead.

He walked toward them. It appeared they were between the ages of eight and fourteen, boys and girls alike. They were dressed in shabby tatters. On the hot summer day, almost none of the boys had shirts. The girls wore boys' overalls, patched up and handed down. Very few of the children had shoes; those who did wore ones that clearly did not fit. "*Wie geht's?*" he asked—"How are you?" It was practically the only German phrase he knew. They responded with a gush of answers, none of which he understood.

They giggled when it became clear he did not speak German. A couple of the children had studied English in school and they began, haltingly, to ask him detailed questions about the planes they were watching land. How much flour did each plane bring? How many loaves of bread would that make? What about the milk? How many planes were there?

They were unlike any children Halvorsen had ever met before, speaking with evident feeling not only about the details of the planes, but about ideas like freedom, about dreams that were not walled in by rubble. They said they wanted to be able to read whichever books they chose, to see places in the world they had only heard about.

Halvorsen had his doubts about the children. They seemed so sincere, so terribly downtrodden, but he kept thinking of the famous "Hitler Youth." He wondered if these children had once worn its tidy uniforms.

As they spoke, Halvorsen grew anxious, realizing that he had to return to the terminal where the sergeant with the jeep would be waiting for him. He began to look over his shoulder, toward the other end of the airport. The children kept staring at him. Finally, Halvorsen said, "Sorry, kids, I have to go," and waved goodbye.

He took a few steps back toward the terminal. As he did, he put his hand in the pocket of his khaki pants and felt two sticks of gum in a green pack of Wrigley's Doublemint he had picked up at the Rhein-

Main base exchange. He wondered if he should go back and give them to the children. He stopped. In front of him was the two-mile walk to the jeep, behind him were the children at the fence.

SOME PEOPLE'S LIVES are like a feather in the wind, carried from breeze to breeze, buffeted by events. Others travel a steady path they lay out for themselves, or one that their fate or family bequeaths to them. But then there are others for whom their entire life comes down to a single instant that makes sense of all that occurred before and shapes everything that happens after. Perhaps this decisive second comes only to a few. Perhaps everyone has one and most just miss theirs. This was what Hal Halvorsen would later call his "moment of truth," the continental divide of his long life.

He headed back toward the fence. It occurred to him that wherever he had gone—in Haiti, in South America, in Africa—children had gathered about him with their hands out for candy or gum. These children had not. He thought it was that they were too polite to beg. In fact, it is likely many of them had never tasted candy in their lives and most had never chewed gum. He pulled the sticks out of his pocket and the children saw the tinfoil flash in the sunlight. Their faces brightened. Halvorsen realized he only had two pieces for the whole group and was afraid the kids might start tussling over them. He tore the sticks in two.

Four children got pieces of gum, the rest passed around the wrapper, tearing off a sliver and sniffing it dreamily. "The expressions on their faces were incredulous, full of awe—as if they were entering a wonderland." Halvorsen watched their eyes grow big "like it was Christmas Day." The children who got the gum worked it over slowly with their jaws as if savoring the taste. The others placed the pieces of tinfoil carefully in their pocket.

If he brought back thirty cents' worth of candy, thought Halvorsen, "I could put these guys on Easy Street." But he realized there was no chance of his being able to give up sleep to walk around the airport again anytime soon. Just then, another plane came in for a landing, roaring out from over the apartment building and flying directly above.

Without thinking, he blurted out to the children that he would drop candy down to them the next day.

"*Jawohl!*" they shouted. Then one asked how they would know which plane was his. There were hundreds of landings every day and each Skymaster looked identical.

He remembered a signal he had used long before. "Watch the wings," he told them. "Mine will be the plane that wiggles its wings."

"Vhat is a viggle?" asked one girl. So with arms outstretched, Halvorsen gave what he considered an Oscar-worthy performance. They nodded, laughing. Halvorsen said goodbye and sprinted back the two miles to the waiting jeep.

HALVORSEN RETURNED TO the Tempelhof terminal building flushed and short of breath. The sergeant with the jeep had been looking for him. Halvorsen apologized for being late. He did not mention the children or his promise to them. There was nothing wrong with talking to some local kids. But to break the stringent rules of the airlift, as Halvorsen by now realized he had impulsively promised to do, could bring him a severe punishment.

The two men—the sergeant at the wheel and Halvorsen by his side— drove past the gates of the airport. Halvorsen listed off a few top spots he was especially interested in seeing. They headed west and north through a landscape of rubble hills and lost chimneys. As the driver moved slowly through quiet streets and Halvorsen craned his neck to look about, what most surprised him was not the distinctiveness of the sights but their uniformity. He had assumed the arresting pictures in *Life* or in the newsreels had been selected for their singular value. Instead, everywhere he looked was the same beige landscape of crumbled ceilings, grimy roads, a weathered board where a wall once stood. The "gutted buildings without roofs or windows" appeared to stare "up at the open sky in an unchanging trance."

They drove to the Tiergarten, now dirty, denuded save for an occasional lonely, small tree, solitary after having once been surrounded, its skeletal branches like the jagged bones of a starving man. There he saw women hunched over collecting twigs to burn for warmth and hoeing small vegetable gardens to augment their rations. Statues of martial heroes, once hidden in alcoves of leafy boughs along the grassy path of Sieges Allee—Victory Avenue—now stood exposed and forlorn. Some had what looked like cannonball holes right through them. The wind would whip past their large, grave Teutonic heads perched on chests decorated with medals of victories in forgotten battles on some unfortunate field. Berliners called this path "Lollipop Lane."

Past the victory column that towered over the city, past the memorial to the Soviet dead, they came to the stately Brandenburg Gate—the border between the Soviet and western sectors. Halvorsen got out of the jeep to take a picture of its great columns. On either side of it were bombed-out buildings and empty lots. It was afternoon on a summer day and they were in the center of the city, but the scene was silent. The only sound was the low rumble of the idling jeep and the *shush* of a girl, her pants rolled up to her knees, pulling a wagon behind her as she walked slowly from noplace to nowhere.

A couple hundred yards away was the Reichstag, its great dome now an iron skeleton, its gray walls an easily decipherable Rosetta stone of Berlin's recent history—charred from the fire that had brought Hitler to power, blasted by American and British bombs, riddled by Russian bullets in the final encounter of the Second World War, forsaken in a divided country forbidden from governing itself. Halvorsen climbed the steps. Inside the vacant hull, where Germany's brief flicker of democracy had extinguished itself, crows cawed.

The sergeant drove them into the Soviet sector and as they crossed the border he hunched closer to the wheel and scanned their surroundings. Halvorsen was too engrossed to notice. They drove past the once luxurious Adlon Hotel, where the postwar menu was cabbage soup and cooked turnips. They swung south past Goebbels's garden and came to Hitler's bunker. Halvorsen got out of the jeep again and tilted his head up to take in the scorched walls. Sallow children with glazed eyes wordlessly hawked worthless trinkets. The sergeant seemed impatient, shaking his leg nervously. Halvorsen ignored him. He felt omnipotent, a true conqueror, standing on top of the rubble of his enemies. He stepped toward the roofless marble-paneled entrance hall.

Suddenly the sergeant started screaming, "Jump in the jeep, quick! Let's get going!" Halvorsen ran back and, while he was still pulling his leg in, the jeep leapt forward, spraying gravel and dirt behind it. Halvorsen looked over his shoulder. Behind them were two Russian soldiers in another jeep, closing fast. Their guns were drawn.

"Why are they chasing us?" Halvorsen yelled.

The sergeant said they were not supposed to be in the Soviet sector. "They have a couple of Americans in jail over there now."

The Russian jeep was approaching them. The soldiers were shouting. The sergeant tried to lose them, turning through the twisting rubble-strewn streets. The Soviets remained hot on them. Near Potsdamer Platz, they crossed over into the American sector, but the soldiers did not give up the chase. The roads were unpaved and the jeep bounced along through bomb craters that pocked the streets like scars of a childhood disease.

Finally, the Russians pulled back with a final trail of unintelligible expletives. The sergeant did not slow down until they were safely back inside Tempelhof's gates.

IT WAS TEN o'clock by the time Halvorsen climbed into his cot at Rhein-Main. He would have to be up before midnight, but that night sleep came reluctantly. He thought of his day and what the next one would bring. He felt he had just closed his eyes when he awoke to Pickering shaking him. "Glad you made it back, Hal. Have a good trip?" he whispered, not waiting for an answer. Halvorsen felt woozy as he pulled his clothes down from the nails in the barn's sloping ceiling on which they hung.

As they prepared for their 2 A.M. flight on July 20, he began to tell Pickering and Elkins about what had happened and the promise he had made. He planned on dropping the candy to the kids on their second flight of the day, when they were scheduled to come in over Berlin shortly before noon.

Halvorsen's crew members were unhappy. "You're going to get us in one big mess of trouble," Pickering grumbled repeatedly during that nighttime flight to Berlin. Though he would not admit it, Halvorsen himself had felt the nagging tug of second thoughts as soon as he had made the pledge. The more time that passed, the more he realized how serious a punishment he and the others would face for breaking the airlift's rules. He was upset with himself for his rashness, but felt he had no choice but to follow through. Every time he thought back to his conversation with the children, he knew he could not renege.

The two pilots—usually chattering the entire trip—stewed in an uncomfortable silence during the flight. The younger Elkins sat quietly behind them in the cockpit like a seven-year-old whose parents were bickering on a family car ride.

They unloaded their cargo at Tempelhof and raced back to Rhein-Main with the sunrise on their backs. By seven they were on the ground. Halvorsen had begun to assemble the rudimentary elements of a plan. He had three hours before they were to take off again. He went first to the base exchange, open twenty-four hours a day, and there he bought up his weekly allowance of candy and gum. Pickering and Elkins had grudgingly let him have their allotment as well. He bought a bag full of Wrigley's gum and chocolate bars—Hershey, Lyons, Mounds.

He poured the bag out onto his cot in the barn. Even the previous night, he had realized that one of the biggest problems with his plan was that while showering candy on starving kids seemed like a good and noble idea in theory, actually dropping it on them from a moving airplane was a little more complicated. A Hershey bar traveling 110 miles per hour was dangerous. And even if the chocolate did not hit them, there would be little left by the time they scraped it off the hot summer soil.

But sitting on his cot, he hit on an idea. Halvorsen pulled out a handkerchief from the full barracks bag he had brought to treat his running nose. He found a length of junk twine amid the discarded machinery. With a few cuts and pokes from his pocket knife, he fashioned a miniature parachute. Tying some small stones to the twine, he practiced dropping it down the grain chute at the far end of the loft. It seemed to work. He dropped it again and again. He became so wrapped up in his success that he failed to notice the two pilots from his squadron staring up at him in incredulous silence from the lower level of the barn. One of them tapped his temple: "Better watch it, Halvorsen, or they'll ship you back to the States."

"Well, you know how easily a guy can get lift-happy," he chuckled meekly.

Dividing up the rations into three parts, he made a parachute for each. They would not only slow the fall, but they would be markers, making the plummeting candy visible to the children below.

They took off toward Berlin a little after ten. When they entered the corridor over Soviet airspace, Halvorsen scanned the horizon. The Russians had begun to play a dangerous game of harassment with the American cargo planes. Repeatedly, Soviet Yak fighters would buzz the big, lumbering transports, missing a collision by only a few feet. Other times they would fire their guns. The pilots thought they were sitting ducks, or as they called themselves, "Clay's pigeons." Just days earlier, something had hit Halvorsen's plane, taking out the number-two engine. They had put out the fire and just managed to limp into Tempelhof without being forced to throw the fresh milk bottles overboard to get rid of weight.

There was no sign of Russian activity on this flight. The Soviet bases directly below the air corridor—Köthen, Dessau, Zerbst—were quiet. It was a clear day, without a cloud to hide Soviet aircraft. There was just the pale cerulean glow of the skies at 6,500 feet. The sun was bright, beating down on the cockpit. The day was still. Peaceful. Calm. And with Pickering and Elkins silent, Halvorsen battled to stay awake.

His fatigue was deep—burrowed down into him far below where exhaustion lives. He, like all the pilots, had already been tired. Now he had given up most of his sleep time the previous day with his trip to Berlin. This was now his ninth flight between Rhein-Main and Berlin with only a short rest. It was only the anticipation that kept him from falling into a slumber.

Forty minutes after they entered the corridor, Pickering was close enough to Berlin to radio in: "Tempelhof, this is Big Easy 495 requesting clearance for initial approach at 2,000 feet." Halvorsen slowed the plane and began the long circle over the city. As they dropped toward Tempelhof, he excitedly pointed out to Pickering and Elkins all the places he had been to the day before.

The peculiarities of the approach into the airport meant that Halvorsen's plan would have a small chance of success. With him and Pickering at the controls, Elkins would have to drop the tiny parachutes and their contents out of the plane. There was only a narrow moment when he could do so and reach the grassy area where the children gathered to watch the planes land. If Elkins dropped the candy too late, the parachutes would drift down on the wrong side of the fence. If he released the parachutes too early, they would fall on top of the apartment building and never be found.

"Big Easy 495," crackled the voice of the tower, "you are clear for landing." Halvorsen swung around the airport for the final loop before landing, and as he waited to clear the apartment building, it occurred to him that there was a chance the children might not even be there. They had no real reason to trust an American soldier, especially one with preposterous promises of sweets dropping from the military planes that had bombed their city.

Then he wondered the reverse. What if they had become so excited that they had told every child in Berlin? Hundreds or thousands of children might be massed on the barbed-wire fence waiting for three little packages of candy. He considered the possibility that he was about to incite a food riot among nine-year-olds.

As he whipped around the apartment building, he had his answer. "Looks like they haven't told another soul," he said, grinning at Pickering. "Reckon there is about the same number as yesterday." Pickering nodded and breathed in deeply. Halvorsen pulled the plane to the right. As soon as it began to turn, he pulled it back to the left. Then to the right again, and then the left. The Skymaster shook as he went back and forth—at low altitude under the weight of 20,000 pounds of coal. He could see the children jumping and cheering as they saw him wiggle from down below.

As he pulled into the final approach, Halvorsen yelled back to Elkins and once again carefully went over the timing. He said there was no room for error. Elkins said he was ready. Halvorsen was not so sure.

The mood grew even more tense. Pickering just couldn't help himself one more time. "What if an aircraft waiting for takeoff happens to see the parachutes and gets our tail number?"

Halvorsen didn't respond. "Give me full flaps," he said.

The apartment building grew ever bigger as they approached—filling up their windshield. The moment was coming. Their nose peaked over the top of the building. "Now, Elkins!" Halvorsen shouted. The engineer hesitated. "Now!" Elkins pushed the bunched bundles of handkerchiefs, twine, and candy out of the small emergency flare chute in front of the plane's left wing.

A few seconds later they bumped down the runway and slowed to their landing. As usual, the yellow jeep with the large "Follow Me" sign whipped in front of them and led them to the unloading area. Thin German workers swarmed onto the plane to rush the cargo out. Halvorsen and the others were parked on the other end of the airport from the apartment building. Until they taxied down the second sod runway to take off again, there was no way to see the children or to find out if the parachutes had landed anywhere near them at all.

On July 20, around noon, Lucius Clay was sitting in a Skymaster on the runway at Tempelhof waiting to begin the journey that would take him back to Washington. He was tense, and as he spoke with Murphy about their trip and the important meetings ahead, he was discouraged. He had asked Washington repeatedly for more planes for the airlift and pleaded for permission to send the armed convoy to Berlin. On both subjects, he had been put off, disregarded.

Clay and Murphy still believed that the convoy—for all its problems—was the only real solution to the crisis. "The present action of supplying Berlin by air is spectacular and dramatic. The psychological effect in Central Europe is excellent. But everyone recognizes that it is an expedient and not a solution," Murphy had told Marshall and Lovett in a "Top Secret" cable the previous week.

Clay himself had been even more forceful in a cable to the Pentagon the day before his departure for Washington. To him, he said, there were only two real options: armed force or retreat. "It does appear that we cannot do otherwise than retreat with possible fateful consequences to our role as a world leader unless we are prepared and without too long delay to risk a showing of force." If the Soviets were bluffing, they would let the convoy through. If they wanted war, then it was better to have one now than after the humiliation of a withdrawal from Berlin. "The choice before us is a hard choice. However, if we decide to retreat now, this retreat will not save us from again and again having to choose between retreat and war. With each retreat we will find ourselves confronted with the same problem but with fewer and fewer allies on our side."

The last words of his message were terrifying: "I cannot but feel that the world today is facing the most critical issue that has arisen since Hitler placed his policies of aggression in motion. In fact, the Soviet Union has more force immediately at its disposal than did Hitler to accomplish his purpose. Only America can exert the world leadership, and only America can provide the strength, to stop this policy of aggression here and now. The next time may be too late. I believe determined action will stop it short of war. It cannot be stopped without the risk of war." He did not bring up the airlift once in the cable. It was not a relevant enough long-term answer to even mention.

The plane started down the runway to begin heading west. Clay looked out the window, weary. He must have wondered if he would be returning to Berlin in a few days' time to start the process of handing the western sectors over to the Soviets and evacuating American troops. His ulcer churned away inside. His neck throbbed. His body ached from exhaustion. His doctor had begged him to take a few days off before heading across the Atlantic. Clay had waved him away. He felt beleaguered, hopeless. But as his Skymaster bounced off the runway and began to climb over Berlin, Clay saw something peculiar. The children who regularly gathered by the apartment building at the edge of Tempelhof were jumping up and down and waving at his plane. And three of them were holding what appeared to be handkerchiefs.

CLAY'S PLANE HAD crossed the Atlantic and was nearing Washington on Thursday, July 21, when the meeting Forrestal had requested the previous week, to settle control of the atomic bomb, began in the White House. Forrestal's belief that with the Berlin blockade bringing America closer to war it was time for the military to retake possession of the weapons was challenged by the Atomic Energy Commission's chairman, David Lilienthal, one of the original New Dealers, who was determined to keep the power in civilian hands.

Instead of the quiet discussion Truman had expected, both Forrestal and Lilienthal kept adding officials to the meeting's manifest to match those of the other side, setting off an attendance-list race that ended up with each having half a dozen men on their side for the argument. Truman, who had not wanted to hold the meeting and detested the subject, only grew more irate as he watched a seemingly never-ending stream of dark suits enter his office, looking like the endless ribbon a magician pulls from his mouth.

Truman would usually smile and put visitors at ease with a few jocular remarks. Today, there was none of that. "The President greeted us rather solemnly," Lilienthal noted in his diary. "He looked worn and grim."

The group sat in chairs arranged in an arc in front of Truman's desk. "A kind of seriousness hung over" the room, Lilienthal noted, "that wasn't relieved a bit, needless to say, by the nature of the subject and the fact that even at that moment some terrible thing might be happening in Berlin that would put this group into the hands of forces that might sweep our desires and wishes away, while the tides of force took over."

Each side had prepared a letter stating its position. The meeting began with bickering over which side would read its position first. After going back and forth over this while Truman seethed, they came to an agreement. Donald Carpenter, the Remington gun company executive on loan to Forrestal to handle atomic issues, began to read to Truman, in a condescending tone, a long memo laying out the point of view of the military. Truman glared at Carpenter as he prattled on obliviously. When he finished, Carpenter said there were accompanying memos from the various service secretaries and the Joint Chiefs of Staff. He began to read those as well.

Truman held his hand out for the letters. "I can read," he said sharply.

Lilienthal knew better than to recite his own side's position verbatim and instead simply told Truman he should exercise his own discretion. The law, Lilienthal pointed out, already gave the president the power to transfer control of the bombs to the military "from time to time" as situations warranted.

Truman was doleful and contemplative. The strain of the previous weeks had clearly taken its toll on him. That day the prominent columnists Joseph and Stewart Alsop had written that "everyone in a position to know the facts, from President Truman and Secretary of State Marshall on down, is grimly aware that the Russian blockade of Berlin might lead to war before next winter." The *Los Angeles Times* upped the ante with an article sketching out the military scenarios of the early days of a war that would begin by August 1—within the next ten days.

All his life, Truman would maintain that he had "never lost any sleep" over his decision to bomb Hiroshima and Nagasaki, but as this discussion continued—the first airing of the consideration of atomic attacks since the end of the war—he betrayed the possibility that there had been haunted nights. "I don't think we ought to use this thing unless we absolutely have to," he said when both sides had finished stating their case. "It is a terrible thing to order the use of something that . . ." He stopped and stared down at his desk. The room was still. "That is so terribly destructive, destructive beyond anything we have ever had."

He looked up at the group, almost beseeching them to comprehend his burden. "You have got to understand that this isn't a military weapon. It is used to wipe out women and children and unarmed people, and not for military uses. So we have got to treat this differently from rifles and cannon and ordinary things like that."

Truman told the men he would read over the memos, but that with the situation in Berlin, "I have got to think about the effect of such a thing on international relations. This is no time to be juggling an atom bomb around." He stood up. The meeting was over. The men got up as well and one by one they walked out of the room.

WHEN LUCIUS CLAY stepped out of the Skymaster at National Airport, flashbulbs exploded. His return to Washington to meet with Truman on Berlin was front-page news around the country. Bradley and Royall were there to greet him for the cameras. The press shouted for a statement on what would happen in the crisis. "I have returned from Germany for a quick trip at the request of Kenneth C. Royall to report to the Department of the Army on the German situation," he said. "There is nothing else I can say at this time."

From the airport, Clay went to have dinner at Forrestal's house. The men talked late into the night. Forrestal had been shaken by his meeting with Truman that afternoon. As he spoke, his conversation would slip off its track and veer into thickets of tangents; his words would become jumbled up in their sentences, tossed like tomatoes in a salad. Clay was nervous and tense as well. His whole body ached from the long flight, as well as from apprehension.

Forrestal and Clay had been at odds for years. The secretary of defense had been the first to see the dimensions of the Soviet threat, while the general had held on to the dream of friendship with the Russians long after most others in the Truman government had given up. Forrestal, more than anyone else in the highest ranks, believed war was coming; Clay seemed so confident the Soviets were bluffing that he was willing to use a military incursion into their territory to force them to show their hand.

Yet that night, eating dinner in Forrestal's dining room, they met at the crossroads of their obsessions. Forrestal feared a nuclear war; he could taste the ashes in his mouth. That day he had sought to secure control over the atom bomb. Clay was terrified that America would abandon Berlin. It very well might have already had he not put up such a fight over the past months. The next morning's meeting would be decisive.

As their conversation went on in Forrestal's big echoing house, they managed to scare each other like boys telling ghost stories around a campfire. But they were not trading in phantasms. Clay, who had advocated so forcefully for the armed convoy based on the Soviets' reluctance to go into battle, admitted to Forrestal that he thought there was a one-in-four chance of war—an awesomely high likelihood given his past assurances. Forrestal must have looked stricken. Clay, the commander of American forces in Europe, tried to reassure him. If war did come, he did not believe that all of Western Europe would be immediately conquered by the Red Army. "Twenty good divisions could hold up the Russians at the Rhine." Forrestal stared at him squarely. They did not have twenty divisions. They had one.

Forrestal walked up the curved staircase to his bedroom. He laid his head on his pillow but did not fall asleep. That night he thought of mushroom clouds.

Clay slept uneasily as well. The next morning, the day of the meeting of his life, he woke from restless dreams to find he could not move his neck.

THE NATIONAL SECURITY Council meeting began at 11 A.M. on July 22. Truman, who almost never attended the meetings, was sitting in the center of the Cabinet Room's long table. Sunlight streamed through the shutters on the big glass doors that led out to the Rose Garden. Models of military aircraft decorated the room. Half an hour earlier, Truman had told a press conference that the chances of world peace were "as good as they have ever been." Now, with the doors closed, the time for pleasing words had passed. Berlin's decisive hour had come.

Truman welcomed Clay and asked him to report on the situation in

Berlin. Clay, who had for three years been sending increasingly frantic cables to the Pentagon about the state of affairs in Germany, took to the invitation with the glee of a paleontologist when cocktail party chatter turns to dinosaurs. He began by again emphasizing that the "abandonment of Berlin would have a disastrous effect" on plans for a West Germany and would mean the "loss of our position in Europe." Just two days earlier, he had said that the choices were an armed convoy or retreat. But sitting in the White House, he delivered a dramatically different message. The "use of armed convoys obviously could create an act which might lead to war. It is, therefore, desirable not to use them until all other ways have been tried and failed." Instead, he repeated his request for more planes. "The airlift has increased our prestige immeasurably," he said. "It has been impressive and efficient and thrown the Russian timetable off." They had 52 Skymasters and 80 of the smaller C-47s and they were making 250 trips to Berlin a day. With more planes, he believed they could hold out until winter came. To do that, he needed another 75 C-54s. There was a gasp in the room when he gave the number. It was more than half of the Air Force's entire transport fleet.

Despite the crick in his neck, Clay was compelling in his presentation. But what stood out was his discussion of a factor that had not really been considered in all the previous meetings on the siege of Berlin in Washington: the commitment of the Berliners themselves to democracy and freedom. Bradley and the others in the Pentagon, the architects of victory in World War II, saw the conflict over Berlin through a military prism—American forces would be decimated by superior Russian numbers. The diplomats viewed the crisis in terms of relations between the great powers of the world. But Clay told Truman, Forrestal, Marshall, and the rest about Reuter and Jeanette Wolff—"The Trumpet"—and how she had told Berliners of the six years she spent in Hitler's prison and the equivalent amount of time she was willing to spend in a Soviet prison rather than allow the Russians to dominate Berlin. He kept returning to the human dimensions of the choice before the National Security Council—of the body blow to the faith of Europeans in America if the allies were to withdraw from Berlin, of the powerful asset that Berliners' willingness to live through hardship would be in the months ahead. And though he did not say it, his moving presentation made clear he believed America had a moral duty to stand with those who were willing to embrace democracy amid the ruins of the Reich— and that this duty should be part of their deliberations. What he would later say of Truman was true of Clay himself: He realized they were in a new kind of conflict, "a political war, not a physical military war."

But the point was lost on the National Security Council that day. No sooner had Clay finished than the new Air Force chief of staff, General Hoyt Vandenberg, opposed the request for more transport planes. Doing so would cause a immense disruption of normal military operations and "would adversely affect our capabilities to wage strategic warfare"—the real work of an air force. He did not reveal it then, but he and the other military chiefs, including Bradley, had prepared a report for Forrestal imploring that, despite Truman's repeated assertion, "the withdrawal possibility should at least be borne in mind," since "neither air transport nor armed convoy in themselves offer a long-range solution to the problem."

The cabinet members took turns expressing their doubts about Clay's plans for the airlift. The pinched nerve in Clay's neck prevented him from turning to look at his antagonists. Truman let the conversation run its course, saying little other than to agree with Clay that "if we move out of Berlin we have lost everything we are fighting for." The group came to a consensus on beginning to move dependents out of the city and on making a diplomatic overture to Stalin. Walter Bedell Smith, along with envoys from Britain and France, would be sent to negotiate with the Soviet leader. But there was still no agreement on more planes for Berlin. The clock on the mantel, under the portrait of Woodrow Wilson, ticked away.

After an hour, Truman rose from the table and excused himself to deal with other matters. Clay was crestfallen. There had been no decision to provide the additional C-54s. Unable to turn his head, he shifted his whole body to watch Truman walk out of the room. In the last moment, as Truman opened the door to leave, he turned back to Clay with a smile and said, offhandedly, "Oh, drop in by my office before you leave, General."

THREE HOURS AFTER the National Security Council meeting ended in the White House, a World War II veteran named Stephen Supina, despondent over the situation in Berlin, decided, as his brother would explain it, that "he didn't want to go through another war" and that "somebody ought to blast the United Nations into action." So he took off in his little red-and-yellow Piper Cub and dropped a bomb over the UN headquarters in New York. It exploded in the air and no one was hurt.

CLAY WAS DEJECTED. That night, he was in such pain that the man who never took a day off thought of checking into a Washington hospital.

The next morning, Clay arrived at the White House with his bags packed. "You look like you feel bad, General," Truman prodded mischievously.

"Mr. President," Clay burst out, "I'm very disappointed. Without those planes I just don't think we're going to make it in Berlin."

Truman let him continue in this fashion before interrupting with a Missouri smile that was so wide that Clay thought it was the most dazzling thing he had ever seen. "You're going to get them. I just overruled the Joint Chiefs." Truman—facing political pressures on all sides in the midst of the presidential campaign—had settled on the airlift as a way to avoid the shoals of appeasement and a disastrous war.

Clay discovered that his neck felt much better. He went, naturally, to Capitol Hill to pay his respects to the members of the Foreign Affairs Committee. Before returning to National Airport to begin the journey back to Berlin, he went to the Pentagon for a press conference—one of the largest yet held in the building. Clay announced that the airlift would be getting more planes. He was reassuring. "I don't believe this crisis is a move toward a military showdown," he said. "Obviously in a tight situation you get a situation where hotheads would cause war but I don't think it will happen." Bradley's reaction to this statement must have been unprintable.

It had been a difficult few days for Clay. He had seen Berlin's fate hanging by the slenderest thread, and he had beaten back the assembled wisdom of America's national security leadership. As he was finishing the news conference, a reporter yelled, "How are your nerves standing it in Berlin?"

Clay gave a small laugh: "It's a lot better on the nerves in Berlin than it is in Washington."

As he rushed through the Pentagon's halls trying to get to the airport, Clay ran into Cardinal Spellman, the archbishop of New York. They shook hands. The prelate asked him to speak at the Al Smith Dinner in October. Clay, courtly, polite, did not think much of it and hurriedly agreed.

The growing threat of war seemed to be fuel for Wallace's candidacy. "The Berlin crisis doubtless has increased war fears and added pacifist votes for him," wrote the *New York Times*. On July 24, with reports of Truman's decision to send more military planes to Germany splashed across the nation's front pages, Wallace, the self-declared tribune of the "frightened and dissatisfied," took his turn at accepting his party's nomination for president.

The Progressives were the third party to hold their convention in Philadelphia that summer, but their convention was unlike any other. The delegates were young—the average age was thirty and many were in their teens. Three-quarters of the delegates were new to politics—Americans like George McGovern, who was so inspired by the cause he spent his twenty-sixth birthday traveling to Philadelphia from Mitchell, South Dakota. Two out of five were labor union members—the "Auto Workers for Wallace" pushed a slogan-draped car up and down the center aisle. The mood was merry. Each day began with a sing-along of folk music. "I had them all singing," Pete Seeger would remember. "And they didn't just mumble it. They were singing out." He led them in "The donkey and the elephant go 'round and 'round on the same old merry-go-round." Yip Harburg, the famous songwriter of "Over the Rainbow" and "Brother, Can You Spare a Dime?" had written a tune called "Friendly Henry Wallace." Paul Robeson, one of Wallace's most impassioned supporters, sang "The House I Live In," "Ol' Man River," and a song with the lyrics: "From the Bay of Massachusetts, out into the Golden Gate, Henry Wallace leads his army, against destruction, fear, and hate." At any moment during the proceedings, there would be numerous huddles on the convention floor forming around young men and women who had spontaneously begun strumming a guitar.

But for all the jollity, the delegates took their work, and themselves, seriously. They believed that their campaign was the last chance to head off a cataclysm—or as they chanted throughout the week, it was "Wallace or War." The party platform called for an increase in the minimum wage, strong action against racial discrimination, national health insurance, a Department of Peace, higher levels of farm supports, guaranteed pensions for older Americans, better-paying jobs, and more protections for labor unions, but, said Taylor in his vice presidential acceptance speech, "the only issue" is "whether we shall live out our lives and the lives of our children in peace or whether we shall perish." It was, he said, "as simple and straightforward as that. It is life or death. It is peace or war." He and Wallace would win "because I do not believe that God in his mercy will inflict this terrible atomic ordeal on mankind."

With a giant portrait of Franklin Roosevelt hanging from the rafters, every mention of Harry Truman or James Forrestal or Lucius Clay was met roundly with catcalls and boos. Wallace saw the administration's moves against domestic Communists as more of a threat than Soviet encroachments abroad. "We are in the midst of a fierce attack upon our freedom," he said. The steps to jail those suspected of preparing domestic attacks were being taken to distract Americans from "the stupid bungling in Berlin." Wallace was asked at a news conference in Philadelphia about the lack of free elections in Soviet-dominated areas in Europe. "I'd like to have a free election in this country, too," he harrumphed.

But while they found great fault in America's government, the Progressives would not brook the slightest criticism of the Soviets or any Communist. A platform plank stating, "Responsibility for ending the tragic prospect of war is a joint responsibility of the Soviet Union and the United States" was voted down. A Vermont delegate proposed an amendment to say, "Although we are critical of the foreign policy of the United States, it is not our intention to give blanket endorsement to the foreign policy of any nation." Even this oblique refusal to endorse all Soviet policies was met with boos and ultimately rejected.

"I have never heard worse speeches on this earth, nor seen more hideous lady politicians," H. L. Mencken muttered to a fellow journalist during the convention, shaking his head. Later that year, the curmudgeonly "Sage of Baltimore" would suffer a massive stroke from which he would never recover, but that he was saved to cover the Progressive Party convention of 1948 is evidence of a higher power. It was, he wrote, a "paranoiac confection" of "grocery store economists, mooney professors in one-building universities, editors of papers with no visible circulation, preachers of lost evangels and customers of a hundred schemes to cure all the sins of the world." For this, the Maryland delegation to the convention, after considered debate, voted to issue him a formal censure.

WHEN IT CAME time for Wallace to deliver his acceptance address, the Progressive Party convention moved to Shibe Park, home of the Philadelphia Phillies, to accommodate all those who wanted to be on hand. The crowd of 32,000 dwarfed the audiences that had seen Truman and Dewey deliver their nomination speeches that same summer. What's more, each person had to pay an entrance fee ranging from $2.60 for a seat behind home plate to a quarter for a spot out in left field. Those seats were packed.

Wallace himself spoke from a stand just off second base. When he appeared in the stadium, "the demonstrators nearly tore down the house," wrote one reporter. For fifteen minutes straight, "shouts, screams, cheers and in some cases sobs came from the throats of the crowd," marveled the *Philadelphia Bulletin*.

When they quieted enough for Wallace to speak, he began his address with Franklin Roosevelt's vision and the spirit of the Elbe. Four years earlier, when he was vice president, "every one of us dreamed of a time when the sound of peace would again be heard in the land, and there would be no more fear, and men would begin to build again." But then, "in Hyde Park they buried our President—and in Washington they buried our dream." Now, "instead of the dream, we have inherited disillusion."

Wallace promised the ecstatic delegates that he would return to what he claimed were Roosevelt's policies and told them "a new frontier awaits us." Instead of pouring billions of dollars into defense industries, he would use that money to "build new schools" and "end the murderous tyranny of sickness and disease."

The heart of the speech, a full third of the text, was a single topic: "The world's eyes today focus upon the burning spot of the Cold War—Berlin. Berlin need not have happened. Berlin did not happen. Berlin was caused. When we were set on the road of 'get tough' policy, I warned that its end was inevitable. Berlin is becoming that end. There is no reason why the peace of a world should hang on the actions of a handful of military men stationed in Germany! In all earnestness, I assure you that if I were president, there would be no crisis in Berlin today."

"We hear it said," he continued, "that we should have a showdown at Berlin. But what is the showdown about? What is the American public interest which will be served by a showdown? There may be some private interests"—he paused—"some interests of Dillon, Read and international bankers." He spat out the name of the bank at which Forrestal had been president. "But there is no public interest." In all his travels, he had "yet to meet the American in shop or field or college or independent business who wants to give up his life to defend Dillon, Read or to obtain the privilege of feeding two million people in Berlin." America "can't lose anything" by retreating from Berlin "in a search for peace."

Wallace's support had held steady in the six months since he announced his candidacy. If it continued to do so, he would deny Truman any chance at reelection—especially now that South Carolina governor Strom Thurmond was also running for president as a pro-segregation candidate backed by the Southern delegates who had walked out of the Democratic convention. Truman's defeat would, Wallace's followers believed, send a clear signal that Democrats could no longer act as what he called the "carbon-copy" of the Republicans. The tension over Berlin had drawn new adherents to his cause. "I say the lives of our children, and our children's parents, are far too precious to be left to the tempers of second lieutenants at road barriers where zone meets zone—or to the generals who are quoted calmly as favoring a 'show of strength,'" he told the cheering delegates as he stood beside an enormous sign that read "The Time Is Now." That night, in the biggest speech of his campaign, he staked his candidacy on the success or failure of the airlift attempting to supply Germany's besieged capital. "I say the peace of the world is far too fragile to be shuttled back and forth through a narrow air corridor in freighter planes."

W allace was not alone in turning the focus of his campaign on Berlin. All of July, Republican heavyweights such as vice-presidential nominee Earl Warren, John Foster Dulles, Arthur Vandenberg, Harold Stassen, and even the nonpartisan Dwight Eisenhower trooped up to pay their respects to Dewey at his upstate New York farm. After each meeting, Dewey would tell the press that he would not make an issue over the crisis in Berlin—and then proceed to cast aspersions on Truman's abilities to handle the situation. On July 24, the same day Wallace was nominated, Dewey read a prepared statement to reporters from the veranda of his white farmhouse. The blockade, he said, had occurred because Democrats had "fundamentally neglected" the principles of firmness, diplomacy, and competence that he was pledging to bring to Washington, but, he indicated, he was too high-minded to mention such "past lapses."

It was beginning to become clear that the 1948 election would circle around the siege of Berlin. Truman's plan to call Congress back into session to deal with unmet domestic needs had been carefully formulated—for all of Truman's claims at spontaneity—by the political masterminds at the Democratic National Committee to embarrass the Republicans. But by the time the "Turnip Day" Congress convened, it had been overshadowed by events in Germany. Polls at the time showed Americans far more concerned with the threat of war than the issues of wages and education Truman said had been ignored by the "Do Nothing Congress." The Republican chairman of the House Foreign Affairs Committee said it was the Berlin blockade that the summer session should be addressing: "That is the supreme issue confronting not only the nation but the world. It is a world conflict between Christ and the devil, between freedom and slavery."

Truman, too, was thinking of little else. "It's all so futile," he wrote to his sister the week after Clay's visit and the Progressives' convention. "Dewey, Wallace, the cockeyed Southerners and then if I win—which I'm afraid I will—I'll probably have a Russian war on my hands."

If Berliners had been obsessed with food and the pangs of their hunger before the blockade, the siege had made them fanatical. There was, wrote Ruth Andreas-Friedrich in her diary, "No light, no radio, no electricity to cook. Fortunately it is summer, we think every day. The days are longer, and it doesn't matter so much that for days on end one eats nothing but bread with margarine and chives." Berliners slipped into the Russian sector to trade away some of their belongings for a potato. They sneaked out into the country to traipse through the woods to collect vegetables. They pulled wooden carts through town with them wherever they went, picking up twigs for fire. They sarcastically referred to these carts as "Volkswagen."

With electricity severely limited, RIAS sent twelve sound trucks on rounds through Berlin, making dozens of stops each day to read the news. Newspapers carried the schedule of the routes. Hundreds of people would surround the newscasters at each stop, hungry to learn about the latest tidings. The crowds were so large that their trucks' travel had to be coordinated with the police. In Berlin's churches, attendance more than doubled in July. Some that had seen empty pews for years were now filled to capacity.

It was at this fretful moment that the Russians closed their trap. Almost exactly one month after they had blockaded the western sectors of the city, the Soviet-controlled *Neues Deutschland* newspaper carried a front-page headline: "Airlift Has No Purpose—In the Future All Berliners Can Buy Their Rations in the East Sector." West Berliners would receive fresh produce and meats. All they had to do was to trade in their own sector's ration card for a new Soviet card—in effect, deliver their loyalty to the Communists. The food would be available beginning August 1.

Railway cars from Wismar, Rostock, and Stettin on the Baltic headed toward Berlin filled with grain, American intelligence agents learned. In the Soviet sector, the Russians prepared to open registration offices to process the paperwork and distribute the food—thirty-one in the city center alone to accommodate the expected rush. They neatly stacked provisions of food. And then they waited.

The airlift "has gripped the imagination of the Western world," announced Edward R. Murrow's familiar voice in mid-July. Every day, newspapers across the United States carried the tonnage figures and number of flights for the previous twenty-four hours—usually on the front pages. Americans charted the course of their ups and downs as if they were following a pennant race. Reporters rushed to Germany to cover the excitement of the airlift. Someone, it was unclear who and under whose orders, had chalked "LeMay Coal and Feed Company—Round-the-clock service—Delivery guaranteed" on the side of some of the planes and the name began to stick. Profiles of LeMay—an ever-green of the news business—began to appear anew. *Time* magazine wrote that the continuation of the airlift after a full month was "a kind of 20th Century miracle play representing both the West's humanitarian purpose and its military strength." The *New York Times* noted, "We were proud of our Air Force during the war. We're prouder of it today."

The truth was, however, that, for all the excitement, the airlift was failing. By the beginning of August, even with drastically limited rations, Berlin had less than two weeks of milk, meat, and flour on hand. This was the case even though food, not coal, had been the priority. The coal situation was even worse. During the first month of the airlift, 86 million pounds of coal had been flown in, compared with the usual July consumption of 650 million pounds. Operation Vittles had only a two-day supply of tires and engine and propeller parts.

This was during the summer. Once winter came—when flight conditions would plummet and the city's needs would grow—continuing the airlift would be impossible. Forrestal and the others in Washington knew this to be the case. Most Berliners did as well. It was "obvious that Operation Vittles could not be carried on" when winter came, wrote *Time* in July. That same month, columnist Walter Lippmann wrote that continuing the airlift past the summer was "a technical absurdity." A cartoon in the Soviet-operated Berlin newspaper *Tägliche Rundschau* showed a little boy in the future year of 1949 asking his grandmother to tell him again the fairy tale of supplying Berlin by air. Another Communist Berlin paper mocked the airlift as an idea "built largely on clouds." Despite the American promises, it continued, supplying people from the air "cannot be done. Apparently they regard the Berliners as dumb-bells. Once before, the supply of 200,000 Germans was guaranteed through the air—namely the Paulus army at Stalingrad. The result is known."

It was. In the forty-five-year history of flight, airplanes had been used successfully in many ways—bombing runs, dogfights, air patrols. But airlifts—attempts to fly supplies to stranded people—had amassed a record of failure almost completely unblemished by a hint of success.

In 1918, 9,000 British troops were trapped by Turks in the town of Kut, 100 miles south of Baghdad along the banks of the Tigris. An attempt was made to save them by the primitive biplanes of the Royal Flying Corps. Pilots flew over the tiny town to drop 200-pound packages of food and supplies to the troops. It was not enough. The British held out for 147 days before surrendering to the Turks. They were sent on forced death marches, beaten savagely, and put into hard-labor camps where more than half of them died. Seven decades later, a British historian would describe it as "the most abject capitulation in Britain's military history."

During World War II, 250,000 German soldiers under the command of Field Marshal Friedrich Paulus were surrounded in Stalingrad. Reich Marshal Hermann Göring personally promised Hitler they would be supplied by air. For two and a half months, six hundred planes were devoted to the effort of airlifting 600,000 pounds per day. They were able to provide only 10 percent of that amount. The trapped Germans ate dogs and cats. When Göring had Iron Crosses dropped as a morale booster, the soldiers left them to rust in the snow. Ninety thousand survived to surrender. Six thousand made it back to Germany alive.

In fact, only once had there been a large-scale airlift that succeeded: the World War II supply of 60,000 American troops in China trapped on the far side of the Himalayas. And the man responsible for that success—the one man in the world who knew how to organize an airlift on the scale necessary to save Berlin—was now stuck as a mid-level bureaucrat in the Pentagon.

10

AUGUST

The skies were once the home to the last remaining knights of battle. When armies no longer faced off in chivalric contests but slogged through mud and cowered in trenches, pilots still had a whiff of romance to their efforts. They were golden warriors—jaunty, wisecracking, plucky heroes who went wherever, and did whatever, they pleased.

When Bill Tunner arrived at Rockwell Field in San Diego as a fresh West Point graduate in 1929, the uniform of an American army pilot was the same as that of a horse-mounted cavalry officer, with tall brown leather boots and riding breeches. The only differences were that when the pilot climbed into the cockpit of a biplane—they would call what they did "riding" a plane instead of "flying" it—he wore a leather helmet instead of the broad-rimmed campaign hats that would later be called "Smokey the Bear hats," and the sword he otherwise wore slung over his hip was left back on the ground.

One day, Tunner was given the chance to fly to Sacramento in a bigger plane—a three-engined Fokker with a single straight wing perched above the fuselage. There was no need to file "a flight plan, there was no weather information, and the only map available was a Rand McNally California State map." He performed a preflight check on the plane and then stepped in, "looked into the cabin, and immediately froze. A dozen pallid faces were looking back at me." Tunner had never flown passengers before and nobody had told him that there would be any on this flight. The passengers, some of whom were elderly and had never previously been in an airplane, had reason to blanch as well at the sight of the slight twenty-two-year-old who needed a mechanic to show him where the plane's ignition switches, oil temperature, and gas gauges were. "We stared at each other for a long moment."

Nevertheless, they took off, and the foldout map guided him past the palm-lined boulevards of 1920s Los Angeles, over the orange groves of the San Fernando Valley, then on to Bakersfield, Tulare, and Fresno and above the verdant fields of California's farmland. In that era, he would recall, "a flight was not so much from San Diego to Sacramento as it was from this pasture here to that cornfield there to whatever that flat place was up ahead. You felt as though you were trying to steal second base when you lost sight of a field." They landed at the Sacramento Depot after a five-hour trip at an average speed of about 85 miles per hour.

"Only in retrospect does that pleasant afternoon over California become symbolic," he would write. "For there was certainly no way for that young bomber pilot to know that he was going on to fly, as commanding officer directly responsible for the operation, more men and more cargo over greater distances than anyone else in the history of aviation, past, present, and for a long time to come."

It was important for another reason as well. As much as any one person, it would be Bill Tunner who ended that light and cavalier spirit of a military pilot casually flying an airplane he didn't truly understand to a destination he was unsure how to reach. He had thrived on that spirit of adventure—and he would banish it from the skies forever. Bill Tunner brought airpower—a twentieth-century invention—into the twentieth century. And he did it by organizing the largest air transport operation in history over the skies of Berlin.

TUNNER'S FATHER HAD come to New Jersey from the ancient mountain village of Leoben in Austria. As one of five children in a struggling immigrant family, he knew "it would take some kind of a miracle to put me through college." He was panicked by the thought that he would be unable to attend college, that he would live out his days with his horizons crimped. Then one day, at age fifteen, reading a textbook in his high school civics class, he found his miracle. He would describe the buoyancy he felt at that moment in grandiloquent terms: "The book said that the United States of America maintained a military academy on the Hudson River where a boy could get a free college education if he was appointed by his congressman. I looked up from the page with a new hope." Years later he choose to illustrate the sensation with the experience that had come to signify a feeling of relief: "It was like coming out of the clouds to find a landing field right ahead."

Discovering that appointments to West Point were made by his congressman on the basis of merit, Tunner, as he would many times in the years to come, put himself to work on a strenuous schedule. He already exhibited the lack of comprehension for human frailty that would drive his accomplishments and fuel his critics. "I never thought it at all unusual that I would work so hard for a free education; if I thought about it at all, I probably wondered why everybody else did not."

Flying was the province of daredevils and risk takers when Tunner first took to the skies as a cadet. Because of the danger, he was paid $62 extra in flight pay—more than half again as much as he would otherwise receive. He did not inform his parents of his decision to join the Army Air Corps until after he had been flying for a year and could prove to them that he had already survived that long.

The source of the danger was not just the planes—primitive contraptions often built of fabric and wood—it was the pilots. In describing a stereotypical pilot of the era, Tunner would paint a portrait of a leathery, grizzled cowboy: "a cool and nonchalant old-timer with a weather-beaten face and piercing eyes, narrowed, with crow's feet in the corners from years of peering into the blue." It was no accident. Air had the sensibility and the rules of the Wild West. The public avidly followed brutally dangerous air races and thrilled to stunts of pilots who would hang from planes in flight or step from the wings of one plane to those of another.

It was this approach to flight Tunner would come to disdain. But in San Diego, Tunner began to discover there was another aspect to airpower, what he would call "the secret of paper work." While his fellow officers spent sunny southern California afternoons cavorting in the swimming pool or playing a round of golf, Tunner took pride in sitting behind a desk working through a stack of military documents. "I found that if I got right down to my papers, dull as they were, and did the job instead of moaning about it, I could accomplish in an hour or less the work other officers were spending the entire morning on."

What Tunner failed to realize was that, despite the delight he took in his own diligence, his dedication to performing the routine mind-numbing tasks that his more flippant colleagues dismissed was advancing his career down a lonely, lackluster branch of the growing Air Corps. Years after leaving Rockwell Field, after serving for nearly a half decade as a flight instructor at a base in Texas and then being transferred to the Panama Canal Zone, he was still known more for his facility in filling out forms than for his dexterity at flight. "Thanks to my reputation with paper work back at Rockwell Field, I was rewarded with more of it in Panama," he would recall cheerfully. "At Rockwell I had done a dull job efficiently in order to get it over with; in Panama I gave it my best because it was fascinating."

Where other officers sought more opportunities to get time in the sky, Tunner headed for his desk. "Even after starting out at 7 A.M. in the morning with close-order drill, I didn't mind coming to the office, unbuckling my saber, and working the rest of the day on operations. I found out there was a lot more to flying than simply boring holes through the sky. Neither planes nor men could fly constantly. Planes required maintenance, men required rest. Schedules of both had to be planned assiduously in order to have planes ready to fly at the same time crews were available to fly them." Tunner had found his calling—a peculiar and particular set of skills that few others possessed.

When World War II began, Tunner was assigned to the Ferrying Division of the Air Transport Command—the organization charged with delivering the new airplanes that were coming off assembly lines by the thousands. He worked out of a cleared space in a "smelly basement office" of the Munitions Building in Washington, a gargantuan structure along Constitution Avenue directly north of the Reflecting Pool and Lincoln Memorial, on what is now the site of the Vietnam Veterans Memorial.

He devoted himself completely to his mission. Searching for more pilots who could do the dreary work of flying transport missions without, as he would put it, acting like "cowboys," he hit on the idea of using women flyers. Unaware that such a proposal had been rejected at higher ranks, he established what became the Women's Auxiliary Ferrying Squadron (WAFS) and Women Airforce Service Pilots (WASP), putting women to work flying military planes for the first time, not because he believed in women's equality but because he was committed to doing whatever was necessary to accomplish his mission. He allowed a thousand women to fly military air missions, provided they had almost twice as much flying experience as required of men.

Tunner reveled in life at his desk in the decrepit basement. Though he had two young boys with his wife, Sarah, he took pride in working "twelve to fifteen hours a day, seven days a week." It was not until more than two years after Pearl Harbor that he took his first day off, Christmas Day 1943. He worked even when he didn't have to. Three times a month, instead of cutting orders for someone else to ferry a plane across the country, he would order himself to go. Leaving Washington at 6 P.M. on a Friday, he would take an American Airlines sleeper plane to Los Angeles and arrive there by 8 A.M. A factory representative would pick him up, show him around the plane if it was unfamiliar, and by 9 A.M. Tunner would be on his way, hopping across the country until sometime Sunday evening, when he reached whichever base back East was his final destination. He would take a commercial flight home, be "in bed by midnight, and back at my desk at eight o'clock Monday morning."

"I made these trips entirely for fun," he would recall blithely of the three times a month he chose to miss entire weekends with a wife and sons, who hardly ever saw him as it was.

BY THE SPRING of 1944, Tunner's division was delivering 10,000 planes a month to bases around the United States and a thousand more overseas, but in Asia the effort to supply Chiang Kai-shek's soldiers and American troops fighting in China was flailing. Provisions had originally been transported over the treacherous Burma Road, which twisted over teetering precipices deep into China. But as the forces of the Empire of Japan had advanced, Allied posts on the road had fallen before them: the port of Rangoon, Bhamo, and Myitkyina along the banks of the Irrawaddy. Therefore, in 1942 it was finally decided to airlift everything that U.S. forces in China would need from northeast India to Kunming in the Yunnan Province—every gun, every bullet, every morsel of food rations, every drop of gasoline. In between lay some of the world's densest jungles and the snowy peaks of the Himalayas.

From their base at Chabua along the Brahmaputra, planes would fly out over the Naga Hills and the tribes of headhunters who lived there. They flew above jungles so thick that if a pilot and copilot bailed out of a falling plane and landed 150 feet apart they could neither see nor hear each other, and so deadly that, if they landed hurt, they would turn their guns on themselves to end the pain of being consumed by red ants. Their flight route rose toward the mountains, and they could navigate by the "aluminum trail" of wrecked planes that marked their way across the craggy peaks. Heavy hail would tear the serial numbers from the airplanes' skin. Monsoons with winds of hundreds of miles per hour would toss planes around like leaves, sending them cartwheeling past the mountain peaks. Cliffs rose thousands of feet above wild river rapids. There was a higher rate of fatalities over the open skies of what was called "the Hump" than in bombing raids over Nazi Germany. The journey over the Hump was so difficult that the Army did something unusual to calm the pilots' shaky nerves. After each round trip, the airmen were given a slip of paper to be turned in immediately for two ounces of whiskey. Most pilots scurried off to drown their worries. For some, two ounces was not enough to do the job. They would save up their vouchers until they could accumulate enough to buy an ocean of Wild Turkey or Old Crow and forget about the terrors at the edge of the sky.

By 1944, the Hump had come to be known as the "graveyard for commanders." No man sent there to run the operations had ever advanced in his career again. One colonel physically broke down under the strain. A general had been demoted, his stars ripped from his shoulders. They had immense challenges and little to work with. Supplies ran low on everything from wiring to food to toilet paper—when newspapers and magazines arrived from the States, they were handed out with the quip "read 'em and wipe." The Hump had been where "you exiled officers you wanted to get rid of," recalled Tunner, who had sent his share there. It was a home of misfits and miscreants, the mediocre and the middling.

In August of that year, Tunner was sent to take command. As his plane approached, he saw "huge black blotches" on the runway where Americans had crashed and burned. As he walked through the base, he saw GIs lolling about unshaven and unwashed. Languid in the sticky Indian summer, they were sitting around playing cards or simply lazing away under the jungle sun. As he approached, his rank clearly visible, they would grunt in his direction. "Weren't you trained to stand up when your boss comes around to see you?" he snapped. To another group of Hump pilots, he yelled that they looked like a "bunch of damn taxi drivers."

Tunner began to hold the men in his command to his own exacting standards of organization. He mandated daily inspections of living quarters and, before long, the bamboo huts with dirt floors were "kept as clean as the decent American homes from which these boys came." He ordered a parade every Saturday. Some threatened to refuse to follow what they saw as a silly requirement during a time of war. "Bitching was rampant," Tunner recalled, reveling in it. He dared anyone to cross him. "I knew none of them would carry out their threats, and as for the bitching, let them." He became resented and despised, known to the men as a "cold, hard driver." They gave him the nickname "Willie the Whip." He was less than concerned: "I didn't lose any sleep over it." What he wanted, needed, was order. He was satisfied only when everyone was marching in lockstep to the beat he set.

The military bearing and regulation translated into better performance and safety in flight. Tunner established a "jungle indoctrination program" to teach pilots and crews about how to survive and find their way out of the jungle, how to communicate with natives, the plants they could eat, the wild beasts—large and small—they had to avoid. But most important, he brought his demand for regimentation and "rigid standards of excellence" to the operations of the entire endeavor. "We were a big business, and to run a big business successfully we had to know what was going on. I wanted to know just exactly what every airplane on every base was doing every minute of the day." He expected his staff to work the same hours he did. "If the days did not offer enough hours to perform our tasks and to sleep, too," he informed them, "well, we had not come to India to sleep."

Tunner's approach worked. When he arrived in August 1944, the record for the Hump had been 308 flights per day, carrying 2.6 million pounds to China. By the time the war was over a year later, they were flying 1,118 flights a day and transporting over 10 million pounds—more than in some entire months of 1943.

WHEN THE WAR ended and everyone else had headed home, Tunner remained behind, keeping his men there with him. He was consumed by a new dream of tying the nations of Asia together with air transport. He called it the "Orient Project."

His wife had, by then, taken their sons home to her mother's house in Mississippi. One day, she took the boys to a dentist in New Orleans and suddenly collapsed unconscious. Tunner received a telegram with the news—accompanied with a personal message from his commander, General Harold George, reminding him that the war was long over, that it was now time for him to come home, and that he should go immediately to

Louisiana. He flew three days and nights straight to New Orleans. By that time Sarah had regained consciousness, but the doctors were unable to find out what the problem had been. They thought it might well be a brain tumor, but warned that it would take months to make a full diagnosis. Tunner took Sarah and the boys back to Mississippi and managed to spend the rest of the day with them before leaving for Washington. He had not seen them for more than a year. In Washington, General George was doubtful about the Orient Project—the cry of "bring the boys home" was rising and military demobilization was quickening in pace. But he told Tunner he would let him go ahead with it for now. Tunner returned immediately to India. He had been gone nine days—seven in travel, two in the United States, one of those with his family.

A month later, he was flying to Beijing when his plane received a message informing him that Sarah had fallen again. This time the doctors were sure it was a tumor, but they would not operate until he arrived. Tunner would recall that "again" General George "advised me to come home," which raises the question of what he would have done were it not for that recommendation. Once more, he traveled home over three days and nights. The doctors operated the next day, but the tumor had spread over a large area of her brain. Sarah never awoke. In his memoir he would describe what happened: "She lingered on for a year and a half, still comatose. Then she died."

The next sentence he wrote was "And the Orient Project collapsed. The boss had run out on his own project, and those who had volunteered lost faith." He, of course, had not run out but gone to a dying wife and small children who needed him. But there is more between those two sentences than the empty space of a white page. It was not just the Orient Project that collapsed, but the career of its creator.

IN DESCRIBING THE years after the war, Tunner would choose words of physical pain. They were a period of "cutting the military establishment to the bone, quickly and effectively. No part of that establishment was hit harder than air transport." As "the nation stripped its great military machine to the bone, I was shunted from place to place." He accepted a civilian position as president of a new global delivery service called World Air Freight, which would have had renowned general Henry "Hap" Arnold as its chairman. At the last minute, he backed out and stayed in the Air Force because of Sarah's comatose condition. Without Tunner to lead it, the business did not get off the ground. Postwar demand was so high that had it gone forward, Tunner would probably have become a multimillionaire.

Instead, he was appointed as deputy in the new Military Air Transport Service—a position similar to the one he had held seven years earlier during a great world war. He was assigned a desk and a few assistants in a small office on a long hallway in the Pentagon. He moved into Walter Reed Hospital and lived in his comatose wife's room until she died. "I was plunged from the peak of accomplishment and the glory of success to the depths of grief and despair."

Then, in June 1948, Berlin was blockaded. An airlift began. General Bill Tunner, the hero of the Hump, squared his shoulders and waited for the call. It did not come.

As the airlift began to grow in early July, Tunner was away on an inspection tour of facilities around the country. He had an assistant, Colonel Ross Milton, snoop around the Pentagon in search of tidbits of information. "He called each night and he was not happy with my news, for there appeared to be no sentiment for a major effort and no mention of Tunner going over to run it," Milton recalled.

"Air transport is a science in itself," Tunner would argue repeatedly to anyone who would listen. "To be carried out at its maximum efficiency air transport must be run by men who know the techniques of air transport and who are dedicated to air transport—*professionals!*" The men in charge of the airlift simply did not know what they were doing. He had the expertise. They did not. "The capability of an airlift was unknown in Europe. It was generally unknown in our military. It is not strange that it was unknown to Clay. I knew both General LeMay and the actual commander of the Airlift, Joe Smith, and admired and respected both of them as combat officers. But this was not combat. In

air transport everything is different—rules, methods, attitudes, procedures, results."

Tunner was "beginning to get restless. With an airlift taking place in
the world, I did not enjoy warming the bench back in Washington." He
marched into the office of his commanding officer—General Laurence
Kuter—and said that the Military Air Transport Service should take
control of the airlift. He put it "in writing to show him I was dead serious." As if there were any doubt. Kuter "read my memorandum and
calmly told me to relax."

"I did," Tunner said, "but I didn't feel that it was right." All the pain
and disappointments and grief of the past years seem to have come to the
fore. Tunner's entire sense of himself was now built on the reputation he
thought he had established as the world's expert on air transport. He had
sacrificed a great deal to achieve that status. Now with Europe's—indeed,
perhaps the world's—fate depending on the success of an airlift, he was not
only on the sidelines, but in fact forgotten. He learned about what was happening at his breakfast table while reading the newspaper like a civilian.

Yet where the rest of the world thrilled to the initial stories of long
hours, urgency, caffeine, and bedlam, of the fly-by-the-seat-of-their-
pants pilots with the can-do attitude, Tunner was disgusted. "To any of
us familiar with the airlift business, some of the features of Operation
Vittles which were most enthusiastically reported by the press were con-
tradictions of efficient administration. Pilots were flying twice as many
hours per week as they should, for example; newspaper stories told of
the way they continued on, though exhausted. I read how desk officers
took off whenever they got a chance and ran to the flight line to find
planes sitting there waiting for them. This was all very exciting, and
loads of fun, but successful operations are not built on such methods,"
he would recall superciliously. "If the Airlift was going to succeed and
Berlin to remain free, there must be less festivity and more attention to
dull details, such as good, steady, reliable maintenance." These criti-
cisms were all valid, but if there had not been cause for critique, he
would have had to invent it just to go on through the day.

But unbeknownst to him, Tunner had an ally. General Albert Wede-meyer, the Army's chief of plans and operations, had been commander of American forces in China during the war. It was his troops that had been supplied by Tunner's planes. Soon after the airlift began, he proposed to General Hoyt Vandenberg that Tunner be put in charge. Vandenberg said it would not be necessary, that "any of his best officers could easily handle the matter." But as July had gone on, Vandenberg had watched the airlift falter. When Truman decided to send the additional C-54s, Vandenberg decided a change was needed. He and Wedemeyer lived next door to each other in large houses on the base at Fort Myer. One night, Vandenberg was visiting for a predinner drink. "He sheepishly admitted," Wedemeyer would remember, "that he had made a mistake in not" sending Tunner to Berlin from the very beginning. He told Wedemeyer he would remedy the error.

LeMay, however, put up a fight. Never publicity-shy, he was soaking up accolades and swimming in positive clippings. "He had a good thing going," Tunner would write, "and it was perfectly understandable that he would prefer to remain in control of it rather than have some hotshot come in to throw his weight around." Finally, Vandenberg prevailed. He called Tunner into his office. "O.K., Bill. It's yours. When can you leave for Berlin?"

"Right away, sir," Tunner answered. He asked to be able to pick out his own team, going over the head of General Kuter, who was away on an inspection trip in the Pacific.

"Get going, but be reasonable," Vandenberg said. "Tell Personnel the names of the people you want, and their orders will be cut right along with yours." Kuter would arrive back in Washington to find his deputy and many of his officers gone.

Tunner handpicked twenty officers, most of whom had served with him in India. When his C-54 left for Germany, the other men's wives were on hand to say goodbye. Tunner had told his housekeeper he would be back in ninety days. He put one son in boarding school and another was left with the wife of one of his aides.

In the days after their candy drop, Halvorsen, Pickering, and Elkins watched nervously as the group of children by the Tempelhof fence, growing larger every day, waved excitedly at every plane that went by. "You didn't give them your name, did you?" a worried Pickering asked Halvorsen.

"No, I didn't," Halvorsen replied, adding he had kept his cover on so the children hadn't realized he was almost bald. "They don't know who we are."

But it felt like everywhere they went—in the rest room, on the flight line, in the mess hall, at the base operations center—other pilots were talking about the increasing number of children and their strange behavior.

Despite the risk, a week after their first drop, the three men got a new round of rations and decided to parachute their candy again. This time, Pickering and Elkins were enthusiastic participants. Again the drop hit its mark, the children waved, and in the days to come their ranks swelled even more.

A week later, they dropped candy a third time.

A few days after this, a thick fog swept across the skies of Germany. To Halvorsen, en route to Berlin, it looked like "a down comforter." When they reached the ground at Tempelhof, Halvorsen told the other two he would go into base operations to check on the weather forecast. He walked quickly across the apron through the haze and up the ten steps that led to the operations center's double glass doors. Inside, pilots lounged on mismatched chairs—some plain wood, others ragged armchairs—in front of a big bay window that now was wrapped in mist.

As Halvorsen stepped through the door, he saw a large planning table that usually held maps and charts. But it seemed to be covered with dozens of letters thrown haphazardly into a pile one atop another. He thought this was strange and took a closer look.

Many of the envelopes had been addressed in crayon. In red and green, they were letters to "*Onkel Wackelflugel*" (Uncle Wiggly Wings) or the "*Schokoladen Flieger*" (the Chocolate Flyer), all care of Tempelhof Air Base.

Stunned, Halvorsen backed out the door and rushed to the plane to tell his crewmates that "there is a whole post office full of mail in there for us." They feared a court-martial. They decided they had to stop.

Tunner put his staff to work on the flight over to Germany. He had begun to develop a diagnosis of what was wrong with the airlift. The "hustle and bustle and excitement" got pilots' adrenaline flowing, but "the last place you should find this type of activity is in a successful airlift." By the time their plane landed in Wiesbaden, the airlift's headquarters, at dusk, Tunner's secretary had filled up a notebook with shorthand dictation.

Tunner went immediately to report to LeMay at his 102-room mansion. Upon arriving, he was ushered into a drawing room stuffed with beautiful Oriental rugs and the finest antique furniture, and asked to wait. Eventually LeMay appeared, his ever-present cigar clenched in his lips to mask the fact that the right side of his mouth drooped because of Bell's Palsy.

Vandenberg had taken away operational control of the airlift from LeMay and the Air Force's European command and given it to a special task force under Tunner's direction. To save face, LeMay's office preemptively put out a press release stating that Tunner had been "made available by the air staff to head air lift operations to Berlin." Tunner was given a formal order that limited which officials, other than LeMay, he could even speak to.

The two men dispensed with the pretense of pleasantries. They were the same age, but LeMay was famous around the world and Tunner was all but unknown outside a small circle. Yet it was now the transport expert who was in charge of the airlift.

LeMay "wasn't very pleasant, he was cold," remembered Tunner. In fact, he fairly growled at Tunner. "Well, you better get started."

"Tell Smith I'm here and taking over," Tunner replied.

"Goodbye," LeMay said.

"Goodbye," said Tunner. "And," he would recall, "that's about all the conversation we ever had."

FROM LEMAY'S MANSION, Tunner went to the quarters he had been assigned in Wiesbaden's nearly five-hundred-year-old Schwarzer Bock Hotel. The elevator was broken, so Tunner dragged his trunks and belongings up the stairs to the third floor. His apartment door opened up directly into a dirty bathroom and, through there, a single room that looked out onto a block of burned-out buildings. He sat on the edge of his bed and his whole body slumped.

The next morning, Tunner walked up another three flights of rickety wooden stairs in a residential building down the street from his hotel to reach the small offices he and his staff had been given to run the airlift. The floor was covered with trash. There was not a desk or phone to be found. A naked lightbulb swayed overhead. As one of his officers went off to scrounge for office furniture, others tried using toilet paper for adding-machine tape. Tunner found a chair and steamed with rage.

Moments later, a cheery, fresh-faced young airman sauntered in to schedule appointments that afternoon for everyone to pick up their shopping cards for the post exchange and commissary. Tunner exploded. "We came here to do work," he told his aides. "I'm not asking you to put in twenty-four hours a day, but dammit, if I can do eighteen hours a day, you can do fifteen. We didn't come to Germany to go shopping at the PX or the commissary, so I think we can just skip that little cere-mony this afternoon. Inasmuch as we don't have chairs, desks, or phones, I'll expect you to go to the air bases we will operate from and start learning this business." With a final charge to "Get off your tails and get out on the road," he sent them off with instructions to report back that night.

TUNNER FLEW TO Berlin to examine the situation himself. What he saw confirmed his own confidence that he alone knew how to run an airlift. "The situation was just what I had anticipated—a real cowboy operation." At Tempelhof, there was "confusion everywhere" and "a lot of milling around. In the Operations room I'd seen a dozen pilots and copilots crowding around the Operations desk, waiting for clearance. From there I'd followed the crowd into an adjoining room, a kind of snack bar. Here more crew members were drinking coffee, munching on doughnuts, smoking, talking, and laughing," he observed with scorn.

It was all exactly wrong. "The actual operation of a successful airlift is about as glamorous as drops of water on stone. There's no frenzy, no flap, just the inexorable process of getting the job done. In a successful airlift you don't see planes parked all over the place; they're either in the air, on loading or unloading ramps, or being worked on. You don't see personnel milling around; flying crews are either flying, or resting up so that they can fly again tomorrow." It was the very opposite of what was happening on the airlift. "The real excitement from running a successful airlift comes from seeing a dozen lines climbing steadily on a dozen charts."

The terrain below the corridors to Berlin—small hills and rolling countryside—was more favorable than the Himalayas, but otherwise the airlift to Berlin was much more difficult than that over the Hump. In Asia, they had had 450 Skymasters, use of nine alternative airfields for landing, and near total freedom of the sky. If bad weather intervened, the airlift could be placed on hold for days. In the Berlin operation, the flights were limited to three 20-mile-wide air corridors over the Soviet zone and two crumbling landing fields in Berlin—and a few days off would spell catastrophe. The entire American and British fleets put together did not have 450 Skymasters. Most of all, the maximum the Hump mission had been able to haul was still less than half of the minimum Berlin required to endure.

But Tunner had spent the years since the war—the years of a dead-end career and a dying wife—refining his theory of what made an airlift work. He had not only looked at the Hump's success but studied the failure at Stalingrad. In that airlift, "the number of planes available was more than adequate to do the job," he determined. "The problem lay in organization and in planning." He concluded that what he characteristically called the "essential denominator" of an airlift's success was not the quantity of planes thrown into the operation. The most important figure, in his mind, was "the number of hours each day the plane is in the air carrying cargo to its destination and returning home." As he summed it up, "The trouble with all airplanes is that they spend too much time on the ground."

By nine that evening, he and his staff had reconvened in their dingy offices and began to formulate a plan. Three days later, Tunner issued new instructions to all airlift personnel. From now on, pilots landing at Tempelhof were no longer allowed to leave the side of their aircraft. Instead of wandering off into the terminal and the offices, they would have everything they needed brought to them. Upon landing, they were to hold up a color-coded panel to show whether they needed oil or fuel. The bright yellow jeep with the "Follow Me" sign would swing in front of them. The unloading crew would arrive as soon as the plane came to a halt. Next came a jeep carrying the operations officer to take care of the paperwork. Another jeep followed with the weather officer to give the pilots a forecast of conditions. Finally, as added incentive for the pilots to stay put, came a Volkswagen bus converted into a mobile snack bar serving doughnuts and sandwiches. A ham sandwich was 20 cents, a hamburger was 15 cents, coffee or cocoa was a nickel. A red Coca-Cola cooler was attached to the van's side. The pilots would complain about having to pay for the food: "We haul it and they sell it back to us." But Tunner's final order for the mobile snack bar ended any grousing among the pilots about the new rules. It was very specific and was followed precisely: He instructed the German Red Cross to staff the snack van with the most beautiful young women in Berlin.

TUNNER DID MORE than change the airlift's rules, he began to slowly change its culture. He had a large "Howgozit" board put up at the air bases for all the personnel to see each squadron's performance for the day. Announcing the figures on these boards, and in the airlift's own single-sheet newspaper, the *Task Force Times,* engendered a spirit of competition very different from the aerial races of the airlift's early days. The editor of *Air Transportation* magazine walked into an operations room on a base to hear an enraged officer shouting into a telephone. "What's he yelling about?" the editor asked a sergeant. "Figures," he was told profoundly. "Everybody's tonnage-wacky. He's claiming the tonnage high for the day. Somebody in Wiesbaden gave it to the 313th or some other group. You'd think this was the Kentucky Derby." Tunner was re-creating the airlift in his own image. He was replacing the cowboys of the sky with number crunchers.

Tunner's idea of broadly releasing the official statistics of the airlift's daily performance encountered enormous resistance from the upper echelons of the Air Force. Their natural impulse was to keep such sensitive and often embarrassing numbers secret. "I not only wanted them unclassified," wrote Tunner, "I wanted to publicize them, shout them from the housetops." He knew what a powerful goad to competition over higher cargo transport levels the information could be. Besides, he noted, "a heavily loaded four-engine plane is not something you can smuggle into a city." It was well documented that the Soviets were watching from windows all around Tempelhof, keeping close tabs.

There were some crucial differences between the worldviews of Tunner and the Air Force brass that accounted for the divergent approaches. Tunner—like Truman and Clay, but unlike LeMay, Bradley, Marshall, Vandenberg, and the rest—understood instinctively that the airlift's psychological dimension was as important as any other aspect. The operation's goal had to be to bring not just provisions to the Berliners but inspiration to their struggle.

There was another decisive distinction that explained why Tunner wanted to announce the airlift's daily totals and the rest of the military establishment tried to stop him from doing so. It was the most central divergence of all. All involved believed that sharing this information would tell the Soviets, the Berliners, and the rest of the world how the airlift was doing. The difference was that Tunner believed the airlift would succeed even when winter came; the others were certain it was doomed to failure.

———

Tunner's new rules did not solve all the airlift's problems, but they began to have an immediate effect. Within a few days, the amount of time planes spent on the ground at Tempelhof dropped from an hour and fifteen minutes to only half an hour. The airlift's tonnage levels began to rise, but to the Berliners, the immediate result of the faster turnaround could be seen and heard before it was tasted. The steady dribble of planes into Berlin became a stream. Berliners began to refer to planes overhead as the "parade in the heavens." "One evening," an elderly woman recalled a few years later, "I was looking out the window and counted twenty airplanes, one after the other. I said to myself: 'Now we certainly don't have to go hungry.'"

Berliners were still not sure how they felt about the Americans—and fairly certain about how the Americans felt about them—and they had an initial ironic, snarky response to the can-do élan and effectiveness of the airlift. Some of the first people to receive the dehydrated potatoes called "Pom" invited neighbors over to see whether the dried flakes provided by the inventive Americans would actually turn into a potato paste. By mid-July, an announcer on RIAS joked that in order to ensure a warm Christmas, the bureaucrats in the American military govern-ment had decided to reschedule the holiday for July 25. Decorations would be no problem. The airlift would fly in powdered Christmas trees—just add water.

Berliners were impressed by the operation—by the vast air bridge built of men and machines—but felt like they were pawns in a global power play. On the street they would joke that they were lucky it was not the efficient Americans blockading the city and the bungling Rus-sians flying in supplies—as if the two sides of the conflict were inter-changeable. They were glad the allies were bringing in supplies, but it all seemed disconnected from any sense of humanity. When the airlift began, a City Assembly member would later recall, "people thought, 'Why shouldn't it work?' They had dropped so many bombs on Berlin—they should be able to drop potatoes."

BUT THEN SOMETHING started to happen. It began with Berlin's children. By the beginning of August, as word of the candy drops spread, the pack of children gathered at the Tempelhof fence had grown to hundreds every day. Adults were mystified. An Associated Press reporter filed a story on the phenomenon that made no mention of parachute handkerchiefs bearing sweets. "They never tire of watching the operation," complained one irate Berlin parent. "I've got to go out to Tempelhof, spank my children, and drag them home crying when darkness comes—else they would stay there all night." The children bequeathed a name on the pilots and their planes: "*Rosinenbomber*"—"Raisin Bombers." One boy, who was seven years old at the time, would, fifty years later, remember watching those planes land at Tempelhof as "the beginning of a love affair with the Americans."

Soon mothers and the few fathers joined their children. More than a thousand Berliners started to stand outside Tempelhof every day. On warm days, the number would reach ten thousand. Only a few years earlier, wrote Berlin's *Telegraf*, "the sound of aircraft engines had a distinctly unpleasant undertone, and it was advisable to take cover as rapidly as possible." Now the American planes were "no longer a cause for anxiety. No, quite the contrary. Their roar is deep, good and had a quieting effect."

When a C-47 crashed near Tempelhof, killing the two American lieutenants on board, residents of the neighborhood put up a plaque commemorating the loss: "Once we were enemies yet you now gave your lives for us. We are now doubly in your debt."

Berliners began to come to the airport's gates and present small gifts as tokens of appreciation for the pilots. "Seems to me I've met every German in Berlin," said the Air Force captain charged with handling the callers. Children showed up bearing flowers or a prized, tattered picture book. Older Berliners knitted scarfs and sweaters. In early August, a Sunday edition of *Der Tagesspiegel* mentioned a pilot named Lt. Keller and the two children he had left back home to come fly the airlift. A few days later, Tempelhof received a box addressed to "Lt. Keller, Greenfield, Iowa," containing two handmade children's rag dolls.

The people of Berlin were coming to see they had a chance for the world to think of them as something other than the perpetrators of history's most heinous crime; that, in the airlift, they were joined together with the allies in a common endeavor. In her diary, Ruth Andreas-Friedrich described the feeling of waiting for the night's two hours of electricity to come. "We grope our way around the apartment as if blind. We yawn and talk about the blockade. Whether the airlift will work and whether Berlin will be able to hold out." Then it comes on and "we suddenly call out as if with one voice, 'light!' We start running about laughing, as noisy as if we had been drinking wine. To the light switch, to the stove, to the radio. To cook, to wash some stockings, to iron a blouse, to listen to the news." It was, she wrote, "a question of nerves. Between midnight and two in the morning, we feel our nerves are very strong. Not doormats but heroes. Called upon to defend freedom in Europe."

Ever since the war ended, American public opinion researchers had asked Berliners whether, if forced, they would chose "economic security" or "freedom." The Berliners had been clear and consistent in their response. As recently as the month the blockade began, they had picked a full stomach over a right to vote by a margin of 61 to 34. Never in all the terrible cold months of the years after the war in Berlin had economic security been as precious a commodity as during the blockade. But by the time the Russians sprang their trap in the beginning of August, the outlook had started to shift. The colossal effort to feed them from the sky, the candy being dropped to their children for no motive other than human kindness, were slowly beginning to transform the way Berliners looked at America and the allies, and thought about their own plight. "We want under no circumstances to sell our birthright of freedom for ten days of lentil stew," proclaimed Reuter at a July 27 rally. Berliners agreed. By the time the August 4 deadline to trade in their western sector ration cards for a Russian card and its promise of a cornucopia of fresh meat and vegetables arrived, 22,000 Berliners had made the switch—less than one percent. At one ration office, 20 people out of 285,000 eligible Berliners swapped allegiances to the Communists. In other neighborhoods, not a single Berliner went over to the other side. In the western sectors, Berliners, weak with hunger, let the food stacked in Russian stockrooms rot.

O n August 2, Walter Bedell Smith, along with envoys from Britain and France, arrived at the Kremlin for a late-night meeting with Joseph Stalin on the future of Berlin. They had already talked at length when Stalin sat back in his chair, took a puff of his cigarette, and with a beguiling smile asked, "Would you like to settle the matter tonight?"

Smith tried not to betray his excitement. Stalin offered a deal: the blockade would be lifted in exchange for reopening negotiations over the future of Germany and allowing Berlin to run exclusively on Soviet currency. Smith, who believed "time is still working entirely in favor of the Soviets if they desire to make the position of the Western powers untenable," took the offer.

In the following days, Smith and the other representatives met regularly with Molotov to work out the details. Even Marshall, who had tried to put Smith in Clay's place, thought his ambassador had gone too far. He ordered that any final agreement had to allow for all four powers to control Berlin's currency and could not, under any circumstances, link new discussions over Germany with the lifting of the blockade.

Clay, furious at his longtime rival's willingness to trade away Berlin's future, wrote to him in Moscow. "There are so many kibitzers on this negotiation now that I hesitate to bother the piano player." Nevertheless, he went on to remind Smith that the allies were the "plaintiff," not the "defendant," and should act accordingly.

One day in early August an old man showed up at Tempelhof's gates. He was a skeletal sight—"so thin you could see through him," noted the Air Force captain who spoke to him. He had come bearing a gift. He opened up a velvet-lined wooden box and inside was a magnificent gold pocket watch encrusted with jewels. By any measure, it was priceless. It was an heirloom, the old man said, once the possession of his great-grandfather in the early nineteenth century. What's more, thought the captain, the watch could have "fed him for months on the black market"—probably for years. He insisted on giving it to the airlift in appreciation for what the Americans were doing.

Tunner decided he would have a great ceremony to present the watch to the airlift pilot who had flown the most flights—an eager, unfortunate glutton named Lieutenant James Lykins. The old man's gesture had been real and spontaneous, but Tunner knew that, in the competition for the loyalty and love of Berliners and others watching around the world, it was a story that could be milked for its propaganda value. The ceremony was to take place at Tempelhof on August 13. The thirteenth fell on a Friday.

A speakers' platform was assembled with bunting and flags. A marching band tuned their tubas. The honor guard stood bedecked in full dress uniform. Tunner, en route from Wiesbaden, had a speech prepared—he had written and rewritten it—full of praise for Lykins on behalf of "our great leader, General Clay" and "every freedom-loving citizen of the world."

Then, without warning, a violent storm moved in. The rain was so heavy the Tempelhof controllers couldn't see the runway. Incoming planes were being stacked in a holding pattern, but the tiny air corridor above Berlin could not safely contain the pileup of plane after plane arriving every few minutes.

Circling above Berlin himself as he tried to reach the ceremony, Tunner could only listen over the radio as his airlift descended into chaos.

Below, one plane landed in the wrong place, bouncing across the rubble like a skipped stone. Minutes later, another plane overshot the runway and exploded into flames. A third plane swerved to avoid the fire and blew out its tires. Aboard his plane, Tunner barked, "This is a hell of a way to run an airport," along with a stream of more colorful invective. His aides, Sterling Bettinger and Red Forman, a Hump veteran, cringed. "At that moment, I could have snapped my grandmother's head off," he would admit.

Then, over the Tempelhof aircraft controllers' earphones came an authoritative voice: "This is 5549—Tunner talking, and you listen. Send every plane in the stack back to its home base."

There was a pause. "Please repeat?"

"Send everybody in the stack below and above me home." Now it was Tunner who paused to let it sink in. "And then tell me when it's O.K. to come down."

Tunner turned to Bettinger and Forman. "As for you two, I want you to stay in Berlin until you've figured out a way to eliminate any possibility of this mess ever happening again—ever! I don't care if it takes you two hours or two weeks, that's your job. I'm going to give this guy his watch and then I've got some business to attend to with those monkeys in the tower."

BETTINGER AND FORMAN locked themselves away. Two days after what came to be called "Black Friday," they opened the door to reveal a cat's cradle of string stretching back and forth across the length of the room. It held wire hangers to which were attached model airplanes; more than that, it held the solution to the airlift's problems. Their plan was not difficult for Tunner to embrace—it was an encapsulation of his most basic principles of running an airlift.

With an array of checkpoints and beacons, the airlift would be timed with such precision that it would make the Rockettes look like a first-grade dance recital. Every ninety seconds—precisely every ninety seconds—a plane would take off or land. As each plane passed over a beacon at the city of Fulda, on the border of the Soviet zone, the pilot would call out his tail number over the radio, and the planes behind him would adjust their speed to ensure that there was a gap of exactly three minutes between them. If they were more than three minutes behind, they sped up; if they were less than three minutes away, they slowed down. Tunner's system transformed airplanes from independent agents in the air into cogs in a machine. Each plane's speed would control the next plane, one moving the other like the teeth of a gear.

Furthermore, there would be no stacking or circling of planes over Berlin. A plane would have one chance to land. If it missed its approach because of weather or for any other reason, it would have to head back to western Germany and start all over again.

Finally, pilots would fly using their instruments, not on their own vision. The same procedures would be followed whether the view was clear or impenetrable.

The entire operation was transformed from one that functioned on the energy and enthusiasm of individuals to a large-scale structured mechanism. The airlift became the Airlift.

The system would only work, Tunner believed, if it had a "steady, even rhythm with hundreds of airplanes doing exactly the same thing every hour, day and night, at the same persistent beat." He had to hear it pulsing, at a fixed tempo, "constant as the jungle drums." To accomplish this, the procedures were important, but useless unless stringently enforced. The greatest danger to his system would be a pilot exercising his own judgment. "I insisted on complete regimentation in every aspect of flying," he would note. The new rules, a reporter in Berlin noted, "were the Ten Commandments. There was no room on the airlift for a Lawrence of Arabia. There was no room, even, for a General Custer. Everyone had to fly by the book and it had to be the same book. Otherwise you were lost and, worse, the flow of freight into Berlin would be interrupted." Like Industrial Age prophet Frederick Taylor's "one best way" for assembly lines, Tunner believed "there was only one best technique for each flying maneuver—take-off, climb out, cruise, descent, and landing. No variations. I wanted no experimenting on anyone's part."

It was not until August that Halvorsen received his first letter from Alta while in Germany. It had been forwarded from Alabama—she had written him there, not knowing he was on the airlift. "Things happen rather fast as you can see," he replied to her on August 8. "Got the urge to join this Berlin air lift last month and was on my way in about two hours. One way to get away from Mobile heat." The letter was, despite his new locale, unremarkable. "Darn how time flies—seems I stand still and get nowhere while another year drops off. I don't know how long I'll be over here." Referencing the negotiations taking place in Moscow, he pointed out that the "Ruskies seem to hold the answer." He told her that the 20,000 pounds of flour he flew "sure should make a couple of pancakes." But he did not mention anything about dropping candy to children in Berlin.

By the middle of August, it had been two weeks since they had last dropped the small parachutes outside of Tempelhof. On board their plane, Pickering, Elkins, and Halvorsen no longer even mentioned the drops, as if the very discussion of what they had done could get them in trouble. They would talk away on flights into Berlin, but then grow silent when they came in sight of the apartment building. Despite the passage of two weeks without a drop, the crowd of children had not abated. Indeed, it was continuing to grow.

Finally, a few days after Tunner's precise strictures became the Airlift's law, Elkins, no longer able to contain himself, blurted out to the other two, "What are you guys doing with your rations these days?"

Despite their resolution to stop the candy drops, each of the three men had been quietly hoarding their chocolate and gum rations, unable to bring themselves to use them. They decided to make one more drop—the last one, they swore—that would combine all their candy rations for the past two weeks.

The next day, with six handkerchiefs laden with their accumulated sweets, they made another approach over the apartment building.

Halvorsen wiggled the plane's wings. He saw the children cheer and hold up their hands. "Bombs away!" yelled Elkins as he dropped the parachutes.

It had not been the march of the Red Army but Soviet coups that had overthrown the governments of Eastern Europe. If the allies could not be scared out of Berlin, then, the city's residents feared, the Russians would simply knock off the capital's leadership and take control. By the summer of 1948, Berliners were well acquainted with the warning signs of an impending coup, and these were all present in Berlin that August.

Berlin's city government was hanging on by the slenderest of threads. In mid-August, Acting Mayor Louise Schroeder's health collapsed under the strain of the blockade and the constant pressure of Communist intimidation tactics. She fled to the West, leaving the city in the hands of her deputy, Ferdinand Friedensburg, a member of the Christian Democratic Party. With Reuter disqualified by the Soviets and Schroeder gone, Friedensburg—a finicky, plodding lawyer with clumps of gray hair growing over his ears—was the last hope for democracy in Berlin. If he too stepped down, for whatever reason, the next in line for the mayoralty was a Communist Party leader who would immediately hand over power to the Soviets. The Communists wasted no time in turning up pressure on Friedensburg in every way they could. Nearly every night, he was summoned at midnight for long interrogations in Soviet military offices. The papers were full of blasphemous attacks on his character. On the streets, Russian agents trailed him everywhere he went.

Friedensburg was mayor of a city slowly splitting apart. The blockade of the western sectors had begun to divide Berlin between East and West. Since the end of the war, the experiences of Berliners had been similar irrespective of which military government controlled their area of the city. With half the city under siege, Berlin started to feel, for the first time, like two cities.

Soon after the blockade had been put in place, Berlin's police chief, Paul Markgraf, the pliant servant of the Soviets, began to purge all non-Communists from the ranks of those in the force's high positions. By the end of July, 590 top officers had been fired. Berlin's city government did not have the power to fire Markgraf since he had been put in his position by the military occupiers, but Friedensburg could and did suspend him indefinitely for failing to follow orders as well as for "his undemocratic and un-German practices." Assistant Police Chief Johannes Stumm was named to take Markgraf's place.

Kotikov demanded that Berlin's government back down, and he refused to recognize Stumm as legitimate. Overnight, Berlin had two police forces. On August 4, Stumm called on all officers loyal to the city government to report to a new headquarters in the western sectors. The Communists demanded the cops remain under the command of Markgraf. Of the 2,000 officers, 1,500 showed up for duty at Stumm's offices.

The day after the drop he had sworn would be his last, Halvorsen landed at Rhein-Main on a return from Berlin. A stern-looking officer was waiting for him on the flight line with a summons to immediately report to his commander, Lieutenant Colonel James R. Haun. The crewmates exchanged worried looks as Halvorsen was led away.

He was ushered in to see Haun without delay. The colonel held a pipe in his jutting jaw. He had a thin moustache, large broad shoulders, and his hair was closely cropped. "Halvorsen, what in the world have you been doing?" he yelled as soon as the meek-looking pilot entered the room.

"Flying like mad, sir" was the best he could muster.

"I'm not stupid. What else have you been doing?" Haun reached for something under his desk. Halvorsen thought he might be going for a whip. Instead, he spread out that day's newspaper. "You almost hit a reporter on the head with a candy bar yesterday. He's spread the story all over Europe." The reporter had seen the tail number on Halvorsen's plane. As Halvorsen stared at the paper in disbelief, Haun asked why he had kept the drops a secret.

"I didn't think you'd approve it, sir."

"You're right," barked Haun. "General Tunner wants to see you. Fit him into your schedule."

HALVORSEN TOOK A transport from Rhein-Main to Tunner's offices in nearby Wiesbaden. As he glided past the dark German forests, he wondered about his fate. He had never met Tunner, but the reputation of "Willie the Whip" was well known. Stories of his cruel treatment of pilots on the Hump were now traded in the German bases, growing more callous with each retelling. Everything in Tunner's past methods— every logistical and disciplinary requirement of the Airlift—pointed to a court-martial for Halvorsen, or at least a severe penalty.

Halvorsen walked slowly, deliberately along the cobblestones of Tannusstrasse and up the three flights of wobbly stairs to the Airlift's headquarters. He could feel his heart pounding as he stepped into Tunner's office. The first thing he noticed was the iciness of the general's blue eyes.

Halvorsen approached Tunner and introduced himself with full military decorum. Tunner looked over the young pilot, sizing him up quickly. He beckoned him forward. And then, rather than giving him a court-martial, he offered his congratulations. He had realized immediately the enormous psychic boost the candy drops could provide to Berliners. In the new kind of war they were fighting, a battle for affections and allegiance as much as for territory, Halvorsen's actions could be a powerful weapon. So despite all his determination to enforce the Airlift's strict rules, Tunner did not send Halvorsen to the brig. He sent him to go speak to the press.

It was a sticky, humid day in Wiesbaden. In the press offices, a single gray metal electric fan hummed away in a corner. Halvorsen shyly poked his head in the door. "I'm Gail Halvorsen. I understand you want to see me?" The reporters, in their shirtsleeves, looked up from their typewriters and set upon him. Word had spread of the mysterious pilot dropping candy attached to handkerchief parachutes to Berlin's children.

For a half hour, they peppered him with every question they could think of. He seemed to know instinctively the kind of nuggets of information they were looking for. Asked for the name of his effort, Halvorsen said it was called "Operation Little Vittles," a stretch for what had simply been a few dozen pieces of candy dropped over the course of a month. He told the reporters he was running out of handkerchiefs, but contemplating it out loud, said, "Come to think of it, I have an old shirt I could cut up." The reporters could not take down the colorful quotes fast enough.

With the split between Markgraf's and Stumm's officers, Berlin now had two rival police forces—each claiming power over the western sectors. The clash between them was inevitable. It came first on August 19, the same day Halvorsen was meeting the reporters. In Potsdamer Platz, the crossroads where the American, British, and Russian sectors intersected, Markgraf's police crossed into western territory to break up the square's flourishing black market. Stumm's police arrived on the scene to turn them back. Each claimed to be the official force of the entire city and considered the other side to be illegitimate. They prepared to do battle. Soviet, American, and British army units appeared to offer backup. The various forces arrayed themselves around Potsdamer Platz with arms drawn. It was not until 10 P.M. that they withdrew.

The following day, Markgraf's forces conducted raids throughout the city, with two into the western side of Potsdamer Platz. In all, they arrested 2,500 Berliners, including some officers from Stumm's forces.

On August 21, the Soviet forces arrived at Potsdamer Platz for the third day. They came en masse—260 officers under Markgraf's command and 400 Red Army troops. This time, the allies were there first. The Russians arrived to find 600 American soldiers there with rifles and submachine guns at the ready. After a decent interval, they slinked away.

Three days later, Berliners, standing in Potsdamer Platz beside rubble piles and a big sign declaring "You Are Leaving the American Sector" in three languages, watched in bafflement as a worker—hunched over a small brush dipped into a small can of paint—worked his way across the cobblestones. With paint spattering his shoes, he was drawing a white line through the middle of the square. It was the first physical demarcation of the division of Berlin.

On August 20 newspapers around America carried a story about Halvorsen from the Associated Press. It was nothing more than a small squib, the kind of human-interest nugget that once populated the extra inches left over in the layout when the real news did not fill the page. But as a break from the tidings of angst and worry, it was memorable and appreciated. The story reported that Berlin's "boys and girls" were regularly gathering by Tempelhof to receive tiny parachutes of candy from Halvorsen, who was dubbed the "lollypop bomber." That evening, ABC News recounted Halvorsen's story and presented him and his "Operation Yum Yum," as they called it, with their "Kelvinator Tribute." Many papers revealed that pilots at Brookley Air Force Base, informed of Halvorsen's undertaking, were starting a collection of candy to provide for his "handkerchutes." The first person in line to donate a candy bar at Brookley was eight-year-old James R. Haun, Jr.

The stories were brief. At any other moment in the country's history, Americans might have smiled and turned the page of the paper or been left with a warm feeling that lingered on into the news program's extended refrigerator commercial. But the days of the cowboy aviators and wartime bombardiers had passed. Since the end of World War II, America had not had a military hero. Now, with a sense that the nation was again on the verge of conflict, here was a new type of military man in a new kind of military operation. Halvorsen became the public face of the otherwise anonymous pilots flying the airlift. And in an America still struggling to come to terms with the mission to feed the Berliners, his example of unalloyed goodness represented a larger idea: that— whatever the conflicting election-year views over how to respond to the

Berlin crisis—America had a moral responsibility to help the humans caught in the middle of the struggle. There could be no clearer example of this than offering candy to starving children.

ON HIS NEXT trip to Tempelhof, Halvorsen brought along a large bag and filled it with all the letters that had been waiting for him on the big table in the operations center. He began to read through the notes—many written in the same crayon as their envelopes—and found, as he had expected, that they were thank-you notes from Berlin's children.

Halvorsen was dizzy from the events. But little that he experienced would make a bigger impression on him than what he found when he returned to the barn on his first day flying after his identity had been revealed. He climbed up the ladder into the loft and found that other pilots had covered the balding gray blanket on his cot with a huge pile of candy.

As negotiations in Moscow continued under cover of secrecy and apprehension grew in Berlin, the situation threatened to careen out of control. On August 26 and 27, the City Assembly tried to meet. The agenda featured the question of new elections for the Berlin government due that fall. On both days the members gave up in the face of Communist mobs gathered outside City Hall carrying signs that read "One administration, one currency, one food supply," "No Marshall Plan," and "No more airfields."

On the evening of August 27, American military police ran a Soviet jeep caught in the U.S. sector off the road and fired on the Russian troops inside. The Soviets, in turn, arrested an American journalist.

Pessimism and despair were rising among already dejected Berliners. That August, with spotty electricity in the western sectors and a dark mood, receipts at west Berlin movie theaters were down 85 percent compared with the previous year. The suicide rate more than quadrupled.

With Tunner's permission, Halvorsen could now make regular drops to the children gathered outside Tempelhof. He did so almost daily. The mass of children continued to grow. Some came because of the spreading legend of the Candy Bomber; others, like the children of Hamlin, followed the sound of the planes to see what was happening.

Eleven-year-old Rainer Baronsky remembered of the first months of the blockade that "we were always hungry, always cold." One day in August, intrigued by the sight of airplanes flying overhead, he and his younger brother sneaked into the elevated S-Bahn train, since they could not afford the fare. They got off at Tempelhof and found a large group of other children standing atop a mountain of rubble watching the planes come in. As they gazed upward, they saw tiny parachutes fall from the sky as a Skymaster passed above them. Rainer and his brother did not know what this meant—word had not reached their neighborhood—but the other children ran toward the parachutes, yelling with glee, so he and his brother did as well. "One parachute got snagged in a tree, so we took a long stick and jarred it loose. My little brother and I opened up the package dangling from the bottom of the chute and found candy! What was candy? We would later find out about its sweet chocolate taste—Hershey bars, Butterfingers—it all looked so good." They took their treasure home, where their father explained that it was a gift from an American. They unwrapped the candy bars and cut them into five pieces for the entire family; they carefully chewed the gum, then dipped it into sugar the next day to give it some taste, and chewed on it again.

Soon Halvorsen ran out of handkerchiefs and could find no more shirtsleeves to tear into parachutes. His supply officer was able to acquire twelve three-foot silk squares. "The *fräuleins* will have them for panties," another pilot said, to laughter. "You will never see them again," said Bill Christian. Halvorsen had his secretaries write a message in German on the fabric: "Please return this parachute to any American Military Policeman that you see so that it may be used again." In English, Halvorsen wrote a message to the MPs: "Please return this parachute to Tempelhof Base Operations for Operation Little Vittles." He dropped them in the morning. By 4 P.M., nine of the twelve had already been returned to the office at Tempelhof addressed to "Uncle Sam Who Wiggles His Wings," "The Chocolate Pilot," and "The Bon Bon Flier."

THE TROOP OF children outside Tempelhof grew so large as Halvorsen's drops became a daily occurrence that he began to worry about setting off a mob stampede at the sight of the few handkerchiefs coming out of his plane. Though the entire Airlift operation under Tunner's command was predicated on each pilot flying in lockstep, obeying precisely the steady beat of the "jungle drums," Halvorsen asked for and received special dispensation to break the rules of the airlift and fly his own pattern. As he approached Tempelhof with a regular load of coal or flour, Halvorsen would pilot the plane over schoolyards or children's hospitals or the soccer fields where tiny figures ebbed in unison like blades of grass in the breeze. He would toss out the parachutes and wait for permission to rejoin the regular traffic pattern. He was gone by the time the candy reached the ground.

But, unbidden, the letters from Berlin's children came in a torrent.

Dear Candy Bomber,

Some days ago I read in the morning paper something about Americans throwing sweets for German kids. How lucky I was last Sunday. I played at a ruin with some friends of mine opposite of our house. Suddenly we saw about ten white parachutes coming out of the sky! One of them set down at the roof of our house. There were three stripes chocolate in the parachute. My sister, mother, and grandma were very glad about the chocolate too! I want to thank you for your love to the German kids. And I want you to

say all your friends many thanks. Please tell them we were very
glad.

Your little friend,
Hans Loewy, 14 years
Berlin

Another read:

August 29, 1948

Dear Uncle Wiggly Wings,
When yesterday I came from school, I had the happiness to get
one of your sweet gifts. First I did not know what do of joy and I
could not come home quickly enough, to look at your wonderful
things. You cannot think how big the joy was, they all, my brother
and parents stood about me when I opened the strings and fetched
out all the chocolate. The delight was very large!

Gratefully,
Lieselotte Müller

These children had been Hitler's last hope, inculcated since birth
with a hatred for Americans and their wickedly egalitarian democracy.
When the war had ended, they had been so scarred by the American
aerial attacks that the sight of a lit match sent them into convulsions of
terror. An American in a uniform—even a Salvation Army uniform—
caused them to burst into tears. They had been the children who played
the game of "rape." Now social workers observed that a new game was
dominant amid the craters and rubble-strewn streets of Berlin. The
city's children were playing the game of "Airlift."

Clay would concede that on at least one point Sonny Whitney and
Hoyt Vandenberg had been right: Tempelhof and the British airfield in Berlin, Gatow, did not have the capacity to handle the number

of flights needed to bring both the food and coal the city would need when the weather grew cold. Though journalists and the members of Truman's cabinet still believed that supplying Berlin by air in the winter was a laughable impossibility, Clay—watching the effects of Tunner's new rules on the rising graphs of airlift cargo totals—began to think otherwise. A new air base would be needed to handle all those planes.

An open piece of land was surveyed in the French-sector neighborhood called Tegel. It had been from towers that still stood on these grassy hills, in the northwest of the city, that the last broadcast of Nazi radio had been transmitted at 1:55 A.M. on May 2, 1945: "The Führer is dead. Long live the Reich." Now this meadow, with the radio towers controlled by the Soviets, was to be the site of a new airport.

On August 17, LeMay wrote to Clay. The "present estimate of the Tegel Airfield is February 1949, of course dependent to a great extent on the severity of the coming winter."

Three days later, Clay responded. "I don't accept this February 1949 estimate for Tegel. It is much too long." They did not have until February. Besides, Clay knew something about building airports.

With the conventions over, presidential politics in the United States came to a summer pause. There were no train trips or rallies or speeches. But all during August, each of the campaigns thought ahead, planning and strategizing.

The most ironclad law in politics is that of unintended consequences. Certainly, when Truman and his political handlers had concocted their plan to bring Congress back into a summer session, they had never considered that it would give the House Un-American Activities Committee a chance to convene. On August 11, freshman representative Richard Nixon from California took the train up to New York to meet with Dulles in order to coordinate with the Dewey campaign his plans for a public confrontation between Whittaker Chambers and the former State Department adviser he had accused of spying, Alger Hiss.

The inquiry was a sensation. For the first time, television cameras broadcast a congressional hearing to the public, and the threat of a creeping encroachment of Communist peril entered Americans' living rooms. The Dewey campaign decided that it would pick up on the theme of a Communist infiltration of Truman's administration. The premise offered a way to address the fear of the Russians without referring directly to Berlin and the threat of war.

Dewey himself spent time that August planning, as well. He exchanged letters with his mother discussing the accommodations that would be available to the family at the inauguration in Washington in January.

Truman and his advisers also used the still, sticky Washington August to organize themselves. Clark Clifford presented the president with a detailed memo explaining their strategy for the coming campaign. There were three "main objectives": The first was to win over the independent vote. The second was to capture the large blocs of voters who tended to move in unison: "workers, veterans, and Negroes." The last of the main objectives was not about constituencies but an encapsulation of a campaign message that was intended to stave off the challenges from both Dewey and Wallace: "The third objective is to cut through all party lines by showing that the President's party had kept the nation on a road leading to peace, and that changes in this policy may lead to war."

With Americans fearful of an approaching conflict with Russia, Truman would raise the specter of danger if he was replaced. The 1948 election would be the first of the atomic age—the first where voters had to make a decision on who was fit to protect America and prevent the annihilation of large swaths of the world in an instant. Like Wallace, Truman would stake his campaign on American attitudes toward the aerial defense of Berlin.

ALL DURING AUGUST, negotiations in Moscow over Berlin's fate had continued. The Soviets were alternatively quarrelsome and cooperative, changing their attitude and their bargaining position on a daily basis, and often more frequently than that. Just when the Western envoys were prepared to quit the discussions and admit failure, the Russians gave ground. They would agree to lift the blockade and have the Soviet's mark, under four-power control, serve as the currency for Berlin. They even gave up on a guarantee that the creation of a West Germany come to a halt. On August 30, the four governments released a communiqué announcing their accords, "subject to agreement being reached among the four Military Governors in Berlin for their practical implementation." All that was left was for Clay, Sokolovsky, and the rest to work out the details. They were given until September 7 to do so.

In Washington, Truman's political advisers prepared for a declaration of victory if the blockade was indeed lifted. William Batt of the Democratic National Committee told the White House that Truman should personally announce the news to the nation. Batt went so far as to draft a speech with ringing, utopian phrases straight from Clifford's memo: "our goal must be—not peace in our time—but peace for all time."

Berlin's fate, the fate of peace in the world, and perhaps of Harry Truman's election as well, all appeared to rest in the hands of Lucius Clay and the other battling military governors in Berlin. One of Truman's campaign speechwriters would recall waking up in the middle of the night during that clammy August, sweating and panicked over the doom that would face his young wife and infant son if war over Berlin came. Truman's sleeping routine was upset that month as well. The floor under Margaret's piano had given way. His bathroom was about to tumble into the Red Room below. Truman was forced to move into the Lincoln Bedroom. The White House was literally crumbling around him.

11

SEPTEMBER

"The blockade will be lifted," wrote Ruth Andreas-Friedrich in her diary on September 1. "One hardly dares to believe it, but they say it is true." At Helmstedt, on the border between western Germany and the Soviet zone, trains filled with food were said to be preparing to head toward Berlin. They would need only "several hours of paperwork" before they could begin to roll, reported the *Los Angeles Times*. The Airlift would be called off within ten days, predicted a United Press dispatch. "Berliners are jubilant," noted Andreas-Friedrich. "No more dehydrated potatoes and canned meat. No more power cuts, no tiresome conversion acrobatics between East marks and West marks. Paper for the magazines and, what is most important, no more enmity and unrestrained hatred between Berliners." She and her daughter splurged that night, lighting four candles instead of their usual one. "Who knows, perhaps already by tomorrow we shall have light again by just switching it on."

At Kleist Park, where the four military governors had once worked together harmoniously in the Allied Control Council, they now met on August 31 to begin haggling over the final pieces of minutia needed for an accord ending the blockade. Every day, dozens of Berliners gathered outside the gates. Children sat on their fathers' shoulders to watch the big black cars glide past the intricately corniced colonnades that led to the great sweeping driveway. There was an air of expectancy, a hope that the terrible fate that had seemed to be set for the city might not come to pass.

Clay was the last to arrive at the opening day's sessions. The other military governors were already seated, waiting for him. He walked in glowering, refusing to shake Sokolovsky's hand. Given the rotation of the chairmanship of the old Allied Control Council, it was Clay's turn to run the meeting. He said he would not preside. Koenig, the French military governor, agreed to do so. Clay sat in silence, not saying a word, leaving little doubt about his disdain for the proceedings. "I am not going to be the war monger which plunges defenseless France and UK as well as US into war," he had told Draper in a teleconference the night before. "On the other hand, I have no hope of reaching a solid agreement which protects our position." The Russians too evinced little desire to re-create the spirit that had once characterized the four-power meetings. On their second day of meetings, as a remembrance of times past, Koenig prepared a buffet of refreshments for the conclusion of the session. The Soviet delegation got up at once upon adjournment and left without saying farewell.

With their September 7 deadline looming, the four military governors met every day, as did a series of subcommittees of experts they established. The substance of their conversations was complicated, involving the operations of a "Bank of Emission," which would issue the currency, and the powers of a "Financial Commission," which would control it. They argued at length about which restrictions on travel into Berlin would be rolled back. But it quickly became clear that the obstacles to agreement could be boiled down to two main differences: The Soviets would not allow the allied powers to have any real say over the economic life of Berlin, and they would not commit themselves to completely lifting the blockade.

If this were not enough, Sokolovsky added another hitch. With the sound of airplanes on their final approach into Tempelhof droning above continuously, he announced that the air corridors were being overused, and demanded that part of their agreement limit the number and type of planes flying into Berlin from the west—in effect, shutting down the Airlift. Sokolovsky's insistence on this point should have indicated immediately that the Russians were not serious about coming to an accord.

Nevertheless, the meetings continued. They would end late at night, and Clay would then have to stay up till almost dawn on teleconferences with the officials in Washington or connect with them early in the morning while it was still dark in America. There had been numerous conversations between Forrestal, Lovett, and Royall about how to handle Clay. They agreed that they did not trust him in these negotiations. Lovett especially felt Clay would not be able to "preserve his calm and poise." He told Forrestal that Clay was "now drawn as tight as a steel spring." Forrestal seemed to understand and suggested someone, perhaps Royall, should go to Berlin to oversee Clay's actions. It was quickly agreed, however, that such a move would send a strong signal of lack of confidence. Instead, Pentagon and State Department officials slogged through hours of discussions with Clay on a daily basis, going over everything that had occurred in the four-power talks. Forrestal, Bradley, Royall, Lovett, and Bohlen all took part. When a decision was needed from someone who was not there, Clay would be asked to hold while the official would be called by phone, no matter the hour. The late nights and early mornings took their toll. Everyone involved in what they called the "telecon nightmare" was fatigued. "For God's sake," exploded Lovett at the blameless teleconference operator at one point, "it's time to stop. We're not making any sense anymore." But every day, the intercontinental reports continued.

ON SATURDAY, SEPTEMBER 4, after five days of discussions and with only three more remaining before their deadline, the four military governors finished another day of fruitless meetings in the early evening. Just as they adjourned, Sokolovsky said he had an announcement to make. Beginning on Monday, September 6, the Russians would be conducting extensive air maneuvers that would run into the narrow allied air corridors over the Soviet zone. The other three military governors stood there, mouths agape. Sokolovsky reassured them. It was only the "normal maneuvers for this time of year for the Soviet forces." Clay reported to Washington that night that he found this "amusing since in the four summers we have been in Berlin we have never heard or seen these maneuvers previously."

Robertson was mannerly. He thanked Sokolovsky for sharing the information and said he hoped it would not interfere with traffic in the air corridors.

"Certainly," answered Sokolovsky.

"I am not sure," reported Clay, "whether this meant 'Certainly, yes' or 'Certainly, no.'"

Clay too thanked Sokolovsky for notifying them; however, he said, he "must point out" to the marshal that, in case he had not noticed, "the air corridors to Berlin and in Berlin were now crowded with" hundreds of aircraft traveling through on a daily basis to bring food to the city. Speaking "in the interests of the American airmen," he asked that such maneuvers not be conducted in the corridors. "Sokolovsky insisted they must use the corridors."

Afterward, Clay met with Robertson and Koenig. The other two governors were holding on to hope. They still believed "that agreement was quite possible," Clay notified the Pentagon. "I must admit that I am completely unable to diagnose the events which lead to such conclusions on their part."

3 September 1948

Dear Chocolate Uncle!

The oldest of my seven sons had on this day his sixteenth birthday. But when he went out in the morning we were all sad because we had nothing to give him on his special day. But how happily everything turned out!

A parachute with chocolate landed on our roof! It was the first sweets for the children in a very long time. Chocolate cannot be

bought even with money. My oldest son, a student, came home at
eight o'clock and I was able, after all, to give him some birthday
happiness.

I will gladly return the handkerchief parachute if necessary but I
would pray for you to let me keep it as a memento of the Airbridge
to Berlin.

> *With deepest appreciation,*
> *Frau Helga Mueller*

Twice in late August, the Berlin City Assembly had attempted to meet and was shouted down by mobs. They were to try again on Monday, September 6. All sides were aware of the meeting's importance. Another failure would demonstrate to Berliners that their city's government was no longer functioning. The democratic party leaders wrote to General Kotikov asking him for police protection at City Hall from Markgraf's forces in the Soviet sector. He never answered. Instead, Markgraf's deputy publicly promised that their police forces would not impede any mob actions by the Communists against Berlin's elected government. On Sunday evening, Otto Suhr, the chairman of the Assembly, went on the radio to plead with all parties to declare a truce from rioting so that the council could do its work, especially at that moment, when the military governors were undertaking their sensitive negotiations.

Unbeknownst to the military governors, Acting Mayor Friedensburg took an extra step for protection. He had forty-six of the Stumm western sector police, in plainclothes, come over the sector boundary to guard City Hall.

ON SEPTEMBER 6, it was raining again in Berlin. Outside City Hall, black umbrellas popped up like caps on mushrooms. By 11 A.M., as many as three thousand Communist protesters had arrived in trucks draped with red flags and by foot in long marching columns. "There then followed," Howley wrote in his diary, "a series of events which would be incredible anywhere except Berlin."

At noon, by a prearranged signal, the mob moved forward. The metal outer gates to City Hall were knocked down. The building's janitors tried to hold the glass-paned front doors closed, but after a few moments of struggle these were kicked in, sending shards of glass into the entry hall. The Communists grabbed a wooden bulletin board and used it to break down what remained of the doors. The Soviet police, at the vanguard of the surging throng, proceeded to arrest the janitors for defending the building and then stood in the corridors singing the "Internationale" as the mob poured by. The protesters occupied the Assembly hall and its galleries, chanting and demanding that the city government accede to the Communists' proposals. Otto Suhr and other democrats watched fretfully. In the crowded hallways, political factions met in heated debates, shouting past one another and the din. Markgraf himself, reeking of schnapps, roamed the corridors personally pointing out targets for the crowd to attack. Ernest Leiser, an American wire correspondent, spotted a demonstrator who had broken his camera earlier in the day and began to argue with the man. The German, in turn, grabbed at young Marguerite Higgins of the *Herald Tribune*. Leiser walloped him, and the two men got into a fistfight. The Markgraf police came to the German's aid. Joe Evans of the *Wall Street Journal* dove into the fray to help Leiser and was thrown down a staircase.

Markgraf learned that there were officers of the breakaway Stumm police force in the building, and his men began combing the halls for them. The western sector police officers hurried to the doors of the offices maintained by the American, British, and French military governments asking to be sheltered inside. The Americans immediately agreed and took in twenty of them. The French let ten into their offices. The British liaison officer called Robertson for instructions on what to do. Robertson, in turn, called Bevin in London, who approved providing shelter to the remaining sixteen Stumm police.

In the assembly chamber, the mob broke the microphones of the RIAS reporters on hand to record the day's proceedings. At 2 P.M., with most of the democratic members of the City Assembly having fled the building, one of the leaders of Berlin's Communist Party was escorted through the crowd, up to the rostrum. He called the Assembly session to order, denounced the misdeeds of the democrats, and moved to enact the Communists' "Winter Emergency Program." By 2:30, the meeting was ended and the mob marched back out the shattered doors of the City Hall, singing and chanting along their way.

Once the crowd had cleared the building, more than 550 Soviet sector police formed a cordon around the City Hall. No one would be let in or out. Now hostages, the American, French, and British soldiers—along with the western sector police they were sheltering—looked out from their office windows to see Russian troops armed with tommy guns standing below.

IN WASHINGTON, IT was Labor Day. The city was quiet. In backyards, families had their last cookouts of the summer. Children played on the Mall. Forrestal used the holiday to hold a long meeting about Berlin with Lovett and Bradley in his office. They had no inkling of the events taking place at City Hall that afternoon, but Lovett came to the meeting armed with a hunch. "He reiterates that it was only a hunch," Forrestal wrote in his diary. "There are no intelligence estimates to support this conclusion." What Lovett wondered was whether the negotiations with the Soviets—beginning in Moscow at the end of July, dragging on through August, now hopelessly mired down in Berlin in September—had all been simply a ruse. The shifting attitudes of the Russians had been so erratic, so outside the scope of what logic could imagine. "The sheer duplicity of the Soviets during these negotiations is beyond the experience of the experts in the State Department," Forrestal noted. Was it possible that Stalin had led the Western governments down a rabbit hole for more than a month of conferences in Moscow and Berlin that skillfully alternated hope with ultimate despair, keeping the allies from taking any steps beyond continuing discussions, and then deposited them into September with winter and the necessary end of the Airlift now fast approaching? Forrestal and the men in his office pondered the possibility. Again, Lovett emphasized, it was just a hunch.

———————

AT 8 P.M. IN Berlin, a troop of Markgraf police under the direction of a Russian major Otschkin reentered the City Hall. They banged on the door marked "Secretariat of American Liaison Officers" and shouted "Police!" The American junior lieutenant inside opened the door a crack to tell them they had to go speak to his major down the hall. The moment he did, the police forced their way into the offices. A brief fistfight ensued between the Markgraf officers and the Stumm police hiding in the room, but the west Berliners were quickly overpowered by superior numbers. They were each handcuffed to two Soviet sector police—men who only months earlier had been their colleagues on the unified police force of Berlin—and marched out the front door of City Hall into waiting trucks. Some cursed as they were being led away. Others, knowing what lay ahead for them, cried.

American major John Davisson, who had been helplessly caught down the hall when his country's offices were invaded, went, along with the French and British liaison officers, to confront Major Otschkin. Davisson objected to the German police breaking into an American office—especially since it had been done under Soviet command. The Americans were hiding criminals, Otschkin replied.

It was "a violation of official allied territory," said the French officer, Captain Victor Siegelmeyer. "In the name of the French military government, I protest the Nazi methods used here tonight."

The British liaison, Colonel Whitefoord, added that he also protested the "intimidation of Russian soldiers running about this building and outside."

"Are you scared?" taunted Otschkin.

"No," said Whitefoord.

"Then it is none of your business. I didn't come to arrest you. If you are afraid, you can stay here overnight, but we are going to eat." At that, he and his minions turned and walked away.

Inside the British and French offices, twenty-six western sector police still waited in hiding.

———

THE ATTACK ON City Hall was not unexpected. In the six months since Beneš was banished from the Prague Castle and Masaryk plunged from his window, Berliners had been awaiting a putsch against their government. Now it had come. The Soviets had caused the democrats to flee from the City Assembly meeting and then called it to order under Communist control.

But that night, in the dormitory of a technical school in the British sector, Suhr also held a city council session. With the members of Berlin's democratic parties in attendance, he began to carefully follow the agenda that had been prepared for the day's session at City Hall. Standing about without desks or chairs, they approved plans to prepare the city for the winter ahead and to hold new elections at the end of the year. They decided to meet in the west from then on.

With limited radio access, word of the events at City Hall traveled through the city by rumor. When electricity came to her neighborhood that night, Ruth Andreas-Friedrich learned over the RIAS broadcast on the radio that the democrats, instead of giving up to the Communists, had held their own meeting in the western sector. She knew immediately that this one decision was critical to defeating the Communist attempt to overthrow Berlin's government. "So they failed! Or at least they didn't succeed in pulling off a *coup d'état.* As of today we not only have two city police forces, but also two city parliaments. Perhaps by tomorrow we will have two city governments and along the sector boundary a Chinese wall with battlements and watchtowers." She thought she was exaggerating.

CLAY WAS IN the evening's negotiation with Sokolovsky when the Soviets ordered the invasion of the American offices in City Hall. His first impulse was to send American troops to the scene in the Soviet sector "to restore order." He quickly thought better of it. Instead, as he reported to Bill Draper at the Pentagon that night, he had restrained himself and done nothing as "Soviet sector police broke into our office and led about twenty of the poor devils off to death or worse." It was one in the morning in Berlin. Clay, sitting in the quiet, windowless teleconference room in his headquarters, was despondent. "Pride is a cheap commodity, thank God, or I could never hold my head up. We are being pushed around here like we were a fourth-class nation."

The deadline for an agreement with the Soviets on lifting the blockade was upon them and they were "getting nowhere. I have tried every tactical method I know of." The Soviets were "making only those proposals which would give them complete control so as to make our acceptance impossible. They are then willing to discuss their proposals interminably but never to yield an inch." He did not know what else he could do. "I feel like I am failing you."

He resolved he would not continue to take the abuse. The next time his soldiers were so harassed, Clay informed Draper, who immediately notified Royall and Bohlen by phone, he would send American troops into the Soviet sector. "I'll let you know in advance though."

AROUND THE TIME Clay was giving Washington its latest scare, Hal Halvorsen landed back at Rhein-Main after his second round trip to Berlin of the day to receive his own fright. He had finished his flight debriefing and was about to leave to return to the barn when the operations officer mentioned, in an offhand way, "I've got a note for you, Halvorsen." The message read, "I want to see you as soon as possible." It was signed by Tunner. The same cold rain that had fallen on City Hall came down on Rhein-Main as well and, in the middle of the night, added to Halvorsen's "nervous chill." Like all the pilots, he was terrified of Tunner. He wondered if the children had been caught selling his candy on the black market. It would have netted them a fortune.

The next morning, Halvorsen traveled again to Wiesbaden and again climbed the rickety stairs. The Airlift's offices were a hive of activity. Tunner, naturally, was reviewing tonnage figures on a chart when Halvorsen approached. Seeing Halvorsen, Tunner told him to sit down. "I haven't got time to visit long. The Air Force has requested that you proceed to New York for interviews on the *We the People* television program. They want to hear about what we are doing and the details of your operations. Do you want to go?"

"When do I leave?" replied Halvorsen, as relieved to not be in trouble as he was excited about the journey.

In two days, Tunner told him. "By the way, Halvorsen," he added, "don't get a big head about this thing."

THAT NIGHT OF September 6, Harry Truman was on board a train speeding home to Washington through a sloe-black Midwest. He looked out the window. A caliginous mist hung over the terrain of farmhouses and village crossings. He had chosen Labor Day to kick off his presidential campaign. In what would become a ritual for Democratic candidates, Truman had traveled to Detroit's Cadillac Square to address a throng of unionized workers and a radio audience listening in at home, or in their cars, on that holiday. The coffers of the Democratic National Committee were nearly empty. They had been able to afford only a limited amount of radio time to broadcast the Labor Day address. As he read the speech to launch his campaign, Truman, far behind in the polls, with his party split, had been forced to frantically drop entire sections of his written text to complete as much of his remarks as he could before the country heard the plug being pulled on the president of the United States.

Yet it was not only the hopelessness of his campaign that Truman was thinking of as the train shook down the tracks that night. It was the situation in Berlin. Together with the British and French, he and his advisers had decided that there was no use in seeking an extension on the September 7 deadline for the Berlin talks. The search for a negotiated solution to the blockade crisis had ended in failure. The idea of sending a tank column guiding a convoy of supplies into the Soviet zone had been shelved. All that remained now was to wait and see what the Airlift could do.

In the sixty years since the 1948 campaign, it has become an article of faith that the election was decided on the basis of domestic concerns such as crop prices or workers' wages, and that national security issues played little role. "Though conducted against the backdrop of the Cold War, the election of 1948 saw remarkably little debate between Dewey and Truman over it," wrote a recent chronicler of that campaign. Two of the most acclaimed historians of twentieth-century America concluded that "foreign policy had not been an issue between the major parties in the 1948 campaign." Yet the truth is that the conflict with the Soviet Union, the fear of an approaching war, and the siege of Berlin shaped almost every aspect of that election and were subjects of vociferous argument between the candidates. They determined the strategies of each of the various contenders—with the exception of the single-issue campaign of the segregationist Strom Thurmond. The daily banner headlines of dire news from Berlin dominated newspapers' front pages and weighed on the minds of the voters. And it was the issue of war and peace that would ultimately decide the election.

Having rushed through the night, Truman's train pulled into Union Station in Washington at 1 P.M. on Tuesday, September 7. Two hours later, an emergency session of the National Security Council was convened to discuss the state of affairs in Berlin. The news was all bad. Futile negotiations. Soviet air maneuvers in the corridors. Riots in City Hall. Time, George Marshall said, was on the side of the Soviets. The longer the blockade dragged on, the worse conditions in Berlin would be. He advocated taking the matter to the United Nations. Few, if any, at the meeting thought this would lead to a solution; it had not taken that institution long to develop a reputation as an ineffectual, splintered debating society. However, as those in the room understood, public opinion would demand a failed attempt at utilizing the route of the United Nations before any eventual military action was initiated.

As they discussed the situation, Royall informed Truman that General Bradley was going to talk to Clay to make sure that any protective measures taken against Soviet misdeeds were not unduly provocative. They wished, if possible, to avoid a skirmish. But it must be recognized that anything could happen, the Army secretary said. He told Truman that plans were being finalized to evacuate Reuter, Suhr, Friedensburg, and the rest of the city's democratic leaders if the need came. Lovett chimed in to propose distributing pistols and rifles to west Berliners so that they could protect themselves in case of Soviet invasion.

WHEN THE NATIONAL Security Council meeting ended, it was night again in Berlin. Inside the British and French liaison offices in City

Hall, western sector police were still hiding from the Soviet troops and Markgraf police that were waiting for them in the corridors and encircling the building. They began to come down with cabin fever. Several had attempted to escape, but were immediately arrested when they stepped outside. That afternoon, the trapped British soldiers sent out an urgent request for tea, milk, and sugar.

As the night wore on, the ranks of the Red Army troops and Soviet-controlled police grew. At 9 P.M., Captain Siegelmeyer, the French liaison officer, returned to City Hall from a night at the theater, bearing champagne for the men inside his office. He was told he could not enter. "This is the French way in," he shouted as he pushed past the guards and jumped through the broken glass doors. As he landed on the floor, a few of Markgraf's police approached. Siegelmeyer lifted himself off the ground with one hand and kicked one of his assailants. He delivered a roundhouse to the jaw of another. But when he reached his office, he found sixty Soviet policemen standing outside. Siegelmeyer gave up and went back out the building. He had the Germans hiding inside his office lower him a basket by rope so that he could deliver them the champagne.

At two in the morning, Kotikov called Jean Ganeval, the French commandant in Berlin, and promised to end the standoff. He would guarantee safe passage out of the Soviet sector to the nineteen western police officers remaining in City Hall. At four, two French trucks arrived to retrieve the men. They were awoken and—after forty hours of being held hostage—walked bleary-eyed out of the building. The trucks pulled away.

They had traveled only four blocks when they were flagged down at a roadside barricade by two Soviet jeeps. When the trucks pulled to a stop, nearly a hundred Red Army soldiers emerged from the shadows of nearby buildings. With submachine guns in hand, they surrounded the two trucks, dragging the men out and taking them off to prison.

Within minutes, Ganeval was calling Kotikov. The Russian answering the phone told him that he could not be put through. Ganeval tried to reach Kotikov for the rest of the day, unsuccessfully. Beset by a strong Communist tide at home, a series of unstable governments that fell throughout the summer, a deep-seated hatred for the Germans, and a fear of the Soviet army's strength, the French had been weary partners in confronting the blockade. They had contributed almost nothing to the Airlift effort. But now, deceived, Ganeval was incensed. He would bide his time for a response, but in the meanwhile, he sent Kotikov a cable. "I still am unable to believe that an agreement reached under your personal guarantee could have been violated in such a flagrant fashion," he wrote the Russian. "The facts were such as I have reported them. I hold it important to establish them in a formal way.

"And I know that no one will doubt my word."

A FEW HOURS later, at midday in Berlin on Wednesday, September 8, Clay was in a teleconference with Forrestal, Bradley, Royall, and Draper. They reviewed the status of the Airlift, the events at City Hall, and the end of the negotiations with Sokolovsky. As Royall had told Truman he would, Bradley pressed Clay on his vow to send troops into the Soviet sector to halt the disturbances. Clay told him not to worry. "Sometimes I let off steam," he revealed to no one's surprise. He promised he would not make such a move without getting prior approval. He pointed out, however, that the time when he made such a request might soon come. "You cannot live surrounded by force and bluff without showing that you have no fear of the first and only contempt for the latter."

When the teleconference ended after two hours, it was still mid-morning in Washington, but already Forrestal's head was swimming. As he left the room to make his way into a Pentagon meeting with Marshall and the Joint Chiefs of Staff regarding their military options in Berlin, Forrestal confided to Royall that the pressure on him was staggering. The negotiations were "of a nature that requires almost continuous attendance in order to follow the threads between State and the Defense Departments." To understand what was happening in Berlin meant one "had to maintain daily and almost hourly familiarity" with the "minutiae of detail in connection with the Bank of Emission, with trade arrangements, etc." Forrestal admitted he felt he was falling further behind. He was feeling overwhelmed.

His own intransigence had created a position of secretary of defense with broad responsibility and little formal power or personal staff. "Clark, I was wrong," he admitted to Clifford that summer. "I cannot make this work. No one can make it work." All summer he had been battling with the generals and admirals to try to bring them to agreement on a budget that fit within Truman's parameters of no more than $15 billion for the next year. He would plead with them, cajole them, summon them to a weekend retreat up at Newport, but there was little budge.

The longer the struggle wore on, the more consumed by it he became. If it had been simply a bureaucratic disagreement, it would have weighed on Forrestal and troubled him, but would not have had the psychological impact that it ultimately did. However, the argument was not merely about dollars. It was fundamentally about the nature of the war Forrestal believed lay ahead. In August, the Pentagon had given final approval to HALFMOON, the first war plan that envisioned an all-out nuclear assault on Russia. The plan was built on the assumption that war would begin in Germany and the Soviets would quickly engulf the rest of Western Europe. The Americans would launch atomic bombers carrying their entire nuclear arsenal from air bases in Okinawa, Egypt, and England. It was Forrestal's nightmare scenario. With a budget of $20 billion, there would be enough manpower and equipment to try to slow a Soviet advance and to hold the Mediterranean—countries like Greece, Turkey, and perhaps Italy. At $15 billion—Truman's firm figure—Soviet troops would brush past the tiny, ill-prepared American forces and there would be no choice but to implement HALFMOON and launch the atomic attack on Russia and Eastern Europe at the outbreak of fighting.

Forrestal became fixated on trying to find a way out of the knot. He pored over the minor trivia of the budget. In one meeting, he hounded Bradley about the Army giving its soldiers too many pairs of pants. Forrestal ate almost all his meals at his desk. The lights in his office would be seen burning at four or even five in the morning. That week, the *Saturday Evening Post,* in a cover story entitled "If War Comes—," carried a picture of Forrestal sitting at his desk, his lips pressed together so tightly they vanished. The caption under the photo read, "Your fate is in his hands."

THAT SAME DAY, September 8, Frank Howley, under instructions from Clay, went to confront Kotikov about the events at City Hall. With his face reddened, as it would when he grew angry, Howley sneered at the brazen outrage of Markgraf's forces directing a mob action and invading the American offices. Kotikov calmly replied with an hour-and-a-half-long address he had prepared in response. Howley sat squirming as he listened to Kotikov explain that "the mob was really a group of workers legitimately proceeding to their City Hall to petition their elected city government." One could hardly blame them, Kotikov pointed out. "It is well known to you that the Berlin population is quite alarmed by the unsatisfactory preparation of the city for the coming winter." The western police had been on hand, undercover, to create a fracas, he said. The allied military personnel had been "drunk, disorderly, and aiding and abetting the disturbance." Kotikov went on in this vein, as if, wrote Howley in his diary, "all Americans are bad angels and all Russians are from the waiting room of Jesus Christ." By the time Kotikov was done, Howley's face had grown so flushed it appeared as if he might spontaneously combust.

Howley asked for assurances that the Russians would release the western policemen seized at City Hall. Kotikov was evasive. He claimed that Soviets were treated far worse in the American sector than was true the other way around. After all, when had General Clay been detained in the Russian sector as Marshal Sokolovsky had been in the American? "I ask you, dear Colonel, is this fair?"

Howley said he wanted to remind his colleague that there were "large numbers of Soviet citizens freely moving in the American sector in complete security." The Americans would, "of course, in view of the unsatisfactory replies, reexamine our own policy in the administration of our own sector."

Was this an ultimatum or a threat? Kotikov asked, mopping at a suddenly glistening brow.

It was neither, Howley said. It was "simply a statement of fact."

Kotikov's demeanor changed. His voice dropped. He began to massage his fingers. He asked Howley to notify him in advance if the Americans were going to make a move. And the situation with the police arrests, he promised, "would be untangled quickly."

On September 8, the leaders of Berlin's democratic parties requested permission to hold a rally the following day on the steps of the Reichstag to protest the Soviet actions at City Hall. At first, the British, whose sector the area was in, refused, unwilling to further ignite an incendiary situation. The Reichstag lay just on the border of the Soviet zone. Yet when the decision was appealed to Robertson, he reversed it. The rally was scheduled for 5 P.M. on Thursday, September 9.

That morning at dawn, RIAS sound trucks began to wind their way through the city. "Berliners from East and West," the announcers intoned, "to the Reichstag! Your city is in danger. Today at 5 P.M., Berlin calling the world! Against the blockade, against the Markgraf police, against Communist terror! The decision lies in your hands." The western sector labor unions convinced businesses to close for the day at two and arranged for transportation home after the public systems closed at six.

All afternoon, the square at the foot of the Reichstag filled with Berliners. They came not in a trickle but in a flood. It was warm and cloudy, with temperatures hanging in the upper seventies, the kind of day that pits a dying summer against a bracing fall. Men wore hats, women their best dresses; boys had on their ties. Blind and sundered veterans of the Wehrmacht hobbled along, swept up in the flow of the crowd. "Housewives ran away from their stoves, the hairdresser abandoned his customer under the drying hood, the news vendor closed his newsstand," observed Ruth Andreas-Friedrich in her diary. "Everybody came running, thinking: I must demonstrate. We belong to the West. We are Berliners. We are a community of fate. It is a great thing to feel a part of a community of fate."

In the midst of terrible conditions, they had come to ask not for peace but for justice. They were there to plead with the allies to continue to resist the blockade, to stand firm against food and warmth and electricity for Berlin if it meant a sacrifice of the city's freedom. It was a remarkable statement in that time and place—a testament to the power of the allied answer to the siege. The Airlift had provided more than flour and coal; Halvorsen had shared more than candy. The kindness and determination of those who had once been Germany's enemies had brought, as the Berliners would invariably explain to anyone who asked, a sense of hope, of the possibility that after Nazism and war and its brutal aftermath, a better life might be possible, that a world still coming to grips with the horrors of the Holocaust might treat them not as pariahs but as heroes. By five o'clock, there were 300,000 Berliners gathered in protest. From the steps of the Reichstag, they stretched out for more than a mile. It was the largest gathering since the end of the war.

Even Reuter and the other organizers were taken aback by the size of the assemblage. But it was the palpable spirit of purpose amid hardship that was most poignant. The *New York Times*' Drew Middleton, looking back over a full life a quarter of a century later, would write of that day, "I have seen and been moved by many crowds. But none, not even the people of London bidding goodbye to Winston Churchill, has moved me as much as that vast throng." Otto Suhr's Jewish wife, Susanne, would recall standing up near the speakers' podium, gazing out on the gathering. "I never cried during all the war—but I cried then."

The display of oratory from Berlin's leaders that late summer eve was by turns affecting, stirring, and defiant. Franz Neumann, his shirtsleeves rolled up, began the rally by calling for a moment of silence for victims of Nazi totalitarianism. Friedensburg and Suhr and other politicians followed, but the crowd was waiting for Reuter. He spoke last and did not disappoint. His words would become part of his city's lore. He wore a light suit and dark checked tie, his jowls hung loosely, and the dark rings under his eyes gathered like ripples. "While there is a recess in the four-power discussions on Berlin, this demonstration gives allied statesmen an opportunity to find out what the Berlin people really stand for," he said, clutching the podium, and speaking to Truman and Clay and the other allied leaders as much as the multitudes gathered before him. "We know what is going on at negotiations in the building of the Control Council and in the stone palaces of the Kremlin. We cannot be bartered, we cannot be negotiated, we cannot be sold. All political discussions in Berlin are backed by the will of the people determined to maintain their freedom. Whoever would surrender this city, whoever would surrender the people of Berlin, would surrender a world. More, he would surrender himself.

"Today no diplomat or general will speak or negotiate. Today the people of Berlin will make their voice heard. You peoples of the world, you peoples in America, in England, in France, in Italy: Look at this city and see that you may not abandon this city, that you *cannot* abandon this city. There is only one possibility—for us to stand together united until this battle is won, until this fight is finally settled with victory over our enemies, with victory over the powers of darkness. The people of Berlin have spoken. We have done our duty and we will keep on doing our duty. People of the world: now do your duty. In the time to come, help us not only with the roar of your planes, not only with the transport equipment you send here, but with staunch and indestructible support for the common ideals that solely are capable of assuring our future and that solely are capable of assuring your future. People of the world: look at Berlin!"

FOR ALL THE eloquence of the speakers, the crowd had been much larger than expected and the sound system was rudimentary and weak. Most could not hear a word that was said, but stood in silence for the hour and a half of speeches gazing at the hulking mass of the Reichstag before them. Shelled and charred and battered, it was riddled with bullet holes. More than anything the politicians could say, it served as a reminder of what Berlin had lived through and what it had wrought on the world.

The speeches ended and the Berliners began to trudge home. They walked past the Tiergarten, its sparse trees bent over as if they were too weakened and weary to stand upright. At the Brandenburg Gate, directly southeast of the Reichstag, the border between the British and Soviet sectors, an open cattle car filled with Soviet sector police stood by. The crowd began to jeer them. "Pfui on Communism," "Back to Moscow," "Markgraf pigs," "Kotikov get out." Thousands strong, they were able to shout at the officers with impunity. It emboldened them. Someone threw a rock. And then another. From the ruins, people grabbed bricks and began to hurl them at the Soviet police. The truck's glass was shattered. One officer was hit in the face. He brought his hands to his head to try to hold back the gusher of blood.

The officers began to fire into the crowd. A fifteen-year-old boy, diving to protect a female nurse standing behind him, was shot in the groin. He lay on the pavement bleeding to death. The Berliners began to scurry away in panic. Mothers grabbed their children by the hand and pulled them as they raced away. A tired-looking man in a worn blue suit stood his ground. "Traitors! Communist swine!" he yelled. He was struck in the head, hard, with a club. Still he stood. He turned to the retreating crowd. "They can beat us, but don't run away. Stand fast! Drive them back to Moscow!" An officer lifted a gun and shot him in the chest at point-blank range.

Someone spied a young man scaling the massive columns of the Brandenburg Gate, and as if with a single mind, everyone stopped to watch him reach the top of the grimy, burnt arch and make his way to the Red Flag flying high above. The sun was setting over the Tiergarten, and the lone silhouetted figure was bathed in a warm orange glow. He pulled at the flag but it did not give. Two shots were fired at him but missed. He tugged at it again and again and it finally tore free. The flag and its pole fell slowly in the breeze like the last crinkly leaf fluttering from a barren tree. The Berliners leapt on it ravenously, tearing at it with a delight that looked almost maniacal. The cry of "Burn it!" swept through the crowd. Lighters and matches were produced. The wind blew them out at first. They tried again. The throng moved in closer to see what would happen. A single individual, a young boy, no more than twelve, pushed against the flow of the crowd. He had the wooden flagpole, ten feet long, thrown over his shoulder and he was dragging it behind him. "I'm taking this to my uncle," he shouted joyfully. "We need fuel for the stove."

A jeep with five Soviet soldiers brandishing machine guns came on the scene and began to fire in the air. A British officer arrived soon after and stepped in front of them. He tapped lightly on their guns and gestured for them to turn and leave. They lowered their weapons and drove off. A light summer rain began to fall and the angry crowd melted away.

At the same moment Reuter was reaching his peroration in Berlin, David Dubinsky, the president of the International Ladies' Garment Workers' Union, was meeting with Truman in the White House, at the president's request. Dubinsky had been a founder of the American Labor Party but had bolted when it was captured by Communists. Now the party was firmly in the Wallace camp. It was critical to Truman's election that Dubinsky work energetically against his old allies.

The two men discussed politics at length. But there was something else on Dubinsky's mind. "I am worried. I think we will ultimately be pushed out of" Berlin, he told reporters, recounting his conversation with Truman when he stepped out of the West Wing. "Hitler put the trade union leaders in concentration camps, but Stalin will chop their heads off. I told the president that in the event we are pushed out of Berlin, we should protect them and not leave them there."

"What did the president say to that?"

"He said, 'We will not be pushed out of Berlin.'"

It had been that kind of day for Truman. Berlin was dominating most every conversation. At a morning news conference, he had been pressed nine times to comment on the situation in Germany. He stuck by his policy of avoiding public statements on the crisis. "I know you are limited on this thing, but that thing hangs awfully heavy on people's hearts and minds," a reporter beseeched him. "With that in mind, is there anything you could say that would be cheering or hopeful or optimistic?"

"We are still standing up for our rights in Berlin" was the most he would offer.

At 5 P.M. that evening, Truman hosted a reception for the Finance Committee of the Democratic National Committee. These were the party's most loyal financial backers. In the Red Room of the White House, he climbed atop an elegant chair to give these men a blunt message. He understood their attitude toward his chances for victory, but would they not at least agree that the president of the United States should be able to make his case to the American people? If those in the room did not come up with $25,000 soon, the cross-country campaign trip he planned on taking beginning next week would not get past Pennsylvania. Two men there immediately committed to donating $10,000.

Many others, even in this crowd of committed partisans, held back. That morning, Elmo Roper had announced that "Thomas E. Dewey is almost as good as elected" and that his firm would discontinue its polling of the 1948 presidential race. Roper was the savant of the young science of election polling. When the *Literary Digest* predicted Alf Landon would be elected in 1936, he had been off by only 1.1 percent in his forecast of Roosevelt's margin of victory. In 1944, he had been off by 0.3 percent from the final tally. It was an inviolable political axiom that whoever was ahead on Labor Day would win the election, and Roper determined that Dewey had a lead of 44 to 31 percent over Truman. Further polling was pointless, he said. He could "think of nothing duller or more intellectually barren than acting like a sports announcer who feels he must pretend he is witnessing a neck and neck race."

Forrestal, the wealthiest man in the cabinet, had been named to the Finance Committee but did not attend the Red Room reception. A spokesman said he was out of town.

THE FOLLOWING MORNING, Friday, September 10, with news of the Soviets killing one Berliner and wounding twenty-two more dominating the front pages, Truman met with the cabinet in the White House. Forrestal was in his usual seat. Marshall, usually the stoic, complained that everyone involved in the Berlin discussions was in a state of exhaustion.

They had been in teleconferences until 2 A.M. the previous night and had resumed at 8:30 A.M. that morning. With the negotiations in Berlin over, the Americans wanted to now take the matter to the United Nations immediately. The British and French shied away from the finality of such a move and wanted to try another approach to Moscow. As Bevin kept pointing out, Washington was thousands of miles away from the consequences, while in London they were "in the front line." It was determined by the cabinet that to present a unified front, and in light of their commitment to working with their allies, they would wait on the United Nations and again try a final appeal to Stalin.

As the meeting broke up, Forrestal spoke to Marshall. The secretary of state could not have been surprised about what was on Forrestal's mind. He was wondering again about whether Truman would be ready to drop atomic bombs if war came. In his diary, Forrestal could not even bring himself to spell out the word. "Talked with Marshall this morning on use of A and a conference with the President. He suggested a meeting with the President at twelve Monday."

Hal Halvorsen, having left Germany on the day of the Reichstag rally, arrived in New York City on September 11. The producer of *We the People* took him around town and checked him into a hotel. On Monday morning, September 13, Halvorsen showed up at CBS Studios No. 51, just south of Times Square, to begin two days of rehearsals for the popular scripted interview show.

Nineteen forty-eight was the year that television, as a part of Americans' lives and not just a technological novelty, was born. There were 6,000 television sets in America in 1946. In 1947, 175,000 would be produced. In 1948, there would be 977,000 televisions shipped to consumers. That September was the last month that fewer than a hundred thousand televisions were built. But what was more important than selling the mammoth wooden boxes with their seven-inch screens was the production of programs that would make Americans want to spend the

$98.50 (payable in easy installments) to buy the contraptions. In 1948, *Puppet Playhouse,* featuring Howdy Doody, aired on NBC five times a week from 5:30 to 6:00—the first program of the day's schedule. *Kukla, Fran, and Ollie* and *Hopalong Cassidy* joined it that fall. Over the summer, professional wrestling and the nightly news had made their first television appearances. The *Texaco Star Theater* with Milton Berle bowed that June, with critics declaring its host "television's first real smash!" Another variety show, *Toast of the Town,* was less well received. The *New York Times* declared the show's choice of a somewhat stiff New York *Daily News* columnist named Ed Sullivan "as master of ceremonies seems ill-advised." *Candid Microphone* debuted in August, but did not gain much popularity until after it was renamed *Candid Camera* the next year.

With a still relatively small number of Americans owning television sets, they were set up for public viewing in restaurants and community centers and shop windows. In October, during the 1948 World Series, a hundred sets were placed in Boston Common so that fans could watch the hometown Braves. The following month, when television's first opera, *Otello,* was broadcast at the 750 Bar and Grill on Third Avenue, a television set was positioned by the sign reading "Not responsible for hats, coats, umbrellas or lost weekends." Every so often, the bartender with the dirty apron would slap the hand of a dozing drunk: "Hey, wake up. This is opera." Needless to say, baseball had a brighter future in the medium.

We the People combined interviews, musical selections, and dance numbers with automobile advice brought to viewers by the show's sponsor, Gulf Oil. Halvorsen had his first dry run for the broadcast on Monday afternoon. On Tuesday, he had three more. That night, his face painted in heavy makeup, Halvorsen appeared live at 9 P.M.

Halvorsen immediately became one of television's first sensations. Here was a young man in uniform—the kind of person hardly heard from in the years since the war—who was a representative of the Airlift that had so captured America's imaginations, as well as a singular figure with a heartwarming story of his own to tell. He was earnest and humble. In a time of worry, he symbolized the possibility that war could be averted and reconciliation achieved.

The morning after his *We the People* appearance, Halvorsen arrived at the Wings Club in the Biltmore Hotel for a 10 A.M. news conference. The room was packed with reporters. He handled their questions with aplomb. He mused about flying over east Berlin: "I'd like to drop some in the Soviet sector, too, but they might complain we were dropping bombs or something." He spoke of Berlin's children: "I think it helps them a little bit just to have something to look forward to every day." He made clear to the reporters, and to the Americans who would read their stories in the days to come, that though he had not intended any grand impact from his candy drops when they had begun, he recognized that there was a power in convincing these children that America stood by them and cared about what happened to them. "One cannot tell of the future effect on the thinking of those children," he said, "but I am certain that the majority of them would never allow a Hitler-type dictator to turn them against the United States."

Then, in a response to another question, Halvorsen summed up his life, and his answer would make him a star: "My car is in Mobile, all my handkerchiefs are in Berlin, and my heart is in Utah. How I'm ever going to get out there and remain long enough to talk her into marriage, I don't know. And I've practically got no hair left to tear out worrying about it, big as the problem is." With those words, he took his story from one of war and peace to the affairs of the heart. Of the hundreds of newspaper articles that would appear about Halvorsen in the months to come, almost all referred to his plight as a lovesick pilot far from his true love. Reporters would be sent to crack the mystery of her identity. The combustible mix of television, international drama, and personal soap opera made Hal Halvorsen, in that moment in American life, a national celebrity.

Over the next days, his photograph appeared in papers around the country in all manner of poses, a large number of them involving chocolate bars. The *New York Times* dubbed his project "Operation Gum Drop." The headline in the *New York Post* was "Got Any Spare Hankies? This 'Lift' Pilot Can Use Them." The other networks demanded their turn. The afternoon of his press conference he was asked to come to the Mutual Broadcast Network studios to appear on the *Human Side of the News* at 4 P.M. and *Mutual Newsreel* at 10. That Friday, he helped write the script for a radio play about the Airlift starring Henry Fonda and Joe E. Brown. On Saturday, he had back-to-back appearances on ABC and NBC television. When, on the air, he told Tex McCrary that he was running low on handkerchiefs, the television host untucked his shirt from his pants, ripped off his shirttail, and said "Here, use this as a parachute."

"YOU'D HAVE THOUGHT I was the president or somebody, the way they gave out with the old VIP treatment," Halvorsen would say that September. "Every time I turned around there was somebody new at my elbow asking about Little Vittles." He would admit he was "tuckered out, broke and getting slightly allergic to candy bars," but would maintain "I sure had a heck of a good time." His New York visit was exciting. The transport pilot was received as a hero, drenched with accolades that the most accomplished wartime bombers could not even imagine. His nights were filled with television appearances or trips out on the town. But back at the scene of his happiest moments with Alta since he had left for war, he could not help but remember her every time he turned around. "Busy as _____ with Big + Little Vittles," he wrote to her before returning to Germany. "Get mail in bags instead of letters. Still watch for yours though. . . . Lonely? Me too." Yet it was more than just the memories of Alta that left him empty and disoriented. Whether he was being squired about around New York or walking the streets alone in his free moments, he felt out of place.

The days were bright and clear, the kind of crisp September in New York that fairly crackles with possibility. But everywhere he looked he was reminded of the contrast with Berlin. Trim men in smart suits wore their hats doffed ever so slightly to the side. With hemlines lower, long skirts fluttered around the shapely ankles of women who clucked their heels happily down Park Avenue. He went to the Polo Grounds to see the Giants beat the Dodgers and watched as boys hawked armfuls of peanuts and hot dogs. At the City Center, he gazed at ladies in their finery at a performance of *Show Boat*. As he wandered through Manhattan, sleek skyscrapers rose above him; rushing taxicabs bleated in frustration; chubby, irritated businessmen pushed past him on their way to meetings they no doubt considered as matters of "life or death."

"Fresh from the bombed and desolate landscape of a ravished city to the sidewalks of New York was like coming out of the darkness into the light," Halvorsen would recall. It was no figure of speech. Where Berlin after sunset was largely enveloped in sable, the office buildings of midtown Manhattan left their lights burning all night—illuminated beacons delivering brash declarations of prosperity. Double-decker buses crowded the city streets. El trains rumbled above Third Avenue. Every night, from Grand Central Station, right by the Hotel Biltmore, the 20th Century Limited left at 6:01 to Utica, Erie, Waterloo, and points beyond. On the day after Halvorsen's press conference, the *New York Times* opined that it was only at the site of the United Nations building now being constructed, "a wasteland of dirt and rubble level with the sidewalks" that "a bombed-out Berliner suddenly transported" to New York might find his surroundings familiar. The Manhattanites exulted in their plenty. They measured their bounty against the yardstick of Halvorsen's new world. In the postwar years, they would frequently brag, "Why, the garbage thrown away in this city every day—*every day*—would feed the whole of Europe for a week."

Rather than a homecoming, his trip to America felt like a journey to a foreign land. After years of wandering from base to base, of flying countless transport flights across distant frontiers, Halvorsen had finally found his place in far-off Berlin.

ON FRIDAY AFTERNOON, while working on the script for the radio play, Halvorsen received an invitation to dine that evening with John Swersey of the Huyler Candy Company. He arrived at the Manhattan Hotel and a maitre d' escorted him to a linen-draped table with fine china and a large bouquet in the center. Swersey, a plump man with a bulbous nose, rose to meet him. He was warm and friendly. "Have a seat," he beckoned.

As they discussed their dinner order, Swersey peppered Halvorsen with detailed questions about the candy drops. Halvorsen answered as best he could, but was distracted by the sight of four forks by his plate. He could not fathom what they were all for. Swersey interrupted Halvorsen's confusion with a blunt question: "How much candy could you use, Lieutenant?"

Halvorsen did a quick calculation of how much candy everyone in the squadron could possibly drop on a daily basis for a period of months. He answered "three tons" in an offhand way and went back to worrying about the forks.

AFTER DINNER, SWERSEY took Halvorsen to the Upper East Side home of Harry Orland King, the owner of Huyler's. On the way, as Halvorsen looked out the car window at the luminous windows of well-stocked stores, Swersey confided that he was Jewish and somewhat conflicted about helping the Germans. But the children of Berlin, he said, were that country's future, and if a little bit of candy could improve their lives, he would do whatever he could to make that possible. When they arrived at King's house, the tycoon promised to help round up donations from Hershey's, Mars, Lyons, and other confectioners. King's wife, former Arizona congresswoman Isabella Greenway, immediately promised Halvorsen a thousand tiny parachutes a week.

Halvorsen would board the Skymaster headed back to Berlin with two large duffel bags filled with 368 pounds of candy and 50 pounds of handkerchiefs. *We the People* arranged to ship him another 40,000 candy bars and 25,000 pieces of gum. "We're getting enough candy to satisfy the sweet tooth of every kid in Berlin," he crowed to the press. He had no idea.

This . . . is Berlin," said William Shirer over the Mutual Radio Network, and any American who had lived through World War II could not help but be terrified by his familiar reedy voice once again intoning those words. He continued, "I came to Berlin this time for the same reason that often seemed to make it important to be in this particular place. A new crisis had threatened the peace and made men talk of war again. I've covered a number of world crises from here, it seems, and one war that was the worst of all. When I left here the last time at the end of 1945, it seemed incredible that war could ever come from anything that happened in these ruins. Yet three or four days ago in New York and Washington, many seemed fearful that the situation in Berlin had become so ugly that anything could happen. And by anything"—and here his voice dropped for emphasis—"they meant war. So I departed New York Wednesday evening to find out. And thanks to our Air Force, I landed here in Berlin a day and a half later."

The situation in Berlin looked increasingly bleak. Over a single week, the full horror of what the allies had feared might come in Berlin was previewed to them. The four-power talks—the seeming last hope for a negotiated settlement—had broken down, and soon after there had followed a riotous attempted coup at City Hall, a massive rally at the Reichstag, and a bloody altercation between Berliners and the Soviet sector police. It was a taste of where Berlin was headed, especially as the food and coal situation grew more critical. What's more, winter was approaching. Within days of the warm summer evening at the Reichstag, a chill had set in all over the country. Germans wore long trench coats reaching almost all the way to the ground. Military Police wore gloves as they stood guard. When the blockade had begun, Forrestal and the others in Washington predicted that if an agreement were not reached, the moment of reckoning would come in October. And September was slipping away.

What Shirer found most remarkable about Berlin was not its sights—they were almost unchanged since he had left after that postwar visit in 1945—but its sounds. He had heard descriptions of the overhead clamor of the landing airplanes, but they had not captured what it was like to live with their unremitting hum. "I've gone through many a bombing, both here and in London, but this—this constant roar of planes overhead, every minute of your existence, night and day—is quite a new experience."

The man responsible for that experience, Bill Tunner, was still struggling daily to maintain the steady beat of planes landing in Berlin every three minutes. The friction between him and LeMay had not abated, but he had been given a relatively free hand. He still strained to make do with limited resources and poor working conditions—the German janitor who washed the Airlift headquarters used so much water on the floor that Tunner had to wait each morning until the phone wires dried to make calls, and no one in the office spoke enough German to be able to tell him to stop. But the day after the protests in Berlin, Tunner, in his office reviewing the latest figures, determined that September 10 was the first day that the Airlift had delivered more than 10 million pounds of supplies.

That same day, the Soviets carried out Sokolovsky's threat and sent their fighter planes and bombers flying through the allied air corridors, usually against the flow of traffic, aiming directly at the slow Skymasters before pulling away at the last moment. Under the guise of military exercises, the Russians fired antiaircraft explosives into the air corridors. Soviet planes flew patterns over Berlin leaving vapor trails in their wake. Taken together, it was the largest show of Russian military strength since the war's end.

As soon as the wrangling with Sokolovsky had ended, Clay realized that the Soviets were clearly committed to seeing the blockade through to its end. The Airlift was now Berlin's only hope. Yet if it were to not simply stave off starvation, but also provide fuel for energy and heat during the winter, it would need more planes than the 125 Skymasters Truman had granted back in July.

Clay asked LeMay how many C-54s the Airlift needed to fully supply

Berlin at the reduced ration levels. The bomber did not know the answer, but would not admit to Clay that, with Tunner in charge of the Airlift, he had little awareness of the operation's day-to-day functions. Nor would he allow Tunner to provide the answer to Clay directly. So LeMay said he would let Clay know the answer shortly and then called for Tunner.

Tunner, just as bullheaded, instead sent his young aide, Ross Milton, to see what LeMay wanted. When Milton arrived, LeMay asked him how many C-54s would be required to achieve full capacity. Milton said he would hurry back to Airlift headquarters and find out the answer. No, said LeMay, sit down right here and figure it out. Milton was given some paper and a slide rule and sat down by a coffee table in a corner of LeMay's office. While LeMay was boisterously greeting a delegation of foreign visitors, Milton scratched out some rough calculations, taking into account "some weather factors and various other guesses," and came up with the number 222. LeMay took the paper, got back on the phone to Clay, and rounding up, said they would need exactly 225 Skymasters to make the Airlift work.

On September 10, three days after the four-power talks had collapsed, Clay cabled Bradley to say they needed another 107 Skymasters—60 by October 1 and another 47 in place by December 1. Bradley told him all he could get was 50 more.

UNDER CLAY'S WATCH, construction on the airport at Tegel was getting under way. A call for workers went out over RIAS and 17,000 Berliners showed up. Most were ordinary women who labored alongside barefoot peasants, onetime professors, and maimed veterans of Hitler's army, in three shifts, around the clock. The wages being offered were low, though the daily warm meal of a ladle of potato soup and a hunk of black bread was appreciated. But many of the workers, when asked, said that what really brought them out to the deserted field of rolling sand hills was the chance to contribute to the survival of their city. Often, workers would stay after their shift—when they were no longer on the clock—to finish up a job they had begun that day.

An airfield able to handle the steady beating of heavy cargo planes landing all hours of day and night would need runways built with foundations of a minimum depth of two feet. Such an amount of concrete was not available in Berlin, nor was it feasible to fly it into the city without a huge impact on the Airlift's normal freight. The Americans were momentarily stymied until Ken Swallwell, an engineer whom Tunner had worked with on the Hump and brought with him to Germany, had a realization. Looking around Berlin, he said, "Our own Air Force had the foresight to provide all the material we need over three years ago. There's enough brick rubble from bombed-out buildings in Berlin to build a dozen runways." It was calculated that to build the Tegel runway would require 10 million bricks. These had to be picked up by hand, one at a time, from rubble piles or wrung out of decrepit walls. The only vehicles available to move the bricks were broken-down trucks the Russians had left behind three years earlier. The Americans made one of them run and used it to pull three others through the city, collecting the blocks from various sites and bringing them to Tegel. There, they were carried into place to be pulverized.

—

Weary from his journey back to Germany, Halvorsen arrived at the barn at Rhein-Main. He found the loft filled with more than 800 pounds of candy and more than a thousand handkerchiefs donated from individuals across America who had read of his candy drops or seen him on television. It was one of the first demonstrations of the power of this new medium to touch people on a visceral level.

From Solvang, California, came 525 handkerchiefs collected by the local newspaper. The editor assured Halvorsen that "the residents of the Santa Ynez Valley, Calif. are 100 percent behind" his efforts. In his hometown of Garland, Utah, American Legion Post #43 had placed a sign reading "Put Candy & Gum Here for the Lollipop Bomber" above a constantly filling box.

The publicity begat more publicity. The *Boston Sunday Globe* declared him "a veritable 'king' to the kids of Berlin" and said his candy drops were "a fairy tale that has come true to youthful Berliners." The *Washington Post* wrote that because of Halvorsen, Berlin was the place "where candy drops as if from heaven." The elementary school newspaper the *Weekly Reader* featured an article about the "candy pilot" and donations arrived from classrooms across America—from Mrs. M. M. Anderson's Sunday school class in Tenafly, New Jersey, to the seventh-grade class of Marietta Borough School in Marietta, Pennsylvania. Radio stations from Los Angeles to Boston offered to play listeners' favorite songs if they sent in a donation for Little Vittles.

The Saturday night after he returned to Germany, dozens of the men involved with the Airlift—pilots, ground crew workers, radiomen—gathered at Halvorsen's loft to tie parachutes. There were all sorts of handkerchiefs. Some were silk, some were lace (Halvorsen came to call those "Screaming Mimis," because they dropped so quickly.) Some had Mickey Mouse on them. One was in honor of the fiftieth anniversary of the creation of greater New York City. Others had a special message written to Halvorsen—often from young women. Those were black lace and perfumed. Halvorsen dropped them all. Only the brightly colored ones were put aside. These would come in handy when the snow came.

That Monday was the biggest day of candy drops thus far. Halvorsen, joined by the other pilots in his squadron, dropped 425 parachutes with four chocolate bars each all over the western sectors of Berlin.

At noon, on Monday, September 13, just as Marshall had promised, Forrestal had the meeting with Truman he had been demanding: a full discussion of plans to use atomic bombs on Russia and Eastern Europe if war came over Berlin. Forrestal was not the only person worried about this subject. While nuclear war had steadily receded as a subject of national conversation in the years since Hiroshima, the showdown with Russia had returned it to the center of public debate.

The percentage of leading political columns that discussed the atom bomb in the fall of 1948 was double what it had been a year earlier. But among those in the highest ranks of government, no one was as absorbed by the question of nuclear war as Jim Forrestal.

That day, Forrestal, along with Lovett, Royall, Air Force secretary Stuart Symington, and Generals Bradley and Vandenberg, briefed Truman on the detailed plans of where the bombs would be dropped. Truman was irritated as Forrestal repeatedly pressed him for an answer as to whether he was ready to give the order to drop the bomb. He finally relented. Truman told the men he prayed that he would "never have to make such a decision," but that "if it became necessary no one need have a misgiving but that" he would do so.

Forrestal seemed satisfied, and so, with his campaign tour of the country scheduled to begin at the end of the week, Truman shuffled them out of his office to return to matters of politics. As Forrestal was walking out of the Oval Office, Louis Johnson was walking in. The next day, Truman would announce that Johnson, a West Virginia lawyer who had served as Roosevelt's assistant secretary of war, had agreed to serve as the finance chair of his almost insolvent presidential campaign.

Throughout the day, Truman alternated meetings about Berlin with those about his campaign—within an hour he met with both George Marshall and the new head of Tammany Hall. But it was the conversations about the blockade, especially the meeting with Forrestal about the bomb, that weighed most heavily on him.

The situation in Berlin was bad, his budget director and confidant, Jim Webb, told the Atomic Energy Commission's Lilienthal that afternoon after seeing Truman. Anything could happen. *"Anything,"* he emphasized. "They might walk in tomorrow and shoot General Clay." Truman "has always been optimistic about peace," Webb said, "but he is blue now, mighty blue. It is very hard on him, coming right now particularly."

The country in which he was about to begin campaigning was consumed with concern over Berlin as well. That day, stocks dropped again in a sell-off fueled, wrote the *Los Angeles Times'* financial editor, by "reports that the Russians are prepared to make a final drive to grab control of" Berlin. The public was "acutely apprehensive over the prospect of a 'hot' war," he pointed out, though he believed this was a product of "rabble-rousing radio commentators" whose "persistent outpourings that we are about to be enveloped in World War III have served in no small measure to keep public psychology at hysterical levels."

Yet it was no radio commentator who frightened Harry Truman that night. It was the facts of the circumstances he saw before him. He would publicly talk down the possibility of war at every opportunity, but in the dark of the White House, he thought it might well be imminent. "A terrific day," he wrote sarcastically in his diary before going to bed. "Forrestal, Bradley, Vandenberg, Symington brief me on bases, bombs, Moscow, Leningrad, etc." He could not bring himself to make more than an oblique reference to the atomic targeting information they had shared with him. "I have a terrible feeling afterwards that we are very close to war. I hope not. Discuss situation with Marshall at lunch. Berlin is a mess."

———

That Friday, Truman left Union Station on his whistle-stop tour of the nation. With only two short breaks, he would campaign almost continuously for the six weeks before the November 2 election. Through it all, in ways large and small, it was a campaign shadowed by the crisis in Berlin.

On his first full day of campaigning, Truman gave thirteen speeches as he raced across Illinois, Iowa, and Missouri. All but one were delivered from the caboose of his train. He began speaking at 5:45 in the morning and went until 8:10 at night—literally from before dawn until after dark. But his big speech of the day, the first speech of his campaign tour, was at the National Plowing Match in Dexter, Iowa. Along with the 80,000 people in the crowd, a nationwide audience listened in on the radio.

He was there to discuss his farm policy, yet even this subject was introduced through the prism of Berlin. "The abundant harvests of this country are helping to save the world from Communism," he announced, and then, as if someone else had introduced the topic, said, "and while I'm on that subject—I know that the war talk which is so prevalent today is causing all of you deep concern. It is plain enough that we are facing a very disturbing international situation. I should like every American to realize that this country is making every possible effort to preserve the peace. In this critical situation, my motto has been: 'Keep your temper and stand firm.'" It was as good a summation of Truman's policy in Berlin as any. He had, instinctively, sometimes clumsily, avoided both the disastrous retreat pushed on him by his military and diplomatic advisers as well as the belligerent convoy option presented by Clay. He had not shied away from using military force to advance American interests, but had not blundered into a tragic war. The balance he had struck would yield political benefits as well. Truman had showed himself to be neither the "soft on Communism" caricature of the Republicans nor the warmonger of Wallace's charges. He would need the votes of both Americans worried about the Soviet march and those fearful of war in order to win in November. As Clifford had argued in his memo in August, the goal of his campaign was to convince Americans of the virtue of this middle ground.

DEWEY AND HIS staff had spent August and most of September crafting the campaign speeches he was to give on his own swing through the nation. The collapse of the Berlin negotiations, however, caused them to reassess their strategy. A meeting of his top advisers was called in Albany on September 15 to discuss how they would respond to the deepening crisis. Dewey's innate decency, and certainty that the Berlin problem would be his to deal with by January, limited how harshly he could attack the Democratic blunders that he believed had led to the blockade. But he was constrained by politics as well. With voters on edge because of the fear of war, he could not be seen as attempting to take partisan advantage of the situation. Moreover, with the Airlift having excited the admiration of Americans, Truman was no longer perceived as the weak figure he had appeared to be in the spring. Though voters still seemed certain to deny the president another term, they had plainly come to approve of America's response in Berlin.

Dewey also kicked off his fall electioneering in the swing state of Iowa, three days after Truman's speech in Dexter. "We live in a world where tyranny is on the march," Dewey proclaimed before referring one by one to Jan Masaryk and the other democratic leaders of Eastern Europe who were now dead, exiled, or imprisoned. But in this speech, almost entirely about the face-off with the Soviet Union, he did not, even indirectly, mention Harry Truman.

He would rely on surrogates to deliver harsher attacks that eschewed any subtlety. The following day, the former Democratic governor of Pennsylvania and Roosevelt's ambassador to Austria publicly endorsed Dewey with a statement decrying "President Truman's vacillation between appeasement and halfway measures." The chairman of the Republican National Committee accused Truman of accepting the support of the Communist Party and forging a "working arrangement" with Communists who wanted to overthrow the government. The Republican Party broadly distributed a leaflet stating that Truman had direct "knowledge of spying in the Government" and that in his and Roosevelt's administrations, 1,700 federal employees "were Communists or members of Communist-controlled groups." Earl Warren, Harold Stassen, and others all delivered full-frontal blows against Truman's policy toward Russia. Here, however, Truman did Dewey one better. In mid-September, at the height of the campaign, instead of barnstorming in the small towns of Pennsylvania or Minnesota, his running mate, Alben Barkley, went on a well-publicized trip to Berlin to discuss the Airlift with Lucius Clay.

WALLACE TOO WAS campaigning strenuously, lashing Truman for bringing America to the brink of war. "Peace is the basic issue of the presidential campaign," he told a crowd of 48,000 people who had paid between 50 cents and $3.60 for the privilege of seeing him speak at

Yankee Stadium. When, the previous night, a thunderstorm soaked the crowd and rained out the rally, the Wallaceites—men in suits, women with bobbed haircuts and horn-rimmed glasses—sang together as they walked back to the subway station, and then happily returned the next day.

At the start of his rallies, the houselights dimmed, drums rolled, and then a single spotlight would find Wallace at the door, following him as he made his way through the crowd with the beat crescendoing as he reached the podium. "All of you who are within the sound of my voice tonight have been called to serve," he would intone, and people would scream until their voices rasped away.

A diet faddist and devotee of astrology and quack mysticism, Wallace fit right in among the Hollywood celebrities and New York literati who flocked to his campaign. He was not of them—Lillian Hellman, the bon vivant head of "Women for Wallace," was horrified when she visited him at his home and he served her a lunch of shredded wheat, eggs, and a glass of water—but he could campaign in Spanish among Mexican day laborers in the morning and dazzle a ritzy Beverly Hills fund-raiser at night, and this the celebrities ate up.

Over the summer, Wallace nobly went to the South to inveigh against racial injustice, only to be bitterly scorned. As September passed, the animus directed at him seemed to be increasing wherever he went. His call for abandoning Berlin and suing for peace with the Soviets was met with ever greater derision. In Boston, hundreds booed him and chanted "Give our regards to Stalin." In Charlotte, Pete Seeger began to play the "Star-Spangled Banner" on his banjo at a rally, but so many eggs were thrown from the crowd of 3,000 gathered in front of the Mecklenburg County Courthouse that even a heckler shouting "Go back to Russia" was pelted from behind. One of the signs said, "Peddle Your Junk in Moscow, Henry." All across the country, he was bombarded with a gastronomically diverse fusillade from angry mobs. The Associated Press listed the ammunition as "tomatoes (ancient), eggs (very ancient) and ice cream cones (fresh)." But Wallace would soldier on through his speeches, standing in a puddle of yolks, pieces of shell stuck to his jacket.

IN LOS ANGELES, home of nearly half the voters in electoral-rich California, the three campaigns crossed paths. Truman's and Dewey's trains passed within three miles of each other outside of town. California was a critical state, hotly contested by both Democrats and Republicans, and a home to many of Wallace's most fervent supporters.

On September 23, Truman confronted Wallace's candidacy for the first time since his St. Patrick's Day address. To a sparse crowd at Gilmore Stadium, at the corner of Beverly Boulevard and Fairfax Avenue, Truman delivered a stemwinder of an attack on Dewey's policies, declaring Republicans to be the party of "big business first." He made subtle allusions to Dewey's lack of military service during World War I. But as he drew to his close, with Lauren Bacall, Humphrey Bogart, and Ronald Reagan sitting on stage behind him, Truman made a direct appeal to the liberals considering voting for Wallace. "Most of the people realize that the Democratic administration is doing everything that can be done to preserve the peace," he said. "There are, however, some people with true liberal convictions, whose worry over the state of the world has caused them to lean toward a third party. To these liberals I would say in all sincerity: 'Think again.'" He charged that Wallace's party was being guided by Communists, but if this did not bother the liberals, there was a "very practical reason" why they should not vote for the Progressives: They would split their votes and elect the Republicans. Wallace could not win, Truman pointed out. "Don't waste your vote." As his speechwriters knew it would, the call to the liberals to come home dominated the news coverage of Truman's Los Angeles visit.

The following day, Dewey spoke at the Hollywood Bowl to a crowd twice the size of Truman's. Preceded on stage by dancing chorus girls and a marimba band, flanked by Gary Cooper and Ginger Rogers, under the starlit quiet of the Hollywood hills, Dewey delivered his most detailed policy address thus far on the nature and strength of the Communist threat. Truman, he charged, "has been giving aid and comfort to the enemies of our system." But the tough charge was undermined as he admitted that "at this moment, planes built in the great aircraft factories of this West Coast are shuttling back and forth, day and night, in all kinds of weather to keep the torch of freedom lit in tense and explosive Berlin. While they carry the freight of peace, we are proving our determination to stand by the free peoples of Europe." The success of the Berlin Airlift was making it difficult to continue credibly accusing Truman of having abandoned freedom-loving people or running an incompetent foreign policy. "In Berlin," Dewey conceded that night, "our planes and our men are giving the world fresh proof that America has what it takes."

A week later, Wallace came to Los Angeles. He purposely delivered his speech at Gilmore Stadium, the same place where Truman had spoken. Four thousand more people showed up than had been there for Truman, each giving a campaign contribution to get in. They found it well worth the price to hear Wallace call for ending the occupation and bringing the troops home from Germany "as soon as possible."

The Golden State and its crucial votes seemed out of reach to Truman because of Wallace's appeal to the left of the Democratic Party. When they finally left California, Clifford told Lilienthal, he felt he was ready "to crawl in a hole and die."

ON SEPTEMBER 25, the Soviets turned down the renewed allied plea to lift the blockade. There was now no choice but to go to the United Nations—a last step before deciding to go to war. Even while barnstorming the country, both Truman and Dewey closely monitored the situation. Aboard the *Ferdinand Magellan,* the train car built for Roosevelt during the war, Truman had a phone in the wood-paneled office that he could have hooked up to an outlet by the side of the train tracks when he pulled into the station. Dewey had a similar system on his train and, through the assistance of the State Department, was in touch with Dulles, who was part of the United Nations delegation meeting in Paris, as often as once a day.

In Texas, Truman said he had "thoroughly approved" the decision to take Berlin to the Security Council. Campaigning in the Pacific Northwest, Dewey proclaimed, "This is too sober a moment in our history for threats or recrimination. It is a time instead for a real and solemn reassertion of what we believe, what we hope for and what we will endeavor, against whatever odds and difficulties to achieve." An aide was sent out to tell confused reporters that this meant he backed Truman's decision to go to the United Nations.

Truman's campaign was constantly searching for shrewd ways to carefully keep the issue of Berlin at the forefront of voters' minds. When one of his press aides in the White House, Eben Ayers, discovered that Walter Bedell Smith was in Washington from Moscow to join in the deliberations on Berlin, he pounced. "It struck me that if the president could ask Smith to meet him at some point on the trip to report on the Moscow talks, etc., it would get smash play in the papers," Ayers wrote in his diary. He called the political operatives aboard the train with his pitch. They and Truman jumped at the idea. It was Saturday in El Paso and Truman said he wanted Smith to meet him in San Antonio on Sunday. Ayers called Bob Lovett to tell him that the president wanted to see his ambassador to Moscow the next morning. "My God," said Lovett. "I don't know where he is." Smith had gone fishing in the Catoctin Mountains for the weekend. Ayers, Lovett, and others began a round of phone calls trying to track him down. Throughout the day, from stops in small towns in Texas, political aides called in to the White House to check on their progress.

In San Antonio on Sunday, Truman again played up the virtue of his moderate course, summarizing his approach to the Soviet threat as "keep your bullets bright and your powder dry," but Smith was still nowhere to be found. Finally, that afternoon, the phone on Ayers's desk rang. Ambassador Smith is on the line, the White House operator announced. Smith said he had heard from General Bradley that Ayers was looking for him. Yes, Ayers said breathlessly, the president wanted him in Texas. Smith, surprised, agreed to fly out the next day on Truman's plane.

The following afternoon, Smith climbed on board Truman's train in Dallas under cover of secrecy. As the train headed toward Bonham, stopping for Truman to give remarks in Greenville and Bells, the two men discussed Berlin. Nearby sat Sam Rayburn, the Democratic leader in the House of Representatives, and Lyndon Johnson, whose 87-vote margin of victory in the recent Democratic primary for Senate was still tied up in the courts.

When his meeting with Truman concluded, Smith was sent into the press car. He walked in quietly, and as the reporters saw him, they gasped. They had not known Smith had returned to the United States, much less that he was on board their train rumbling through rural Texas. At a time when intercontinental travel was still rare, when more people still went to Europe by sea than by air, it was a bombshell. The reporters stood on chairs or held on to overhead luggage racks in what the correspondent of the *Christian Science Monitor* termed "one of the most unusual press conferences in history." Asked whether the United States was going to go to war, Smith replied, "That's too deep for me to answer." He said to the reporters that relations with Russia had never been at a more critical stage, and when they asked, he assured them that this was on the record and that Truman shared his views. Smith had told the men in the Kremlin, he informed the reporters, that Truman's foreign policy was backed "by 90 percent of the American people."

Ayers was pleased: "It got pretty good play in the papers."

THE TRIBUNE OF the 10 percent that did not agree with Truman's hard line against the Soviets arrived in Dallas that same day. It surprised no one that Wallace opposed the move to bring the Berlin issue to the United Nations. Both parties, he charged, were manufacturing a crisis for political reasons and for the benefit of their backers in big business. He aimed especially at Forrestal, whose hands he said were "stained with blood."

But it would have surprised Wallace, it would have simply floored him, to know that Smith and the military men in the Pentagon shared his conviction that America should retreat from Berlin. Back in Washington, behind closed doors at the State Department, Smith railed at Clay's and Truman's policies. "I regret very much that we are in Berlin at all," he said. "I know some of our people in Berlin do not agree with me"—everyone knew he was referring to his rival—"but for what it's worth I have always felt that we should never have let ourselves get into an exposed salient like Berlin under such conditions." Now his hope was that the United Nations would offer a cover "for us to get out of Berlin," abandoning the city to the Russians. He saved his sharpest scorn for the Airlift and the idea that they should treat Berliners as people whose hopes were integral to America's own interests. "Our present hysterical outburst of humanitarian feeling" about the Berliners, he scoffed, "keeps reminding me that just three and a half years ago, I would have been considered a hero if I had succeeded in exterminating those same Germans with bombs."

Amid the gale forces of history, it would have taken only the slightest, imperceptible shifts of breezes for Wallace to have been in Truman's place and Smith to have been in Clay's. It boggles the imagination to consider the course of events if Roosevelt had died a year earlier or if Marshall's order to fire Clay had not been rescinded in March of 1948. There was never a clearer refutation of the canard that it is simply the current and not the captain that guides humanity past the shoals.

T he press was filled with coverage of the decision to go to the United Nations. "The climax of the cold war is at hand," opined the *Hartford Courant*. "There's no fooling this time," wrote the *Minneapolis Star*. "The events being set in motion could lead to war." The *Cleveland Plain Dealer* believed that "the most explosive issue of the post-war era is placed in the hands of an agency ill-prepared and poorly qualified to handle it." The newsreel *News of the World* announced that "the grim struggle for Berlin may be the UN's acid test." A decision was needed quickly, its announcer continued, as "Communist-inspired riots make terrorism the order of the day in besieged Berlin." The *Boston Globe* dissented from the march toward a showdown. "Berlin's currency, and Berlin for that matter," its editors wrote, "are very poor issues on which to launch a world-shattering conflict."

With such roiling emotions, any notion that the 1948 election would avoid being shaped by the fight over Berlin was obliterated by the end of September. In Bonham, Texas, after Smith got off the campaign train, Sam Rayburn, the Democratic leader in the House of Representatives, announced, in introducing Truman to his hometown, that a vote for Dewey was a vote for war. "What would our enemies throughout the world think if we replaced our great leader now? Would they think we were going back on our policy of world peace, of world concord, of world order? I am afraid they might."

The next day, in Oklahoma City, Truman answered Dewey's charges of being soft on Communism. It was, his political advisers believed, the "Administration's most vulnerable point." Clark Clifford drafted a rebuttal, and last-minute contributions from New York businessman Abe Feinberg and Ed Kaufmann, the founder of Kay Jewelers, paid for the speech to be repeatedly broadcast nationwide. Truman's train was forty minutes late, and to get to the fairgrounds to deliver the address, his car had to race through the packed streets of Oklahoma City, whizzing by puzzled spectators who had gathered to wave to him. He arrived at the grandstands ten seconds before the live broadcast began.

Truman turned Dewey's attacks around, charging that it was the Republicans who were the tools of the Communists. It was they whose congressional investigations into domestic Communism had undermined the secret work of the FBI. It was their "rank and file" that had opposed the Marshall Plan in Congress, the plan that had halted "Communist encroachment throughout the world." The Communists were backing Wallace because they wanted Dewey to win so that he could enact "reactionary policies" that would "lead to the confusion and strife on which Communism thrives." The logic was somewhat convoluted, but it was a theme Truman would return to throughout the rest of the campaign.

Dewey could, and did, attack Truman's competence and decry the decisions that had led to the crisis, but other than finger-pointing, he had little to offer. He did not have an alternative to Truman's Airlift and pursuit of diplomacy, so his charges rang hollow. Preparing to assume power, he often spoke, by his campaign's own admission, to Stalin more than the American electorate. The night of Truman's Oklahoma City attack, Dewey gave a speech in Missoula, Montana. "Tonight, a dark cloud hangs over the future of every one of us. A ruthless aggression that has mankind's enslavement as its goal is abroad in the world. In Berlin, where by solemn agreement we have every right to be, we are confronting that aggressive power face to face. In Paris, at the meeting of the United Nations, our representatives and those of other free nations, are laboring mightily against great odds to bring about a peaceful settlement even at this late hour." He painted, wrote the *New York Times*, "a bleak picture of avoiding a clash with Russia."

September 30, 1948

Mister Lieutenant Gale S. Halvorsen,

My mother told me of you, dear uncle, that you had thrown handkerchiefs with sweets for the children in Berlin. Please tell me where that is, because I want to go there too with my sister Jutta. Oh please, dear uncle, write me the place that I can catch me some sweets.

With warm regards
We are Yours,
Christa and Jutta Kühnel

On the last day of September, the one hundredth day of the blockade, a Russian lieutenant on a motorbike pulled into the American sector of Berlin to visit his German girlfriend. An older woman, seeing an armed Russian, believed that the invasion had begun. She called the Stumm police, who alerted American troops. Two jeeps filled with GIs arrived on the scene and the Russian, drunk, began to fire. He missed them, but shot a German bystander in the leg before he was apprehended.

The situation in Berlin was combustible. Around the city, fistfights between Berliners and Markgraf police were breaking out as the Soviet-sector officers tried to enforce a ban on Berliners reading Western news-papers while using public transportation in the Russian-controlled areas. Inspectors moving through the subway were confiscating the smallest amount of food, from Berliners of all ages, to make sure not an extra morsel made it into the western sectors.

As September ended, the Airlift's figures were rising, but slowly. The planes were still bringing in only 40 percent of the meager amount that had been delivered before the blockade. Berlin was receiving only a quarter of the trickle of medical supplies that had arrived before June. Stocks were being depleted instead of being built up for the winter. Royal Air Force experts predicted that once the cold weather arrived and the fog blanketed northern Europe, the cargo numbers would drop by a further 30 to 40 percent. In a bad omen, it had been the coldest September in thirty years.

"Can the American fliers feed you through storm and sleet?" the Com-munist press asked Berliners. The answer was clear. The American consul general in Germany reported that among the Berliners "who think and talk in clear and unsentimental fashion" there was the "definite opinion that Berlin cannot be adequately supplied by the air bridge during the coming winter. The winter requirement will be too great, for not only must the millions of Berlin's inhabitants be fed; they must be kept warm and occupied." It was the consensus of unsentimental people—those too sophisticated to be taken in by the maudlin and fanciful—everywhere.

Clay, once seen as the most tough-minded of men, was no longer among them. But he did need more C-54s and needed them immedi-ately. Once the days of good weather passed, the opportunity to build up the stockpiles would not return.

The fifty more Skymasters Bradley had promised Clay had not come and would not be enough. On September 23, he again pressed Bradley for more planes: "Our average Airlift capacity to date has not sufficed to stockpile for the winter months and in fact we are not quite holding our own." A week went by with no reply. Finally, on September 30, Bradley informed Clay that his "request for additional aircraft has been referred to the Joint Chiefs of Staff." Clay had been down this road before.

12

OCTOBER

When, on October 3, Hal Halvorsen's plane landed in Berlin in the midst of a driving storm, seven hundred children were waiting for him on the tarmac. It was "Lieutenant Gail Halvorsen Day" at Tempelhof Airport.

The children were held back by a rope as Halvorsen parked the *Island of Christmas,* the plane he was flying that day. The rope was dropped and they ran and skipped toward the Skymaster, yelling "*Rosinenbomber*" and "*Onkel Sam.*" Halvorsen poked his head out the window, flashed his enormous grin, and waved. The children screamed with excitement. With a great heave, he threw a big handful of handkerchiefs into the air and they floated down to the children. A boy who managed to grab one of the parachutes tore open the twine-wrapped treats and stuffed a chocolate bar whole into his mouth, sticking all five fingers into his maw to make sure his prize was eaten before anyone tried to grab it away from him.

It was an event staged for the newsreel cameras, but the emotion behind it was real. Halvorsen emerged from the plane and the children mobbed him, pulling at his sleeve, hoping to touch him. Children brought him great bunches of flowers and drawings they had made; a boy gave Halvorsen his toy fire truck. Five-year-old Lutz Otrember was lifted up by his mother so he could see. "A parachute down by my house came with chocolate," he yelled to Halvorsen. "Thank you!" The boy's eyes filled with tears.

"Halvorsen smiled in embarrassment and mumbled, 'This is kind of too much,'" the *Los Angeles Times* reported in its front-page story on the event the next day.

BY EARLY OCTOBER, Operation Little Vittles was more than a cute moniker for Halvorsen's daily candy drops, it was truly a complicated undertaking. Though Halvorsen still directed the efforts, twenty-five to thirty other pilots were now also delivering the small parachutes. At Rhein-Main base operations, Halvorsen stuck a large map of Berlin onto a wall with numbers marking areas along the flight path in and out of the city where drops should be made. Below, he placed cardboard boxes filled with premade parachutes. When the parachutes were not prepared for the pilots, the results could be uneven. One pilot, wanting to help but too tired to bother tying up the handkerchiefs, simply tossed a whole box of O'Henry bars out of the plane as he flew over a group of kids.

Overwhelmed by donations, Halvorsen and the others could not keep up. The town of Chicopee, Massachusetts, home to Westover Air Force Base, the launching point of planes headed to the Airlift, volunteered to take charge of gathering the candy and tying the parachutes. On October 14, each of the twenty-two schools in the town, from grade schools to colleges, sent representatives to an organizing meeting. Mayor Edward Bourbeau assigned the abandoned Grape Street Fire Station for their use. Chicopee's children formed a committee, elected officers, and began volunteering when not in school, every weekday from 2 to 5 P.M. and Saturdays from 9 to noon.

Contributions began to come in to Chicopee from across America— candy from Walla Walla, Washington, and Corpus Christi, Texas. The Connecticut chapter of the Veterans of Foreign Wars provided 3,000 handkerchiefs. Walgreens drug stores provided 200 pounds of candy and gum. The Budd Company of Philadelphia donated 11,000 yards of linen. Chicopee schoolchildren cut it up into 18-inch squares, attached the twine and candy, and on each parachute stamped, in German, "This candy is sent to you from the school children of America." In the course of their efforts, the Chicopee students would be responsible for collecting, sorting, and preparing 36,000 pounds of candy attached to 100,000 handkerchief parachutes for Halvorsen and the other Candy Bombers.

A month after his television appearances in New York, the press coverage of Halvorsen's activities had not abated, it had increased. Over a two-day period in the middle of October, a photograph of children watching C-54s, waiting for a candy drop, was carried in the *New York Times,* the *Washington Post,* the *Boston Herald,* the *Memphis Commercial Appeal,* the *Baltimore Sun,* the *Detroit News,* the *Dallas Morning News,* and dozens of other papers. *Newsweek,* stating the obvious, called Halvorsen the most popular Airlift pilot. That same week in mid-October, *Time* reported that several thousand kids were now gathering in the graveyard by the apartment building waiting for the drops for hours on end.

Almost every day, Halvorsen would find a heaving bag of mail had been left for him on his cot by the mail clerk. Contributions came from Australia and Panama, requests for candy from war-ravaged Denmark. Two secretaries—one German, one American—were assigned to him by the Rhein-Main base commander, and they sent out one of four form responses to most letters. While much of the candy now went through Chicopee, Halvorsen was still being deluged with donations. In October, students in Buellton, California, held a school dance to collect handkerchiefs for him. The hall was decorated with a frieze showing ruined Berlin and planes dropping tiny parachutes. Handkerchiefs tied to candy were hung from the lights and from a model airplane suspended from the ceiling. The Life Savers Corporation donated 4,000 rolls to take part in "the very unique brand of thoughtfulness you are showering on the Berlin children." They shipped a thousand rolls a week "in order that our share of the cargo be distributed at peak freshness" and promised to send more. "We join all others the world over who have heard of your enterprise in hoping for its continuance," wrote a company executive.

But the letters that made the biggest impression on Halvorsen came from Berlin. From nine-year-old Peter Zimmerman, Halvorsen received a crudely made parachute, a map, and instructions so that he could drop candy at the Zimmerman home: "Fly along the big canal . . . at the second bridge, turn right. . . . I live in the bombed out house on the corner. I'll be waiting in the backyard at 2 P.M." On his next flight, Halvorsen searched for the house in vain. Soon after, he received another note from young Peter: "No chocolate yet! . . . You're a pilot! . . . I gave you a map! . . . How did you guys win the war anyway?" Halvorsen put a chocolate bar in the mail.

Ten-year-old Helma Lurch wrote that she and her little brother were unable to compete in the scramble for chocolate with some of the older, faster children, "so please drop some chocolate on our street." She closed: "Take care of yourself, and remember us children and we will remember you our whole life."

When Truman returned to Union Station in Washington from his two-week trip across the country on October 2, he had the beginnings of a plan: a dramatic October gambit to avert war and win the election. Two of his speechwriters, apprehensive over both the international situation and the sinking prospects for the campaign, had come up with an idea that would address both difficulties. Truman, they proposed, should send a personal emissary to meet with Stalin face-to-face and offer a message of peace. To undertake this sensitive mission, they suggested a name sure to appeal to the president: the poker buddy he had installed as chief justice of the Supreme Court, Fred Vinson. Though Clark Clifford and other political advisers thought it was a terrible idea, Truman immediately grabbed on to it.

The next day, "Lieutenant Gail Halvorsen Day" in Berlin, Truman summoned Vinson to the White House. Vinson was appropriately reluctant. He knew nothing more about the Berlin crisis than what he had read in the newspapers; he had no experience in foreign policy and no relationship with Stalin. He told Truman that Supreme Court justices should be wary of undertaking tasks at the behest of the executive branch, particularly a highly political undertaking a month before a presidential election. Truman insisted to his friend that it was his patriotic duty to bring to Stalin the president's personal hopes for peace. After much cajoling, Vinson agreed.

Truman told his press secretary, Charlie Ross, to secure a half hour of nationwide airtime for a special announcement from the White House on the night of Tuesday, October 5. Ross predicted, correctly, that the networks would be hesitant to provide such an audience so close to the election. He would have to tell them what it was about. Truman allowed him to do so, but insisted that "every possible precaution" be taken to prevent the news from leaking out. Ross swore the broadcasters to secrecy. Truman's speechwriters prepared an address to the nation that ended with a triumphant pledge to solve the Berlin crisis: "We shall spare no effort to achieve the peace on which the entire destiny of the human race may depend." But despite all the activity, the rest of Sunday, October 3, passed with Truman neglecting to inform any of his foreign policy advisers about his plan.

Unlike Franklin Roosevelt, who had guided America's foreign policy with the flighty improvisations of a jazz soloist, Truman had, throughout his administration, insisted on a relatively orderly national security apparatus. He had delegated broad latitude to his cabinet secretaries and aides and carefully considered every move in Berlin before making a commitment. He had insisted that America work in concert with its allies, even that it walk in lockstep with them. Marshall was in Paris, at the meeting of the United Nations, and, on October 4, formally put the issue of Berlin on the agenda of the Security Council. But October 4 passed as well without Truman informing Marshall in Paris or Forrestal at the Pentagon or Smith in Moscow of his blockbuster plan. He made no attempt to alert the governments of Britain or France that he was about to strike out on his own and junk their previous agreements. Bob

Lovett, in charge of the State Department in Marshall's absence, came to the White House to meet with Truman that day. It was just the two of them. Still, Truman failed to mention that he was planning on upsetting weeks of careful negotiations over Berlin with a far-fetched scheme to achieve peace.

On Tuesday, October 5, Lovett was sitting at his desk at the State Department when an aide walked in with a draft of Truman's message to Stalin that had been received in the code room. Lovett's hand trembled as he read the document. He picked up the phone and called Truman, asking to see him at once. Truman invited him to come right over, and though he did not let on, he must have known what it was about. Lovett ran downstairs and got in his black official car. For the first time, he asked his driver to turn on the car's siren and flashing red lights and speed to the White House. He went straight to see Truman and told him he could not send Vinson to Moscow. Truman appeared surprised. He asked why. Lovett told him it would undermine American foreign policy, split the allies, and destroy the credibility of his administration. If this was not enough to convince him, Lovett added a blunt warning: If Truman went forward, there was no doubt Marshall would resign.

Truman and Lovett reached Marshall in Paris by teleconference. Truman broached the idea and Marshall said it would be a disaster. Truman quickly backed down. To make sure, Marshall began to compose a message to Truman that charged that sending Vinson to Moscow in the midst of the United Nations deliberations would be a bungle of historic proportions. Yet his exquisite sense of etiquette returned and, regaining his composure, he threw the draft away. He ended up apologizing for not doing more to keep the president informed on the state of the Paris negotiations while Truman had been on the campaign trail. He asked permission to return to Washington that weekend to fully brief Truman on the status of the diplomatic discussions regarding Berlin. Truman quickly agreed.

THAT SAME MORNING, Truman met with Forrestal for the first time in the weeks since he had departed on his cross-country tour. The mood between them was frosty. Rumors were racing through Washington that the defense secretary was making overtures to Dewey. In fact, he was. Desperate to remain in office, Forrestal had traveled in secret to visit the Republican nominee two or three times that summer and fall. Forrestal had complained to Dewey about Truman being unwilling to spend enough on national defense. And while he did not come out and say he wanted to stay in his post, and Dewey did not say he was considering it, both men knew the nature of the dance they were choreographing.

Forrestal, however, never the silkiest of politicians, had not done a particularly good job of keeping his disloyalty quiet. Word that he was trying to win Dewey over had made it into numerous newspaper stories during September and October. Forrestal himself had told Clifford, Truman's closest political adviser, that he was certain Dewey would win. Waiting in the anteroom of Treasury secretary John Snyder for a meeting to begin, Forrestal saw Louis Johnson emerging from the office with a broad smile. Johnson said he had just collected a $10,000 check for the president's campaign from Snyder and would be coming to see Forrestal soon. "Don't come to see me," Forrestal replied sharply. "I'm not going to give a dime to the campaign." Later that month, he finally did have a Marine sergeant deliver an envelope containing a personal donation to Truman-Barkley headquarters. Inside the envelope was $100 in cash.

Perhaps it was guilt over his betrayal or perhaps there had been a steady change in the man, but, whatever the reason, Forrestal seemed a diminished figure that Tuesday afternoon in October. He was shaky in manner and haggard in appearance. "His mood struck me as a strange combination of suppressed emotion, courage, and a sense of defeat," recalled Clifford. To a president so full of cocksure confidence, Forrestal made a startling admission. He told Truman he had been wrong to oppose the creation of a Department of Defense and a secretary position with real statutory powers. The strain of the Berlin deliberations and the swirling budget battles in response had convinced him that the job he held required a staff and greater authority. Truman accepted his admission equably and without reproach.

Forrestal tried again to convince Truman to accept a higher ceiling on the defense budget. At $18.5 billion, he argued, the United States would be able to hold part of Mediterranean Europe from the onslaught of the Red Army as a staging ground from which to wage a conventional war to retake the continent. Truman would not budge.

Truman and Clifford were not the only ones who were becoming exasperated with the secretary of defense. Forrestal was becoming compulsive, retreading the same ground in conversation over and over again. That day, Stuart Symington, the Air Force secretary, reported to Forrestal, as he had promised he would do the previous night, that he had asked Vandenberg about the Air Force's atomic capabilities. Vandenberg told him to reassure Forrestal, once again, that "as he had already told" him, "he was absolutely certain" the atom "bomb could be dropped where, how and when it was wanted."

THE FOLLOWING MORNING, October 6, Truman returned to the campaign trail for a swing through Pennsylvania and New Jersey. During the course of that day, the White House announced that Truman was canceling planned campaign stops that weekend to meet with Marshall and review the situation in Berlin. The meeting was so important that the president was personally sending his plane, the *Independence,* to Paris to retrieve the revered secretary of state. Newspapers were filled with coverage of Marshall's upcoming visit. Then, on October 8, the eve of Marshall's arrival, the inevitable occurred and word of the Vinson ploy leaked, allegedly from one of the broadcast networks that had been told the presidential speech to the nation was now canceled. Truman was coming home on an overnight train from a late rally in Buffalo as word spread through the capital. When he arrived at Union Station, reporters shouted questions to him about the dissension in his administration and the scrubbed peace mission. The speculation was that Marshall had arrived to resign. After dropping off Bess at the White House, Truman raced to National Airport. The *Independence* was circling overhead, waiting for him to arrive so that he could be on hand when it landed.

Marshall was grim as he descended from the airplane. Truman was sunny. As Truman grabbed Marshall's hand, Secret Service agents had to hold back a crush of reporters. The two men got into the back of Truman's waiting car. Bob Lovett sat between them. As the cameras caught them before they pulled away, of the three, only Truman was smiling.

When they arrived at the White House, Truman worked to smooth over Marshall's anger. They spent a long while crafting the carefully worded statements from the president and the secretary of state describing their discussions over the Vinson mission and the reasons for Marshall's return to Washington. Truman claimed he had simply been "wondering" aloud to Marshall about whether Vinson's traveling to see Stalin might clear up any "misunderstandings" the Soviets might have. He made no mention of the fact that he had already alerted the networks of his announcement at that point. Marshall was equally disingenuous, claiming he had forgotten all about the Vinson idea until he stepped off the plane in Washington and saw it mentioned in the day's newspapers.

The next day, Marshall returned to Paris amid a growing chorus of attacks on the Vinson scheme. Truman was accused of playing politics with the nation's security and of seeking to appease Stalin in search of an appeal to the Wallace voters. The *Washington Post* reported that British diplomats maintained the Vinson plan "could have wrecked the United Nations." Columnist Walter Lippmann, who was quietly helping Dewey, maintained that the incident showed that "in plain words, Mr. Truman does not know how to be President." Clifford himself would later call it "the worst mistake of the Truman campaign," and presidential historian Robert Ferrell would note "the result was a fiasco."

It is possible, however, that this conventional view is wrong, that the Vinson affair was not a bungled stunt but the wiliest move of a canny politician. What if Truman never intended to actually go through with the plan? It was completely out of character for Truman to take such a momentous step in foreign policy without the advice of his top advisers—indeed to do so while purposely hiding it from them. Furthermore, he had spent his entire presidency insisting that the United States craft its international stance in conjunction with its European allies, and this had been especially true during the Berlin crisis. Truman must have known that the mission would eventually be canceled because of the inevitable opposition, and must have guessed that Marshall would not go through with a resignation (before departing for Paris, Marshall had informed Truman that doctors at Walter Reed had discovered his kidney had grown to twice its normal size and that he would be resigning after the election, whatever the outcome, giving him little incentive to do so in October, no matter how angry he was). Finally, Truman must have realized that once the broadcast networks learned of the nature of his announcement, the news would leak. It was the way of Washington. For all the opprobrium heaped on him by politicians and diplomats, the bombshell news—combining war, politics, and the hint of scandal—ensured that the Berlin crisis continued to dominate the public conversation. Dewey was pushed further out of the spotlight, and Wallace voters saw Truman making enormous efforts to find peace. It could not have turned out better if Truman had planned it—which means perhaps he did.

For weeks to come, rather than shying away from the controversy, Truman would bring up the Vinson peace mission to audiences large and small along the campaign trail—including in a "nonpolitical" address to the American Legion in Miami ten days later. Just when press attention for the supposed debacle began to die down, Truman would defend it again and a new round of commentaries would appear. He would never admit—never even hint—that he knew what he had done by creating and milking the rumpus over the Vinson plan, but once, a short while after Marshall returned to Paris, he had reacted to a discussion of the matter with a comment that stuck in his advisers' minds. Clifford and the speechwriters were in the Oval Office wringing their hands with dismay over the botched scheme. Truman listened to them for a while and then broke into an impish grin. "I don't think it's that bad," he said with a twinkle.

DEWEY WAS NOT similarly hesitant. Like those in the press and official Washington, he saw the Vinson farce as a disaster for American diplomacy and a final guarantee of his victory. Publicly, Dewey said he would not deign to comment on this national embarrassment. "I'd rather lose the election than add to the damage this country had already suffered from this unhappy incident." But he continued to make little pinprick references, slipping lines into speeches saying the country needed an administration that "knows where it is going," that would let "its right hand know what its left hand is doing," that is "not going to weave, wobble and wiggle." He accused Truman of "clumsiness" and "weakness" in "undercutting" the work of his United Nations delegation.

Privately, Dewey dropped the mealymouthed code words. To the reporters covering his campaign, he exploded with anger, griping, off-the-record, that President Truman had little right to be taking such a major initiative on his way out the door. "If Harry Truman would just keep his hands off things for another few weeks! Particularly, if he will keep his hands off foreign policy, about which he knows considerably less than nothing!"

"Jesus, my eyes began to pop out," Edwin Lahey of the *Chicago Daily News* recalled of his reaction. "Here was this man saying that the President of the United States should keep his hands off foreign policy until this bum was elected—the world would be safe.

"That's the night the angels switched. Somebody in heaven said, 'We gotta flatten this bum.' And that's what happened."

October 2, 1948

The Dear Lollypop Uncle,
  My dear mother says that she wished one of you could fly very low over Siemensstadt-Berlin and drop some of your Lollypop parachutes as there are many children here that would like to know what they taste like.

Ursela Schmidt

William Shirer found that everywhere he went in Berlin, he heard "expressions of gratitude." The night of "Lieutenant Gail Halvorsen Day," October 3, he was "sitting with a group of Germans in a little candlelit café. It was cold, miserable weather, but Airlift planes kept roaring in on schedule." One of the Germans sitting at the table turned to him and said, earnestly, "We'll gladly sit here in the cold by candle light as long as your people keep delivering supplies. The little sacrifices we make are nothing compared to those you are making."

That those planes continued to deliver supplies was largely a product of the efforts of Bill Tunner, a man most Berliners had never heard of. The question facing him now was whether the Airlift would defeat, or be defeated by, the coming winter.

He had thrown himself fully into the work of the Airlift, setting up a cot in his office so he would not have to walk the two hundred steps back to his room in the Schwarzer Bock Hotel. At 3 A.M., he was often looking over the shoulder of men on the night watch, asking detailed questions about the status of various planes. Each morning, he held a full staff meeting at seven. He developed a persistent hacking cough that would not go away and he lost so much weight that it drew medical attention.

But in those fifty analytical charts in his headquarters, being updated twenty-four hours a day, Tunner had solved the riddle that had bedeviled airmen since the birth of flight. He had made an airlift work, and done so on the largest scale ever attempted. *Newsweek*'s John Thompson had hitched a ride on the airlift into Berlin in the beginning of July and found it to be "a magnificent, confused, slapdash performance." Three months later, in the beginning of October, he flew it again and saw that it had been transformed: "Today Operation Vittles is Big Business, organized and operated with typical American commercial efficiency." The commentator Joseph Alsop had a similar experience. "The airlift is no longer stirring," he observed, "as a brave, dramatic and dangerous last-minute expedient, such as it was in the early days of the 'LeMay Coal & Food Co.'" There was "no more flavor of emergency about the present airlift operation than there is about the operations of the New York Central Railroad." What Tunner had done was toss "out the window" all "romance of the 'wide blue yonder' variety" and instead "bring the effort to organize air transport like an assembly line to a sort of peak of completeness." At Tempelhof, what stood out to those who observed the Airlift was the "effortless quiet." They would point out that "no one runs or shouts. No loudspeakers blare and almost no lights flash." The process of landing the planes in Berlin—with the bright yellow "Follow Me" jeeps and the *fräulein*-stocked Red Cross snack truck—became so smooth that some pilots who arrived in Germany that fall maintained that, in their months of flying the Airlift, they never even set foot on the tarmac at Tempelhof. Ross Milton, Tunner's aide, was charged with escorting the endless stream of distinguished visitors who came to see the Airlift. He found them to be visibly disappointed when they arrived at the flight line. "There would be a few airplanes on the ramp being unloaded, one landing, one taking off, and that was it, an unvarying pattern any time of the day or night." It was Tunner's vision realized—a dull, steady rhythm "constant as the jungle drums."

Coal and food combined for 90 percent of the Airlift's total cargo, but the Airlift planners learned that the variety of needs in a city of millions was almost endless. By the end of September, the Airlift had transported 2,000 rolls of newsprint, weighing 500 pounds each. It carried special shipments of food for the animals in Berlin's zoo, saccharin for diabetics, kosher meat for the small number of remaining Jews, medicines for hospitals, and supplies for nursing mothers. Civilian airlines—including Pan American Airways, Alaska Airlines, and American Airlines—and their pilots were pressed into service ferrying passengers and cargo.

The level of tonnage and the Airlift's metronome-like quality required more than Tunner's charts and graphs. It demanded constant creativity and improvisation. Just as each minute mattered on the Airlift, each pound entered into the calculations. Carrying the dehydrated potatoes called Pom cut weight requirements by 80 percent over the real thing. Boning and canning meat saved 25 percent of the weight. Baking bread in Berlin rather than preparing it in the West made sense because the excess weight of water in a loaf and its bulky, light nature made it difficult to transport, so flour and yeast were flown into the city to be delivered to bakeries. Beans and dried pea soup were both filling and full of calories and protein, but took too long to cook and therefore used up too much coal, so shipments were stopped. Each plane was required to carry exactly 19,500 pounds. Every bag of coal was weighed to make sure that the planes were not overburdened. Conversely, to ensure that the planes did not fill up with items such as paper napkins or cereal, which took up much room but did not weigh much, these types of cargo were married with heavier freight like coal or flour. "Otherwise," said the European Command's logistics chief, "we could jam a plane with noodles until they ran out of the pilot's ears and we still would be carrying no more than three tons."

It was through these daily prosaic decisions, the exertions of thousands of mechanics and cargo loaders, the exhausting flights of pilots in slow planes the size of railroad boxcars, that three-quarters of one of the largest cities in the world was fed. The achievement was staggering. That fall, primitive Tempelhof, with its cracking pierced-steel and sod runways, was handling 50 percent more traffic than New York's LaGuardia Airport, which, just a few months earlier, had been the busiest airport in the world.

"I NEVER HAD," Tunner would admit later, "what you would call a 'happy' relationship with General LeMay." The tension between the two men had real consequences. LeMay's attempt to retain some control over the Airlift had severely hampered Tunner's authority. He had no jurisdiction over personnel, no ability to make promotions or seek replacements. He could not request parts and equipment. They "were going through engines like a cavalry goes through hay," recalled one Airlift veteran, but at one point, with no spare starters at Tempelhof, crews had to start broken engines with bungee cords. "We didn't have enough spare parts in Europe to rebuild the ass end of a Piper Cub," recalled an operations officer.

An even more crucial shortage was that of airplane mechanics. By the time the Airlift had 160 Skymasters, it only had enough personnel to service 50 of them. Tunner wanted to enlist the help of the veterans of the legendary Luftwaffe—many of them now hungry Berliners—but official military government policy prevented him from hiring them.

The only person who could overturn that policy was Clay himself. Since Tunner was barred from speaking to Clay, asking for a special dispensation, "presented an interesting problem," he admitted. But LeMay could not prevent Clay from speaking to Tunner. So one afternoon, Tunner made sure he just happened to be at Tempelhof when Clay arrived for a flight. He parked himself right in the general's line of sight. "Any problems, Tunner?" Clay asked.

Tunner replied that, come to think of it, he desperately needed help in repairing the planes. He described the poor state of the aircraft and the strains on his crews. "I think I can whip it if you will allow me to hire some skilled German mechanics."

Clay hardly waited a beat. "Go ahead and do it," he said. "And tell Curt I said it's O.K.," he added slyly as he walked off.

LeMay's staff members told Tunner he had made a mistake that he would regret, that the Germans would throw things into the aircrafts' machinery or put bombs in bags of coal. "Nonsense," Tunner replied. "They are just as interested as I am in getting those people in Berlin fed." He set out to find the best mechanics he could, but discovered that the Luftwaffe veterans were initially nervous to cooperate with the American Air Force. One decision changed their attitude dramatically. To oversee the German mechanics, Tunner hired not just any technician, but Major General Hans-Detlef Herhundt von Rohden, who had been one of the highest-ranking officers of the failed attempt to supply Stalingrad by air. The German mechanics—including one who had formerly been the chief engineer of Lufthansa airlines—flocked to work by his side.

AS CONSTRUCTION ON the new airport at Tegel continued, it became apparent that while much of the work could be done by hand, heavy machinery would be needed to move earth and lay down the runway. Tractors, bulldozers, and steamrollers were almost nonexistent in the western sectors, and there was no way such large pieces of equipment could fit in an airplane to be flown into Berlin. One of the Airlift staff remembered that, during the war, a civilian employee of the Army named H. P. Lacomb had developed a method of cutting apart machinery and then flying the parts to construction sites in Brazil. The FBI was put to work tracking him down, and he was discovered working an ordinary engineering job at a small airport in the Midwest. Within days, he was on his way to Germany. At Rhein-Main, he would take his oxyacetylene torch to the body of an earthmover and skillfully carve it up so that it could be flown to Berlin in pieces and then be easily welded back together. Eighty-one earthmovers were brought to Berlin in this way, and all through October thousands of Berliners walked alongside the giant machines, sewn together like Frankenstein monsters, as they built the new airport together.

IT WAS NO accident that LeMay received much of the credit for the Airlift—he courted reporters and gave them the colorful quotes they loved. In contrast, Tunner was publicity-shy. Indeed, when *Life* magazine wanted to put him on their cover in October, he pleaded with them not to do so. But in one of the rare interviews he gave during the Airlift, he revealed himself more than he knew. The interview was about the morale problem plaguing the operation. Pilots, the reporter pointed out to Tunner, were bored, tired, and drained. In response, Tunner "whipped out reams of performance reports," telling the reporter that the way to solve such human issues was the same way one built the apparatus of an airlift, by "breaking it down into small problems, taking them one at a time, and trying to solve them."

Tunner could grapple with cargo combinations, shortages of engine parts, or a lack of trained mechanics, but no problem so bedeviled him as providing for the care and sustenance of the air and ground crews that made up the Airlift. Try as he might to search his charts for the answers, they were not there. Yet in an operation so precisely timed, so dependent on concentration and discipline and exertion, nothing was more important to success than the efforts of the men who flew, loaded, fixed, and guided the planes.

They were under severe strain. By the middle of October, 10,000 of those on the Airlift were veterans of the Second World War—weary men, now military reservists, who had started new lives believing that the victory they had won would bring with it peace, only to be yanked out of their ordinary existence and returned to flying shaky planes over foreign lands. They would often wear their children's miniature baby shoes clipped to their chest beside their medals. Others were young—in their teens or early twenties, they had just missed being old enough to go to battle in the last war. They had been thrown into an edgy situation, one whose nature and gravity they sometimes failed to grasp. One young pilot, soon after arriving on base in west Germany, asked if he might take a plane to Berlin when he had time off. When he was told this was not allowed, he followed up by asking, "Well, then, could you give me a copy of the train schedule to Berlin?" In another instance, one night in the control tower in Berlin, as planes were coming in fast and the weather was worsening and the blips on the radar traveled across the screen like perfectly spaced pearls, a baby-faced tower operator tuned frequency dials and advised incoming airplanes. Whenever he had a second, he would dive under the counter, fumble about agitatedly, and then come back up again to respond to the worries of another approaching pilot. Finally, he gave up looking under the desk and blurted out, "Has anyone seen my yo-yo?"

By October, duty tours, which had originally been 45 days, had been extended to 90 and then 180 days. Halvorsen sold the red car he had parked under the pines in Mobile, uncertain whether and when he would get to drive it again. Airmen deployed to Germany had often been permitted only 45 or 65 pounds of baggage, and many had to transport tool kits, which counted against this limit. Therefore, much of their clothing, and all of their winter wear, had to be sent as "unaccompanied baggage"—traveling on slow boats that took three to six months to reach them. They would have purchased more, but there had been too little winter clothing ordered for sale in stores on German bases. No one had thought that the Airlift would still be going on as winter approached.

A steady influx of new pilots began arriving for duty in October. Many had been trained at Great Falls, Montana. There, in a spot specifically chosen because its bad weather and poor visibility resembled Berlin when winter came, an exact replica of the flight patterns of the Airlift had been laid out in the prairie. Runways were built to mirror the length of those in Berlin, and at Rhein-Main and the other western German bases. Planes were loaded up with 20,000 pounds of steel drums filled with sand to simulate the weight of a fully loaded Skymaster, and then sent out along routes identical to those of the corridors into Berlin. After three weeks at Great Falls, the crews would be transferred directly to Germany knowing how to fly the Airlift and obey all its stringent procedures.

Crews came to Germany from Australia, New Zealand, Canada, and South Africa, but the vast majority were from America and Britain, and their airmen had to learn not only to fly together but to adapt to one another's peculiarities. One of Tunner's men, stationed at Fassberg in the British zone, complained indignantly that he was being served "two slices of tomato and a kipper" for breakfast instead of an American meal of eggs and bacon. Tunner was moved to order that different rations be distributed to each air force. The movie theater at Fassberg showed American films three nights a week, British films another three nights a week, and, on the seventh, a German stage show. On American movie nights, patrons were charged a 20-cent flat ticket price and told they could sit where they chose. On British nights, according to their custom—and their film distributors' requirements—there were three different-tiered ticket prices and assigned seats. Invariably, American GIs would sit where they wanted and had to be convinced to move by the usher. Eventually most Americans adapted to life on a British base. As the months wore on, they would even become ornery if they missed their afternoon tea.

Flying through the corridors could be nerve-racking. Russian Yaks and MiGs shrieked out of a corner of the sky and missed the lumbering C-54s by only a few feet. The Russians would shoot off rockets in the direction of the planes, drop bombs down from above the air traffic, and fire bullets at the Skymasters. At Gatow Airport in Berlin, which butted up against Soviet territory, the Russians shined bright searchlights straight into the direction of planes taking off at the end of the runway. Pilots covered up their cockpit window with newspapers and maps, and flew using only their instruments.

But of all the difficulties faced by the crews, especially the pilots, the greatest was fatigue. It was not just the long hours, it was the tedium and stultifying boredom of the endlessly repeating routine. It got so bad that they didn't dread a Yak barreling out at them from the wisps, they almost longed for it. They did anything they could to stay awake. They listened to Armed Forces Radio's *Midnight in Berlin* broadcast where Bill Perkins promised "hillbilly, semi-classical, sweet stuff, jazz but not too much jive." Some would suck on bitter Alka-Seltzer tablets. One crew maintained an ongoing game of bridge. Others played poker. The air crews would hang beer outside the window of the plane in flight so they could pop open a cold bottle as soon as they landed. A number of pilots took up knitting and put the plane on autopilot while they made ankle socks. A newlywed pilot methodically studied a sex manual in preparation for the day he would be reunited with his young bride.

But more often than Tunner ever knew, the crews would lose their battle with exhaustion and just nod off. Sometimes pilots and copilots took turns sleeping and tested their skills to see whether they could land without waking up their partner. Often all aboard would fall asleep. If this happened while the planes were parked, waiting to take off, ground operations officers kept a fishing pole ready and would whack the windshield to wake those inside. But when the crews fell asleep in the air, they would drift away until somehow one of them was roused. The lucky ones would fall asleep on the flight home from Berlin. They'd awaken over France or Belgium or the English Channel and race back to Germany. The less fortunate fell asleep when they were heading in the other direction, ending up over Soviet-controlled Eastern Europe and trying to make it back to Berlin before the fuel ran out.

The strain—the lack of sleep, the monotony, the homesickness, the clash of cultures, the Russian harassment, the pressure of the crisis—all proved too much for some. In Wiesbaden, some men hurled themselves through windows to break their bones so that they would no longer have to fly. At Fassberg, a pilot fired a shotgun at a cuckoo clock that was keeping him from sleeping. In Berlin, GIs monitoring the unloading prayed for bad weather to relieve the constant demands. Lieutenant Joe Wisdom, known as "Bearded" Wisdom, vowed he would not shave his moustache until he was sent back to the States. It took longer than he had expected and his whiskers grew to more than six inches, curling up when they stopped growing out. At Tempelhof, a Skymaster crashed on the runway. Rescuers rushed to the burning wreckage only to find the pilot and copilot gone. They had broken through the window, hopped the airport fence, and, finally cracked, fled into the streets of Berlin.

THE MAN WHO had been nicknamed "Willie the Whip" on the Hump would seem ill-equipped to deal with these psychological breakdowns. And in commanding the Airlift, Bill Tunner retained his hard-charging ways. He would still explode in anger if he arrived on a base and saw more than five planes on the ground at a time. He still, in the words of his secretary, "wanted everything done as of yesterday." He was still obsessed with slide rules and logarithms and big sheets of numbers. In the middle of October, LeMay returned to the United States to take over the Strategic Air Command. On his last day, he sent out dozens of letters of commendation on the occasion of his departure. They were essentially form letters. He used identical language over and over, praising the recipient's "industry and able management." In Tunner's, he added another word to the formulistic phrase. Writing to Tunner, LeMay praised his "industry, zeal and able management."

Yet while Tunner retained that uncompromising fervor, the man who showed up in Germany was different from the one who arrived in India. In the intervening years, he had watched helplessly as his wife slowly faded from life, he had raised two young boys alone, and he had seen his career stall out. At night, unable to sleep, Tunner would walk around the German bases wearing a crumpled baseball cap and a weathered, olive-green flight jacket shorn of any insignia. Airlift personnel would not even notice him at first. A young radar operator would simply feel Tunner's hand resting softly on his shoulder, reassuring him with a bare nod. Tunner, who had to be practically ordered to return to his dying wife and young children after the war, set up "ham" radio links so that airmen could talk to their families back home. On the Hump, he had said, "As for the bitching, let them." Now, he invited a group of pilots to a meeting room on the ground floor of the Schwarzer Bock. They arrived at 10 A.M. to find a table of cold cuts and a keg of dark German beer. Tunner greeted them warmly and chatted with them about nothing in particular as they ate their salami and bratwursts and finished off a couple of steins. Then he said, "I called you men here today to ask you some questions—and I want to hear some biased answers." He proceeded to press them on their opinions of how the Airlift was working and how it could be improved. With his staff arrayed around the room, Tunner listened to the pilots' suggestions about the placement of the radio beacons or the procedures for enforcing airspeed or the arrangement of space in the barracks, and immediately issued orders putting them into effect. All day the beer flowed and the session went on, delving deeply into every aspect of the Airlift, with Tunner continuously engrossed. Finally, around seven P.M., one pilot, draining what was left in his stein, made another suggestion: "How about getting the Red Cross or somebody to send over a couple of hundred beautiful American girls" to act as secretaries?

Ken Swallwell, Tunner's deputy for operations, looked up from his notepad, aghast. "We don't have enough housing as it is. Where would they sleep?" Tunner and the pilots burst into laughter and the meeting ended. They walked out of the hotel and off into the night.

Not long after he returned to Paris from meeting with Truman in Washington, Marshall had a private, secret conversation with John Foster Dulles. The outcome of the presidential election was clear. "Almost everyone else but Harry S. Truman seems to agree that Dewey will probably be chosen to lead the United States in this testing time," wrote Joseph and Stewart Alsop in a story in the October 16 *Saturday Evening Post* titled "What Kind of President Will Dewey Make?" With the Berlin crisis so volatile, Marshall told Dulles, it was important they have a smooth transition. Indeed, the situation was so dangerous that Marshall said he was prepared to take a step that had never been done before and transfer authority to Dulles as soon as the election was over. He told Dulles that he was telling him this "in utmost confidence." Dulles practically ran out of the room to tell Dewey, sending a special intercontinental courier to deliver the message to the governor on the campaign trail.

In the hallways at the United Nations, in column after column in American newspapers, there was rampant speculation on what steps Dulles would take once he became secretary of state. But there was little suspense about one decision he was expected to make the moment he took office. "It is generally assumed," wrote Frank Howley in his diary that month, "that the first act of Dewey, if Dewey wins the election and if Dulles becomes Secretary of State, would be the removal of General Clay from his present assignment." With this in mind, Bill Draper, Clay's friend and liaison in the Pentagon, presented the military governor on October 13 with a suggestion. "It may well be," he wrote gingerly, "that the new Administration will have its own ideas as to commanders as well as Cabinet members." In order "to save you possible future embarrassment," Draper advised Clay, he should submit his resignation to Bradley "now before the election." Perhaps, he wrote, the time had finally come for Clay "to go catfishing for a few months." Trying to soften the blow, he hoped they "might do a little catfishing together—I personally would like nothing better."

Clay did not argue with the assumptions that Dewey would win or that this meant he would be fired. But he had been fired once before and yet was still serving in Berlin. He replied to Draper that he could not "voluntarily leave with Berlin still in blockade as to do so would be running out." He had tried to resign approximately a dozen times in his first three years in Germany, but would not do so in the midst of a crisis. "No soldier can request retirement and be consistent with his life-principles under present conditions." He too tried to lighten the tone. "As to the catfishing," he replied to Draper, "it's a date."

Two days later, Clay had a taste of what was to come when Dulles arrived for a preelection publicity tour of Germany. The trip was intended to capture press attention and demonstrate that Dewey's team was ready to take control, even amid the Berlin siege. Neither Clay nor Dulles was looking forward to spending time with the other. The mutual antipathy between them stretched back to their vicious debates over Germany's future. It had been stoked by Dulles's statement, ten days earlier, that the American position in Berlin might soon be "untenable" if German morale weakened as winter under the blockade wore on. Yet Clay had no choice but to host the visiting Dulles, first in the American zone in the west and then, on Sunday, October 17, at his home in Berlin.

That Sunday morning, Howley received a call inviting him to lunch at Clay's house. He arrived to find Clay standing with his back to the crackling fireplace. Dulles stood in front of him. But "the atmosphere," Howley noted in his diary, "was anything but warm." Neither man was talking to the other. Howley barged into the silent room and tried to strike up some banter. No one else joined in. They stood about, stiffly, for ten minutes. Dulles hardly said three sentences the entire time.

Lunch was served and they walked into the dining room. Clay sat at the head of the table. Dulles was on his right. Murphy was on his left. Howley was seated at the other end. "Ice existed between Dulles and Clay," he observed. The meal was served but no one spoke. Howley decided to try to make conversation. "I did considerable talking since no one hated me and I was, after all, a nonbelligerent at the table." He started by spending "five or ten minutes condemning the Communists." It happened to be his second favorite topic. He managed to weave in his favorite subject as well by talking about how he thought himself to be a potential target of assassination. He had clearly given this a lot of thought. He went into excruciating detail about how the Soviets would go about shooting him in such an attempt as he was driving in his open Horch. He explained what he believed were the Russian preferences for shooting targets in the heart instead of the head, and their theories on the assassination of top leaders over lower-level officials. The others listened as he went on; they pushed their food around their plates. When someone finally managed to change the subject, things brightened, somewhat. "The best discussion at the table between Dulles and Clay was over the subject of Rhine wines, on which they seemed to have perfect agreement."

As the painful lunch wore on, it was clear that Dulles was, in Clay's description, "very lukewarm to the airlift." They were sitting drinking their coffee when Clay suggested that, in that case, perhaps Dulles would like to meet Ernst Reuter. Dulles, who saw little use in talking to a German municipal official about such a sensitive matter of global grand strategy, looked to his aide for a way out. He asked him if there might be any political difficulties from holding such a meeting. "I have the greatest respect for the opinions of General Clay and Mr. Murphy," the aide said. "If they think it is all right, I think so too."

"I might as well have left you in Paris if that's all the advice you are able to offer me," Dulles snapped.

Reuter arrived a short while later. Clay had had enough. "This is your problem," he whispered to Reuter and then left him and Dulles alone, sitting three feet apart. Dulles's eye twitched behind his glasses, his face convulsing in small spasms, a tic he had contracted as a young man on a business trip to the West Indies. Reuter looked haggard, his features were drawn. The hum of Skymasters on their approach into Tempelhof could be heard continuously overhead. Instead of offering Reuter his encouragement, Dulles launched immediately into an interrogation. "Will the Germans stand fast during the winter?" he wanted to know. "Or will they give up, accept Russian aid, and get us out of Berlin rather than take more suffering?"

Reuter, who had spent time in two concentration camps, had little patience for being lectured on fortitude by a prosperous corporate lawyer. He replied evenly. "The people of Berlin are accustomed to suffering," he began. "We are willing to suffer a great deal more to escape Russian domination."

No one will ever know exactly what Reuter went on to say in the meeting, but after that conversation, there is no record of Dulles ever again expressing a public or private doubt about the Airlift. When he and Reuter were done, Dulles and Clay went to go speak to the press together. Howley, who acted as though the unexpressed thought was not worth having, marveled at the show. "It is to me a great thing that privately two men may differ completely but present a different picture at public appearance," he wrote in his diary. Nevertheless, Dulles's attitude had noticeably changed from what he had been telling reporters only days earlier. The Soviets, the presumed secretary of state–in–waiting said, had imposed the blockade "doubtless hoping that starvation would break men's resistance, drive the Western powers from their agreed position, and subject another 2,225,000 people to Soviet rule." Instead, America and its allies had responded "by bringing into being an Airlift so spectacular that all the world marveled." Because of this Airlift, it was clear, he pointed out, that "the morale in western Berlin and western Germany has risen to a new high." Clay could only nod.

Clay knew he was being exploited on behalf of the Dewey campaign. He did not like it, and not only because of his antipathy for Dulles or the likelihood he would be instantly fired in a Dewey administration or the long-standing Democratic roots of his family. His admiration for Truman's response to the blockade, for overruling all his top advisers in order to stay in Berlin and provide planes for the Airlift, made him passionate for the president's victory in November. Though constrained by his uniform, Clay would later admit that "in 1948, I was very much for President Truman." So were most of the American soldiers in Germany. Every time a Russian fighter buzzed their C-54, Hal Halvorsen later said, "we cast a mental vote for Harry Truman."

Clay—the cunning bureaucratic fighter, the son of a senator—would not be outmatched by Dulles. When asked by a reporter, at that press conference with Dulles, whether he soon intended to resign, his response was a masterpiece of rhetoric. "I am not requesting retirement," he replied. "As long as Berlin is under blockade, I wouldn't think of voluntarily asking to leave. I'd be a damn poor soldier if I requested to leave." By emphasizing that he would not "request" to retire and would not "voluntarily" resign, he made it clear that if Dulles wanted to be rid of him, he would have to fire the popular symbol of the American resistance in Berlin. And even having delivered this shiv of revenge, Clay was not done. Dulles had used his visit with Clay to promote Dewey's campaign. Clay would do him one better.

The Soviets continued to try to lure Berliners into trading in their western sector ration cards for Russian-issued documents. They introduced simplified registration procedures and evening hours of operation to make it easier for Berliners to pick up Soviet-provided food. They offered to throw in home heating oil. In October, they offered 175 pounds of real, fresh potatoes—an alluring prospect for Berliners sick of the paste of Pom. In reply, the Berliners who had lived through the plunder of the city's women by the Russian invaders three years earlier jibed, "Better Pom than 'Frau Komm.'" The number of residents of the blockaded western sectors who gave in to the blandishments and their hunger rose as winter approached, but it never reached above 5 percent of the population. "We have done our best," announced Howley in October, "to help the people of Berlin to keep from selling their souls for the sake of a noonday meal."

All summer and into the fall, west Berliners had been helped by the fact that the blockade was not airtight. On October 8, for instance, a twenty-six-year-old American sergeant with big ears and a wide grin drove his car from western Germany to Berlin, getting past Russian guards, whose post was littered with spent cognac bottles, by convincing them his automobile insurance paperwork was a special pass. Though he was the first American to make it to Berlin on land since the beginning of the blockade in June, he succeeded in proving that it was impossible to hermetically seal off one half of a large city. Elevated trains still moved between sectors. Tens of thousands of people lived in the west and worked in the east and vice versa. Smugglers and black marketeers plied their trades. The besieged Berliners engaged in large-scale foraging, sneaking out into the countryside by foot or on bicycles, and returning with baskets full of potatoes or berries. On average, Berliners were able to augment their rations by 150 calories a day through these means—the rough equivalent of a couple of slices of bread.

But on October 19, just as winter approached, the Soviets began to physically divide the city and seal off the western sectors. At ninety-two street crossings on the border of western Berlin and Soviet territory, the Russians erected checkpoints and barricades. Soviet-sector workmen dug up cobblestones from the street and stacked them in piles to form barriers to stop people from driving across the sector line. Berliners stood about shocked, baffled at what was happening to their city. Police at the roadblocks searched every car and pedestrian crossing the border and confiscated food or coal or even non-Communist newspapers. Special summary courts were set up at the checkpoints to immediately sentence to forced labor anyone found with contraband in their truck or handbag. On the first day, 15 vehicles entering west Berlin from the Soviet zone were impounded, their contents confiscated, and their drivers arrested. By the end of the month, 286 vehicles had been seized, along with an untold number of individuals. Even trucks carrying humanitarian supplies from the Red Cross were banned. The Soviets' "intent has been complete and total blockade from the start," Howley observed in a statement on the new Russian moves. They had now come about as close to this goal as they could. The amount that Berliners were able to augment their official rations dropped precipitously to negligible levels, to an average of 50 to 75 calories a day—about two-thirds less than it had once been. The Airlift was now western Berlin's last link to the outside world.

The same day that the barricades went up in Berlin, Clay departed for America from Tempelhof. He was making the voyage home, for only the second time since the blockade began, in order to keep the hasty commitment he had made to Cardinal Spellman to speak at the annual Al Smith Dinner in New York. But the trip would also provide him the opportunity to again lobby Harry Truman for more planes.

In September, Clay had asked for more than a hundred additional Skymasters. By the end of that month, Bradley had promised fifty, delivered none, and told Clay that the matter was under consideration. Impatient as ever, Clay waited only four days before he tried once more. "While I hesitate to bother you again," he cabled Bradley on October 4, "I am seriously disturbed over delay to send additional C-54s with corresponding delay in their arrival. Bad weather is almost upon us and our present lift is only slightly exceeding our minimum needs. It will not meet bad weather conditions." He received no further reply. Unbeknownst to Clay, Bradley, General Vandenberg of the Air Force, and the other top military leaders were not only ignoring his pleas, they were again pushing to have the United States pull out of Berlin. "It is the considered opinion of the Joint Chiefs of Staff," they wrote in an October 13 memorandum to the members of the National Security Council, "that our present military power cannot effectively support the supply of Berlin by air lift on an indefinite basis without such a diversion of military effort as has affected and will continue progressively to affect seriously and adversely the ability of the National Military Establishment to meet its primary national security responsibilities." They believed they simply could not continue to waste time and sacrifice their airpower to this type of aerial charity work. Bradley and the others urged the National Security Council to decide whether they planned to fight for Berlin. If they did, then they should begin "full-out preparations for the early eventuality of war." If they did not, they should begin steps "leading to our withdrawal from Berlin." Either way, the monkeying around with a flying convoy should come to an end.

The Chiefs of Staff were not alone in their disdain for the Airlift. While Clay's plane was in the air, heading to Washington, the CIA sent a secret "Review of the World Situation" to the White House. The intelligence analysts concluded that the United States was now worse off than if the Airlift had never been attempted. The huge effort had resulted in "making Berlin a major test of U.S.-Soviet strength in the eyes of

Germany and of Western and Eastern Europe, and reaffirming a direct U.S. responsibility for the welfare and safety of the German population of the western sectors of the city." These were, in their estimation, negative consequences. The very fact that the Airlift had so caught the imagination of Germans, Americans, and, indeed, people around the world meant that "the U.S. is now committed, in Berlin, to maintaining a strategic outpost on political grounds when, in the final analysis, that outpost can be maintained only by force or with Soviet tolerance." Like the military chieftains, the CIA analysts were certain that the Airlift itself was fated to fail. They too concluded that "a choice will have to be made between a planned withdrawal or the eventual maintenance of the Berlin position by force."

Clay arrived in Washington at night on October 20. The next morning, he had breakfast with Forrestal. Clay reacted angrily to word of the new calls for retreat. "The only thing that has kept Europe stable has been the presence of the American Army and the Airlift. Withdraw that," Clay said, according to Forrestal, "and you practically turn the show over to Russia and the Communists without a struggle."

Forrestal found the situation bleak. "The most dangerous spot is our own country," he told Clay, "because the people are so eager for peace and have such a distaste for war that they will grasp any sign of a solution of a problem that has had them deeply worried."

If Forrestal was thinking of Wallace, he was not alone. That same morning, Truman was locked away for hours with his political advisers. They were drafting a series of speeches that Truman would deliver in the remaining ten days of the campaign. For most of October, their campaign had appealed to voters' pocketbooks, painting Dewey's Republicans as enemies of labor unions, farmers, and the New Deal. But by all accounts, Truman was still behind. In his final appeal, he would turn to the issue foremost on Americans' minds—the question of war or peace. Truman's ability to raise doubts about Dewey, isolate Wallace, and win over the surging, fretful middle class to his approach in Berlin would make the difference between a shocking victory and his already assumed defeat.

This was Truman's mind-set when Clay, along with Forrestal, Murphy, Royall, and Draper, arrived at 11 A.M. Truman warmly welcomed the general back to the White House. They delved immediately into the business at hand. Clay reported to Truman on the progress of the Airlift, but his briefing went further than the quantities of daily tonnage or rationed calories. The general from the Corps of Engineers once again told Truman that the importance of the Airlift was also its effect on the German psyche. Berliners had come to embrace the Americans who had arrived as conquerors and occupiers only three years earlier. In a nation with only the scantest, saddest experience with democracy, there was evidence the people were rejecting the comfort of a totalitarian ideology. As Clay said to a meeting of the National Security Council immediately after leaving Truman's office, the Airlift's success had "made Germany one of the most anti-Communist countries in the world."

Clay repeated his request for more planes. Truman needed little convincing. He too saw the power of the Airlift—not only in the minds of Berliners but in those of the voters he was courting at home as well. He approved Clay's full request for 116 more Skymasters. They agreed to announce the decision at once.

BY 5 O'CLOCK THAT evening, Clay was in a room at New York's Waldorf-Astoria Hotel, changing his shirt while visiting with his old friend Dwight Eisenhower. Downstairs, the ballroom was filling with two thousand guests and a swarm of reporters, all twittering with anticipation for Clay's appearance as the featured speaker of that evening's annual Al Smith Memorial Dinner. As the *New York Times* would opine the next morning, "Since the Russian blockade of Berlin was put into effect last summer it is no exaggeration to say that General Clay's job has been just about the most important in the world." In his absence from America, he had become a major figure in the nation's conversation. His name could be found on the front pages almost every day. His visage often graced the covers of magazines. "If we had in this country the British system of awarding titles to our military men," continued the *New York Times* editorial, "it is possible our commander in Germany would be known to history as Viscount Clay of Berlin." But through the months of tension, Clay's had been a distant voice. This night would be, as *Time* put it, "his first direct report to the U.S. people on the Battle for Berlin." It was an important event, one made all the more significant, as Clay had known it would be, by the presence of the other prominent guest that night, the secondary figure of the evening, New York's governor, Thomas E. Dewey.

Dewey spoke first but said little. Clay's speech was twice as long and it was not only a paean to the Airlift but also a defense of the American policies in Germany since the war—the very policies Dewey had been traveling the country claiming had led to the blockade. The Soviets had chosen the German capital for their showdown with the West, he said, because "if the Western allies could be forced from Berlin, then the impression would be created that they could be forced out elsewhere. The voices of freedom would become weak and lose their strength through fear." But the Russians had "failed to recognize our strength in the air. They did not understand the determination of the Western allies to fulfill their obligation to the peoples under their charge. They did not reckon with the will of several million Germans in Berlin to resist being placed under a police state." And, implicitly, though he did not come out and say it, they had not counted on the strong response of America's president, Harry Truman. With Dewey sitting directly on his right, Clay stood at the podium and said, "The Airlift can—it must—be continued until there is stability in Europe that assures peace."

Eleven days before the election, Dewey was overshadowed and his campaign charges that Truman was weak and wobbly had been gleefully undercut. All eyes were on him to see his reaction. He had no choice but to join in a prolonged standing ovation. Then, when Clay was done, Dewey had to listen again to Clay praise the Airlift for the sake of the newsreel cameras and pose with his head cocked in interest so that the photographers could get the shot. The picture of Clay speaking and Dewey gazing at him approvingly was seen all over the country, appearing in hundreds of newspapers. Clay had turned Dewey, on the verge of being elected president, into a prop in demonstrating national support for Harry Truman's foreign policy.

By midnight, twenty-seven hours after he landed in America, Clay was on his way back to Berlin.

———

13 October 1948

Mr. 1st Lt. Halvorsen,

I have already read in the Telegraf that little parachutes with candy dropped is by your airplane. We live in Charolottenburg and can not to Tempelhof come. My sister and I like so much chocolate to eat but our mother can us not buy and our father is dead. Please perhaps one time something for us to bring?

Healthy greetings,
Gertraud and Brigitte Schuffelhauer

———

The next day, Truman's train pulled out of Union Station on the swing that would take him to election day. Campaigns begin with the best of intentions, but along the way inevitably lead to something more honest, laying bare candidates for who they are and a moment in time for its essential character. There was a romance in Truman's seemingly quixotic scurries around the rural corners of America. Truman would speak wherever he could find a crowd. If it was late at night, he would appear at the train's rear platform in his bathrobe, inveigh against privileged plutocrats, promise peace, and shuffle off back to bed. For his part, Dewey set out to be responsible in his remarks. He bravely told voters he could not offer easy answers and vowed never to tell one audience one thing and another audience something else. He often ended up saying nothing at all. "America's future—like yours in Arizona—is still ahead of us," he told a crowd in Phoenix. But as the campaign entered its final week, something rawer and uglier came to the fore. The 1948 election would end in an all-out brawl over Berlin, Communism, and war.

All through October, Dewey had repeated his charge that Truman had vacillated in confronting the Soviets. Truman had waited to respond. When he did, it came in one of the nastiest attacks in the history of twentieth-century American politics. On October 25, Truman headed to Chicago to make the first of the carefully crafted speeches he and his advisers had drafted to finish the campaign. He set the tone that morning in a whistle-stop address in Garrett, Indiana. Five thousand people and three brass bands were on hand. "The Republicans are trying to pretend that my administration has been friendly to Communism. That bit of campaign propaganda reminds me a lot of the stories we heard during the war and are now hearing from the Communists in Russia. They believe that if you tell a big enough lie, somebody is bound to believe it." In fact, he charged, the opposite was true. He alleged that some Republicans had tried to help get Henry Wallace onto the ballot in order to split the vote. "If anybody in this country is friendly to the Communists, it is the Republicans," who "have joined up with this Communist-inspired Third Party to beat the Democrats."

Truman arrived in Chicago that afternoon, driving slowly past two miles of waving supporters in an open car, on his way to a nighttime address at the city's stadium. The arena—the site of Truman's nomination, and Wallace's defeat, for the vice presidency—was filled, and a television audience watched from home. Truman began by recalling the world as it had been during that Democratic convention in 1944. "We were fighting a terrible war then. We won that war for freedom, and we are now engaged in an even greater struggle—the struggle to preserve freedom and peace all over the world. Now, the principal objective of my administration as President has been to create worldwide conditions of a just and lasting peace. I have never turned from that objective."

He spoke of Woodrow Wilson's dream and Franklin Roosevelt's United Nations, but said, "We must do more than just avert war. We must also preserve here in the United States the kind of life we believe in and want to keep." He went on: "The American way of life which most of us have been taking for granted is threatened today by powerful forces of which most people are not even aware." That threat did not hail from "the contemptible Communist minority" or from "the crackpot forces of the extreme right wing." Instead, there was a darker and even more dangerous group at large. If they were allowed to "continue to work unchecked, this nation could awaken a few years from now to find that the Bill of Rights had become a scrap of paper." This insidious cabal was known as the Republican Party.

The Republicans, Truman charged at this moment of heated worry about war and despotism, had "opened the gate to forces that would destroy our democracy." He pointed out that "again and again in history, economic power concentrated in the hands of a few men has led to the loss of freedom." And there was always one invariable constant to the rise of despotism. "When a few men get control of the economy of a nation, they find a 'front man' to run the country for them. Before Hitler came to power, control over the German economy had passed into the hands of a small group of rich manufacturers, bankers, and landowners. These men decided that Germany had to have a tough, ruthless dictator who would play their game and crush the strong German labor unions. So they put money and influence behind Adolf Hitler. We know the rest of the story. We also know that in Italy, in the 1920s, powerful Italian businessmen backed Mussolini, and that in the 1930s, Japanese financiers helped Tojo's military clique take over Japan." Truman did not need to reveal the identity of this front man he was claiming was a would-be American Hitler—right down to his moustache. If anyone failed to pick up the analogy, the next day's papers did it for them.

When Dewey came to Chicago Stadium the very next day, he lamely accused Truman of "mud-slinging." He and his advisers, however, knew he needed to do more. So in a special radio address, he charged that under Truman, "millions of people have been delivered into Soviet slavery while our own administration has tried appeasement one day and bluster the next. Our country desperately needs new and better leadership in the cause of peace and freedom. It needs a government that will lead from strength to build peace in the world so that your sons and men will not have to go through another war." If Truman was charging that Dewey would bring fascism, Dewey claimed that Truman was costing America its hard-won peace.

The day after this, October 27, the Wednesday before the election, Harry Truman's campaign reached its apogee. The 1948 election had played out against the backdrop of the real possibility of world war. "The presidential campaign," wrote *Newsweek,* was "taking place in the midst of the greatest diplomatic crisis in American history." Polls showed most Americans expected war within ten years, nearly half within three years. Though Truman had spoken to this concern, even stoked the fears of what would happen if Dewey was elected, he had not mentioned Berlin in a single public address since the blockade and Airlift began—a remarkable reminder of the political etiquette of a campaign caught between the eras of torchlights and television. Now, in Boston, Truman would finally do overtly what he had done implicitly all along: claim credit for the Airlift and position the Berlin crisis as the foremost concern of voters preparing to enter the ballot booths.

After arriving at South Station, Truman and his party checked into the old Statler Hotel. Despite the approach of election day, Truman's mood was light. He played a waltz on the piano in his room and, when he was done, rose and said, "Let's go, boys. We can't keep a crowd of good Democrats waiting." He made his way through a packed lobby of well-wishers and traveled to Mechanics Hall, near Copley Square.

"Yesterday, the free peoples of the world were threatened by the black menace of fascism. The American people helped to save them," Truman said before a crowd of 15,000. "Today, the free peoples of the world are threatened by the red menace of Communism. And again, the American people are helping to save them." He began to gather steam. "I want you to get this straight now: I hate Communism. I deplore what it does to the dignity and freedom of the individual. I detest the godless creed it teaches. I have fought it at home. I have fought it abroad, and I shall continue to fight it with all my strength. This is one issue on which I shall never surrender."

He repeated his accusation that Wallace's Progressive Party was a tool of the Communists and that they were trying to split the vote to elect Dewey. "You may wonder why the Communists, with their supposed hatred for capitalism, are working night and day for the victory of the party of big business. Well, I'll tell you why. The Communists don't want me to be President, because this country, under a Democratic administration, has rallied the forces of all the democracies of the world to safeguard freedom and to save free people everywhere from Communist slavery." Indeed, "it is clear why the Communists would like to bring about my defeat, and elect a Republican President. . . . Let me remind you that the Communist Party in this country reached its maximum strength in 1932, under a Republican President. Communism thrives on misery. Human suffering nourishes the Communist menace. That menace withers away where there is prosperity, justice, and tolerance."

Truman recounted the steps his administration had taken to combat the Communist tide—from aid to Greece and Turkey to the Marshall Plan. And then he added, "In Germany, we have taken the frank and firm position that Communism must not spread its tentacles into the Western Zone." The crowd cheered. "We shall not retreat from that position." The applause grew. "We shall feed the people of Berlin." They broke into a tumultuous roar. Truman had claimed the popular Airlift as his own, countered the Republicans' most powerful charge against him, and accused the Republicans of standing with America's enemies. "You can fight Communism on November 2nd with a Democratic vote," he assured the cheering throng.

Two days after returning to Berlin from America, Clay sent a classified cable to Draper in the Pentagon. "Harry King, president of Huyler's, has obtained ten tons candy for Airlift to Berlin with parachutes," he wrote. The confectioners would begin moving the candy in installments to Westover Field in Massachusetts. "I hesitate to ask Air Forces for any more help but morale value here and at home would be real if candy could be flown over. Will you see what Air Forces can do perhaps to put a small amount in each plane coming over here? Then will you telephone Mr. King in my name and advise him what can be done?"

With cargo allotments so tight, there was little extra space, but special exceptions were constantly being made for Halvorsen and Little Vittles. Though Tunner's entire Airlift was built around the principle that a minute delay in landing a plane was a catastrophe, the growing ranks of Candy Bombers were given dispensation to break away from the ironclad pattern, fly about Berlin to drop their parachutes, and then return to the conveyor belt. Planes were stripped down to their bare essentials and no unneeded weight was allowed on board. An extra 33 pounds on each plane over the course of a year added up to a full day's supply for Berlin, but the couple of dozen regular Candy Bombers were routinely allowed to bring 600 or 700 pounds of excess weight in chocolate bars, gum, and handkerchief parachutes on their flights. The military brass allowed the candy drops to continue, but, naturally, they created regulations. As the Airlift went on, official requirements were issued for the creation of the parachutes specifying lightweight cloth in a 15-inch square connected by four 16-inch-long pieces of string.

The gratitude the Berliners had for the candy bombing was not limited to Halvorsen. It extended to all the pilots—and through them to all Americans. One day in October, Halvorsen was standing on the tarmac at Tempelhof, not far from the terminal building, waiting to take off. A young girl, perhaps eight or nine years old, approached him, holding on to her mother with one hand and a frayed teddy bear with the other. Halvorsen was just another pilot, waiting in line, getting ready to climb back into his plane. The girl, he realized, "didn't know I was the Candy Bomber from Adam."

"Please take my bear," she said, haltingly, her brown eyes filled with grief as if she were mourning the passing of a loved one. Halvorsen tried to refuse. The mother explained that the bear, clearly fashioned from scraps found at home, had been the girl's favored treasure during the war. She would never let go of it on those nights in the bomb shelters when the Allied planes were overhead, and she believed it had saved her life. Now she was convinced it would save the life of an American pilot. As much as Halvorsen attempted to convince her to keep her bear, the girl insisted. He thanked her and she curtsied in her little dress before she turned to leave.

The Soviets too saw the power of what Halvorsen had done. Their Berlin newspapers criticized the candy drops for causing thousands of Berlin children to daily tromp through the graveyard by the apartment building. This, the articles stated, showed disrespect to the dead and taught the youngsters to emulate American boorishness. When several children from east Berlin wrote to Halvorsen asking him to drop candy to them as well, he did so. After two weeks, he was told to stop. The Soviet Union had filed an official complaint against Halvorsen's encroachment on their airspace.

All during October, at the United Nations session in Paris, ambassadors from around the world sought to find a way to end the dangerous standoff in Berlin. Neutral nations from South America and Asia worked to find a compromise. The best they could come up with was a proposal for lifting the blockade while commencing talks on introducing Soviet control over the entire economy of Berlin. It was, in large part, similar to the failed deal that had been struck in Moscow two months earlier. With winter soon upon Berlin, the Soviets had little reason to resume the charade of negotiation. The neutral nations introduced their plan to the Security Council on Friday, October 22. On Monday, October 25, the Soviet ambassador vetoed it. The American representative to the United Nations, Philip Jessup, sounded a note of resignation: "There is no evidence that the Russians wished to reach an agreement." At the same time, he left the door to talks open, just enough so that a shaft of light could shine through the crack. "We are members of the Security Council and if the Russians are willing to reach an agreement, they will find us ready."

It had been the last, slim chance for a resolution before the cold and fog of November set in. The veto, said Ferdinand Friedensburg, "means for Berlin a new testing will be met by the population." Preparations for the winter continued. "The nights are getting longer, the days are getting cooler," noted Ruth Andreas-Friedrich as October came to an end. "Whenever one runs into an acquaintance on the street, he asks: 'Do you have any coal? Do you know where there is any coal?'" There was not much to be had. On October 29, it was announced that the average Berlin household in the western sectors would receive a special distribution of 50 pounds of coal—perhaps all that they would get for the entire winter. The previous winter, Berliners had shivered and frozen with 550 pounds of coal per household. The Dickensian-named chief of the American military government's Berlin public health branch, Major R. S. Paine, tried to reassure Berliners. "The coming winter will be stiff, there's no doubt about that. But contrary to some wild predictions, there will be no dying in the streets." It was a wan attempt to offer comfort.

To the press, Clay attempted to be encouraging. "The reports we get indicate that the morale of the population is surprisingly good," he said at a news conference. "Of course," he added, "it hasn't gotten very cold yet." At the end of October, Clay announced a new food ration for Berlin—an increase to 2,000 calories a day for the average Berliner. For some, the increase was small. Children between the ages of six and nine would receive only an additional 14 calories daily. Older children got 284 more calories a day. In all, the new ration level was an amount far beyond the ability of the Airlift to deliver even under the best conditions. It was meant as a reassurance that all would be well, a whistle past the graveyard up ahead. For everyone involved—Tunner and his pilots, Clay in his headquarters, the Berliners fretting over the future—knew that the coming conditions would be anything but their best.

At 8:30 P.M., on Tuesday, October 26, a week before the election, voters tuned in to the popular ABC show *America's Town Meeting of the Air,* to find the week's program devoted to "the most urgent question of the moment, perhaps the most crucial question before the world today." It was not Truman versus Dewey but rather "the conflict between East and West in Berlin. Are we headed toward another World War?"

Like bands of Bedouins, the candidates and their campaigns had traveled the country, sleeping in a different place every night, setting off again the next morning. The last weekend, they all converged on the same place, New York, America's largest city, whose votes would decide the biggest electoral prize. Half of the city's police force was put on assignment protecting Truman, Dewey, or Wallace. At one point, the caravans carrying Truman and Wallace nearly collided. Wallace's motorcade had to take three left turns to avoid running into Truman's.

On Thursday, October 28, after a nine-mile parade through the city under a raging downpour of ticker tape, Truman spoke at Madison Square Garden. He mocked Dewey for a schedule that seemed to be constantly following in Truman's wake. Dewey had spoken at Chicago Stadium the day after Truman and in the same auditorium in Cleveland the day after Truman, and had even stayed in the same suite at the Statler Hotel in Boston, arriving just hours after Truman left (Dewey's entourage took up 70 rooms in the hotel compared with 40 for the president's; 115 members of the press trailed him to Boston as opposed to 55 who had come with Truman). With an air of mock seriousness, Truman said, "Now, I have a confession to make to you here tonight. For the last two or three weeks I've had a queer feeling that I'm being followed, that someone is following me." He said it gravely, as if revealing he was suffering from a psychological ailment. "I felt it so strongly that I went into consultation with the White House physician. And I told him that I kept having this feeling, that everywhere I go there's somebody following behind me. The White House physician told me not to worry. He said: 'You keep right on your way. There is one place where that fellow is not going to follow you—and that's in the White House.'" The huge crowd laughed. It was so ludicrous it was funny. After all, who would ever imagine that someone this powerful—when the fate of the world was on the line—could have gone raving mad?

The next day, in an off-the-record press conference, Dewey told reporters he was planning to keep Forrestal in his job. "President Truman was constantly fouling Forrestal up," he supposedly said. The news leaked the day before the election.

ON OCTOBER 29, the Friday before election day, the lead story was the astonishing news of a rare public statement from Joseph Stalin. In a message, released the previous day, in the form of answers to a series of questions posed by *Pravda,* Stalin accused Truman of "a policy of aggression, a policy of unleashing a new war." He went on to predict that Truman would follow Churchill into electoral oblivion. "The horrors of the recent war are still too fresh in the memories of peoples, and the public forces favoring peace are too strong," he said, for Truman to succeed.

Truman did not respond. That day he campaigned in Harlem—the first president, indeed the first candidate, to ask for votes in what the Associated Press story on his visit called "the teeming Negro district." The Cold War permeated even his discussion of civil rights. "Democracy's answer to the challenge of totalitarianism is its promise of equal rights, and equal opportunity for all mankind," he said. That night, in Brooklyn, in his final formal speech of the campaign, Truman gave another address highlighting his strong stand against the Soviets while at the same time appealing to Wallace voters concerned by the peril of war. "I had hoped that we would get through this political campaign without the Republican candidate dragging American foreign policy into party politics," he said, disingenuously, before accusing Dewey of dashing that aspiration. "He has seen fit to attack the Democratic Party's record on foreign policy. He has attacked my conduct of foreign affairs in unmeasured terms. He has torn off his mask of bipartisanship and revealed the ugly partisan passion underneath." Again, Truman charged collusion between Dewey, Wallace, and the Communists. He defended the Vinson mission and said that those, like Dewey, who criticized it "have made up their minds that war is inevitable." It all added up to a single conclusion, to the words he wanted to linger in the thoughts of voters going to the polls: "Our foreign policy is safer in Democratic hands than in Republican hands."

On October 30, Dewey, in his closing appeal at Madison Square Garden, with Gloria Swanson and Rube Goldberg showing support, expressed confidence in victory. "The Democratic Party is totally a splintered and divided party. Its own house is divided and at the point of collapse."

The following day, October 31, as many as a million people in Brooklyn lined 80 miles of streets, standing several deep on the sidewalks, to watch Henry Wallace's fifty-car procession parade by. Their votes on Tuesday, Wallace announced in a rally that afternoon, would "determine whether we have war or peace in 1949."

THAT WEEKEND IN Berlin, the Communist newspaper *Tägliche Rundschau* wrote it was certain that Dewey would win. "The elections will put the Republicans into the White House," announced Radio Moscow, adding that the results would "aggravate the crisis in the Democratic Party." In Albany, Dewey's legal counsel, Charles Breitel, and a large staff burned the lights in their Capitol offices late into the night as they pored over heavy, leather-bound volumes of federal statutes and regulations, studied elaborate charts of the executive branch's structure and configuration, and outlined the duties and reach of every agency, board, and commission that they needed to be prepared to stock with loyal Republican functionaries ready to serve after nearly two decades in the wilderness. The head of the United States Secret Service decided he should be in New York for the election rather than Missouri. The reference book *Who's Who* sent its 1949 edition to the printer listing Dewey's address as 1600 Pennsylvania Avenue. For its first election-night coverage on television, NBC News built a large cardboard model of the White House with a tiny treadmill inside that would spin miniature elephants around for the camera once the results had been called. There were no miniature donkeys on hand. "The first post-election question is how the government can get through the next ten weeks," wrote Joseph and Stewart Alsop in their column that would run in newspapers across America on Wednesday morning. "Events will not wait patiently until Thomas E. Dewey officially replaces Harry S

Truman. Particularly in the fields of foreign and defense policy, somebody somewhere in Washington must have authority to give answers that will still be valid after January 20."

Yet, though it is stunning in retrospect, there was almost no discussion in the press during the weeks leading up to the November 2 election about how those foreign policy events might play on voters' minds. Each day, the nation's radio and television news broadcasts, its newspapers' front pages, were split between stories about the swirling crisis in Berlin and the presidential election at home. They were treated as two parallel lines that would never intersect. Stalin's preelection attack on Truman, Clay's triumph at the Al Smith Dinner, the public's fascination with the Airlift, its approval of America's stand in Berlin, and its apprehension over war and the Communist threat were almost never mentioned in any story covering the presidential race. But voters, seeing the articles side by side every day, drew their own conclusions. On Saturday, October 30, newspapers carried accounts, usually above the fold, of Army secretary Royall's announcement the previous day that, for the first time since the end of World War II, the Army was restructuring its operations to a semi-wartime footing. Americans read the news as Harry Truman headed toward his Missouri home to await the verdict of his countrymen.

13

NOVEMBER

"There is nothing poetic about Berlin winters," observed Frank Howley. Perched as far north as Alaska, where the northern European lowlands give way to glacial gashes of cliffs and valleys that march out to the Baltic Sea, Berlin is defenseless against the cold winds that roll across the Russian steppes. And even more than its frigidity, the city in winter has long been notorious for its fogs—deep and enveloping, they swaddle the city for days on end. Indeed, if some poet had been moved to describe Berlin's winters in verse, it would be with words like those that were used in discussions of the subject, there and in Washington, from the first days of the blockade, terms appropriate not to a sonnet, but a dirge.

All through the months of the siege, winter had been the land beyond the edge of the map, the place all feared to even consider. Every challenge the Berliners had met, every obstacle the Airlift had surmounted, was discounted because of the conviction that when November, the traditional start of Berlin's winter, arrived all would be finally and irretrievably lost. So, in July, Forrestal had set a final deadline of October for the American government to make a decision between war and retreat. In September, on the exultant day of the Reichstag rally, Gustav Pietch, a railroad union leader, growled to the crowd, "The blockade has failed—and now the Communists can only wait for the help of General Hunger and Generalissimo Winter," commanders many believed were almost unbeatable. Even in October, Clay had begged for more planes to allow him to stock up on the supplies he knew would not get through once the shroud fell over Berlin. Now November had come. If the Airlift were to flounder, if Berlin's spirit were to fail, this would be the moment. November and December, wrote Howley, would be "the acid test of the airlift."

ON NOVEMBER 1, the fog came in. Conditions were so poor that Tempelhof Airport shut down. The next night, the fog was so bad in Wiesbaden that an Airlift plane, making its second approach as it tried to land, could not see the runway and instead plowed into the ground. Five men died. That night, the fog closed Tempelhof for another ten hours. The sound of descending planes overhead had become such a constant that when, in the dead of night, there was silence, Lucius Clay bolted up awake in bed. "At that time, the word 'Tempelhof' meant deliverance," Hans-Karl Berhrend, then nineteen years old, would recall years later. "When, as sometimes happened because of the weather, the noise of the airplanes suddenly disappeared—that was terrifying. Normally, the roar of airplanes is unwelcome. At that time, it was the exact opposite. When it became silent, we were afraid." Another Berliner remembered the sensation as well. "Suddenly, outside the windows and above the roofs, there is a paralyzing silence. It weighs on one like the silence of a corpse. All at once a whole city is listening to stillness, and in the breasts of hundreds of thousands, terrible uncertainty begins to arise."

They were right to be afraid. On November 1, the Airlift ferried into Berlin less than 6 million pounds for the first time since August 20. By November 3, there was a backlog of thirty-five planes sitting on the runway at Tempelhof. That day, only 4 million pounds of cargo were flown into Berlin, a level not seen since Black Friday, August 13.

It was the middle of the night in Germany when the first returns began to come in from early reporting precincts on the East Coast. The staff of the European edition of *Stars and Stripes* had resolved to work around the clock to put out multiple editions of the Wednesday, November 3 paper as results of the presidential election were released. Each new run of newspapers was distributed to American occupation troops and Airlift crews. They were even flown aboard Skymasters to soldiers stationed in Berlin. There did not seem to be much possibility of a surprise. Each edition carried an article revealing that last-minute public opinion polls from the *Chicago Tribune,* the *Philadelphia Inquirer,* the New York *Daily News,* and the Gallup organization all showed Dewey with significant leads. The first edition's headline was dull, noncommittal: "Nation Storming Polls." By the second edition, results had begun to come in and the banner proclaimed what all expected, "Dewey Has Early Lead." Almost all the states had reported by the time of the third edition, and while Dewey was within a breath of capturing the White House, he was still not there. "Election Race Is Close," read the headline, and the story stated that Dewey had won 24 states and 258 votes in the Electoral College. Truman had 18 states and 227 electoral votes. There were 266 needed to win. "Truman Leads Dewey; Deadlock Is Possibility," shouted the fourth and final edition. Neither candidate had won enough votes. It was possible the election would be thrown to the House of Representatives. Both sides were waiting on Ohio.

It was not until the Thursday-morning edition of *Stars and Stripes* that the men on the Airlift read the news: "TRUMAN WINS."

DEWEY FACED REPORTERS the next day at Republican headquarters at the Roosevelt Hotel. He said he wouldn't run a third time; he did not know what had happened, but did not believe there had been an error in strategy. He assured all that Mrs. Dewey, who was not there, was taking the defeat "fine." It was all bland and unremarkable, predictable. He sounded tentative and stunned. Then he was asked, "Do you think it is essential we continue a bipartisan foreign policy?" Immediately, he grew firm. It was "most essential that we do." He referred to Truman's attacks on him over the last days of the campaign, the accusations that the Republican Party was colluding with the Communists, that only the Democrats could be trusted to stand up to the Soviet threat in Berlin and elsewhere. "The past weekend," he said, somewhat dramatically, considering the era, "was one of the blackest in the recent history of the world."

Dewey slunk off to two weeks in the sun of Tucson. Truman was welcomed back to Washington by one of the largest crowds in the city's history. Expectations were for 200,000, but 750,000 showed up. They sang and cheered as his motorcade passed, sometimes overwhelming the Secret Service and encircling his car. The staff of the *Washington Post* hung a sign outside their building reading, "Welcome Home from the Crow Eaters." As Truman rode by, he threw his head back and laughed.

The following day, he would sign a directive instructing the State Department to begin the negotiations Lovett had postponed for a North Atlantic Treaty to guarantee America would defend Western Europe from Soviet attack.

Four days after the election, Wallace made his first public appearance—at a reception held at the Soviet embassy in honor of the thirty-first anniversary of the Russian Revolution.

IN POPULAR MEMORY, Truman's victory in 1948 is attributed to a "Give 'Em Hell" campaign that emphasized populist economic positions and defended the progress of the New Deal. Dewey's defeat is blamed on an aloof, imperious nature; on vague, platitudinous statements; and on the fact that he looked like "the little man on the wedding cake." All these certainly played a role in the results. But in 1948, had it not been for the Berlin crisis, Thomas Dewey would have been elected president of the United States.

Truman's response to the Berlin blockade—the wildly popular Airlift—transformed his image from an accidental president often seen to be overcome by events to a strong commander in chief taking decisive action at a moment of alarm. His campaign deliberately capitalized on, though it did not encourage, that palpable sense of public dread. "In times of crisis, the American citizen tends to back up his president," Clark Clifford would observe, a truth noticed by a White House for neither the first time nor the last. Clifford's counterpart on Dewey's staff—Elliott Bell—agreed that the Russian threat diminished the Republicans' chances. "The bear got us" was how he put it after the election.

Yet as critical as the Berlin Airlift was to Truman's defeat of Dewey, it was decisive in the other race that was essential to his victory: the battle of Franklin Roosevelt's vice presidents—Truman against Wallace. From the beginning of 1948, the widespread confidence in Republican prospects was predicated on Wallace draining a large number of votes from Truman. If he had ended up with support anywhere near the level polls predicted before the siege of Berlin began, Truman would have lost the election. But all fall Wallace was under withering attack from Democrats for being a Communist tool at a time when war with the Soviets appeared on the horizon.

Confronted by a Soviet Union that had set out to starve millions into submission and bearing witness to Truman's efforts to use American power to save lives while preserving peace, liberal voters blanched at supporting Wallace and returned to Truman's column instead. As Karl Schmidt, the chronicler of Wallace's campaign, wrote, the Berlin Airlift was "the tombstone for Progressive hopes." On election day, Wallace won only 2.5 percent of the vote. Half of his votes, just over 500,000 ballots, came from a single state—New York. Nearly twice that many had come out in Brooklyn alone to see him the Sunday before the election. But the Halloween crowds had proved to be phantom supporters, there for the show, not the man.

Wallace had thrown New York to Dewey. But in California, where in the spring he had been predicted to get 800,000 votes, only 190,000 cast their ballots for him. Truman won the state with a margin of only 18,000 votes. In 1948, Henry Wallace received 1.15 million votes nationally. With only 25,000 more votes—the 18,000 in California and a little over 7,000 in Ohio—the election would have been sent to the House of Representatives. If Wallace had done just a little bit better than that, if he had received another 69,000 votes—a pittance distributed among five states—Dewey would have been elected outright. If Wallace's vote had not collapsed to the extent it did, all of Truman's fiery, folksy speeches from the back of the caboose would have been in vain. And Wallace's vote collapsed—and Truman won the election—because of Berlin.

On November 5, after less than three months of construction, the first plane landed at Tegel Airport. It carried Bill Tunner and ten tons of cheese. Clay and Howley were there to welcome it. The French provided an honor band, which played the "Star-Spangled Banner," "God Save the King," and the "Marseillaise." The runway, 5,500 feet long, was the longest in Europe. It was stronger than the average runway in American airports at the time. It had been built almost entirely by hand, by 17,000 hungry Berliners working day and night.

Within days, the new airport in the French sector was operational. There was, however, one major problem. The two towers of Soviet-controlled Radio Berlin were still standing and in use about 400 yards from the runway, presenting a danger to pilots, particularly in the fog. One was 390 feet tall, the other 260 feet; neither was illuminated, and both lay directly in the Skymasters' flight path.

The successive French governments that autumn were still wary of overly antagonizing the Soviets. They feared the Red Army and faced domestic political pressures as well. On November 11, Communists rioted in Paris, hurling café chairs at police lines along the Champs-Élysées. Yet French commandant Jean Ganeval's relations with Kotikov had ruptured after the Russian had betrayed him by arresting the Stumm police hiding in the French liaison offices during the City Hall riot. Ganeval had sent Kotikov a letter requesting that the Soviets immediately pull down their two radio towers in the French sector. The Americans were offering to pay for the rebuilding of the towers in a different location. He received no response. Ganeval called to make an appointment to see Kotikov on the matter. Kotikov did not return his call. Ganeval then simply showed up at Kotikov's headquarters and asked to see the Russian commandant in person. He was told Kotikov would be unable to see him. This, Ganeval found quite rude.

He wrote Kotikov another letter on November 20. Ganeval told the Russian that he had until December 16 to pull down the towers or action would be taken. As Ganeval had informed Kotikov back in September, he hoped no one would doubt his word.

Shortly after the election, Philip Jessup, the Columbia professor of international law who served as America's primary representative on the United Nations Security Council, ran into Jacob Malik, his Soviet counterpart, outside the council chamber. Malik taunted Jessup about the embarrassment of America's pollsters in predicting Truman's defeat. "Dr. Gallup should transfer his activities to your country," Jessup said, smiling. "It would be much easier for him to predict the results of elections there." The response was classic Jessup: an ironic wink with a touch of iron. Jessup would be criticized by other diplomats for maintaining open communication—even occasional banter—with the Russians in the midst of the Berlin crisis. He failed to realize, Robert Murphy charged, that "Soviet negotiators cannot be influenced by personal friendships." But it was not a friendship that Jessup had established with Malik, it was the possibility of a conversation.

There was little to talk about in November of 1948. The neutral nations on the UN Security Council—and the secretary-general, Trygve Lie—were still trying to develop a middle-ground position that both East and West could embrace. They were discovering such terrain did not exist. In fact, the American position was hardening as time went on.

Jessup had made a highly publicized trip to Berlin in late October. He had spent many hours with Clay, addressed the German people over the radio, and even met with Tunner to review the Airlift's operations. He came back to Paris enormously impressed with what he had seen. He was convinced that, with the Airlift, Berlin could hold out through the winter. Jessup returned from Berlin, Trygve Lie would note, less willing to compromise in order to end the blockade of the city than he had been before he left.

November 12, 1948

Mr. Halvorsen, Lt.

I request you to distribute the attached 12 bags of tiny toy motors to American boys of your native town and hope that they will have much joy on them, just as the Berlin children by your parachute-gifts.

In the enterprise of my brother-in-law, who manufactures the constructive parts, I obtained some by begging. I am sorry to have got no more as in this moment I am unemployed.

Please regard the mail as a sign of my greatfull acknowledgement of your disinterested action.

Yours truly,
Hans Drewemann

Three hundred well-wishers had boarded Truman's train when it arrived at Union Station for his triumphant return to Washington. A band struck up "I'm Just Wild About Harry." A red-haired woman on board tried twice to kiss Truman, but he successfully dodged her both times. James Forrestal was one of those who boarded Truman's train, but he must have realized he was climbing on too late. The former boxer, who still bore a crooked nose as a mark of his youthful rebelliousness, marveled at the upset. "The President sure swung one from the floor this time," he shouted over the tumult. It was Forrestal who felt staggered by the results. He had been asked repeatedly for donations to the Democratic campaign, right up to the days before the election. He sent a contribution of $250, but not until a week after Truman's victory. In the 1948 election, Forrestal, who had made a fortune in the stock market, had bet wrong.

Forrestal, his closest friend Ferdinand Eberstadt noticed over the years, would swing between troughs of despair and peaks of euphoria. But all through 1948, especially after the Berlin blockade began, and particularly after Dewey's defeat ended his chances for remaining in power, Forrestal's mood tumbled in a single direction, ever deeper into a valley of shadows. In one of the most dangerous moments in American history, Forrestal, with more total responsibility for the national defense than any other cabinet member ever before, was losing his last chance to prepare the nation for a war he believed was coming. He asked Eisenhower to return to the Pentagon on a part-time basis to help him address the preparedness crisis. Eisenhower was shocked to find Forrestal suffering from what the general would call, in his diary, a "terrific, almost tragic disappointment." Forrestal was flogging himself mercilessly, noted Eisenhower. "He gives his mind no recess and he works hours that would kill a horse." The day after the president returned to the White House, Forrestal asked for an appointment with Truman. As soon as the election results were known, there had been a daily drip of newspaper articles predicting Forrestal would quickly step down. As Forrestal entered the White House that Saturday, November 6, photographers standing outside the door shouted a request that he pose for pictures. "We're starting another four years, you know?" one yelled. Forrestal replied, "Yes—but not for me."

The news stories were clearly a hint from Truman's advisers that the defense secretary should resign. Forrestal chose to ignore them. He had determined that he would fight for his job. Truman himself was not yet willing to ask him directly to quit. But, perhaps even more than the disloyalty, the president was growing exasperated with his defense secretary's unpredictability. That Saturday in the White House, Forrestal told Truman he wanted to go to Europe to assess the situation in Germany firsthand. He planned to leave in three days.

Were it not for the election, Forrestal would have been in Berlin long before, but it was appropriate he went when he did. Something in him drew Forrestal to places when they were at their most anguished and anxious. It was what brought him to those islands in the Pacific—Iwo Jima and Bikini—at the moments when calamity appeared. It was what took him to Berlin in November when the fog came in and would not leave. Wearing a three-piece tan suit and a wide-brimmed hat, Forrestal waited in the western zone until the pall covering the city lifted enough for him to fly in. Clay was at Tempelhof to greet him and they returned to the general's house for dinner. While they ate, Clay repeated his argument that America had to hold Berlin—even if it meant battling the most severe weather. "If we get out of Berlin under duress," Forrestal recorded Clay as saying, the Soviets "will walk through Europe, and at least gain such power and prestige in France that France will crumble." And if war did come, Clay told Forrestal, he "would not hesitate to use the atomic bomb."

At a news conference before departing from Tempelhof the next morning, Forrestal, surrounded by what the *New York Times* called an "impenetrable fog," tried to provide some inspiration to the men of the Airlift. "I have been deeply impressed with the fine spirit of Airlift personnel in what must be a dreary task," he said, unable to escape the tug of the roiling melancholy waters deep within him. He retreated behind cold rationality. "I have always wanted to see the Airlift and the condition of affairs in Europe. This statistical presentation today was extremely clear that the Airlift is a cyclical development in the use of air transport." He responded to a question about whether he would stay in his position by pointing out it was "a matter to be determined by the President." He served at Truman's pleasure. Or, as he put it, "The date of termination is at his disposal."

WHILE FORRESTAL WAS in Europe, Senator Howard McGrath, the chairman of the Democratic National Committee, was asked how Truman would treat those members of his administration who had exhibited disloyalty during the election. Everyone knew who the question was referring to. "There are some the President can't help but forgive," McGrath answered, focusing on the positive. "I'm sure that he will forgive venial sins."

"Do you mean venial as opposed to mortal sins?" said a reporter.

McGrath agreed with the distinction. He was asked to define what Truman would consider a mortal sin of disloyalty. He said it was one that "kills the soul."

The day Forrestal returned from Europe, Truman was asked directly, at a news conference, whether he would keep his defense secretary on the job. All he could offer was, "I have no comment."

The following day, Forrestal phoned Truman, on vacation in Key West, requesting to brief him immediately. Truman wearily agreed, and Forrestal flew down the next day, November 18. The press speculated, correctly, that the trip had more to do with Forrestal campaigning to keep his job than the need for an immediate discussion of the situation in Berlin.

Forrestal arrived determined and full of brio. But Truman welcomed him with little warmth and did not bother to spend any time speaking alone with his defense chief. Forrestal was wearing a tightly knotted tie among the easygoing, lounging men in Hawaiian shirts; his self-confidence fled and he grew silent, worried, withdrawn. He arrived at 12:30 and joined Truman and his friends in a chicken-à-la-king lunch, and by 3:30 he was already gone. If Truman was expecting Forrestal to respond to the clear suggestions that he quit, he was disappointed. Later that day, the White House press secretary was asked whether Forrestal would stay. He replied, "I don't know what is in Mr. Forrestal's mind."

FORRESTAL REMAINED THE most brilliant and farsighted member of Truman's cabinet—that fall, for instance, concerned that government agencies were not sharing files and information, he proposed a single, centralized department to coordinate the domestic security efforts of the immigration service, Coast Guard, Federal Bureau of Investigation, and others. But his moments of furious activity and deep thinking were now matched with long periods of stultifying lethargy. Papers that needed immediate action languished on Forrestal's desk. He would often stay in his office long into the night, past the time his work was done, unable to bring himself to move. Late one evening, an aide said, "Hadn't you better go home, Mr. Secretary?" Forrestal blinked at him. "Go home? Home to what?"

His wife Jo's erratic behavior had continued to spiral into tempests of rage and loathing fueled by alcohol and mental instability. Earlier that year, at a dinner the Forrestals were hosting in honor of Winston Churchill's son, Randolph, Josephine appeared at the top of the staircase as the guests were milling about and slurred, "Good Lord, what in the world do all of you people have to say to each other?" By the end of the year, she was often gone, traveling to visit friends in sunnier climes, and Forrestal was frequently left alone in the large house in Georgetown. He would ask acquaintances to come over for lonely meals and they would listen to him mutter about the rising power of the Russians. His friends, including Eberstadt, pleaded with him to resign with dignity from an administration that clearly no longer had much use for him, but the loss of office and the loss of peace had become wrapped together in his mind. He saw himself as a lone defender, as all that stood against the onslaught of a horde and war. Without power, he indicated to others, all would be lost.

Three times in the latter part of 1948, an artist hired to paint Forrestal's official portrait almost finished the job only to step back from the canvas and, each time, find that, in spite of his efforts, he had portrayed Forrestal's face as pinched into a pained twist.

In the first week of November, the tonnage carried into Berlin by the Airlift dropped 20 percent from the level of the last week of October. The next week, it dropped 5 percent more. By November 13, the day Forrestal arrived in Berlin, the worst fog in many years descended on the city. The next day, when he held his press conference at Tempelhof, the Airlift was almost completely shut down from 3 A.M. to 9 P.M. It was the worst day of the Airlift since it had gathered steam in July, and the following day, November 15, was even worse—in twenty-four hours, there were only 197 landings in Berlin.

The visibility was so bad that, in western German cities such as Frankfurt, even buses could not run. But though the dire nature of the situation was apparent, the need to keep up morale among the pilots and reassure Americans and Berliners alike about the continuing capabilities of the Airlift led the military leaders to attempt to convince the press that all was well. On November 9, Tunner sent a secret memo to all his base commanders asking them to forbid their officers from expressing personal opinions to reporters who "are interested in the effect of present bad weather on the success of the Airlift." The official line, in case they were asked, was to be "optimistic within reason." Sometimes the effort to head off panic reached preposterous levels. On the day after Forrestal departed, with less than 4 million pounds of supplies arriving daily in Berlin, a city whose siege had lasted nearly five months and convinced millions that the world was on the brink of war, Clay was asked by a reporter whether he believed "a solution of the Berlin crisis can be achieved by the end of this year." He responded, "I don't know what you mean by Berlin crisis. There isn't any crisis that I know of."

In fact, the brume would come sweeping across Berlin's airports so that it looked like what a control operator called a "perpendicular wall of fog." The tower could not see the tarmac. Once, a "missing in action" report was being prepared for a Skymaster. It had landed at Tegel but wandered around lost in the mists for half an hour. When a jeep was sent out to find the plane, it got lost too. Such events happened frequently. Paul Curtis, then nineteen years old, would remember how he and his fellow mechanics would ride out into the fog looking for planes on the apron. They would sit on the hood of a jeep and hold their hands out above them. When they touched a plane's nose, they knew they had found one. One pilot, turning his plane to park it off the runway, was seized by a strange feeling and pulled to a sudden stop. He would discover his plane's nose was seven feet from that of another aircraft.

On November 9, the Navy's own C-54s began to join the Airlift. Tunner was on hand at Rhein-Main to welcome the first crew. It was raining so hard that he would remember the water at the hardstand reaching up to his knees. When the plane door opened, a Navy officer wearing his blue double-breasted dress uniform with a shiny gold braid on the coat and a big gold stripe, poked his head out and asked the wet, frowzled Tunner, "Are we at land or sea?" Tunner laughed: "Why, we ordered this just for you. We wanted the Navy to feel at home." Like all the other pilots arriving in Germany, the Navy fliers were immediately sent off to Berlin with a full load. Making those first flights without any visibility presented a special difficulty—or perhaps was a blessing. "I was just a dumb ensign flying copilot and with the fog I had no idea where we were landing," remembered Alfred Cave. "Then one afternoon the fog lifted a bit as we were coming in. I glanced to my side and saw people looking back at me from fifth floor apartment windows. It was not until then that we realized our approach was down a corridor on both sides with apartment houses. Where we stopped was only a stone's throw from more tall buildings in front of us. It was a revelation." In his spare time, Royal Air Force pilot Lieutenant "Frosty" Winterbottom would draw sketches on the canteen walls poking fun at their situation. One had a frightened crew making an emergency approach into Berlin, guided by a Ground Control Approach (GCA) operator saying, "Hello York 274. Understand you are lost in cloud on three engines, icing up, hydraulics jammed and short of fuel. Visibility here is 800 yards. Cloud base 200 feet. Repeat after me: 'Our Father who art in heaven . . .'"

But if the men of the Airlift prayed for the weather to clear, their entreaties went unanswered. Tunner began to spread the planes out for safety, sending them to Berlin at a pace of every five minutes instead of every three. To load the planes, sacks of coal or flour were passed in human chains where one man's left toe touched up against another man's right heel so they would not lose one another in the fog. Pilots were ordered not to land unless the fog hung at least 200 feet off the ground and there was visibility of 400 yards. Every pilot landing reported just that: "200 feet ceiling—400 yards visibility." One later admitted, "We couldn't even see the bleeding runway."

Amid so much necessity, inventions were born. The Westinghouse Electric Corporation sent forty-two of "the world's brightest lights," filled with krypton gas and flashing with the brilliance of 50 million 60-watt bulbs. A double row of these strobe lights was placed atop the apartment building on the approach to Tempelhof and in the cemetery below. The Soviets used the construction for propaganda purposes. The Americans would "not leave the dead alone," an eastern sector newspaper charged, stating that the lights added to the already heavy damage done to graves being defiled by the "hundreds of children chasing after candies dropped by American pilots." But the innovation worked and was adopted beyond the Airlift. Within a few years, air travelers around the world would become accustomed to the sight of strobes used to guide landing planes to the runway. Another invention would also become a familiar part of air travel: When the beam of his flashlight bounced helplessly against the fog, a young man on the flight line glued colored cones of Plexiglas on top of the lens to create a bright wand with which he could direct the taxiing planes and point the pilots to the right place to park.

Berlin's winters had such a horrible reputation for fog and rain that when the Airlift began, it had been assumed that the flights could not continue in any real numbers into November. Yet for all the pessimism, the weather turned out to be even worse than it had been feared. November of 1948 was not just another foggy month for Berlin. In only 63 of the month's 720 hours—9 percent—were conditions good enough for pilots to fly by visual flight rules. The amount of cargo lifted that month was the lowest it had been since July—back before the arrival of Tunner's organization and the additional Skymasters. By the middle of November, just when clear skies mattered more than at any moment in Berlin's history, meteorologists had made a stunning determination: 1948 was to be the foggiest winter since the 1860s.

The legendary Hatfield and McCoy feud came to an official end on its 67th anniversary yesterday when two survivors of the original families shook hands amid popping flashbulbs and corks from bottles of corn whiskey, but no gunfire," reported the United Press on November 8. Paul McCoy and Miss Toney Terry Hatfield shook hands and "the two then sent a telegram to Premier Joseph Stalin asking him to 'shake hands with the rest of the world and lift the Berlin blockade.'"

For the first time since the darkest years of World War II, there was no Nobel Peace Prize awarded for 1948. It did not seem appropriate. But that November, the Nobel Prize in Literature went to T. S. Eliot. In Berlin, this seemed fitting; the open question was whether the blockade would end with a bang or a whimper.

In a survey that month, three out of four Berliners agreed that the confrontation over the blockade was "serious enough to cause a war in the near future." For many, at least in the moments when their nerves gave way, a final conflagration seemed to hold out relief, a better alternative than listening anxiously for the whir of the Skymasters overhead or watching the planes sit for entire days on the runway at Tempelhof waiting for the fog to break. "It's a little bit like the last months of the war. You kept on doing what you were supposed to, but you knew it was hopeless," a west Berliner, sitting in his overcoat in his frigid office, told a reporter that month. "I'm not a defeatist, but when I ask myself how we're going to get through this winter, I just don't know." If the end was coming anyway, some reasoned, it would be easier if it came quickly. "To be living here among the ruins seems equivalent to already be lying in one's own coffin," wrote the poet Gottfried Benn in a letter to a friend.

The Berliners had most every imaginable reason to lose hope. In the years since the end of the war, their city had been beset by blow after blow—cold, hunger, rape, black markets, destruction of their homes, a disintegration of order, rampant crime, a pervasive sense of despondency. Now, surrounded, besieged, with winter having arrived, with their only possibility of deliverance blocked by the gray haze that hung over the city, they found their situation had grown even worse.

The days were growing shorter. By 4 P.M., even without the fog, the sun would begin to set. By six, when the public transportation shut down for the night, Berlin—a city almost completely without working streetlights—was nearly pitch black. Before the war, there had been more than 4,000 taxicabs in Berlin. Now there was not one. In the hours before they stopped running, the trams were packed an average of 40 percent beyond their maximum capacity. Those Berliners who did not manage to cram themselves on board in time trudged home in an enveloping gloom.

When they reached their small, crowded, often ruined apartments, their situation did not brighten. With candles a rarity, they would feel their way around the room to find a chair to sit on. And then they would wait. When the two hours of electricity for the night began, neighborhoods would spring to life, busier at three in the morning than they had been in the early evening. Housewives would heat up water and place it in thermoses so their husbands could better shave the next morning. They would iron their husband's one shirt so that he could look proper and presentable when he left for work. It was an entire city of people trying to fool one another, pretending that life was all right.

But no one was deceived. Men would still not leave the house without a hat, but it would be tatty and ill-fitting. Women wore patches on their dresses. The children who had scampered about the city on bare feet in June found it less comfortable to do so in November. When each flight's cargo was precious, few supplies other than the most essential made it into Berlin. In the last five months of 1947, more than 14,000 blankets and more than 4,000 towels had been brought to the city. In the same period a year later, there were less than 2,000 blankets and a total of 70 towels to fill the needs of the entire city. There was not a single new blouse or pair of socks or raincoat for Berlin. The city's hospitals did not have enough diapers for sick children. They used paper to band-age wounds. They went without any painkillers, even for those recovering from surgery. The hospitals had five hours of electricity a day. For emergency surgeries, they had to make a special request of power from the central plant to turn on the lights. Almost everything else a city of two and a quarter million people required was put on hold so that the Airlift could bring food to alleviate the hunger and coal to fend off the cold.

And yet it was not enough, not even close. In Berlin they joked, "I can't freeze. I'm shivering too much." A family's entire coal ration for that winter could be carried in a single paper shopping bag. That same winter, residents of southern Britain, a much warmer climate, received a ration of coal thirty-four times as large. At night, a cold wind would whip its way through the ruins, dragging the thermometer down below 20 degrees, shrieking as it pushed aside the soiled rags and cardboard wedges that had covered up the broken apartment windows. Inside, Berliners sat, bundled up, exhaling frost like puffs of smoke from a train. "When we go to bed we dress as if heading for an expedition to Greenland," wrote Ruth Andreas-Friedrich in her diary. When water splashed on the wall above the sink, it would freeze on contact and stay as ice for months.

It was so cold that even in the warmest places, the relatively well-provided-for offices of the American military government, workers brought blankets and quilts to wrap around themselves during the day. Robert Murphy cabled Marshall in November requesting that the Foreign Service diplomats working in Berlin during the blockade receive hardship pay, as if they had been posted to a dusty consulate in the bush. "Although we cannot complain of inadequate housing accommodations, our fuel and light are certainly inadequate, our former cultural and recreational facilities have been greatly restricted, our transportation has likewise been severely curtailed and private cars are allowed only five gallons of gasoline per month. As to geographic isolation, this factor is too well known to require additional comment."

The Americans set up 180 "warming centers" around Berlin in shuttered restaurants, air-raid shelters, and barracks. These heated rooms were open from 10 A.M. to 8 P.M. and offered reading material, sewing classes, and entertainment—along with heat—but they could accommodate a total of only 36,000 Berliners at a time. Instead, Berliners resorted to any means they could think of to stay warm. The city, which had been so proud of its awning of boughs before the war, decided it had no choice but to cut down half of its remaining trees. Berliners would feed pages of their family Bible into potbelly stoves. One woman burned old love letters, saying she preferred the brief warmth of a fire to the words of her old flame.

While they shivered, they also starved. Clay had promised to increase the official ration so that the average daily distribution that November would be a quarter of a stick of margarine, a two-ounce slice of Spam, six tablespoons of Pom or flour, four tablespoons of noodles, an ounce of sugar, and six slices of bread. But this promise had been too ambitious to actually fulfill. Even when it had been made, at the end of October, the Airlift was not hitting its minimum levels, and of course November was so much worse. Berliners would line up in front of butcher shops at four in the morning to get a bowl of hot broth made from boiled bones. Sometimes the stores carried only Pom or cabbage for days on end. Frostbitten apples were being sold on the black markets. To entice customers with nothing to spend to come into stores with nothing to sell, shopkeepers would put cardboard hams on display in the window. Cafés remained open, but regulations stated that one pound of coffee had to be spread among 50 cups. The brew was so watery that Berliners dubbed it "flower coffee," because, while drinking it, they could see the floral pattern on the bottom of the china cup.

After more than three years of misery, Berliners, now pressed to their limit, turned desperate. When a plane crashed approaching the British Gatow Airport in Berlin that winter, killing all on board, Germans picked through the wreckage, gathering coffee beans scattered through the debris one by one. They built small fires, cooked the topsoil in pans, and with a sieve drained out useful lard that had seeped into the dirt. At Tempelhof, when bags of Pom spilled some of their contents while being unloaded, German workers would stuff the dehydrated potatoes into their mouths, giving themselves horrible cramps when the uncooked flakes expanded in their stomachs. After the third worker was taken away from Tempelhof in an ambulance, the American corporal overseeing the unloaders told them they could put all the flakes they could grab in their pockets and take them home as long as they did not eat them raw.

By November, industrial production had dropped by 80 percent from its levels before the blockade. Nearly 16,000 factories shut down or had drastically limited schedules. Hungry workers would stare at the same piece of paper for minutes on end, trying to make sense of—or even remember—the simple task before them. Schools became optional, because there was not enough heating to keep them warm. Inge Gross would remember sitting in those cold classrooms: "We had trouble concentrating and our reactions were slow. The simplest math problems seemed like advanced calculus. We had trouble staying awake." The toll extended far beyond a lack of focus. As the winter went on, though the allied and German authorities made every effort to hide the truth and cover up the numbers by pointing to other maladies, dozens of Berliners began to be found dead of starvation.

The purpose of the blockade, however, was not to kill the Berliners, nor even to inflict physical pain. What the Soviets were counting on, the one element they needed for the siege to work, was a psychological breakdown in the city. Berliners would not give in and rise up against the allies just because of hunger. They would, the Russians knew, do so only because of fear and despair. That November, with fog encasing the city in misery, Berliners began to give in to the dejection. Two out of five Berliners said they were completely unable to bathe or shower. More than two-thirds of Berliners said their dirtiness led to feelings of inferiority and irritability. But it was nothing compared with the tricks hunger played on their minds. Reality became warped into a twisted convulsion of paranoia. The hungrier they became, the less the Berliners trusted even those closest to them. Families would find themselves arguing viciously about whether one of them had received a thicker slice of stale bread. Children and parents would keep their rations separate from one another, with the awful suspicion that someone was going to eat their food.

The blockade had made Berlin's terrible situation immeasurably worse. The Airlift was grounded as an operation that could provide anything near what the city required. The winter, so dreaded since the blockade's beginning, had arrived with a vengeance unseen in nearly a century. By any measurement of logic, by any analysis of the German capital's history, by any examination of its people's clearly expressed attitudes, this was the moment when Berlin would fold.

AND YET . . .

In later years, Berliners would look back on that winter and remember the hardship—the hunger, the lethargy, the freeze, and the deprivation. But they would also remember those months at the end of 1948 as among the most special of their entire lives, as a time when they treasured the small pleasures of life, rejoiced in the company of their family, celebrated a spirit of fellowship, and drew together in community tighter than they ever had before and ever would again.

"In the evening we sat together in a group with several people who lived in the same building," recalled a sixty-one-year-old man just three years after that winter. "Jokes and songs always came into their own, and the Airlift planes roaring through the night sang the bass in perfect time. . . . We would stay together cheerfully until almost eleven o'clock. The tiny light in the radio, which was already turned on, lighted up punctually, and all sharperned their ears to hear the evening broadcast. The electric light shone wonderfully bright, even though we had only half the bulbs on for the sake of economy. The candle, of which we were so proud, was blown out with huge puffs, and the evening magic was over." Berliners came to cherish those hours in the middle of a jet-black night when the lights came on. They would go to movie theaters, which showed all they could of a film in the two hours of electricity available. Some would heat up a brick and watch the movie with it wrapped up in their overcoat. A once-stylish shop held a late-night fashion show where six models paraded in low-cut gowns before an overflowing crowd bundled in their heaviest coats. When the two hours were up and the lights went out, the show went on by candlelight. The ticket price for Berlin's cabarets amounted to about one-tenth of an average couple's earnings for the month, but the seats at the Kabaretta Komica were filled every night. Comedian Walter Gross found the audiences receptive that winter: "They applauded like crazy. They wanted to keep warm."

Berliners, despite all their privations, kept five daily newspapers going and listened avidly when the radio came on. "RIAS was our daily food" was how Herbert Krüger, then a young boy, would put it nearly sixty years later. Eight out of ten Berliners listened regularly to the station. Every morning, RIAS would announce the tonnage figure of the previous day. That September, they had, appropriately, broadcast a radio version of George Orwell's *Animal Farm*. One popular program simply read off the names and descriptions of missing persons being sought by family members since the end of the war. The theme song of another show looked forward to the day "when the lights are on and the trains are moving." Satirist S. S. von Várady's defiant broadcasts were especially beloved. He began each of his five-minute spots with the Berlin Philharmonic's stirring rendition of "Who's Afraid of the Big Bad Wolf?"

THE BERLINERS DID not fold under the pressure of the blockade. Instead, that pressure, a pressure of incomprehensible force, transformed them into something beautiful and pure and able to withstand the hardest blows. Clay had been convinced, since he first came to Germany, that he "could not hope to develop democracy on a starvation diet." So the Americans, for the three years since the war, had tried to feed the German people. They did it without any demonstration that they actually cared about what happened to their defeated enemy. Clay crowed he "had no desire to do things because it was for their good." And for those three years the attitudes about democracy among Berliners, the people who had heiled and fought for Hitler, had barely budged. Every time they were asked, they had replied, by wide margins, that if forced to choose, they would pick economic security without liberty over freedom and democracy with hunger. The month the siege began, they had repeated their verdict: 61 to 34. In November, when the decision was not abstract but real in a way that no one could have ever guessed it would be, they were asked the question again. For the first time since the end of World War II, perhaps for the first time in the seven-hundred-year history of Berlin, their attitude had changed. Berliners now chose "free elections, free speech, a free press, and freedom of religion" over "economic security and good employment opportunities" by 54 to 40.

Clay and the other Americans had been wrong. A commitment to democracy had come to Berlin—a devotion so fierce it would awe those who took its comforts for granted—at precisely the city's most trying moment. The years of effort in trying to revive Berlin's economy had not only failed, they had failed to lead Berliners to embrace the ideas of freedom. What had been needed was an experience of metamorphosis, a common endeavor to bring the victors and vanquished together, and—most of all—a touch of humanity and kindness.

The Airlift fed and warmed Berlin as much as it could, but Berliners might well have buckled that winter if the endeavor had been only a movement of machines in the sky with the aim of maintaining America's options in a strategic outpost. Instead, Hal Halvorsen's candy drops had been a catalyst that had transformed the character of the Airlift and the way Berliners thought about it. He had "really started something," the *New York Times* wrote on the last day of October, which was more true than they knew. Halvorsen was "the one person who won the hearts of the Berliners—adults and children alike," wrote Inge Gross, who was fourteen at the time. As he came to represent the Airlift and America to the Berliners, through him America became a country that cared enough about the defeated Germans to, in those months of strain, deliver candy to children—an act without any ancillary benefit or ulterior motive, a gift of plain compassion.

And while, to him, kindness may have been its own reward, the candy drops—and the Airlift in general—paid dividends that changed the psychology of the German capital. A fifteen-year-old girl wrote during the Airlift that it reminded her "that in this world there are higher things than national egoism—namely humanity and the existence of all peoples in human dignity." Berliners came to feel they had to live up to the faith the world was putting in them. Three years after the blockade ended, the West Berlin evening newspaper *Der Abend* asked its readers to answer the question "What do you remember about the blockade?" Results poured in. A stonemason wrote that the "people who for a long time had been opposed to us in battle suddenly stood at our sides as if they were our own brothers." Another Berliner found it a wonder that "things turned out in a way that nobody could easily believe. The enemies of yesterday became the friends of today." A laborer recalled, "Early in the morning, when we woke up, the first thing we did was listen to see whether the noise of aircraft engines could be heard. That gave us the certainty that we were not alone, that the whole civilized world took part in the fight for Berlin's freedom." So the Berliners resolved not to "betray the Airlift pilots who were helping us without interruption, trusting in our steadfast behavior." Despite their troubles, they were unbowed. "I walked proudly through the streets," wrote another. "I was helping to write a proud page in the history of Berlin's housewives."

It is easy to dismiss the psychological impact of Halvorsen and even the Airlift as mere sentimentality. But something real happened in Berlin that winter of the blockade—the mind-set of Berliners changed dramatically—and it had real consequences. In July, when they thought the blockade was only, could only be, temporary, 43 percent of Berliners in the western sectors said they would leave the city if they could. By October, with winter approaching, war a real possibility, their city splintering, the number had dropped by a third. In the years after the war, Berlin had become "Crime Capital of the World"—it was racked with gang warfare, violent robberies, and brutal murders. But as the blockade wore on, as Berliners should have, by all rights, grown more desperate, crime began to drop. Indeed, it plummeted. Overall, crime rates fell by 20 to 30 percent during the blockade. There were 39 percent fewer robberies in 1948 than there had been the year before. Berliners were assigned plots of land to cultivate, tiny strips of soil where they could plant a few vegetables. "It is one of the most inspiring phenomena of the present time," observed a *Christian Science Monitor* reporter that November, "that not a single leaf of lettuce, not a single cabbage head, is taken by strangers from these unprotected beds." Crime fell so far, so fast that dire winter that the place that had been "Crime Capital of the World" only a year earlier now had the lowest crime rates of any big city in the Western world.

But it was not just the Berliners that had been transformed. The attitudes of the Americans had changed as well. They had come to Berlin determined to punish the Germans so that they would never turn to totalitarianism again. Yet neither harsh reprisals nor detached efforts at providing for Germans' well-being and security had done much to foster devotion to the principles of democracy. Halvorsen, intuitively, had understood that the way to change Berliners' outlooks was to treat them as people, not as pawns in a global chess match. Without intending to, without even knowing it, Halvorsen had provided a lesson to the eminent foreign policy experts and imposing generals in Washington. The Cold War was a new kind of war, one that would be fought and won not primarily with bullets and armaments but with ideas and appeals; it would be waged, for the most part, not by great powers battling over territory but by a competition for the affections and convictions of people on every continent. Hal Halvorsen and the Airlift had showed that in a new type of conflict there was a different use for armed might, that for democracy to take root it required a change in minds and hearts more than in economic conditions, that America's strength was not just military muscle but an undisputedly moral voice.

All during those months of the blockade there were some—John Foster Dulles, Omar Bradley, Curtis LeMay, Walter Bedell Smith—who could never see the Airlift and the candy drops as anything other than humanitarian relief efforts, charitable aid that was at best a distraction from the real work of diplomacy or arms. Once Clay, Howley, perhaps even Truman himself would have seen things similarly. But they had changed. One winter day, Marjorie Clay was being driven through Berlin when her car passed a girl who was walking in the cold with only tattered strips of leather on her feet. She told her driver to pull over and beckoned for the young woman to approach. Mrs. Clay traced the girl's feet on a piece of paper and, without identifying who she was, told her to come that afternoon to a certain address in the leafy district of Zehlendorf. The girl trudged to the address to find it was a big three-story house, surrounded by poplar and beech trees, with a sloping roof leading down to ivy-covered walls. At the door, waiting for her, were two pairs of shoes and several secondhand dresses. She was overcome with happiness, and when she learned that the stately woman with deep-blue eyes who had knelt in the cold to trace her dirty feet had been the wife of the general who commanded the armies that had conquered and now ruled her nation, she gasped and nearly fainted. Asked about the story by a reporter, Marjorie Clay smiled. "My husband says this is the best way to defeat Communism." It was America's "unselfish devotion in helping the Germans," she continued, that had "shown them the meaning of a real democracy."

Hal Halvorsen had started out as one man. The Berliners—the children and then the adults—called him "the Candy Bomber." But his spirit and example had proved catching. Other pilots joined in and looked at their mission in Germany in a different way. Clay and Howley came to regard the people they ruled over with great affection instead of cold detachment. In Washington, the hard-nosed, practical men in the Pentagon and the State Department, the foreign policy theorists who had thought deeply about the affairs of nations, learned that simple acts of human kindness could unleash powerful forces. As the Airlift went on, they all became Candy Bombers.

November 13, 1948

Angel from the Heavens,

You have given us a great joy: today my father watched a Skymaster, which a small parachute of pocket-handkerchief with a piece of chocolate cast down. He picked it up and brought it to us. We were very joyful because we have eaten long time no chocolate.

We think always of this, that the American pilots bring a great offering for our town and our life.

The best respects and thanks to all the men of the Skymaster from Uta Ryll, thirteen years old.

It was one thing to pledge fealty to democracy in public opinion surveys or in response to the questions of American newspapermen, but still another to actually embrace it in practice, especially when the very act of voting brought with it the possibility of danger. Berlin's municipal elections—the second election since the end of the war—were scheduled for December 5. The first, in 1946, had—by setting in motion the events that resulted in Ernst Reuter's selection as mayor being vetoed by the Soviets—contributed to the breakdown of the harmony between the occupying powers. These new elections, under much more trying circumstances, would test whether Berliners would risk everything for the freedom to cast a ballot.

Early on, the Soviets decided they would not participate in the election. As they were at that moment in the process of attempting to starve three-quarters of the city's population into submission, it was, from their standpoint, a wise decision. Kotikov had announced on October 20 that the Soviet sector would not take part in the balloting because of "terrorism, political persecution, and Fascist war propaganda" coming from the West. While they knew that, particularly given the circumstances, the Communists would not have won many votes, the Russians also realized that a massive turnout in the western sectors would buoy the wintertime morale they were seeking to undermine. On the other hand, if Berliners stayed home, it would send a signal to the world that it was time for the Western allies to withdraw and end the suffering in the capital.

To convince the Berliners to sit the election out, the Russians worked to sow fear and distrust in the western sectors, to convince the Germans of the evil of America and the West. Communist newspapers carried appeals to the Berliners: "HOUSEWIVES IN THE WEST! Do you want to indicate by voting that you approve of the present conditions? Do you want people to think that you are satisfied with electricity rationing, with the tiny gas ration, with the dark and cold homes into which the rain still comes, with the eternal canned food, and with all the difficulties brought on by the West marks? On December 5, get even with those who want to split Berlin. Don't vote." The Russians attacked the Airlift itself. The Soviet-sector *Berliner Illustrierte Zeitung* ran a two-page photo spread showing Western bombers dropping a barrage on Berlin and dead Germans lying in the street. The caption read, "Five years ago, November 23, 1943, the Berlin air bridge began." A preelection pamphlet distributed by the Russians claimed, "Yesterday phosphorus, today raisins, tomorrow atom bombs." The Soviet-sector radio stations played a jingle:

> *Don't be lured by promises sweet.*
> *Think of the dried potatoes you've had to eat.*
> *Think of all the cut down trees*
> *And the dark, cold rooms in which you freeze.*
> *Don't vote for the candidates, like a dunce,*
> *Whose parties have already betrayed you once.*

"Whoever votes, votes for the splitting of Berlin," the Communists claimed, and in this they were correct. By going forward with elections in the West that were not recognized in the East, Berliners would be creating a situation where their city had two governments. Already this had been slowly happening. It had begun with the police department and its split into the Markgraf and Stumm forces. Other departments in the municipal structure had also been fragmented. The City Assembly was meeting in the west while a rump group carried on sessions at City Hall in the east. In mid-November, the fire department broke apart, and the French arrested its Communist chief for attempting to move western sector firetrucks over the boundary. But there was still officially one government for all of Berlin. Acting Mayor Ferdinand Friedensburg still went to his City Hall office every day—even though since October he had been subject to arrest on Soviet charges of "fascist provocation" for his speech at the Reichstag rally. On November 17, the Communist *Tägliche Rundschau* listed the consequences if there were two governments for Berlin—one recognized by the allies, the other by the Soviets. Those in the west who worked in the east would be unable to travel back and forth for their jobs. Gas lines, water mains, and sewers would shut down while they were being rebuilt to run no farther than the new border. Telephone and mail services would be interrupted. Criminals would run loose by crossing over city lines. Even more than the practical impact was the psychic meaning of sundering a once proud center of civilization. As one Communist city councilor put it, "Berlin, after the elections, will as surely be divided as if there were two cities instead of one."

THE WEEK OF Thanksgiving, the fog broke, and as if it had been a dam holding back the energies of the Airlift, there was a flood of supplies flown into Berlin. With the new planes that Truman had authorized in October now having arrived, the Airlift carried record levels of cargo. On Thanksgiving Day, November 25, the mobile canteens on the runway at Tempelhof served turkey to the pilots as they waited the few minutes for their freight to be unloaded. Then they were on their way. That day, for only the second time since the Airlift had begun, more than 12 million pounds of supplies were flown to Berlin. "Never anywhere, at any time, have Americans more to be thankful for than those of us privileged to serve in Germany today," said Clay in his Thanksgiving message to his troops.

That weekend, Clay announced that the Airlift had overcome the worst of the winter fog. November had been so bad—so much worse than anyone could have predicted—that he could be excused for thinking that the bright skies of Thanksgiving meant that the trial was over. As if on cue, the skies over Berlin darkened. Before midnight that Friday, the fog rolled in like an oncoming freight train. And it did not lift.

At the end of what had been the foggiest month in Berlin in eighty years came the worst fog to hit Europe ever recorded. It stretched from Manchester to Warsaw and from Stockholm to Milan. In Paris, pedestrians could not see 30 yards in front of them. Sailors on board the *Queen Elizabeth,* stuck in port because of fog since the middle of the month, could not even see the end of the gangplank. In London, a train accident killed twenty-one people. Nine ships went aground on the coast of Norway. Airports shut down from Dublin to Prague. On November 30, the last day of the month, the Airlift came to a virtual stop.

MORE THAN ANYTHING the Soviets could have said or done, the fog—which dragged on longer than anyone had ever experienced—scared the people of west Berlin. And as if to capitalize on that terror, the Russians chose this moment to seize the initiative. Rather than wait for the elections to go forward, that foggy November 30 they brought the coup that Berliners had long expected. In a hastily called convention at the Admiral's Palace, a theater that usually showcased musical comedies, Communist delegates unanimously elected a new regime for the city and called on the current government to disband. Fritz Ebert, the fat, short, bald, bland son of the first president of Weimar Germany, was chosen as the new mayor of Berlin. He declared the upcoming elections "have hereby become null and void" and promised that his government would hold its own elections at some future date. In one of the opera house's boxes, fifteen Russian officials looked on. Outside, on Babelplatz, where the Nazi youth had undulated around a fire of crackling books, a crowd of 100,000 held signs aloft in the fog. "Whoever Voted for Hitler Voted for War—Whoever Votes Now Votes for War," read one slogan. "Boycott the Election of the City Splitters," read another. When Ebert came out to speak to them, the fog was so thick that most in the square could not even see him.

Berlin was now formally divided. There were two governments—each claiming sovereignty over the entire city, each having power over only half. The allies were outraged. Clay called Ebert "worthless." Ganeval—with withering Gallic disdain—called the attempted coup "the most stupid putsch ever made." The next morning, when Acting Mayor Friedensburg attempted to enter City Hall, police guards informed him he had been barred from the building by Ebert, Berlin's "new Lord Mayor." He walked away muttering "usurper" under his breath. It fell to Howley to assure Berliners that the elections scheduled for that coming Sunday in the western sectors would go on and that "democratic rights and liberties will be safeguarded."

Not all were as sanguine about the upcoming balloting as Howley was. At the end of November, Marshall cabled Robert Murphy expressing grave doubts about whether the election should go forward. It was not the right time for partisan politicking in Berlin, he told his chief diplomat in Germany. The campaigning would merely exacerbate the tensions in the city and—he wrote a few days before the coup—it would permanently split Berlin.

Murphy waited two days to respond to his boss, but he still had not cooled down. If the Americans canceled the election, he wrote, it would earn them "richly deserved contempt not only of German population but of Russians themselves who would see in it confession of weakness which they would exploit to the full." Piqued, he continued that "in my opinion, if we are to go to that extent to appease Soviet authorities, it would be better to immediately announce our withdrawal from the city of Berlin."

Marshall still did not understand what was truly at stake in Berlin and what the stand there had come to mean to people who were watching closely in distant nations. The elections, Murphy explained to him, "have become for Berliners and Germans in general, more and more with every Soviet effort to stop them, an eagerly awaited opportunity to show the world by the volume of their vote which side they stand on, and have become for much of West world, in spite of all anti-German feelings, a demonstration of free men's determination to defend their freedom."

Murphy would not, he told the secretary of state, show Marshall's telegram to Clay or even tell him that Marshall was "entertaining such a notion unless you instruct me specifically do so because I think it will elicit some explosive reaction and there would be justified criticism of last-minute vacillation and lack of courage." It was about as hard a charge as one could lay at the feet of the revered Marshall. But even a diplomat like Murphy could be excused for cracking under the strain. At midnight on the last day of November, the day of the coup, Berlin had been enshrouded in fog for ninety-nine hours. That day, a total of ten planes made it through to the city, carrying the least supplies of any day since that first makeshift day of flights in June. And the elections were only five days away.

14

DECEMBER

The new government of East Berlin went to work immediately. On its third day in power, a reporter from West Berlin, poking around on the other side of the border, was seized by one of Markgraf's police. He asked what his crime had been. The officer pointed at the reporter's mouth. "Chewing gum is American. It is now against the law here."

That same week, the man who had introduced chewing gum to so many Berliners, who had made it a political statement, received a surprise of his own. Halvorsen had landed at Rhein-Main when, once again, an officer was waiting for him on the flight line. Again, he wondered if he had done something wrong.

"Halvorsen, jump in the jeep—I want to show you something," the officer said. They drove out to the base's railway spur. There, a boxcar was being guarded by heavily armed soldiers. Halvorsen wondered who the prisoner was. "Who have you got in the car?" he asked.

"It isn't who, it's what," replied the officer. He said the boxcar was full of chocolate bars, candy, and gum, "almost enough stuff to buy King Ludwig's castle on the black market." Halvorsen stood silent in shock. The officer continued on. "Three and a half tons of candy. From some guy named Swersey in New York."

ANDREI CHERNY

HALVORSEN HAD NOT thought much about his answer when, over dinner in New York, he had told Swersey, the man from Huyler's Candy, that he could distribute up to three tons of candy. And in the months since, as donations came in from across America, a big shipment of candy became less vital. The Candy Bombers were dropping about all the chocolate and lollipops and gum they could handle. Other Airlift pilots were constantly chipping in as well. By mid-November, the post exchange at the Wiesbaden base was chronically out of Hershey and Nestlé bars. But now Halvorsen had 7,000 pounds of candy all at once; a few days later, a similar shipment of 6,000 pounds arrived in another railroad car. Swersey and his boss, Harry King, had collected donations from all the major confectioners in America; Clay had arranged for their delivery through the Pentagon.

Halvorsen had no idea what to do with so much candy. It was far too much to shower on Berlin through the normal parachute drops. But another pilot had a suggestion: "It's almost Christmas. Let's give them a Christmas party."

After more than a hundred hours, the fog that had engulfed all of Europe temporarily lifted on December 1. That day it began to snow. It was only a light dusting, but it was taken as a sign of what was to come in Berlin's winter, and it was seen, by the pessimists, as a symbol of the mounting odds against the Airlift's continuing success. As such, it could not have come at a worse time. What was unknown in the December 5 election was not the results, but the turnout: How many Berliners would take the proactive step of casting a ballot, of showing their fidelity to democracy? The press, as it is wont to do, set the expectations. If 80 percent of Berliners voted, every major paper determined, it would be a sign that they were willing to stand up for the allies despite all the hardships of the blockade. "If, on the other hand, only 70 or 60 percent go to the polls," wrote Ferdinand Kuhn, the correspondent for the *Washington Post,* "Moscow will conclude that the people of Berlin have begun to lose faith in the West, have decided not to expose themselves to possible Soviet reprisals, and have started to reconcile themselves to eventual Soviet control."

In the days leading up to the December 5 election, the Soviets used every means of blandishment and intimidation they could muster to convince Berliners to stay away from the polls. West Berlin housewives received form letters—addressed "Dear Neighbor"—that reminded them they should take up the "generous offer" of the Soviets to provide them with food. Few Berliners had accepted the Soviet ration cards since they were offered in July, but in that first week of December, the Russians kept improving their offer. On December 2, they offered nearly a ton of coal to each household. The next day, it was unlimited amounts of electricity. The Soviets announced they would cut income taxes by one-third. They promised up to 350,000 Christmas trees for those who signed up for their card. And they offered each school-age child half a pound of candy.

It still did not take. So the Russians turned to fear. "If you vote on the 5th, you vote for war," went a frequently heard Communist slogan. Sometimes the propaganda was tone-deaf. Western sector election placards were pasted over with Soviet posters. One had a picture of the aftermath of an Allied air raid, and read, "Whoever elects the warmongers votes for the return of nights of bombing." But American planes flying overhead and making drops now had a different meaning to Berliners.

Other aspects of the Soviet campaign were more nimble and displayed a greater understanding of how the blockade and the Airlift had changed Berlin. On December 3, East Berlin's *Neues Deutschland*'s headline was "Washington Dissatisfied with General Clay." The story said that his dismissal was imminent. It was a claim pitched to further undermine Berliners' sense of security. The American general, once a symbol of oppression and occupation, had become a source of confidence. The following day, the Soviets went even further. The *Tägliche Rundschau* asserted that "West Powers Want to Leave Berlin in January."

Clay and Howley already knew, it wrote, but were trying to cover up the truth. For years, since long before the blockade, the Soviets had been claiming the Americans were about to retreat from Berlin. But as the election approached, the accusation carried special weight. Handbills with big black lettering appeared on commuter trains: "Stay away from the polls. Don't endanger your future." The danger being raised was now personal more than political. If—or rather *when,* insisted the Communist newspapers with a growing vehemence that seemed plausible in the days of snow and fog—the allies quit Berlin, those who had participated in the election would be publicly recorded as having opposed the Soviets. Placards pasted on walls near the Brandenburg Gate eschewed all subtlety: "Those who vote will be duly noted."

RUMORS SPREAD THROUGH the city of Soviet heavy artillery and troop regiments massing on the outskirts of Berlin, of Markgraf police being armed with machine guns, of Wehrmacht veterans being trained in the tactics of street combat. When Howley assured West Berlin's leaders that there were enough American troops on hand to protect them, he was accused by the Communists of fomenting a civil war and using the Airlift to stock Berlin with weapons. "Propaganda poppycock," Howley responded. "Western Berliners know what happened in Prague," he said, "and some are fearful. However, we have plenty of soldiers to ensure that no such smash play can be made here by the Russians using armed German Communists. Berlin's December 5 election will be an election of ballots and not bullets."

But though the campaign would not be waged with arms, it did not lack for fists. In the first few days of December, gangs of hundreds of Communist thugs roamed the fog-streaked streets of West Berlin, searching for election rallies. When they came upon one, they would heckle the speakers, throw stink bombs, and loudly chant their slogans. Before long, the shoving would start, a punch would be thrown, and a general melee would begin. Reuter began to welcome the appearance of the teams of agitators at his rallies. "We know who our foe is," he would say as the Communists dove into the crowd, "but he does not know how tough we are." The fights came to have a kabuki quality. A cordon of brawny trade unionists would be waiting for the East Berliners. Their clash would ensue and, when they were done, both sides—the bullies and the bouncers—repaired to have their wounds treated at first-aid stations set up in advance outside of the hall.

THAT WEEK OF the election the fog was again so thick that only a trickle of Airlift planes made it through the corridors. Clay, in Frankfurt for meetings, had been waiting for days to get back to Berlin. It was crucial that he be back in the city for the election, he told Tunner: "We must let the flag be seen." His absence was only offering support to Soviet charges that he was about to leave Berlin. Tunner said it was far too dangerous for him to fly, but Clay persisted. With no other choice, Tunner approved the flight as long as Clay signed a waiver releasing the Air Force from responsibility if the worst occurred.

They waited for the slightest break in the fog. It finally came at 2 A.M. on December 4, the day before the election. Clay, his wife, Robert Murphy, and a couple of others were driven to Rhein-Main. A jeep brought them through the mist until they came upon a plane having ice scraped violently off its wings. The crew invited Mrs. Clay to sit in the cabin so she would be more comfortable. Everyone else sat in bucket seats in the cargo hold. Clay tried to sleep; Murphy and the others played a loud game of gin rummy.

When they reached Berlin, the fog was so bad that the tower at Gatow refused to accept the plane. They tried Tempelhof, and there too the control operators said the conditions made it impossible to land. They were told to turn around and head back to west Germany. Clay barged into the cockpit and grabbed the microphone from the pilot. It took only a few words from him before permission to land was granted. Once the plane had skidded to a stop, it was enveloped in the haze. The visibility was 100 feet. Clay's pilot could not see down the taxiway so two airmen were dispatched to escort the plane to its hardstand. They walked out in front of the slowly rolling Skymaster, each shining a flashlight up ahead.

Dawn came over a city on the edge. In the final hours before the balloting, Berliners saw the blur and heard the blare of an all-out political campaign. "Berlin is worth a fight," shouted the Western parties. "Berlin is worth peace," answered the Communists. Under huge banners with the slogan "Berlin answers the Russian blockade," the democrats pressed their case. "It's cold in Berlin," they argued to those who groused about the lack of coal during the blockade, "but it's colder in Siberia."

On election eve, the leaders of all three democratic parties—men who often bitterly disagreed—joined hands together on a single stage. Berlin's infant democracy was marked by the backbiting, factionalism, and parochialism to which democracies are prone, but in this moment the city's leaders were able to rally the people in a way that only democracies can. That night none of the party leaders campaigned for themselves—something larger was at stake. Acting Mayor Friedensburg, from the Christian Democrats, said, "Anyone who stays home tomorrow is giving a vote for Communism against freedom." The head of the Liberal Democrats defiantly announced, "The Communists will never smash our will, even if they resort to the use of those cannon which ring our city." Ernst Reuter, a Social Democrat, told the crowd, "The Soviets are pressing us with all means short of war. They want to press us to our knees but they will never achieve it."

To reassure voters, 4,500 officers from the Stumm police were dispatched to guard against violence at the polling stations. "There are enough freedom-loving men available on election day to protect the ballot boxes if the police forces are not sufficient," said the charismatic Franz Neumann in one of the last rallies. That same day Paul Markgraf addressed an assembly of five hundred of his officers: "It depends on you whether all reactionary agents will be driven out of Berlin or whether American imperialism will conquer Germany's capital." The stage for election day was set.

THE SOVIETS DECLARED that election day, Sunday, December 5, was a "day of reconstruction." Instead of having the day off, every Berliner who worked in the East—including the 125,000 who lived in the West—was required to show up to their jobs for an extra weekend shift. In retaliation, the democratic labor unions declared a transit strike lasting until 10 A.M. on election day so that the workers would be able to vote before heading off to their jobs.

When the polls opened at 8 A.M., there was understandable apprehension about how many voters would show up. After clearing somewhat the previous day, "a fog as heavy and dank as a soaked sponge settled on the city's streets," reported the *New York Times'* Drew Middleton. Police officers guarding the voting locations had to stand closer than planned to the entrances so that they could actually see the door. That morning's Communist *Berliner Zeitung* announced that "whoever refrains from voting has chosen life over death." East Berlin radio again trumpeted all the benefits that came from accepting the Soviet rations. But all day long, Berliners—suffering under the blockade, surrounded by Soviet territory for at least a hundred miles in every direction—lined up to cast their ballots.

They voted in beer halls and bombed-out buildings. In hospitals, to maintain secret voting, nurses would work their way down rows of beds, holding up towels around patients as they filled out their ballots. In Zehlendorf, the neighborhood near Clay's headquarters, a frail old man made his way down the street toward the polling place with his arms wrapped around the shoulders of his two sons, one of whom who had lost an arm. Every forty steps or so, the father had to sit down and rest for a while. Then the three of them would get up and take another forty strides closer to the ballot booth. In another neighborhood, Charlottenburg, a middle-aged woman arrived near the end of the day with her makeup streaked with tears. She explained that her husband had just been offered a better-paying job in the Soviet sector and had told her not to jeopardize it by voting. "I don't mind living with a rascal," she said after dropping her ballot into the box, "but I do mind living with a dumb rascal. I told him I am getting a divorce."

A mob of Communist youth with clubs entered the French sector but was quickly turned back. At Polling Place No. 87, two Russian soldiers barged in and tried to make off with the ballot box, but the voters inside overpowered them and threw them out of the building. Otherwise the day was peaceful. Markgraf's threatened interference never happened. In fact, all day there was only one incident of gunfire in anger. At sunset, a Russian army sentry by the Tiergarten saw someone on top of the Brandenburg Gate pulling down the Red Flag. He fired once and missed. He fired two more times but missed again. The man continued to pull down the flag. It turned out to be another Soviet soldier, putting the flag away for night.

That day, more than 86 percent of Berliners cast their ballots. It was, recorded Ruth Andreas-Friedrich in her diary, "an admirable result considering that this decision most likely will have to be paid for with an intensification of the blockade, a winter without coal, nights without light and a permanent diet of dehydrated potatoes, dehydrated vegetable and canned meat. We feel as if we had wings. We feel it's great to be a Berliner. It is wonderful to live in a city that prefers death to slavery, that has decided to suffer more deprivations rather than dictatorship."

Reuter's Social Democrats—the most extreme of the parties in their anti-Communism—won more votes than the other parties combined. Reuter was publicly jubilant. It was "a great victory for Germany and the whole world. We may look forward to the future with great confidence." Two days later, the City Assembly once again chose him as mayor—and this time there was no Soviet veto in the Kommandatura. That day, the fog in Berlin lifted. Reuter accepted the news of his election with a private somberness. He looked out the window of his office in a new City Hall in West Berlin and said, "Now I am Lord Mayor of rubble."

On December 16, shortly after nine in the morning, the telephone lines to the broadcast station of Soviet-run Radio Berlin were cut. Within moments, a hundred French military police offers broke into the station offices just off the Tegel runway and ordered the Soviet and German technicians to board buses that would take them to East Berlin. The buses took the long way.

A short while later, the American and British officers at Tegel were welcomed into French general Ganeval's conference room for a special, hastily called reception. They thought it strange when, after they had all entered, the door was locked shut behind them. But the French had provided a bountiful spread of pastries and drink, so the officers shared in the feast without considering whether there was an occasion. At 10:45 the room rattled with an explosion. They all rushed to the large windows to see the two Russian radio towers at Tegel jump into the air and then collapse into a tangled web of steel. After the gasps had settled into a stunned silence, they looked back over their shoulder to hear Ganeval say softly, "You will have no more trouble with the tower."

Ganeval announced to the press that he had given the Soviets a December 16 deadline, which they chose to ignore. "I could no longer accept responsibility for possible accidents" on the Airlift from the towers. With the Russian radio station knocked off the air, the manager of RIAS sent a note to the Soviets offering to let them broadcast over the American station for an hour that afternoon. There was no reply.

At a news conference, Clay—who for years had been exasperated with France's refusal to confront the Soviets—could barely contain himself as he expressed gratitude for the French "action in removing a real source of danger to our pilots on the Airlift." He was asked whether he knew what the Russian reprisal might be. He said he did not.

"Do you care?"

"No."

By 2:30 on the afternoon the towers were demolished, Kotikov called Ganeval asking for a meeting. He was at the Frenchman's office by 4. The two men had not spoken since Kotikov had betrayed him in September.

"How could you do it?" Kotikov demanded.

Ganeval delighted in his revenge: "With dynamite—from the base."

y the way, I got us some fir sprigs," Ruth-Andreas Friedrich's daughter told her mother on December 24. The Berlin diarist was, at first, confused. "I completely forgot. It is Christmas." When the electricity came on, her daughter prepared a punch of brandy and sugar. "'Cheers,' she mumbled. We do not look at each other." That night a storm laid a blanket of snow over the city, draping its ruins in white. Berliners rushed home to their apartments, stepping carefully so they did not slip on icy streets. With their shoulders hunched and their chins digging into their torsos, they looked like they were contracting into themselves, and they had the distinct feeling that all their innards were huddling up against one another for warmth. When they stepped in their front doors and shook off the snow, there were no lights in the windows or Christmas trees in their parlors. When the radio turned on, RIAS played "Silent Night" and, despite a steady rumble in the sky, it had never sounded more mournful.

BUT IN CORNERS of the city that Christmas there was happiness when a man named "Berlin" and a man named "Hope" arrived together to celebrate the Airlift. In the first of what would be a Christmas tradition that would last more than forty years, Bob Hope came to entertain the troops. He did not come to Germany alone. He brought with him a cavalcade of popular actresses, singers, and models, six statuesque Rockettes, and a composer born Israel Baline who had gained fame under the adopted name of Irving Berlin.

The entertainers traveled around Germany to half a dozen bases over the course of five days. On Christmas they were in Berlin—arriving in a C-54 along with 20,000 pounds of canned corn. At 3 in the afternoon and again at 8:30 that night, they performed in the center of the city to a cheering crowd of American servicemen. Lucius Clay sat in the front of the auditorium. Army secretary Royall and Air Force secretary Symington had come along with the troupe, as had Vice President–elect

Barkley. "Your success," Barkley told the Airlift men there for the show, "may give a pattern to the world for the democracy in which we believe." He declared the six-month-old Airlift "the greatest filibuster of all time."

Fortunately, most of the jokes were left to Hope. The show, mixing humor and saccharin, was broadcast on RIAS to all of Berlin. It played over the radio in operations centers and was piped into planes flying in the corridors. And it was recorded and then aired to an American audience on NBC's *The Bob Hope Show* the Tuesday after Christmas.

Hope introduced the program to those at home by explaining that he had gone to Germany for "the boys who have given up their Christmas to strengthen the cause of humanity. Because of these men, a child eats who might otherwise go hungry—the light of freedom burns more brightly in the world." He reminded Americans that "most of these fellows, a couple of years ago, were carrying cargoes that were a lot hotter, but none that were any more important to the welfare of the world." The Airlift was "not only lifting the morale of the German people but it's also lifting a cloak of hatred that has existed since World War I. Our American guys are flying a plane into Berlin every three minutes all the way around the clock, and every plane is loaded with food, fuel, and faith in man's humanity to man."

To the troops, he served up the rat-a-tat banter that was his trademark. He came on stage to his theme song, "Thanks for the Memory," and said he had "had a nice trip in from America. You know, America? That's where if you get a couple of cigarettes, you smoke 'em." He joked that the pilots flew "so close to the Russians" they could "hear 'em singing 'I'm Dreaming of a Red Christmas.'" And that the fog was so bad, "even the birds here check with the control tower before they take off."

The Rockettes shimmied onto the stage with top hats and long legs, rendering salutes to the cheering troops. Actress, model, and tennis star Jinx Falkenburg came out in a glowing white strapless gown and hit balls out into the audience. Squeaky-voiced Irene Ryan (who would gain her greatest fame as "Granny" on *The Beverly Hillbillies*) offered up some jokes of her own. Flaxen-haired big-band vocalist Jane Harvey was greeted with wolf calls and then a deep and poignant silence as she sang of "chestnuts roasting on an open fire" and "tiny tots with their eyes all aglow."

Hope called Irving Berlin out on stage. "Bob, I wish you'd do that introduction over again," Berlin said, reading stiffly off a piece of paper.

"Why? Is there something wrong, Irving?"

"Yes, you know you've got the name wrong. It's Irving Jones."

"Irving Jones?"

"I changed it. Anything over here named Berlin they cut up into sectors."

But for all the laughs, the meaning of the Airlift was clear that Christmas. "I only wish the Statue of Liberty could talk," Hope said in conclusion. "She'd take one look at the job you're doing and say, 'Men, you're not only lifting coal, you're lifting men's hearts. You're raising the Iron Curtain. And the torch in my right hand? You're putting it in every heart in Europe."

WHEN THE SHOW was over, Clay invited the visitors—Barkley, Royall, Symington, and the entertainers—to come to his house and join him and Marjorie in their Christmas dinner. A great big Christmas turkey was carved for the guests and they gathered around an enormous tree singing Irving Berlin's "White Christmas."

It was almost midnight by the time Hope and his troupe reached their hotel. In the lobby, their escort officer finally worked up the courage to say what he had been thinking for hours. He approached Hope and told him that the men who were actually working the Airlift at Tempelhof that Christmas night had not been able to see the show. Hope's prominent chin dropped and he appeared, the officer recalled, "like a doctor just come home on a winter night from a difficult call being told that another emergency is waiting for him on the far side of town."

A young member of Hope's entourage, who had overheard the escort's request, was appalled. "He wants us to go out to the airport and do it all over?" Hope glowered at the young man. Within ten minutes, the escort officer was in a car on the way back out to Tempelhof with Bob Hope and Irving Berlin sitting beside him.

At the air base, Hope shook hands with the pilots and then mounted a coal truck to deliver an impersonation of Alben Barkley orating. Within minutes, the show was interrupted by the shriek of sirens as fire engines approached. In the middle of the night, the blasts from photographers' flashbulbs had looked like the explosion of a crashed plane.

TO CELEBRATE CHRISTMAS, CBS News recorded a unique broadcast of the flight into Berlin with correspondent Bill Downs, one of Edward R. Murrow's reporters during World War II, reporting from the cockpit. They called it "Santa Flies the Airlift."

Oil leaked from the number 3 engine as plane number 42, carrying 16,000 pounds of coal, took off from Rhein-Main. RIAS lent CBS its recording equipment—a big, brown box that did not need an electrical outlet, and a heavy metal microphone. "In Europe, the holiday season of 1948 will be known as 'The Christmas they had the Airlift to Berlin,'" Downs shouted over the rumble of the plane in flight. "We hope it will be the only Christmas thus identified."

The flight that CBS had chosen to highlight was a special one. "The pilot of this Christmas flight on the Berlin Airlift is a very famous man," reported Downs. "I know you've heard of him and heard about him before. He's Lieutenant Gail Halvorsen of . . . where?"

"Garland, Utah," Halvorsen interjected, his voice shaking with nervousness.

"Lieutenant Gail Halvorsen of Garland, Utah—the man who originated Operation Little Vittles."

Every day during the first weeks of December, five to ten flights had notified the Tempelhof control tower that they were arriving carrying a special cargo. The planes were met on the runway by a security officer, who personally removed a set of boxes and took them to a heavily fortified city jail. There, empty cells had been set aside to guard the boxes and their precious contents. It was in this fashion that, 100 pounds at a time, Halvorsen and others had transported Swersey's chocolate and candy to Berlin for the children's Christmas parties. The last shipment arrived in Berlin on December 23 carrying thousands of chocolate bars, 218,000 rolls of fruit drops, 4,140 packages of gum drops, and 3,000 sticks of chewing gum.

On the afternoon of December 24, before the sun set, the Americans held 4,000 parties for children throughout West Berlin. At a few, Lucius Clay personally greeted the grubby kids. At one celebration in the Zehlendorf district, Willie Williams, among Halvorsen's most active disciples, distributed candy bars to 1,600 children. He then went to visit the three hundred sick youngsters at the Okcar-Helene-Heim Hospital. They, as with every hospitalized child in Berlin, were given a gift of chocolate. At another party, the Airlift pilots delivered fresh fruit along with the sweets. When the children were given oranges, they were uncertain what they were. They began to try to bounce them as if they were balls.

But that night, the six-month anniversary of the blockade, Hal Halvorsen was not distributing candy at the Yuletide parties in Berlin. His Christmas dinner consisted of hot turkey between two pieces of bread. He was on duty flying eight tons of coal into Berlin.

Over that Christmas, Halvorsen received 1,400 Christmas cards. Letters from children in Berlin regularly came in at a rate of 30 a day. The *Weekly Reader* had made a special follow-up pitch for its young readers in American schools to send candy for Christmas, the Boy Scouts of Boston organized a holiday collection, and—along with the 5.5 million chocolate bars that had arrived from the American confectioners and were distributed at the parties—Operation Little Vittles was flush. Aboard plane 42 that Christmas Eve, Halvorsen had 800 pounds of candy in 4,000 parachutes ready for a special delivery to the quiet city below.

Halvorsen put the plane on autopilot, and his copilot that night—a veteran of the air war in the Pacific—played a song he had prepared for the occasion:

Jingle Bells, Jingle Bells, jingle every day,
We have a ten ton present and it's well upon its way.

We drive in this C-54 all night and half the day,
What fun it is in Tempelhof and a Christmas GCA.

Dashing through the night, along the corridor,
Going to Berlin gets to be a bore.
Santa's GCAs will get us down all right.
When I see that apartment house, I nearly die of fright.

Carrying beans, carrying coal, sometimes it is gas,
It'll be a Merry Christmas when we're on the ground at last.

As they approached Berlin, they removed the escape window on the port side of the plane to throw out the candy parachutes made of "handkerchiefs which the kids can use to blow their noses—and believe me, they need them," reported Downs. The fog laid over the city and they could not see the streets as they dropped the candy down below into the "dangerous, vision-killing haze."

"Christmas on the Airlift," the CBS listeners were told, "is not a story of silent nights, of lighted windows and quiet towns and firesides at home. As you have heard, it's a story of engines roaring, men sweating, and giant planes cutting through the atmosphere, night and day, in a constant food and fuel transfusion over the Russian blockade. The purpose? To keep alive this island city that has become a symbol of determined democracy. For Berliners, St. Nicholas doesn't come down the chimney. He roars down the three corridors over Soviet-occupied territory."

WHEN AIRLIFT PERSONNEL had first arrived in Germany they were warned to not walk on the streets alone. "We were afraid of getting our throat slit and ending up in the river," remembered Jim Spatafora, the young airman who had dropped extra helpings of food into the trash bins for the nuns. "But from July 1948 to December 1948," he saw that "a miracle took place." The antipathy and disdain with which the Americans and Germans had once considered each other had melted away.

That winter, Navy lieutenant commander Eugene Lawrence, newly arrived on the Airlift, was sightseeing in Frankfurt when he noticed two Germans shooting him dirty looks. He assumed that this was the hatred of the conquering Americans he had heard so much about. "Finally, I heard one of them whisper to the other, *'Ruskie.'*" He realized they had not recognized his uniform. "I didn't want them to keep that impression, so I got out my ID card and showed them where it said 'U.S. Navy.' Their frowns turned to grins." Another Navy pilot, Arlie Nixon, had been in Germany before the blockade. During that time, as he would tell it almost fifty years later, when he and other "servicemen went to a German restaurant to get something to eat, the voices would all stop and everybody would get up and walk out." His voice breaking as he struggled to hold back tears after half a century, he told of the change: "After that Airlift started you couldn't drink all the beer they sat down on your table." He gulped hard. "We won the war." That Christmas eve, air bases throughout the country received phone calls from ordinary Germans inviting American soldiers to come to their homes and join in their meager holiday dinners.

Dear Candy Bomber,

On the morning of the day after Christmas when I entered the kitchen, I noticed a handkerchief-parachute lying on the roof of the house next door. While I was wondering if the parachute was still carrying its load, and how I could get hold of it, my three daughters, 8, 10, and 13 years old entered the kitchen and discovered right away the object I had in mind. They urged me to get the parachute for them, and even so I did not know how to get hold of it, I decided to try it.

I went over to the house next door and like a thief I creeped up the stairs. . . . But the parachute could not be reached and I did not want to risk my life. A look at my kitchen window where I could see my three girls standing gave me again the courage to do something to get hold of the parachute. After a long search I found a pole which was a bit too short, but lengthened with courage and closed eyes, it did the job. I hurried down the stairs with my sweet load. . . . Happy voices greeted me at home and I looked upon it as an award for the dizzy minutes on the roof.

What happened next did not take as long as the perspiration and recovering of the parachute did. The handkerchief was a little bit damaged but my wife took it with the happy remark that the handkerchief stock now had increased. The children unwrapped the chocolate, distributed and ate it up. Satisfied they declared that this was a real—though a little late—Christmas present. . . . I received the string on which the parachute carried its load and my mother-in-law (81 years old) was happy with the children.

I want to thank you very much and wish you a happy New Year and good luck on all you flights which help the Western Sectors to live. I remain with best regards,

Adolf Kuhtz

James Forrestal spent that Christmas season making appearances at the many receptions on his schedule. He would arrive at the cocktail party, greet the host and hostess with a thin smile, shuffle his feet for a few minutes of stilted small talk, down a martini, and be out the door and on his way all in eight minutes flat. When he showed up at the deserted country club to play golf, while all the other members were at home celebrating the holiday with their families, he finished the course at a record-setting pace. Forrestal gave every indication that he was a man running out of time.

In the years since Iwo Jima, Forrestal had changed, first slowly, and now, in the last weeks of 1948, at a quickening rate. The sardonic humor was gone; the man who had been a locomotive in pinstripes was no more. He puttered about at his desk as if he were chained to it and unable to leave. Before delivering a speech, he would feel the need to make an infinite number of minute tinkers to the text. Once a decision was made, he would continue to reconsider his judgment. "Jim has trouble making up his mind," Truman remarked to Clifford, an assessment no one would have made of Forrestal before the crisis over Berlin.

Over the course of 1948, Forrestal had begun to falter, and by the end of the year his dithering was the least worrisome of his symptoms. For so long, he, almost alone, had seen the rising Soviet threat in its full dimension. With a fearsome war seemingly hovering black on the horizon, he was unable to see any future other than a grim atomic holocaust. On December 9, he had made his final bid for a higher defense budget, arriving at the White House for a meeting with Truman with graphs and grids and the Joint Chiefs of Staff in tow. Bill Draper, who had worked with Forrestal for more than twenty years on Wall Street and in Washington, would say that the defense secretary was "more concerned than I had ever seen him in my life." But Truman would not change his mind.

Now, even as all of Forrestal's fears and delusions and feelings of failure fed off one another, it was clear even to him that his time in office was coming to an end. That fall, Louis Johnson, who had done so much to raise the campaign funds for Truman's election and who had so long coveted the post of defense secretary, was directing a sophisticated effort to drive Forrestal out of the job. Built like a bulldozer, a connoisseur of fat Havana cigars, an Elk, a Mason, and a former president of Rotary International, Johnson was a boisterous, backslapping joiner, as crass as he was ambitious. He was already angling for the Democratic presidential nomination in 1952 and believed that the Defense post would be the perfect stepping-stone. Convincing Truman of Forrestal's perfidy had not been hard. In this, Johnson had the help of having the facts on his side. But with all the White House hints that Forrestal resign being ignored, and with Truman exhibiting a reluctance to outright fire his defense chief, Johnson pressed on. He distributed trickles of leaked information and outright lies to scandalmongers such as Drew Pearson, who published them in his widely read newspaper column. Forrestal, in the stories, was accused of duplicity, deceit, incompetence, and even personal cowardice. As Forrestal's friend, Supreme Court justice William O. Douglas, would recall a quarter-century later, "Louis Johnson's friends in the press were laying down a barrage on Jim and he could not stand that kind of pressure." The two men spoke frequently in those weeks, with Forrestal at loose ends. Finally, Douglas came to Forrestal's office in the Pentagon. They talked for hours. The justice, an old Washington hand, proposed a public relations counterattack, with professional press assistants hired to fight back. "This is war, Jim. It's like Iwo Jima, but it's newsprint, not bullets, that's being used against you." Forrestal stiffened. Douglas could not have imagined the images then running through his friend's mind.

Forrestal had been through nearly a decade of the fantastic pressures of war—hot and Cold; of bureaucratic assaults and political maneuvers in Washington; of the onslaughts of newspaper articles, congressional inquiries, and sharply pointed memos. It was death by a thousand paper cuts. And as 1948 ended, Forrestal was bleeding. He told friends he believed he was being followed. John McCone, who was serving as a *de facto* deputy secretary of defense, arrived for lunch one day at Forrestal's Georgetown home. On the agenda were the latest reports of their preparations for war. As they sat down to eat, Forrestal, very naturally, pulled down two of the shades in the dining room and placed himself in a chair away from the window. He told McCone equably that it was to avoid giving a sniper a clear shot. McCone searched his boss's eyes for a hint that the secretary of defense was making a joke. He found none.

Word of such incidents reached Truman, and he ordered the Secret Service to find out whether Forrestal truly was being followed. Their investigation revealed something even more terrifying. America's secretary of defense had gone mad. Forrestal's butler told the agents that just a few days earlier, for instance, Forrestal had walked into the kitchen wearing his fedora, clearly having forgotten it was on his head. He looked directly at his longtime servant and asked, "Where's my butler?" By the end of December, the breakdown was not confined to Forrestal's home or the sanctuary of his office. During a cabinet meeting to plan the administration's foreign policy initiatives for the coming term, Clifford, sitting against the wall, watched as Forrestal, sitting beside Truman at the table, scratched at a raw spot on the back of his scalp. As the meeting went on, Forrestal dug his fingernails in deeper as if he were trying to pry something out. The red spot grew to the size of a silver half dollar. As Clifford watched in horror, blood began to ooze out from Forrestal's head.

THAT DECEMBER, FORRESTAL was by no means alone in his worries. A committee of the House of Representatives issued a report announcing that there was a secret army, based in America, with eight hundred officers, that was drilling in preparations to overthrow the federal government through sabotage, bombing, kidnapping, infiltration, espionage, "and other methods of wrecking a country." When, that month, Eric Blair, writing under the pen name of George Orwell, completed *1984* on the remote Scottish island of Jura, the dystopian world he feared seemed to loom as a real possibility.

Yet as 1948 came to a close, there were, if one looked hard, signs of hope. The situation in Berlin was still dismal—on December 31, the weather was 30 degrees with rain and snow. But after six months of blockade, democracy had not crumbled in West Berlin and war had not come. *Time* magazine declared the Berlin Airlift the "symbol of the year." Against all the pressure that a nation could face, the United States had stood its ground. "In the year 1948—a fitful year—in a nervous century," declared the magazine's editors, "the world's greatest nation of free men finally resolved to meet Communism's deadly challenge with every weapon of peace that it possessed; and if the struggle against Communism required war, the U.S. would fight. . . . Major General William H. Tunner's airlift blazed a roaring, dramatic demonstration of U.S. determination across Europe's troubled skies."

Frank Howley gave the credit not to his fellow Americans but to the people he had once ruled over in a spirit of vengeance. "The year 1948 has been the most significant in the history of Berlin," he announced in a New Year's message to the city's residents. "Its people not only made important advances in democracy but affirmed their belief in spiritual values above shoddy materialism. The people of this front-line metropolis showed clear evidence of their self-respect, of their dignity and their right to a place among the free communities of the world. . . . By the courage of their votes they refused to sell out to one-party tyranny, knowing it could have brought no real gain, for Soviet communism produces nothing but confusion." He looked ahead with a sense of promise. The tonnage levels for the Airlift in December were still below those of September and October, but higher than they had been in November. And with the end of December, Berlin's foggy season was coming to a close. "The new year," Howley predicted, "will witness the same unswerving courage and determination on the part of the people of Berlin, which in the long run will bring plenty with freedom, instead of misery with slavery."

15

SPRING AGAIN

On the last day of 1948, an American plane flew from a British base in Germany to a landing field in the French sector of Berlin to become the 100,000th flight of the Airlift. As the pilot, Lieutenant Robert McGuire, turned over the 20,000 pounds of coal he had carried, he grinned at the hubbub around him and exulted, "Now I can go back to Alaska." The next day, January 1, 1949, his tour of duty in Berlin was over and he was en route to Fort Richardson, Alaska, to be reunited with his family.

The men on the Airlift had come to Germany expecting to be there for a few weeks. That soon grew into ninety days. And when the Air Force planners realized that the operation would continue beyond the point they had expected it could not—into Berlin's winter—the tour for the pilots and others was stretched out to six months.

For those who had been on the Airlift the longest—the men who had been gathered from distant bases around the world and thrust into the exciting, disorganized "LeMay Coal and Feed Company" in July of 1948—the six-month tours were ending in January of 1949. The first train of soldiers from the Fassberg Air Base to the waiting ship home at the port of Bremerhaven was dubbed the "Rotation Special." It left the base with its exterior chalked with graffiti. The airmen had scrawled:

"Miami Bound," "PA, Here we come," "Slow boat to Jersey," and "Texas." One of them described not where they were going, but where they had been. He simply wrote: "It *Did* Happen."

On January 11—one day past six months since he had stepped in for Pete Sowa on that flight out of Mobile—Hal Halvorsen was preparing to fly a load into Berlin. Just moments before he was to take off, a personnel officer walked up to tell him that this was to be his last flight. It was his turn to go home. Halvorsen quickly scurried to gather all the parachutes he had ready—about 250 of them—and departed for one more trip down the corridor and one final candy drop over the ruins of the German capital.

In Berlin, after the handkerchiefs with their chocolate and gum had been delivered, he stood on the tarmac at Tempelhof and looked around, trying to emblazon the sights into his mind, worried that he might forget. He craned his neck to look at the huge terminal building— Hitler's monument to hubris—which dwarfed the tiny planes and the people scampering in its shadow. He watched pilots make their listless attempts at flirting with the girls in the mobile snack bar. He looked down to the end of the runway. The apartment building hovered out past the fence. In front of it, a knot of children were gathered. The Candy Bombers no longer dropped their parachutes at that spot. The children were simply there, as they were every day, to watch the planes.

A few days later, he was at Rhein-Main, sitting as a passenger onboard a C-54. He was leaving Germany with decidedly mixed emotions. There, for the first time in what had been a life of aimless wandering, he had found a sense of purpose. An indecisive young man, always allowing himself to be pulled along by events, he had resolved to do something—to break the rules of the Airlift and drop candy to the children he met—and this had smashed the pattern of his life. Halvorsen had dedicated himself to organizing the candy bombing with a passion he had never exhibited for anything before. Ninety thousand candy parachutes had been dropped on Berlin. He had made arrangements for Little Vittles to continue under the leadership of his fellow pilot from Brookley, Larry Caskey, and, once he, in turn, left in February, Willie

Williams. But the candy bombing would never feel quite the same without the Candy Bomber—and Halvorsen would miss the joy and importance of his mission.

Yet as Halvorsen sat in that Skymaster on the Rhein-Main runway, he now had a new calling—one he would, at long last, pursue with the same single-minded doggedness with which he had organized Little Vittles. During the Airlift, separated by an ocean and by poor mail service, but even more by the all-encompassing nature of his work, the sporadic rate of his and Alta's letters to each other had slowed even further. But he had written her on January 11—mailing the letter just before he was told he was being sent home—and in the letter he addressed the bombshell Alta had delivered to him in her Christmas card: She had decided to go abroad on a church mission.

For a Mormon woman, a mission was optional and a much less common undertaking than for men. It had been his dithering, the liberties he had taken with her heart for years, that had led Alta to consider such a step. "Guess you never knew such a darn chick as me," he wrote her. "I'm disgusted with myself, too. Just as well tell you this as feel it all the time: when you told me you were leaving on a two year mission you made me kinda weak in the knees. Leaving? Guess I've always kinda leaned on you subconsciously all the time and can't quite place you being gone. Seems like your being around all the time there out west was just like company in my similar status back east somehow. Just seems empty to know you're going somewhere away for a long time. Would like to see you before you left. If I could work foresight like hindsight I'd like to have traded those two very brief visits in N.Y. and W. P. B. [West Palm Beach] for a long daily association like if you had a job in New Orleans or Mobile. That's if we had it to do over." After waiting for Halvorsen through six years of war and peace, Alta was looking for something more than "a long daily association." But nevertheless, Halvorsen asked her to put off the mission for at least a little bit longer: "Don't be in too big of a hurry. Stall 'em a couple of months." Though he had not yet shared it with Alta, Halvorsen had finally made up his mind. "There's a girl back in Salt Lake City I've got to convince on this marriage business," he told reporters in Germany before he left.

Now the Skymaster began to crawl down the Rhein-Main runway. Halvorsen's big duffel bag was lighter without the handkerchiefs he had brought to Germany to fight his head cold, but some of the extra room was taken up by a tattered teddy bear. He caught sight of the barn where he had lived in the second-floor loft. A light snow was drifting through Rhein-Main, and he watched the ground crews preparing the planes, the cargo loaders heaving the heavy bags, the pilots making their final checks. The Airlift was continuing, as busy and hectic as ever. The C-54 in front of them in line took off and headed to the east, toward Berlin. Halvorsen's plane followed right behind down the runway, but, once aloft, it banked to the west. Hal Halvorsen was going home.

WHEN THE SKYMASTER carrying Halvorsen landed at Westover Air Base in Massachusetts, he looked out its window to see a large crowd gathered on the tarmac with a clearly distinguished welcoming committee eagerly waiting for a visiting dignitary. He disembarked quickly, rushing off to the side so that he could avoid interrupting the ceremony. Halvorsen was halfway to the operations center before someone grabbed him and said the ceremony was for him.

His homecoming continued in that vein. From Westover, he went to nearby Chicopee to meet the young people who had worked for months to supply the Candy Bombers. He received a key to the city and a banquet was held in his honor at the famous Red Barn restaurant. He was taken to the Savage Arms Factory and allowed to pick out any gun he wanted. At the Spalding sporting goods company, he was presented with a set of Bobby Jones golf clubs in a leather bag. When he was next brought to a baby clothes manufacturer, he protested: "Just a minute. There is something I have to tell you. I'm not married yet." The company representative said she was well aware of that. But, she added, "We hear there are prospects."

From Chicopee, Halvorsen headed to New York. There he was a

guest on *Hi Jinx*—the program hosted by Jinx Falkenburg and Tex McCrary that was pioneering the morning-talk-show format. John Swersey took him around town again, including a night out at the Copacabana. And Halvorsen held another press conference for the city's reporters, this time at the Roosevelt Hotel. He passed out lollipops to them and when they asked him about his plans, he had his ready answer: "My car is in Mobile, all my handkerchiefs are in Berlin, and my heart is in Utah." Once again, the quote made it into newspapers all around America.

It looked like curtains," remembered Army undersecretary Bill Draper of the awful fog that choked Berlin in November and December. "If that fog had stayed another three weeks we probably would have had to run up the white flag. We probably couldn't have gone on. You can't have people starving, and keep on with the occupation. But the weather lifted about the fifth of January . . ." When it did, the Berlin Airlift had won.

There would still be days of all-encompassing haze that brought operations to a standstill, the snow and cold would still charge through the wide-open air bases and break into Berliners' homes on dark nights, and the hunger and cold would abate only slightly. Industrial production was still down 60 to 70 percent. Unemployment was more than three times what it had been at the beginning of the blockade. A third of the city was living on public assistance. Yet after November and December had done their worst, the Airlift was still going and Berlin still stood.

Of the 225 American C-54s assigned to the Airlift at its full strength, there were—once maintenance and bad weather, fueling and refueling, loading and unloading were taken into account—only 48 in the air at any one time. But those small planes were, as the spring of 1949 approached, able to bring Berlin not only its bare necessities but, with Tunner's precise organization, even a little bit more. By the end of February, the Airlift would fly 16 million pounds of supplies to Berlin in a single day—double the minimum required amount. Ration levels were raised again by a couple of hundred calories—and the Airlift was able to consistently deliver them. And that was not all. For the first time since June, tiny amounts of fresh meat began to appear in Berlin's stores. Tins of liverwurst were available on occasion. Limburger cheese was hauled until the American pilots—willing to put up with cold and fog and dust from coal, but not a terrible smell—refused to fly any more. In March, the American and British Air Forces brought ten tons of matzah and 3,000 liters of Passover wine to the 4,600 Jews remaining in Berlin. That spring, the Airlift flew in doorknobs and Ping-Pong balls and more than a million cigars a week.

WITH THE FEELING of crisis having passed, life in Berlin became something approximating normal. Berliners made the best out of the shambles they lived in. When the winter broke, they sunbathed out in the open air of what had once been the living rooms of second-floor apartments. Children made seesaws out of discarded beams, played inside bomb craters, and built sand castles out of rubble and dirt. The vegetable gardens that now took up the Tiergarten blossomed and bloomed in a carnival of colors.

The feeling of crisis—the fear of starvation and war—had passed to such an extent that even Lucius Clay returned to his old habits. Over-ruled by Washington on a relatively minor economic measure, he sent a two-sentence cable to Bill Draper in the Pentagon at the end of December: "I shall of course carry out the measure on equalization which will greatly damage military government's prestige as it makes its word meaningless. When I have done so, I shall request relief." A few days into January, he sent a message to Bradley: "As the representative of the United States, I have understandably become associated in the German mind with our determination to remain in Berlin. Hence, I have been apprehensive that my departure would give both satisfaction and propaganda opportunities to the Soviet Military Administration and to the Communist Party. However, the airlift has now proved its capability." He went on to complain again about being second-guessed by policymakers in the State Department. "I now feel definitely that it is in the best interests of the Army that I be permitted to retire." When George Marshall announced his retirement a few days later and was replaced as secretary of state by Dean Acheson, Clay decided he could wait to leave a little bit longer, but by February, all agreed that the situation in Berlin had stabilized enough for Lucius Clay to come home. The date of his return was set once again. Though Berlin was still blockaded, he would step down as the military governor of Germany on May 15.

Visiting Americans could mistake the sense of normalcy in Berlin for a flagging of the city's determination. "The most extraordinary thing about the airlift today is that it is no longer extraordinary," wrote the *New York Times* columnist Anne O'Hare McCormick on a trip to Germany. "It is taken for granted by the population and the occupying forces that it can be continued indefinitely if necessary." That spring, a writer for *The New Yorker* observed that "the airlift has been taken as a matter of course, and a freight-carrying plane has attracted no more attention here than a United Parcel Service truck does in Westchester." But the visitors missed something. The pilots saw a very different view. Approaching Tempelhof in March 1949, a pilot pointed to a mass of Berliners standing out by the apartment building, beyond the fence, at the edge of the runway. "Notice those people down there?" he shouted to a reporter along for the ride. "They're always there, watching—day and night." They were still there in the spring as they had been in the summer, fall, and winter.

"It must be obvious to even the most dense Communist that their tactics have failed," Frank Howley told reporters in March. "Neither the blockade at the Elbe nor the ice of winter stopped the Airlift. It must be obvious that it would be to their own interests to discontinue these tactics, which have caused more trouble to them than to us." The siege of Berlin had not only failed, it had backfired. Berliners had become rabidly pro-democratic; Western European nations under threat were banding together and seeking a defense treaty with a United States that was turning its back on isolationism; and all around the world the Berlin Airlift had become a symbol of an America that was not only strong but good. Newspapers in nearly every country in the world gave in-depth coverage to the dramatic story. The State Department released stirring photos on plastic plates so they could be printed on presses in provincial cities as well as in the world's capitals. In the Turkish town of Giresun, on the Black Sea, the city's daily dedicated an entire page to images of the Airlift. A picture exhibition about blockaded Berlin drew 200,000 on a single day in Guangzhou, China.

Ironically, though public opinion around the world was turned dramatically against the Soviets, the huge amount of attention focused on the siege made it hard for them to simply back down. The blockade had become more than a temporary negotiating tactic that could be lifted at any time with the announcement that long-awaited bridge repairs had been completed. Abandoning it now would be a disastrous admission of defeat. The Americans, having come so close to retreat, were willing to wait. Howley announced that any peace would be up to the Russians. "Let them shake the hand which we've never refused to give them."

From its very inception, the United Nations was held to be a failure. In its first four years, it had never lived up to the hopes imparted by Franklin Roosevelt and its founders as a force for peace in the world. As the Cold War arose between the United States and the Soviet Union, it had been sidelined and fractured, made feckless, toothless, and frail. All during the fall of 1948, often well-meaning ambassadors from neutral nations had held long, earnest negotiating sessions to attempt to forge a compromise over Berlin that would spare the world from war. The Soviets, preferring to allow the blockade to take its course, had vetoed every compromise. But the course of the blockade had turned in a surprising direction, and now it was the Russians who were seeking a way to end it. And in the spring of 1949, the United Nations would become more than just a stage for harangues and tirades. It would play a positive role in securing peace in the world—not by imposing it as Roosevelt had imagined, but in a more modest fashion: It proved its worth as a forum where representatives of the world's nations could talk to one another, where they could grab that extended hand of which Howley had spoken.

Since his blast just before the American presidential election, Stalin had remained largely quiet on matters of world affairs. But on January 27, he released his written answers to a series of four questions put to him by Hearst news correspondent Joseph Kingsbury-Smith. It was routine practice for Western newsmen to submit such questions to Stalin, and it was almost as routinely his practice to ignore them. But in this instance Stalin provided answers almost within a few days, and while most of his pronouncements were anodyne, his response to a query about the possibility of ending the Berlin standoff was notable— for what it did not say. Stalin indicated that if the ongoing work to create a West Germany was put on hold until the four-nation Council of Foreign Ministers could meet, the blockade would be raised. The Western allies would not accept such a deal, but it was immediately apparent that Stalin's position was softening. He had made no mention of the currency question in Berlin and had dropped all pretense of "technical difficulties."

Truman and Acheson hatched a two-part strategy. A week after Stalin's announcement, Acheson held a press conference where he, in a manner as relaxed as the occasionally pompous diplomat was capable of, signaled that the new stance had been noticed. "There are many ways in which a serious proposal by the Soviet government to" lift the blockade could be made, he concluded. "All channels are open for any suggestion to that end." But, Acheson said to the reporters, "I hope you will not take it amiss if I point out that if I, on my part, were seeking to give assurance of seriousness of purpose, I would choose some other channel than the channel of a press interview." The United States government was willing to talk, Acheson was telling Stalin, but not by means of announcements in newspapers.

Two more weeks passed until the second part of Truman and Acheson's plan fell into place. While the United Nations delegations were waiting for the body's permanent home to be built in Manhattan, they were meeting in a reconfigured gyroscope factory on Long Island. There, on February 15, Philip Jessup ambled over to Jacob Malik in the delegates' lounge as they were milling about before a debate over the admission of Korea to the United Nations began. He casually remarked on the weather, "finding it was a subject on which" they could usually agree. The two men chatted for a short time before Jessup said that, by the way, he had noticed that Stalin's statement had made no notice of the currency disagreement and was wondering if the omission was accidental. Malik, usually affable, became immediately formal. He told Jessup he had no information about that question. Jessup made every effort to appear as if he was not much concerned one way or another, but, he replied, if Malik should happen upon any information perhaps he would let Jessup know. The two men shook hands and went their separate ways.

AS 1949 BEGAN, the world seemed to be closing in on James Forrestal. He felt surrounded by prying eyes, by men in dark suits who had come to watch his every move. He called the attorney general, Tom Clark, and accused him of sending FBI agents to invade his home. "You've got your men over here. . . . They've been all over the house. . . . They've tapped my wires. They're trying to get something on me." He continued to lean on his friend Justice William O. Douglas, who would recall spending "night after night, pacing the floor, trying to help him untangle the imaginary skein of troubles and woes that seemed to encompass him." Forrestal implored his friend for help: "Bill, something awful is about to happen to me."

On January 11, Forrestal met with Truman at the White House. Though no detailed account of their conversation exists, it is apparent that the president, alarmed by the reports he was receiving about Forrestal's behavior, told his secretary of defense that it was time to step down. Forrestal emerged from the meeting dazed, unable to fully accept that he was to be forced out of power and replaced by a devious gladhander like Louis Johnson. A hydra of reporters was waiting for him in the West Wing lobby. Forrestal, a gaunt, aging man, shriveled so that his collar hung around his neck like a noose, stepped hesitantly into the room.

The reporters demanded to know whether he would resign. As Truman was not ready to announce the change, Forrestal attempted to dissemble. He said it was routine for all cabinet members to offer to vacate their posts at the beginning of a new term. "Do you want to and expect to continue as secretary of defense?" a reporter pressed.

Forrestal—shaken, ashen—replied mournfully. "Yes. I am a victim of the Washington scene."

FORRESTAL'S RESIGNATION WAS announced by the White House on March 3. He was to step down at the end of the month. On March 17, Forrestal traveled to New York to speak at the annual dinner of the Friendly Sons of St. Patrick. His speech at the event, the site of Truman's breakthrough address the previous year, would serve as his valedictory. "Two weeks from today, I will leave my job as Secretary of Defense," he told an audience of 2,500 in the Astor Hotel's ballroom and those watching on television at home. "I have held that our national security is paramount and is the best insurance for world peace." Once Forrestal had stood largely alone in the councils of government in believing that the United States faced an all-encompassing threat from Soviet aggression. But since the end of World War II, the nation's policies had shifted in the direction Forrestal had been advocating. There was no more dramatic example of this than the Airlift in the skies over Berlin. A nation on its heels in the spring of 1948 was standing firm in the spring of 1949. "I believe we have made it plain that the United States will not disassociate itself from the future of Western Europe. I believe that by making our intentions so clear that no one can misread them, we have advanced and not retarded our progress toward a real peace. No other interpretation, to my mind, can explain the economic progress and the change in the international political climate during the past twelve months."

What Forrestal told the Friendly Sons of St. Patrick was true:

American foreign policy had changed dramatically in the course of the year. The day following his address, March 18, one year and one day after the quivering European ambassadors had gathered around a radio to listen to Truman's speech to Congress, the North Atlantic Treaty was unveiled in Washington, pledging mutual assistance if any member nation was attacked. That day, when Secretary Acheson was asked about what was envisioned as the type of "armed attack" that would compel NATO members to respond, he said an example would be a strike on Berlin Airlift planes by Soviet aircraft.

The Soviet siege of Berlin and the allied response had helped convince Americans to make this unprecedented military commitment. It brought America closer to Europe. It brought Europeans closer to one another. Together with the Marshall Plan, the Russian threat helped bring about the economic alliances that led to the European Union. In western Germany, the demonstration of American commitment in the Airlift gave the men forging a new constitution the confidence to go forward. And the showdown in Berlin—and coinciding breakdown of James Forrestal—would lead to the creation of the Department of Defense, to the position of chairman of the Joint Chiefs of Staff, and the unified structure of the modern military.

In those final days in office, Forrestal believed he had failed to sound the alarm over the Soviet threat in enough time, with enough force. But America's foreign policy had been reshaped in Forrestal's image. And Forrestalism would live on after he left government. No official in Truman's government—not George Marshall or Dean Acheson or George Kennan—would do more to shape the outlook and attitude of Americans toward the Soviet Union during the decades of the Cold War than James Forrestal. While others saw Russia as simply another of history's expansionist powers, he saw the threat of Communism as that of an insidious ideology at odds with the basic promises of democracy. When future presidents would speak of "a long twilight struggle" or "an evil empire," some foreign policy experts cringed. Forrestal would have nodded, even if grimly.

THE MORNING OF March 28, the day scheduled for Forrestal's farewell ceremony at the Pentagon, the phone rang in the Oval Office. Truman lifted the receiver and listened quietly before saying, "Yes, Jim, that's the way I want it." He hung up the phone and looked over at his naval aide, standing nearby. "That was Forrestal. He wanted me to tell him whether I really wanted him to be relieved by Louis Johnson today."

After watching Johnson get sworn in as America's second secretary of defense, Forrestal went to the White House to formally say goodbye to Truman. The president had a surprise for him. The cabinet, the Joint Chiefs of Staff, and other high officials were waiting for Forrestal in the Oval Office. To their applause, Truman, grinning, pinned a medal on the lapel of Forrestal's suit and read aloud a citation honoring his "meritorious and distinguished service." Forrestal tried to respond. "It's beyond me . . . beyond my . . ." he stammered. "There you are," Truman comforted him. "You deserve it, Jim."

The following morning, Forrestal traveled to Capitol Hill to receive the thanks of the House Armed Services Committee. It was the last public event on his schedule. When the meeting was over, Air Force secretary Stuart Symington—who had been Forrestal's friend during those golden summers on Long Island in the 1920s, but then had become a bitter rival in the Pentagon—turned to Marx Leva, Forrestal's aide. "Marx, old fellow," he said, "would you mind if I rode back to the Pentagon with Jim? There's something I want to talk to him about." Forrestal and Symington climbed into the backseat of the waiting black car and drove off, alone.

What happened in that car will probably never be known. Though Forrestal's aides insisted on it, Symington would deny even that the ride occurred. Whatever it was that was said, Leva arrived back at the Pentagon to find his boss sitting in the tiny, empty office he had been given to prepare for his departure. Forrestal was staring at an empty wall. His fedora was perched on his head. "Mr. Secretary, is there anything I can do for you?" Leva asked.

Forrestal did not respond. Leva tried again. "He was almost in a coma, really," he would recall. Finally, Forrestal looked at him and said, "You are a loyal fellow." He would repeat the phrase over and over.

Leva secured a car and took Forrestal home. He then tracked down Ferdinand Eberstadt, Forrestal's best friend, who was testifying before a Senate committee. Eberstadt and Forrestal spoke every day, but when Eberstadt called over to the house, Forrestal refused to come to the phone. "You tell James," Eberstadt said to the housekeeper, "that he can get away with that with a lot of people, but not with me." Forrestal came on the line and Eberstadt said, "I'll be right over."

"For your own sake, I advise you not to," Forrestal said slowly.

"I'm on my way."

When Eberstadt arrived, the house was dark and the blinds were drawn. The servant said Forrestal was upstairs and Josephine Forrestal was vacationing in Hobe Sound, Florida. Forrestal appeared at the top of the stairs and Eberstadt saw "the skin of his neck and face was hanging loosely, and his loss of weight was even more noticeable." Forrestal wrapped his arms around his friend. Eberstadt squeezed him back, gave him a light pat, and after a few moments tried to pull away. Forrestal would not let go. The Russians, he whispered into Eberstadt's ear, had bugged the house and were hiding in the garage.

Forrestal pointed through the blinds at two shady characters standing about on the street corner. At just that moment, the doorbell rang. Eberstadt opened it to find a man who claimed he had been an alternate delegate to the 1948 Democratic convention and was looking for Forrestal's support in his bid to be postmaster of his hometown in North Carolina. Eberstadt told him to write a letter. Forrestal watched as he walked off and began speaking to the two men on the corner.

Seeing Forrestal's condition, Eberstadt quickly decided that his friend needed to leave Washington. He asked Leva to arrange for a plane to take Forrestal to Florida. There, Josephine, and Bob Lovett, would meet him. The house servant quickly packed a suitcase and retrieved Forrestal's golf clubs. A few hours later, he landed in Florida. Lovett too was shocked at the sight of the "wizened, shrunken man" who climbed down a ladder from the plane. He took Forrestal by the arm to make sure he did not crumple. "I'm glad you brought your golf clubs," Lovett said, smiling, trying to be light, "because I'm going to take every dollar you've got." Forrestal stared at him squarely in the eyes. "I must talk to you," he said in a low whisper, his eyes darting across the empty flat land. "The Russians are after me, the FBI is watching me, the Zionists are after me."

When he arrived in the house where he would stay, Forrestal searched under the bed for microphones. When he and Lovett went for a walk on the beach, he pointed to the metal sockets sticking out of the sand that were used to hold up sun umbrellas. "We had better not discuss anything here. Those things are wired, and everything we say is being recorded."

The illustrious William Menninger, who six months earlier had been the first psychiatrist to be featured on the cover of *Time,* arrived to examine Forrestal a couple of days later. His diagnosis was that Forrestal was suffering from symptoms very similar to those faced by the World War II soldiers returning from combat who were being treated at the Menninger facility in Topeka. Menninger advised that Forrestal be transferred to Kansas immediately. But speaking by phone to Josephine Forrestal, Truman disagreed. There was the stigma of admitting that Forrestal was suffering from mental illness to consider. And Truman had other worries: that Forrestal might reveal national security secrets to the civilian doctors, as well as that the revelation that a madman had been in charge of America's military forces and been shaping its national security policies in the midst of an international crisis might destroy confidence in the United States government at home and abroad. So instead, on April 2, Forrestal was sent to the Bethesda Naval Hospital, a tall tower outside of Washington. He was placed in a room on the sixteenth floor.

On March 14, a month after he had broached the subject of Berlin with Jacob Malik, Philip Jessup—now based in Washington as ambassador-at-large—received word from the Russian asking to see him the next time he was in New York. He replied that he would be there the next day.

When Jessup arrived at the Soviet mission at 680 Park Avenue—a red brick building across the street from the Council on Foreign Relations—Malik delivered a message from Moscow: Stalin's failure to mention the currency issue was "not accidental." If a meeting of the Council of Foreign Ministers to discuss Germany's future was scheduled, the blockade would end. Jessup asked if the blockade could be lifted in advance of a meeting of the four nations' top diplomats. Malik said this was a new question. He would have to get back to Jessup once again.

This time only a week passed. Three days after the NATO Treaty was unveiled, Malik informed Jessup that the Berlin blockade could end before the foreign ministers gathered. Malik then asked if the allies would "call off" formation of a new West Germany in advance of such a meeting. Jessup said he could make no such promises.

Their conversations continued. That month, Stalin replaced Marshal Sokolovsky as Russian military governor in Germany and Vyacheslav Molotov as foreign minister after ten years—personnel moves that traditionally indicated major shifts in Soviet policy. But when Jessup and Malik met again on April 10, the Russian read a prepared statement from Moscow stating that even if preparations for West Germany would not stop, the Soviets understood that the new government would not be put in place until after the foreign ministers met. It was a simple request whose only effect would be to help the Soviets save face. Jessup replied that if this was what the Soviets believed, they were mistaken. With the Airlift working, the Americans saw little need to compromise. If the blockade was lifted, it would be in such a way that all the world would know the Russians had suffered a total defeat.

As the months of fog ended and the Airlift gained more strength, the candy drops over Berlin became even more plentiful. In his one month on the job as Halvorsen's replacement as chief Candy Bomber,

Larry Caskey supervised the delivery of 6 million pounds of candy. But the operation had changed. It had evolved past Halvorsen's makeshift use of rags and handkerchiefs, and even past the crateloads of premade parachutes arriving from the United States. Now the majority of the candy delivered to Berlin's children was not dropped from above but was distributed through Berlin welfare agencies and hospitals and youth centers. With the need to stuff every plane full of coal and flour having passed, boxes of candy and chocolate could be flown in on the Airlift on a regular basis. Many more children got treats in this manner—when Willie Williams took over from Caskey, he pledged to "put a candy bar in the pocket of every kid in Berlin"—but they somehow tasted less sweet than they had when they fell from the sky.

As for the original Candy Bomber, his return stateside, the *Task Force Times* decided, was "largely a transfer from the candy circuit to the knife-and-fork circuit." Halvorsen, the Airlift newspaper announced, "has been wined, dined and feted from the moment he landed." He traveled in loops around the country giving after-dinner speeches to industry conventions and other groups in which he described his experiences in "making life a little sweeter for Berlin children." He would sit at the head table in a hotel ballroom, in Chicago or New York, flanked by plump businessmen—their pink necks warring with their tight shirt collars—and pick at his food while they shoved steaks down their gullets. Photos would catch him surrounded by their mirth, gazing off thousands of miles away.

Halvorsen spoke at the National Geographic Society in Washington, where he was given a new sixteen-millimeter Filmo camera. He returned to New York for two days of speeches. He made low flights and dropped candy parachutes over Salt Lake City and over Ogden, where all traffic was stopped and the mayor was moved to declare, "Why, that was the biggest thing ever to hit Ogden. I'll bet that was more exciting than the presidential inauguration!" His hometown of Garland had a "Welcome Home Lt. Halvorsen Day" at which Utah's secretary of state was the featured speaker. Restaurants across America sent him invitations to be their guests for a free meal. Back at Brookley, Mobile's press association awarded him with its "Scroll of Merit." In gratefully accepting, he said he could not stay in town for long. "There's a gal in Salt Lake City who must be sold on the idea of matrimony. I've got to get out there and do a super selling job." Reporters pressed him to find out the identity of his sweetheart. Articles speculated as to who she might be. He would not divulge her name. "I've been up in the air too long. I've got a lot of ground work to do before I know just where I stand." In fact, Halvorsen had been up in the air with Alta for longer than he had been in the cockpit. But now he had decided.

It was a month and a half after his return to America that Halvorsen was finally reunited with Alta. She was living with her parents in Nevada. The moment they saw each other for the first time in nearly three years, they both knew instantly that any talk of her leaving for a mission was over. They went skiing together on Mount Charleston outside of Las Vegas. At the bottom of the hill, he took the diamond he had bought in Rio and carried with him for years out of the folded wax paper in his wallet. He had had it mounted on a ring. Halvorsen asked Alta to marry him. She did not say yes until he managed to convince her he was not joking.

News of their engagement, along with staged photos—one of Alta feeding him a Baby Ruth bar, another of him handing her the teddy bear he had received from the girl at Tempelhof—appeared in dozens of newspapers around America, from the Utica, New York, *Observer-Dispatch* to the Zaneville, Ohio, *Times Recorder* to the Kingsport, Tennessee, *News*. "Berlin 'Bonbon Bomber' Wins Own Sugar Plum" was the headline in the *Los Angeles Times*.

Two days after they were engaged, it was time for Halvorsen to return to Mobile. He set off on the three-day drive before six in the morning and sent her postcards every few hours along the way. "I've never missed anyone or anything so much as I've missed you these past days," the once-reticent Halvorsen wrote her when he made it to Alabama. But this time their separation would be brief.

A week later, they met in Los Angeles to attend the Academy Awards. Halvorsen was representing the Air Force, whose short movie, *Operation Vittles,* was nominated for a best documentary award. It was a hokey piece of propaganda ("One of our gang, Lieutenant Halvorsen, loved the small fry. He instituted Little Vittles. It wasn't much, just candy bars on tiny handkerchief parachutes dropped to the Berlin kids. A great guy! We all gave Little Vittles candy and handkerchiefs. Good flying, chum!"). Though it went down to defeat, Halvorsen and Alta loved walking down the red carpet, sitting alongside a bare-shouldered Elizabeth Taylor, and watching Barbara Stanwyck, Douglas Fairbanks, and Jane Wyman pass by. (Wyman was awarded Best Actress; her former husband, Ronald Reagan, whom she had divorced the week the Airlift began, was not there.) But as the evening wore on, Halvorsen fidgeted uncomfortably. "The dress of the three men who came from the shadows to scrape garbage barrels flashed before me and I struggled to reconcile my participating in this operation so soon after being in another so totally different."

On April 16, the day before Easter, they were married at the Little Church of the West in Las Vegas. "I'm not nervous," Halvorsen said as the ceremony was about to begin, "but my knees are knocking and I'm flat on my back." But when he saw Alta walking toward him down the aisle, in her cream-colored satin dress, carrying a bouquet of purple orchids surrounded by white carnations, he felt a sense of calm. "Gail Halvorsen," asked the bishop, "do you take Alta Jolley by the right hand in the covenant you now enter into to become her companion and husband, to love, honor and cherish her as long as you both shall live, and do you hereby propose to observe all the laws, covenants, and obligations pertaining to the holy state of matrimony?" Halvorsen licked his lips and swallowed hard as the question was being asked, but his reply was firm and strong: "I do."

They drove to the Grand Canyon for their honeymoon. The next day, Halvorsen and Alta watched Native Americans do a "Hopi war dance" for the visiting tourists. With a $10-a-head charge for a mule ride on the 7½ miles to the floor of the canyon, Halvorsen decided they should hike down the Bright Angel Trail in order to save the $20. Alta wore blue shorts and Halvorsen had a cap. The flying hero developed vertigo as he looked over the edge along the way and he nearly lost his balance. Alta laughed. They put out a picnic lunch. The desert flowers were in full bloom. It was so quiet that Easter Sunday on the floor of the Grand Canyon that the passing breeze seemed almost like a roar.

On April 1, one of West Berlin's newspapers carried a banner headline announcing that the Airlift would no longer be needed, since the Americans had completed digging a tunnel between western Germany and the besieged city. It was a prank, but the faith that Americans could accomplish just about anything had taken hold. The Airlift was working without the pilots seeming to strain themselves. By the first week of the month, as spring broke through and the weather warmed after the long winter, they were playing touch football on the ramp at the Celle Air Base while waiting for their planes to load. To Tunner, it was a problem, a sign the operation was going so smoothly that the pilots thought "they could rest on their laurels." While getting a massage from a 200-pound German woman in the basement of the Schwarzer Bock Hotel, Tunner developed a solution.

Tunner announced his plan to his top officers: Over Easter weekend, the Airlift would make a one-day, all-out effort to set a new record of 20 million pounds. Tunner would call it the "Easter Parade." The idea was kept a secret until, at noon on Friday, April 15, each base's quotas were unveiled. The pilots let out gasps when they saw the goals. Over the next twenty-four hours, everyone on the Airlift worked with a single, common purpose; pilots, air traffic controllers, and mechanics all stayed up through the night. Even cooks were put to work on the tarmac, loading coal. "It's tons for Tunner" was the slogan of the men on the flight line. Most every plane—no matter what its condition—was sent up into the sky. One pilot took off in an airplane without an oil pressure reading. Another crew flew an entire round trip with their cabin filled with billowing smoke from a busted hydraulic system.

Tunner raced around Germany to personally oversee every part of the effort. He approached one pilot about to take off from Tempelhof and asked for a ride. With his flight jacket hiding his insignia, the general went unrecognized by the pilot. "You'll have to shake your tail and get aboard. We're in a hurry," he was told. Tunner grinned—and hustled onto the plane. When he arrived to inspect the Fassberg Air Base, Tunner was met by its commander, Colonel John Coulter, who bounded toward him with the news that the base was 10 percent ahead of its quota. "That's fine," said Tunner, deadpan. "Of course, it's not up to what they are doing at Celle. They're really on the ball over there." Coulter crumpled and then rushed back to the flight line to speed up the loading even more. Tunner proceeded to the Celle Air Base and repeated the same act.

In twenty-four hours of the "Easter Parade," on 1,398 flights, the Airlift transported more than 26 million pounds of coal and supplies including 2,000 rubber hot-water bottles, tobacco, a plane full of manhole covers, condoms, dried apricots, and cuckoo clocks. The coal alone was the equivalent of a freight train six hundred cars long. A plane landed in Berlin once every 63 seconds. At the four-power Berlin Air Safety Center, the Russian air traffic monitor threw his hands up in the air. "Your planes are coming in and out too fast. I cannot keep track of them," he yelled at the other three controllers as he stormed out of the room.

Tunner had kept the Easter Parade a secret from even the other generals in Germany. But when Howley realized what was happening, he arrived at Tempelhof to welcome the crews. He declaimed to the reporters about the importance of freedom and the inhumanity of the blockade. His words were drowned out by the aircraft engines. Clay too had not been told about the big push in advance. He was at home for an Easter meal, about to tuck into a slice of fresh blueberry pie, when it dawned on him that the buzz of the planes overhead was continuing without even a pause. He looked up from his plate and said, "You know, I think we've licked them."

Ten days after the Easter Parade, the Russians privately indicated that they would raise the Berlin blockade without conditions. Jessup and Malik only had to meet a few more times to finesse the details of which restrictions would be lifted, and to set the timing for the end of the blockade and the meeting of the Council of Foreign Ministers.

On May 3, Lucius Clay was on board a special train heading toward the American army installation at Grafenwöhr in western Germany. A ceremony was being planned there for the next day to mark his May 15 departure from Germany, but Clay was still waiting for the White House to publicly reveal the news. It was late that night when word reached Germany of Harry Truman's announcement that, after four years, Clay was stepping down.

The following morning, Clay stood up in a jeep with his hand at his temple in a stiff salute as he inspected a line of 11,000 GIs at attention for his review. Many still had not heard the news of his resignation until Truman's statement was read aloud. Then Clay addressed his troops. "You have inherited the tradition of the Allied armies who fought their way into Europe," he told them. He spoke of the hopes they once had for a world united in peace, a world unbesmirched by the troubles of war. "Unfortunately, it is still a troubled world. However, our Army stayed in Europe and continues to stay in Europe to guarantee the peace and stability which was attained at such great sacrifice." Looking out on the assembled soldiers he declared, "My heart is filled with pride and joy." He stepped back from the microphone on the reviewing stand and the troops paraded before him for the next hour and a half. As the parade ended, forty-two P-47 Thunderbolt fighters flew overhead in a formation that spelled out the letters C-L-A-Y. Then they swooped in low over the reviewing stand in a final salute, wiggling their wings above him.

Clay was on his way back to Berlin after the ceremony when Jessup and Malik, joined by the French and British ambassadors to the United Nations, announced their final accord. In the capital, Berliners had gathered expectantly around a RIAS sound truck. The announcer began to read: "Agreement has been reached between the three Western powers and the Soviets regarding raising the Berlin blockade and the holding of a meeting of the Council of Foreign Ministers. All communications, transportation and trade restrictions imposed by both sides"—a frisson of excitement raced through a crowd stirring in anticipation—"will be lifted on May 12." The announcer continued with the statement, but no one heard another word he said as they hollered and jumped and grabbed at one another in celebration.

On board the train back from Grafenwöhr, Clay welcomed the news of the end of the blockade and the meeting of the Council of Foreign Ministers in Paris eleven days later. Looking back on his time in Europe, he admitted to reporters that "only the future can reveal our successes or failures," but "if the Germans prove to have learned to believe in and to respect the basic rights of human beings, we will have achieved much." He was asked if he himself had learned anything, and it took him only a moment to answer. "I hope I have learned humility," said the man who had once been celebrated for his certitude. With so many lives in his hands, it "made one quickly realize that you cannot always be right in every decision."

"Can you tell us something about your personal plans?" a reporter asked a short while later.

"I am retiring from the Army on June first, and I have no plans beyond that," he replied.

"What is the date, General, for the catfishing?"

"It would start, I should think, about June first."

ON CAPITOL HILL, the proponents of the NATO Treaty were forced to argue that the pact was still needed now that the Berlin crisis had passed. Though its ratification was no longer in doubt, it was under consistent attack by those on both the left and right who opposed the American crusade against international Communism. Robert A. Taft stood against the treaty in the well of the Senate, and Henry A. Wallace was on a fifteen-day nationwide tour decrying it as "a pact of destruction."

On May 5, the day after the announcement that the blockade would be lifted, Wallace was the leadoff witness in opposition to the treaty at the hearings of the Senate Foreign Relations Committee. He accused the Truman administration of deliberately concealing from the American people the negotiations over Berlin that had taken place since

February in order to continue scaring them so as to "assure the ratification and implementation of the Atlantic pact."

In three and a half hours of testimony, he argued that the NATO treaty "substitutes for the one world of the United Nations the two hostile worlds of a Divided Nations." The treaty was the product of men of "evil actions" trying to "enforce our will by force in all parts of the world." The result would be that "there is a very grave danger that we will make Russia into what we say she is: into a wild and desperate cornered beast."

Old Tom Connally of Texas, the committee's chairman, leaned down over the rostrum. "Did you say corned beef?"

Wallace sighed. "Cornered beast, Senator. Cornered beast."

IN MOSCOW THAT spring, the hit movie was titled *Meeting on the Elbe*. Four years after the April day when American and Russian soldiers embraced in the center of a divided Germany, two out of five Muscovites saw the film depicting the event. It was the feature on twenty-two of the capital's fifty movie screens. The movie began with reenactments of those hopeful scenes, but then depicted what happened next: hardworking, honest Russians thwarting the attempts of the drunk Americans to enrich themselves off the black market, return the Nazis to power, and spread "Wall Street imperialism."

"Two worlds have met on the Elbe's shores," said one of the movie's characters. "Germany cannot just stay in between. The time to make a choice has come."

ON MAY 8, the German Parliamentary Council in Bonn, after eight months of drafting, was ready to vote on a constitution for the new nation of West Germany. In contrast to the constitution of the Weimar Republic, the new document recognized "inviolable and inalienable human rights" such as equality before the law, the right to assemble, and freedom of faith, press, and speech.

The council met for seven hours that day so that they could adopt the final draft on this, the four-year anniversary of the fall of Hitler's regime. The date, Konrad Adenauer, the council's president, declared, should mark not only the death of Nazism, but the birth of freedom. Yet the delegates' speeches in favor and in opposition ran so long that midnight was approaching and the document still had not been approved. It was decided that the vote should be taken and the speeches could then continue afterward. The constitution of the Federal Republic of Germany was approved at 11:55 by a vote of 53 to 12. The speeches by the politicians then went on, irrelevantly, long into the night. Democracy had come to Germany.

FOR THE SECOND time in a year and a half, Lucius and Marjorie Clay packed up their belongings—their clothes and mementoes and furniture—to leave Germany. But the place Clay was departing from in May of 1949 was fundamentally changed from that of March of 1948. The fear of a war that he had worried could come with "dramatic suddenness" had receded. A sense of community and camaraderie had emerged in what had once been the "Crime Capital of the World." The citizens of the city that had been Hitler's capital, the people who were to have populated his showcase metropolis, had embraced ideas of liberty and equality that they had eschewed only a year earlier. Berliners were now 30 percent more likely to believe American efforts to spread democratic ideas would have a favorable effect on the German way of life than their countrymen under American occupation in the west.

That last week of the blockade—the week between the announcement of its end on May 4 and the opening of the gates on May 12—found Berliners reveling in joyous anticipation, savoring the excitement of the approaching moment when they would no longer be shut off from the world. "With the end of the blockade approaching, Berlin's mood varied from that of a front line just before battle to that of a circus day in a small town," wrote Drew Middleton for the *New York Times* on May 10. Defeated by force of arms, beaten down by the sad years after the war, guilty over their part in inhumanity, Berliners had now won a great victory. "The German people, who had been somewhat apathetic ever since their defeat, came back to life during the Airlift. This was especially true of Berliners," observed Robert Murphy. After 321 days of siege, it was the Soviets, not the Berliners, who had been crushed, their defeat laid bare for all the world to see. They had been reduced to finding any means they could to save face. The allies believed they had an agreement with the Russians to lift the blockade at midnight on the twelfth. No, insisted Vasily Chuikov, Sokolovsky's replacement in Berlin, in formally announcing the procedures under which trucks and trains would be allowed to travel through the Soviet zone: It would be a minute past midnight.

There were no more teleconferences to keep Clay up late into the night. On May 11, he worked in his office until 10 P.M., went home, and was long asleep by midnight. At that hour, in Helmstedt, at the western border of the Soviet zone, hundreds of Germans had gathered to watch the first cars and trucks pass through the checkpoint heading down the autobahn toward Berlin. The mood was raucous. Seemingly the entire town had come out to the border crossing, along with many other Germans who had hiked with backpacks from miles away to be part of the event. The milling crowd had "the air of a county fair," reported the *Task Force Times.* "It was like carnival night," said the radio correspondent for CBS News. *Stars and Stripes* described the line of eager Americans and British waiting to race to Berlin as like something out of the "Oklahoma land rush." The plump moon hanging overhead, the flashbulbs of dozens of cameras popping, the floodlights for the newsreels, the magnesium flares sending sparks into the night, all bathed the midnight scene in radiance. There was enough jostling and photographing going on, wrote still another newsman, to "have done justice to a Hollywood premiere."

At exactly one minute past midnight, the Russians lifted the barrier separating their zone from West Germany. Four minutes later, Corporal Hector Cluff lifted the white bar on the allied side of the border. Six automobiles and two British trucks loaded with hay rolled the 100 yards toward the Soviet checkpoint with the electrically illuminated red star on its roof. The crowd of Germans and reporters followed behind them on foot. Russian lieutenant Nicholas Petrovich walked over to the lead jeep and asked for the soldiers' documents. The British captain handed over their paperwork and Petrovich made a great show of inspecting it. As he stood there officiously, an old German woman walked past him and thrust a big bouquet of flowers into the hands of the driver. The Red Army guards standing at the post tried to look stern, but helplessly broke into grins as American newsmen climbed aboard the Soviet sentry boxes to get a better shot and popped camera bulbs into their faces. "Gentlemen, gentlemen," Petrovich shouted in English, "I must ask you to be keeping the order. Otherwise you cannot go at all." But after two minutes of staring at the travel orders, Petrovich gave a slight signal, and the barrier across the highway to Berlin was lifted.

The line of jeeps and cars and trucks trying to get to Berlin that night grew so long that the Russians eventually gave up on examining their documents and simply waved more than seventy-five of them through. The American and British soldiers and journalists raced one another to Berlin, traveling in excess of ninety miles an hour down the moonlit autobahn. Over the previous ten months, grass and weeds had grown up in the cracks of the unused highway and between the cobblestones of its off-ramps. At the Elbe, they saw the remnants of the metal bridge, destroyed in the war, still hanging out over the river, and crossed the new Russian structure, whose "technical difficulties" had evidently been solved.

The crowd of revelers the cars left behind at Helmstedt receded during the night, but in Berlin a throng of about six hundred was at the checkpoint when the first truck—carrying 16 tons of cucumbers—made it the 110 miles from Helmstedt. They were there for the second truck, with its 13 tons of leeks. They were still there when the sun came up. All that night, with the Airlift planes still audible overhead, they danced and cheered as the food trucks made it through. Parents lifted children onto their shoulders to get a better look. The Berliners gave the drivers bottles of schnapps and draped them in lilacs. Those who could not afford flowers presented them with garlands made of leaves.

The truck drivers enjoyed the merriment, but it was not what stirred them most that night. The most moving sight of those first hours after the end of the blockade was their first view of the city. Driving down a dark and deserted highway across the German countryside they would spy a glow in the distance. As they approached, it grew more brilliant, and then its source became clear: electricity had returned to the city. After nearly a year, the lights were on all over Berlin.

IT WAS NOT until 1:23 a.m. that the first train left Helmstedt for Berlin. The shades were ordered to be lowered for the entire ride in case the train was attacked and stoned. On board, British Tommies sang "It's a Long Way to Tipperary" as they crossed the border into the Soviet zone. The Russians insisted that trains could pass through their territory only if they were pulled by Soviet locomotives, and so it was their own engines that finally broke the blockade, pulling fifteen trains overflowing with food and supplies into Berlin. On the side of the freight cars, someone had written, in German, "Faith for Faith" and "Berlin, We Greet You."

The trains carried lemons, oranges, cucumbers, potatoes and fresh meat. The goods made their way immediately into the stores. All day long Berliners gathered and stared through shop windows at cakes, butter, cuts of pork, seemingly endless links of sausage. Some women would stand there and break down in tears—sobbing from relief and joy. Berliners did their shopping and exited the stores past long lines of those waiting to get in. They happily showed off their groceries as if they were modeling furs. In the crowd, big-eyed young girls were pulled back by their mothers when they curiously leaned too far in the direction of the passing strangers' shopping bags. Those farther back in the swarm stood on their tiptoes in order to catch a glimpse into the bags full of food. Proprietors of Nordsee fish markets held boxes of fresh fish on ice up to assembled crowds just as they would works of art—and the Berliners applauded. Children grinned while licking chocolate ice-cream cones, and ate oranges with expressions of pure delight—though the younger ones grimaced at the unfamiliar sensation of the taste and texture of citrus.

"Berlin is the happiest city in the world today," wrote one correspondent. The day was declared a public holiday, and the city's streets, which for years had so often felt eerily deserted, teemed with life and laughter. Berliners carried signs reading, "Hurray! We're still alive!" and "Berlin Lives Again" and "Hail to the New Era." Those who had been stranded in the west for nearly a year had joyful reunions with their families. At home, Berliners switched their lights on and off all day in amazement.

CLAY'S AIDE AND interpreter, Robert Lochner, had been on the first train to Berlin when it pulled into the station at a few minutes past five A.M. He made his way back to the office around 6:15 and found Clay at his desk going over papers. "How did it go?" Clay asked.

"Well, surely you've received reports," Lochner said.

"No, I put a pillow on my phone."

That morning, Clay rode to West Berlin's City Hall for a special session of the City Assembly. Amid the elation, there was solemnity. Ernst Reuter called for the creation of a stockpile of food and coal in case the Russians ever attempted to cut off the city again. Franz Neumann read out the names of the forty-eight American and British men who had died in the Airlift, and the Germans rose in silence to honor them. The square in front of Tempelhof was renamed Plaza of the Air Bridge.

Then Reuter spoke again to close the ceremony. On this day of celebration, he looked forward. "The Red Flag," he declared, "will someday be removed from the Brandenburg Gate and replaced by the flag of the German republic." And he harked back to that overcast September day eight months earlier when hundreds of thousands of Berliners had gathered at the Reichstag. "In our great demonstrations in the summer of the past year, we called on the world for help. The world heard our cry. We are happy to have here in our midst as a guest the man who, together with his two colleagues"—all eyes turned on Clay sitting at Reuter's side—"took the initiative in organizing the Airlift in the summer of last year. The memory of General Clay will never fade in Berlin. We know for what we have to thank this man," Reuter shouted over a roar of applause, "and we take advantage of this hour in which he bids farewell to Berlin to say that we will never forget what he has done for us."

Clay stepped to an array of microphones. "The end of the blockade does not merely mean that trains and trucks are moving again," he said. "It has deeper meaning." Something even more terrible than hunger and cold had been plaguing Berlin. "By the physical breaking of the blockade, there has also been a breaking of the spiritual and moral blockade which may have gripped this city before." Now, "the people of Berlin have earned their right to freedom and to be accepted by those who love freedom everywhere. The people of Berlin ranked with the American and British pilots who fed the city as the real heroes of the blockade."

"I shall not use the English word 'goodbye' but rather try to say to you *'Auf Wiedersehen'*"—Until we meet again. Lochner, translating, had to share the microphones with his boss and, when he leaned in, he saw what no one in the audience could. General Lucius Clay's eyes were welled up with tears.

CLAY'S FINAL DAYS in Germany passed quickly. That same afternoon of the day the blockade was lifted, he flew to Frankfurt to sign off on the German constitution and end the military occupation. When John McCloy, Roosevelt's original choice, arrived to take over from him, it would be as a civilian high commissioner. Two days later, Howley arranged for Clay—the military governor of Germany, the man who had barely deigned to speak to Germans in his first years in Berlin—to make a courtesy call on Ernst Reuter in City Hall. Clay had come as a conqueror determined to be strict. That morning, the day before he departed, Berlin's *Telegraf* wrote that "He is a German hero."

On May 15, it was time for Clay to leave. He and Marjorie said goodbye to his staff. He pulled down the red nameplate of "General L. D. Clay" that had hung above his office door, took one last look at his battleship of a desk, and walked out of the room, leaving it redolent of tobacco and stale coffee.

It was raining that Sunday afternoon as Clay, with a car waiting to take him to Tempelhof, stepped outside the front of American headquarters to watch a final military parade. Several thousand Americans, British, French, and Germans were gathered, standing side by side in his honor. They were silent as the members of the Berlin Military Post marched in review past the general for the last time.

Four years earlier, Clay had stood in that same spot as Harry Truman came "to raise the flag of victory over the capital of our greatest adversary." That day, Truman had declared they were "not fighting for conquest" but rather for a vision of what America's role in bringing peace and freedom to the world should be. The peace had proved elusive, but the democracy had come to a place where some had thought it could never thrive. "I'd like to think that during the years our flag was flown in Germany, it stood for something more than military power," Clay would later note and, during those years, for millions of Germans—and for untold millions more who watched from other nations—it did.

Clay had admitted to growing emotional as he listened to Truman recite the creed of America in the world. Now he was affected again as he watched the flag being slowly lowered for the night from atop the tall pole in front of the big gray building. He looked at the vast, mixed assembly gathered to pay him tribute. The 298th Army Band marched out and played "Dixie" in honor of the man who had been a boy among the charred remains of war. And they played another song. He knew its lyrics well, and they ran through his mind:

> *I gets weary, an' sick of tryin',*
> *I'm tired of livin', an' scared of dyin',*
> *But Ol' Man River, he just keeps rollin' along.*

COMING HOME

When the flag had come down and the band marched off the field, Clay and his wife climbed into the car to take them to Tempelhof. The rainy streets were choked with half a million Berliners standing in silent respect for the American general. At Tempelhof, Reuter and others were on hand to wish him well. Clay climbed the stairs to the plane, turned, and yelled "Goodbye everyone!" He waved from the window as the Skymaster taxied down the runway, wedged in with the Airlift flights.

Louis Johnson and Omar Bradley were among those on hand to meet him at National Airport in what one newspaper termed "the most stirring official welcome Washington has lavished on a returning hero in many a day." Drummers in Revolutionary War garb trilled. Rifle butts clacked against the pavement. A seventeen-gun salute was fired as Clay was led toward a waiting car.

He was brought straight to the White House, where more than two hundred of the most important men and women in Washington were gathered to greet him in the Rose Garden. The blooms were full, and their perfume mixed with the scent of fresh-cut grass. Truman presented Clay with a medal for distinguished service. Clay, he said, had "proved himself not only a soldier in the finest tradition of our

American arms, not only an administrator of rare skill, but a statesman of the highest order—firm, courageous, dedicated to the cause of peace. His entire administration was marked by a deep devotion to our democratic ideals of justice and freedom." Truman pinned the medal on Clay, who whispered his thanks, telling Truman it was his "greatest honor." Truman turned to the press and assembled dignitaries. He rattled off the names of the World War II heroes he had decorated—Eisenhower, Nimitz, and others—but, he said, "I take as much pleasure in handing General Clay this medal as I did in handing any of the others."

"Mr. President," Clay said in response, "to a soldier there can come no higher honor than receiving a decoration for service from his commander in chief. I am humbly grateful." A solitary plane wandered overhead, almost drowning out his words. Clay stepped back next to Marjorie. He dug his hand into his left pocket and pulled it out. He dug his hand into his right pocket, pulled out a handkerchief, and brought it to his face. Truman beckoned Marjorie to give him a congratulatory kiss. She demurred shyly. Clay stepped forward and kissed her instead. The cameramen missed it and shouted for him to do it again. Clay waved them off with a laugh. They would not give up and continued to clamor until he gave in and—beaming—kissed her once more. She flushed with self-consciousness. "Are you passing those out?" drawled Vice President Barkley. "Yes, come and get it," she answered, brightly. He leaned in and she planted a big kiss on his lips.

"I NEVER HAD more pleasure in my life in presenting anyone than I do in presenting our guest today," said Speaker Sam Rayburn in introducing the man he had first known as a young officer in the Rivers and Harbors Division of the Corps of Engineers. "An old friend has come home from his labors, which have been stupendous and great. His imprint will be left on world history." Clay, having learned that he was invited to address both chambers of Congress only the night before, had not had time to write remarks. He stepped to the podium in the House chamber without a note.

Clay accepted the tribute in the name of the soldiers and airmen of the occupation and the Airlift. He noted the time that had passed since the end of the war. "It is impossible to forget, and it is difficult to forgive. We all remember that Germany started the aggressive war which has brought the world to the conditions which we have seen during the past four years. One has only to revisit Buchenwald or Dachau to remember the extreme cruelty of the Nazi regime." But he had witnessed a transformation. "I saw in Berlin the spirit and soul of a people reborn. . . . Men and women and children in that city took their stand."

He then walked to the other side of the Capitol and delivered a completely different speech to the Senate. In the chamber where, as a young boy in the galleries, he had watched his father serve, he briefly recounted his experiences in Germany. "At the risk, perhaps, of saying something here that sounds sentimental, I do wish to recall two personal incidents," he noted in concluding his remarks. "Almost four years ago . . . the American flag was raised over our headquarters in Berlin in the presence of the president of the United States. At that time, in a short and simple speech, he said that out of victory we had no desire for territorial or material gain; that the United States wanted only a world in which there could be peace and freedom. I saw the people of Berlin—two and one-half million strong—have their second choice, their second opportunity to choose freedom, and this time they did not repeat the error they first made. They decided they would live by Airlift; that they would undertake the discomforts of a cold without electricity, and with employment for only a few. They had decided to cast their lot with those who loved freedom."

There was a second event, as well. "Sunday, two days ago, I saw my last retreat in Berlin. I saw our flag being lowered with the full knowledge that it would be raised again on the following morning. I felt that in these four years it had become a symbol of firm justice and not of oppression, of a rule of law and not arbitrary law, and that indeed it had become to millions of people not of our land, the same symbol of freedom and of the dignity of man that it means to us."

TWO DAYS LATER, New York City honored Clay with a ticker tape parade. The number of individuals so celebrated had trailed off after World War II, and those processions that did take place had been poorly attended, desultory affairs. But on May 19, a quarter of a million New Yorkers came to cheer the gaunt, fatigued man racked with ulcers who rode up Broadway from the Battery to City Hall. "City officials were frankly amazed at the turnout," a newspaper account pointed out, "as the season for hero-welcoming passed several years ago."

The parade of 1,600 was led by thirty-nine men on horseback carrying brightly colored flags. It featured firefighters, police officers, and sanitation workers who were veterans of World War II; a fife-and-drum corps; soldiers, sailors, and marines. Clay had Robert Murphy sit next to him in the open car as they crawled up the Canyon of Heroes. Walter Bedell Smith, back from Moscow, followed behind in the rear of Clay's parade. "As I came up your streets," Clay told Mayor O'Dwyer and the 10,000 others jammed into the plaza outside City Hall, "I could not but think of the many parts of the world today where there is no freedom and where people walk in fear and trembling and where people cheer those whom they are told to cheer."

A few days later, there was yet another parade in Clay's honor. On May 26, all the stores in Marietta, Georgia, were closed. For days, posters tacked up around town had promised "Big Parade, Speaking, Barbecue, Dance." And when the day came, 8,000 people pressed against one another in the town square to see the man they had known as a boy return after many years. Clay climbed atop a float with a sign that read, "Let's Go Catfishing, General." A pole, a pail of live bait, and a jug of corn whiskey were placed nearby.

He retired that week as the most famous, revered, and honored general in history never to have seen—much less served in—combat. Had he served for another year, he likely would have fulfilled his ambition and led troops into battle in Korea.

On Saturday, May 21—nine days after the end of the blockade, two days after Clay's triumphant ride up Broadway—James Forrestal had a big steak lunch in his room at the Bethesda Naval Hospital and talked cheerfully with his attendants. His condition appeared to have improved, but in his seven weeks at the hospital, he had been continually racked by nightmares and visions. He still spoke often of the dangers to the country and, in the words of one of his doctors, "whether or not people were as alert to these potentialities as they should be." Visitors began to be allowed on a limited basis—but evidently not with any consideration of who Forrestal actually wanted to see. Truman came in late April with a bottle of bourbon, and afterward his spokesman said the two men had "quite a chat." Louis Johnson arrived a few days later and announced to reporters that he and Truman wanted to help Forrestal's recovery by sending him on an around-the-world inspection trip of military bases. Senator Lyndon Johnson showed up at the hospital and barged into Forrestal's room. But when Forrestal asked for a Catholic priest he knew to come see him for a confession, the request was denied.

That night of May 21, the Navy corpsman who was scheduled to watch over Forrestal failed to show up for duty. It would later be claimed he had been drunk. Instead, another lieutenant—who had never performed a full watch before—was assigned to sit in Forrestal's room and guard him through the night. At 1:45 A.M., Forrestal was in bed, apparently sleeping. The room was dark. The corpsman went down the hall to the nurse's station to make an update in the patient's chart. He returned at 1:50. He stepped quietly into the room and sat back down in his chair. When his eyes adjusted to the darkness, he realized Forrestal was gone.

JAMES FORRESTAL'S DEAD body, clad in pajamas, was found a few minutes later on a cement awning jutting out from the hospital tower's third story, thirteen floors below an open pantry window across the hall from his room. He was wearing his watch. The sash of a bathrobe was tied tightly around his neck. Inside his room, the sheets were turned back off his mattress. There were pieces of broken glass in his bed, shards of a glass ashtray on the room's Persian rug, and an unused razor lying on the floor by his slippers. A red leather-bound anthology of poetry, its spine decorated in gold, was opened to Sophocles's "The Chorus of Ajax." Between the back cover and the last page were sheets of hospital memo paper on which that poem had been copied:

Fair Salamis, the billows' roar
Wanders around thee yet;
And sailors gaze upon thy shore
Firm in the Ocean set.
Thy son is in a foreign clime,
Where Ida feeds her countless flocks,
Far from thy dear remembered rocks,
Worn by the waste of time—
Comfortless, nameless, hopeless—save
In the dark prospect of the yawning grave. . . .

Woe to the mother, in her close of day,
Woe to her desolate heart, and temples gray,
When she shall hear
Her loved one's story whispered in her ear!
"Woe, woe!" will be the cry—
No quiet murmur like the tremulous wail
Of the lone bird, the querulous nightingale—

Only "night" of "nightingale" had been copied before the papers were put away. The handwriting was noticeably different than Forrestal's had been, as if it were the pen of a completely different man. The stanza that came after the copying stopped read:

When Reason's day
Sets rayless—joyless—quenched in cold decay,
Better to die, and sleep
The never-waking sleep, than linger on
And dare to live, when the soul's life is gone

There were deep scratches in the sill below the outside of the pantry window from which Forrestal had plunged—as if in terrible terror, he had dug his fingernails into the limestone, struggling frantically to hold on and climb back into the tower, to pull himself away from the fate that lay below. If so, it was his final failure.

Josephine Forrestal was in Paris, staying at the Ritz, at the time of her husband's death. She was flown back to Washington on Truman's plane, which happened to be in France after having brought Secretary of State Acheson to the meeting of the Council of Foreign Ministers.

Many observers expected these four-power sessions to yield no more progress than the previous conferences had. But some held out hope that after the Soviets' unambiguous defeat in the blockade, the path to a real peace had been cleared. "Red Bid to End the Cold War Seen," ran a headline in the *Los Angeles Times*. The Paramount News announcer said the meeting "may point the way out of the Cold War." Even a secret CIA "Review of the World Situation" sent to Truman in mid-May speculated that the Soviets might have been forced into attempting to "reach a *détente* with the West in Europe."

But that term would not enter into common usage for another twenty years. The Paris meeting proved to be as unproductive as every previous diplomatic minuet with the Russians had been in the years since the end of the war, and the Cold War would rage on for four more decades.

Yet the face-off in Berlin would be the closest the United States and Soviet Union ever came to World War III. After the Berlin block-ade, the conflict between the Americans and the Soviets settled into a dangerous but somewhat stable balance of terror. As Paul Nitze, the Forrestal aide who went on to be a foreign policy adviser to seven presi-dents, would write in 1999, "I still consider the Berlin crisis of 1948 to be the most parlous moment for America, far closer, in my view, to drawing us into conflict with the Soviet Union than the later Cuban mis-sile crisis."

But despite the danger, Truman's policy of avoiding both aggression and appeasement worked. Before the blockade, Soviet Communism had been a force that was on the move, creeping across the map of Europe and toppling free governments one by one. After the blockade was defeated, the Communists would not gain another inch of territory in Europe. In fact, they would never again even try.

THOUGH NO ONE knew it at the time, the victory of the Airlift would mark the sunny apex of the American Century—before the slow slog of Korea, before the shock of Sputnik, before Americans had even heard of places such as the Bay of Pigs or Khe Sanh. Never again—not even amid the hula hoops and sock hops of the seemingly placid 1950s—would Americans be as brashly self-confident, as free from doubts over their nation's goodness as in those months when the highest tensions gave way to the rampant conviction that all was possible and within their reach.

"There was never a country more fabulous than America," wrote the British historian Robert Payne after a long journey through the nation in 1948 and 1949. "She bestrides the world like a Colossus: no other power at any time in the world's history has possessed so varied or so great an influence on other nations." The United States, he pointed out, had "half of the wealth of the world, more than half of the productivity, nearly two-thirds of the world's machines."

But the moment at the summit, like all such moments, was short-lived. That August of 1949, three months after the end of the blockade, America's nuclear monopoly ended when the Soviets tested an atomic bomb in the desert of Kazakhstan. In October, Chinese Communists emerged victorious in their civil war and Mao Zedong proclaimed the birth of the People's Republic of China. In February of the following year, Senator Joseph McCarthy, in a speech to the Wheeling, West Virginia, Republican Women's Club claimed to have in his hand a list of members of the Truman State Department who were closet Communists, thus beginning one of the ugliest chapters of American history. On June 25, 1950, almost two years to the day of the beginning of the Berlin blockade, North Korean troops swarmed past the 38th parallel, setting off the first war to end in stalemate for the United States in nearly a century and a half.

Though the blockade was lifted in May of 1949, the Airlift continued on until the end of September in order to build up Berlin's stockpiles. Sixty years later, its more than 277,000 flights and 4.6 billion pounds of food and supplies dwarfs the size of any such operation since. In the massive undertaking of the Airlift, pulled together haphazardly and uncertainly, the average monthly accident rate was 50 percent less than it was during that same period in the Air Force overall.

"Moosburg, Germany was bombed yesterday in a surprise raid by an American B-17 Flying Fortress," announced the American Air Force on September 15, 1949. Hearing a low-flying plane approach, Germans in the small Bavarian town scrambled from their houses, and soon the village's streets were filled. It was the last candy bomb run of Operation Little Vittles. Willie Williams dropped thousands of candy parachutes from the open doors of the plane. The pilot at the controls of the plane, Lieutenant Harry Bachus, knew the target well. He had spent five months as a prisoner of war in a barbed-wire enclosure on the outskirts of town. "We can show the German people, and particularly these youngsters, who will be the leaders of tomorrow, that the airplane can be an instrument of mercy and good will as well as a machine that can destroy mankind," Bachus said afterward.

Howley left Berlin on September 6, 1949. The Russians had been celebrating for weeks. "General Howley is glad he is going home. So is Berlin," read the photo caption in a Soviet morning paper. Berlin radio played "Deep in the Heart of Texas" in his honor even though he was from Philadelphia. "Back to Texas!" jibed the announcer. "Never come back, General Texas!"

He was replaced in Berlin by General Maxwell Taylor—later a chairman of the Joint Chiefs of Staff. Howley's departure was as acrimonious as his arrival. In his last days, he, along with the British and French commanders, met with Kotikov in order to try to reestablish a dialogue. At the end of the meeting, Kotikov offered a toast to Howley on his departure from the city. He spoke words of praise, but said his terrible ulcers prevented him from drinking any strong alcohol. Even champagne, he said, was far too potent. "Have a martini," Howley suggested.

"What's a martini?" Kotikov asked. Howley didn't answer, but presented him with a glass from a waiting tray.

"To a successful journey to the United States," sniggered Kotikov before swallowing his drink—olives and all. He turned gray with pain. Howley smiled and proposed another toast, handing Kotikov another martini. And then a third toast and a fourth. Howley asked if they should drink one more. Kotikov stumbled away whimpering, "Nyet." Cheerfully, Howley walked out the door for the last time.

And as he had through most of his time in Berlin, Howley would continue to war with his own government. He publicly accused the State Department of sending a representative to Kotikov after his departure to say that "now that General Howley is gone we want to start off with a clean slate." For his part, Taylor would pledge to continue Howley's "firm" policies. "However," he added, "everyone has a somewhat individual method of conducting negotiations."

Howley had come to Berlin in a black Horch, with two squealing pigs, and his heart full of hatred. On the day he left, a farewell ceremony was held in his honor. When McCloy finished his words of praise, How-ley said goodbye and began to walk to his car. The 15,000 assembled Berliners burst through the barriers and mobbed him. As he waded through the crowd, reaching for the outstretched hands, a gaunt woman whose deep wrinkles hid her youth thrust her blue-eyed baby toward Howley. In broken English, she shouted above the din, "This is my baby. You saved when the Russians would not give us milk." Howley merely nodded and made his way to the big automobile that would take him and his family to a special train waiting for them. As the driver slowly pushed the car through the surging crowd, "Howlin' Mad" Howley turned to his wife and began to cry.

Back home, he became a frequent commentator on television news programs and wrote a syndicated newspaper column, which he called "Shooting Straight." He would find himself getting into arguments with cabdrivers, railing against Communism from the backseat of a taxi stuck in traffic.

Tunner left two days after Howley, slinking out of Germany in silence, without any recognition that he was departing save for a brief blurb in the paper after he was already gone. He boarded a midday plane in Wiesbaden, with his Airlift still bustling around him, and took off. Returning home, he was assigned to the exact same position as deputy director of the Military Air Transport Service from which he had been saved thirteen months earlier.

Tunner would watch as his rival, Curtis LeMay, rose to become among the most famous and reviled generals in twentieth-century America while passing himself off as the architect of the successful Air-lift. LeMay would claim credit for hiring the German mechanics, for bringing the operations jeeps out to the planes, even for the mobile snack van where pilots could buy "a little coffee and a Nabisco or some-thing." He was the youngest four-star general since Ulysses Grant, and his threat to bomb the North Vietnamese "back into the Stone Age" made LeMay the model for Air Force General Buck Turgidson in Stanley Kubrick's *Dr. Strangelove.* In 1968, he served as running mate to Alabama governor George Wallace in his third-party campaign for president. The week before the end of the blockade was announced, the *Washington Post* wrote, "To Clay goes the credit for organizing the airlift, but LeMay made it technically possible." As LeMay's star ascended, each successive round of newspaper profiles would give him even more credit for the organization of the Airlift. Tunner would be steadily forgotten. On the occasion of the Airlift's fiftieth anniversary, *Newsweek* would recall the importance of a General "Turner."

As his own minor fame faded, Tunner would grow increasingly perturbed at the acclaim LeMay was receiving, telling others he found LeMay's glory-seeking "disgusting." He would write a memoir in which hardly a page passed where he did not feel the need to remind readers of his achievements and importance. In it, he would return continually to the theme that air transport was vitally important but consistently overlooked. It was no great leap to conclude he felt similarly about the field's most prominent exponent and practitioner. The book dripped with the resentment of being slighted. It was only after years of rejections for his proposal that the book found a publisher.

In 1961, twelve years after he left Germany, when the Berlin Wall went up and many feared a new blockade would begin, Tunner, by now retired, wrote to LeMay and Maxwell Taylor offering to assist in contingency planning for a possible new airlift. Both replied cordially that they would keep him in mind.

Tunner remarried (to a woman who had been one of his WAC pilots during World War II) and they had a daughter together. They bought a farm and a big white house along the banks of the Ware River where the grass flowed to the water's edge. From the bough of a great oak, he hung a rope swing. The man who had so rarely seen his boys, disappearing for weekends on cross-country trips for no reason at all, would spend hours pushing his daughter on that swing. She would giggle with delight. He found it comforting as well, making her swing back and forth, in an even rhythm, like the steady beat of a jungle drum.

Hal Halvorsen would not be the last celebrity created by television's ability to convey flickering intimacy who would then recede into a life of relative anonimity. The first time he went to a movie after having returned to Alabama, his engagement to Alta was featured in the newsreel. Within a few years, however, he would be only dimly remembered by his countrymen, an offhand sentence in most histories of the era, a memory clattering about in America's consciousness.

But in Germany, and especially in Berlin, the pilot from Utah would become part of the national lore. At Berlin's commemorations of the fiftieth anniversary of the Airlift in 1998, he arrived in a Skymaster, as he had long before. It was parked on the tarmac at Tempelhof to accept visitors the next day. The crowd began to gather before dawn. When he and the other Airlift veterans arrived at the airport at 7 A.M., the line had already grown to more than two hundred people. The Berliners approached him all day, nodding a few words of thanks or silently, tearfully grasping his hand. They brought their children and bewildered, uncomprehending grandchildren. They came with bottles of wine and boxes of cookies. Sixty-year-old men broke down as they told him what a parachute that fell to their feet as they walked through ruined streets had meant to them as children. A man came to him hesitantly and asked for forgiveness: He pulled from his pocket a handkerchief he had found as a boy and held on to instead of returning to Tempelhof as the instructions directed. When night fell, the line was still there, stretching out toward the Tempelhof fence and the apartment building beyond.

Halvorsen spent more than thirty years in the Air Force, during which time he and Alta raised their five children. She passed away in 1999, three months before they were to celebrate their fiftieth wedding anniversary.

But in 1949, all that lay ahead of him. Halvorsen returned to Brookley Air Force Base in Alabama. He went back to flying C-74 transport missions to Puerto Rico. His life was much as it had been before he left.

But he was no longer lost or alone. He found a small house for Alta and him to live in, "a fairly new, plain, five room frame house (has water piped in, too) that isn't too far from the field but not in a very glamorous setting," he wrote her. "It will take a lot of hard work together but that I look forward to—It will be fun with you." He thought it would be more cost-effective to rent it unfurnished. In May, the same day Clay arrived in Washington, he was given an award from General Vandenberg. He and Alta used the $500 to buy bedroom furniture.

Halvorsen was finally allowed by the Air Force to apply to enter college. In the meantime, they made a home together. Their house was small, but they were happy. They would watch the clouds roll in off the Gulf. They planted seeds for a garden out back. And there, where the Mobile River empties into the bay, every so often, to return a kindness from long before, Hal and Alta Halvorsen would invite Pete Sowa and his wife—and the twins—over for Sunday dinner.

OCTOBER 1990

*On October 3, 1990—the anniversary of "Lt. Gail Halvorsen Day"—
Germany became one nation again with a reunified Berlin its one capital.
A year earlier, the wall that split the city had been torn down, not by
bombs or armies but with the bare hands and garden tools of unknown
Berliners. During the reunification ceremony, a lone C-47 buzzed overhead, making slow circles above the Reichstag and the Brandenburg Gate,
a reminder of a distant moment.*

*In the forty years after the blockade, as America and Russia stood at
nuclear sword tips, West Berliners had—as Ernst Reuter had called upon
them to do—built up and carefully maintained a stockpile of supplies in
case their city was ever besieged again. By 1990, they had secretly squirreled away 132 million pounds of wheat, 52 million pounds of canned
meat, 15 million pounds of butter, 11 million cans of sardines, and 18 million rolls of toilet paper. Now, no longer on an island split off from the rest
of West Germany, Berliners had no need for the accumulated provisions.*

*At the same time, the Soviet Union was crumbling. Shorn of their
empire, with their economy in rubble, the Russian people were hungry.
Some were even starving. There was no milk in the stores; potatoes were
becoming rare. Severe rationing was being introduced in their biggest*

cities. Black markets and bartering were becoming prevalent. Winter was approaching.

West Berliners, imprisoned behind a wall by Russian soldiers and policies for forty years, might have been expected to look toward their defeated foes with something approaching hatred. Instead, they decided they would turn over their hoarded food and supplies to the very people who had made that stockpile necessary.

It was a wonderful gesture, a resonant rhyme of something that had happened long before, but there were difficulties. Long journeys by land were impractical. "The big problem will be transporting it in winter as the cold could destroy the tinned food," said an official of Berlin's economic department. Even if this could be surmounted, breakaway Soviet republics were, a newspaper pointed out, "blockading rail lines and roads to prevent goods from being transported" into Russia.

Berliners were willing to put aside their enmity and anger, and deliver food and supplies to those who had just months before been their enemies. "The only trouble is," the New York Times observed, "they don't know how to deliver it."

NOTES

Prologue: September 2001

xiii *Hundreds of Londoners:* New York Times, September 14, 15, 2001; *Time,* September 24, 2001.

xiii *The crowd felt young:* San Francisco Chronicle, December 30, 2001; interviews with Steve Kettmann, November 2005 and June 2007.

Introduction: June 24, 1948

1 *Harold Stassen:* William Manchester, *The Glory and the Dream* (Boston: Little, Brown, 1973), p. 452; *Los Angeles Times,* June 20, 1948; Joseph Goulden, *The Best Years* (New York: Atheneum, 1976), p. 378.

1 *With a pained:* James T. Patterson, *Mr. Republican: A Biography of Robert A. Taft* (Boston: Houghton Mifflin, 1972), p. 410; Gary A. Donaldson, *Truman Defeats Dewey* (Lexington: University of Kentucky Press, 1999), p. 153.

2 *His campaign:* Los Angeles Times, June 20, 1948; Joseph C. Goulden, ed., *Mencken's Last Campaign: H. L. Mencken on the 1948 Election* (Washington, D.C.: New Republic Book Company, 1976), pp. 29–30; Richard Norton Smith, *Thomas E. Dewey and His Times* (New York: Simon & Schuster, 1982), p. 495.

2 *The air of abundance:* Irwin Ross, *The Loneliest Campaign: The Truman Victory of 1948* (New York: New American Library, 1968), p. 105.

2 *The statuesque sailor:* Richard Norton Smith, p. 498; *Los Angeles Times,* June 24, 1948.

2 *To make the speakers':* Goulden, *Mencken's Last Campaign,* p. 25.

2 *The new phenomenon:* New York Times, April 17, 1988.

2 *Ten million:* Harold I. Gullan, *The Upset That Wasn't: Harry S Truman and the Crucial Election of 1948* (Chicago: Ivan R. Dee, 1998), pp. 89, 96; author's calculations.

2 *The Democratic Party:* Ross, pp. 2, 103.

3 *But in the pivotal year:* Author's calculations of 1948 newspaper headlines using ProQuest database.

3 *At 6 A.M.:* Lucius Clay, *Decision in Germany* (Garden City, N.Y.: Doubleday, 1950), p. 365; *Los Angeles Times,* June 24, 1948.

3 *Two and a quarter million people:* National Council for Geographic Education, "World's 25 Largest Cities in 1950 and 2000," http://www.ncge.org/resources/geoclub/activities/DataSets-25Cities_1950and2000.pdf. Berlin was largest by area, not population.

3 *To Colonel Frank Howley:* Frank Howley, *Berlin Command* (New York: Putnam, 1950), p. 3.
3 *That morning, a gentle drizzle:* Richard Collier, *"Bridge Across the Sky"* (New York: McGraw-Hill, 1978), p. 50.
3 *He thought there was a chance:* Howley, *Berlin Command,* p. 197.
3 *It was a city: Stars and Stripes,* March 10, 1948.
4 *Since dawn:* Howley, *Berlin Command,* pp. 203, 200, 10.
5 *However, "withdrawal would snuff: Christian Science Monitor,* June 26, 1948.
5 *As the* New York Times*: New York Times,* July 6, 1948.
5 *"All the Russians need":* Robert Cowley, ed., *The Cold War: A Military History* (New York: Random House, 2005), p. 25.
5 *If this had occurred:* Walter Isaacson and Evan Thomas, *The Wise Men* (New York: Simon & Schuster, 1986), p. 447.
6 *The general in charge:* Eugene Davidson, *The Death and Life of Germany* (New York: Knopf, 1957), p. 203.

Part I: The Banks, Spring 1945
1: The End

11 *Crossing a rough ocean:* Elbert H. Duncan, "Steadily Advance: A History of the 273rd Infantry Regiment," http://69th-infantry-division.com/histories/273.html.
11 *Now, behind:* Clay, pp. 15–16.
11 *In front of him:* Mark Scott and Semyon Krasilshchik, eds., *Yanks Meet Reds* (Santa Barbara, Calif.: Capra Press, 1988), pp. 25, 123–24, 23.
12 *It was said:* Studs Terkel, *The Good War* (New York: Random House, 1986), p. 445.
12 *The morning:* Scott and Krasilshchik, p. 144.
12 *The dirt roads:* Terkel, p. 445.
12 *White flags bowed:* Cornelius Ryan, *The Last Battle* (New York: Simon & Schuster, 1966), p. 470.
13 *Soon they ran:* Scott and Krasilshchik, pp. 19, 25, 26, 117; Terkel, pp. 445–46; Toland, p. 452; Ryan, p. 471.
15 *In the winter:* Michael Haydock, *City Under Siege* (Washington, D.C.: Brassey's, 2000), p. 8.
15 *Kotzebue "couldn't talk:* Terkel, p. 446.
16 *"We couldn't understand:* Scott and Krasilshchik, p. 118.
16 *So they simply:* Ryan, p. 471.
16 *Three hours later:* Scott and Krasilshchik, pp. 43, 48, 50, 51, 61, 145; Nancy Caldwell Sorel, *The Women Who Wrote the War* (New York: Arcade Publishing, 1999), p. 342.
17 *"Men on both sides:* Scott and Krasilshchik, pp. 15, 155.
17 *The Russians broke into:* Andy Rooney, *My War* (New York: PublicAffairs, 2000), p. 273.
17 *Ann Stringer, a journalist:* Scott and Krasilshchik, p. 79.
17 *It was "the best: New York Times,* April 28, 1945.
17 *The language differences:* Scott and Krasilshchik, pp. 15, 172; Goulden, *The Best Years,* p. 252.
18 *"We waited for them:* CNN "The Cold War, Episode 1," http://www.cnn.com/SPECIALS/cold.war/episodes/01/script.html.
18 *"You get the feeling: Time,* April 28, 1985.
18 *It was a "mad scene:* Scott and Krasilshchik, p. 84.
18 *Freed from a German:* Lilya Wagner, *Women War Correspondents of World War II* (New York: Greenwood Press, 1989), pp. 85–88.
18 *Americans taught the Russians: New York Times,* April 28, 1945.
18 *At one Elbe celebration:* Sorel, p. 344.
19 *"We've been waiting:* Toland, p. 456.
19 *"East and West:* Frank Gillard, British Broadcasting Company, April 27, 1945, http://news.bbc.co.uk/onthisday/hi/dates/stories/april/27/newsid_3563000/3563723.stm.
19 *In Moscow, the maximum: New York Times,* April 28, 1945.
19 *In New York:* Martin Gilbert, *The Second World War: A Complete History* (New York: Henry Holt, 1989), p. 673.
19 *Over the radio:* American Presidency Project, "Statement by the President Announcing the - Junction of Anglo-American and Soviet Forces in Germany," April 27, 1945, http://www.presidency.ucsb.edu/ws/index.php?pid=12369&st=&st1=.
19 *His skin was caked:* Scott and Krasilshchik, p. 125.

2: Tombstones

20 *As assistant secretary,* John H. Backer, *Winds of History* (New York: Van Nostrand Reinhold, 1983), p. vii; Michael Beschloss, *The Conquerors* (New York: Simon & Schuster, 2002), p. 198.

20 *The door swung open:* Isaacson and Thomas, p. 202.

20 *With a broad smile:* Interview with John McCloy, January 16, 1971, Jean Edward Smith Papers.

21 *One, former senator:* Beschloss, p. 191.

21 *Mr. President:* Interview with John McCloy, January 16, 1971, Jean Edward Smith Papers.

22 *McCloy noticed that:* Robert Murphy, *Diplomat Among Warriors* (New York: Doubleday, 1964), pp. 277–78. FDR had lost 36 pounds in the preceding months.

22 *After a week of warm:* National Climate Data Center, http://climvis.ncdc.noaa.gov/cgi-bin/fsod_xmgr.

22 *"McCloy, I'm too tired:* Interview with John McCloy, January 16, 1971, Jean Edward Smith Papers.

22 *As a young boy:* Beschloss, pp. 9–12, 23–26.

23 *Returning from Tehran:* American Presidency Project, "Fireside Chat," December 24, 1943, http://www.presidency.ucsb.edu/ws/index.php?pid=16356&st=&st1=.

24 *En route to Tehran:* Beschloss, pp. 23, 77, 106.

25 *"If I had my way":* Douglas Botting, *From the Ruins of the Reich* (New York: Crown, 1985), p. 194.

25 *Election-year statements:* Beschloss, pp. 95, 167.

25 *Roosevelt himself:* Ibid., p. 83.

25 *He often arose:* Gregor Dallas, *1945* (New Haven: Yale University Press, 2005), p. 254.

26 *His plan was:* Jean Edward Smith, *Lucius D. Clay* (New York: Henry Holt, 1990), p. 215.

26 *Leaving the Yalta:* Beschloss, p. 188.

26 *"Who?" Roosevelt pressed:* Interview with John McCloy, January 16, 1971, Jean Edward Smith Papers.

26 *He hardly knew:* Backer, p. vii.

27 *McCloy left the Oval Office:* Smith, *Lucius D. Clay,* pp. 212, 191.

27 *Instead, when McCloy recounted:* Interview with John McCloy, January 16, 1971, Jean Edward Smith Papers.

28 *Byrnes, who had:* James F. Byrnes, *Speaking Frankly* (New York: Harper & Row, 1947), p. 47.

28 *His office:* Smith, *Lucius D. Clay,* p. 191.

28 *Clay and Byrnes:* Ibid., pp. 194–95.

29 *He enforced brownouts:* Arthur Settel, ed., *This Is Germany* (Freeport, N.Y.: Books for Libraries, 1950), p. 28.

29 *He shut down:* Smith, *Lucius D. Clay,* pp. 199–200.

29 Time *magazine: Time,* March 19, 1945.

29 *His thoughts were interrupted:* Clay, p. 2.

29 *The so-called:* Thomas Parrish, *Berlin in the Balance* (Reading, Pa.: Addison-Wesley, 1998), pp. 145–46; Rick Atkinson, *An Army at Dawn* (New York: Henry Holt, 2002), p. 45.

29 *Clay instructed:* Murphy, p. 276.

30 *Where most offices: The New Yorker,* January 13, 1951.

30 *He later would joke:* Smith, *Lucius D. Clay,* pp. 27–31, 21–22; Columbia Oral History interview of Lucius Clay, 1973, pp. 49, 59.

32 *He would run: Marietta Daily Journal,* May 25, 1949.

32 *The Clays owned:* Columbia Oral History, pp. 15, 21.

32 *But of all the happy memories: The New Yorker,* January 13, 1951.

32 *Their small suite:* Smith, *Lucius D. Clay,* pp. 22–23.

33 *But much of the time:* Backer, p. 45.

33 *He ran around town: Time,* June 25, 1945; Smith, *Lucius D. Clay,* p. 31.

33 *"He was strong-willed:* Backer, p. 46.

33 *In the summer of 1914:* Smith, *Lucius D. Clay,* pp. 31, 34–35.

34 *He made some:* Jean Smith Interview, C-SPAN *Booknotes,* November 18, 1990.

34 *Ignoring his prescribed studies:* Smith, *Lucius D. Clay,* pp. 34–39.

35 *"I thought we ought:* Backer, p. 46.

35 *"The greatest thrill:* Smith, *Lucius D. Clay,* p. 41.

35 *He contacted the War Department:* Columbia Oral History, p. 84.

35 *He reported in:* Smith, *Lucius D. Clay,* p. 43.

35 *As Marjorie McKeown:* Backer, p. 47; Smith, *Lucius D. Clay,* p. 44.

35–36 *While efficiency reports:* Backer, p. 49.

36 *In 1929:* Smith, *Lucius D. Clay,* pp. 55–59.

36 *From his office:* Backer, pp. 49–50.

36 *He made the acquaintance:* Smith, *Lucius D. Clay,* pp. 505, 171, 67–71, 89–91.

37 *The airports:* Clay Interview, Eisenhower Administration Project, Columbia University, p. 22.

37 *He did not even wear:* Jean Edward Smith Papers, Box 7.

37 *On Sunday, December 7:* Smith, *Lucius D. Clay,* pp. 97–99, 113–114, 155. That night in a confused meeting called by the commander of the Army Air Corps, Clay was told to ground all civilian airplanes from taking off the next day. He argued such a step was too extreme. Instead, they agreed to check the pilots' identification before takeoff.

38 *A lipstick manufacturer: Reader's Digest,* October 1948.

38 *Looking back: The New Yorker,* January 13, 1951.

39 *Byrnes recounted:* Byrnes, p. 47.

39 *John Kenneth Galbraith:* Smith, *Lucius D. Clay,* p. 2.

39 *"He had a mind:* Backer, pp. 46, 56.

39 *"Clay has incurred: New York Times,* July 15, 1945.

39 *His own grown sons:* Clay, p. 71.

39 *"Day after day":* Backer, p. 50.

40 *In the spring of 1943:* Smith, *Lucius D. Clay,* p. 160.

40 *That December:* Jean Edward Smith Papers, Box 1.

40 *When Dwight Eisenhower:* Smith, *Lucius D. Clay,* pp. 169, 171.

40 *Then, just as the winter:* Ibid., pp. 180–183; Howley, *Berlin Command,* p. 17.

40 *About a week:* Backer, p. 51.

41 *Clay arrived back:* Clay, pp. 3–4.

41 *The phone rang:* Smith, *Lucius D. Clay,* p. 189.

41 *"I am afraid that I failed:* Clay, p. 4.

41 *"I never saw:* Backer, p. 51.

41 *All that kept:* Clay, p. 4.

42 *Murphy smiled broadly:* Murphy, p. 276.

42 *A few minutes:* Clay, pp. 2–4.

42 *The following day:* Beschloss, pp. 202–3; Smith, *Lucius D. Clay,* pp. 215–16; Byrnes, p. 48.

43 *A month later: Time,* May 7, 1945.

3: Visions

44 *On his desk:* Ryan, p. 317.

44 *At the hour: New York Times,* April 13, 1945.

44 *"The mere conquest:* American Presidency Project, "Undelivered Address Prepared for Jefferson Day," April 13, 1945, http://www.presidency.ucsb.edu/ws/index.php?pid=16602.

45 *For six years:* Martin Gilbert, *The Day the War Ended* (New York: Henry Holt, 1995), p. 1.

45 *On the night: New York Times,* November 6, 1912; Townsend Hoopes and Douglas Brinkley, *Driven Patriot* (New York: Knopf, 1992), p. 21.

46 *When the Great War:* Henry Kissinger, *Diplomacy* (New York: Simon & Schuster, 1995), p. 45.

46 *Captain Harry S Truman:* Beschloss, p. 228.

46 *In his last, sad days:* David Fromkin, *In the Time of the Americans* (New York: Knopf, 1995), p. 363.

46 *In March 1921:* Isaacson and Thomans, p. 125.

46 *Born in the working-class:* Hoopes and Brinkley, pp. 22–29.

47 *He became a successful:* Arnold Rogow, *James Forrestal* (New York: Macmillan, 1963), p. 67.

47 *Forrestal's boss:* Hoopes and Brinkley, pp. 51, 13–15.

48 *By the 1920s:* Rogow, p. 61.

48 *They frequently:* Hoopes and Brinkley, pp. 38, 41, 34.

48 *At a cocktail party:* Ibid., pp. 42–48; Thomas Boettcher, *First Call* (New York: Little, Brown, 1992), p. 28.

49 *He first went:* Rogow, pp. 91–92.

49 *He cultivated:* Hoopes and Brinkley, p. 120.

50 *When the* New York Times: *New York Times,* December 7, 1941.

50 *Roosevelt announced: Time,* May 22, 1944.

50 *Jo's move to Washington:* Hoopes and Brinkley, pp. 131–35, 216.

51 *He was offshore:* Ibid., pp. 195–97.

52 *The Japanese waited:* James Bradley with Ron Powers, *Flags of Our Fathers* (New York: Bantam, 2000), p. 154.

52 *On the fourth day:* Hoopes and Brinkley, p. 199.

52 *The landing craft:* James Forrestal, *The Forrestal Diaries*, edited by Walter Millis (New York: Viking, 1951), p. 30.

52 *As they scurried:* Hoopes and Brinkley, p. 199; James Bradley, pp. 172, 205, 207. This was the first flag-raising on Iwo Jima, not the second immortalized in Joe Rosenthal's famous photograph. Indirectly, however, Forrestal was responsible for that second flag. He had been so excited, perhaps relieved, by the scene of joy he had witnessed when the flag went up that he asked to take the flag back to the United States. Colonel Chandler Johnson, whose men had put the flag up, wanted it for the battalion. In order to make sure that Forrestal or someone else did not get to keep it, he ordered it taken down himself. He sent his assistant operations officer to find a suitable replacement. "And make it a bigger one!" he called after the lieutenant.

53 *In the weeks:* Hoopes and Brinkley, p. 201.

53 *Shortly after he returned:* Forrestal, pp. 32–33.

54 *Indeed, on the Fourth:* Mudd Library Unedited Diaries, p. 6.

54 *Forrestal felt most:* Graham White and John Maze, *Henry A. Wallace: His Search for a New World Order* (Chapel Hill: University of North Carolina Press, 1995), pp. 1–2.

54 *Among the comfortable:* Mayne, p. 29; Daniel Yergin, *Shattered Peace* (Boston: Houghton Mifflin, 1977), p. 246.

54 *He once told a friend:* Alonzo Hamby, *Beyond the New Deal: Harry S. Truman and American Liberalism* (New York: Columbia University Press, 1973), p. 23.

54 *When, as vice president:* White and Maze, p. x.

55 *In his* Wallace's Farmer: Goulden, *The Best Years,* p. 217.

55 *He believed that the future:* Ibid., p. 218; Jules Abels, *Out of the Jaws of Victory* (New York: Henry Holt, 1959), p. 114.

55 *More than half:* Clifford, p. 113.

55 *"When Henry looks:* Hoopes and Brinkley, p. 263.

55 *But at ten to six:* Forrestal, pp. 42–43; David McCullough, *Truman* (New York: Simon & Schuster, 1992), pp. 346–47; Harry S Truman Library Photograph, Accession number 73-1909.

56 *As the cabinet:* Hoopes and Brinkley, p. 204.

56 *Wallace appreciated the sentiment:* Yergin, pp. 69–70.

4: Flight

57 *On that tragic:* Gail Halvorsen "Personal History," unpublished, February 14, 1985, p. 23.

57 *But shortly after noon:* Ibid., p. 23.

58 *Gail S. "Hal" Halvorsen:* Ibid., pp. 1–2, 58, 60. Halvorsen's parents named him Gail, but he did not like the feminine-sounding name. In high school, his teachers called him by his middle name, Seymour, which was not much better. His close friends then began to call him Hal, and once he went to college it was the name he went by. Later he would use the name Gail more often.

58 *The Halvorsens grew:* Ibid., pp. 3–21; Gail Halvorsen, *The Berlin Candy Bomber* (Springville, Utah: Horizon Publishers, 1997), pp. 14–15; *Mobile Register,* January 24, 1949; Halvorsen interview, August 2005.

60 *In his spare time:* Halvorsen, *The Berlin Candy Bomber,* pp. 16–20; Halvorsen interview, February 3, 2007.

60 *At the time:* Isaacson and Thomas, p. 203.

61 *His high school:* Halvorsen, *The Berlin Candy Bomber,* p. 15.

61 *In the meantime:* Halvorsen, "Personal History," p. 23.

61 *It was there:* Gail Halvorsen, "Personal History, Part Three," unpublished, July 24, 1990, p. 10.

62 *It was, significantly:* Halvorsen, "Personal History," p. 24.

62 *"The chemistry seemed:* Alta Halvorsen, "Alta's Story in Her Own Words," in "Alta Jolley Halvorsen," Halvorsen family volume.

62 *In March 1943:* Halvorsen, "Personal History," p. 24; Halvorsen, "Personal History, Part Three," p. 11; Halvorsen interview, February 3, 2007.

63 *Seven out of ten:* Goulden, *The Best Years,* p. 7.

63 *They traveled:* Halvorsen, "Personal History," p. 27.

63 *"This is it!":* Gail Halvorsen to Alta Jolley, August 13, 1943, Halvorsen Private Papers.

63 *At the beginning:* Roger Launius and Coy Cross, *MAC and the Legacy of the Berlin Airlift* (Scott Air Force Base, Ill.: Military Airlift Command, 1989), p. 1.

63 *And though other:* Otha C. Spencer, *Flying the Hump: Memories of an Air War* (College Station: Texas A&M University Press, 1992), p. xiv.

64 *Transport pilots:* Frank Donovan, *Bridge in the Sky* (New York: David McKay, 1968), p. 106.

64 *Halvorsen had set out:* Halvorsen interview, February 3, 2007.

64 *One pilot remembered:* Spencer, p. xvii.

64 *Even while still:* Halvorsen, "Personal History," pp. 26, 29; Halvorsen, "Personal History, Part Three," pp. 29–32; Spencer, p. 41.

64 *He would be stuck:* Gail Halvorsen interview, August 8, 2005.

66 *They had not seen each other:* Halvorsen, "Personal History, Part Three," p. 27.

66 *Alta had joined:* Mary Jensen, "Our Season in New York," in "Alta Jolley Halvorsen," Halvorsen family volume.

66 *Within an hour:* Halvorsen, "Personal History, Part Three," pp. 27–29.

66 *He bought a big, brown:* Halvorsen, "Personal History," p. 32.

66 *She wore a bright red:* Gail Halvorsen interview and family video footage, August 8, 2005.

67 *On the morning:* Backer, p. 18.

67 *On some days:* Robert Sickels, *The 1940s* (Westport, Conn.: Greenwood Press, 2004), p. 25; Collier, p. 19; "Boots on the Ground," http://www.third-way.com/data/product/file/12/boots_on_the_ground.pdf.

67 *Those who wanted:* Halvorsen, "Personal History, Part Three," pp. 32–34; Halvorsen, "Personal History," p. 33; Halvorsen interview, February 3, 2007.

5: The Descent

70 *Lucius Clay:* Clay, pp. 8–9.

70 *The scholars had "lived:* Letter to General John Hildring, May 7, 1945, Jean Edward Smith, ed., *The Papers of General Lucius D. Clay* (Bloomington: Indiana University Press, 1974), pp. 11–12.

71 *It was 6 P.M.:* Smith, *Lucius D. Clay,* p. 236.

71 *Jodl asked:* Botting, *From the Ruins of the Reich,* p. 87.

71 *Clay stayed up:* Smith, *Lucius D. Clay,* p. 236.

71 *As the clock neared:* Botting, *From the Ruins of the Reich,* p. 90; *Stars and Stripes,* May 8, 1949.

72 *Big Ben:* New York Times, May 8, 9, 1945; Botting, *From the Ruins of the Reich,* p. 94; Richard Mayne, *Postwar: The Dawn of Today's America* (London: Thames and Hudson, 1983), p. 8; Isaacson and Thomas, p. 272; Roy Hoopes, *Americans Remember the Home Front* (New York: Hawthorn Books, 1977), pp. 343–44; *Time,* May 14, 1945.

73 *In the White House:* McCullough, p. 382.

73 *"The flags of freedom:* American Presidency Project, "Broadcast to the American People Announcing the Surrender of Germany," May 8th, 1945, http://www.presidency.ucsb.edu/ws/index.php?pid=12241&st=&st1=; *New York Times,* May 9, 1945; Goulden, *The Best Years,* p. 8.

73 *The morning after:* Smith, *Lucius D. Clay,* p. 237.

74 *"Life will be hard:* Foreign Affairs, July/August 1998.

74 *Time magazine concurred:* Time, June 25, 1945.

74 *"General Clay's exceedingly:* Backer, p. 6.

74 *The Baltimore Sun:* Smith, *Lucius D. Clay,* p. 6.

75 *In the days before:* Backer, pp. 285–86.

75 *In fact, he left:* Smith, *Lucius D. Clay,* pp. 5, 217; Clay, pp. 5–7.

75 *A week after:* Backer, pp. 15–16.

77 *No one was quite:* Otto Friedrich, *Before the Deluge* (New York: Harper & Row, 1972), p. 6.

77 *When General George Patton:* Botting, *From the Ruins of the Reich,* p. 12. The debate over whether Eisenhower should have tried to take Berlin instead of letting the Soviets sack the city is one of historians' favorite parlor games. It is also among the most fatuous. Eisenhower had some very good reasons for not making the advance: other targets, such as Dresden and Leipzig, had much more of what was left of Germany's heavy industry. Americans were 285 miles away, as opposed to the Soviets who had only 35 miles to go. American troops and supplies were needed

in the Pacific in what was expected to be a brutal invasion of the Japanese home islands. Bradley's estimated figure of a cost of 100,000 troops was more than half of the total American troops lost in battle in the European theater. Despite all this, an American and British capture of Berlin may still have been worth it, were it not for a central fact: Bending to accommodate Stalin at every turn, they would have given the conquered parts of Berlin over to the Soviets as they did with large swaths of what became the Soviet zone of Germany. It would have been, without a doubt, all for naught.

77 *Making its way:* Howley, *Berlin Command,* pp. 16–17.
78 *A member of Philadelphia's:* *Life,* June 5, 1944; *Stars and Stripes,* December 14, 1947; Howley, *Berlin Command,* p. 19; *Who's Who,* 1972–1973 entry, in Papers of Frank L. Howley.
78 *He joined the Army:* Papers of Frank L. Howley.
78 *When his unit:* Haydock p. 22; Frank Howley, *Your War for Peace* (New York: Henry Holt, 1953), p. 4.
78 *He landed on Omaha Beach:* Ibid., pp. 17–25; Papers of Frank L. Howley; Personal Diary of Colonel Frank L. Howley, in Papers of Frank L. Howley.
79 *Soon after dawn:* Howley, *Berlin Command,* pp. 20, 22, 26–27; Personal Diary of Colonel Frank L. Howley; Haydock, p. 23.
80 *"It was my intention:* Parrish, p. 79.
81 *As his column:* Howley, *Berlin Command,* p. 11.
81 *On the Russian side:* Ibid., pp. 28–32; Personal Diary of Colonel Frank L. Howley; *Stars and Stripes,* December 11, 1948.
83 *"The road to Berlin:* Howley, *Berlin Command,* pp. 42, 32; Personal Diary of Colonel Frank L. Howley.
84 *"As I rode:* Howley, *Your War for Peace,* p. 69.
84 *He was someone who:* For example, see transcript of William Heimlich interview conducted for CNN's 1998 series, *The Cold War,* http://www.gwu.edu/~nsarchiv/coldwar/interviews/episode-4/heimlich2.html. William Heimlich, a top intelligence official who came into Berlin with Howley and later became head of RIAS, when asked to describe Howley, called him "dramatic" three times in nine sentences.
84 *"Two years of war:* Petra Goedde, *GIs and Germans: Culture, Gender, and Foreign Relations, 1945–1949* (New Haven: Yale University Press, 2003), pp. 42, 5, 47; Allied Museum permanent exhibit, Berlin; Franklin M. Davis, *Come as a Conqueror: The United States Army's Occupation of Germany, 1945–1949* (New York: Macmillan, 1967), p. 143.
85 *On April 12:* Beschloss, p. 212.
85 *Two weeks later:* Gilbert, *The Day the War Ended,* p. 29.
86 *During the war:* National Archives, Record Group 44, ARC identifier 513988.
86 *Howley looked:* The Editors of the *Army Times, Berlin: The City That Would Not Die* (New York: Dodd, Mead, 1968), p. 31.
86 *When Hitler was still:* Lowell Bennett, *Berlin Bastion* (Frankfurt: Fred Rudl, 1951), p. 10; Alexandra Richie, *Faust's Metropolis* (New York: Carroll & Graf, 1998), p. 331; Otto Friedrich, pp. 5, 11.
87 *The city had:* Richie, p. 331; Bennett, p. 140.
87 *There, in 1931:* Stephen Van Dulken, *Inventing the 20th Century* (New York: New York University Press, 2003), p. 110.
87 *With 149:* Robert P. Grathwol and Donita M. Moorhus, *American Forces in Berlin* (Washington, D.C.: Department of Defense, Legacy Resource Management Programs, 1994), p. 2.
87 *"There is no city:* Brian Ladd, *The Ghosts of Berlin* (Chicago: University of Chicago Press, 1997), p. 117.
87 *Berlin was the home:* Sherill Tippins, *February House* (New York: Houghton Mifflin, 2005), p. 40.
87 *It was Berlin:* Otto Friedrich, pp. 89, 204, 219; Max Jammer, *Einstein and Religion* (Princeton: Princeton University Press, 1999), p. 19.
88 *"This city is a melting pot:* Dorothy Rowe, *Representing Berlin* (Burlington, Vt.: Ashgate Publishing, 2003), p. 138.
88 *If, in later years:* John Mander, *Berlin: The Eagle and the Bear* (Westport, Conn.: Greenwood Press, 1959), p. 139; Antony Beevor, *The Fall of Berlin 1945* (New York: Viking, 2002), p. 2; Eric Johnson and Karl-Heinz Reuband, *What We Knew: Terror, Mass Murder and Everyday Life in*

Nazi Germany (London: John Murray, 2005), p. 330. Even half a century later, a 1999 study of Germans born before 1930—those who would have been fifteen and older at the war's end—revealed that 54 percent of those living in Berlin admitted to once having believed in Nazism and 65 percent of Berliners admitted to once sharing Nazi ideals.

88 *It was Berliners:* Richie, pp. 424, 415.

88 *At night, after the work:* Susanne Everett, *Lost Berlin* (New York: Galley Books, 1979), p. 186.

89 *"These buildings of ours":* Ladd, p. 126.

89 *Under Speer:* Richard Brett-Smith, *Berlin '45: The Grey City* (London: Macmillan, 1967), pp. 138–39; Paul Steege, *Black Market, Cold War* (New York: Cambridge University Press, 2007), p. 192.

89 *Speer designed:* Richie, p. 471.

89 *Hitler and Speer:* Robert Conot, *Justice at Nuremberg* (New York: Carroll & Graf, 1984), p. 240; Beschloss, p. 291.

89 *In 1934:* Ladd, p. 145.

89 *When, in 1909:* Haydock, pp. 30–31; Wolfgang Huschke, *The Candy Bombers: The Berlin Airlift 1948/49, A History of the People and the Planes* (Berlin: Metropol, 1999), p. 121; *Air Force Times,* April 30, 1979.

90 *Stretching out:* Grathwol and Moorhus, p. 15.

90 *In case the point:* Parrish, p. 236.

90 *It had 5,000:* Haydock, p. 31; *Chicago Tribune,* August 14, 2004; Richie, p. 418.

90 *As befitted its place:* Air Force Times, April 30, 1979.

90 *By 1938:* T. H. Elkins with B. Hofmeister, *Berlin: The Spatial Structure of a Divided City* (London: Methuen, 1988), p. 111.

91 *On the nights:* A. C. Grayling, *Among the Dead Cities* (New York: Walker, 2006), p. 62.

92 *American and British:* Otto Friedrich, p. 6.

92 *"Each mother:* Beevor, *The Fall of Berlin 1945,* p. 180.

92 *"This youth of ours":* Guido Knopp, trans. Angus McGeoch, *Hitler's Children* (Gloucestershire: Sutton Publishing, 2000), pp. vii, 153–54.

92 *Another word problem:* Lynn H. Nicholas, *Cruel World: The Children of Europe in the Nazi Web* (New York: Knopf, 2005), p. 77.

92 *Beginning in September:* Emmy Werner, *Through the Eyes of Innocents* (Boulder, Colo.: Westview Press, 2000), pp. 48–58.

93 *In Berlin, on April 20:* Knopp, p. 9.

93 *But by that time:* Botting, *From the Ruins of the Reich,* pp. 50–51.

93 *One out of every ten:* Eric Morris, *Blockade* (New York: Stein and Day, 1973), p. 37.

93 *By early April:* Botting, *From the Ruins of the Reich,* pp. 51–54.

94 *When a shell exploded:* Beevor, *The Fall of Berlin 1945,* p. 310.

94 *At the city clerk's office:* Anthony Read and David Fisher, *The Fall of Berlin* (New York: Norton, 1992), p. 317.

94 *Exactly sixteen years:* Beevor, *The Fall of Berlin 1945,* pp. 196–97; Ryan, p. 387; Richie, p. 572.

94 *On April 25:* Botting, *From the Ruins of the Reich,* p. 57.

94 *Of the males:* Ryan, pp. 26–27.

95 *But by the end of April:* Eric Morris, p. 34.

95 *When the Russians approached:* Nicholas, pp. 421–42; Read and Fisher, *The Fall of Berlin,* p. 197.

95 *Others would go home:* Nicholas Stargardt, *Witness of War: Children's Lives Under the Nazis* (London: Jonathan Cape, 2005), p. 294.

95 *One out of every nine:* Botting, *From the Ruins of the Reich,* pp. 103, 68.

95 *Five thousand:* Nicholas, p. 422.

96 *The Russians used:* Otto Friedrich, p. 6.

96 *A German Panzer officer:* Botting, *From the Ruins of the Reich,* p. 62.

96 *Babies would die:* Ryan, p. 422.

96 *At Tempelhof:* Haydock, p. 23; Henry H. Arnold, *American Air Power Comes of Age,* volume 2 (Birmingham, Ala.: Air University Press, 2002), p. 399.

96 *One shell hit:* Otto Friedrich, p. 6.

96 *A lion escaped:* Botting, *From the Ruins of the Reich,* p. 75.

96 *The Russians would lose:* Robert Ostergren and John Rice, *The Europeans* (New York: Guilford

Press, 2004), p. 353; Henrik Bering, *Outpost Berlin: The History of the American Military Forces in Berlin, 1945–1994* (Chicago: edition q, 1995), p. 6; http://siadapp.dior.whs.mil/personnel/CASUALTY/WCPRINCIPAL.pdf.

96 *Of the 125,000:* Botting, *From the Ruins of the Reich,* p. 84.
96 *"These men have come:* Richard Brett-Smith, *Berlin '45: The Grey City* (London: Macmillan, 1967), p. 42.
97 *The Siberians:* Botting, *From the Ruins of the Reich,* p. 66.
97 *Over the course:* The Guardian, May 1, 2002. Antony Beevor writes, "Estimates of rape victims from the city's two main hospitals ranged from 95,000 to 130,000." But it seems likely that, given the conditions in Berlin at the time, and the societal stigma attached not only to rape but to rape by Russians, only a fraction of the victims would have brought themselves to a hospital.
97 *"Frau, komm!":* Botting, *From the Ruins of the Reich,* pp. 66, 189; Richie, p. 564.
98 *"Poison or bullet:* Ruth Andreas-Friedrich, *Battleground Berlin* (New York: Paragon House, 1990), p. 17.
98 *In fact, it was by:* The Guardian, May 1, 2002.
98 *For some, the rapes:* Botting, *From the Ruins of the Reich,* p. 69.
98 *In the weeks after:* Richie, p. 591.
98 *"Better a Russian:* Read and Fisher, *The Fall of Berlin,* p. 440.
98 *"Ruins, craters:* Time, May 14, 1945.
99 *Ernest Leiser:* Gilbert, *The Day the War Ended,* p. 70.
99 *World War II ended:* Botting, *From the Ruins of the Reich,* p. 76; Richie, p. 596.
99 *In those final:* Time, April 25, 1985.
100 *Rather the moment:* Ryan, p. 318.
100 *The Soviets told the Americans:* Ann Tusa and John Tusa, *The Berlin Airlift* (New York: Sarpedon, 1988), p. 28.
100 *They rode in wearing:* Howley, *Berlin Command,* pp. 43–44; Personal Diary of Colonel Frank L. Howley, in Papers of Frank L. Howley.
101 *"I had managed:* Botting, *From the Ruins of the Reich,* p. 114.
101 *The next day:* Howley, *Berlin Command,* p. 45.
101 *Howley said he needed:* Personal Diary of Colonel Frank L. Howley, in Papers of Frank L. Howley.
102 *They entered the city:* Donovan, p. 15.
102 *"It didn't look:* Personal Diary of Colonel Frank L. Howley, in Papers of Frank L. Howley.
102 *The apartment buildings:* East European Quarterly, Fall 1995. In a survey that counted apartments where the interior walls were destroyed as "lightly damaged," 70 percent of central Berlin was considered to have been utterly destroyed.
102 *It was a dark city:* Haydock, p. 6.
102 *The debris was piled:* Howley, *Your War for Peace,* p. 69.
102 *As Howley rode:* Haydock, p. 2.
102 *"Berlin is a shambles":* Howley, *Berlin Command,* p. 41.
103 *"Wretched, walking:* Howley, *Your War for Peace,* p. 69.
103 *"Were these the crack:* Botting, *From the Ruins of the Reich,* p. 130.
103 *As July of 1945:* Andreas-Friedrich, p. 40; Personal Diary of Colonel Frank L. Howley, in Papers of Frank L. Howley.
103 *Bodies floated:* Arnold-Forster, p. 22.
103 *They would be wrapped:* Botting, *From the Ruins of the Reich,* p. 130.
103 *There was no water:* Mark Arnold-Forster, *The Siege of Berlin* (London: Collins, 1979), p. 22.
103 *Raw sewage:* Richie, p. 607.
103 *Only 9,300:* Grathwol and Moorhus, p. 35.
103 *In the months:* Botting, *From the Ruins of the Reich,* p. 130.
104 *Of babies born:* Howley, *Your War for Peace,* p. 69.
104 *Many had not survived:* Jean Edward Smith, *The Defense of Berlin* (Baltimore: Johns Hopkins Press, 1963), p. 67.
104 *Fifty-three thousand orphans:* Botting, *From the Ruins of the Reich,* pp. 130, 133,135; Grathwol and Moorhus, p. 34.
104 *"The hollow-eyed:* Howley, *Your War for Peace,* p. 69.
104 *Doctors in 1945:* Grathwol and Moorhus, p. 60.

104 *When they saw:* Botting, *From the Ruins of the Reich,* p. 130.

104 *The sight:* Davis, p. 219.

104 *"Enjoy the war":* Ryan, p. 30.

104 *On the Fourth:* Howley, *Berlin Command,* pp. 47–49; Personal Diary of Colonel Frank L. Howley, in Papers of Frank L. Howley.

105 *"Wherever we looked:* Clay, p. 21.

105 *When his car passed:* Stars and Stripes, May 14, 1949.

105 *Robert Murphy:* Wolfgang Schivelbusch, *In a Cold Crater: Cultural and Intellectual Life in Berlin, 1945–1948,* translated by Kelly Barry (Berkeley: University of California Press, 1998), p. 19.

105 *To Clay:* Clay, p. 21.

105 *"Something that is worse:* Isaacson and Thomas, p. 288.

105 *By July 7:* Murphy, p. 295.

106 *An "Inter-Allied:* Smith, *The Defense of Berlin,* p. 87; Personal Diary of Colonel Frank L. Howley, in Papers of Frank L. Howley.

106 *Before the meeting:* Howley, *Berlin Command,* pp. 53–56; Personal Diary of Colonel Frank L. Howley, in Papers of Frank L. Howley; Jean Edward Smith Papers, Box 7.

108 *Along with him:* National Archives, March 16, 1945, letter from Forrestal to Lieutenant John F. Kennedy, ARC number 192727. "The Secretary of the Navy regrets that your disability has terminated your service on the active list of the Navy, and wishes you many years of happiness."

108 *"Went into Berlin":* Mudd Library Unedited Diaries, p. 412.

108 *After the tour:* John Kennedy, *Prelude to Leadership* (Washington, D.C.: Regnery, 1995), pp. 106, 59.

108 *The smell:* Beschloss, p. 255.

108 *"A more depressing sight:* Smith, *The Defense of Berlin,* p. 67.

108 *He looked at them:* McCullough, p. 414.

108 *"This is a hell:* Harry Truman to Bess Truman, July 20, 1945, Harry S Truman Library.

108 *"The Russians have recognized:* Personal Diary of Colonel Frank L. Howley, in Papers of Frank L. Howley.

108 *"The coming months:* Botting, *From the Ruins of the Reich,* p. 137.

109 *The defeated Germans:* Time, June 25, 1945.

109 *When the Americans had arrived:* Grathwol and Moorhus, p. 11.

109 *Under a big sun:* McCullough, p. 428; Clay, p. 44.

109 *Speaking without notes:* Beschloss, p. 257.

109 *They were there:* American Presidency Project, "Remarks at the Raising of the Flag Over the U.S. Group Control Council Headquarters in Berlin," July 20, 1945, http://www.presidency.ucsb.edu/ws/index.php?pid=12171&st=&st1=.

110 *It was, wrote:* McCullough, p. 429.

110 *That day he was awed:* Clay, p. 45.

110 *In Berlin, as spring:* Botting, *From the Ruins of the Reich,* p. 50.

110 *When Thornton Wilder's:* Ralph Willett, *The Americanization of Germany, 1945–1949* (London: Routledge, 1989), pp. 67, 12.

110 *Kennedy wrote:* Kennedy, p. 53.

110 *"We are on very good: Manchester Guardian,* July 9, 1945.

111 *In a public opinion:* Isaacson and Thomas, p. 270.

111 *On June 8:* Charles Bohlen, *Witness to History* (New York: Norton, 1973), p. 222.

111 *Without any Soviet:* Walter Bedell Smith, *My Three Years in Moscow* (Philadelphia: Lippincott, 1950), p. 23.

111 *The day was warm:* David Eisenhower, *Eisenhower: At War, 1943–1945* (New York: Random House, 1986), pp. 819–20.

111 *While Zhukov:* D. M. Giangreco and Robert E. Grffin, *Airbridge to Berlin* (Novato, Calif: Presidio, 1988), p. 40.

112 *Zhukov in his toast:* Walter Bedell Smith, p. 23.

112 *Eisenhower responded:* Stephen E. Ambrose, *Eisenhower,* volume 1 (New York: Simon & Schuster, 1983), p. 429.

112 *It had been fought:* Eisenhower, pp. 819–20.

112 *Now "we are going:* Walter Bedell Smith, p. 23.

112 *The lunch came:* Clay, p. 47.

Part II: The Bend, Spring 1948
6: Chasm

115 *Belowdecks:* National Archives, *Germany: Handle With Care,* March of Time series, 1947, ARC identifier 23820; 97648

117 *Soon after the war:* Lance Morrow, *The Best Year of Their Lives* (New York: Basic Books, 2005), p. 34.

117 *"The year's harvest:* Time, January 3, 1949.

117 *The late 1940s:* William Graebner, *The Age of Doubt: American Thought and Culture in the 1940s* (Boston: Twayne, 1991), p. 65.

117 *"At last:* Eric Goldman, *The Crucial Decade—and After* (New York: Random House, 1956), pp. 11–12.

117 *The first couple of years:* Sickels, pp. xxiii–xxiv, 113.

117 *Bob Hope:* Box Office Report, "Top 20 Films of 1948 by Domestic Revenue," http://www.boxofficereport.com/database/1948.shtml.

117 *The Oscar:* Academy of Motion Picture Arts and Sciences, "Awards Database," http://awardsdatabase.oscars.org/ampas_awards/DisplayMain.jsp?curTime=1166167115324.

117 *The editors:* Stars and Stripes, January 1, 1948, December 23, 1947; *Time,* January 3, 1949.

118 *When the Associated Press:* Stars and Stripes, February 29, 1948.

118 *"Zip-A-Dee-Doo-Dah":* Charles Panati, *Panati's Parade of Fads, Follies, and Manias* (New York: HarperCollins, 1991), p. 230.

118 *That spring:* Stars and Stripes, May 9, 1948.

118 *"I can look back:* Goulden, *The Best Years,* p. 6.

119 *"It's all very well:* Goldman, p. 10.

119 *"Get Germany:* Shlaim, p. 27.

119 *Americans could be forgiven:* Isaacson and Thomas, p. 348.

119 *Dawn came late:* Saturday Evening Post, May 10, 1947.

120 *While he fed:* Haydock, p. 167; Smith, *Lucius D. Clay,* p. 325.

120 *He "contrived:* Mark Arnold-Forster, *The Siege of Berlin* (London: Collins, 1979), p. 21.

120 *And as he smoked:* National Archives, *Battle for Berlin,* March of Time series, 1948; Backer, p. 137; Robert Lochner interview, George Washington University National Security Archive, http://www.gwu.edu/~nsarchiv/coldwar/interviews/episode-4/lochner4.html.

120 *Clay's home in Berlin:* Backer, p. 103; author's observations; *Washington Post,* May 18, 1949.

120 *Seven days a week:* Jean Edward Smith Papers, Box 7; *Saturday Evening Post,* May 10, 1947; Richard Collier, *Bridge Across the Sky* (New York: McGraw-Hill, 1978), p. 1.

120 *Upon his arrival:* Backer, p. 182; National Archives, *Paramount News,* May 18, 1949.

121 *Reporters would note:* Time, July 12, 1948.

121 *"He looked up at you:* Annelore Slater in "Berlin Airlift," WETA documentary, 1998.

121 *When he became enraged:* Backer, pp. 136, 56.

121 *"You couldn't help:* Edloe Donnan interview, George Washington University National Security Archive, http://www.gwu.edu/~nsarchiv/coldwar/interviews/episode-4/donnan2.html.

122 *"It was the nearest thing:* Interview with John McCloy, January 16, 1971, Jean Edward Smith Papers. After Eisenhower's return to the United States, General Joseph T. McNarney held the title of military governor from November 1945 to March 1947, with Clay holding the official title of deputy military governor for military government. However, McNarney concentrated on overseeing American forces in Europe, did not consider himself to be the military governor, and left such matters almost entirely to Clay at his discretion.

122 *In Tokyo:* William Manchester, *American Caesar* (Boston: Little, Brown, 1978), p. 607.

122 *When he made his way:* Ibid., pp. 558–60.

122 *Clay's home:* The New Yorker, January 13, 1951.

122–123 *At night:* Jean Edward Smith Papers, Box 7.

123 *Clay would drink:* Saturday Evening Post, May 10, 1947.

123 *When he first:* Backer, pp. 31, 106, 56.

123 *A friend would recall:* Smith, *Lucius D. Clay,* p. 13.

124 *"There is no parallel:* Cable to Draper, November 3, 1947, *Papers of General Lucius D. Clay,* p. 475.

124 *Two million:* Beschloss, p. 274.

124 *Clay was unembarrassed: New York Times,* July 4, 1948.

124 *By the beginning:* Clay, pp. 283–305; Smith, *Lucius D. Clay,* pp. 332, 393; Backer, p. 139; Parrish, p. 84; Howley, *Berlin Command,* p. 119.

125 *The Americans tried everything: Stars and Stripes,* March 22, 1948.

125 *"Anyone who seriously:* Backer, p. 58.

125 *Indeed, professional public opinion:* Merritt and Merritt, eds., *Public Opinion in Occupied Germany: The OMGUS Surveys, 1945–1949,* pp. 146, 171.

126 *Around the country:* Eugene Davidson, p. 151.

126 *In survey:* National Archives, Record Group 260, Office of Military Government, Information Control Division, Report #82, "German Sentiment for Peace and Security," 12/8/47. The margins were 57 percent to 29 percent on February 3, 1947, 62 to 26 on May 12, 1947, 62 to 26 on July 14, 1947. In Berlin, as late as April 15, 1948, the margin was 64 to 29. George Gallup, intrigued by the question, decided to take the same poll in the United States in May 1948. The results were that 12 percent of Americans chose "economic security" and 83 percent chose "freedom" (*Washington Post,* May 9, 1948).

126 *Of this Clay:* Backer, p. 59.

126 *Clay usually ate:* Robert Lochner interview, George Washington University National Security Archive, http://www.gwu.edu/~nsarchiv/coldwar/interviews/episode-4/lochner4.html; Jean Edward Smith, *Lucius D. Clay,* p. 425.

126 *During the Great Depression: Arizona Republic,* June 30, 2006.

126 *After the war:* Brett-Smith, pp. 111–12.

127 *In the first few:* Howley, *Berlin Command,* p. 86.

127 *For the unemployed:* Tusa and Tusa, p. 91.

127 *Housewives received:* Botting, *From the Ruins of the Reich,* p. 134.

127 *In the first six:* Russell Hill, *Struggle for Germany* (New York: Harper & Brothers, 1947), p. 84.

127 *Even by 1947:* Jenkin Lloyd Jones, *Flight to Germany,* May 1947 pamphlet; Dennis Bark and David Gress, *A History of West Germany,* vol. 1 (Oxford: Basil Blackwell, 1989), pp. 130–31. The infant mortality rate in Berlin in 1947 was twice that of Sudan's during its terrible 2006 (*CIA World Factbook,* "Rank order—infant mortality rate," https://www.cia.gov/cia/publications/factbook/rankorder/2091rank.html).

127 *The military government's:* National Archives, Record Group 260, Information Control Division.

128 *When, in early:* Jean Edward Smith Papers, Box 2; *Stars and Stripes,* May 24, 1998; Joseph Werner, p. 77; author interview.

128 *Many—an estimated:* Douglas Botting, *The Aftermath: Europe* (Alexandria, Va.: Time-Life Books, 1983), pp. 58–59; Richie, p. 639.

129 *Berliners created:* Andreas-Friedrich, p. 194.

129 *In the summer of 1947:* Davis, pp. 155–56.

129 *By early 1948, the standard price:* Jenkin Lloyd Jones, *Flight to Germany,* May 1947 pamphlet; Theodore H. White, *Fire in the Ashes* (New York: William Sloane, 1953), p. 135; Robert Jackson, *The Berlin Airlift* (Wellingborough: Patrick Stephens, 1988), p. 33. At least part of what drove this phenomenon was that the supply of available women outran the demand of Berlin's few men. In the area around Tempelhof Airport, there were 717 women between the ages of eighteen and twenty-one—and 71 men of those years. In Lichtenfelde, not far from Clay's headquarters, there were 81 males between sixteen and twenty-one among a population of 15,000 (Botting, *From the Ruins of the Reich,* p. 253).

129 *Women in their twenties: New York Times,* April 2, 1948.

129 *A GI would cruise:* Interview with Larry Gelbart, April 2007.

129 *"I know very fine people:* Richie, p. 640.

130 *What Clay saw around him:* Backer, p. 2.

130 *An estimated: Stars and Stripes,* March 11, 1948.

130 *Some worked:* Donovan, p. 19.

130 *Hurled down:* Ibid., p. 18; Daniel Harrington, *The Air Force Can Deliver Anything* (Ramstein Air Base: United States Air Force Office of History, 1998), p. 83; Jean Edward Smith, *The Defense of Berlin,* p. 67.

131 *A visiting correspondent:* Donovan, p. 19.

131 *At the going rate: Stars and Stripes,* March 4, 1948.

131 *"It seemed as if:* Davison, p. 13.

131 *The winter of 1947:* Collier, p. 15; Patricia Meehan, *A Strange Enemy People: Germans Under the British, 1945–1950* (London: Peter Owen, 2001), p. 239; Richie, p. 638; Eric Morris, p. 79.

131 *Even with a puny:* Eugene Davidson, p. 138.

131 *Every day:* Botting, *From the Ruins of the Reich,* pp. 145–46.

132 *The Germans "looked:* Curtis LeMay with MacKinlay Kantor, *Mission with LeMay* (Garden City, N.Y.: Doubleday, 1965), p. 402.

132 *As Lucius Clay sat:* Stars and Stripes, December 23 and 30, 1947.

132 *One ice-cold:* Botting, *From the Ruins of the Reich,* p. 148.

133 *Berliners, Melvin Lasky:* Willett, p. 3.

133 *From his first:* Settel, p. 25; *Reader's Digest,* October 1948.

134 *"We are not here:* Stars and Stripes, May 14, 1949.

134 *Neither he:* Murphy, p. 327; Robert Lochner interview, George Washington University National Security Archive, http://www.gwu.edu/~nsarchiv/coldwar/interviews/episode-4/lochner4.html.

134 *Soon after: The New Yorker,* January 13, 1951.

134 *"In heart:* Botting, *From the Ruins of the Reich,* p. 248.

134 *Beginning a year:* Information and Education Division, United States Forces European Theater Headquarters, "The 6 Hour Troop Information Program," April 1946, Air Force Historical Research Agency.

134 *American soldiers were told:* Interview with Jim Spatafora, October 2005.

135 *They had arrived:* Joseph Werner, *Berlin Airlift: Brides and Grooms Created* (Stony Brook, N.Y.: Water Edge Publishing, 1999), p. 29.

135 *Major Everett S. Cofran:* Botting, *From the Ruins of the Reich,* p. 210.

135 *A small group of soldiers: Chicago Daily Tribune,* December 1, 1945.

135 *On mess walls:* Eugene Davidson, p. 86.

135 *Outside the mess:* Hill, p. 80.

135 *Most had never tasted: Chicago Daily Tribune,* February 9, 1947. During the brutal winter of 1947, hot chocolate was served to 435 children in an unheated classroom in the American sector of Berlin. Since the drink seemed foreign to so many, the children—aged six to ten—were asked if they had ever had it before. Almost two-thirds—280 of the 435—had never in their lives tasted cocoa.

135 *"In the midst:* Botting, *From the Ruins of the Reich,* pp. 216, 211; Schivelbusch, p. 27; George Kennan, *Memoirs, 1935–1950* (Boston: Little, Brown, 1967), pp. 428–29.

136 *On Severino DiCocco's:* Joseph Werner, p. 28.

136 *Instead of destroying:* Nicholas, p. 535.

136 *Jim Spatafora, a young airman:* Interview with Jim Spatafora, September 2005.

137 *In the months ahead:* Letter to McCloy, June 16, 1945, *Papers of General Lucius D. Clay,* p. 24.

137 *Six months after:* Merritt and Merritt, *Public Opinion in Occupied Germany: The OMGUS Surveys, 1945–1949,* p. 192.

137 *The Germans fully realized: Papers of General Lucius D. Clay,* p. xxix.

137 *He would proclaim:* Jean Edward Smith, *Lucius D. Clay,* p. 239.

137 *Most afternoons: Time,* July 12, 1948; *Battle for Berlin,* March of Time series, 1948.

138 *Perched at the edge:* Clay, p. 35; Collier, p. 4; Haydock, pp. 37, 123; *Stars and Stripes,* March 16, 1948.

138 *On the occasion:* Parrish, p. 92.

138 *Six foot:* Collier, pp. 3–4.

138 *He was the son of poor:* Mark Arnold-Forster, p. 157; Backer, p. 88; *Los Angeles Times,* April 15, 1948; Jean Edward Smith, *Lucius D. Clay,* p. 262

139 *When one of Clay's:* Clay, p. 136.

139 *The two men:* Jean Edward Smith, *Lucius D. Clay,* pp. 262, 550.

139 *They would insult:* Backer, pp. 87–88.

139 *Iran and Greece:* Haydock, p. 118.

140 *As one Communist: Time,* August 25, 1952.

140 *In January:* Jackson, p. 28.

140 *In June:* William I. Hitchcock, *The Struggle for Europe: The Turbulent History of a Divided Continent, 1945–2002* (New York: Doubleday, 2002), p. 88; Joseph Held, *The Columbia*

History of Eastern Europe in the Twentieth Century (New York: Columbia University Press, 1992), p. 212.

140 *When antipathy:* Backer, p. 166.

141 *Between the end:* Foreign Affairs, July–August 1998.

141 *Of the top:* Haydock, p. 115.

141 *"He could indeed:* Bering, p. 72.

141 *The men under:* William Heimlich interview, George Washington University National Security Archive, http://www.gwu.edu/~nsarchiv/coldwar/interviews/episode-4/heimlich5.html.

141 *His harsh treatment:* Howley, Berlin Command, p. 87.

141 *"If we bring food:* Time, August 15, 1949.

141 *A few months after:* Saturday Evening Post, February 2, 1946.

142 *"I was in closer:* Howley, Berlin Command, pp. 54, 14.

142 *"We came here:* Haydock, p. 81.

142 *The Russians "have:* Howley, Berlin Command, pp. 138, 14–15.

143 *Kotikov would arrive:* Time, May 17, 1948.

143 *In the privacy:* Personal Diary of Colonel Frank L. Howley.

143 *It is likely:* New York Times, December 20, 1946.

143 *"The Russians are the world's:* Howley, Berlin Command, pp. 11–12, 17.

143 *Soviet-controlled radio:* Howley, Your War for Peace, p. 2.

144 *"It would take:* Parrish, p. 152.

144 *At one point:* Report by Office of Military Government, US Sector, Berlin, July 1, 1945–September 1, 1949, Papers of Frank L. Howley.

144 *In one session:* Haydock, p. 63.

144 *In the last:* Stars and Stripes, March 18, 1948.

144 *Sometimes their "crime":* Knud Krakau interview, October 2005. In this instance, the young man was released by the Soviets a decade later.

144 *Cars would come:* Howley, Berlin Command, p. 165.

144 *Sometimes, an agent:* Arthur Smith, Kidnap City: Cold War Berlin (Westport, Conn.: Greenwood Press, 2002), pp. 10–11.

145 *Howley issued:* Arthur Smith, p. 10.

145 *The city's newspapers:* Andreas-Friedrich, p. 210.

145 *The "reign:* Stars and Stripes, March 18, 1948.

145 *Life in the city:* Andreas-Friedrich, p. 193.

145 *A few days:* Haydock, p. 15.

145 *The Americans:* Howley, Berlin Command, pp. 119–21.

145 *As the October 1946:* Davison, pp. 46–47.

146 *Two Western-leaning:* Howley, Berlin Command, pp. 131, 144.

146 *Born in a tiny:* Saturday Evening Post, February 5, 1949; Arnold-Forster, pp. 35–36; Haydock, pp. 72–73.

149 *"Do you want:* Haydock, p. 110.

149 *Three days later:* Howley, Berlin Command, p. 149.

149 *Letters to "Mayor:* Jackson, p. 30.

149 *But she refused:* Smith, The Defense of Berlin, p. 98.

149 *A convert's zeal:* Collier, pp. 8–9.

150 *Since 1945, Howley:* Personal Diary of Colonel Frank L. Howley.

150 *By the fall:* Howley, Berlin Command, p. 156.

151 *Thirty-five years:* Jean Edward Smith, Lucius D. Clay, pp. 426–27.

152 *Another freshman:* Jean Edward Smith Papers, Box 6.

152 *Occasionally, Clay:* Backer, p. 103.

152 *A buzzer was installed:* The New Yorker, January 13, 1951.

152 *At a guesthouse:* Jean Edward Smith, Lucius D. Clay, pp. 416–18; Wolfe, p. 106. Dulles had little faith in Germany and little consideration for Germans. As a young lawyer attached to the committee handling reparations, he had written into the Treaty of Versailles the provision assigning to the German people as a whole—not simply to their kaiser and his regime—the blame of plunging the world into war (Fromkin, p. 328).

154 *"General Clay, there has been:* National Archives, Record Group 260, Office of Military Government Files, Clay Memoir Files, Clay Press Conferences and Speeches.

154 *Clay had returned:* Jean Edward Smith, *Lucius D. Clay,* pp. 423, 9.

155 *Often the threats:* Backer, p. 103.

155 *After one such episode:* Letter to Byrnes, August 19, 1946, Letter to McNarney, August 21, 1946, *Papers of General Lucius D. Clay,* pp. 255, 259.

155 *After another threat:* Cable to Eisenhower, July 28, 1947, *Papers of General Lucius D. Clay,* pp. 389–90.

156 *It would be eleven:* Backer, p. 194. Before leaving the military to take the presidency of Columbia University, Eisenhower wrote a final efficiency report for Clay's file on February 6, 1948: "While his work has not brought him actual battle command experience I believe that his work as the American Administrator in Germany will come to be recognized, when that work is once fully understood, as one of the outstanding contributions to our country. If he has a fault, it is a too acute sensitiveness" (Jean Edward Smith Papers, Box 4).

156 *The truth was:* Jean Edward Smith, *Lucius D. Clay,* p. 439.

156 *Clay announced:* National Archives, Record Group 260, Office of Military Government Files, Clay Memoir Files, Clay Press Conferences and Speeches.

156 *For years:* Backer, pp. 103, 136.

156 *Once, on a Saturday:* Jean Edward Smith, *Lucius D. Clay,* pp. 326–27; Jean Edward Smith Papers, Box 7.

157 *Subsisting on cigarettes:* Jean Edward Smith, *Lucius D. Clay,* p. 425.

157 *On his way back:* Forrestal, p. 183.

157–158 *"Secretary Marshall's announcement:* Teleconference with Draper, January 9, 1948, *Papers of General Lucius D. Clay,* p. 533.

158 *Clay could only purse:* Jean Edward Smith, *Lucius D. Clay,* p. 457.

7: March

159 *The lights in the garret:* Marcia Davenport, *Too Strong for Fantasy* (New York: Charles Scribner's Sons, 1967), pp. 394–441; Mayne, pp. 118–35; *Time,* March 22, 1948; Haydock, pp. 119–22; interviews with Susan Eisenhower and Ernest Kolowrat; *Saturday Evening Post,* February 5, 1949; *Stars and Stripes,* February 27, 1948, March 6, 1948.

163 *"All winter:* Goldman, p. 79.

164 *He viewed himself:* Robert Donovan, *Conflict and Crisis* (New York: Norton, 1977), p. 188.

164 *America was facing:* Isaacson and Thomas, pp. 355, 384.

164 *On a winter weekend:* Kennan, pp. 292–93, 557.

165 *Forrestal distributed thousands:* Hoopes and Brinkley, p. 272; Yergin, pp. 212–13; Fromkin, p. 632.

165 *With the backing:* Boettcher, p. 101.

165 *"I greatly appreciated:* Hoopes and Brinkley, pp. 274–76.

166 *As he later:* Kennan, p. 358.

166 *On the day:* Isaacson and Thomas, pp. 403, 404.

167 *That same year:* Clark Clifford with Richard Holbrooke, *Counsel to the President* (New York: Random House, 1991), pp. 162–63.

168 *The secretary of defense would oversee:* Stars and Stripes, March 7, 1949.

168 *"This office will probably:* Forrestal, pp. 299, 300; Hoopes and Brinkley, p. 132.

169 *It was already:* Mudd Library Unedited Diaries, p. 1121.

169 *The same week:* Haydock, p. 122.

169 *In France:* Hitchcock, p. 90; Botting, *The Aftermath: Europe,* p. 134.

170 *He became obsessed:* Rogow, pp. 343, 132.

170 *"He arrived in his:* Omar N. Bradley and Clay Blair, *A General's Life: An Autobiography by the General of the Army* (New York: Simon & Schuster, 1983), p. 476.

170 *He lost his appetite:* Rogow, p. 306; *Stars and Stripes,* May 23, 1949.

170–171 *"I pray to God:* Rogow, p. 125.

171 *His office:* Stars and Stripes, May 23, 1949; Avi Shlaim, *The United States and the Berlin Blockade, 1948–1949* (Berkeley: University of California Press, 1983), p. 67.

171 *Within two years:* Raymond P. Ojserkis, *"Beginning of the Cold War Arms Race: The Truman Administration and the US Arms Build-up* (Westport, Conn.: Praeger, 2003), p. 7; *Historical Tables, Budget of the United States Government, Fiscal Year 2005* (Washington, D.C.: Office of Management and Budget, 2004), pp. 45–52.

172 *"There are no innocent:* Lynn Eden, *Whole World on Fire* (Ithaca, N.Y.: Cornell University Press, 2004), pp. 46–47.

172 *When victory: New York Times,* October 5, 1945, and November 20, 1945.

172 *"No one was getting:* Curtis LeMay, United States Air Force Oral History Interview #736, March 9, 1971, p. 3; John Man, *Berlin Blockade* (New York: Ballantine Books, 1973), p. 46; Haydock, p. 105; Jackson, p. 39.

173 *"At a cursory:* LeMay, p. 411.

173 *The same month:* Hoopes and Brinkley, p. 370.

173 *It was not just:* Randall Woods and Howard Jones, *Dawning of the Cold War* (Athens: University of Georgia Press, 1991), p. 190.

173 *At the end of 1947: Air University Review,* July–August 1981.

174 *"Ike had left me:* Omar Bradley, p. 474.

174 *As early as October: New York Times,* October 29, 1945.

175 *Wallace had fought:* John Culver and John Hyde, *American Dreamer* (New York: Norton, 2000), p. 365.

175 *"How I wish:* Goulden, *The Best Years,* p. 212.

175 *It was, in the phrase:* Hitchcock, p. 45. Harold Nicolson was describing Clement Attlee succeeding Winston Churchill.

175 *By August:* Culver and Hyde, p. 418–19.

176 *"I approved:* Clifford, p. 117.

176 *America had "no:* Culver and Hyde, p. 422.

176 *"Whether we like it:* Hoopes and Brinkley, p. 258.

176 *The firestorm:* McCullough, pp. 515–17.

176 *"Henry is the most:* Margaret Truman, pp. 317–18.

177 *There were low whistles:* Yergin, p. 254.

177 *The next day:* Harry Truman, *Memoirs,* Volume 2 (Garden City, N.Y.: Doubleday, 1956), p. 560.

177 *The chaos surrounding:* Robert G. Kaiser, *Cold Winter, Cold War* (New York: Stein and Day, 1974), p. 146.

177 *When Truman took office:* Goulden, *The Best Years,* p. 10.

177 *A year later:* Donaldson, p. 6.

177 *By the first week:* Kaiser, p. 43.

177 *National chairman B. Carroll Reece:* Morrow, pp. 40–41.

178 *Wallace responded:* Ross, p. 147.

178 *That same day:* Margaret Truman, p. 343.

178 *The rallies required:* Culver and Hyde, pp. 444–45; Federal Reserve Bank of Minneapolis, Consumer Price Index Calculator, http://www.minneapolisfed.org/research/data/us/calc/?year.

179 *In early April:* Forrestal, pp. 261–62.

179 *That fall:* Isaacson and Thomas, p. 422.

179 *His candidacy:* Culver and Hyde, p. 457.

179 *"The bigger the peace:* Allen Yarnell, *Democrats and Progressives* (Berkeley: University of California Press, 1974), p. 2.

179 *Democrats had abandoned:* White and Maze, p. 257.

180 *Taylor had been:* Karl M. Schmidt, *Henry A. Wallace: Quixotic Crusade 1948* (Syracuse, N.Y.: Syracuse University Press, 1960), p. 56.

180 *Known as "The Crooning Cowboy":* Zachary Karabell, *The Last Campaign* (New York: Random House, 2000), p. 118; *Stars and Stripes,* February 25, 1948; McCullough, p. 645; *Time,* March 1, 1948.

180 *He had come:* F. Ross Peterson, *Prophet Without Honor: Glen H. Taylor and the Fight for American Liberalism* (Lexington: University Press of Kentucky, 1974), pp. 25, 78.

180 *In 1947: Stars and Stripes,* February 25, 1948.

180 *In his announcement:* Yarnell, p. 65.

180 *Throughout 1947:* "General Approval Trend for President Truman (1945–1952)," Roper Center for Public Opinion Research, University of Connecticut, http://www.ropercenter.uconn.edu/cgi-bin/hsrun.exe/Roperweb/PresJob/PresJob.htx;start=HS_fullresults?pr=Truman.

180 *When asked:* Robert A. Divine, *Foreign Policy and U.S. Presidential Election, 1940–1948* (New York: New Viewpoints, 1974), p. 173.

181 *The same week: Stars and Stripes,* December 24, 1947. When asked who the Democrats' most

likely vice presidential nominee was, 25 of the correspondents picked Jim Forrestal—far and away the most often mentioned choice.

181 *It was because:* Yarnell, p. 126.

181 *That same February: Stars and Stripes,* February 14, 1948.

181 *The young, vigorous:* Karabell, p. 77.

181 *As the Republicans':* Gullan, p. 91.

181–182 *He began his campaign: Stars and Stripes,* February 14, 1948.

182 *"We should not be:* Clarence E. Wunderlin, Jr., ed., *The Papers of Robert A. Taft,* Volume 3, *1945–1948* (Kent, Ohio: Kent State University Press, 2003), p. 387.

182 *"Before an election":* Wunderlin, pp. 402–4.

182 *Harry Truman was on vacation:* Log of President Truman's Trip to Puerto Rico, the Virgin Islands, Guantánamo Bay, Cuba, and [Fourth] Key West, Florida, February 20–March 5, 1948, Truman Presidential Library, http://www.trumanlibrary.org/calendar/travel_log/documents/index.php?documentdate=1948-03-01&documentid=7&studycollectionid=TL&pagenumber=64; American Presidency Project, "The President's News Conference at Key West," March 1, 1948, http://www.presidency.ucsb.edu/ws/index.php?pid=13118&st=&st1=; *Stars and Stripes,* March 2, 1948.

183 *Two days after:* Margaret Truman, pp. 358–60.

185 *At the beginning:* Richie, p. 662; Parrish, p. 175; Collier, p. 11; Giangreco, p. 91; Caroline Kennedy-Pipe, *Stalin's Cold War: Soviet Strategies in Europe, 1943–1956* (Manchester: Manchester University Press, 1995), p. 134.

185 *A few days after:* Cable to Department of the Army, January 13, 1948, *Papers of General Lucius D. Clay,* p. 542.

185 *Americans who crossed:* Clay, pp. 372, 353.

185 *Beginning in January:* Jackson, p. 34.

186 *With tension rising:* Collier, p. 3; William Harris, "March Crisis 1948, Act I," *Studies in Intelligence,* Fall 1966, pp. 4–7; Clay, p. 354; Woods and Jones, p. 188.

187 FROM CLAY EYES ONLY: Forrestal, p. 387. In later years, when it became clear that a Soviet attack had not been imminent and that he had overreacted, Clay would assert that he had sent the cable to Chamberlain—at the lieutenant's request—as a prod to be used to influence recalcitrant members of Congress who were blocking President Truman's national security initiatives that March (Jean Edward Smith, *Lucius D. Clay,* p. 467). Though Clay's biographer endorsed this view, it is a dubious explanation. First, Chamberlain's own reaction to the cable shows that he was not in on any such plot. Second, Clay's own words contradict this rationalization. Two days before the "dramatic suddenness" cable, General Floyd Parks, chief of the Army's Public Information Division, wrote to inform Clay that Socialist peace activist Jerome Davis was quoting him as having said, in a meeting in Berlin, "There isn't the slightest danger of war with Russia. But we have to circulate the story . . . so we can put over the Marshall Plan." Clay responded to Parks in much the same vein as in his cable to Chamberlain, albeit with less dramatic language. He "did not think there was an immediate danger of war with Russia," he wrote. However, "this did not mean that we do not face this danger at some time unless we take measures to make it most unlikely. In point of fact, I now doubt if we have as much time as I once thought" (cable to Parks, March 3, 1948, *Papers of General Lucius D. Clay,* p. 564). In an interview on May 18, 1976, just months before he died, Clay, in retelling the story of the blockade, repeated the words of his March 5 cable almost verbatim in describing the hunch he had in the spring of 1948: "Some months before the Berlin blockade came about, I felt I recognized a change in attitude on the part of the Soviet High Command in Berlin. I so reported to my government. I said I have no intelligence to back this up, but I see a very real change in the attitude of the High Command and it could lead to very serious trouble; I wouldn't put war beyond possibility" (Jean Edward Smith Papers, Box 7).

187 *Chamberlain was handed:* Harris, "March Crisis 1948," *Act I,* p. 8; Omar Bradley, p. 477.

188 *On Saturday, March 6:* Cray, p. 625

188 *Truman scribbled:* Isaacson and Thomas, pp. 439–40.

188 *"I feel I could:* Morrow, pp. 130–31.

188 *Marshall was silver-haired:* Isaacson and Thomas, pp. 390–91.

188 *When they met:* Stephen Ambrose, *The Victors* (New York: Simon & Schuster, 1998), p. 18.

188 *When Truman nominated:* Mark A. Stoler, *George C. Marshall: Soldier-Statesman of the American Century* (Boston: Twayne Publishers, 1989), p. 147; Cray, p. 586.

189 *That March:* Cray, p. 650.
189 *Testifying before:* J. Samuel Walker, *Henry A. Wallace and American Foreign Policy* (Westport, Conn.: Greenwood Press, 1976), p. 186; Haydock, p. 114.
189 *Taft opposed:* Isaacson and Thomas, pp. 432–34.
189 *His ally, John Taber:* Parrish, p. 132.
189 *The very day that Clay:* Patterson, *Mr. Republican,* p. 388; Frank Kofsky, *Harry S. Truman and the War Scare of 1948,* (New York: St. Martin's Press, 1993), p. 124; Michael J. Hogan, *A Cross of Iron: Harry S. Truman and the Origins of the National Security State, 1945–1954* (Cambridge: Cambridge University Press, 1998), pp. 90–91. Congressional Democrats thought that, in a moment of crisis, an enormous tax cut was rash, but their principled stance was to counter Taft's plan for a $4.8 billion tax cut with a more reasonable $4 billion cut of their own (*New York Times,* March 17, 1948).
190 *By Wednesday:* Harris, "March Crisis 1948, Act I," p. 9.
190 *At a press conference:* Forrestal, p. 389; Boettcher, p. 149.
190 *"Recent developments:* Papers of General Lucius D. Clay, p. 569.
191 *He had dropped:* Haydock, p. 48; Forrest C. Pogue, *George Marshall: Statesman* (New York: Viking, 1987), p. 175.
191 *Weighing in:* Hitchcock, p. 46.
191 *Instead of the elegant:* Allan Bullock, *Ernest Bevin: Foreign Secretary, 1945–1951* (London: Heinemann, 1983), p. 82.
191 *While the foreign ministers:* Smith, *Lucius D. Clay,* pp. 408–9.
192 *He was an instinctive:* Allan Bullock, *Ernest Bevin: A Biography* (London: Politicos, 2002), p. xi.
192 *Bevin would routinely:* Bullock, *Ernest Bevin: Foreign Secretary, 1945–1951,* p. 82.
192 *"If it became known:* Don Cook, *Forging the Alliance* (New York: Morrow, 1989), pp. 117–22.
193 *He returned to Washington:* Forrestal, p. 393.
193 *The previous day:* "Memo to Omar Bradley from Lt. Gen. Chamberlin," March 14, 1948, National Archives, Army Plans & Operations Files, Record Group 319.
193 *In contrast:* Davison, p. 74.
193 *As preparedness stood:* Yergin, p. 353.
193 *He had already:* Forrestal, p. 394.
194 *Since the early days:* Kofsky, p. 86.
194 *Pres.* must: Yergin, p. 352.
194 *He had intended:* Forrestal, pp. 394–95.
195 *As he squirmed:* Hoopes and Brinkley, p. 57. Forrestal drank large amounts of water when he was nervous, a trait that was noticed in his Wall Street days but undoubtedly continued as he hurtled on toward his end. Nearly every photograph of him from 1947 onward shows his lips pressed together tightly.
195 *"All last week:* Time, March 22, 1948.
195 *In overthrowing:* Christian Science Monitor, March 16, 1948.
195 *For his part:* Washington Post, March 17, 1948.
195 *Truman believed:* Yergin, p. 353.
196 *As if to buttress:* Harris, "March Crisis 1948, Act I," p. 21.
196 *Forrestal arrived:* Forrestal, p. 397.
197 *No sooner:* National Climatic Data Center, http://www4.ncdc.noaa.gov/cgi-win/wwcgi.dll ?wwDI~StnSrch~StnID~20027254.
197 *The climate:* Time, March 22, 1948.
197 *"Almost three years:* American Presidency Project, Special Message to Congress on the Threat to the Freedom of Europe, March 17, 1948, http://www.presidency.ucsb.edu/ws/index.php? pid=13130&st=&st1=.
198 *He had "entered:* Cray, p. 645.
198 *One of the foreign ministers:* David Childs, *Britain Since 1945* (London: Routledge, 2001), p. 41.
198 *With little ceremony:* Cook, pp. 127–28.
198 *Truman went straight:* New York Times, March 18, 1948.
199 *Earlier that week:* New York Times, March 15, 1948.
199 *He offered to fix:* Jean Edward Smith, *Lucius D. Clay,* pp. 457–59.
199 *That evening:* Collier, p. 19.

200 *Bradley's deputy:* Teleconference with Department of the Army, March 17, 1948, *Papers of General Lucius D. Clay*, pp. 579–83; Parrish, p. 135; Jean Edward Smith, *Lucius D. Clay*, pp. 325, 551.

201 *In the Grand: New York Times*, March 17–18, 1948; Abels, p. 32; American Presidency Project, St. Patrick's Day Address in New York City, March 17, 1948, http://www.presidency.ucsb.edu/ws/index.php?pid=13131&st=&st1=#.

203 *On Friday, March 19:* Isaacson and Thomas, p. 441.

203 *"He looked tired:* Yergin, p. 357.

203 *"There was scarcely:* Ross, p. 71; Hogan, pp. 120–58; *The Papers of Robert A. Taft*, Volume 3: *1945–1948*, p. 397. Taft would eventually feel forced to back the draft. It should also be noted that while the draft and universal military training were enormously unpopular on the far left and right, the vast majority of Americans supported the moves. In an April 1948 Gallup poll, 63 percent of Americans approved of a new draft and only 23 percent disapproved. The age group most strongly in favor of universal military training was those between twenty-one and twenty-nine, who supported it by an 80 percent to 16 percent margin (*Washington Post*, April 9, 1948).

204 *"The simple fact:* McCullough, pp. 608, 613.

204 *The House majority:* Frank Kelly, *Harry Truman and the Human Family* (Santa Barbara, Calif.: Capra Press, 1998), p. 41.

204 *The right-wing: Chicago Tribune*, March 18, 1948.

204 *A couple of weeks:* "Job Performance Ratings for President Truman (1945–1952)," Roper Center for Public Opinion Research, University of Connecticut, http://137.99.36.203/CFIDE/roper/presidential/webroot/presidential_rating_detail.cfm?allRate=True&presidentName=Truman.

204 *The fall of Prague: Christian Science Monitor*, March 15, 1948.

205 *On March 14:* "Robert Murphy Memo to George Marshall," March 22, 1948, National Archives, Berlin Political Section Files.

205 *On the radio:* Edwin Gere, *The Unheralded* (Shutesburg, Mass.: Andrus Publishing, 2005), p. 42.

205 *When, the same week: New York Times*, February 26, 1948.

205 *"The ugly sound:* Andreas-Friedrich, pp. 192, 198.

205 *The chairmanship:* United States Department of State, *Foreign Relations of the United States, 1948*, Volume 2: *Germany and Austria,*" (Washington, D.C.: U.S. Government Printing Office, 1973), p. 885; Collier, pp. 5–6; Jean Edward Smith, *Lucius D. Clay*, pp. 470–71; Backer, p. 225; Giangreco, p. 78.

207 *Finally, Clay:* Settel, p. 321.

207 *"Nearly every hour:* Andreas-Friedrich, p. 204.

207 *"I don't know: Los Angeles Times*, March 23, 1948.

208 *Two days after:* Jean Edward Smith, *Lucius D. Clay*, pp. 458–59.

208 *"It is very:* Teleconference with Royall, Bradley, and Noce, March 23, 1948, *Papers of General Lucius D. Clay*, p. 596.

208 *Clay went home: The New Yorker*, January 13, 1951.

208 *On March 24:* William Harris, "March Crisis 1948, Act II," *Studies in Intelligence*, Spring 1967, pp. 10–19; *New York Times*, March 26, 1948.

209 *It sounded:* Harris, "March Crisis 1948, Act II," pp. 23–26.

210 *Two hours later:* Teleconference with Bradley and Noce, March 31, 1948, *Papers of General Lucius D. Clay*, pp. 597–600.

210 *"Had I enough hair:* Omar Bradley, p. 478.

211 *By 11:40:* Harris, "March Crisis 1948, Act II," p. 27.

211 *Someone proposed:* Forrestal, p. 408; Harris, "March Crisis 1948, Act II," p. 29.

211 *They summoned:* Richard Rhodes, *Dark Sun: The Making of the Hydrogen Bomb* (New York: Simon & Schuster, 1995), p. 320.

212 *But the others: New York Times*, August 29, 1948; Rogow, p. 306. It is not certain that Forrestal wetted his lips in this fashion at the March 31 lunch, but he did so repeatedly in moments of stress at lunches and dinners throughout that month and thus it seems more than likely that he would do so at this stressful meeting.

212 *At 1 P.M.:* Harris, "March Crisis 1948, Act II," p. 27; Teleconference with Bradley, Royall, Wedemeyer, and Collins, March 31, 1948, *Papers of General Lucius D. Clay*, pp. 600–604.

213 *"If our action now:* Teleconference with Bradley, Royall, and Wedemeyer, March 31, 1948, *Papers of General Lucius D. Clay,* pp. 604–7. "During this teleconference I thought I detected some apprehension on the part of Secretary Royall and his advisers that a firm stand on our part might develop incidents involving force which would lead to war," Clay would write in his memoirs in a masterpiece of understatement (Clay, p. 369).

213 *Three Western trains:* Cable to Bradley, April 1, 1948, *Papers of General Lucius D. Clay,* p. 607.

213 *Onboard the "Berliner":* Collier, pp. 17–21; Tusa and Tusa, pp. 107–8.

214 *In the middle: Washington Post,* April 18, 1948.

214 *At the end:* Yergin, p. 357.

214 *The speaker: Stars and Stripes,* February 2, 1948.

215 *"The men who speak:* Yarnell, p. 59.

215 *Six days:* Peterson, pp. 110, 100.

215 *He had been worried:* Yergin, p. 357.

216 *With the Italian Communists:* Hoopes and Brinkley, pp. 315–16.

216 *On April 2:* National Archives, "Possibility of Direct Soviet Military Action During 1948," April 2, 1948.

216 *"April!:* Gail Halvorsen to Alta Jolley, February 22, 1948, April 4, 1948, May 8, 1948, Halvorsen Private Papers; Halvorsen interview, February 2007. "BOQ" stands for "Bachelor Officers' Quarters."

218 *Five days after:* Cook, pp. 128–34; Rhodes, p. 319.

220 *As the United States:* Davison, pp. 200, 83.

220 *In a city:* Richie, p. 662.

220 *That spring, high-ranking:* Davison, p. 64.

220 *Howley would receive:* Jackson, p. 88.

220 *"We are receiving:* Cable to Wedemeyer, April 2, 1948, *Papers of General Lucius D. Clay,* p. 611; cable to Bradley, April 2, 1948, *Papers of General Lucius D. Clay,* pp. 611–12; Teleconference with Bradley and Royall, April 2, 1948, *Papers of General Lucius D. Clay,* pp. 613–15.

220 *With Clay refusing:* Omar Bradley, p. 481.

221 *On April 10:* Teleconference with Bradley, April 10, 1948, *Papers of General Lucius D. Clay,* pp. 621–23. It is interesting to note that, in his memoirs, Clay reproduces a few sentences of the teleconference but leaves off the last three words of the sentence "I believe the future of democracy requires us to stay until forced out" (Clay, p. 361).

Part III: The Bridge, 1948–1949
8: June

225 *One by one:* Parrish, pp. 128–29.

226 *It was, wrote: Christian Science Monitor:* May 8, 1948.

226 *On May Day: New York Times,* May 2, 1948; UCLA Film Archives, VA14393; National Archives, "Classified Cable to State Department," Office of Political Advisor Germany, May 6, 1948, Record Group 84, Entry 2536.

227 *By the middle:* Jackson, p. 33.

227 *German students:* Willett, p. 3.

227 *Health officials: Chicago Daily Tribune,* July 5, 1948.

227 *Since the beginning:* Jackson, p. 24.

227 *Six days a week:* National Archives, "Cable from Hays to Voorhees," March 16, 1948, and "Child Feeding Program in Germany," February 28, 1948, Office of Military Government, Record Group 84, Entry 2531B, Box 243.

228 *"For six weeks:* Personal Diary of Colonel Frank L. Howley in Papers of Frank L. Howley, May 3, 1948; Tusa and Tusa, p. 99.

228 *"They can load us: Washington Post,* June 2, 1948.

228 *In May, the French:* Cable to Draper, May 31, 1948, *Papers of General Lucius D. Clay,* p. 661.

228 *"It would be far more ignominious:* Tusa and Tusa, p. 121.

228 *"Don't make it too hard:* Yergin, p. 370.

229 *"The United States does not plan:* James McAllister, *No Exit: America and the German Problem, 1943–1954* (Ithaca, N.Y.: Cornell University Press, 2002), pp. 147–48.

229 *The legislation:* Divine, pp. 210–11.

230 *"The Nations of Europe: New York Times,* June 7, 1948.

230 *Smith met with Molotov:* Shlaim, pp. 145–47.

230 *On May 11:* Culver and Hyde, pp. 475–77.

230 *"The policies of Truman:* Divine, p. 205.

231 *In early June:* Jean Edward Smith, *Lucius D. Clay,* p. 480; Yergin, p. 372.

231 *Forrestal would be allowed:* Boettcher, pp. 154–55.

231 *It was ten:* Howley, *Berlin Command,* pp. 157–60, 179–84; Murphy to Marshall, June 17, 1948, *Foreign Relations of the United States, 1948.* Volume 2: *Germany and Austria,* 908–9; Collier, p. 37–40; Tusa and Tusa, pp. 46, 136–37; Haydock, pp. 130–32; Personal Diary of Colonel Frank L. Howley, in Papers of Frank L. Howley, June 30, 1948; May 17, 1949, interview transcript in Papers of Frank L. Howley; *Stars and Stripes,* June 18, 1948; National Archives, "Soviet Licensed Press version of June 16 Kommandatura," Record Group 84, Office of the US Political Advisor to Germany, Berlin, Classified General Correspondence files.

235 *On June 18:* Cook, p. 150; *New York Times,* June 20, 1948.

235 *"We are in the process:* Peterson, p. 119.

235 *Omar Bradley: New York Times,* June 21, 1948.

235 *Marshall announced: Los Angeles Times,* June 18, 1948.

235 *He invited Taft:* Mudd Library Unedited Diaries, p. 2279. It was not the first such act of disloyalty on Forrestal's part. In late April, Truman told his White House aides—after a meeting with Forrestal—that he was "getting damn sore" at Forrestal for continually going behind his back to Republicans in Congress. If he does not stop, Truman said, "I'll get someone else." Robert H. Ferrell, ed., *Truman in the White House: The Diary of Eben A. Ayers* (Columbia: University of Missouri Press, 1991), p. 253.

236 *It was past: Los Angeles Times,* June 20, 1948.

236 *Later that night: New York Times,* June 20, 1948.

236 *On Saturday, June 19:* Murphy to Marshall, June 19, 1948, *Foreign Relations of the United States, 1948,* Volume 2: *Germany and Austria,* pp. 910–11; Davison, p. 91.

237 *The State Department:* National Archives, Plans and Operations files, June 21, 23, 1948, Record Group 319; Marshall to Embassy in Soviet Union, June 23, 1948, *Foreign Relations of the United States, 1948,* Volume 2: *Germany and Austria,* p. 916.

237 *Curtis LeMay:* LeMay Diary, June 20, 1948, Air Force Historical Research Agency.

237 *"Campaign to be fought: New York Times,* June 20, 1948.

237 *"Good old Joe!:* Ross, p. 97.

237 *Roosevelt and Truman's: Los Angeles Times,* June 22, 1948.

238 *A huge inflatable:* Donaldson, p. 150.

238 *The little tinkle: New York Times,* June 22, 1948.

238 *In the hall: New York Times,* June 22, 1948; *Los Angeles Times,* June 24, 1948; *Chicago Daily Tribune,* June 26, 1948.

238 *In January:* Ross, pp. 148, 157.

238 *"The fact" was: Los Angeles Times,* June 22, 1948.

238 *That same day:* Davison, pp. 93–94.

239 *"Something dangerous:* Andreas-Friedrich, pp. 225–26; Davison, pp. 95–96; Personal Diary of Colonel Frank L. Howley in Papers of Frank L. Howley; Steege, pp. 199–200.

241 *"Communist demonstrations:* Murphy to Marshall, June 23, 1948, *Foreign Relations of the United States, 1948,* Volume 2: *Germany and Austria,* pp. 914–15.

241 *It was shortly:* Collier, pp. 48–50; Donovan, pp. 36–37.

241 *"Here it is":* Bennett, p. 39.

241 *Every day:* Man, p. 51.

241 *As soon as the electricity:* "Notes on the Blockade of Berlin 1948," Papers of Frank L. Howley; Haydock, p. 160.

241 *By morning:* Collier, pp. 49–50; National Archives, Murphy to Marshall, June 24, 1948, 8 P.M., Record Group 84, Entry 2536.

242 *Word spread:* Howley, *"Berlin Command,"* p. 199.

242 *On Soviet-controlled radio:* Donovan, p. 73; Collier, p. 51; Howley, *Berlin Command,* p. 199.

242 *American troops: Washington Post,* June 25, 1948.

242 *"There is enough food:* Tusa and Tusa, p. 148.

242–243 *"We shall not let:* Andreas-Friedrich, pp. 229–30.

243 *That evening: Washington Post,* June 25, 1948; Parrish, p. 167; *Time,* July 5, 1948.

243 *At 3:30: Christian Science Monitor,* June 25, 1948.

243 *In the White House: New York Times,* June 25, 1948.

243 *Taft was the clear:* Richard Norton Smith, p. 498.

243 *Dewey, a man who: Time,* March 22, 1948.

244 *Nominated for his: Los Angeles Times,* June 24, 1948.

244 *He turned off: Chicago Daily Tribune,* June 26, 1948; Parrish, p. 169.

244 *As delegation bosses: Christian Science Monitor,* June 25, 1948.

244 *The clouds broke: Washington Post,* June 26, 1948.

244 *A summer storm:* Patterson, p. 414.

244 *The giant elephant:* Karabell, p. 138.

244 *While Dewey made his way:* Ross, p. 107; *Washington Post,* June 26, 1948.

245 *His brief acceptance: Christian Science Monitor,* June 25, 1948; Richard Norton Smith, pp. 499–500.

245 *"The unity we seek: Washington Post,* June 25, 1948.

245 *Berlin was on edge:* Donovan, p. 72.

245 *As Clay descended: Stars and Stripes,* June 25, 1948.

245 *"Do you think:* Elizabeth Lay, *The Berlin Air Lift,* Historical Division, Headquarters European Command, 1952, p. 9.

245 *The Soviets:* Cable to Royall, June 25, 1948, *Papers of General Lucius D. Clay,* p. 699.

246 *Then he said no: Washington Post,* June 25, 1948; Collier, p. 53; Settel, p. 419. Clay originally gave the quote in Frankfurt before he flew to Berlin but then repeated it almost precisely at Tempelhof (Clay Papers, p. 701; National Archives, Murphy to Marshall, June 25, 1948, 11 A.M., Record Group 84, Entry 2536).

246 *"It is absolutely:* Settel, p. 322.

246 *"If your hand:* Jean Edward Smith, *The Defense of Berlin,* p. 107.

246 *"Physically all that:* Collier, pp. 53–55; Jean Edward Smith, *Lucius D. Clay,* p. 495.

247 *He believed:* Clay to Royall, June 25, 1948, *Foreign Relations of the United States, 1948,* Volume 2: *Germany and Austria,* p. 918.

247 *A few hours earlier:* Tusa and Tusa, p. 148.

247 *He called Marguerite Higgins: Washington Post,* June 25, 1948.

247 *"While the eyes: New York Times,* June 25, 1948.

248 *Clay was sitting:* Backer, pp. 237–38; Teleconference with Royall and Collins, June 25, 1948, *Papers of General Lucius D. Clay,* pp. 699–704; Clay, p. 366; Clay to Royall, June 25, 1948, *Foreign Relations of the United States, 1948,* Volume 2: *Germany and Austria,* pp. 917–18; National Archives, Clay Teleconference with Royall, June 25, 1948, Record Group 200, TT 9667.

249 *Royall grabbed:* Memorandum by the Chief of the Division of Central European Affairs, June 28, 1948, *Foreign Relations of the United States, 1948,* Volume 2: *Germany and Austria,* pp. 928–29; Memo regarding June 25 Meeting, National Archives, Plans and Operations File, Record Group 319.

249 *Dewey's victory: New York Times,* June 25, 1948.

249 *The energetic: Los Angeles Times,* June 25, 1948.

249 *After a ten:* The President's Day, June 25, 1948, Harry S Truman Library, http://www .trumanlibrary.org/calendar/main.php?currYear=1948&currMonth=6&currDay=25. Marshall was in bed at Walter Reed Hospital. At age sixty-seven, he had had nineteen days off in the nine years since 1939. He was, by that point, in Dean Acheson's description, "a four-engine bomber going on only one engine" (Pogue, p. 303; Stoler, p. 173).

249 *The press was told: Chicago Daily Tribune,* June 26, 1948.

249 *Other than that:* National Archives, Plans and Operations files, June 25, 1948, Record Group 319.

250 *In London:* Parrish, p. 190; *Washington Post,* June 26, 1948.

250 *That day, French:* Caffery to Marshall, June 24–25, 1948, *Foreign Relations of the United States, 1948,* Volume 2: *Germany and Austria,* pp. 916–17.

250 *"About 2,250,000: New York Times,* June 26, 1948; Donovan, p. 72.

251 *Clay told Reuter:* Jean Edward Smith, *Lucius D. Clay,* pp. 501–2; Robert Lochner interview, George Washington University National Security Archive, http://www.gwu.edu/~nsarchiv/ coldwar/interviews/episode-4/lochner4.html. Clay and Brandt would claim that Reuter was told of the airlift in this conversation, but given that Clay was still wedded to the idea of the convoy at this point, this seems very unlikely.

251 *"We shall, in any case:* Collier, pp. 60–61.

251 *Robertson and Albert Wedemeyer:* Shlaim, pp. 203–5. In the years to come, numerous Americans and Britons would take—and be given—credit for first suggesting that food be sent to a besieged Berlin by air. The truth is that the idea was widely discussed and dismissed even before the airlift of supplies to Western personnel in the city in April. Clay himself had it in his mind long before the blockade began. For instance, in early June he had told reporters that, in case of an "emergency," airplanes could bring food to Berlin "to the fullest extent necessary." This could not be done, however, "on a permanent basis" (*New York Times,* June 13, 1948). This was the same outlook he had when the blockade began. Neither he, nor anyone else involved in the discussions, thought that an airlift could be anything other than a temporary expedient.

251 *"The blockade left the air:* Bill Gilbert, *Air Power* (New York: Citadel Press, 2003), p. 172.

252 *The* New York Times: *New York Times,* June 25, 1948.

252 *Lifting the scrambler phone:* Collier, p. 61; Jean Edward Smith, *Lucius D. Clay,* pp. 495, 500; Cook, p. 152. Historians have long debated when and whether this Clay/LeMay conversation took place. Clay would write that it occurred on June 24, though the documentation contradicts this. Murphy, who was in the room for it, would place it as occurring in late July (Murphy, p. 355). Historian Roger Miller argues that Clay did not even speak to LeMay in that phone call but to his deputy and that coal was likely not even mentioned (Roger Miller, *To Save a City* [College Station: Texas A&M University Press, 2000], pp. 44, 152). The murkiness that surrounds the start of the airlift underlies the most salient feature of its beginning: no one thought twice about it at the time. Clay was not ordering a grand movement of men and machines. He was looking for a stopgap measure that might provide some marginal relief of the pressure on the situation until the Soviets backed down or Washington approved his convoy plan or an ignoble retreat from Berlin was commenced.

252 *In fact, the next day:* Lay, p. 10.

252 *Before the blockade:* Personal Diary of Colonel Frank L. Howley; Tusa and Tusa, pp. 143–44.

253 *"Frank I'm ordering:* Howley, *Berlin Command,* pp. 204–5.

253 *It carried twenty-one:* Stephen Ambrose, *The Wild Blue: The Men and Boys Who Flew the B-24s Over Germany* (New York: Simon & Schuster, 2001), p. 34.

253 *Once the war began:* Grathwol, p. 34; Parrish, p. 194; Howley, *Berlin Command,* p. 205.

253 *Jack Bennett:* Collier, pp. 62–63.

254 *"We ended the week:* National Archives, "Secret Cable to State Department," Office of Political Advisor Germany, June 27, 1948, Record Group 84, Entry 2536; Clay, pp. 372–73; Tusa and Tusa, p. 162; Haydock, p. 162.

254 *The young American soldiers: Los Angeles Times,* June 27, 1948.

254 *The American troops: Time,* July 5, 1948.

255 *That morning Forrestal:* Isaacson and Thomas, p. 457.

255 *But that afternoon:* National Archives, Memorandum for Clay, June 26, 1948, Record Group 319.

255 *That first day:* Office of MAC History, *The Berlin Airlift: A Brief Chronology,* Military Airlift Command, Scott Air Force Base, 1988, p. 3; Donovan, p. 42; *New York Times,* June 27, 1948; Tusa and Tusa, p. 150.

255 *What he saw:* Howley, *Berlin Command,* pp. 204–5.

256 *"Today the two: New York Times,* June 27, 1948.

256 *In Berlin, that weekend:* Davison, p. 107.

256 *The leader of Berlin's: Washington Post,* June 27, 1948.

256 *The* New York Times: *New York Times,* June 25, 28, 1948.

256 *In turn, the* Washington Post: *Washington Post,* June 28, 1948.

256 *The previous day, in England: Stars and Stripes,* June 27, 1948; *New York Times,* June 27, 1948.

257 *Privately, Churchill:* Shlaim, p. 138. Truman would dismiss the idea of preemptive strikes: "Such a war is the weapon of dictators not of free democratic countries like the United States" (Rhodes, pp. 225–26).

257 *"Let us continue: New York Times,* June 28, 1948.

257 *To Omar Bradley:* Parrish, p. 181.

257 *A single wagon train:* Backer, p. 236. Historians now know what the men in the meeting did not: that the Soviets had already decided they would not allow such a convoy through what they considered "holy Soviet borders." Clay's convoy would probably have been met by a hail of gunfire and it can be assumed that it would have led to war (Parrish, p. 176).

257 *Clay was putting:* Jean Edward Smith, *Lucius D. Clay*, p. 496.

258 *"The Soviets would:* Cook, p. 152.

258 *The night before:* National Archives, "Secret Cable to State Department," Office of Political Advisor Germany, June 26, 1948, Record Group 84, Entry 2536.

258 *Whether or not this crisis:* Jean Edward Smith, *Lucius D. Clay*, pp. 496–97.

258 *That morning:* National Archives, Memo to Bradley, June 27, 1948, Record Group 319.

258 *If the city:* Roger Miller, pp. 55–56.

258 *Nevertheless, they decided:* Forrestal, pp. 452–53.

258 *The meeting had begun:* Mudd Library Unedited Diaries, p. 2323.

258 *On Monday, June 28:* Ibid., p. 2327.

258 *His cabinet:* Jean Edward Smith, *Lucius D. Clay*, pp. 507–8; Forrestal, p. 455. Royall was so surprised and incredulous at Truman's decision that he could not bring himself to believe it. "The President indicated his tentative approval of staying in Berlin," he wrote in a memorandum to Bradley. "However, he stated that this was not a final decision" (Mudd Library Unedited Diaries, p. 2328).

259 *He wanted to reinforce:* Collier, p. 67.

259 *These planes:* Yergin, p. 379. The B-29s they sent were actually not equipped to be able to carry atomic bombs.

259 *"For the first time:* Cable to Royall, June 28, 1948, *Papers of General Lucius D. Clay*, pp. 709–10.

260 *But that day:* Man, p. 51.

260 *It was still:* Stars and Stripes, June 27, 1948.

260 *"United States aircraft:* New York Times, June 27, 1948.

260 *His two top military:* Parrish, pp. 183–84.

260 *The director:* National Archives, Memorandum for the President from Roscoe Hillenkoetter, June 28, 1948.

260 *The west Berliners:* National Archives, Memorandum for the President from Roscoe Hillenkoetter, June 30, 1948.

261 *In Berlin, food stockpiles:* Miller, p. 44.

261 *On Saturday:* Gail Halvorsen to Alta Jolley, June 29, 1948, Halvorsen Private Papers.

261 *That Monday evening:* Typed diary of Harry S. Truman, June 28, 1948, Truman Presidential Library, http://www.trumanlibrary.org/exhibit_documents/index.php?pagenumber=10&titleid=177&tldate=1948-00-00%20&collectionid=berlin&PageID=1&groupid=3405; National Climatic Data Center, http://www4.ncdc.noaa.gov/cgi-win/wwcgi.dll?wwDI~StnSrch~StnID~20027254.

9: July

262 *On the morning:* Curtis LeMay Diary, Air Force Historical Research Agency, Maxwell Air Force Base.

262 *LeMay reminded Clay:* Washington Post, July 13, 1948.

262 *Clay's office:* Backer, p. 238.

263 *The British proposed:* Washington Post, July 3, 1948.

263 *The coal was dropped:* Haydock, p. 165.

263 *His officers proposed:* The Bee-Hive, Fall 1948.

264 *With the planes:* Collier, pp. 64, 68.

264 *The alert flashed:* Bill Gilbert, p. 176.

264 *Jeanette Wolff:* Davison, pp. 113, 114, 134.

266 *The only public response:* Shlaim, p. 199.

266 *Winston Churchill sat:* Christian Science Monitor, July 1, 1948.

266 *Later that same day:* Davison, p. 117.

266 *In downtown Honolulu:* Collier, pp. 76–77; Bennett, pp. 55–56.

267 *On Saturday:* Halvorsen inteview, August 2005; Halvorsen personal movie recordings; Halvorsen, *The Berlin Candy Bomber*, pp. 25–27, 36; Halvorsen Private Papers.

268 *In the days after:* Cable to Noce, July 1, 1948, *Papers of General Lucius D. Clay*, pp. 714–15.

269 *They each drove out:* National Archives, Murphy to Caffrey, July 4, 1948, Record Group 84; Clay, p. 367; Cable to Royall and Bradley, July 3, 1948, *Papers of General Lucius D. Clay*, pp. 722–24.

269 *Reporters were informed:* New York Times, July 5, 1948.

269 *At that very moment:* New York Times, July 11, 1948; Cook, p. 172.
270 *They flew through:* Halvorsen, The Berlin Candy Bomber, pp. 36–42; Lindsay, p. 88.
271 *The area had once:* Donovan, p. 43; Parrish, p. 207.
272 *It had been an established:* Gere, p. xii.
272 *Now, overflowing:* Donovan, p. 112.
272 *"I thought for a while:* The Bee-Hive, Fall 1948.
272 *The three combined:* Harrington, p. 27.
272 *The tarpaper shacks:* Halvorsen interview, August 2005; Halvorsen, The Berlin Candy Bomber, pp. 42–46; Leonard Whipple interview, October 2005.
274 *The next morning:* Halvorsen interview, August 2005; Halvorsen, The Berlin Candy Bomber, pp. 47–49.
274 *Early cargo:* Collier, p. 72.
274 *One pilot flew:* Torchy Dames interview, September 2005.
274 *This merlot mission:* The Bee-Hive, Fall 1948.
274 *Halvorsen climbed into:* Halvorsen, The Berlin Candy Bomber, pp. 50–67; Tim Chopp and Ed Ide interviews, June 2005; Giangreco, p. 106; Bering, p. 90; Gere, p. 13; Haydock, p. 165; Naval Aviation News, January–February 1996; Botting, From the Ruins of the Reich, p. 128; Halvorsen letter to the Garland Times, July 18, 1948, Halvorsen Private Papers; Donovan, p. 45; Bill Baker interview, June 2005; The Bee-Hive, Fall 1948; Haydock, p. 31; Grathwol, p. 33; Man, p. 69.
277 *Landing at Tempelhof:* Arnold-Foster, p. 33.
277 *One was simply:* William Tunner, Over the Hump (New York: Duell, Sloan, and Pearce, 1964), pp. 169–70; Collier, p. 82
278 *Women from Berlin:* Grathwol and Moorhus, p. 38.
278 *LeMay ordered:* United States Air Force Europe, Berlin Airlift 50th Anniversary, CD-ROM.
278 *They then ran back:* Halvorsen interview, February 2005.
278 *Hundreds lined up:* Stars and Stripes, May 24, 1998.
278 *Halvorsen acted skittish:* Halvorsen, The Berlin Candy Bomber, pp. 57–63; United States Air Force in Europe Release Number 1766, July 1948; National Archives, CBS News, radio report, ARC number 112094; Donovan, p. 111; Bill Baker interview, June 2005; Arnold-Foster, p. 96; United Press International, December 14, 1948; National Archives, Office of Military Government Files, "Berlin Reactions to the Air Lift and the Western Powers," July 23, 1948.
280 *The apron was made:* Harrington, p. 26.
280 *They saw that many:* National Archives, "Air Transport," newsreel, ARC number 20936.
280 *On the outside:* Parrish, p. 238; National Archives, "Die Luftbrücke," newsreel.
280 *A pilot named Hugo:* United States Air Force Europe, Berlin Airlift 50th Anniversary, CD-ROM.
280 *Pilots were sleeping:* Collier, p. 71; Donovan, pp. 47–48, 110; Unpublished recollections of W. C. "Dub" Southers; Haydock, pp. 155–56; The Bee-Hive, Fall 1948. There were other sources of the exhaustion. At Rhein-Main, when the airlift began, the Army continued its usual practice of firing off a cannon at 6 A.M. to announce reveille. The new pilots' requests to dispense with the practice were ignored. In the dead of night, a group of them used ropes and pulleys to move the cannon to the top of a four-story building. The cannon was brought back down by the Army and not shot off at 6 A.M. again (Giangreco, p. 101).
281 *"Never been as tired:* Harry S Truman, Dear Bess: The Letters from Harry to Bess Truman, 1910–1959 (Columbia: University of Missouri Press, 1998), p. 554.
281 *A disparate group:* McCullough, pp. 632–35.
282 *That July 9:* Tusa and Tusa, pp. 165, 168.
282 *"We are in the midst:* Margaret Truman, pp. 15–16.
282 *Clay had been:* Time, July 12, 1948.
282 *That Saturday, July 10:* Backer, p. 241.
283 *Clay had received:* Miller, p. 43. In fact, the intelligence reports were faulty. Recently declassified documents show that the Soviets had decided they would not let the convoy go through. This probably would have meant that one side or the other would have opened fire (Parrish, p. 176). In 1989, former Soviet foreign minister Andrei Gromyko wrote that Stalin embarked on the Berlin blockade "in the certain knowledge that the American administration was not run by frivolous people who would start a nuclear war over such a situation" (Richie, p. 1060).
283 *I am still convinced:* Cable to Bradley, July 10, 1948, Papers of General Lucius D. Clay, p. 734.

283 *The allies were slowly:* It is a hoary perennial of literature on the early Cold War to point out that the Berlin Airlift worked because air corridors over the Soviet zone had been agreed upon while there was no document delineating access rights for the Western powers by land to Berlin. Only the most literal-minded would make this differentiation. There had been an oral agreement and years of established procedures that guaranteed allied land access to Berlin. Furthermore, there was the inherent logic of being able to supply their own sectors. A written agreement to provide for access rights to Berlin by road or rail could have been broken just as easily as the Soviets voided other agreements regarding the capital when they argued that the allies had lost their privileges in the city. The only real difference between land and sky was a road could be blocked where a plane had to be shot down.

283 *"While I know:* Cable to Department of Army, July 12, 1948, *Papers of General Lucius D. Clay,* p. 736.

284 *"Since the entire reason:* Yergin, p. 399.

284 *"There is no enthusiasm:* Goulden, *The Best Years,* pp. 382–83.

285 *At the city's hotels:* McCullough, p. 636.

285 *Unable to afford:* Manchester, *The Glory and the Dream,* p. 453.

285 *The Democratic National Committee:* Goulden, *The Best Years,* p. 74.

285 *Big, fleshy:* McCullough, p. 636.

285 *To light:* Goulden, *Mencken's Last Campaign,* pp. 25, 31, 34.

285 *"Berlin lies:* Davison, p. 128.

286 *The allies, by their actions:* Shlaim, p. 233.

286 *"Time is still working:* Jean Edward Smith, *The Defense of Berlin,* pp. 103–4.

286 *Truman had already read it:* Bohlen to Marshall, July 14, 1948, *Foreign Relations of the United States, 1948,* Volume 2: *Germany and Austria,* p. 966.

286 *In Berlin, Clay's:* Cable to Bradley, July 15, 1948, *Papers of General Lucius D. Clay,* pp. 739–40.

286–287 *At a rally:* Time, July 26, 1948.

287 *At 7 P.M.:* Margaret Truman, p. 11.

287 *That day Dewey:* New York Times, July 15, 1948.

287 *Truman arrived:* Truman Library, "Trip of the President to Philadelphia, Penn, July 14, 1948," http://www.trumanlibrary.org/whistlestop/study_collections/1948campaign/large/docs/documents/index.php?documentdate=1948-07-14&documentid=23&studycollectionid=Election&pagenumber=1.

287 *The ground below:* Manchester, *The Glory and the Dream,* p. 454.

287 *He thought of:* Margaret Truman, p. 12.

287 *It was 1:30:* New York Times, July 15, 1948; Karabell, p. 151; McCullough, pp. 641–42.

288 *He carried a small:* Margaret Truman, p. 13.

288 *Almost all the men:* Douglas Schoen, *On the Campaign Trail* (New York: Regan Books, 2004), pp. 128–29.

288 *As he stepped:* National Archives, Universal Release, newsreel, Number 160.

288 *"Senator Barkley:* American Presidency Project, "Address in Philadelphia Upon Accepting the Nomination of the Democratic National Convention," July 15, 1948, http://www.presidency.ucsb.edu/ws/index.php?pid=12962&st=&st1=#.

289 *It was 5:30:* Margaret Truman, p. 14.

289 *The National Security Council:* Mudd Library Unedited Diaries, p. 2361.

289 *Marshall argued:* Declassified Documents Reference File, Papers of Harry S. Truman: President's Secretary's Files, July 16, 1948.

291 *As he well knew:* David F. Krugler, *This Is Only a Test: How Washington, D.C., Prepared for Nuclear War* (New York: Palgrave Macmillan, 2006), p. 1.

291 *"Nothing but the 'equalizing':* Washington Post, July 25, 1948.

292 *He and Marshall stayed:* Forrestal, p. 458.

292 *"I feel it essential:* National Archives, Royall to Clay, July 16, 1948, Plans and Operations File, Record Group 319.

292 *"Hold on to:* Divine, p. 216.

293 *The New York Times':* New York Times, July 18, 1948.

293 *That same day:* Shlaim, p. 241.

293 *"The showdown is at hand:* UCLA Film Archives, Hearst Newsreel, VA14390.

293 *On Monday morning:* Shlaim, pp. 247–49.

294 *"Let's keep in mind: Presidential Studies Quarterly,* Summer 1980.

294 *At 11:45:* Forrestal, p. 459.

294 *"I'd made the decision:* Margaret Truman, p. 15.

294 *That day, on the force: Washington Post,* July 20, 1948.

294 *In the city's: Chicago Daily Tribune,* July 5, 1948.

295 *Berliners were now: Washington Post,* July 18, 1948.

295 *On its best day:* National Archives, Murphy to Marshall, July 20, 1948, Record Group 84.

295 *"There is a slow but steady: New York Times,* July 24, 1948.

295 *If the allies deserted: Chicago Daily Tribune,* July 5, 1948.

295 *One German woman: New York Times,* June 26, 1978.

295 *A social worker:* Collier, p. 10.

296 *One morning:* Halvorsen interview, February 2007; Halvorsen, *The Berlin Candy Bomber,* pp. 88–89.

296 *"Berlin wasn't there":* Bill Baker interview, June 2005.

296 *They had been part:* Halvorsen, *The Berlin Candy Bomber,* pp. 92–93.

297 *On July 19:* Halvorsen interviews, February 2005, August 2005, August 2007; Halvorsen, *The Berlin Candy Bomber,* pp. 94–101; *New York Times,* September 16, 1948.

299 *It occurred to him:* Halvorsen interviews, February 2005, August 2005, August 2007; Halvorsen, *The Berlin Candy Bomber,* pp. 101–5; Donovan, p. 87; "The Story of Operation Little Vittles," undated Chicopee newspaper story; *Air Classics,* July 1998; Collier, p. 87. Chewing gum was an Americanism, not well known in many parts of Europe. A Danish airline during that period had been handing out gum labeled "to prevent unpleasant pressure in your ears during start and landing." A passenger flagged down a stewardess: "Help me get this stuff out of my ears. It doesn't help anyways" (*Stars and Stripes,* April 1, 1949).

300 *Halvorsen returned:* Halvorsen interviews, February 2005, August 2005, August 2007; Brett-Smith, p. xi; Halvorsen, *The Berlin Candy Bomber,* pp. 105–9; Collier, p. 10; UCLA Film Archives, VA14391.

302 *It was ten:* Halvorsen interviews, February 2005, August 2005, August 2007; Halvorsen, *The Berlin Candy Bomber,* pp. 109–12; *Air Classics,* July 1998; Collier, pp. 87–88; Haydock, pp. 176–77; Donovan, pp. 58–65; Parrish, pp. 236–37.

306 *On July 20:* National Archives, Murphy to Saltzman and Hickerson, July 19, 1948, Record Group 84; Haydock, p. 177.

307 *"The present action:* National Archives, Murphy to Marshall and Lovett, July 11, 1948, Record Group 84.

307 *"It does appear:* Cable to Draper, July 19, 1948, *Papers of General Lucius D. Clay,* pp. 743–46.

308 *His doctor: Washington Post,* August 20, 1948; Haydock, pp. 177–78.

308 *Clay's plane:* Harry Truman Presidential Library, President's Daily Calendar, July 21, 1948, http://www.trumanlibrary.org/calendar/main.php?currYear=1948&currMonth=7&currDay=21; David E. Lilienthal, *The Journals of David E. Lilienthal,* Volume 2: *The Atomic Energy Years, 1945–1950* (New York: Harper & Row, 1964), pp. 388–92; Forrestal, pp. 460–61.

309 *That day the prominent: Washington Post,* July 21, 1948.

309 *All his life:* Richard Haynes, *The Awesome Power* (Baton Rouge: Louisiana State University Press, 1973), p. 46.

310 *Bradley and Royall:* National Archives, *Paramount News,* newsreel, July 28, 1948.

310 *From the airport:* Forrestal Diary, pp. 459–60; Mudd Library Unedited Diaries, p. 2376.

311 *The National Security Council:* Harry Truman Presidential Library, President's Daily Calendar, July 22, 1948, http://www.trumanlibrary.org/calendar/main.php?currYear=1948&currMonth=7&currDay=22.

311 *Truman, who almost never:* White House, History of the National Security Council, 1947–1997, http://www.whitehouse.gov/nsc/history.html#truman.

311 *Sunlight streamed:* UCLA Film Archives, Hearst Newsreel, VA143977.

311 *Half an hour:* American Presidency Project, "President's News Conference," July 22, 1948, http://www.presidency.ucsb.edu/ws/index.php?pid=12965&st=&st1=.

311 *Truman welcomed:* Declassified Documents Reference System, Papers of Harry S. Truman: President's Secretary's Files, July 23, 1948; Mudd Library Unedited Diaries, p. 2376; Collier, pp. 90–92; Rhodes, pp. 325–26. It is not clear why Clay suddenly changed his stance on the

armed convoy. One possibility is that his discussion with Forrestal and others made him recon-sider the advisability of risking war. This seems unlikely, since previous statements indicated he had thought about this factor and concluded that war would come one way or another if the Russians so desired. More likely is that his brief time in Washington had convinced him that the armed convoy was a dead option—at least at that moment—and that the battle was over whether Berlin should be abandoned. The airlift allowed him to keep Berlin alive until others came to understand the necessity of a convoy.

313 *He did not reveal it:* Shlaim, p. 307.

314 *Three hours after: Washington Post,* July 23, 1948.

314 *That night, he was: Papers of General Lucius D. Clay,* p. 755.

314 *"You look like:* Collier, p. 92. Clay's own recollection in his memoir of the circumstances of Tru-man's decision differs from this account taken from a book written with his cooperation. Given that his memoir is riddled with inaccuracies regarding the meeting of the National Security Council—including the date of the meeting and his laughable assertion that there was "no dis-sent to my recommendations" in the National Security Council meeting—it cannot be safely relied upon.

314 *Clay discovered:* Jean Edward Smith, *Lucius D. Clay,* p. 516.

314 *He went, naturally: Washington Post,* July 23, 1948.

314 *Before returning: Washington Post,* July 24, 1948; *Chicago Daily Tribune,* July 24, 1948.

315 *As he rushed:* Cable to Draper, *Papers of General Lucius D. Clay,* August 28, 1948, p. 789.

315 *"The Berlin crisis: New York Times,* July 25, 1948.

315 *The delegates were young:* Ross, p. 141.

315 *Three-quarters:* Culver and Hyde, p. 485.

315 *Two out of five:* Peterson, p. 126; *Washington Post,* July 25, 1948.

315 *Each day began:* Ross, p. 141.

315 *"I had them all singing":* Iowa Public Television, Pete Seeger interview, http://www.iptv.org/wallace/docs/Trans_PeteSeeger.pdf; *New York Times,* April 17, 1988.

316 *Paul Robeson:* Schmidt, p. 186; *Chicago Daily Tribune,* July 25, 1948.

316 *They believed that:* Abels, p. 118.

316 *The party platform: Washington Post,* July 24, 25, 1948; *New York Times,* July 25, 1948; Peterson, p. 130; *Los Angeles Times,* July 25, 1948; *Christian Science Monitor,* June 29, 1948.

316 *"We are in the midst:* Karabell, p. 15.

316 *The steps to jail: Washington Post,* July 22, 1948.

316 *Wallace was asked:* Abels, p. 118.

317 *A platform plank:* Karabell, p. 180.

317 *"I have never heard:* Goulden, *Mencken's Last Campaign,* pp. 15, 90.

317 *For this, the Maryland:* Richard Norton Smith, p. 507.

317 *The crowd:* Kleinman, p. 262.

317 *What's more:* Goulden, *Mencken's Last Campaign,* pp. 83–86.

317 *When he appeared: Washington Post,* July 25, 1948; Glen H. Taylor, *The Way It Was with Me* (Secaucus, N.J.: Lyle Stuart, 1979), p. 385.

318 *Four years earlier: New York Times,* July 25, 1948.

320 *Truman's plan:* Kelly, p. 47.

320 *The Republican chairman: Washington Post,* July 21, 1948.

320 *"It's all so futile":* Margaret Truman, p. 17.

320 *There was, wrote:* Andreas-Friedrich, p. 234.

320 *They sarcastically:* Donovan, p. 84.

320 *With electricity severely:* National Archives, Murphy to Marshall, June 29, 1948, Record Group 84; Collier, p. 84; Office of Military Government monthly report, July 1948, Papers of Frank L. Howley.

321 *In Berlin's churches: Christian Science Monitor,* July 24, 1948.

321 *Almost exactly:* Davison, p. 165; *Diplomatic History,* Fall 1997.

321 *The airlift "has gripped:* National Archives, CBS News, radio report, ARC number 112094.

321 *Someone, it was:* Haydock, p. 155.

321 Time *magazine: Time,* July 26, 1948.

322 *The* New York Times: *New York Times,* July 4, 1948.

322 *By the beginning:* Tusa and Tusa, p. 177.

322 *During the first:* Arnold-Foster, p. 84.

322 *Operation Vittles:* Haydock, p. 176.

322 *Most Berliners:* Merritt and Merritt, *Public Opinion in Occupied Germany: The OMGUS Surveys, 1945–1949,* pp. 248–49.

322 *It was "obvious:* Time, July 12, 1948.

322 *That same month, columnist: Washington Post,* July 8, 1948.

322 *A cartoon:* Davidson, p. 209.

322 *Another Communist Berlin paper: Chicago Daily Tribune,* July 6, 1948.

322 *In 1918:* Donovan, p. 39.

323 *During World War II:* Richie, pp. 523–24; Catherine Merridale, *Ivan's War: Life and Death in the Red Army, 1939–1945,* (New York: Metropolitan Books, 2006), p. 179; Anthony Beevor, *Stalingrad* (New York: Viking, 1998), p. 292.

10: August

324 *When Bill Tunner arrived:* Tunner, pp. 3–22; Ann Tunner interview, June 2005; Adela Riek Scharr, *Sisters in the Sky* (St. Louis: The Patrice Press, 1986), p. 42.

329 *By the spring:* Tunner, pp. 27, 43–136; Spencer, pp. 138, 141, 170.

331 *When the war ended:* Tunner, pp. 148–49; Ann Tunner interview.

332 *In describing:* Tunner, pp. 9, 151, 155–56

333 *"He called each night:* Miller, p. 90.

334 *Tunner was "beginning:* Tunner, pp. 159–60, 41.

335 *Vandenberg said:* Wedemeyer letter to Nicholas Pasti, January 21, 1974, William H. Tunner Papers, Air Force Historical Research Agency; Parrish, p. 214.

335 *He and Wedemeyer:* Wedemeyer letter to Tunner, November 23, 1960, William H. Tunner Papers, Air Force Historical Research Agency.

335 *"He had a good thing:* Tunner, pp. 162–63.

335 *Kuter would arrive:* Tunner Oral History, Air Force Historical Research Agency.

335 *When his C-54 left:* Robert Rodrigo, *Berlin Airlift* (London: Cassell, 1960), p. 40.

335 *Tunner had told:* Tunner, pp. 165–66.

336 *In the days after:* Halvorsen, *The Berlin Candy Bomber,* pp. 113–16; National Archives, Newsreel, "Berlin: Focal Point of World" (Welt Im Film translation); National Archives, 342 USAF 17643 R 1-4; National Archives, *"Die Brücke*—The Bridge," Archival Research Catalogue 46909; Collier, pp. 87–88; Huschke, p. 232.

337 *Tunner put his staff:* Tunner, pp. 162, 166; Tunner Oral History, Air Force Historical Research Agency, p. 86; Collier, p. 97. LeMay's diary from that period is in conflict with Tunner's recollection. It records Tunner as visiting LeMay the morning after his arrival in Germany (LeMay Diary, Air Force Historical Research Agency).

337 *To save face:* Haydock, p. 181.

338 *From LeMay's mansion:* "505 Years of the 'Schwarzer Bock' in Wiesbaden"; Tunner, pp. 162, 166–70; Collier, p. 100.

340 *In that airlift: Aerospace Historians,* September 1971.

340 *As he summed: Time,* October 18, 1948.

340 *Three days later:* Tunner, p. 171; *Stars and Stripes,* November 20, 1948; Harrington, p. 44; United States Air Force Europe, Berlin Airlift 50th Anniversary, CD-ROM.

341 *The editor:* Tunner, pp. 180–81.

342 *Within a few days:* Harrington, p. 44.

342 *Berliners began:* Davison, p. 140.

342 *By mid-July:* Giangreco, p. 167.

343 *When the airlift began:* CNN "The Cold War, Episode 4," http://www.cnn.com/SPECIALS/cold.war/episodes/04/script.html.

343 *An Associated Press: Christian Science Monitor,* August 13, 1948.

343 *One boy:* Parrish, pp. 256–57.

343 *On warm days:* Donovan, p. 82.

343 *Only a few:* Davison, p. 330.

343 *When a C-47: New York Times,* July 30, 1948.

343 *"Seems to me:* Giangreco, pp. 111–12.
344 *"We grope:* Andreas-Friedrich, pp. 234–35.
344 *As recently:* Davison, p. 339.
344 *"We want: Diplomatic History,* Fall 1997; Donovan, pp. 90–91.
345 *On August 2:* Smith to Marshall, August 3, 1948, *Foreign Relations of the United States, 1948, Volume 2: Germany and Austria,* pp. 999–1007; Tusa and Tusa, pp. 204–11; National Archives, Record Group 84, Top Secret Cables to other missions.
346 *One day:* Tunner, pp. 152–55; Giangreco, p. 116; William H. Tunner Papers, Air Force Historical Research Agency, Maxwell Air Force Base; Harrington, p. 47.
347 *With an array:* Tunner, pp. 172–75; Harrington, p. 44; Arnold-Foster, p. 68.
349 *"Things happen rather fast:* Gail Halvorsen to Alta Jolley, August 8, 1948, Halvorsen Private Papers.
349 *By the middle:* Halvorsen, *The Berlin Candy Bomber,* pp. 116–19; *Stars and Stripes,* October 17, 1948; Halvorsen interview, August 2005; CNN "The Cold War, Episode 4," http://www.cnn.com/SPECIALS/cold.war/episodes/04/script.html.
350 *In mid-August:* Giangreco, p. 137; Collier, p. 9; *Stars and Stripes,* November 1, 1948.
350 *Nearly every night:* Philip Windsor, *City on Leave* (New York: Praeger, 1963), p. 109.
351 *Soon after the blockade:* Richie, p. 670; Giangreco, p. 116; Weekly intelligence report, Papers of Frank L. Howley.
351 *The day after:* Halvorsen interviews, February, August, 2005; Halvorsen, *The Berlin Candy Bomber,* pp. 116–19; *Stars and Stripes,* October 17, 1948; Halvorsen interview, August 2005; CNN "The Cold War, Episode 4," http://www.cnn.com/SPECIALS/cold.war/episodes/04/script.html.
352 *It was a sticky:* Stars and Stripes, May 24, 1998.
353 *In Potsdamer Platz:* Haydock, pp. 191–92; *New York Times,* August 22, 1948.
354 *On August 20:* Los Angeles Times, August 20, 1948.
354 *That evening, ABC News:* Halvorsen Private Papers.
354 *Many papers: Christian Science Monitor,* August 20, 1948.
354 *The first person: Mobile Register,* August 22, 1948.
355 *On August 26:* Haydock, pp. 199–201; Tusa and Tusa, p. 222.
355 *That August:* Office of Military Government monthly report, August 1948, Papers of Frank L. Howley.
355 *The suicide rate:* Andreas-Friedrich, pp. 240–41.
356 *Eleven-year-old:* Gere, p. 174.
356 *Soon Halvorsen:* Halvorsen, *The Berlin Candy Bomber,* pp. 199–20; Collier, p. 106.
357 *By 4 P.M.:* Halvorsen Oral History, Air Force Historical Research Agency; Halvorsen interview, February 2005; *Salt Lake Tribune,* unknown date, Halvorsen Private Papers.
357 *But, unbidden:* Halvorsen Private Papers.
358 *The city's children: Stars and Stripes,* October 29, 1948.
359 *It had been from:* Beevor, *The Fall of Berlin 1945,* p. 385.
359 *On August 17:* Library of Congress, LeMay Papers.
359 *On August 11:* Richard Norton Smith, p. 507.
360 *For the first time:* Morrow, p. 267.
360 *He exchanged letters:* Karabell, p. 189.
360 *Clark Clifford:* Clifford to Truman, August 17, 1948, Truman Presidential Library, http://www.trumanlibrary.org/whistlestop/study_collections/1948campaign/large/docs/documents/index.php?documentdate=1948-08-17&documentid=11&studycollectionid=Election&pagenumber=1.
361 *On August 30:* Tusa and Tusa, p. 217.
361 *William Batt:* Divine, p. 231.
361 *One of Truman's:* Kelly, p. 46.
361 *The floor under Margaret's piano:* McCullough, p. 652.

11: September
362 *"The blockade will be:* Andreas-Friedrich, p. 241; *Los Angeles Times,* September 1, 7, 1948.
362 *Every day:* UCLA Film Archives, VA2686.
363 *"I am not going:* Teleconference with Draper, August 30, 1948, *Papers of General Lucius D. Clay,* p. 794.

363 *On their second day:* Murphy to Marshall, September 1, 1948, *Foreign Relations of the United States, 1948,* Volume 2: *Germany and Austria,* p. 1103.

364 *They would end:* Teleconference with Royall, September 2, 1948, *Papers of General Lucius D. Clay,* p. 803; *Washington Post,* September 15, 1948; *New York Times,* September 10, 1948.

364 *There had been numerous:* Forrestal, p. 480.

364 *On Saturday, September 4:* National Archives, Murphy to Marshall, September 4, 1948, 12 A.M., Record Group 84, Entry 2534.

365 *Dear Chocolate Uncle!:* Halvorsen Private Papers.

366 *The democratic party:* Personal Diary of Colonel Frank L. Howley in Papers of Frank L. Howley.

366 *Instead, Markgraf's deputy:* Haydock, pp. 205–6.

366 *On September 6:* UCLA Film Archives, VA2686; Tusa and Tusa, pp. 226–29; Arnold-Foster, pp. 73–74; *New York Times,* September 7, 1948; Personal Diary of Colonel Frank L. Howley in Papers of Frank L. Howley; National Archives, Murphy to Marshall, September 7, 1948, 2 A.M., Record Group 84, Entry 2536; Haydock, pp. 206–7; Donovan, p. 93; *Stars and Stripes,* September 7, 1948; Davison, pp. 185–87; Howley, *Berlin Command,* pp. 215–17; Davison, pp. 185–87.

368 *Forrestal used the holiday:* Forrestal, pp. 481–82.

369 *At 8 P.M.:* National Archives, Murphy to Marshall, September 8, 1948, 8 A.M., Record Group 84, Entry 2536; Personal Diary of Colonel Frank L. Howley in Papers of Frank L. Howley; *New York Times,* September 7, 1948; *Stars and Stripes,* September 7, 1948.

370 *But that night:* National Archives, Murphy to Marshall, September 7, 1948, 2 A.M., Record Group 84, Entry 2536; *New York Times,* September 7, 1948; Windsor, p. 113; Howley, *Berlin Command,* p. 215.

370 *With limited radio:* Andreas-Friedrich, pp. 242–43.

370 *Clay was in the evening's:* Teleconference with Draper, September 6, 1948, *Papers of General Lucius D. Clay,* pp. 831–35.

371 *Around the time:* "Individual Flight Record," Halvorsen Private Papers; Halvorsen interviews, February and August 2005; Halvorsen, *The Berlin Candy Bomber,* pp. 135–36; Gail Halvorsen to Alta Jolley, September 7, 1948, Halvorsen Private Papers.

372 *As he read the speech:* Karabell, p. 212.

372 *"Though conducted:* Ibid., p. 29.

372 *Two of the most acclaimed:* Stephen Ambrose and Douglas Brinkley, *Rise to Globalism: American Foreign Policy Since 1938* (New York: Penguin Books, 1997), p. 101.

373 *Having rushed through:* New York Times, September 8, 1948.

373 *The news was all bad:* Forrestal, pp. 483–84; National Archives, Papers of Harry S. Truman: President's Secretary's Files, September 9, 1948.

373 *Inside the British:* National Archives, Murphy to Marshall, September 8, 1948, 8 A.M., Record Group 84, Entry 2536; Tusa and Tusa, pp. 227–29; *New York Times,* September 8, 1948; Personal Diary of Colonel Frank L. Howley in Papers of Frank L. Howley; Haydock, p. 207; Donovan, p. 97.

375 *A few hours:* Teleconference with Forrestal, Royall, Draper, Bradley, and Wedemeyer, September 8, 1948, *Papers of General Lucius D. Clay,* pp. 845–49; Forrestal, p. 484; *Washington Post,* September 9, 1948.

376 *"Clark, I was:* Clifford, p. 160.

376 *In August, the Pentagon:* Mudd Library Unedited Diaries, p. 2402; Omar Bradley, pp. 488–89.

376 *The plan was built:* Hoopes and Brinkley, pp. 405–6; Rhodes, p. 321.

376 *With a budget of $20 billion:* Boettcher, p. 160; Forrestal, p. 503.

376 *Forrestal ate almost all:* Stars and Stripes, May 23, 1949; *New York Times,* August 29, 1948.

376 *That week, the* Saturday: *Saturday Evening Post,* September 11, 1948.

377 *That same day:* Cable to Draper and Bradley, September 8, 1948, *Papers of General Lucius D. Clay,* p. 844–45; National Archives, Murphy to Bohlen, September 8, 1948, 9 P.M., Record Group 84, Entry 2536; Personal Diary of Colonel Frank L. Howley in Papers of Frank L. Howley; Howley, *Berlin Command,* p. 109. Howley notes that Kotikov would tug on his fingers whenever he became nervous.

378 *On September 8:* Collier, pp. 116–21; Davison, pp. 188–90; William Heimlich interview, George Washington University National Security Archive, http://www.gwu.edu/~nsarchiv/coldwar/interviews/episode-4/heimlich4.html; Richie, p. 671; Davidson, p. 211; Andreas-Friedrich, p. 243; *Stars and Stripes,* September 10, 1948; *New York Times,* January 12, 1990; Drew Middleton, *Where*

Has Last July Gone? (New York: Quadrangle, 1973), p. 165; Personal Diary of Colonel Frank L. Howley in Papers of Frank L. Howley; National Archives, *Berlin Calls on the World,* Department of Defense film, Record Group 111, ARC number 23886; Andreas Anderhaus and Jack O. Bennett, *Blockade, Airlift, and Airlift Gratitude Foundation* (Berlin: Press and Information Office of the Land Berlin, 1985), p. 34; CNN "The Cold War, Episode 4," http://www.cnn.com/SPECIALS/cold.war/episodes/04/script.html.

380 *For all the eloquence:* National Archives, Murphy to Marshall, September 10, 1948, 6 P.M., Record Group 84, Entry 2536; Arnold-Foster, p. 76; Collier, pp. 120–21; *Chicago Daily Tribune,* September 10, 1948; *New York Times,* September 10, 1948; National Archives, *Berlin Calls on the World,* Department of Defense film, Record Group 111, ARC number 23886; Personal Diary of Colonel Frank L. Howley in Papers of Frank L. Howley; *Stars and Stripes,* September 10, 11, 1948; Jean Edward Smith, *Lucius D. Clay,* p. 522; Steege, p. 239.

382 *At the same moment:* The President's Day, September 9, 1948, Harry S Truman Library, http://www.trumanlibrary.org/calendar/main.php?currYear=1948&currMonth=9&currDay=9; *New York Times,* September 10, 1948; *Washington Post;* September 10, 1948.

382 *At a morning:* American Presidency Project, President's News Conference of September 9, 1948, http://www.presidency.ucsb.edu/ws/index.php?pid=12989&st=&st1=.

383 *At 5 P.M.:* The President's Day, September 9, 1948, Harry S Truman Library, http://www.trumanlibrary.org/calendar/main.php?currYear=1948&currMonth=9&currDay=9; Margaret Truman, pp. 20–21; McCullough, p. 678.

383 *That morning, Elmo Roper:* Goulden, *The Best Years,* p. 398; Ross, pp. 2–3; McCullough, p. 657.

383 *Forrestal, the wealthiest:* *New York Times,* September 10, 1948.

383 *Marshall, usually the stoic:* Forrestal, pp. 485–86; *Historian,* February 1990.

384 *Hal Halvorsen, having left:* Halvorsen to Tunner, "Trip Report," September 29, 1948.

384 *There were 6,000:* Graebner, p. 80.

384 *In 1947:* Radio-Electronics-Television Manufacturers Association, "Television Receiving Set Production, 1947–1953," http://www.tvhistory.tv/1947-53-USA-TV-MonthlyProduction.JPG.

385 *In 1948, Puppet Playhouse:* The Howdy Doody Show Online, "The Howdy Doody Show History," http://www.howdydoodytime.com/hdshow.htm.

385 *Kukla, Fran, and Ollie:* James Trager. *The People's Chronology* (Detroit: Gale, 2005); *New York Times,* July 4, 1948.

385 *In October, during:* David Halberstam, *Summer of '49* (New York: William Morrow 1989), p. 23.

385 *The following month:* *Stars and Stripes,* December 2, 1948; Museum of Broadcast Communications, "Music on Television," http://www.museum.tv/archives/etv/M/htmlM/musicontele/musicontele.htm.

385 *Halvorsen had his first:* Halvorsen to Tunner, "Trip Report," September 29, 1948; *San Francisco Chronicle,* September 16, 1948; *Memphis Press-Scimitar,* September 27, 1948; *The Bee-Hive,* Fall 1948; *New York Times,* September 16, 1948; *New York Post,* September 15, 1948; *Task Force Times,* September 28, 1948.

387 *"You'd have thought:* *Stars and Stripes,* September 30, 1948; Halvorsen to Tunner, "Trip Report," September 29, 1948; Halvorsen, *The Berlin Candy Bomber,* p. 136; Jan Morris, *Manhattan '45* (New York: Oxford University Press, 1987), pp. 52, 53, 174, 184; *New York Times,* September 15, 1948.

388 *On Friday afternoon:* Halvorsen to Tunner, "Trip Report," September 29, 1948; Halvorsen, *The Berlin Candy Bomber,* pp. 136–37; Halvorsen interview, February and August 2005; *Air Force Times,* October 16, 1948; *Stars and Stripes,* September 30, 1948; Gail Halvorsen to Alta Jolley, September 1948, Halvorsen Private Papers; *Boston Sunday Globe,* October 10, 1948; *New York Times,* September 16, 1948.

389 *"This . . . is Berlin":* National Archives, "William L. Shirer—Berlin Airlift," Archival Research Catalogue 111997.

391 *He still strained:* Catherine Gibson letter to Tunner, November 4, 1960, William H. Tunner Papers, Air Force Historical Research Agency.

391 *But the day after:* *The Bee-Hive,* Fall 1948; Parrish, pp. 251–52; Jackson, pp. 129–30; *Los Angeles Times,* September 10, 1948.

391 *Clay asked LeMay:* *Air Force Magazine,* June 1978; Harrington, p. 43. This occurred sometime in August.

392 *On September 10:* Cable to Bradley, September 10, 1948, *Papers of General Lucius D. Clay,* p. 852; cable to Bradley, September 23, 1948, *Papers of General Lucius D. Clay,* p. 878. Clay would claim to have asked for 69, not 60, by October 1. He was originally told he could have 40 more by Bradley, but that number was soon thereafter raised to 50.

392 *A call for workers:* Richie, p. 665; Harrington, p. 55; Donovan, pp. 134–37, 192; Grathwol, p. 42; Collier, pp. 108–9; Tunner, pp. 211–12; Parrish, p. 275.

393 *Weary from his journey: Task Force Times,* unknown date.

393 *From Solvang:* October 22, 1948, letter in Halvorsen Public Papers.

393 *In his hometown:* Unidentified newspaper clip in Halvorsen Public Papers.

393 *The* Boston Sunday Globe: *Boston Sunday Globe,* September 26, 1948.

394 *The* Washington Post: *Washington Post,* October 9, 1948.

394 *The elementary school:* Unidentified newspaper clips in Halvorsen Public and Private Papers.

394 *Radio stations:* Collier, p. 106.

394 *There were all sorts: Magazine Digest,* April 1949; *Christian Science Monitor,* October 12, 1948; Halvorsen Public Papers.

394 *That Monday: Stars and Stripes,* September 30, 1948.

394 *At noon:* The President's Day, September 13, 1948, Harry S Truman Library, http://www .trumanlibrary.org/calendar/main.php?currYear=1948&currMonth=9&currDay=13; Forrestal, p. 487; Paul Boyer, *By the Bomb's Early Light: American Thought and Culture at the Dawn of the Atomic Age* (New York: Pantheon Books, 1985), p. 292; Ross, p. 175.

395 *The situation in Berlin:* Lilienthal, p. 406.

395 *That day, stocks: Los Angeles Times,* September 14, 1948.

396 *"A terrific day:* Yergin, pp. 391–92; Shlaim, p. 338.

396 *On his first full day:* American Presidency Project, "Rear Platform and Other Informal Remarks in Illinois, Iowa, and Missouri," September 18, 1948, http://www.presidency.ucsb.edu/ws/index .php?pid=12999&st=&st1=.

396 *But his big speech:* American Presidency Project, "Address at Dexter, Iowa, on the Occasion of the National Plowing Match," September 18, 1948, http://www.presidency.ucsb.edu/ws/ index.php?pid=13000&st=&st1=; Manchester, "The Glory and the Dream," p. 460.

397 *A meeting of his top advisers: Washington Post,* September 16, 1948.

398 *Dewey also kicked: Stars and Stripes,* September 22, 1948; *Washington Post,* September 15, 1948; *New York Times,* September 21, 1948.

398 *The following day: Stars and Stripes,* September 23, 1948.

398 *The chairman: Stars and Stripes,* September 6, 1948.

398 *The Republican Party: Stars and Stripes,* October 19, 1948.

398 *Earl Warren: Wall Street Journal,* September 7, 1948.

398 *In mid-September: New York Times,* September 15, 17, 1948; *Washington Post,* September 15, 1948.

398 *"Peace is the basic issue: Christian Science Monitor,* September 11, 1948; Ross, p. 226.

399 *At the start:* Goulden, *The Best Years,* p. 391.

399 *"All of you:* Karabell, p. 125.

399 *He was not of them:* O'Neill, p. 91; Karabell, p. 124.

399 *In Boston:* Karabell, pp. 231–34.

399 *The Associated Press: Stars and Stripes,* September 22, 1948. Earlier in September, the Associated Press reported that "two Greensboro, NC youths who accorded Wallace with a egg and fruit reception were ordered by a municipal county court to write several times the famous Voltaire quotation 'I disapprove of what you say but I'll defend to the death your right to say it'" (*Stars and Stripes,* September 6, 1948).

400 *In Los Angeles: New York Times,* September 24, 1948; *New York Times,* September 25, 1948; American Presidency Project, "Address at the Gilmore Stadium in Los Angeles," September 23, 1948, http://www.presidency.ucsb.edu/ws/index.php?pid=13012&st=&st1=; McCullough, p. 665.

400 *The following day:* Ross, p. 196;

401 *A week later: New York Times,* October 3, 1948.

401 *When they finally:* Divine, p. 239.

401 *Aboard the* Ferdinand Magellan: Dallas, p. 283; Manchester, *The Glory and the Dream,* p. 450.

401 *Dewey had a similar system:* Divine, pp. 241–42.

401 *In Texas: Stars and Stripes,* September 29, 1948.

402 *When one of his press aides:* Eben Ayers Oral History Interview, Harry S Truman Library, http://www.trumanlibrary.org/oralhist/ayers4.htm; Ferrell, p. 273; McCullough, p. 677; *Christian Science Monitor,* September 28, 1948; *Stars and Stripes,* September 29, 1948; White, p. 3.

403 *The tribune of the 10: Los Angeles Times,* September 28, 1948; *Chicago Daily Tribune,* September 29, 1948.

403 *"I regret very much:* Minutes of the 286th Policy Planning Staff Meeting, September 28, 1948, *Foreign Relations of the United States, 1948,* Volume 2: *Germany and Austria,* pp. 1194–97. The minutes state that these were not precise quotations but "the gist of his remarks."

404 *"The climax: New York Times,* September 28, 1948; UCLA Film Archives, VA14393.

405 *In Bonham: Christian Science Monitor,* September 28, 1948.

405 *The next day, in Oklahoma City:* Clifford, pp. 230–32; *New York Times,* September 29, 1948; McCullough, pp. 679–80; Abraham Feinberg Oral History Interview, Harry S Truman Presidential Library, http://www.trumanlibrary.org/oralhist/feinberg.htm; American Presidency Project, "Address in Oklahoma City," September 28, 1948, http://www.presidency.ucsb.edu/ws/index.php?pid=13023&st=&st1=.

405 *Preparing to assume: Christian Science Monitor,* September 29, 1948; *Stars and Stripes,* September 30, 1948; *New York Times,* September 29, 1948.

406 *Mister Lieutenant:* Halvorsen Private Papers.

406 *On the last day: Stars and Stripes,* October 1, 1948; *New York Times,* October 1, 1948; *Los Angeles Times,* September 27, 1948; *Christian Science Monitor,* October 2, 1948.

407 *The planes were still:* Tusa and Tusa, p. 235.

407 *Berlin was receiving: Stars and Stripes,* October 15, 1948.

407 *"Can the American: Washington Post,* September 12, 1948.

407 *The American consul general:* National Archives, Edward Groth to Marshall, "Some Thoughts of a German Official," Record Group 84.

407 *On September 23:* Cable to Bradley, September 23, 1948, *Papers of General Lucius D. Clay,* pp. 878–79.

12: October

408 *When, on October 3: Stars and Stripes,* October 4, 1948; *Springfield Daily News,* October 4, 1948; *Los Angeles Times,* October 4, 1948; *Task Force Times,* October 5, 1948; UCLA Film Archive, VA13977.

409 *By early October: Air Classics,* July 1998; Halvorsen, *The Berlin Candy Bomber,* pp. 127–28; Earl Moore interview, October 2005; *Holyoke Transcript,* October 15, 1948; *Chicopee Herald,* October 26, 1989; *Springfield Union,* November 2, 1948; unidentified newspaper clips in Halvorsen Public Papers; "The Story of Operation Little Vittles," undated Chicopee newspaper story.

410 *Over a two-day:* Unidentified newspaper clips in Halvorsen Private Papers.

410 *Newsweek, stating: Newsweek,* October 18, 1948.

410 *That same week: Time,* October 18, 1948.

410 *Almost every day: Stars and Stripes,* October 30, 1948; Huschke, p. 234; Halvorsen, *The Berlin Candy Bomber,* pp. 120–35; *Christian Science Monitor,* October 12, 1948; newspaper clips in Halvorsen Private Papers; John Burnett letter to Halvorsen; October 21, 1948; Halvorsen Public Papers; *Stars and Stripes,* October 10, 1948.

411 *When Truman returned:* The President's Day, October 2, 1948, Harry S Truman Presidential Library, http://www.trumanlibrary.org/calendar/main.php?currYear=1948&currMonth=10&currDay=2; Shlaim, pp. 355–58; Clifford, p. 233; McCullough, pp. 685–88; *Washington Post,* October 10, 1948; Divine, p. 256; Pogue, pp. 407–8; Bohlen, p. 269; *New York Times,* October 9, 1948.

413 *That same morning, Truman:* The President's Day, October 5, 1948, Harry S Truman Presidential Library, http://www.trumanlibrary.org/calendar/main.php?currYear=1948&currMonth=10&currDay=5; Mudd Library Unedited Diaries, p. 2539; Forrestal, p. 498; Rogow, pp. 276, 279; *Chicago Daily Tribune,* October 10, 1948; Clifford, p. 160; Keith McFarland and David Roll, *Louis Johnson and the Arming of America* (Bloomington: Indiana University Press, 2005), p. 139. There was no sense that a secretary of defense should steer clear of partisan politics. During the campaign, both Secretary of the Army Royall and Secretary of the Navy John L. Sullivan had been active surrogates on Truman's behalf (*Washington Post,* November 5, 1948).

415 *The following morning:* The President's Day, October 6, 1948, Harry S Truman Presidential

Library, http://www.trumanlibrary.org/calendar/main.php?currYear=1948&currMonth=10& currDay=6; American Presidency Project, "Address at Convention Hall in Philadelphia," October 6, 1948, http://www.presidency.ucsb.edu/ws/index.php?pid=13035&st=&st1=; Divine, p. 256.

415 *During the course: Stars and Stripes,* October 7, 1948.

415 *Then, on October 8:* Divine, p. 256; *New York Times,* October 10, 1948; *Stars and Stripes,* October 10, 1948; McCullough, p. 688; *Washington Post,* October 10, 1948.

416 *Truman must have known:* Cray, p. 650.

417 *He would never admit:* Ross, p. 214; Divine, p. 259.

417 *Publicly, Dewey said:* Abels, pp. 203–4; Divine, p. 258; *Stars and Stripes,* October 16, 1948; *Washington Post,* October 11–13, 1948; Goulden, *The Best Years,* pp. 414–15.

418 *The Dear Lollypop:* Halvorsen Private Papers.

418 *William Shirer found:* Task Force Times, October 5, 1948.

419 *He had thrown:* Collier, pp. 122–23; author's measurement; Tunner, p. 215.

419 Newsweek's *John Thompson:* Newsweek, October 18, 1948.

419 *The commentator: Washington Post,* December 29, 1948.

420 *The process of landing:* Rhodes, p. 330.

420 *Ross Milton:* Launius and Cross, p. 40.

420 *Coal and food:* Collier, p. 162.

420 *By the end of September:* Task Force Times, September 28, 1948.

420 *It carried special shipments:* Tusa and Tusa, p. 258; Arnold-Foster, p. 82.

420 *Civilian airlines: Wall Street Journal,* October 5, 1948; *Washington Post,* October 2, 1948, Miller, p. 77.

420 *Carrying the dehydrated:* Combined Airlift Task Force Report, 1949, p. 43; Tusa and Tusa, pp. 239–40; Tunner, pp. 203–4; *Task Force Times,* October 20, 1948; *Stars and Stripes,* December 27, 1948.

421 *That fall:* Dudley Barker, *Berlin Airlift: An Account of the British Contribution* (London: Air Ministry and Central Office of Administration, 1949), p. 43; Tusa and Tusa, p. 256.

421 *"I never had":* Tunner Oral History, Air Force Historical Research Agency, p. 101.

421 *They "were going:* Chuck Powell interview, September 2005; Harrington, p. 31.

421 *"We didn't have:* Donovan, p. 56.

421 *By the time:* Tusa and Tusa, p. 310.

422 *So one afternoon:* Tunner, pp. 182–83; Tunner Oral History, Air Force Historical Research Agency, pp. 101–2; *The Bee-Hive,* Fall 1948.

422 *One of the Airlift:* Harrington, p. 55.

423 *Indeed, when* Life*:* Tunner to Major Tilley, United States Air Force in Europe, Public Information Officer, October 22, 1948, William H. Tunner Papers, Air Force Historical Research Agency.

423 *The interview was about: Stars and Stripes,* January 7, 1949.

423 *By the middle of October:* United States Air Force Europe, Berlin Airlift 50th Anniversary, CD-ROM; Miller, p. 80.

424 *They would often wear:* National Archives, *Berlin: Focal Point of the World,* Welt Im Film newsreel series, Archival Research Catalogue 614794.

424 *In another instance:* Major Alden L. Van Buskirk, "The 1946th and the Berlin Airlift," unpublished manuscript, pp. 10, 46.

424 *Airmen deployed:* Combined Airlift Task Force Report, 1949, p. 73.

424 *Many had been trained: Stars and Stripes,* December 27, 1948, January 30, 1949, February 5, 1949; Parrish, pp. 281, 287; Haydock, pp. 226–27.

425 *One of Tunner's men:* Catherine Gibson letter to Tunner, November 4, 1960, William H. Tunner Papers, Air Force Historical Research Agency; Tunner, p. 210.

425 *The movie theater:* Rodrigo, p. 71

425 *Russian Yaks:* Tunner, pp. 185–86; *Reader's Digest,* October 1961; Berlin Airlift Historical Foundation, "Statistics Summary of Russian Harassment Incidents in Air Corridors to Berlin"; John Schuppert interview, September 2005; Parrish, pp. 238–39; Haydock, p. 224.

426 *They listened to: Stars and Stripes,* December 22, 1948, and April 16, 1949; Collier, pp. 139–40; Bill Gilbert, p. 176; John Schuppert interview, September 2005; United States Air Force in Europe Press Release, No.2100-A, October 29, 1948.

426 *Sometimes pilots:* Anderhaus and Bennett, p. 65.

426 *If this happened:* Collier, p. 139.

426 *The strain:* Collier, p. 122; Bill Gilbert, p. 176; *Task Force Times,* October 5, 1948.

427 *He would still explode:* Collier, pp. 107, 123; interview with Charles Church, September 2005.

427 *On his last day:* Library of Congress, Curtis LeMay Papers.

427 *Yet while Tunner:* Harrington, p. 81; *Mobility Forum,* July/August 1999; Tunner, pp. 175–76; Collier, pp. 110–12.

428 *"Almost everyone else: Saturday Evening Post,* October 16, 1948.

429 *With the Berlin crisis:* Pogue, p. 410; Richard Norton Smith, p. 20; Divine, p. 267.

429 *"It is generally assumed:* Personal Diary of Colonel Frank L. Howley in Papers of Frank L. Howley.

429 *With this in mind:* Teleconference with Draper, October 13, 1948, *Papers of General Lucius D. Clay,* pp. 896–900.

430 *Two days later:* National Archives, Record Group 260, Office of Military Government Files, Clay Memoir Files, Clay Press Conferences and Speeches.

430 *It had been stoked: Christian Science Monitor,* October 6, 1948.

430 *That Sunday morning:* Personal Diary of Colonel Frank L. Howley in Papers of Frank L. Howley.

431 *As the painful lunch:* Jean Edward Smith, *Lucius D. Clay,* p. 502.

431 *They were sitting:* Howley, *Berlin Command,* pp. 223–24; Fromkin, p. 78; Clay, p. 391.

432 *"It is to me:* Personal Diary of Colonel Frank L. Howley in Papers of Frank L. Howley.

432 *The Soviets, the presumed: Stars and Stripes,* October 18, 1948.

432 *Though constrained:* Jean Edward Smith, *Lucius D. Clay,* p. 504.

432 *Every time a Russian fighter:* Halvorsen interview, February 2007.

432 *When asked by a reporter: Stars and Stripes,* October 18, 1948.

433 *The Soviets continued: Diplomatic History,* Fall 1997; Collier, pp. 85–86.

433 *"We have done: Stars and Stripes,* October 2, 1948.

433 *All summer: Stars and Stripes,* October 12, 1948; *New York Times,* October 12, 1948; *Washington Post,* October 10, 1948; Miller, p. 53; Davison, pp. 196–98; "Notes on the Blockade of Berlin 1948," HQ British Troops Berlin, Papers of Frank L. Howley; Howley, *Berlin Command,* p. 240.

434 *But on October 19: Stars and Stripes,* October 20, 1948; UCLA Film Archives, VA14393; Howley, *Berlin Command,* p. 240; Parrish, p. 263; "Notes on the Blockade of Berlin 1948," HQ British Troops Berlin, Papers of Frank L. Howley; Davison, pp. 196–98.

434 *The same day: Stars and Stripes,* October 20, 1948.

435 *Impatient as ever:* Cable to Bradley, October 4, 1948, *Papers of General Lucius D. Clay,* p. 890.

435 *"It is the considered opinion:* Shlaim, pp. 361–62.

435 *While Clay's plane:* National Archives, "Review of the World Situation," October 20, 1948, Central Intelligence Agency files.

436 *"The only thing that has kept:* Forrestal, p. 507.

436 *That same morning:* The President's Day, October 21, 1948, Harry S Truman Library, http://www.trumanlibrary.org/calendar/main.php?currYear=1948&currMonth=10&currDay=21.

436 *This was Truman's mind-set:* Declassified Documents Reference System, Papers of Harry S. Truman: President's Secretary's Files, "Memorandum for the President," October 21, 1948.

437 *He approved:* Jean Edward Smith, *Lucius D. Clay,* p. 504. As mentioned previously, Clay's memories on this count are unreliable. In his memoir and in interviews with his biographer, he conflated the two visits to Washington. For instance, he put Truman in the room at the National Security Council meeting in October. He was not, but had been in July.

437 *By 5 o'clock:* Jean Edward Smith, *Lucius D. Clay,* p. 504; *New York Times,* September 20, 1948.

437 *As the New York Times: New York Times,* October 22, 1948.

438 *This night would be: Time,* November 1, 1948.

438 *Clay's speech was twice: New York Times,* October 22, 1948; UCLA Film Archive, VA14431; Personal Diary of Colonel Frank L. Howley in Papers of Frank L. Howley.

439 *Mr. 1st Lt.:* Halvorsen Private Papers.

439 *The next day:* The President's Day, October 22, 1948, Harry S Truman Library, http://www.trumanlibrary.org/calendar/main.php?currYear=1948&currMonth=10&currDay=22.

439 *If it was late:* Goulden, *The Best Years,* p. 393.

439 *"America's future:* Ross, p. 196.

439 *All through October:* Divine, p. 269.

440 *He set the tone:* American Presidency Project, "Rear Platform Remarks in Indiana," October 25, 1948, http://www.presidency.ucsb.edu/ws/index.php?pid=13066&st=&st1=; *Washington Post,* October 26, 1948.

440 *Truman arrived in Chicago: Washington Post,* October 26, 1948; *New York Times,* October 26, 27, 1948; American Presidency Project, "Address in the Chicago Stadium," October 25, 1948, http://www.presidency.ucsb.edu/ws/index.php?pid=13068&st=&st1=.

441 *So in a special radio address:* Gullan, pp. 141–42.

442 *"The presidential campaign:* Divine, p. 266.

442 *Polls showed:* Boyer, p. 335.

442 *After arriving: Christian Science Monitor;* October 27, 28, 1948; Kelly, pp. 74–77.

443 *Two days after:* Cable to Draper, October 26, 1948, *Papers of General Lucius D. Clay,* pp. 908–9.

444 *An extra 33:* Combined Airlift Task Force Report, p. 55; *Stars and Stripes,* October 30, 1948.

444 *As the Airlift went on:* John Provan and R.E.G. Davies, *Berlin Airlift* (McLean, Va.: Paladwr Press, 1998), p. 62.

444 *One day in October:* Halvorsen interview, February 2007; Halvorsen, *The Berlin Candy Bomber,* pp. 147–48.

445 *Their Berlin newspapers:* Jackson, p. 95; *Time,* October 18, 1948.

445 *When several children: Air Classics,* July 1998.

445 *The neutral nations:* Jean Edward Smith, *The Defense of Berlin,* p. 123.

445 *The American representative: Stars and Stripes,* October 30, 1948.

445 *The veto: Stars and Stripes,* October 27, 1948.

446 *"The nights are getting:* Andreas-Friedrich, p. 247.

446 *On October 29: Stars and Stripes,* October 30, 1948.

446 *The Dickensian-named: Stars and Stripes,* October 15, 1948.

446 *"The reports we get:* National Archives, Record Group 260, Office of Military Government Files, Clay Memoir Files, Clay Press Conferences and Speeches.

446 *At the end of October:* Jean Edward Smith, *Lucius D. Clay,* p. 524; Elizabeth Lay, *The Berlin Air Lift* (Historical Division, Headquarters European Command, 1952), p. 119.

446 *At 8:30:* National Archives, Record Group 260, Office of Military Government Files, Clay Memoir Files, Clay Press Conferences and Speeches.

447 *Half of the city's: New York Times,* October 29, 30, 1948.

447 *On Thursday, October 28: New York Times,* October 29, 1948; American Presidency Project, "Address in Madison Square Garden," New York City, October 28, 1948, http://www.presidency.ucsb.edu/ws/index.php?pid=13075&st=&st1=.

447 *Dewey had spoken: Christian Science Monitor,* October 27, 1948.

447 *The next day: Stars and Stripes,* November 2, 1948.

448 *That day he campaigned: Stars and Stripes,* October 30, 1948.

448 *That night, in Brooklyn:* American Presidency Project, "Address at the Brooklyn Academy of Music, New York City," October 29, 1948, http://www.presidency.ucsb.edu/ws/index.php?pid=13079&st=&st1=.

449 *On October 30: Los Angeles Times,* October 31, 1948; *New York Times,* October 31, 1948.

449 *The following day, October 31: New York Times,* November 1, 1948.

449 *That weekend in Berlin: Chicago Daily Tribune,* October 30, 1948.

449 *"The elections will put: New York Times,* October 28, 1948.

449 *In Albany: Saturday Evening Post,* October 16, 1948.

449 *The head of the United States Secret Service:* Karabell, p. 7.

449 *The reference book:* Donaldson, p. 210.

449 *For its first election-night:* Richard Norton Smith, p. 20.

449 *"The first post-election:* Ross, p. 5.

13: November

451 *There is nothing poetic:* Howley, *Berlin Command,* pp. 219, 237; Lowell Bennett, p. 19; Elkins, p. 70.

452 *In September: Time,* September 20, 1948.

452 *On November 1:* Parrish, p. 282.

452 *The sound of descending:* Donovan, pp. 100–101; *Chicago Tribune,* August 14, 2004.

452 *They were right:* Combined Airlift Task Force Report, p. 88; *Chicago Daily Tribune,* November 4, 1948.

453 *The staff of the European: Stars and Stripes,* November 3, 4, 1948.

454 *Dewey slunk off: New York Times,* November 6, 7, 8, 1948; Cook, p. 197.

455 *"In times of crisis:* Parrish, p. 261.

455 *"The bear got us":* Richard Norton Smith, p. 543.

455 *As Karl Schmidt:* Schmidt, p. 78.

455 *On election day:* Yarnell, p. 208; Ross, pp. 229, 246–47. If Dewey, with his 189 electoral votes, had won California and Ohio, with 25 electoral votes apiece, no candidate would have had a majority. He still would have needed 27 more electoral votes to win outright. He could have accomplished this if Wallace had done the slightest bit better in these states: 5,856 more votes in Idaho (4 electoral votes), 28,362 more votes in Iowa (10 electoral votes), 1,934 more votes in Nevada (3 electoral votes), 4,407 more votes in Wyoming (3 electoral votes), and 28,716 more votes in Virginia (11 electoral votes).

456 *On November 5: New York Times,* November 5, 6, 1948; *Chicago Daily Tribune,* November 6, 1948; Harrington, p. 55; Tunner, pp. 211–12; Donovan, pp. 134–37; Haydock, pp. 237–38; Lowell Bennett, p. 138.

456 *On November 11:* Botting, *The Aftermath: Europe,* p. 136.

456 *Yet French commandant Jean Ganeval's:* Huschke, pp. 140–41; Collier, pp. 145–46; Parrish, pp. 276–77; William Heimlich interview, George Washington University National Security Archive, http://www.gwu.edu/~nsarchiv/coldwar/interviews/episode-4/heimlich5.html.

457 *Shortly after the election:* Parrish, p. 315.

457 *He failed to realize:* Murphy, pp. 357–58.

458 *Jessup had made:* Backer, pp. 249–50.

458 *Mr. Halvorsen, Lt.:* Halvorsen Private Papers.

458 *Three hundred: Washington Post,* November 6, 1948; *New York Times,* November 6, 1948.

459 *He had been asked:* Hoopes and Brinkley, pp. 429–30. There is some evidence that Forrestal made a larger contribution of $2,500 as well through a secret account he controlled. If so, the account was so secret that it is unclear whether Truman was aware of the donation.

459 *Forrestal, his closest friend:* Jeffrey M. Dorwart, *Eberstadt and Forrestal: A National Security Partnership, 1909–1949* (College Station: Texas A&M University Press, 1991), p. 166.

459 *He asked Eisenhower:* Hoopes and Brinkley, p. 416.

459 *As Forrestal entered: Stars and Stripes,* November 7, 1948.

459 *That Saturday in the White House: Chicago Daily Tribune,* November 10, 1948.

460 *Wearing a three-piece: New York Times,* November 15, 1948; *Chicago Daily Tribune,* November 15, 1948; Forrestal, pp. 52–57; *Stars and Stripes,* November 15, 1948.

460 *While Forrestal was in Europe: Washington Post,* November 12, 1948; *New York Times,* November 12, 1948.

461 *The day Forrestal returned:* American Presidency Project, "The President's News Conference at Key West, Florida," November 16, 1948, http://www.presidency.ucsb.edu/ws/index.php?pid=13088&st=&st1=.

461 *The following day:* Hoopes and Brinkley, pp. 427–28; *New York Times,* November 19, 1948; Log of President Truman's Fifth Trip to Key West, Florida, November 7–21, 1948, Harry S Truman Presidential Library, pp. 52–53, http://www.trumanlibrary.org/calendar/travel_log/key1947/keywest5th_toc.htm; Forrestal, p. 529.

461 *Forrestal remained: Los Angeles Times,* November 4, 1948; Hoopes and Brinkley, p. 432; Clifford, p. 171; Boettcher, pp. 158–59.

462 *In the first week of November: Washington Post,* November 10, 1948; *New York Times,* November 15, 21, 1948; Collier, pp. 135–36; *Stars and Stripes,* November 15, 16, 1948.

463 *On November 9:* William H. Tunner Papers, Air Force Historical Research Agency; National Archives, Record Group 260, Office of Military Government Files, Clay Memoir Files, Clay Press Conferences and Speeches.

463 *Once, a "missing: The Bee-Hive,* Spring 1949; *Stars and Stripes,* February 17, 1949; Interview with Paul Curtis, October 2005; Collier, pp. 136–37; Tunner, p. 214; Miller, p. 167; Jackson, p. 125.

465 *The Westinghouse Electric Corporation: New York Times,* November 19, 1948; *Christian Science*

Monitor, November 29, 1948; Combined Airlift Task Force Report, 1949, p. 43; Wolfgang W. E. Samuel, *I Always Wanted to Fly: America's Cold War Airmen* (Jackson: University Press of Mississippi, 2001), p. 25; Haydock, pp. 244, 258.

465 *In only 63:* Harrington, pp. 64–65; Miller, p. 168

466 *"The legendary Hatfield: Stars and Stripes,* November 9, 1948.

466 *In a survey: New York Times,* November 14, 1948.

466 *"It's a little bit: Wall Street Journal,* November 16, 1948.

466 *"To be living here:* Andreas-Friedrich, p. 261.

467 *Before the war:* Lowell Bennett, p. 140; Report by Office of Military Government, US Sector, Berlin, July 1, 1945–September 1, 1949, Papers of Frank L. Howley.

467 *In the hours:* "Notes on the Blockade of Berlin 1948," Papers of Frank L. Howley.

467 *Housewives would heat:* Donovan, pp. 72, 86.

467 *In the last five months:* "Notes on the Blockade of Berlin 1948," Papers of Frank L. Howley.

467 *The city's hospitals: Chicago Daily Tribune,* November 10, 12, 1948; Bering, p. 113.

468 *In Berlin they joked:* Donovan, p. 166.

468 *A family's entire coal ration:* Report by Office of Military Government, US Sector, Berlin, July 1, 1945–September 1, 1949, Papers of Frank L. Howley; Anderhaus and Bennett, p. 38.

468 *That same winter:* Tusa and Tusa, p. 244.

468 *At night, a cold:* Collier, p. 131.

468 *"When we go to bed:* Andreas-Friedrich, p. 251.

468 *It was so cold: Chicago Daily Tribune,* November 10, 1948; National Archives, Record Group 84, Entry 2536, Classified Cables to State Department, November 1948, Box 15.

468 *The Americans set up: Wall Street Journal,* November 17, 1948; *Stars and Stripes,* December 11, 1947.

469 *The city, which had been so proud: Chicago Daily Tribune,* November 7, 1948.

469 *Berliners would feed:* Collier, pp. 131–33.

469 *Clay had promised: New York Times,* November 21, 1948; *Christian Science Monitor,* November 13, 1948; "Notes on the Blockade of Berlin 1948," Papers of Frank L. Howley; Collier, pp. 86, 133, 137; Rodrigo, p. 80.

469 *When a plane crashed:* Bering, p. 112.

469 *At Tempelhof, when bags of Pom:* Haydock, p. 173.

470 *By November: Washington Post,* November 10, 1948; *Stars and Stripes,* January 1, 1949; Collier, p. 131.

470 *Inge Gross:* Gere, p. 178.

470 *As the winter:* Collier, p. 137.

470 *Two out of five:* Merritt and Merritt, *Public Opinion in Occupied Germany: The OMGUS Surveys, 1945–1949,* p. 266.

471 *"In the evening:* Donovan, pp. 180–81; Collier, pp. 131–32; *Stars and Stripes,* October 10, 1948, February 17, 1949.

472 *"RIAS was our daily:* Interview with Herbert Krüger, September 2005; *New York Times,* November 3, 1948; Office of Military Government monthly report, September 1948, Papers of Frank L. Howley, Air Force Historical Research Archives; National Archives, National Security Council memo, February 23, 1961, President's Committee on Information Activities Abroad; David Clay Large, *Berlin* (New York: Basic Books, 2001), p. 32.

472 *Clay had been convinced:* Clay, pp. 265–66.

473 *Berliners now chose:* Davison, p. 339.

473 *He had "really started something: New York Times,* October 31, 1948.

473 *Halvorsen was "the one:* Inge Stanneck Gross, *Memories of World War II and Its Aftermath* (Eastsound, Wash.: Island in the Sky, 2005), p. 165.

473 *A fifteen-year-old:* Nicholas, p. 545.

474 *Three years after:* Davison, p. 329.

474 *A laborer recalled:* Donovan, pp. 100, 182–83, 190.

474 *In July:* Anna J. Merritt and Richard L. Merritt, eds., *Public Opinion in Semisovereign Germany: The HICOG Surveys, 1949–1955* (Urbana: University of Illinois Press, 1980), p. 57.

474 *Overall, crime:* Lowell Bennett, p. 145; Report by Office of Military Government, US Sector, Berlin, July 1, 1945–September 1, 1949, Papers of Frank L. Howley; *Christian Science Monitor,* November 13, 1948; Davison, p. 319.

475 *One winter day: Washington Post,* May 18, 1949.

477 *Kotikov had announced:* Giangreco, p. 165.

477 *"HOUSEWIVES IN THE WEST!:* Donovan, p. 185; *Stars and Stripes,* November 20, 1948; Steege, p. 251.

478 *"Whoever votes: Stars and Stripes,* November 11, 1948.

478 *In mid-November: Chicago Daily Tribune,* November 23, 1948.

478 *Acting Mayor Ferdinand Friedensburg:* National Archives, Murphy to Marshall, November 15, 1948, Record Group 84, Entry 2531B.

479 *On November 17:* National Archives, Murphy to Marshall, November 17, 1948, Record Group 84, Entry 2536.

479 *As one Communist: Chicago Daily Tribune,* November 28, 1948.

479 *On Thanksgiving Day: Washington Post,* November 25, 1948; *New York Times,* November 25, 1948; *Los Angeles Times,* November 25, 1948.

479 *That weekend, Clay announced: New York Times,* November 29, 1948.

479 *At the end: Chicago Daily Tribune,* December 1, 1948; *Los Angeles Times,* November 29, 1948, December 1, 1948; Gere, pp. 65–67; *Stars and Stripes,* December 1, 1948.

480 *Rather than wait: Chicago Daily Tribune,* December 1, 1948; *Christian Science Monitor,* December 1, 1948; *Los Angeles Times,* December 1, 1948; *New York Times,* December 1, 1948; *Washington Post,* December 1, 1948.

480 *Clay called Ebert:* Lowell Bennett, p. 164.

480 *Ganeval—with withering:* Davison, pp. 218–19.

480 *The next morning: Stars and Stripes,* December 2, 1948.

481 *It fell to Howley: New York Times,* December 1, 1948.

481 *At the end of November:* Murphy to Marshall, November 26, 1948, *Foreign Relations of the United States, 1948, Volume 2: Germany and Austria,* pp. 1268–70; Murphy to Marshall, November 26, 1948, *Foreign Relations of the United States, 1948,* Volume 2: *Germany and Austria,* pp. 1270–72.

14: December

483 *On its third day: Stars and Stripes,* December 4, 1948.

483 *That same week:* Halvorsen, *The Berlin Candy Bomber,* pp. 141–42.

484 *By mid-November:* Air Force Historical Research Archives, Report of Unavailable Post Exchange Items, November 12, 1948.

484 *But now Halvorsen had:* Halvorsen, *The Berlin Candy Bomber,* pp. 141–42; Huschke, p. 235; Halvorsen Private Papers. A total of 100,700 packages of candy were shipped by the American Confectioners Association. The first shipment of 54,856 packages left from New York on the USS *Greenville Victory* on November 18. A Huyler's executive wrote Halvorsen to tell him the candy was on its way, but the letter did not arrive until after the delivery was already in Germany.

484 *That day it began: Stars and Stripes,* December 2, 1948.

484 *"If, on the other hand: Washington Post,* December 5, 1948.

485 *West Berlin housewives:* Davison, p. 226.

485 *On December 2:* Tusa and Tusa, p. 292; *Christian Science Monitor,* December 2, 1948.

485 *"If you vote: Stars and Stripes,* November 11, 1948.

485 *One had a picture:* Tusa and Tusa, p. 291.

485 *On December 3:* Davison, p. 225.

485 *The* Tägliche Rundschau: National Archives, Record Group 84, Entry 2536, Classified Cables to State Department, December 1948, Box 15.

486 *Handbills with big black:* Collier, p. 142.

486 *Rumors spread:* Davison, p. 225.

486 *When Howley assured:* National Archives, Record Group 84, Entry 2536, Classified Cables to State Department, November 1948, Box 15.

486 *"Propaganda poppycock": Chicago Daily Tribune,* November 11, 1948; *Stars and Stripes,* November 11, 1948.

486 *In the first few: New York Times,* December 2, 1948; *Stars and Stripes,* December 2, 1948; Davison, p. 228; *Los Angeles Times,* December 4, 1948.

487 *That week of the election:* Clay, pp. 382–83; Collier, p. 143.

488 *In the final hours:* National Archives, Record Group 84, Entry 2536, Classified Cables to State Department, October 1948, Box 15; *Washington Post,* December 5, 1948; *Christian Science Monitor,* December 2, 1948; Anthony Read and David Fisher, *Berlin: The Biography of a City*

(London: Hutchinson, 1994), p. 264; *Stars and Stripes,* December 4, 1948; *New York Times,* December 5, 1948.

488 *The Soviets declared: New York Times,* December 5, 1948; Tusa and Tusa, p. 292; *Washington Post,* December 5, 1948.

489 *When the polls opened: New York Times,* December 6, 1948; Collier, p. 143; *Stars and Stripes,* December 6, 1948; *Washington Post,* December 6, 1948; *Chicago Daily Tribune,* December 6, 1948; *Christian Science Monitor,* December 6, 1948; Collier, p. 144.

490 *It was, recorded:* Andreas-Friedrich, pp. 252–53.

490 *On December 16: New York Times,* December 17, 1948; *Washington Post,* December 17, 1948; *Chicago Daily Tribune,* December 17, 1948; *Christian Science Monitor,* December 18, 1948; Huschke, pp. 140–41; Tunner, p. 212; William Heimlich interview, George Washington University National Security Archive, http://www.gwu.edu/~nsarchiv/coldwar/interviews/episode-4/heimlich5.html; Parrish, pp. 276–77.

492 *"By the way:* Andreas-Friedrich, p. 255; Gere, p. 56; UCLA Film Archives, VA2686.

492 *But in corners:* "Bob Hope and American Variety," Library of Congress exhibition, http://www.loc.gov/exhibits/bobhope/uso.html; National Archives, *Paramount News,* newsreel, January 9, 1949; Interview with Larry Gelbart, April 2007; *Chicago Daily Tribune,* December 26, 1948; *New York Times,* December 26, 1948; *Stars and Stripes,* December 25, 27, 1948; Museum of Radio and Television, New York; UCLA Film Archives, VA2686; *Task Force Times,* December 23, 1948.

494 *When the show was over:* Clay, p. 387; *New York Times,* December 26, 1948; *Washington Post,* May 18, 1949; Haydock, pp. 255–56.

495 *To celebrate Christmas:* National Archives, "Santa Flies the Airlift," CBS News, Archival Research Catalogue 112871; *Portland Herald,* January 17, 1949; *Christian Science Monitor,* December 21, 1948; Halvorsen Private Papers; *Chicago Daily Tribune,* January 5, 1949; Halvorsen, *The Berlin Candy Bomber,* pp. 141–42; *Task Force Times,* December 24, 1948; Lowell Bennett, p. 178; Clay, p. 387; Office of Military Government monthly report, November 1948, Papers of Frank L. Howley, Air Force Historical Research Archives; Interview with Earl Moore, September 2005. GCA was the abbreviation for the Ground Control Approach radar.

497 *When Airlift personnel:* Interview with Jim Spatafora, October 2005; Joseph Werner, p. 113; *Navy Aviation News,* March 1949; Robert Frye, *The Berlin Airlift,* television documentary, WETA, 1998.

499 *James Forrestal spent that Christmas:* Rogow, pp. 306–8; Clifford, p. 173; William O. Douglas, *Go East, Young Man* (New York: Random House, 1974), p. 288; Hoopes and Brinkley, pp. 419, 433–36; William Draper Oral History, Harry S Truman Library, http://www.trumanlibrary.org/oralhist/draperw.htm; *Stars and Stripes,* May 2, 1949; Boettcher, p. 169.

502 *A committee of the House of Representatives: New York Times,* December 5, 1948.

502 *When, that month:* D. J. Taylor, *Orwell* (London: Chatto & Windus, 2003), p. 396.

502 *The situation in Berlin: Task Force Times,* December 31, 1948.

502 Time *magazine: Time,* January 3, 1949.

502 *"The year 1948: Stars and Stripes,* January 1, 1949; Miller, p. 170.

15: Spring Again

504 *On the last day: Stars and Stripes,* January 1, 1949.

504 *The first train:* Giangreco, p. 164.

505 *On January 11: Portland Herald,* January 17, 1949.

505 *In Berlin, after the:* Halvorsen, *The Berlin Candy Bomber,* pp. 145–50; *Chicago Daily Tribune,* January 25, 1949.

506 *But he had written her:* Gail Halvorsen to Alta Jolley, December 30, 1948, January 11, 1949, Halvorsen Private Papers; *Los Angeles Times,* January 17, 1949.

507 *Now the Skymaster:* Halvorsen, *The Berlin Candy Bomber,* pp. 151–57; Haydock, p. 260; *Christian Science Monitor,* January 25, 1949; WSPR radio transcript from January 27, 1949, in Halvorsen Public Papers; unidentified newspaper clips in Halvorsen Public Papers; Tex McCrary to Gail Halvorsen, January 26, 1949, Halvorsen Private Papers; *New York Times,* January 25, 1949.

508 *"It looked like curtains:* William Draper Oral History, Harry S Truman Library, http://www.trumanlibrary.org/oralhist/draperw.htm.

508 *Industrial production: Washington Post,* February 20, 1949.

508 *Unemployment was more:* Harrington, p. 84; Eric Morris, p. 139.

508 *A third of the city:* Report by Office of Military Government, US Sector, Berlin, July 1, 1945–September 1, 1949, Papers of Frank L. Howley.

508 *Of the 225:* Jackson, p. 137.

509 *Ration levels:* Giangreco, p. 159.

509 *For the first time:* Tusa and Tusa, p. 304.

509 *Tins of liverwurst:* National Archives, *Operation Vittles,* Department of Defense newsreel, Archival Research Catalogue 65515.

509 *Limburger cheese: Los Angeles Times,* December 7, 1948.

509 *In March: Stars and Stripes,* March 25, 1949.

509 *That spring:* Robert Frye, *The Berlin Airlift,* television documentary, WETA, 1998; *Stars and Stripes,* March 11, 1949.

509 *Children made seesaws:* Emmy Werner, p. 147.

509 *Overruled by Washington:* Cable to Draper, *Papers of General Lucius D. Clay,* December 26, 1948, p. 968.

509 *A few days into January:* Cable to Bradley, *Papers of General Lucius D. Clay,* January 5, 1949, pp. 973–75.

510 *When George Marshall:* Cable to Royall and Bradley, *Papers of General Lucius D. Clay,* January 10, 1949, p. 980; Teleconference with Royall, Bradley, and Voorhees, March 2, 1949, *Papers of General Lucius D. Clay,* pp. 1031–32.

510 *"The most extraordinary thing: New York Times,* March 5, 1949.

510 *That spring, a writer: The New Yorker,* May 14, 1949.

510 *Approaching Tempelhof: Reader's Digest,* April 1949.

510 *"It must be obvious: Washington Post,* March 21, 1949, and April 17, 1949.

512 *But on January 27: Christian Science Monitor,* January 31, 1949.

512 *Truman and Acheson:* Dean Acheson, *Present at the Creation* (New York: Norton, 1969), pp. 267–69; *New York Times,* February 3, 1949.

513 *There, on February 15: Presidential Studies Quarterly,* September 1972.

513 *As 1949 began:* Jack Anderson with James Boyd, *Confessions of a Muckraker* (New York: Random House, 1979), p. 123; Hoopes, pp. 438–40; Douglas, p. 287; *New York Times,* January 12, 1949; *Stars and Stripes,* February 3, 1949.

514 *Forrestal's resignation:* Forrestal, p. 553; *New York Times,* March 6, 18, 1949; *Los Angeles Times,* March 19, 1949; *Stars and Stripes,* March 19, 1949; *Wall Street Journal,* November 3, 1948; Windsor, p. 129.

516 *The morning:* Hoopes, pp. 444–54; Forrestal, p. 554; Marx Leva Oral History Interview, Harry S Truman, Presidential Library, http://www.trumanlibrary.org/oralhist/leva.htm; Dorwart, p. 169; Clifford, p. 174.

518 *On March 14: Political Science Quarterly,* September 1972.

519 *In his one month: Stars and Stripes,* February 15, 16, 1949; unidentified clipping in Halvorsen Public Papers.

520 *As for the original: Task Force Times,* March 9, 1949; unidentified clippings in Halvorsen Private Papers; unidentified clippings in Halvorsen Public Papers; *Salt Lake Tribune,* February 26, 1949; Halvorsen, "Personal History," p. 65; *Los Angeles Times,* March 14, 1949.

521 *Two days after:* Gail Halvorsen to Alta Jolley, March 14, 15, 16, 17, 1949, Halvorsen Private Papers.

521 *It was a hokey:* National Archives, *Operation Vittles,* Department of Defense newsreel, Archival Research Catalogue 24076.

522 *Though it went down:* Academy Awards invitation and parking pass, Halvorsen Private Papers; *Los Angeles Herald-Express,* March 25, 1949; Halvorsen, *The Berlin Candy Bomber,* pp. 159–60.

522 *On April 16: Las Vegas Review-Journal,* April 17, 1949; *Los Angeles Times,* April 17, 1949; home movie and records, Halvorsen Private Papers.

523 *On April 1: New York Times,* April 2, 1949; Rodrigo, pp. 193–94; *Task Force Times,* April 7, 1949; Tunner, pp. 218–22; Proposal for "Airlift: Berlin to the Stars," Tunner Personal Papers; Collier, pp. 151–54; Arnold-Forster, p. 92; *Time,* April 25, 1949; *Stars and Stripes,* April 17, 1949; Report by Office of Military Government, US Sector, Berlin, July 1, 1945–September 1, 1949, Papers of Frank L. Howley; *The Bee-Hive,* Spring 1949; *New York Times,* June 26, 1978.

525 *On May 3:* Clay, p. 242; *New York Times,* May 4, 1949; *Stars and Stripes,* May 5, 1949. Always delicate, Louis Johnson told reporters that he wanted to bring Clay back from Germany because he didn't want another Forrestal breakdown on his hands (Ayers, p. 307).

525 *Clay was on his way: New York Times,* May 5, 1949; Collier, p. 155.

526 *On board the train: Stars and Stripes,* May 5, 15, 1949; National Archives, Record Group 260, Office of Military Government Files, Clay Memoir Files, Clay Press Conferences and Speeches.

526 *On Capitol Hill: New York Times,* May 2, 5, 6, 1949; *Washington Post,* May 6, 1949; *Los Angeles Times,* May 6, 1949.

527 *In Moscow: Time,* May 23, 1949; *Los Angeles Times,* March 13, 1949; *New York Times,* March 8, 1949.

527 *On May 8: New York Times,* May 9, 1949; *Stars and Stripes,* May 10, 1949.

528 *Berliners were now 30:* Merritt and Merritt, eds., *Public Opinion in Semisovereign Germany: The HICOG Surveys, 1949–1955,* pp. 58–59.

528 *"With the end of the blockade: New York Times,* May 11, 1949.

528 *"The German people:* Murphy, p. 355.

529 *No, insisted Vasily Chuikov: Stars and Stripes,* May 10, 1949.

529 *There were no more: Stars and Stripes,* May 12, 13, 14, 1949; *Task Force Times,* May 16, 1949; *New York Times,* May 12, 1949; National Archives, *Paramount News,* newsreel, May 28, 1949, Archival Research Catalogue 99399; *Chicago Daily Tribune,* May 12, 1949; *Sydney Morning Herald,* May 13, 1949; *Los Angeles Times,* May 12, 1949; UCLA Film Archives, VA14393. The competition between the allies and the Soviets continued. The day that the blockade was to be lifted, the British at Helmsted had painted the fence on their side of the border. It had fallen into disrepair after months of disuse. The Russians soon responded by bringing out their own brushes and painting their checkpoint a pale green with bright red stars, golden sunbursts, and a hammer and sickle.

531 *It was not: New York Times,* May 12, 1949; Tusa and Tusa, pp. 356–57; *Stars and Stripes,* May 12, 1949; *Los Angeles Times,* May 12, 1949; *Washington Post,* May 12, 1949; Collier, pp. 156–57; UCLA Film Archive, VA14393; Robert Lochner interview, George Washington University National Security Archive, http://www.gwu.edu/~nsarchiv/coldwar/interviews/episode-4/lochner5.html.

532 *"Berlin is the happiest: Sydney Morning Herald,* May 12, 1949; Jackson, p. 139; Collier, p. 155; Jean Edward Smith, *The Defense of Berlin,* p. 130; *Stars and Stripes,* May 13, 1949; Robert Lochner interview, George Washington University National Security Archive, http://www.gwu.edu/~nsarchiv/coldwar/interviews/episode-4/lochner5.html; CNN "The Cold War, Episode 4," http://www.cnn.com/SPECIALS/cold.war/episodes/04/script.html.

533 *Clay's final days:* Robert Lochner interview, George Washington University National Security Archive, http://www.gwu.edu/~nsarchiv/coldwar/interviews/episode-4/lochner5.html; *New York Times,* May 13, 16, 1949; Clay, p. 391; *Stars and Stripes,* May 14, 16, 1949; Jean Edward Smith, *Lucius D. Clay,* pp. 545, 555.

Afterword: Coming Home

535 *When the flag: New York Times,* May 16, 1949; Jean Edward Smith, *Lucius D. Clay,* p. 555; *Stars and Stripes,* May 16, 1949.

535 *Louis Johnson: Christian Science Monitor,* May 18, 1949; National Archives, *Paramount News,* newsreel, June 1, 1949, Archival Research Catalogue 99400; *Stars and Stripes,* May 16, 1949; National Archives, *General Lucius D. Clay Is Welcomed in Washington,* Department of Defense newsreel, Archival Research Catalogue 21271; *New York Times,* May 18, 1949; *Washington Post,* May 18, 1949; *The New Yorker,* January 13, 1951.

538 *Two days later, New York City: Los Angeles Times,* May 20, 1949; *Stars and Stripes,* May 20, 1949; *New York Times,* May 19, 20, 1949.

538 *A few days later: Stars and Stripes,* May 26, 1949; *Marietta Daily Journal,* May 25, 1949; Blair Family Papers, Kennesaw State College, http://ksuweb.kennesaw.edu/archives/html/Blair/Blair1_box3.htm; Backer, p. 282; *New York Times,* June 1, 2, 12, 1949; *Christian Science Monitor,* June 23, 1949. Over the next month, he received honorary degrees from Harvard, Yale, Columbia, and Rutgers. Then came the job offers. The political leadership of Georgia tried to convince him to run for governor. He was asked to direct the New Jersey Turnpike Authority, to be executive vice president of General Motors, and to be executive vice president of IBM.

Though he and Marjorie had only $3,000 in their savings account, he rejected them all. Finally, that fall, he accepted the job of chief executive officer of the Ecusta Paper Company outside of Asheville, North Carolina. He quit after two months. Eventually he would become head of the Continental Can Company and a managing partner of Lehman Brothers investment house. He spearheaded the building of the interstate highway system, returned to Berlin as Kennedy's special envoy, raised the ransom money for those caught in the Bay of Pigs fiasco, and helped rebuild the Republican Party after the Goldwater debacle on behalf of Dwight Eisenhower (Jean Edward Smith, *Lucius D. Clay,* pp. xi, 556–61).

539 *On Saturday May 21:* Hoopes and Brinkley, pp. 461–65; Mudd Library, Princeton, "Admiral M. D. Willcutts Board of Investigation—Death of James V. Forrestal, civilian," July 13, 1949, Forrestal Papers, http://infoshare1.princeton.edu/libraries/firestone/rbsc/finding_aids/forrestal/willcutts/report1.pdf; *Stars and Stripes,* May 23, 1949; *New York Times,* May 23, 1949; *Washington Post,* April 28, 1949, May 23, 1949. The report of the Board of Investigation into Forrestal's death was declassified in 2004, after fifty-five years.

541 *Josephine Forrestal: New York Times,* May 24, 1949; Hoopes and Brinkley, p. 466; *Los Angeles Times,* April 21, 1949; National Archives, *Paramount News,* newsreel, June 4, 1949, Archival Research Catalogue 99400; National Archives, "Review of the World Situation," May 18, 1949; W. R. Smyser, *From Yalta to Berlin* (New York: St. Martin's Press, 1999), p. xiv.

542 *"There was never a country:* Goulden, *The Best Years,* p. 426; McCullough, p. 733.

543 *Though the blockade: Stars and Stripes,* May 24, 1998; Harrington, pp. 103, 109; Combined Airlift Task Force Report, 1949, p. 44.

543 *"Moosburg, Germany:* United States Air Force Europe, Press Release No. 4865-A, September 15, 1949.

544 *Howley left Berlin: Stars and Stripes,* September 3, 5, 8, 1949; Personal Diary of Colonel Frank L. Howley in Papers of Frank L. Howley; Howley, *Berlin Command,* p. 270; Howley, "Your War for Peace," pp. 1–2; National Archives, "Longines Chronoscope," January 26, 1953, Archival Research Catalogue 95817.

545 *Tunner left: Stars and Stripes,* September 10, 1949.

545 *Tunner would watch: Air Force Magazine,* March 1998; LeMay, p. 417; *Washington Post,* April 28, 1949; Letters in William H. Tunner Papers, Air Force Historical Research Agency; interview with Ann Tunner, June 2005. LeMay would retire to Southern California's San Fernando Valley. Glen Taylor, who lost his Senate seat in the 1950 election, lived out his days as a toupee salesman in Northern California. Henry Wallace's running mate and George Wallace's running mate—the polar opposites of American politics in the Cold War—would die within a few years of each other on opposite ends of the same state.

547 *Hal Halvorsen:* Gail Halvorsen to Alta Jolley, March 17, 1949, April 4, 1949, Halvorsen Private Papers; Halvorsen, *The Berlin Candy Bomber,* pp. 162, 236–37.

Epilogue: October 1990

549 *On October 3: New York Times,* October 4, 1990, November 26, 1990; *Los Angeles Times,* November 21, 29, 1990; *Time,* December 10, 1990.

BIBLIOGRAPHY

Abels, Jules. *Out of the Jaws of Victory.* New York: Henry Holt and Co., 1959.

Acheson, Dean. *Present at the Creation.* New York: Norton, 1969.

Allied Museum, Berlin. *Pioneers of the Airlift.* Berlin: Nishen, 1998.

Almond, Gabriel Abraham. *The American People and Foreign Policy.* Westport, Conn.: Greenwood Press, 1977.

Ambrose, Stephen. *Eisenhower,* Volume 1. New York: Simon & Schuster, 1983.

———. *The Victors.* New York: Simon & Schuster, 1998.

———. *The Wild Blue: The Men and Boys Who Flew the B-24s Over Germany.* New York: Simon & Schuster, 2001.

Ambrose, Stephen, and Douglas Brinkley. *Rise to Globalism: American Foreign Policy Since 1938.* New York: Penguin, 1997.

American Woman in Blockaded Berlin. *Operation Vittles Cookbook.* Berlin: Deutscher Verlag, 1949.

Anderhaus, Andreas, and Jack O. Bennett. *Blockade, Airlift, and Airlift Gratitude Foundation.* Berlin: Berliner Forum, 1985.

Anderson, Jack, with James Boyd. *Confessions of a Muckraker.* New York: Random House, 1979.

Andreas-Friedrich, Ruth. *Battleground Berlin: Diaries 1945–1948.* Translated by Anna Boerresen. New York: Paragon House, 1990.

Annan, Noel. *Changing Enemies: The Defeat and Regeneration of Germany.* London: HarperCollins, 1995.

Armstrong, Anne. *Berliners: Both Sides of the Wall.* New Brunswick, N.J.: Rutgers University Press, 1973.

Army Times, the Editors of. *Berlin: The City That Would Not Die.* New York: Dodd, Mead, 1968.

Arnold, Henry. *American Air Power Comes of Age,* Volume 2. Birmingham: Air University Press, 2002.

Arnold-Forster, Mark. *The Siege of Berlin.* London: Collins, 1979.

Atkinson, Rick. *An Army at Dawn.* New York: Henry Holt, 2002.

Backer, John. *Winds of History.* New York: Van Nostrand Reinhold, 1983.

Bark, Dennis, and David R. Gress. *A History of West Germany,* Volume 1. Oxford: Basil Blackwell, 1989.

Barker, Dudley. *Berlin Airlift: An Account of the British Contribution.* London: Air Ministry and Central Office of Administration, 1949.

Barnouw, Dagmar. *Germany 1945*. Bloomington: Indiana University Press, 1996.

———. *The War in the Empty Air: Victims, Perpetrators, and Postwar Germans*. Bloomington: Indiana University Press, 2005.

Barone, Michael. *Our Country: The Shaping of America from Roosevelt to Reagan*. New York: Free Press, 1990.

Barros, James. *Trygve Lie and the Cold War*. DeKalb: Northern Illinois University Press, 1989.

Beevor, Antony. *The Fall of Berlin 1945*. New York: Viking, 2002.

———. *Stalingrad*. New York: Viking, 1998.

Behrman, Greg. *The Most Noble Adventure*. New York: Free Press, 2007.

Beisner, Robert. *Dean Acheson*. New York: Oxford University Press, 2006.

Bennett, Lowell. *Berlin Bastion*. Frankfurt: Fred Rudl, 1951.

Benns, F. Lee, and Mary Elisabeth Seldon. *Europe, 1939 to Present*. New York: Appleton-Century-Crofts, 1965.

Bering, Henrik. *Outpost Berlin: The History of the American Military Forces in Berlin, 1945–1994*. Chicago: Edition q, 1995.

Beschloss, Michael. *The Conquerors*. New York: Simon & Schuster, 2002.

Bird, Kai. *The Chairman: John J. McCloy, the Making of the American Establishment*. New York: Simon & Schuster, 1992.

Black, Cyril, et al. *Rebirth: A History of Europe Since World War II*. Boulder, Colo.: Westview Press, 1992.

Blum, John Morton. *V Was for Victory: Politics and American Culture During World War II*. New York: Harcourt Brace Jovanovich, 1976.

Boettcher, Thomas. *First Call: The Making of the Modern U.S. Military, 1945–1953*. Boston: Little, Brown, 1992.

Bohlen, Charles. *Witness to History*. New York: Norton, 1973.

Bolles, Blair. *The Big Change in Europe*. New York: Norton, 1958.

Borgwardt, Elizabeth. *A New Deal for the World: America's Vision for Human Rights*. Cambridge, Mass.: Harvard University Press, 2005.

Botting, Douglas. *The Aftermath: Europe*. Alexandria, Va.: Time-Life Books, 1983.

———. *From the Ruins of the Reich*. New York: Crown, 1985.

Bower, Tom. *The Pledge Betrayed: America and Britain and the Denazification of Postwar Germany*. Garden City, N.Y.: Doubleday, 1982.

Boyer, Paul. *By the Bomb's Early Light: American Thought and Culture at the Dawn of the Atomic Age*. New York: Pantheon Books, 1985.

———. *Fallout: A Historian Reflects on America's Half-Century Encounter with Nuclear Weapons*. Columbus: Ohio State University Press, 1998.

Bradley, James, with Ron Powers. *Flags of Our Fathers*. New York: Bantam, 2000.

Bradley, Omar. *A Soldier's Story*. New York: Henry Holt, 1951.

Bradley, Omar, and Clay Blair. *A General's Life: An Autobiography by the General of the Army*. New York: Simon & Schuster, 1983.

Brands, H. W. *The Devil We Knew: Americans and the Cold War*. New York: Oxford University Press, 1993.

Brett-Smith, Richard. *Berlin '45: The Grey City*. London: Macmillan, 1967.

Brooks, John. *The Great Leap: The Past Twenty-five Years in America*. New York: Harper & Row, 1966.

Bullock, Allan. *Ernest Bevin: A Biography*. London: Politicos, 2002.

———. *Ernest Bevin: Foreign Secretary, 1945–1951*. London: Heinemann, 1983.

Byrnes, James. *Speaking Frankly*. New York: Harper & Row, 1947.

Campbell, John. *The United States in World Affairs 1947–1948*. New York: Harper & Brothers, 1948.

Carroll, James. *House of War: The Pentagon and the Disastrous Rise of American Power*. New York: Houghton Mifflin, 2006.

Childs, David. *Britain Since 1945*. London: Routledge, 2001.

Church of Jesus Christ of Latter-day Saints. *The Book of Mormon*. Salt Lake City: Intellectual Reserve, 1981.

Clark, Delbert. *Again the Goosestep*. Indianapolis: Bobbs-Merrill, 1949.

Clay, Lucius. *Decision in Germany*. Garden City, N.Y.: Doubleday, 1950.

———. *Germany and the Fight for Freedom*. Cambridge, Mass.: Harvard University Press, 1950.

Clifford, Clark, with Richard Holbrooke. *Counsel to the President.* New York: Random House, 1991.

Coffey, Thomas. *Iron Eagle: The Turbulent Life of General Curtis LeMay.* New York: Crown, 1986.

Cohn, Beverly. *What a Year It Was! 1949.* Los Angeles: MMS Publishing, 1998.

Collier, Richard. *Bridge Across the Sky.* New York: McGraw-Hill, 1978.

Conot, Robert. *Justice at Nuremberg.* New York: Carroll & Graf, 1984.

Cook, Don. *Forging the Alliance.* New York: William Morrow, 1989.

Cowley, Robert, ed. *The Cold War: A Military History.* New York: Random House, 2005.

Cray, Ed. *General of the Army: George C. Marshall, Soldier and Statesman.* New York: Norton, 1990.

Culver, John, and John Hyde. *American Dreamer.* New York: Norton, 2000.

Dallas, Gregor. *1945.* New Haven: Yale University Press, 2005.

Davenport, Marcia. *Too Strong for Fantasy.* New York: Charles Scribner's Sons, 1967.

Davidson, Basil. *Germany: What Now?, Potsdam—Partition.* London: Frederick Muller, 1950.

Davidson, Eugene. *The Death and Life of Germany.* New York: Knopf, 1957.

Davies, Andrew. *Where Did the Forties Go?* London: Pluto Press, 1984.

Davis, Franklin. *Come as a Conqueror: The United States Army's Occupation of Germany, 1945–1949.* New York: Macmillan, 1967.

Davison, W. Phillips. *The Berlin Blockade: A Study in Cold War Politics.* Princeton: Princeton University Press, 1958.

Diggins, John Patrick. *The Proud Decades: America in War and in Peace, 1941–1960.* New York: Norton, 1988.

Diner, Dan. *America in the Eyes of the Germans: An Essay on Anti-Americanism.* Translated by Allison Brown. Princeton, N.J.: Markus Wiener Public, 1996.

Divine, Robert. *Foreign Policy and U.S. Presidential Election, 1940–1948.* New York: New Viewpoints, 1974.

Donaldson, Gary. *Truman Defeats Dewey.* Lexington: University of Kentucky Press, 1999.

Donner, Jörn. *Report from Berlin.* Translated by Albin T. Anderson. Bloomington: Indiana University Press, 1961.

Donovan, Frank. *Bridge in the Sky.* New York: David McKay, 1968.

Donovan, Robert. *Conflict and Crisis.* New York: Norton, 1977.

Dorwart, Jeffrey. *Eberstadt and Forrestal: A National Security Partnership, 1909–1949.* College Station: Texas A&M University Press, 1991.

Douglas, William O. *Go East, Young Man.* New York: Random House, 1974.

Ebsworth, Raymond. *Restoring Democracy in Germany.* New York: Praeger, 1960.

Eden, Lynn. *Whole World on Fire.* Ithaca, N.Y.: Cornell University Press, 2004.

Eisenberg, Carolyn. *Drawing the Line.* Cambridge: Cambridge University Press, 1996.

Eisenhower, David. *Eisenhower: At War, 1943–1945.* New York: Random House, 1986.

Elkins, T. H., with B. Hofmeister. *Berlin: The Spatial Structure of a Divided City.* London: Methuen, 1988.

Elliot, Michael. *The Day Before Yesterday: Reconsidering America's Past, Rediscovering the Present.* New York: Simon & Schuster, 1996.

Everett, Susanne. *Lost Berlin.* New York: Galley Books, 1979.

Ferrell, Robert. *Harry S. Truman.* Columbia: University of Missouri Press, 1994.

———, ed. *Dear Bess: The Letters from Harry to Bess Truman, 1910–1959.* New York: Norton, 1983.

———, ed. *Truman in the White House: The Diary of Eben A. Ayers.* Columbia: University of Missouri Press, 1991.

Forrestal, James. *The Forrestal Diaries.* Edited by Walter Millis with the collaboration of E. S. Duffield. New York: Viking, 1951.

Fousek, John. *To Lead the Free World: American Nationalism and the Cultural Roots of the Cold War.* Chapel Hill: University of North Carolina Press, 2000.

Friedman, Norman. *The Fifty Years War: Conflict and Strategy in the Cold War.* Annapolis, Md.: Naval Institute Press, 2000.

Friedrich, Otto. *Before the Deluge.* New York: Harper Perennial, 1995.

Fromkin, David. *In the Time of the Americans.* New York: Knopf, 1995.

Gaddis, John Lewis. *The Cold War.* New York: Penguin, 2005.

———. *The Long Peace: Inquiries into the History of the Cold War.* New York: Oxford University Press, 1987.

Gaglione, Anthony. *The United Nations Under Trygve Lie, 1945–1953.* Lanham, Md.: Scarecrow Press, 2001.

Gavin, James. *On to Berlin: Battles of an Airborne Commander, 1943–1946*. New York: Viking, 1978.

Geppert, Dominick, ed. *The Postwar Challenge: Cultural, Social, and Political Change in Western Europe, 1945–1958*. New York: Oxford University Press, 2003.

Gere, Edwin. *The Unheralded*. Shutesbury, Mass.: Andrus Publishing, 2004.

Giangreco, D. M., and Robert E. Grffin. *Airbridge to Berlin*. Novato, Calif.: Presidio, 1988.

Gilbert, Bill. *Air Power*. New York: Citadel Press, 2003.

Gilbert, Martin. *The Day the War Ended*. New York: Henry Holt, 1995.

———. *The Second World War: A Complete History*. New York: Henry Holt, 1989.

Gimbel, John. *The American Occupation of Germany: Politics and the Military, 1945–1949*. Stanford, Calif.: Stanford University Press, 1968.

Glaser, Hermann. *Rubble Years: The Cultural Roots of Postwar Germany, 1945–1948*. New York: Paragon House, 1986.

Glendon, Mary Ann. *A World Made New: Eleanor Roosevelt and the Universal Declaration of Human Rights*. New York: Random House, 2001.

Goedde, Petra. *GIs and Germans: Culture, Gender, and Foreign Relations, 1945–1949*. New Haven: Yale University Press, 2003.

Golay, John Ford. *The Founding of the Federal Republic of Germany*. Chicago: University of Chicago Press, 1958.

Goldman, Eric. *The Crucial Decade—and After*. New York: Random House, 1956.

Gori, Francesca, and Silvio Pons, eds. *The Soviet Union and Europe in the Cold War, 1943–1953*. New York: St. Martin's Press, 1996.

Gorlizki, Yoram, and Oleg Kulevniuk. *Cold Peace: Stalin and the Soviet Ruling Circle, 1945–1953*. New York: Oxford University Press, 2004.

Gormly, James. *The Collapse of a Grand Alliance, 1945–1948*. Baton Rouge: Louisiana State University Press, 1987.

Gottlieb, Manuel. *The German Peace Settlement and the Berlin Crisis*. New York: Paine-Whitman Publishing, 1960.

Goulden, Joseph. *The Best Years*. New York: Atheneum, 1976.

———, ed. *Mencken's Last Campaign: H. L. Mencken on the 1948 Election*. Washington, D.C.: New Republic Book Company, 1976.

Graebner, William. *The Age of Doubt: American Thought and Culture in the 1940s*. Boston: Twayne Publishers, 1991.

Grathwol, Robert, and Donita M. Moorhus. *American Forces in Berlin: Cold War Outpost, 1945–1994*. Washington, D.C.: Department of Defense, Legacy Resource Management Programs, 1994.

Grathwol, Robert, et al. *Oral History and Postwar German-American Relations: Resources in the United States*. Washington, D.C.: German Historical Institute, 1997.

Grayling, A. C. *Among the Dead Cities*. New York: Walker, 2006.

Great Britain. Army. *Notes on the Blockade of Berlin 1948: From a British Viewpoint in Berlin*. Berlin: HQ British Troops Berlin, RAF Gatow, HQ Airlift, BTB; Military Government, BTB, 1949.

Gross, Inge Stanneck. *Memories of World War II and Its Aftermath*. Eastsound, Wash.: Island in the Sky, 2005.

Grosser, Alfred. *The Colossus Again*. New York: Praeger, 1955.

———. *Germany in Our Times*. New York: Praeger, 1971.

Grouse, Peter. *Operation Rollback: America's Secret War Behind the Iron Curtain*. Boston: Houghton Mifflin, 2000.

Gullan, Harold. *The Upset That Wasn't: Harry S Truman and the Crucial Election of 1948*. Chicago: Ivan R. Dee, 1998.

Halberstam, David. *Summer of '49*. New York: Morrow, 1989.

Halvorsen, Gail. *The Berlin Candy Bomber*. Springville, Utah.: Horizon Publishers, 1997.

Hamby, Alonzo. *Beyond the New Deal: Harry S. Truman and American Liberalism*. New York: Columbia University Press, 1973.

———. *Man of the People: A Life of Harry S. Truman*. New York: Oxford University Press, 1995.

Hampton, Mary. *The Wilsonian Impulse: U.S. Foreign Policy, the Alliance, and German Unification*. Westport, Conn.: Praeger, 1996.

Harper, John Lamberton. *American Visions of Europe: Franklin Roosevelt, George F. Kennan, and Dean G. Acheson*. Cambridge: Cambridge University Press, 1994.

Harrington, Daniel. *The Air Force Can Deliver Anything*. Ramstein Air Base: United States Air Force Office of History, 1998.

Hastings, Max. *Armageddon: The Battle for Germany, 1944–45*. London: MacMillan, 2004.

Haun, James. *Spitfire Wingman from Tennessee*. Nashville: Stormwatch Press, 2006.

Haydock, Michael. *City Under Siege*. Washington, D.C.: Brassey's, 2000.

Haynes, Richard. *The Awesome Power: Harry S. Truman as Commander in Chief*. Baton Rouge: Louisiana State University Press, 1973.

Heidelmeyer, Wolfgang, and Guenter Hindrichs, eds. *Documents on Berlin, 1943–1963*. Munich: R. Oldenbourg Verlag, 1963.

Held, Joseph. *The Columbia History of Eastern Europe in the Twentieth Century*. New York: Columbia University Press, 1992.

Hill, Russell. *Struggle for Germany*. New York: Harper & Brothers, 1947.

Hitchcock, William. *The Struggle for Europe: The Turbulent History of a Divided Continent, 1945–2002*. New York: Doubleday, 2002.

Hogan, Michael. *A Cross of Iron: Harry S. Truman and the Origins of the National Security State, 1945–1954*. Cambridge: Cambridge University Press, 1998.

———. *The Marshall Plan*. Cambridge: Cambridge University Press, 1987.

Hoopes, Roy. *Americans Remember the Home Front*. New York: Hawthorn Books, 1977.

Hoopes, Townsend, and Douglas Brinkley. *Driven Patriot*. New York: Knopf, 1992.

Howley, Frank. *Berlin Command*. New York: Putnam, 1950.

———. *Your War for Peace*. New York: Henry Holt, 1953.

Hoyt, Edwin. *The Airmen: The Story of American Flyers in World War II*. New York: McGraw-Hill, 1990.

Huschke, Wolfgang. *The Candy Bombers: The Berlin Airlift 1948/49, A History of the People and the Planes*. Berlin: Metropol, 1999.

Inglis, Fred. *The Cruel Peace: Everyday Life in the Cold War*. New York: Basic Books, 1991.

Isaacson, Walter, and Evan Thomas. *The Wise Men*. New York: Simon & Schuster, 1986.

Jackson, Robert. *The Berlin Airlift*. Wellingborough: Patrick Stephens, 1988.

Jammer, Max. *Einstein and Religion*. Princeton: Princeton University Press, 1999.

Joesten, Joachim. *Germany: What Now?* Chicago: Ziff-Davis Publishing Company, 1948.

Johnson, Eric, and Karl-Heinz Reuband. *What We Knew: Terror, Mass Murder and Everyday Life in Nazi Germany*. London: John Murray, 2005.

Judt, Tony. *Postwar*. New York: Penguin, 2005.

Junker, Detlef, ed. *The United States and Germany in the Era of the Cold War, 1945–1990*. Cambridge: Cambridge University Press, 2004.

Kaiser, Robert. *Cold Winter, Cold War*. New York: Stein and Day, 1974.

Karabell, Zachary. *Architects of Intervention: The United States, the Third World, and the Cold War, 1946–1962*. Baton Rouge: Louisiana State University Press, 1999.

———. *The Last Campaign*. New York: Random House, 2000.

Kaznick, Peter, and James Gilbert, eds. *Rethinking Cold War Culture*. Washington, D.C.: Smithsonian Institution Press, 2000.

Kee, Robert. *1945: The World We Fought For*. London: Hamish Hamilton, 1985.

Kelly, Frank. *Harry Truman and the Human Family*. Santa Barbara, Calif.: Capra Press, 1998.

Kennan, George. *American Diplomacy, 1900–1950*. New York: New American Library, 1951.

———. *Memoirs: 1925–1950*. Boston: Little, Brown, 1967.

Kennedy, John. *Prelude to Leadership: The European Diary of John F. Kennedy, Summer 1945*. Washington, D.C.: Regnery, 1995.

Kennedy-Pipe, Caroline. *Stalin's Cold War: Soviet Strategies in Europe, 1943–1956*. Manchester: Manchester University Press, 1995.

Kinzer, Stephen. *Overthrow*. New York: Times Books, 2006.

Kleinman, Mark. *A World of Hope, a World of Fear: Henry Wallace, Reinhold Niebuhr, and American Liberalism*. Columbus: Ohio State University Press, 2000.

Knopp, Guido. *Hitler's Children*. Translated by Angus McGeoch. Gloucestershire: Sutton Publishing, 2000.

Koch, H. W. *The Hitler Youth: Origins and Development, 1922–45*. New York: Stein and Day, 1975.

Kofsky, Frank. *Harry S. Truman and the War Scare of 1948: A Successful Campaign to Deceive the Nation*. New York: St. Martin's Press, 1993.

Krugler, David. *This Is Only a Test: How Washington, D.C., Prepared for Nuclear War.* New York: Palgrave Macmillan, 2006.

Ladd, Brian. *The Ghosts of Berlin: Confronting the German History in the Urban Landscape.* Chicago: University of Chicago Press, 1997.

Laqueur, Walter. *The Rebirth of Europe.* New York: Holt, Rinehart and Winston, 1970.

Large, David Clay. *Berlin.* New York: Basic Books, 2001.

Launius, Roger, and Coy Cross. *MAC and the Legacy of the Berlin Airlift.* Scott Air Force Base, Ill.: Military Airlift Command, 1989.

Lay, Elizabeth. *The Berlin Air Lift.* Historical Division, Headquarters European Command, United States Air Force, 1952.

Leahy, William D. *I Was There.* New York: Whittlesey House, 1950.

LeMay, Curtis, with MacKinlay Kantor. *Mission with LeMay: My Story.* Garden City, N.Y.: Doubleday, 1965.

Levenson, Thomas. *Einstein in Berlin.* New York: Bantam, 2003.

Lieberman, Joseph. *The Scorpion and the Tarantula.* Boston: Houghton Mifflin, 1970.

Lilienthal, David. *The Journals of David E. Lilienthal,* Volume 2: *The Atomic Energy Years, 1945–1950.* New York: Harper & Row, 1964.

Lindsay, Edward. *American Country Editors Abroad.* Decatur, Ga.: Huston-Patterson, 1946.

Lingeman, Richard. *Don't You Know There's a War On?: The American Home Front, 1941–1945.* New York: Putnam, 1970.

Lukacs, John. *1945: Year Zero.* Garden City, N.Y.: Doubleday, 1978.

McAllister, James. *No Exit: America and the German Problem, 1943–1954.* Ithaca, N.Y.: Cornell University Press, 2002.

McCreary, Edward. *The Americanization of Europe.* Garden City, N.Y.: Doubleday, 1964.

McCullough, David. *Truman.* New York: Simon & Schuster, 1992.

MacDonough, Giles. *After the Reich.* New York: Basic Books, 2007.

———. *Berlin.* London: Sinclair-Stevenson, 1947.

McFarland, Keith, and David Roll. *Louis Johnson and the Arming of America.* Bloomington: Indiana University Press, 2005.

McFarland, Linda. *Cold War Strategist: Stuart Symington and the Search for National Security.* Westport, Conn.: Praeger, 2001.

Maddox, Robert James. *From War to Cold War: The Education of Harry S. Truman.* Boulder, Colo.: Westview Press, 1988.

Man, John. *Berlin Blockade.* New York: Ballantine Books, 1973.

Manchester, William. *American Caesar.* Boston: Little, Brown, 1978.

———. *The Glory and the Dream.* Boston: Little, Brown, 1973.

Mander, John. *Berlin: The Eagle and the Bear.* Westport, Conn.: Greenwood Press, 1959.

———. *Berlin: Hostage for the West.* Westport, Conn.: Greenwood Press, 1962.

Markowitz, Norman. *The Rise and Fall of the People's Century: Henry A. Wallace and American Liberalism 1941–1948.* New York: Free Press, 1973.

May, Arthur. *Europe Since 1939.* New York: Holt, Rinehart and Winston, 1966.

May, Elaine Tyler. *Homeward Bound: American Families in the Cold War.* New York: Basic Books, 1988.

Mayer, Herbert. *German Recovery and the Marshall Plan, 1948–1952.* Bonn: Edition Atlantic Forum, 1969.

Mayne, Richard. *Postwar: The Dawn of Today's America.* London: Thames and Hudson, 1983.

Meehan, Patricia. *A Strange Enemy People: Germans Under the British, 1945–1950.* London: Peter Owen Publishers, 2001.

Merridale, Catherine. *Ivan's War: Life and Death in the Red Army, 1939–1945.* New York: Metropolitan Books, 2006.

Merritt, Anna, and Richard L. Merritt, eds. *Public Opinion in Occupied Germany: The OMGUS Surveys, 1945–1949.* Urbana: University of Illinois Press, 1970.

———. *Public Opinion in Semisovereign Germany: The HICOG Surveys, 1949–1955.* Urbana: University of Illinois Press, 1980.

Merritt, Richard. *Democracy Imposed.* New Haven: Yale University Press, 1995.

Meyers, Jeffrey. *Orwell.* New York: Norton, 2000.

Middleton, Drew. *The Struggle for Germany.* Indianapolis: Bobbs-Merrill, 1949.

————. *Where Has Last July Gone?* New York: Quadrangle, 1973.

Miller, David. *The Cold War: A Military History.* London: John Murray, 1998.

Miller, Merle. *Plain Speaking.* New York: Berkley, 1973.

Miller, Roger. *To Save a City.* College Station: Texas A&M University Press, 2000.

Millman, Chad. *The Detonators.* New York: Little, Brown, 2006.

Milward, Alan. *The Reconstruction of Western Europe, 1945–51.* London: Methuen, 1984.

Miscamble, Wilson. *From Roosevelt to Truman.* Cambridge: Cambridge University Press, 2007.

Montgomery, M. R., and Gerald Foster. *A Field Guide to Airplanes of North America.* New York: Houghton Mifflin, 2006.

Morris, Eric. *Blockade.* New York: Stein and Day, 1973.

Morris, Jan. *Manhattan '45.* New York: Oxford University Press, 1987.

Morrow, Lance. *The Best Year of Their Lives.* New York: Basic Books, 2005.

Moskin, J. Robert. *Mr. Truman's War.* New York: Random House, 1996.

Mosley, Leonard. *Marshall: Hero for Our Times.* New York: Hearst Books, 1982.

Mowat, R. C. *Ruin and Resurgence, 1939–1965.* New York: Humanities Press, 1966.

Murphy, David, Sergei E. Kondrashev, and George Bailey. *Battleground Berlin: CIA vs. KGB in the Cold War.* New Haven: Yale University Press, 1997.

Murphy, Robert. *Diplomat Among Warriors.* New York: Doubleday, 1964.

Naimark, Norman. *The Russians in Germany.* Cambridge: Belknap, 1995.

Neal, Steve, ed. *HST: Memories of the Truman Years.* Carbondale: Southern Illinois University Press, 2003.

Nicholas, Lynn. *Cruel World: The Children of Europe in the Nazi Web.* New York: Knopf, 2005.

Office of MAC History. *The Berlin Airlift: A Brief Chronology.* Scott Air Force Base, Ill.: Military Airlift Command, 1988.

Offner, Arnold. *Another Such Victory: President Truman and the Cold War, 1945–1953.* Stanford, Calif.: Stanford University Press, 2002.

Ojserkis, Raymond. *Beginning of the Cold War Arms Race: The Truman Administration and the US Arms Build-up.* Westport, Conn.: Praeger, 2003.

Olson, James. *Stuart Symington: A Life.* Columbia: University of Missouri Press, 2003.

O'Neill, William. *American High: The Years of Confidence, 1945–1960.* New York: Free Press, 1986.

Ostergren, Robert, and John Rice. *The Europeans.* New York: Guilford Press, 2004.

Panati, Charles. *Panati's Parade of Fads, Follies, and Manias.* New York: HarperCollins, 1991.

Parrish, Thomas. *Berlin in the Balance.* Reading, Pa.: Addison-Wesley, 1998.

————. *Roosevelt and Marshall.* New York: William Morrow, 1989.

Patterson, James. *Mr. Republican: A Biography of Robert A. Taft.* Boston: Houghton Mifflin 1972.

Patton, David. *Cold War Politics in Postwar Germany.* New York: St. Martin's Press, 1999.

Pearcy, Arthur. *Berlin Airlift.* Shrewsbury: Airlife, 1997.

Peters, Charles. *Five Days in Philadelphia.* New York: PublicAffairs, 2005.

Peterson, Edward. *The American Occupation of Germany.* Detroit: Wayne State University Press, 1977.

Peterson, F. Ross. *Prophet Without Honor: Glen H. Taylor and the Fight for American Liberalism.* Lexington: University Press of Kentucky, 1974.

Piantadosi, Claude. *The Biology of Human Survival.* New York: Oxford University Press, 2003.

Poen, Monte, ed. *Letters Home by Harry Truman.* New York: Putnam, 1984.

————. *Strictly Personal and Confidential: The Letters Harry Truman Never Mailed.* Boston: Little, Brown, 1982.

Pogue, Forrest. *George Marshall: Statesman.* New York: Viking, 1987.

Provan, John, and R.E.G. Davies, *Berlin Airlift,* McLean, Va.: Paladwr Press, 1998.

Read, Anthony, and David Fisher. *Berlin: The Biography of a City.* London: Hutchinson, 1994.

————. *The Fall of Berlin.* New York: Norton, 1992.

Rempel, Gerhard. *Hitler's Children: The Hitler Youth and the SS.* Chapel Hill: University of North Carolina Press, 1989.

Rhodes, Richard. *Dark Sun: The Making of the Hydrogen Bomb.* New York: Simon & Schuster, 1995.

Richie, Alexandra. *Faust's Metropolis: A History of Berlin.* New York: Carroll & Graf, 1998.

Rodrigo, Robert. *Berlin Airlift.* London: Cassell, 1960.

Rogow, Arnold. *James Forrestal.* New York: Macmillan, 1963.

Rooney, Andy. *My War.* New York: PublicAffairs, 2000.

Rose, Lisle. *Dubious Victory: The United States and the End of World War II*. Kent, Ohio.: Kent State University Press, 1973.

Ross, Irwin. *The Loneliest Campaign: The Truman Victory of 1948*. New York: New American Library, 1968.

Rowe, Dorothy. *Representing Berlin*. Burlington, Vt.: Ashgate Publishing, 2003.

Ryan, Cornelius. *The Last Battle*. New York: Simon & Schuster, 1966.

Salisbury, Harrison. *The 900 Days: The Siege of Leningrad*. New York: DaCapo, 1985.

Samuel, Wolfgang. *German Boy*. Jackson: University Press of Mississippi, 2000.

———. *I Always Wanted to Fly: America's Cold War Airmen*. Jackson: University Press of Mississippi, 2001.

Schain, Martin, ed. *The Marshall Plan: Fifty Years After*. New York: Palgrave, 2001.

Schapsmeier, Edward L., and Frederick H. Schapsmeier. *Prophet in Politics: Henry A. Wallace and the War Years, 1940–1965*. Ames: Iowa State University Press, 1970.

Scharr, Adela Riek. *Sisters in the Sky*. St. Louis: The Patrice Press, 1986.

Schivelbusch, Wolfgang. *In a Cold Crater: Cultural and Intellectual Life in Berlin, 1945–1948*. Translated by Kelly Barry. Berkeley: University of California Press, 1998.

Schlesinger, Stephen. *Act of Creation*. New York: Westview, 2003.

Schmidt, Karl. *Henry A. Wallace: Quixotic Crusade 1948*. Syracuse, N.Y.: Syracuse University Press, 1960.

Schoen, Douglas. *On the Campaign Trail*. New York: Regan Books, 2004.

Schuffert, John. *Airlift Laffs*. San Antonio, Tex.: Berlin Airlift Veterans Association, 1999.

Scott, Mark, and Semyon Krasilchik, eds. *Yanks Meet Reds*. Santa Barbara, Calif.: Capra Press, 1988.

Settel, Arthur, ed. *This Is Germany*. Freeport, N.Y.: Books for Libraries, 1950.

Sherman, Martin. *A World Destroyed: The Atomic Bomb and the Grand Alliance*. New York: Knopf, 1975.

Shlaim, Avi. *The United States and the Berlin Blockade, 1948–1949*. Berkeley: University of California Press, 1983.

Sickels, Robert. *The 1940s*. Westport, Conn.: Greenwood Press, 2004.

Simbeck, Rob. *Daughter of the Air: The Brief Soaring Life of Cornelia Fort*. New York: Atlantic Monthly Press, 1999.

Simpson, Christopher. *Blowback: America's Recruitment of Nazis and Its Effect on the Cold War*. New York: Weidenfield & Nicolson, 1988.

Simpson, Cornell. *The Death of James Forrestal*. Boston: Western Islands, 1966.

Smith, Arthur. *Kidnap City: Cold War Berlin*. Westport, Conn.: Greenwood Press, 2002.

Smith, Jean Edward. *The Defense of Berlin*. Baltimore: The Johns Hopkins Press, 1963.

———. *Lucius D. Clay*. New York: Henry Holt, 1990.

———, ed. *The Papers of General Lucius D. Clay*. Bloomington: Indiana University Press, 1974.

Smith, Richard Norton. *Thomas E. Dewey and His Times*. New York: Simon & Schuster, 1982.

Smith, Tony. *America's Mission: The United States and the Worldwide Struggle for Democracy in the Twentieth Century*. Princeton: Princeton University Press, 1994.

Smith, Walter Bedell. *My Three Years in Moscow*. Philadelphia: Lippincott, 1950.

Smyser, W. R. *From Yalta to Berlin: The Cold War Struggle Over Germany*. New York: St. Martin's Press, 1999.

Sorel, Nancy Caldwell. *The Women Who Wrote the War*. New York: Arcade Publishing, 1999.

Spalding, Elizabeth Edwards. *The First Cold Warrior: Harry Truman, Containment, and the Remaking of Liberal Internationalism*. Lexington: University Press of Kentucky, 2006.

Spencer, Otha. *Flying the Hump: Memories of an Air War*. College Station: Texas A&M University Press, 1992.

Stargardt, Nicholas. *Witness of War: Children's Lives Under the Nazis*. London: Jonathan Cape, 2005.

Stebbins, Richard. *The United States in World Affairs 1949*. New York: Harper & Brothers, 1950.

Steege, Paul. *Black Market, Cold War*. Cambridge: Cambridge University Press, 2007.

Stoler, Mark. *George C. Marshall: Soldier-Statesman of the American Century*. Boston: Twayne Publishers, 1989.

Strom, Elizabeth. *Building the New Berlin: The Politics of Urban Development in Germany's Capital City*. Lanham, Md.: Lexington Books, 2001.

Tanenhaus, Sam. *Whittaker Chambers*. New York: Random House, 1997.

Taylor, D. J. *Orwell*. London: Chatto & Windus, 2003.

Taylor, Glen. *The Way It Was with Me.* Secaucus, N.J.: Lyle Stuart, 1979.

Taylor, Ronald. *Berlin and Its Culture.* New Haven: Yale University Press, 1997.

Tent, James. *Mission of the Rhine: Reeducation and Denazification in American-Occupied Germany.* Chicago: University of Chicago Press, 1982.

Terkel, Studs. *"The Good War": An Oral History of the World War II.* New York: Pantheon Books, 1984.

Tillman, Barrett. *LeMay.* New York: Palgrave Macmillan, 2007.

Tippins, Sherill. *February House.* New York: Houghton Mifflin, 2005.

Toland, John. *The Last 100 Days.* New York: Random House, 1965.

Trager, James, ed. *The People's Chronology.* Detroit: Gale, 2005.

Truman, Harry. *Memoirs.* Garden City, N.Y.: Doubleday, 1955–1956.

Truman, Margaret. *Harry S. Truman.* New York: Morrow, 1973.

Tsouras, Peter, ed. *Cold War Hot: Alternate Decisions of the Cold War.* London: Greenhill Books, 2003.

Tucker, Todd. *The Great Starvation Experiment.* New York: Free Press, 2006.

Turner, William. *Over the Hump.* New York: Duell, Sloan, and Pearce, 1964.

Turner, Barry. *Countdown to Victory: The Final European Campaigns of World War II.* London: Hodder & Stoughton, 2004.

Tusa, Ann. *The Last Division.* New York: Perseus Books, 1997.

Tusa, Ann, and John Tusa. *The Berlin Airlift.* New York: Sarpedon, 1988.

United States Department of State, *Foreign Relations of the United States, 1948,* Volume 2: *Germany and Austria,* Washington, D.C.: U.S. Government Printing Office, 1973.

Uris, Leon. *Armageddon.* London: William Kimber, 1964.

Van Dulken, Stephen. *Inventing the 20th Century.* New York: New York University Press, 2003.

Wagner, Lilya. *Women War Correspondents of World War II.* Westport, Conn.: Greenwood Press, 1989.

Walker, J. Samuel. *Henry A. Wallace and American Foreign Policy.* Westport, Conn.: Greenwood Press, 1976.

Weintraub, Stanley. *The Last Great Victory.* New York: Truman Talley, 1995.

Werner, Emmy. *Through the Eyes of Innocents.* Boulder, Colo.: Westview Press, 2000.

Werner, Joseph. *Berlin Airlift: Brides and Grooms Created.* Stonybrook, N.Y.: Water Edge Publishing, 1999.

White, Graham, and John Maze. *Henry A. Wallace: His Search for a New World Order.* Chapel Hill: University of North Carolina Press, 1995.

White, Theodore. *Fire in the Ashes.* New York: William Sloane Associates Publishers, 1953.

Whitfield, Stephen. *The Culture of the Cold War.* Baltimore: John Hopkins Universal Press, 1991.

Whiting, Charles. *The End of the War.* New York: Stein and Day, 1973.

Willett, Ralph. *The Americanization of Germany, 1945–1949.* London: Routledge, 1989.

Windsor, Philip. *City on Leave.* New York: Praeger, 1963.

Wolfe, Robert, ed. *Americans as Proconsuls: United States Military Government in Germany and Japan, 1944–1952.* Carbondale: Southern Illinois University Press, 1984.

Woods, Randall, and Howard Jones. *Dawning of the Cold War.* Athens: University of Georgia Press, 1991.

Wunderlin, Jr., Clarence, ed. *The Papers of Robert A. Taft,* Volume 3: *1945–1948.* Kent, Ohio.: Kent State University Press, 2003.

Yarnell, Allen. *Democrats and Progressives: The 1948 Presidential Election as a Test of Postwar Liberalism.* Berkeley: University of California Press, 1974.

Yergin, Daniel. *Shattered Peace.* Boston: Houghton Mifflin, 1977.

Zink, Harold. *The United States in Germany: 1944–1955.* Princeton, N.J.: D. Van Nostrand, 1957.

ACKNOWLEDGMENTS

If you head south from Tucson, down through Green Valley and past the Santa Rita mountains, you can pull off the shimmering highway, follow a wiggle in the road, and take a dirt path that begins where the paved road ends to arrive at the small home where Gail "Hal" Halvorsen lives in the open desert. You'll never find a more gracious host. I thank him for opening his and his wife Lorraine's homes in Arizona and Utah to me, allowing me to literally rummage through his basement for letters and private papers that had gone unexamined for decades, and letting me trail him as he paid a visit to Berlin and gathered with other Airlift veterans in Minnesota. There would be no story to tell—and I would not have been able to tell it—had it not been for his extraordinary kindness.

Writing *The Candy Bombers* took me to two continents and sixteen states, and along the way I have been helped in countless ways by many who shared their time and insights. Ann Tunner answered endless questions while serving me ginger ale and cookies on the veranda of the white house on the Ware River where her husband, Bill, lived his last years. Earl Moore, Dale Whipple, Dub Southers, Fred Hall, and dozens of their fellow Airlift veterans regaled me with enough stories to fill a few more books. Tim Chopp, Ed Ide, Kevin Kearney, and the other members of the Berlin Airlift Historical Foundation took me up aboard *The Spirit of Freedom,* their restored C-54 Skymaster, and allowed me to spend a weekend with them at an air show in Pennsylvania. Tech Sergeant Matthew Summers showed me around Rhein-Main Air Base on a cold day just weeks before it finally closed. Officer Ronnie Powell and "T" Black of the University of South Alabama helped me pinpoint where Pete Sowa must have lived on Brookley Air Force Base, braving the rain as a summer storm rolled in off Mobile Bay.

For me, the writing of this book has been a personal journey of a sort I did not expect when I began the work. My parents were children in Europe in the time period this book describes. The thought of what they and so many innocent others endured in those years was never far from my mind. All four of my grandparents were "guests" of the German government in places named Auschwitz, Terezin, Buchenwald, and Dachau. As I wrote this book, I struggled with questions of how to respond to such evil—questions that were in some ways similar to those that confronted Germany's occupiers after World War II. Walking through Berlin on a gray fall day I would often shudder when turning a corner and coming upon the site of some terrible monstrousness. Sometimes that shudder would turn to anger, and I would begin to wonder whether the Candy Bombers had been right.

But if you ever need a jolt of hope about the world we live in, go to Berlin and see the possibilities history can hold. In Potsdamer Platz, where Hitler and Speer planned for a gargantuan fountain and parking spots for a thousand cars, where Markgraf's police raided the black marketeers, where hundreds of American and Russian troops faced off with machine guns, where a single, stooped man dragged a paintbrush across the pavement to divide the city, there is now an IMAX movie theater, a Sony store, and a Legoland. To be sure, there is still competition in Berlin for the allegiances of its people. On what once was the American side of Checkpoint Charlie, there is a Subway sandwich shop. Mere feet away, on the old Soviet side, there is a Schlotzsky's deli. Some may tut-tut such rampant commercialization, but no one dies or starves in face-offs over cold cuts and condiments. That this is Berlin today is a testament to the strength of allied military power, to the commitment of two generations of Americans to the idea that democracy and freedom can be brought to the most unlikely places, and to the redemptive, transformative power of human goodness.

My debts are plentiful. A number of friends responded to the imposition of reading my manuscript with cheer and thoughtfulness. Ken Baer, my coeditor at *Democracy: A Journal of Ideas,* demonstrated not only his brilliance in his feedback, but his generosity in shouldering extra responsibilities as I took time off to finish the manuscript. The incisive edits of *Democracy*'s managing editor, Clay Risen, demonstrated why he is one of the finest young writers on the scene. Lauren Hammer Breslow somehow found time amid the joys and burdens of new motherhood to lend her razor-sharp intelligence to the editing task. Steve Kettmann shared his ear for language as well as his long experience of working and living in Berlin. Matt Bai—in my opinion the most perceptive political journalist in America today—read the manuscript while completing his own excellent book, and spent long hours struggling with me through the thorniest questions of proportion and pace. Jeffrey Yarbro was right there, as always, when I needed help the most. These brief mentions are wholly inadequate in conveying how much their friendship means to me or how important their thoughts were to this book. I hope they already know.

Laura Capps and Bill Burton put me up in the "Congressional Suite" of their Washington home while I did archival research. Doug Pravda and Sarah Scrogin, the proprietors of New York's Scravda Inn, helpfully located near Carmine's restaurant, opened their doors to me repeatedly—and often late at night. Brad Leupen bought me a copy of James Byrnes's memoirs. Alisa Schlesinger was a great traveling companion in Berlin and accompanied me on my trips to Frankfurt.

Walter Isaacson and Frank Foer made helpful introductions and guided my early thinking on the book's structure and approach. Doug Brinkley and Arianna Huffington went to bat for me and this project.

Two of the preeminent experts on the Berlin Airlift, Air Force historians Roger Miller and Daniel Harrington, generously provided me with context and contacts, both of which were vital. Ron Davies of the Smithsonian National Air and Space Museum gave me access to the museum's archives. Christian Ostermann of the Cold War International History Project provided an overview of current research. Bob Slayton discussed Bill Tunner with me. Susan Eisenhower and Ernest Kolowrat helped me understand the latest theories on the life and death of Jan Masaryk. Larry Gelbart regaled me with tales of his adventures as one of Bob Hope's writers on that Christmas trip to Berlin.

Numerous librarians and archivists aided me on the scavenger hunt that was the research of putting this story together. Thanks go to the staffs of the National Archives, the Library of Congress, the Columbia University Oral History Research Office, the U.S. Army Military History Institute, the Harry S Truman Presidential Library, the Dwight D. Eisenhower Presidential Library, Princeton's Seeley G. Mudd Manuscript Library, the Hoover Institution Archives, the Georgetown University Library Special Collections Division, and Arizona State University's Hayden Library. The staff of the Interlibrary Loan Desk at Burton Barr Central Library in Phoenix was always of assistance. At the Air Force Historical Research Agency in Alabama, Toni Petito and Sylvester Jackson made extra efforts to be helpful and lived up to the reputation of Southern hospitality. Their counterparts at the U.S. Air Force history office in Ramstein, Germany, allowed me to commandeer a microfilm reader in the middle of their office. I think the taxpayers of America deserve a thanks for seeing the need to fund the work of so many of these libraries and archives. And if there is a more inspiring and humbling spot to research and write than the main reading room of the Library of Congress, I look forward to visiting it.

In Berlin, Bernd von Kostka and Helmut Trotnow allowed me to spend days in the offices of the Allied Museum rifling through books and papers. Professor Knud Krakau of the JFK Institute at the Free

University of Berlin bought me lunch and shared his memories and expertise. Dieter Ramthun of the Berlin chapter of the Airlift Historical Foundation joined me for dinner and taught me a painful lesson about the potency of German beer with his persistent demand for "just one more."

Graham Allison appointed me a senior fellow at Harvard's Kennedy School's Belfer Center for Science and International Affairs, giving me space and time when I was beginning to work on this book.

Rafe Sagalyn immediately saw the importance of this story and stuck with it over many months. My editor, Neil Nyren, exhibited unflappable patience and good cheer through mounting delays. His perceptive guidance demonstrated why he's one of the best in the business.

My work on this book has lasted more than three times as long as the Berlin Airlift itself, and through it all my wife, Stephanie, has been a part of it. She did not mind when reams of manuscript pages overtook our kitchen table. Nor did she mind when, three days after our wedding, I was off to catch a plane to do research at archives in Pennsylvania. More than that, though, she has been my best bibliography organizer, sounding board, adviser, editor, and friend. This book, as with my life, is dedicated to her.

INDEX

Americans: attitudes toward Germans,
    84–86, 108–9, 115–16, 119, 134–37,
    152–53, 278–80, 475; and Berlin
    blockade, 6–7
America's Town Meeting of the Air, 446–47
Andreas-Friedrich, Ruth, 205, 207, 320, 492;
    and blockade, 344, 362, 446; and City
    Hall riot, 239; and elections, 489; and
    Howley, 243; and Reichstag rally, 378;
    and Soviet coup attempt, 370; and
    winter, 468
Animal Farm, Orwell, 472
Army, U.S.: decline of, 171–73; supplies for,
    Clay and, 38–40
Army Air Corps, 60–61; Tunner and, 326–27
Arnold, Henry "Hap," 333
Aronson, Al, 18
Atlanta Constitution, 44
Atlee, Clement, and Bevin, 191
Atomic bomb: Bikini test, 169; Forrestal and,
    415; Soviet test, 542–53; Truman and,
    292, 308–10, 395; U.S. and, 212,
    394–95
    threat of, 291–92; and Berlin blockade,
    257, 259
Atomic Energy Commission, 292
Auden, W. H., 87
Auriol, Vincent, 170
Ayers, Eben, 402, 403

Babcock, Colonel (Howley's deputy), 233
Bacall, Lauren, 400
Bachus, Harry, 543
Baltimore Sun, and Clay, 74
Barkley, Alben, 398, 536; at Bob Hope
    Christmas show, 493; at Democratic
    National Convention, 287–88;
    mother of, 36–37
Baronsky, Rainer, 356
Bartz, Frank, 18
Batt, William, 361
Battle of Berlin, 93–100
Beevor, Antony, 559
Bell, Elliott, 455
Beneš, Edvard, 160–62
Benn, Gottfried, 466
Bennett, Jack, 253
Berhrend, Hans-Karl, 452
Berle, Milton, 385
Berlin, Germany, 3, 78–79, 80, 86–90;
    Christmas 1948, 492–97; Communist
    coup attempt, 366–70; Communist
    kidnappings, 144–45, 185, 208–9;

conflict for control of, 104–7, 139–40,
    220–22; contemporary, 606–7;
    devastation of, 98–99, 108, 275,
    299–301, 559; division of, 208–9,
    240–41, 355, 434, 477–81; Dulles's
    view, 153; elections, 145–46, 477–79;
    evacuation proposal, 200–201,
    220–21; fiftieth anniversary of Airlift,
    547; food supplies for, 126–29;
    Forrestal and, 450–60; hunger in, 227,
    320, 469–70; infant mortality rate,
    562; negotiations with Soviets,
    360–61; occupation of, 556–57;
    police forces, 353–54; population,
    gender ratios, 562; postwar years,
    102–5, 130–33; reunification of,
    549–50; Russian Army and, 93–100,
    559; Soviet coup, 480; Soviet
    restrictions, 236–37; Soviet threat to,
    204–5, 208–9, 220, 238–39, 350–51;
    Soviet Union and, 145–46, 184–86;
    winter in, 131, 451–52, 462–72,
    479–80, 484, 508; and World War II,
    90–92. *See also* Berlin blockade; Clay,
    Lucius D.; German people;
    Germany
  crisis in, 211–12, 375–76, 384, 451–52; and
    presidential campaign, 1948, 395–99;
    Wallace and, 318–19
Berlin, Irving, 492, 494, 495
"Berlin Agreement," 82–83
Berlin blockade, 3–6, 241–43, 406–7, 472–74,
    511, 519, 576; blockade conditions,
    294–95, 320–22, 466–72; end of,
    524–26, 528–32; results of, 515;
    negotiations, 362–64; Stalin and, 575;
    United Nations and, 401–2, 445–46;
    U.S. presidential campaign and,
    401–3, 454–56; winter and, 462–72.
    See also Airlift, Berlin; Berlin,
    Germany
Berlin City Assembly. *See* City Assembly,
    Berlin
Berlin Philharmonic, final concert, 94
Berliner Zeitung, 205; and West Berlin
    elections, 489
Berliners, 529; and Airlift, 342–47, 379–80,
    452; and blockade, 433–34, 466–74;
    and Candy Bombers, 444–45; and
    democracy, 312–13, 472–74;
    Howley and, 502–3; and supplies
    for Russia, 550. *See also* German
    people

ABOUT THE AUTHOR

Andrei Cherny is an editor of the idea journal *Democracy.* A former White House speechwriter and senior fellow at Harvard's Kennedy School Belfer Center for Science and International Affairs, he is the author of *The Next Deal* and has written on history, politics, and culture for the *New York Times,* the *Washington Post,* and the *Los Angeles Times.* Cherny is an officer in the Navy Reserve. He and his wife live in Phoenix. For more information, visit www.TheCandyBombers.com.